Lecture Notes in Computer Science 7215

Commenced Publication in 1973
Founding and Former Series Editors:
Gerhard Goos, Juris Hartmanis, and Jan van Leeuwen

Advanced Research in Computing and Software Science

Subline of Lectures Notes in Computer Science

Pierpaolo Degano   Joshua D. Guttman (Eds.)

Principles of Security and Trust

First International Conference, POST 2012
Held as Part of the European Joint Conferences
on Theory and Practice of Software, ETAPS 2012
Tallinn, Estonia, March 24 – April 1, 2012
Proceedings

 Springer

Volume Editors

Pierpaolo Degano
Università di Pisa
Dipartimento di Informatica
Largo Bruno Pontecorvo, 3
56127 Pisa, Italy
E-mail: degano@di.unipi.it

Joshua D. Guttman
Worcester Polytechnic Institute
Department of Computer Science
100 Institute Road
Worcester, MA 01609, USA
E-mail: guttman@wpi.edu

ISSN 0302-9743   e-ISSN 1611-3349
ISBN 978-3-642-28640-7   ISBN 978-3-642-28641-4 (eBook)
DOI 10.1007/978-3-642-28641-4
Springer Heidelberg Dordrecht London New York

Library of Congress Control Number: 2012932616

CR Subject Classification (1998): C.2.0, D.4.6, E.3, K.4.4, K.6.5, D.2, J.1

LNCS Sublibrary: SL 4 – Security and Cryptology

Typesetting: Camera-ready by author, data conversion by Scientific Publishing Services, Chennai, India

Printed on acid-free paper

Springer is part of Springer Science+Business Media (www.springer.com)

Foreword

ETAPS 2012 is the fifteenth instance of the European Joint Conferences on Theory and Practice of Software. ETAPS is an annual federated conference that was established in 1998 by combining a number of existing and new conferences. This year it comprised six sister conferences (CC, ESOP, FASE, FOSSACS, POST, TACAS), 21 satellite workshops (ACCAT, AIPA, BX, BYTECODE, CMCS, DICE, FESCA, FICS, FIT, GRAPHITE, GT-VMT, HAS, IWIGP, LDTA, LINEARITY, MBT, MSFP, PLACES, QAPL, VSSE and WRLA), and eight invited lectures (excluding those specific to the satellite events).

The six main conferences received this year 606 submissions (including 21 tool demonstration papers), 159 of which were accepted (6 tool demos), giving an overall acceptance rate just above 26%. Congratulations therefore to all the authors who made it to the final programme! I hope that most of the other authors will still have found a way to participate in this exciting event, and that you will all continue to submit to ETAPS and contribute to making it the best conference on software science and engineering.

The events that comprise ETAPS address various aspects of the system development process, including specification, design, implementation, analysis, security and improvement. The languages, methodologies and tools that support these activities are all well within its scope. Different blends of theory and practice are represented, with an inclination towards theory with a practical motivation on the one hand and soundly based practice on the other. Many of the issues involved in software design apply to systems in general, including hardware systems, and the emphasis on software is not intended to be exclusive.

ETAPS is a confederation in which each event retains its own identity, with a separate Programme Committee and proceedings. Its format is open-ended, allowing it to grow and evolve as time goes by. Contributed talks and system demonstrations are in synchronised parallel sessions, with invited lectures in plenary sessions. Two of the invited lectures are reserved for 'unifying' talks on topics of interest to the whole range of ETAPS attendees. The aim of cramming all this activity into a single one-week meeting is to create a strong magnet for academic and industrial researchers working on topics within its scope, giving them the opportunity to learn about research in related areas, and thereby to foster new and existing links between work in areas that were formerly addressed in separate meetings.

This year, ETAPS welcomes a new main conference, *Principles of Security and Trust*, as a candidate to become a permanent member conference of ETAPS. POST is the first addition to our main programme since 1998, when the original five conferences met in Lisbon for the first ETAPS event. It combines the practically important subject matter of security and trust with strong technical connections to traditional ETAPS areas.

A step towards the consolidation of ETAPS and its institutional activities has been undertaken by the Steering Committee with the establishment of *ETAPS e.V.*, a non-profit association under German law. ETAPS e.V. was founded on April 1st, 2011 in Saarbrücken, and we are currently in the process of defining its structure, scope and strategy.

ETAPS 2012 was organised by the *Institute of Cybernetics at Tallinn University of Technology*, in cooperation with

▷ European Association for Theoretical Computer Science (EATCS)
▷ European Association for Programming Languages and Systems (EAPLS)
▷ European Association of Software Science and Technology (EASST)

and with support from the following sponsors, which we gratefully thank:

INSTITUTE OF CYBERNETICS AT TUT; TALLINN UNIVERSITY OF TECHNOLOGY (TUT); ESTONIAN CENTRE OF EXCELLENCE IN COMPUTER SCIENCE (EXCS) FUNDED BY THE EUROPEAN REGIONAL DEVELOPMENT FUND (ERDF); ESTONIAN CONVENTION BUREAU; and MICROSOFT RESEARCH.

The organising team comprised:

General Chair: *Tarmo Uustalu*

Satellite Events: *Keiko Nakata*

Organising Committee: *James Chapman, Juhan Ernits, Tiina Laasma, Monika Perkmann* and their colleagues in the *Logic and Semantics* group and *administration* of the *Institute of Cybernetics*

The ETAPS portal at http://www.etaps.org is maintained by *RWTH Aachen University*.

Overall planning for ETAPS conferences is the responsibility of its Steering Committee, whose current membership is:

Vladimiro Sassone (Southampton, Chair), Roberto Amadio (Paris 7), Gilles Barthe (IMDEA-Software), David Basin (Zürich), Lars Birkedal (Copenhagen), Michael O'Boyle (Edinburgh), Giuseppe Castagna (CNRS Paris), Vittorio Cortellessa (L'Aquila), Koen De Bosschere (Gent), Pierpaolo Degano (Pisa), Matthias Felleisen (Boston), Bernd Finkbeiner (Saarbrücken), Cormac Flanagan (Santa Cruz), Philippa Gardner (Imperial College London), Andrew D. Gordon (MSR Cambridge and Edinburgh), Daniele Gorla (Rome), Joshua Guttman (Worcester USA), Holger Hermanns (Saarbrücken), Mike Hinchey (Lero, the Irish Software Engineering Research Centre), Ranjit Jhala (San Diego), Joost-Pieter Katoen (Aachen), Paul Klint (Amsterdam), Jens Knoop (Vienna), Barbara König (Duisburg), Juan de Lara (Madrid), Gerald Lüttgen (Bamberg), Tiziana Margaria (Potsdam), Fabio Martinelli (Pisa), John Mitchell (Stanford), Catuscia Palamidessi (INRIA Paris), Frank Pfenning (Pittsburgh), Nir Piterman (Leicester), Don Sannella (Edinburgh), Helmut Seidl (TU Munich),

Scott Smolka (Stony Brook), Gabriele Taentzer (Marburg), Tarmo Uustalu (Tallinn), Dániel Varró (Budapest), Andrea Zisman (London), and Lenore Zuck (Chicago).

I would like to express my sincere gratitude to all of these people and organisations, the Programme Committee Chairs and PC members of the ETAPS conferences, the organisers of the satellite events, the speakers themselves, the many reviewers, all the participants, and Springer-Verlag for agreeing to publish the ETAPS proceedings in the ARCoSS subline.

Finally, I would like to thank the Organising Chair of ETAPS 2012, Tarmo Uustalu, and his Organising Committee, for arranging to have ETAPS in the most beautiful surroundings of Tallinn.

January 2012

Vladimiro Sassone
ETAPS SC Chair

Preface

The first conference on Principles of Security and Trust (POST) was held 25–27 March 2012 in Tallinn, as part of ETAPS 2012. POST resulted from an alliance among the workshops it will replace: Automated Reasoning and Security Protocol Analysis (ARSPA), Formal Aspects of Security and Trust (FAST), Security in Concurrency (SecCo), and the Workshop on Issues in the Theory of Security (WITS). Some of these events met jointly, affiliated with ETAPS, in 2011 under the name Theory of Security and Applications (TOSCA). The IFIP WG 1.7 on Theoretical Foundations of Security Analysis and Design has long helped to nourish this community.

We are pleased that POST attracted 67 submissions for its first occurrence, from which the committee selected 20. This volume also contains an abstract of the talk given by our invited speaker, Cynthia Dwork, and a paper by Bruno Blanchet, an ETAPS unifying speaker. We would like to thank them for their contributions.

We are grateful to our dedicated and collegial Program Committee, and to the ETAPS Steering Committee for start-up help. We thank the Organizing Committee in Tallinn. Finally, Andrei Voronkov very helpfully ensured that Easychair worked smoothly.

January 2012   Pierpaolo Degano
Pisa and Boston   Joshua Guttman

Organization

Program Committee

Michael Backes	Saarland University and MPI-SWS
Anindya Banerjee	IMDEA Software Institute
Gilles Barthe	IMDEA Software Institute
David Basin	ETH Zurich
Véronique Cortier	CNRS, Loria
Pierpaolo Degano	Università di Pisa
Andy Gordon	Microsoft Research and University of Edinburgh
Joshua Guttman	Worcester Polytechnic Institute
Steve Kremer	ENS Cachan, INRIA
Ralf Küsters	University of Trier
Peeter Laud	Cybernetica AS and University of Tartu
Gavin Lowe	University of Oxford
Heiko Mantel	Technische Universität Darmstadt
Sjouke Mauw	Université du Luxembourg
Catherine Meadows	Naval Research Laboratory
John Mitchell	Stanford University
Carroll Morgan	University of New South Wales
Sebastian A. Mödersheim	Danish Technical University
Mogens Nielsen	University of Aarhus
Catuscia Palamidessi	École Polytechnique, INRIA
Andrei Sabelfeld	Chalmers University of Technology
Nikhil Swamy	Microsoft Research
Luca Viganò	Università di Verona

Additional Reviewers

Aderhold, Markus	Chevalier, Yannick
Arapinis, Myrto	Chong, Stephen
Barletta, Michele	Ciobaca, Stefan
Bartoletti, Massimo	Clarckson, Michael
Bello, Luciano	Cremers, Cas
Berard, Beatrice	Crespo, Juan Manuel
Birgisson, Arnar	De Caso, Guido
Bodei, Chiara	Delaune, Stéphanie
Boreale, Michele	Eggert, Sebastian
Calvi, Alberto	Elsalamouny, Ehab
Chen, Xihui	Ereth, Sarah

Ferrari, Gianluigi

Fournet, Cédric

Garcia, Flavio D.

Gay, Richard

Gibbons, Jeremy

Gibson-Robinson, Thomas

Goldsmith, Michael

Heam, Pierre-Cyrille

Hritcu, Catalin

Jonker, Hugo

Klaedtke, Felix

Kordy, Barbara

Kramer, Simon

Lux, Alexander

Malkis, Alexander

Mezzetti, Gianluca

Morvan, Christophe

Muller, Tim

Murawski, Andrzej

Naumann, David

Nguyen, Long

Perner, Matthias

Peroli, Michele

Petrocchi, Marinella

Radomirovic, Sasa

Rafnsson, Willard

Ryan, P.Y.A.

Schmidt, Benedikt

Seifert, Christian

Smyth, Ben

Sprenger, Christoph

Sprick, Barbara

Starostin, Artem

Strub, Pierre-Yves

Syverson, Paul

Tiu, Alwen

Truderung, Tomasz

Tuengerthal, Max

Van Delft, Bart

Vogt, Andreas

Wang, Rui

Zalinescu, Eugen

Zunino, Roberto

Table of Contents

Differential Privacy and the Power of (Formalizing) Negative Thinking

(Extended Abstract)

Cynthia Dwork

Microsoft Research, Silicon Valley
dwork@microsoft.com

Abstract. *Differential privacy* is a promise, made by a data curator to a data subject: you will not be affected, adversely or otherwise, by allowing your data to be used in any study, no matter what other studies, data sets, or information from other sources is, or may become, available. This talk describes the productive role played by negative results in the formulation of differential privacy and the development of techniques for achieving it, concluding with a new negative result having implications related to participation in multiple, independently operated, differentially private databases.

Keywords: differential privacy, foundations of private data analysis, lifetime privacy loss, independently operated differentially private databases.

In the digital information realm, loss of privacy is usually associated with failure to control access to information, to control the flow of information, or to control the purposes for which information is employed. *Differential privacy* arose in a context in which ensuring privacy is a challenge even if all these control problems are solved: privacy-preserving statistical analysis of data. Here, even defining the goal is problematic, as the data analyst and the *privacy adversary* are one and the same.

The Formal Definition. A database is modeled as a collection of *rows*, with each row containing the data of a different individual. Differential privacy will ensure that the ability of an adversary to inflict harm – of any sort, to any set of people – should be essentially the same, independent of whether any individual opts in to, or opts out of, the dataset. This is done indirectly, by focusing on the probability of any given output of a privacy mechanism and how this probability can change with the addition or deletion of any row. Thus, we concentrate on pairs of databases (D, D') differing only in one row, meaning one is a subset of the other and the larger database contains just one additional row. Finally, to handle worst case pairs of databases, the probabilities will be over the random choices made by the privacy mechanism.

Definition 1. [3,4] *A randomized function $\mathcal{K}$ gives (ε, δ)-differential privacy if for all data sets D and D' differing on at most one row, and all $S \subseteq Range(\mathcal{K})$,*

$$\Pr[\mathcal{K}(D) \in S] \leq \exp(\varepsilon) \times \Pr[\mathcal{K}(D') \in S] + \delta \qquad (1)$$

P. Degano and J.D. Guttman (Eds.): POST 2012, LNCS 7215, pp. 1–2, 2012.
© Springer-Verlag Berlin Heidelberg 2012

where the probability space in each case is over the coin flips of $\mathcal{K}^1$.

Both the definition and the earliest techniques for achieving it were strongly influenced by negative results [2,5].

Consider a differentially private mechanism answering simple "counting queries" of the form "How many people in the database have property P?" Since a differentially private mechanism exhibits a similar probability distribution on answers for neighboring databases D, D', it is clear that the responses given must sometimes be inaccurate; the goal of algorithmic research in this field is to minimize this inaccuracy. The *Laplace method* achieves $(\varepsilon, 0)$-differential privacy for counting queries by adding noise generated according to the Laplace distribution with parameter $1/\varepsilon$ to the true answer, and releasing this "noisy" value [4]. The resulting expected error is on the order of $1/\varepsilon$.

Differential privacy holds regardless of what the adversary knows, now or in the future. In consequence, differential privacy composes obliviously and automatically; the k-fold composition of (ε, δ)-differentially private mechanisms, involing either k operations on a single database or the mutually oblivious operation of k independent databases with arbitrary overlap, is still roughly $(\sqrt{k}\varepsilon, \delta')$-differentially private [7]. It follows that adding independently generated noise with distribution $\mathrm{Lap}(\sqrt{k}/\varepsilon)$ permits k queries to be answered with a total privacy loss of about ε and expected error per query $\sqrt{k}/\varepsilon$.

A series of results beginning with [1] shows one can do much better – with error depending polylogarithmically on the number of queries – using *coordinated noise*. In fact *coordination is essential* to beat the "$\sqrt{k}$" composition bound [6], so we have reached the end of the line for mutually oblivious, independently operated, differentially private mechanisms running against arbitrarily knowledgeable adversaries. Addressing this newly understood limitation is a fundamental challenge in differentially private data analysis.

References

1. Blum, A., Ligett, K., Roth, A.: A Learning Theory Approach to Non-Interactive Database Privacy. In: Proc. 40th ACM Symposium on Thoery of Computing (2008)
2. Dinur, I., Nissim, K.: Revealing Information While Preserving Privacy. In: Proc. 22nd ACM Symposium on Principles of Database Systems (2003)
3. Dwork, C.: Differential Privacy. In: Bugliesi, M., Preneel, B., Sassone, V., Wegener, I. (eds.) ICALP 2006. LNCS, vol. 4052, pp. 1–12. Springer, Heidelberg (2006)
4. Dwork, C., McSherry, F., Nissim, K., Smith, A.: Calibrating Noise to Sensitivity in Private Data Analysis. In: Halevi, S., Rabin, T. (eds.) TCC 2006. LNCS, vol. 3876, pp. 265–284. Springer, Heidelberg (2006)
5. Dwork, C., Naor, M.: On the Difficulties of Disclosure Prevention in Statistical Databases or The Case for Differential Privacy. Journal of Privacy and Confidentiality 2(1) (2010)
6. Dwork, C., Naor, M., Vadhan, S.: Coordination is Essential (working title) (manuscript in preparation)
7. Dwork, C., Rothblum, G., Vadhan, S.: Boosting and Differential Privacy. In: Proceedings of the 51st IEEE Symposium on Foundations of Computer Science (2010)

---

[1] Typcially, the literature considers $\delta < 1/\mathrm{poly}(n)$ on a database of size n.

Security Protocol Verification: Symbolic and Computational Models

Bruno Blanchet

INRIA, École Normale Supérieure, CNRS, Paris
blanchet@di.ens.fr

Abstract. Security protocol verification has been a very active research area since the 1990s. This paper surveys various approaches in this area, considering the verification in the symbolic model, as well as the more recent approaches that rely on the computational model or that verify protocol implementations rather than specifications. Additionally, we briefly describe our symbolic security protocol verifier ProVerif and situate it among these approaches.

1 Security Protocols

Security protocols are programs that aim at securing communications on insecure networks, such as Internet, by relying on cryptographic primitives. Security protocols are ubiquitous: they are used, for instance, for e-commerce (e.g., the protocol TLS [110], used for https:// URLs), bank transactions, mobile phone and WiFi networks, RFID tags, and e-voting. However, the design of security protocols is particularly error-prone. This can be illustrated for instance by the very famous Needham-Schroeder public-key protocol [161], in which a flaw was found by Lowe [148] 17 years after its publication. Even though much progress has been made since then, many flaws are still found in current security protocols (see, e.g., http://www.openssl.org/news/ and http://www.openssh.org/security.html). Security errors can have serious consequences, resulting in loss of money or loss of confidence of users in the system. Moreover, security errors cannot be detected by functional software testing because they appear only in the presence of a malicious adversary. Automatic tools can therefore be very helpful in order to obtain actual guarantees that security protocols are correct. This is a reason why the verification of security protocols has been a very active research area since the 1990s, and is still very active. This survey aims at summarizing the results obtained in this area. Due to the large number of papers on security protocol verification and the limited space, we had to omit many of them; we believe that we still present representatives of the main approaches. Additionally, Sect. 2.2 briefly describes our symbolic verification tool ProVerif.

1.1 An Example of Protocol

We illustrate the notion of security protocol with the following example, a simplified version of the Denning-Sacco public-key key distribution protocol [109].

P. Degano and J.D. Guttman (Eds.): POST 2012, LNCS 7215, pp. 3–29, 2012.

$$\text{Message 1. } A \rightarrow B : \{\{k\}_{sk_A}\}_{pk_B} \quad k \text{ fresh}$$
$$\text{Message 2. } B \rightarrow A : \{s\}_k$$

As usual, $A \rightarrow B : M$ means that A sends to B the message M; $\{M\}_{sk}$ denotes the signature of M with the secret key sk (which can be verified with the public key pk); $\{M\}_{pk}$ denotes the public-key encryption of message M under the public key pk (which can be decrypted with the corresponding secret key sk); $\{M\}_k$ denotes the shared-key encryption of message M under key k (which can be decrypted with the same key k). In this protocol, the principal A chooses a fresh key k at each run of the protocol. She signs this key with her signing key sk_A, encrypts the obtained message with the public key of her interlocutor B, and sends him the message. When B receives it, he decrypts it (with his secret key sk_B), verifies the signature of A, and obtains the key k. Having verified this signature, B is convinced that the key was chosen by A, and encryption under pk_B guarantees that only B could decrypt the message, so k should be shared between A and B. Then, B encrypts a secret s under the shared key k. Only A should be able to decrypt the message and obtain the secret s.

In general, in the literature, as in the example above, the protocols are described informally by giving the list of messages that should be exchanged between the principals. Nevertheless, one must be careful that these descriptions are only informal: they indicate what happens in the absence of an adversary. However, an adversary can capture messages and send his own messages, so the source and the target of a message may not be the expected one. Moreover, these descriptions leave implicit the verifications done by the principals when they receive messages. Since the adversary may send messages different from the expected ones, and exploit the obtained reply, these verifications are very important: they determine which messages will be accepted or rejected, and may therefore protect or not against attacks. Formal models of protocols, such as [5, 7, 73, 118] make all this precise.

Although the explanation above may seem to justify its security informally, this protocol is subject to an attack:

$$\text{Message 1. } A \rightarrow C : \quad \{\{k\}_{sk_A}\}_{pk_C}$$
$$\text{Message 1'. } C(A) \rightarrow B : \{\{k\}_{sk_A}\}_{pk_B}$$
$$\text{Message 2. } B \rightarrow C(A) : \{s\}_k$$

In this attack, A runs the protocol with a dishonest principal C. This principal gets the first message of the protocol $\{\{k\}_{sk_A}\}_{pk_C}$, decrypts it and re-encrypts it under the public key of B. The obtained message $\{\{k\}_{sk_A}\}_{pk_B}$ corresponds exactly to the first message of a session between A and B. Then, C sends this message to B impersonating A; above, we denote by $C(A)$ the dishonest participant C impersonating A. B replies with the secret s, intended for A, encrypted under k. C, having obtained the key k by the first message, can decrypt this message and obtain the secret s.

The protocol can easily be fixed, by adding the identity of B to the signed message, which yields the following protocol:

$$\text{Message 1. } A \to B : \{\{B, k\}_{sk_A}\}_{pk_B} \quad k \text{ fresh}$$
$$\text{Message 2. } B \to A : \{s\}_k$$

When he receives the first message, B verifies that his own identity appears as first component. After this change, in a session between A and C, the adversary C receives $\{\{C, k\}_{sk_A}\}_{pk_C}$. It cannot transform this message into $\{\{B, k\}_{sk_A}\}_{pk_B}$, because it cannot transform the signature that contains C into a signature that contains B instead. Therefore, the previous attack is impossible. However, this point does not prove that the protocol is correct: there may be other attacks, so a security proof is needed.

1.2   Models of Protocols

In order to obtain proofs that security protocols are correct, one first needs to model them mathematically. Two models of protocols have been considered:

– In the *symbolic model*, due to Needham and Schroeder [161] and Dolev and Yao [111] and often called Dolev-Yao model, the cryptographic primitives are represented by function symbols considered as black-boxes, the messages are terms on these primitives, and the adversary is restricted to compute only using these primitives. This model assumes perfect cryptography. For instance, shared-key encryption is basically modeled by two function symbols, enc and dec, where $\text{enc}(x, y)$ stands for the encryption of x under key y and $\text{dec}(x, y)$ for the decryption of x with key y, with the equality:

$$\text{dec}(\text{enc}(x, y), y) = x. \tag{1}$$

Hence, one can decrypt $\text{enc}(x, y)$ only when one has the key y. More generally, one can add equations to model algebraic properties of the cryptographic primitives, but one always makes the assumption that the only equalities that hold are those explicitly given by these equations.

– In the *computational model*, developed at the beginning of the 1980s by Goldwasser, Micali, Rivest, Yao, and others (see for instance [124, 125, 181]), the messages are bitstrings, the cryptographic primitives are functions from bitstrings to bitstrings, and the adversary is any probabilistic Turing machine. This is the model generally used by cryptographers.

In this model, the length of keys is determined by a value named security parameter, and the runtime of the adversary is supposed to be polynomial in the security parameter. A security property is considered to hold when the probability that it does not hold is negligible in the security parameter. (A function is said to be negligible when it is asymptotically smaller than the inverse of any polynomial.) This probability can also be bound explicitly as a function of the runtime of the adversary and of the probability of breaking each cryptographic primitive; this is called exact security.

For instance, shared-key encryption can be modeled by two functions enc and dec with the same equality (1) as above, but the security of encryption is expressed (informally) by saying that the adversary has a negligible probability of distinguishing encryptions of two messages of the same length [39]. Equalities other than (1) may exist, even if they are not made explicit.

The computational model is much more realistic, but complicates the proofs, and until recently these proofs were only manual. The symbolic model, however, is suitable for automation, essentially by computing the set of all messages the adversary can know. Starting in the 1990s, the proof of protocols in the symbolic model has been an important application field for formal verification methods.

We emphasize that even the computational model is just a model, which ignores many important aspects of reality. In particular, it ignores physical attacks against the devices: side-channel attacks exploit power consumption, timing, noise, ... and fault attacks introduce faults in the system in order to break its security. As protocols are better studied and verified formally, physical attacks become increasingly important and are an area of active research, with some workshops, such as FTDC (Fault Diagnosis and Tolerance in Cryptography) and CHES (Cryptographic Hardware and Embedded Systems), focusing mainly on this area. This survey will not deal with physical attacks.

1.3   Security Properties

Security protocols can aim at a wide variety of security goals. The main security properties can be classified into two categories, *trace properties* and *equivalence properties*. We define these categories and mention two particularly important examples: secrecy and authentication. These are two basic properties required by most security protocols. Some protocols, such as e-voting protocols [105], require more complex and specific security properties, which will not be discussed here.

Trace and Equivalence Properties. Trace properties are properties that can be defined on each execution trace (each run) of the protocol. The protocol satisfies such a property when it holds for all traces in the symbolic model, except for a set of traces of negligible probability in the computational model. For example, the fact that some states are unreachable is a trace property.

Equivalence or indistinguishability properties mean that the adversary cannot distinguish two processes. For instance, one of these processes can be the protocol under study, and the other one can be its specification. Then, the equivalence means that the protocol satisfies its specification. Equivalences can be therefore be used to model many subtle security properties. In the symbolic model, this notion is called process equivalence, with several variants (observational equivalence, testing equivalence, trace equivalence) [5–7], while in the computational model, one rather talks about indistinguishability. Equivalences provide compositional proofs: if a protocol P is equivalent to P', P can be replaced with P' in a more complex protocol. In the computational model, this is at the basis of the idea of universal composability [71]. However, in the symbolic model, their proof is more difficult to automate than the proof of trace properties: they cannot be expressed on a single trace, they require relations between traces (or processes). So most equivalence proofs are still manual, even if tools begin to appear as we shall see in Sect. 2.1.

Secrecy. Secrecy, or confidentiality, means that the adversary cannot obtain some information on data manipulated by the protocol. In the symbolic model, secrecy can be formalized in two ways:

- Most often, secrecy means that the adversary cannot compute exactly the considered piece of data. In case of ambiguity, this notion will be called syntactic secrecy. For instance, in the protocol of Sect. 1.1, we may want to prove that the adversary cannot obtain s nor the key k shared between A and B. These properties hold only for the fixed protocol of Sect. 1.1.
- Sometimes, one uses a stronger notion, strong secrecy, which means that the adversary cannot detect a change in the value of the secret [1, 49]. In other words, the adversary has no information at all on the value of the secret. In the fixed protocol of Sect. 1.1, we could also show strong secrecy of s.

The difference between syntactic secrecy and strong secrecy can be illustrated by a simple example: consider a piece of data for which the adversary knows half of the bits but not the other half. This piece of data is syntactically secret since the adversary cannot compute it entirely, but not strongly secret, since the adversary can see if one of the bits it knows changes. Syntactic secrecy cannot be used to express secrecy of data chosen among known constants. For instance, talking about syntactic secrecy of a bit 0 or 1 does not make sense, because the adversary knows the constants 0 and 1 from the start. In this case, one has to use strong secrecy: the adversary must not be able to distinguish a protocol using the value 0 from the same protocol using the value 1. These two notions are often equivalent [92], both for atomic data (which are never split into several pieces, such as nonces, which are random numbers chosen independently at each run of the protocol) and for probabilistic cryptographic primitives.

Strong secrecy is intuitively closer to the notion of secrecy used in the computational model, which means that a probabilistic polynomial-time adversary has a negligible probability of distinguishing the secret from a random number [9].

Syntactic secrecy is a trace property, while strong secrecy and computational secrecy are equivalence properties.

Authentication. Authentication means that, if a participant A runs the protocol apparently with a participant B, then B runs the protocol apparently with A, and conversely. In general, one also requires that A and B share the same values of the parameters of the protocol.

In the symbolic model, this is generally formalized by correspondence properties [149, 180], of the form: if A executes a certain event e_1 (for instance, A terminates the protocol with B), then B has executed a certain event e_2 (for instance, B started a session of the protocol with A). There exist several variants of these properties. For instance, one may require that each execution of e_1 corresponds to a distinct execution of e_2 (injective correspondence) or, on the contrary, that if e_1 has been executed, then e_2 has been executed at least once (non-injective correspondence). The events e_1 and e_2 may also include more or fewer parameters depending on the desired property. These properties are trace properties.

For example, in the fixed protocol of Sect. 1.1, we could show that, if B terminates the protocol with A and a key k, then A started the protocol with B and the same k. The injective variant does not hold, because the adversary can replay the first message of the protocol.

The formalization is fairly similar in the computational model, with the notion of *matching conversations* [41] and more recent formalizations based on session identifiers [9,40], which basically require that the exchanged messages seen by A and by B are the same, up to negligible probability. This is also a trace property.

2 Verifying Protocols in the Symbolic Model

A very large number of techniques and tools exist for verifying protocols in the symbolic model. We first present a survey of these techniques, then provide additional details on the tool that we have developed, ProVerif.

2.1 Verification Techniques

The automatic verification of protocols in the symbolic model is certainly easier than in the computational model, but it still presents significant challenges. Essentially, the state space to explore is infinite, for two reasons: the message size is not bounded in the presence an active adversary; the number of sessions (runs) of the protocol is not bounded. However, we can easily bound the number of participants to the protocol without forgetting attacks [85]: for protocols that do not make difference tests, one honest participant is enough for secrecy if the same participant is allowed to play all roles of the protocol, two honest participants are enough for authentication.

A simple solution to this problem is to explore only part of the state space, by limiting arbitrarily both the message size and the number of sessions of the protocol. One can then apply standard model-checking techniques, using systems such as FDR [148] (which was used to discover the attack against the Needham-Schroeder public-key protocol), Murφ [159], Maude [107], or SATMC (SAT-based Model-Checker) [16]. These techniques allow one to find attacks against protocols, but not to prove the absence of attacks, since attacks may appear in an unexplored part of the state space. (One can indeed construct a family of protocols such that the n-th protocol is secure for $n-1$ sessions but has an attack with n parallel sessions [154]. More generally, an arbitrary number of sessions may be needed [85].)

If only the number of sessions is bounded, the verification of protocols remains decidable: protocol insecurity (existence of an attack) is NP-complete with reasonable assumptions on the cryptographic primitives [171]. When cryptographic primitives have algebraic relations, the verification is much more difficult, but the complexity class does not necessarily increase. For instance, exclusive or is handled in the case of a bounded number of sessions in [79,80,87] and the Diffie-Hellman key agreement in [78], still with an NP-complexity. Practical algorithms have been implemented to verify protocols with a bounded number of sessions, by constraint solving, such as [155] and CL-AtSe (Constraint-Logic-based Attack Searcher) [81], or by extensions of model-checking such as OFMC (On-the-Fly Model-Checker) [35].

The previous results only deal with trace properties. The verification of equivalence properties is much more complex. First, decision procedures were designed for a fixed set of basic primitives and without else branches [113, 135], but their complexity was too large for practical implementations. Recently, more practical algorithms were designed for processes with else branches and non-determinism [76, 77] or for a wide variety of primitives with the restriction that processes are determinate, that is, their execution is entirely determined by the adversary inputs [82, 88]. Diff-equivalence, a strong equivalence between processes that have the same structure but differ by the terms they contain, is also decidable [36]; this result applies in particular to the detection of off-line guessing attacks against password-based protocols and to the proof of strong secrecy. These techniques rely on symbolic semantics: in a symbolic semantics, such as [65, 104, 147], the messages that come from the adversary are represented by variables, to avoid an unbounded case distinction on these messages.

For an unbounded number of sessions, the problem is undecidable [115] for a reasonable model of protocols. Despite this undecidability, many techniques have been designed to verify protocols with an unbounded number of sessions, by restricting oneself to subclasses of protocols, by requiring user interaction, by tolerating non-termination, or with incomplete systems (which may answer "I don't know"). Most of these techniques deal with trace properties; only the type system of [1] and ProVerif [55] deal with equivalence properties. Next, we present a selection of these techniques.

- Logics have been designed to reason about protocols. Belief logics, such as the BAN logic, by Burrows, Abadi, and Needham [70], reason about what participants to the protocol believe. The BAN logic is one of the first formalisms designed to reason about protocols. However, the main drawback of these logics is that they do not rely directly on the operational semantics of the protocol.

  Another logic, PCL (Protocol Composition Logic) [101, 116] makes it possible to prove that a formula holds after some participant has run certain actions, by relying on the semantics of the protocol. It allows systematic and rigorous reasoning on protocols, but has not been automated yet.
- Theorem proving was used for proving security properties of protocols [165]. Proofs in an interactive theorem prover typically require much human interaction, but allow one to prove any mathematically correct result.
- Typing was also used for proving protocols. Abadi [1] proved strong secrecy for protocols with shared-key encryption. Abadi and Blanchet [2] designed a type system for proving secrecy, which supports a wide variety of cryptographic primitives. Gordon and Jeffrey [126–128] designed the system Cryptyc for verifying authentication by typing. They handle shared-key and public-key cryptography.

  In all these type systems, the types express information on the security level of data, such as "secret" for secret data and "public" for public data.

Typing is better suited for at least partly manual usage than for fully automatic verification: type inference is often difficult, so type annotations are necessary. Type checking can often be automated, as in the case of Cryptyc. Types provide constraints that can help protocol designers guaranteeing the desired security properties, but existing protocols may not satisfy these constraints even if they are correct.

– Strand spaces [118] are a formalism that allows to reason about protocols. This formalism comes with an induction proof technique based on a partial order that models a causal precedence relation between messages. It was used both for manual proofs and in the automatic tool Athena [175] which combines model checking and theorem proving, and uses strand spaces to reduce the state space. Scyther [100] uses an extension of Athena's method with trace patterns to analyze a group of traces simultaneously. These tools sometimes limit the number of sessions to guarantee termination.

– Broadfoot, Lowe, and Roscoe [67, 68, 170] extended the model-checking approach to an unbounded number of sessions. They recycle nonces, to use a finite number of nonces for an infinite number of executions.

– One of the very first approaches for protocol verification is the Interrogator [156, 157]. In this system, written in Prolog, the reachability of a state after a sequence of messages is represented by a predicate, and the program runs a backward search to determine whether a state is reachable or not. The main problem of this approach is non-termination. It is partly solved by making the program interactive, so that the user can guide the search. The NRL Protocol Analyzer (NPA, which evolved into Maude-NPA) [117, 151] considerably improves this technique by using narrowing in rewrite systems. It does not make any abstraction, so it is sound and complete but may not terminate.

– Decidability results can be obtained for an unbounded number of sessions, for subclasses of protocols. For example, Ramanujan and Suresh [169] showed that secrecy is decidable for a class of tagged protocols. Tagged protocols are protocols in which each message is distinguished from others by a distinct constant, named tag. Their tagging scheme prevents blind copies, that is, situations in which a message is copied by a participant of the protocol without verifying its contents. Extensions of this decidability result include [14, 83]. In general, these decidability results are very restrictive in practice.

– Several methods rely on abstractions [99]: they overestimate the attack possibilities, most often by computing a superset of the knowledge of the adversary. They yield fully automatic but incomplete systems.

  • Bolignano [64] was a precursor of abstraction methods for security protocols. He merges key, nonces, ... so that a finite set remains. He can then apply a decision procedure.

  • Monniaux [160] introduced a verification method based on an abstract representation of the knowledge of the adversary by tree automata. This method was extended by Goubault-Larrecq [129]. Genet and Klay [123] combine tree automata with rewriting. This method lead to the implementation of the verifier TA4SP (Tree-Automata-based Automatic Approximations for the Analysis of Security Protocols) [63].

This approach abstracts away relational information on terms: when a variable appears several times in a message, one forgets that it has the same value at all its occurrences in the message, which limits the precision of the analysis. However, thanks to this approximation, this method always terminates.

- Weidenbach [179] introduced an automatic method for proving protocols based on resolution on Horn clauses. This method is at the heart of the verifier ProVerif and will be detailed in Sect. 2.2. It is incomplete since it ignores the number of repetitions of each action of the protocol. Termination is not guaranteed in general, but it is guaranteed on certain subclasses of protocols, and it can be obtained in all cases by an additional approximation, which loses relational information by transforming Horn clauses into clauses of the decidable subclass $\mathcal{H}_1$ [130]. This method can be seen as a generalization of the tree automata verification method. (Tree automata can be encoded as Horn clauses.) With Martín Abadi [2], we showed that this method is equivalent to the most precise instance of a generic type system for security protocols.
- Other abstraction-based techniques for security protocol verification include control-flow analysis [60–62], Feret's abstract-interpretation-based relational analysis [119], Heather and Schneider's rank functions verifier [134], Backes et al.'s causal graph technique [19], and the Hermès protocol verifier [66]. While most verifiers compute the knowledge of the adversary, Hermès computes forms of messages, such as encryption under certain keys, that guarantee preservation of secrecy.

Platforms that group several verification techniques have also been implemented:

- CAPSL (Common Authentication Protocol Specification Language) [108] provides a protocol description language, which is translated into an intermediate language, CIL (CAPSL Intermediate Language), based on multiset rewriting (or equivalently on Horn clauses with existentials in linear logic) [73]. This intermediate language can be translated into the input languages of Maude, NPA, Athena, and of the constraint solving verifier of [155].
- AVISPA (Automated Validation of Internet Security Protocols and Applications) [17] provides, like CAPSL, a protocol description language HLPSL (High-Level Protocol Specification Language), which is translated into an intermediate language based on multiset rewriting. Four verifiers take as input this intermediate language: SATMC for a bounded state space, CL-AtSe and OFMC for a bounded number of sessions, TA4SP for an unbounded number of sessions.

Even if it is rather long, this survey of protocol verification techniques in the symbolic model is certainly not exhaustive. It still shows the wide variety of techniques that have been applied to protocol verification, and the interest generated by this problem in the formal method community.

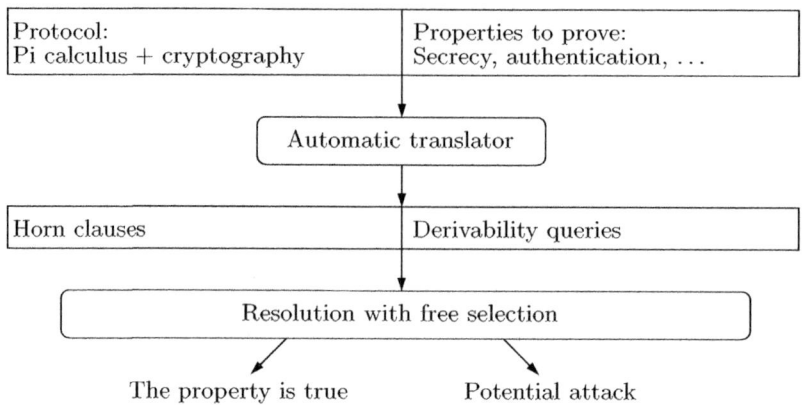

Fig. 1. The verification method of ProVerif

2.2   ProVerif

As mentioned above, the protocol verifier ProVerif is based on an abstract representation of the protocol by a set of Horn clauses, and on a resolution algorithm on these clauses. This tool has the following features:

- It is fully automatic. The user gives only the specification of the protocol and the properties to verify.
- It can handle a wide variety of cryptographic primitives, defined by rewrite rules or by certain equations.
- In contrast to finite state techniques, it can verify protocols without arbitrarily bounding the number of executed sessions (even in parallel) of the protocol or the size of messages. This makes it possible to obtain actual proofs of the security properties.
- It can verify secrecy, correspondence, and some equivalence properties.

Of course, there is a price to pay for these advantages: ProVerif does not always terminate and it is not complete (it may find false attacks). It is still precise and efficient in practice, as demonstrated by case studies, such as [3, 4, 53, 56].

The verification method is summarized in Fig. 1. The Horn clause verification technique is not specific to any formalism for representing the protocol. Among the many existing formalisms, we focused on extensions of the pi calculus with cryptographic primitives. The pi calculus itself [158] is a minimal programming language that models systems communicating on channels. Its cryptographic extensions are particularly well-suited for specifying cryptographic protocols. This line of research was pioneered by the spi calculus [7], which adds encryption, signatures, and hash functions to the pi calculus. It was considerably extended by the applied pi calculus [5], which provides a generic treatment of cryptographic primitives, defined by an equational theory. In our work, we first focused on a simpler case in which cryptographic primitives are defined by rewrite rules. This case can still represent many cryptographic primitives. We distinguish two kinds of primitives: constructors and destructors. Constructors, such as encryption enc, build new terms, while destructors, such as decryption dec, compute on terms. Destructors are defined by rewrite rules. For example, shared-key decryption can be defined by the rewrite rule: $\mathsf{dec}(\mathsf{enc}(x, y), y) \to x$. Decrypting a ciphertext $\mathsf{enc}(x, y)$ with the encryption key y yields the cleartext x.

We then extended the tool to support some primitives defined by equations, by translating these equations into rewrite rules automatically [55]. Hence resolution, on which ProVerif relies, can still use ordinary syntactic unification (instead of unification modulo the equational theory), and thus remains efficient. In particular, this technique supports block ciphers, for which decryption never fails (it may return junk), and a simple model of Diffie-Hellman key agreements. It still has limitations; in particular, it cannot handle associativity, so it does not support XOR (exclusive or). Extensions have been proposed for supporting XOR [140] and for improving the treatment of Diffie-Hellman key agreements [141]. Support for associative-commutative symbols can be offered by unification modulo the equational theory, as in Maude-NPA [117].

The protocol represented in this calculus is automatically translated into a set of Horn clauses (a logic program). This translation is defined in [2]. The main idea of the Horn clause representation is to use a predicate attacker, such that attacker(M) means "the attacker may have the message M". For example, the fact that the attacker can encrypt, resp. decrypt, when it has the key is represented by the following two clauses:

$$\mathsf{attacker}(x) \wedge \mathsf{attacker}(y) \Rightarrow \mathsf{attacker}(\mathsf{enc}(x, y))$$
$$\mathsf{attacker}(\mathsf{enc}(x, y)) \wedge \mathsf{attacker}(y) \Rightarrow \mathsf{attacker}(x)$$

When the attacker has the cleartext x and the key y, it can built the ciphertext $\mathsf{enc}(x, y)$, and when the attacker has the ciphertext and the key, it can obtain the cleartext. The messages exchanged by the honest participants of the protocol can also be represented by similar clauses. The participants are considered as oracles that the attacker can call to increase its knowledge. When a participant A sends a message M after receiving messages $M_1, \ldots, M_n$, we have a clause:

$$\mathsf{attacker}(M_1) \wedge \ldots \wedge \mathsf{attacker}(M_n) \Rightarrow \mathsf{attacker}(M)$$

Indeed, when the attacker has $M_1, \ldots, M_n$, it can send them to A; A replies with M, which the attacker can intercept. For instance, in the original protocol of Sect. 1.1, B receives a message of the form $\{\{y\}_{sk_A}\}_{pk_B}$, modeled by the term $\mathsf{penc}(\mathsf{sign}(y, sk_A), \mathsf{pk}(sk_B))$, where penc represents the public-key encryption, sign the signature, and pk computes the public key from the corresponding secret key. Then, B replies with the secret s encrypted under the key y, $\{s\}_y$, modeled by the term $\mathsf{enc}(s, y)$. Hence, we obtain the clause:

$$\mathsf{attacker}(\mathsf{penc}(\mathsf{sign}(y, sk_A), \mathsf{pk}(sk_B))) \Rightarrow \mathsf{attacker}(\mathsf{enc}(s, y))$$

More details on this representation as well as the complete coding of the protocol of Sect. 1.1 can be found in [54].

This representation of protocols is approximate in that the application of Horn clauses can be repeated any number of times, while the real protocol repeats each step only once per session. So, the state of the participants is only partly modeled. A model that does not make such an approximation can be obtained by using clauses in linear logic instead of classical logic, to control the number of repetitions of each step [114]. The Horn clause model can be seen as a sound abstraction, in the abstract interpretation sense [99], of the linear logic model, obtained by ignoring the number of repetitions of each action [50]. Hence, our technique is sound (when it says that a security property is true, then it is actually so), but not complete (false attacks can be found). However, in our tests, false attacks rarely occur. In fact, false attacks occur typically for protocols that first need to keep data secret, then publish them later in the protocol. In that situation, the Horn clause model considers that the attacker can re-inject the secret in the early part of the run, which is not possible in reality (V. Cortier, personal communication). Ignoring the number of repetitions of each action is a key to verify protocols without bounding the number of sessions.

Using this representation, secrecy can be inferred from non-derivability: if attacker(M) is not derivable, then the attacker cannot have M, that is, M is secret. Even if derivability is undecidable in general, several techniques can be used to determine whether a fact is derivable from a set of clauses. However, the simplest techniques, such as SLD-resolution used in Prolog, would never terminate. (For example, the clause for decryption given above immediately leads to a loop.) More elaborate resolution techniques succeed in this task:

- Ordered resolution with selection has been used in [179] and is implemented in the theorem prover SPASS (http://www.spass-prover.org/).
- Ordered resolution with factorization and splitting terminates on protocols that blindly copy at most one message at each step [84]. (This class of protocols results in clauses with at most one variable.)
- ProVerif uses resolution with free selection (without ordering) [18]. This strategy terminates on *tagged protocols* [58]: in these protocols, each application of a cryptographic primitive is distinguished from others by a constant (the tag). For example, we use enc($(c_0, m), k$) for encrypting m under k, instead of enc(m, k). It is easy to add tags, and it is also a good design practice: it can make protocols more secure, in particular by avoiding type flaw attacks [133]. When we verify a tagged protocol, the implemented protocol should of course also be tagged, since the security proof for the tagged protocol does not imply the security of a non-tagged version. A key to obtain termination is to avoid resolving on facts of the form attacker(x). Indeed, these facts resolve with all facts of the form attacker(M), which leads to non-termination in almost all examples coming from protocols.

These three techniques terminate on numerous practical examples, even outside the decision classes mentioned above.

In case attacker(M) is derivable from the representation of the protocol, ProVerif cannot prove secrecy. In this case, ProVerif uses the derivation of attacker(M) to reconstruct an attack automatically [13]. (Such a reconstruction fails if a false attack has been found.)

We have extended this technique to more complex security properties:

– ProVerif can verify complex non-injective and injective correspondence properties [53], which can in particular model authentication.
– It can also verify a limited class of process equivalences: it verifies a strong equivalence between processes that have the same structure, but differ only by the terms they contain [55] (named diff-equivalence in [36]). This equivalence is useful, for instance to prove strong secrecy [49] and to detect guessing attacks against password-based protocols. ProVerif is so far the only tool that can prove process equivalences for an unbounded number of sessions.

Using our tool, we verified numerous protocols from the literature, finding known attacks or proving the correctness of the protocols. Most examples were verified in less than 0.1 s [53]. We also used ProVerif for verifying a certified email protocol [3], the protocol JFK (a proposed replacement for the key exchange protocol of IPsec) [4], and the cryptographic filesystem Plutus [56]. ProVerif was also used by other authors, for instance for verifying Web services, by translating XML protocols to ProVerif using the tool TulaFale [47, 150], e-voting protocols [21, 105, 139], zero-knowledge protocols [23], RFID protocols [69], and the TPM (Trusted Platform Module) [75, 106]. An extension was proposed for supporting protocols with mutable global state [15]. ProVerif can be downloaded at http://www.proverif.ens.fr/.

3   Verifying Protocols in the Computational Model

Proving protocols automatically in the computational model is much more difficult than in the symbolic model. Still, much research tackled this task. This section presents these approaches.

3.1   Computational Soundness

An attack in the symbolic model directly leads to an attack in the computational model. However, the converse is not true in general: a protocol may be proved secure in symbolic model and still be subject to attacks in the computational model. Following the seminal work by Abadi and Rogaway [8], many computational soundness results have been proved. These results show that, modulo additional assumptions, if a protocol is secure in the symbolic model, then it is also secure in the computational model. They provide a way of obtaining automatic proofs of protocols in the computational model, by first proving them in the symbolic model, then applying a computational soundness theorem. Some work following this line follows.

– Abadi and Rogaway [8] showed that, if two messages are indistinguishable in the symbolic sense, then they are also indistinguishable in the computational sense, if the only primitive is shared-key encryption, assuming a few additional technical restrictions.

– This initial result was followed by considerable extensions. In particular, Micciancio and Warinschi [152] showed that states and traces in the computational model match (up to negligible probability) states and traces in the symbolic model, for public-key encryption in the presence of an active adversary. Therefore, authentication in the symbolic model implies authentication in the computational model. This result was further extended to signatures [93, 136], hash functions [90, 137], non-malleable commitment [122], and zero-knowledge proofs [29]. Cortier and Warinschi [93] also showed that syntactic secrecy in the symbolic model implies secrecy in the computational model for nonces. A tool [89] was built based on [93] to obtain computational proofs using the symbolic verifier AVISPA, for protocols that use public-key encryption and signatures.

   While the previous results dealt with traces, Comon and Cortier showed a computational soundness result for observational equivalence, for protocols that use authenticated shared-key encryption [86].

   These results consider a fixed protocol language and a few primitives at a time, limiting the scope of the results. Frameworks were designed to make computational soundness proofs modular, by encoding many input languages into one [20, 24] and by allowing to compose proofs obtained independently for several primitives [94].

– Backes, Pfitzmann, and Waidner [25–27] developed an abstract cryptographic library including authenticated shared-encryption, public-key encryption, message authentication codes, signatures, and nonces, and have shown its soundness with respect to computational primitives, under arbitrary active attacks. This work relates the computational model to a non-standard version of the Dolev-Yao model, in which the length of messages is present. It has been used for a proof of the Needham-Schroeder protocol fixed by Lowe [148] verified in a proof assistant [176].

– Canetti and Herzog [72] showed how a symbolic analysis in the style of the Dolev-Yao model can be used to prove security properties of protocols in the framework of universal composability [71] for a restricted class of protocols that use only public-key encryption. They then use ProVerif [49] to verify protocols in this framework.

We refer the reader to [91] for a more detailed survey of computational soundness results. This approach enjoyed important successes, but also has limitations: additional hypotheses are necessary, since the two models do not match exactly. The cryptographic primitives need to satisfy strong security properties so that they match the symbolic primitives. For instance, encryption has to hide the length of messages, or the symbolic model must be modified to take into that length. These results often assume that all keys (even those of the adversary) are generated by the correct key generation algorithm. Moreover, the protocols need to satisfy certain restrictions. Indeed, for shared-key encryption, there must be no key cycle (in which a key is encrypted directly or indirectly under itself, as in $\{k\}_k$ or $\{k\}_{k'}, \{k'\}_k$) or a specific definition of security of encryption is necessary [10, 28]. (The existence of key cycles for a bounded number of sessions is a NP-complete problem [95].) These limitations have lead to the idea of directly automating proofs in the computational model.

3.2   Adapting Techniques from the Symbolic Model

Another way of proving protocols in the computational model is to adapt techniques previously designed for the symbolic model.

For instance, the logic PCL [101, 116], first designed for proving protocols in the Dolev-Yao model, was adapted to the computational model [102, 103]. Other computationally sound logics include CIL (Computational Indistinguishability Logic) [30] and a specialized Hoare logic designed for proving asymmetric encryption schemes in the random oracle model [96, 97].

Similarly, type systems [98, 144, 146, 173] can provide computational security guarantees. For instance, [144] handles shared-key and public-key encryption, with an unbounded number of sessions. This system relies on the Backes-Pfitzmann-Waidner library. A type inference algorithm is given in [22].

3.3   Direct Computational Proofs

Finally, the direct approach to computational proofs consists in mechanizing proofs in the computational model, without relying at all on the symbolic model. Computational proofs made by cryptographers are typically presented as sequences of games [42, 172]: the initial game represents the protocol to prove; the goal is to show that the probability of breaking a certain security property is negligible in this game. Intermediate games are obtained each from the previous one by transformations such that the difference of probability between consecutive games is negligible. The final game is such that the desired probability is obviously negligible from the form of the game. The desired probability is then negligible in the initial game. Halevi [132] suggested to use tools for mechanizing these proofs, and several techniques have been used for reaching this goal.

CryptoVerif [51,52,57,59], which we have designed, is the first such tool. It generates proofs by sequences of games automatically or with little user interaction. The games are formalized in a probabilistic process calculus. CryptoVerif provides a generic method for specifying security properties of many cryptographic primitives. It proves secrecy and authentication properties. It also provides a bound on the probability of success of an attack. It considerably extends early work by Laud [142, 143] which was limited either to passive adversaries or to a single session of the protocol. More recently, Tšahhirov and Laud [145, 178] developed a tool similar to CryptoVerif but that represents games by dependency graphs; it handles public-key and shared-key encryption and proves secrecy properties.

The CertiCrypt framework [31,32,34,37,38] enables the machine-checked construction and verification of cryptographic proofs by sequences of games. It relies on the general-purpose proof assistant Coq, which is widely believed to be correct. EasyCrypt [33] generates CertiCrypt proofs from proof sketches that formally represent the sequence of games and hints, which makes the tool easier to use. Nowak et al. [11, 162, 163] follow a similar idea by providing Coq proofs for several basic cryptographic primitives.

4   Verifying Protocol Implementations

The approaches mentioned so far verify specifications of protocols in models such as the applied pi calculus or its variants. However, errors may be introduced when the protocol is implemented. It is therefore important to prove security properties on the implementation of the protocol itself. Two approaches to reach this goal can be distinguished.

A simple approach consists in translating the model into an implementation by a suitable compiler which has been proved correct. This approach was used in tools such as [153, 166, 168, 174]. A limitation of this approach is that the protocol modeling language offers less flexibility in the implementation of the protocol than a standard programming language.

A more flexible, but more difficult, approach consists in analyzing the implementation of the protocol. Results in this approach differ by the input language they consider. Analyzing C code is obviously more difficult than analyzing languages such as F# and Java, in particular due to pointers and memory safety. However, it allows one to verify practical implementations, which are generally written in C. We can also distinguish two ways of analyzing implementations:

– One can extract a protocol specification from the implementation, and verify it using existing protocol verification tools. For instance, the tools FS2PV [46] and FS2CV [121] translate protocols written in a subset of the functional language F# into the input language of ProVerif and CryptoVerif, respectively, so that protocol can be proved in the symbolic model and in the computational model. These techniques were applied to an important case study: the protocol TLS [44]. They analyze reference implementations written in F# in order to facilitate verification; one verifies that these implementations interoperate with other implementations, which provides some assurance that they match practical implementations; however, it is very difficult to analyze the code of implementations written without verification in mind.

  Similarly, Elijah [164] translates Java programs into LySa protocol specifications, which can be verified by the LySatool [60].

  Aizatulin et al. [12] use symbolic execution in order to extract ProVerif models from pre-existing protocol implementations in C. This technique currently analyzes a single execution path of the protocol, so it is limited to protocols without branching. Furthermore, computational security guarantees are obtained by applying a computational soundness result.

– One can also adapt protocol verification methods to the verification of implementations or design new methods for verifying implementations. The tool CSur [131] analyzes protocols written in C by translating them into Horn clauses, yielding a model fairly similar to the one used in ProVerif. These clauses are given as input to the $\mathcal{H}_1$ prover [130] to prove properties of the protocol. Similarly, JavaSec [138] translates Java programs into first-order logic formulas, which are then given as input to the first-order theorem prover e-SETHEO.

The tools F7 and F* [43, 45, 177] use a dependent type system in order to prove security properties of protocols implemented in F#, therefore extending to implementations the approach of Cryptyc [126–128] for models. This approach scales well to large implementations but requires type annotations, which facilitate automatic verification. This approach is also being extended to the computational model [120]: one uses a type system to verify the conditions needed in order to apply a game transformation. Then, the game transformation is applied, and the obtained game is typed again, with a different typing judgment, to justify the next game transformation, and transformations can continue in this way until security can be proved directly by inspecting the game.

Poll and Schubert [167] verified an implementation of SSH in Java using ESC/Java2: ESC/Java2 verifies that the implementation does not raise exceptions, and follows a specification of SSH by a finite automaton, but does not prove security properties.

ASPIER [74] uses software model-checking, with predicate abstraction and counter-example guided abstraction refinement, in order to verify C implementations of protocols, assuming the size of messages and the number of sessions are bounded. In particular, this tool has been used to verify the main loop of OpenSSL 3. Dupressoir et al. [112] use the general-purpose C verifier VCC in order to prove both memory safety and security properties of protocols, in the symbolic model. They use "ghost state" in order to relate C variables and symbolic terms.

5   Conclusion and Future Challenges

This survey shows that research in the field of security protocol verification has been very active, and has enjoyed unquestionable successes. Progress has been made in all directions: verification both in the symbolic model and in the computational model, as well as verification of implementations. We believe that the verification of protocols in the symbolic model has reached a fairly mature state, even though some aspects still need further research, for instance the proof of process equivalences or the treatment of some complex equational theories. However, there is still much work to do regarding the verification of protocols in the computational model and the verification of implementations. We are still far from having a push button tool that would take as input a practical implementation of the protocol and would prove it secure in the computational model. Even if this goal may be out of reach, more progress is undoubtedly possible in this direction. Taking into account physical attacks is a challenging area in which formal methods just start to be used, and in which much research will certainly be done in the future.

Acknowledgments. We thank Pierpaolo Degano for helpful comments on a draft of this paper. Sect. 2.2 is updated from [48]. This work was partly supported by the ANR project ProSe (decision ANR-2010-VERS-004-01).

References

1. Abadi, M.: Secrecy by typing in security protocols. Journal of the ACM 46(5), 749–786 (1999)
2. Abadi, M., Blanchet, B.: Analyzing security protocols with secrecy types and logic programs. Journal of the ACM 52(1), 102–146 (2005)
3. Abadi, M., Blanchet, B.: Computer-assisted verification of a protocol for certified email. Science of Computer Programming 58(1-2), 3–27 (2005)
4. Abadi, M., Blanchet, B., Fournet, C.: Just Fast Keying in the pi calculus. ACM TISSEC 10(3), 1–59 (2007)
5. Abadi, M., Fournet, C.: Mobile values, new names, and secure communication. In: POPL 2001, pp. 104–115. ACM, New York (2001)
6. Abadi, M., Gordon, A.D.: A bisimulation method for cryptographic protocols. Nordic Journal of Computing 5(4), 267–303 (1998)
7. Abadi, M., Gordon, A.D.: A calculus for cryptographic protocols: The spi calculus. Information and Computation 148(1), 1–70 (1999)
8. Abadi, M., Rogaway, P.: Reconciling two views of cryptography (the computational soundness of formal encryption). Journal of Cryptology 15(2), 103–127 (2002)
9. Abdalla, M., Fouque, P.A., Pointcheval, D.: Password-based authenticated key exchange in the three-party setting. IEE Proceedings Information Security 153(1), 27–39 (2006)
10. Adão, P., Bana, G., Herzog, J., Scedrov, A.: Soundness of Formal Encryption in the Presence of Key-Cycles. In: de Capitani di Vimercati, S., Syverson, P., Gollmann, D. (eds.) ESORICS 2005. LNCS, vol. 3679, pp. 374–396. Springer, Heidelberg (2005)
11. Affeldt, R., Nowak, D., Yamada, K.: Certifying assembly with formal cryptographic proofs: the case of BBS. In: AVoCS 2009. Electronic Communications of the EASST, vol. 23. EASST (2009)
12. Aizatulin, M., Gordon, A.D., Jürjens, J.: Extracting and verifying cryptographic models from C protocol code by symbolic execution. In: CCS 2011, pp. 331–340. ACM, New York (2011)
13. Allamigeon, X., Blanchet, B.: Reconstruction of attacks against cryptographic protocols. In: CSFW 2005, pp. 140–154. IEEE, Los Alamitos (2005)
14. Arapinis, M., Duflot, M.: Bounding Messages for Free in Security Protocols. In: Arvind, V., Prasad, S. (eds.) FSTTCS 2007. LNCS, vol. 4855, pp. 376–387. Springer, Heidelberg (2007)
15. Arapinis, M., Ritter, E., Ryan, M.D.: StatVerif: Verification of stateful processes. In: CSF 2011, pp. 33–47. IEEE, Los Alamitos (2011)
16. Armando, A., Compagna, L., Ganty, P.: SAT-Based Model-Checking of Security Protocols Using Planning Graph Analysis. In: Araki, K., Gnesi, S., Mandrioli, D. (eds.) FME 2003. LNCS, vol. 2805, pp. 875–893. Springer, Heidelberg (2003)

17. Armando, A., Basin, D., Boichut, Y., Chevalier, Y., Compagna, L., Cuellar, J., Drielsma, P.H., Heám, P.C., Kouchnarenko, O., Mantovani, J., Mödersheim, S., von Oheimb, D., Rusinowitch, M., Santiago, J., Turuani, M., Viganò, L., Vigneron, L.: The AVISPA Tool for the Automated Validation of Internet Security Protocols and Applications. In: Etessami, K., Rajamani, S.K. (eds.) CAV 2005. LNCS, vol. 3576, pp. 281–285. Springer, Heidelberg (2005)

18. Bachmair, L., Ganzinger, H.: Resolution theorem proving. In: Handbook of Automated Reasoning, vol. 1, ch. 2, pp. 19–100. North-Holland (2001)

19. Backes, M., Cortesi, A., Maffei, M.: Causality-based abstraction of multiplicity in security protocols. In: CSF 2007, pp. 355–369. IEEE, Los Alamitos (2007)

20. Backes, M., Hofheinz, D., Unruh, D.: CoSP: A general framework for computational soundness proofs. In: CCS 2009, pp. 66–78. ACM, New York (2009)

21. Backes, M., Hritcu, C., Maffei, M.: Automated verification of remote electronic voting protocols in the applied pi-calculus. In: CSF 2008, pp. 195–209. IEEE, Los Alamitos (2008)

22. Backes, M., Laud, P.: Computationally sound secrecy proofs by mechanized flow analysis. In: CCS 2006, pp. 370–379. ACM, New York (2006)

23. Backes, M., Maffei, M., Unruh, D.: Zero-knowledge in the applied pi-calculus and automated verification of the direct anonymous attestation protocol. In: IEEE Symposium on Security and Privacy, pp. 202–215. IEEE, Los Alamitos (2008)

24. Backes, M., Maffei, M., Unruh, D.: Computationally sound verification of source code. In: CCS 2010, pp. 387–398. ACM, New York (2010)

25. Backes, M., Pfitzmann, B.: Symmetric encryption in a simulatable Dolev-Yao style cryptographic library. In: CSFW 2004, pp. 204–218. IEEE, Los Alamitos (2004)

26. Backes, M., Pfitzmann, B.: Relating symbolic and cryptographic secrecy. IEEE Transactions on Dependable and Secure Computing 2(2), 109–123 (2005)

27. Backes, M., Pfitzmann, B., Waidner, M.: A composable cryptographic library with nested operations. In: CCS 2003, pp. 220–230. ACM, New York (2003)

28. Backes, M., Pfiztmann, B., Scedrov, A.: Key-dependent message security under active attacks—BRSIM/UC soundness of symbolic encryption with key cycles. In: CSF 2007, pp. 112–124. IEEE, Los Alamitos (2007)

29. Backes, M., Unruh, D.: Computational soundness of symbolic zero-knowledge proofs against active attackers. In: CSF 2008, pp. 255–269. IEEE, Los Alamitos (2008)

30. Barthe, G., Daubignard, M., Kapron, B., Lakhnech, Y.: Computational indistinguishability logic. In: CCS 2010, pp. 375–386. ACM, New York (2010)

31. Barthe, G., Grégoire, B., Lakhnech, Y., Zanella Béguelin, S.: Beyond Provable Security Verifiable IND-CCA Security of OAEP. In: Kiayias, A. (ed.) CT-RSA 2011. LNCS, vol. 6558, pp. 180–196. Springer, Heidelberg (2011)

32. Barthe, G., Grégoire, B., Heraud, S., Zanella Béguelin, S.: Formal Certification of ElGamal Encryption. A Gentle Introduction to CertiCrypt. In: Degano, P., Guttman, J., Martinelli, F. (eds.) FAST 2008. LNCS, vol. 5491, pp. 1–19. Springer, Heidelberg (2009)

33. Barthe, G., Grégoire, B., Heraud, S., Béguelin, S.Z.: Computer-Aided Security Proofs for the Working Cryptographer. In: Rogaway, P. (ed.) CRYPTO 2011. LNCS, vol. 6841, pp. 71–90. Springer, Heidelberg (2011)

34. Barthe, G., Grégoire, B., Zanella, S.: Formal certification of code-based cryptographic proofs. In: POPL 2009, pp. 90–101. ACM, New York (2009)

35. Basin, D., Mödersheim, S., Viganò, L.: An On-the-Fly Model-Checker for Security Protocol Analysis. In: Snekkenes, E., Gollmann, D. (eds.) ESORICS 2003. LNCS, vol. 2808, pp. 253–270. Springer, Heidelberg (2003)

36. Baudet, M.: Sécurité des protocoles cryptographiques: aspects logiques et calculatoires. Ph.D. thesis, Ecole Normale Supérieure de Cachan (2007)

37. Béguelin, S.Z., Barthe, G., Heraud, S., Grégoire, B., Hedin, D.: A machine-checked formalization of sigma-protocols. In: CSF 2010, pp. 246–260. IEEE, Los Alamitos (2010)

38. Béguelin, S.Z., Grégoire, B., Barthe, G., Olmedo, F.: Formally certifying the security of digital signature schemes. In: IEEE Symposium on Security and Privacy, pp. 237–250. IEEE, Los Alamitos (2009)

39. Bellare, M., Desai, A., Jokipii, E., Rogaway, P.: A concrete security treatment of symmetric encryption. In: FOCS 1997, pp. 394–403. IEEE, Los Alamitos (1997)

40. Bellare, M., Pointcheval, D., Rogaway, P.: Authenticated Key Exchange Secure against Dictionary Attacks. In: Preneel, B. (ed.) EUROCRYPT 2000. LNCS, vol. 1807, pp. 139–155. Springer, Heidelberg (2000)

41. Bellare, M., Rogaway, P.: Entity Authentication and Key Distribution. In: Stinson, D.R. (ed.) CRYPTO 1993. LNCS, vol. 773, pp. 232–249. Springer, Heidelberg (1994)

42. Bellare, M., Rogaway, P.: The Security of Triple Encryption and a Framework for Code-Based Game-Playing Proofs. In: Vaudenay, S. (ed.) EUROCRYPT 2006. LNCS, vol. 4004, pp. 409–426. Springer, Heidelberg (2006)

43. Bengtson, J., Bhargavan, K., Fournet, C., Gordon, A., Maffeis, S.: Refinement types for secure implementations. ACM TOPLAS 33(2) (2011)

44. Bhargavan, K., Corin, R., Fournet, C., Zălinescu, E.: Cryptographically verified implementations for TLS. In: CCS 2008, pp. 459–468. ACM, New York (2008)

45. Bhargavan, K., Fournet, C., Gordon, A.: Modular verification of security protocol code by typing. In: POPL 2010, pp. 445–456. ACM, New York (2010)

46. Bhargavan, K., Fournet, C., Gordon, A., Tse, S.: Verified interoperable implementations of security protocols. ACM TOPLAS 31(1) (2008)

47. Bhargavan, K., Fournet, C., Gordon, A.D., Pucella, R.: TulaFale: A Security Tool for Web Services. In: de Boer, F.S., Bonsangue, M.M., Graf, S., de Roever, W.-P. (eds.) FMCO 2003. LNCS, vol. 3188, pp. 197–222. Springer, Heidelberg (2004)

48. Blanchet, B.: Automatic verification of cryptographic protocols: A logic programming approach. In: PPDP 2003, pp. 1–3. ACM, New York (2003)

49. Blanchet, B.: Automatic proof of strong secrecy for security protocols. In: IEEE Symposium on Security and Privacy, pp. 86–100. IEEE, Los Alamitos (2004)

50. Blanchet, B.: Security protocols: From linear to classical logic by abstract interpretation. Information Processing Letters 95(5), 473–479 (2005)

51. Blanchet, B.: Computationally sound mechanized proofs of correspondence assertions. In: CSF 2007, pp. 97–111. IEEE, Los Alamitos (2007)

52. Blanchet, B.: A computationally sound mechanized prover for security protocols. IEEE Transactions on Dependable and Secure Computing 5(4), 193–207 (2008)

53. Blanchet, B.: Automatic verification of correspondences for security protocols. Journal of Computer Security 17(4), 363–434 (2009)

54. Blanchet, B.: Using Horn clauses for analyzing security protocols. In: Cortier, V., Kremer, S. (eds.) Formal Models and Techniques for Analyzing Security Protocols. Cryptology and Information Security Series, vol. 5, pp. 86–111. IOS Press, Amsterdam (2011)

55. Blanchet, B., Abadi, M., Fournet, C.: Automated verification of selected equivalences for security protocols. Journal of Logic and Algebraic Programming 75(1), 3–51 (2008)
56. Blanchet, B., Chaudhuri, A.: Automated formal analysis of a protocol for secure file sharing on untrusted storage. In: IEEE Symposium on Security and Privacy, pp. 417–431. IEEE, Los Alamitos (2008)
57. Blanchet, B., Jaggard, A.D., Scedrov, A., Tsay, J.K.: Computationally sound mechanized proofs for basic and public-key Kerberos. In: ASIACCS 2008, pp. 87–99. ACM, New York (2008)
58. Blanchet, B., Podelski, A.: Verification of cryptographic protocols: Tagging enforces termination. Theoretical Computer Science 333(1-2), 67–90 (2005)
59. Blanchet, B., Pointcheval, D.: Automated Security Proofs with Sequences of Games. In: Dwork, C. (ed.) CRYPTO 2006. LNCS, vol. 4117, pp. 537–554. Springer, Heidelberg (2006)
60. Bodei, C., Buchholtz, M., Degano, P., Nielson, F., Nielson, H.R.: Automatic validation of protocol narration. In: CSFW 2003, pp. 126–140. IEEE, Los Alamitos (2003)
61. Bodei, C., Buchholtz, M., Degano, P., Nielson, F., Nielson, H.R.: Static validation of security protocols. Journal of Computer Security 13(3), 347–390 (2005)
62. Bodei, C., Degano, P., Nielson, F., Nielson, H.R.: Flow logic for Dolev-Yao secrecy in cryptographic processes. Future Generation Comp. Syst. 18(6), 747–756 (2002)
63. Boichut, Y., Kosmatov, N., Vigneron, L.: Validation of Prouvé protocols using the automatic tool TA4SP. In: TFIT 2006, pp. 467–480 (2006)
64. Bolignano, D.: Towards a Mechanization of Cryptographic Protocol Verification. In: Grumberg, O. (ed.) CAV 1997. LNCS, vol. 1254, pp. 131–142. Springer, Heidelberg (1997)
65. Borgström, J., Briais, S., Nestmann, U.: Symbolic Bisimulation in the Spi Calculus. In: Gardner, P., Yoshida, N. (eds.) CONCUR 2004. LNCS, vol. 3170, pp. 161–176. Springer, Heidelberg (2004)
66. Bozga, L., Lakhnech, Y., Périn, M.: Pattern-based abstraction for verifying secrecy in protocols. International Journal on Software Tools for Technology Transfer (STTT) 8(1), 57–76 (2006)
67. Broadfoot, P.J., Roscoe, A.W.: Embedding agents within the intruder to detect parallel attacks. Journal of Computer Security 12(3/4), 379–408 (2004)
68. Broadfoot, P., Lowe, G., Roscoe, B.: Automating Data Independence. In: Cuppens, F., Deswarte, Y., Gollmann, D., Waidner, M. (eds.) ESORICS 2000. LNCS, vol. 1895, pp. 175–190. Springer, Heidelberg (2000)
69. Brusó, M., Chatzikokolakis, K., den Hartog, J.: Formal verification of privacy for RFID systems. In: CSF 2010, pp. 75–88. IEEE, Los Alamitos (2010)
70. Burrows, M., Abadi, M., Needham, R.: A logic of authentication. Proceedings of the Royal Society of London A 426(1871), 233–271 (1989)
71. Canetti, R.: Universally composable security: A new paradigm for cryptographic protocols. In: FOCS 2001, pp. 136–145. IEEE, Los Alamitos (2001)
72. Canetti, R., Herzog, J.: Universally Composable Symbolic Analysis of Mutual Authentication and Key-Exchange Protocols. In: Halevi, S., Rabin, T. (eds.) TCC 2006. LNCS, vol. 3876, pp. 380–403. Springer, Heidelberg (2006)
73. Cervesato, I., Durgin, N., Lincoln, P., Mitchell, J., Scedrov, A.: A meta-notation for protocol analysis. In: CSFW 1999, pp. 55–69. IEEE, Los Alamitos (1999)
74. Chaki, S., Datta, A.: ASPIER: An automated framework for verifying security protocol implementations. In: CSF 2009, pp. 172–185. IEEE, Los Alamitos (2009)

75. Chen, L., Ryan, M.: Attack, Solution and Verification for Shared Authorisation Data in TCG TPM. In: Degano, P., Guttman, J.D. (eds.) FAST 2009. LNCS, vol. 5983, pp. 201–216. Springer, Heidelberg (2010)
76. Cheval, V., Comon-Lundh, H., Delaune, S.: Automating Security Analysis: Symbolic Equivalence of Constraint Systems. In: Giesl, J., Hähnle, R. (eds.) IJCAR 2010. LNCS (LNAI), vol. 6173, pp. 412–426. Springer, Heidelberg (2010)
77. Cheval, V., Comon-Lundh, H., Delaune, S.: Trace equivalence decision: Negative tests and non-determinism. In: CCS 2011, pp. 321–330. ACM, New York (2011)
78. Chevalier, Y., Küsters, R., Rusinowitch, M., Turuani, M.: Deciding the Security of Protocols with Diffie-Hellman Exponentiation and Products in Exponents. In: Pandya, P.K., Radhakrishnan, J. (eds.) FSTTCS 2003. LNCS, vol. 2914, pp. 124–135. Springer, Heidelberg (2003)
79. Chevalier, Y., Küsters, R., Rusinowitch, M., Turuani, M.: An NP decision procedure for protocol insecurity with XOR. In: LICS 2003, pp. 261–270. IEEE, Los Alamitos (2003)
80. Chevalier, Y., Küsters, R., Rusinowitch, M., Turuani, M.: An NP decision procedure for protocol insecurity with XOR. Theoretical Computer Science 338(1-3), 247–274 (2005)
81. Chevalier, Y., Vigneron, L.: A tool for lazy verification of security protocols. In: ASE 2001, pp. 373–376. IEEE, Los Alamitos (2001)
82. Ciobâcă, Ş.: Automated Verification of Security Protocols with Appplications to Electronic Voting. Ph.D. thesis, ENS Cachan (2011)
83. Comon, H., Cortier, V.: Tree automata with one memory, set constraints and cryptographic protocols. Theoretical Computer Science 331(1), 143–214 (2005)
84. Comon-Lundh, H., Cortier, V.: New Decidability Results for Fragments of First-Order Logic and Application to Cryptographic Protocols. In: Nieuwenhuis, R. (ed.) RTA 2003. LNCS, vol. 2706, pp. 148–164. Springer, Heidelberg (2003)
85. Comon-Lundh, H., Cortier, V.: Security properties: two agents are sufficient. Science of Computer Programming 50(1-3), 51–71 (2004)
86. Comon-Lundh, H., Cortier, V.: Computational soundness of observational equivalence. In: CCS 2008, pp. 109–118. ACM, New York (2008)
87. Comon-Lundh, H., Shmatikov, V.: Intruder deductions, constraint solving and insecurity decision in presence of exclusive or. In: LICS 2003, pp. 271–280. IEEE, Los Alamitos (2003)
88. Cortier, V., Delaune, S.: A method for proving observational equivalence. In: CSF 2009, pp. 266–276. IEEE, Los Alamitos (2009)
89. Cortier, V., Hördegen, H., Warinschi, B.: Explicit randomness is not necessary when modeling probabilistic encryption. In: Dima, C., Minea, M., Tiplea, F. (eds.) ICS 2006. ENTCS, vol. 186, pp. 49–65. Elsevier, Amsterdam (2006)
90. Cortier, V., Kremer, S., Küsters, R., Warinschi, B.: Computationally Sound Symbolic Secrecy in the Presence of Hash Functions. In: Arun-Kumar, S., Garg, N. (eds.) FSTTCS 2006. LNCS, vol. 4337, pp. 176–187. Springer, Heidelberg (2006)
91. Cortier, V., Kremer, S., Warinschi, B.: A survey of symbolic methods in computational analysis of cryptographic systems. Journal of Automated Reasoning 46(3-4), 225–259 (2011)
92. Cortier, V., Rusinowitch, M., Zălinescu, E.: Relating two standard notions of secrecy. Logical Methods in Computer Science 3(3) (2007)
93. Cortier, V., Warinschi, B.: Computationally Sound, Automated Proofs for Security Protocols. In: Sagiv, M. (ed.) ESOP 2005. LNCS, vol. 3444, pp. 157–171. Springer, Heidelberg (2005)

94. Cortier, V., Warinschi, B.: A composable computational soundness notion. In: CCS 2011, pp. 63–74. ACM, New York (2011)
95. Cortier, V., Zălinescu, E.: Deciding Key Cycles for Security Protocols. In: Hermann, M., Voronkov, A. (eds.) LPAR 2006. LNCS (LNAI), vol. 4246, pp. 317–331. Springer, Heidelberg (2006)
96. Courant, J., Daubignard, M., Ene, C., Lafourcade, P., Lakhnech, Y.: Towards automated proofs for asymmetric encryption schemes in the random oracle model. In: CCS 2008, pp. 371–380. ACM, New York (2008)
97. Courant, J., Daubignard, M., Ene, C., Lafourcade, P., Lakhnech, Y.: Automated Proofs for Asymmetric Encryption. In: Dams, D., Hannemann, U., Steffen, M. (eds.) de Roever Festschrift. LNCS, vol. 5930, pp. 300–321. Springer, Heidelberg (2010)
98. Courant, J., Ene, C., Lakhnech, Y.: Computationally Sound Typing for Noninterference: The Case of Deterministic Encryption. In: Arvind, V., Prasad, S. (eds.) FSTTCS 2007. LNCS, vol. 4855, pp. 364–375. Springer, Heidelberg (2007)
99. Cousot, P., Cousot, R.: Systematic design of program analysis frameworks. In: POPL 1979, pp. 269–282. ACM, New York (1979)
100. Cremers, C.J.F.: Scyther - Semantics and Verification of Security Protocols. Ph.D. thesis, Eindhoven University of Technology (2006)
101. Datta, A., Derek, A., Mitchell, J.C., Pavlovic, D.: A derivation system and compositional logic for security protocols. Journal of Computer Security 13(3), 423–482 (2005)
102. Datta, A., Derek, A., Mitchell, J.C., Turuani, M.: Probabilistic Polynomial-Time Semantics for a Protocol Security Logic. In: Caires, L., Italiano, G.F., Monteiro, L., Palamidessi, C., Yung, M. (eds.) ICALP 2005. LNCS, vol. 3580, pp. 16–29. Springer, Heidelberg (2005)
103. Datta, A., Derek, A., Mitchell, J.C., Warinschi, B.: Computationally sound compositional logic for key exchange protocols. In: CSFW 2006, pp. 321–334. IEEE, Los Alamitos (2006)
104. Delaune, S., Kremer, S., Ryan, M.D.: Symbolic Bisimulation for the Applied Pi Calculus. In: Arvind, V., Prasad, S. (eds.) FSTTCS 2007. LNCS, vol. 4855, pp. 133–145. Springer, Heidelberg (2007)
105. Delaune, S., Kremer, S., Ryan, M.D.: Verifying privacy-type properties of electronic voting protocols. Journal of Computer Security 17(4), 435–487 (2009)
106. Delaune, S., Kremer, S., Ryan, M.D., Steel, G.: Formal analysis of protocols based on TPM state registers. In: CSF 2011, pp. 66–82. IEEE, Los Alamitos (2011)
107. Denker, G., Meseguer, J., Talcott, C.: Protocol specification and analysis in Maude. In: FMSP 1998 (1998)
108. Denker, G., Millen, J.: CAPSL integrated protocol environment. In: DISCEX 2000, pp. 207–221. IEEE, Los Alamitos (2000)
109. Denning, D.E., Sacco, G.M.: Timestamps in key distribution protocols. Commun. ACM 24(8), 533–536 (1981)
110. Dierks, T., Rescorla, E.: RFC 4346: The Transport Layer Security (TLS) protocol, version 1.1 (2006), http://tools.ietf.org/html/rfc4346
111. Dolev, D., Yao, A.C.: On the security of public key protocols. IEEE Transactions on Information Theory IT-29(12), 198–208 (1983)
112. Dupressoir, F., Gordon, A.D., Jürjens, J., Naumann, D.A.: Guiding a general-purpose C verifier to prove cryptographic protocols. In: CSF 2011, pp. 3–17. IEEE, Los Alamitos (2011)
113. Durante, L., Sisto, R., Valenzano, A.: Automatic testing equivalence verification of spi calculus specifications. ACM TOSEM 12(2), 222–284 (2003)

114. Durgin, N.A., Lincoln, P.D., Mitchell, J.C., Scedrov, A.: Undecidability of bounded security protocols. In: FMSP 1999 (1999)
115. Durgin, N., Lincoln, P., Mitchell, J.C., Scedrov, A.: Multiset rewriting and the complexity of bounded security protocols. Journal of Computer Security 12(2), 247–311 (2004)
116. Durgin, N., Mitchell, J.C., Pavlovic, D.: A compositional logic for proving security properties of protocols. Journal of Computer Security 11(4), 677–721 (2003)
117. Escobar, S., Meadows, C., Meseguer, J.: A rewriting-based inference system for the NRL protocol analyzer and its meta-logical properties. Theoretical Computer Science 367(1-2), 162–202 (2006)
118. Fábrega, F.J.T., Herzog, J.C., Guttman, J.D.: Strand spaces: Proving security protocols correct. Journal of Computer Security 7(2/3), 191–230 (1999)
119. Feret, J.: Analysis of mobile systems by abstract interpretation. Ph.D. thesis, École Polytechnique (2005)
120. Fournet, C., Kohlweiss, M.: Modular cryptographic verification by typing. In: FCC 2011 (2011)
121. http://msr-inria.inria.fr/projects/sec/fs2cv/
122. Galindo, D., Garcia, F.D., van Rossum, P.: Computational Soundness of Non-Malleable Commitments. In: Chen, L., Mu, Y., Susilo, W. (eds.) ISPEC 2008. LNCS, vol. 4991, pp. 361–376. Springer, Heidelberg (2008)
123. Genet, T., Klay, F.: Rewriting for Cryptographic Protocol Verification. In: McAllester, D. (ed.) CADE 2000. LNCS, vol. 1831, pp. 271–290. Springer, Heidelberg (2000)
124. Goldwasser, S., Micali, S.: Probabilistic encryption. Journal of Computer and System Sciences 28, 270–299 (1984)
125. Goldwasser, S., Micali, S., Rivest, R.: A digital signature scheme secure against adaptative chosen-message attacks. SIAM Journal of Computing 17(2), 281–308 (1988)
126. Gordon, A.D., Jeffrey, A.: Typing One-to-One and One-to-Many Correspondences in Security Protocols. In: Okada, M., Babu, C.S., Scedrov, A., Tokuda, H. (eds.) ISSS 2002. LNCS, vol. 2609, pp. 263–282. Springer, Heidelberg (2003)
127. Gordon, A., Jeffrey, A.: Authenticity by typing for security protocols. Journal of Computer Security 11(4), 451–521 (2003)
128. Gordon, A., Jeffrey, A.: Types and effects for asymmetric cryptographic protocols. Journal of Computer Security 12(3/4), 435–484 (2004)
129. Goubault-Larrecq, J.: A Method for Automatic Cryptographic Protocol Verification (Extended Abstract). In: Rolim, J.D.P. (ed.) IPDPS 2000 Workshops. LNCS, vol. 1800, pp. 977–984. Springer, Heidelberg (2000)
130. Goubault-Larrecq, J.: Deciding $\mathcal{H}_1$ by resolution. Information Processing Letters 95(3), 401–408 (2005)
131. Goubault-Larrecq, J., Parrennes, F.: Cryptographic Protocol Analysis on Real C Code. In: Cousot, R. (ed.) VMCAI 2005. LNCS, vol. 3385, pp. 363–379. Springer, Heidelberg (2005)
132. Halevi, S.: A plausible approach to computer-aided cryptographic proofs. Cryptology ePrint Archive, Report 2005/181 (2005), http://eprint.iacr.org/2005/181
133. Heather, J., Lowe, G., Schneider, S.: How to prevent type flaw attacks on security protocols. In: CSFW 2000, pp. 255–268. IEEE, Los Alamitos (2000)
134. Heather, J., Schneider, S.: A decision procedure for the existence of a rank function. Journal of Computer Security 13(2), 317–344 (2005)
135. Hüttel, H.: Deciding framed bisimilarity. In: INFINITY 2002, pp. 1–20 (2002)

136. Janvier, R., Lakhnech, Y., Mazaré, L.: Completing the Picture: Soundness of Formal Encryption in the Presence of Active Adversaries. In: Sagiv, M. (ed.) ESOP 2005. LNCS, vol. 3444, pp. 172–185. Springer, Heidelberg (2005)

137. Janvier, R., Lakhnech, Y., Mazaré, L.: Relating the symbolic and computational models of security protocols using hashes. In: Degano, P., Küsters, R., Viganò, L., Zdancewic, S. (eds.) FCS-ARSPA 2006, pp. 67–89 (2006)

138. Jürjens, J.: Security analysis of crypto-based Java programs using automated theorem provers. In: ASE 2006, pp. 167–176. IEEE, Los Alamitos (2006)

139. Kremer, S., Ryan, M.D.: Analysis of an Electronic Voting Protocol in the Applied Pi Calculus. In: Sagiv, M. (ed.) ESOP 2005. LNCS, vol. 3444, pp. 186–200. Springer, Heidelberg (2005)

140. Küsters, R., Truderung, T.: Reducing protocol analysis with XOR to the XOR-free case in the Horn theory based approach. In: CCS 2008, pp. 129–138. ACM, New York (2008)

141. Küsters, R., Truderung, T.: Using ProVerif to analyze protocols with Diffie-Hellman exponentiation. In: CSF 2009, pp. 157–171. IEEE, Los Alamitos (2009)

142. Laud, P.: Handling Encryption in an Analysis for Secure Information Flow. In: Degano, P. (ed.) ESOP 2003. LNCS, vol. 2618, pp. 159–173. Springer, Heidelberg (2003)

143. Laud, P.: Symmetric encryption in automatic analyses for confidentiality against active adversaries. In: IEEE Symposium on Security and Privacy, pp. 71–85. IEEE, Los Alamitos (2004)

144. Laud, P.: Secrecy types for a simulatable cryptographic library. In: CCS 2005, pp. 26–35. ACM, New York (2005)

145. Laud, P., Tšahhirov, I.: A User Interface for a Game-Based Protocol Verification Tool. In: Degano, P., Guttman, J. (eds.) FAST 2009. LNCS, vol. 5983, pp. 263–278. Springer, Heidelberg (2010)

146. Laud, P., Vene, V.: A Type System for Computationally Secure Information Flow. In: Liśkiewicz, M., Reischuk, R. (eds.) FCT 2005. LNCS, vol. 3623, pp. 365–377. Springer, Heidelberg (2005)

147. Liu, J., Lin, H.: A Complete Symbolic Bisimulation for Full Applied Pi Calculus. In: van Leeuwen, J., Muscholl, A., Peleg, D., Pokorný, J., Rumpe, B. (eds.) SOFSEM 2010. LNCS, vol. 5901, pp. 552–563. Springer, Heidelberg (2010)

148. Lowe, G.: Breaking and Fixing the Needham-Schroeder Public-Key Protocol using FDR. In: Margaria, T., Steffen, B. (eds.) TACAS 1996. LNCS, vol. 1055, pp. 147–166. Springer, Heidelberg (1996)

149. Lowe, G.: A hierarchy of authentication specifications. In: CSFW 1997, pp. 31–43. IEEE, Los Alamitos (1997)

150. Lux, K.D., May, M.J., Bhattad, N.L., Gunter, C.A.: WSEmail: Secure internet messaging based on web services. In: ICWS 2005, pp. 75–82. IEEE, Los Alamitos (2005)

151. Meadows, C.A.: The NRL protocol analyzer: An overview. Journal of Logic Programming 26(2), 113–131 (1996)

152. Micciancio, D., Warinschi, B.: Soundness of Formal Encryption in the Presence of Active Adversaries. In: Naor, M. (ed.) TCC 2004. LNCS, vol. 2951, pp. 133–151. Springer, Heidelberg (2004)

153. Milicia, G.: χ-spaces: Programming security protocols. In: NWPT 2002 (2002)

154. Millen, J.: A necessarily parallel attack. In: FMSP 1999 (1999)

155. Millen, J., Shmatikov, V.: Constraint solving for bounded-process cryptographic protocol analysis. In: CCS 2001, pp. 166–175. ACM, New York (2001)

156. Millen, J.K.: The Interrogator model. In: IEEE Symposium on Security and Privacy, pp. 251–260. IEEE, Los Alamitos (1995)
157. Millen, J.K., Clark, S.C., Freedman, S.B.: The Interrogator: Protocol security analysis. IEEE Transactions on Software Engineering SE-13(2), 274–288 (1987)
158. Milner, R.: Communicating and mobile systems: the π-calculus. Cambridge University Press (1999)
159. Mitchell, J.C., Mitchell, M., Stern, U.: Automated analysis of cryptographic protocols using Murφ. In: IEEE Symposium on Security and Privacy, pp. 141–151. IEEE, Los Alamitos (1997)
160. Monniaux, D.: Abstracting cryptographic protocols with tree automata. Science of Computer Programming 47(2-3), 177–202 (2003)
161. Needham, R.M., Schroeder, M.D.: Using encryption for authentication in large networks of computers. Commun. ACM 21(12), 993–999 (1978)
162. Nowak, D.: A Framework for Game-Based Security Proofs. In: Qing, S., Imai, H., Wang, G. (eds.) ICICS 2007. LNCS, vol. 4861, pp. 319–333. Springer, Heidelberg (2007)
163. Nowak, D.: On Formal Verification of Arithmetic-Based Cryptographic Primitives. In: Lee, P.J., Cheon, J.H. (eds.) ICISC 2008. LNCS, vol. 5461, pp. 368–382. Springer, Heidelberg (2009)
164. O'Shea, N.: Using Elyjah to analyse Java implementations of cryptographic protocols. In: FCS-ARSPA-WITS 2008 (2008)
165. Paulson, L.C.: The inductive approach to verifying cryptographic protocols. Journal of Computer Security 6(1-2), 85–128 (1998)
166. Pironti, A., Sisto, R.: Provably correct Java implementations of spi calculus security protocols specifications. Computers and Security 29(3), 302–314 (2010)
167. Poll, E., Schubert, A.: Verifying an implementation of SSH. In: WITS 2007 (2007)
168. Pozza, D., Sisto, R., Durante, L.: Spi2Java: Automatic cryptographic protocol Java code generation from spi calculus. In: AINA 2004, vol. 1, pp. 400–405. IEEE, Los Alamitos (2004)
169. Sarukkai, S., Suresh, S.P.: Tagging Makes Secrecy Decidable with Unbounded Nonces as Well. In: Pandya, P.K., Radhakrishnan, J. (eds.) FSTTCS 2003. LNCS, vol. 2914, pp. 363–374. Springer, Heidelberg (2003)
170. Roscoe, A.W., Broadfoot, P.J.: Proving security protocols with model checkers by data independence techniques. Journal of Computer Security 7(2, 3), 147–190 (1999)
171. Rusinowitch, M., Turuani, M.: Protocol insecurity with finite number of sessions is NP-complete. Theoretical Computer Science 299(1-3), 451–475 (2003)
172. Shoup, V.: Sequences of games: a tool for taming complexity in security proofs. Cryptology ePrint Archive, Report 2004/332 (2004), http://eprint.iacr.org/2004/332
173. Smith, G., Alpízar, R.: Secure information flow with random assignment and encryption. In: FMSE 2006, pp. 33–43 (2006)
174. Song, D., Perrig, A., Phan, D.: AGVI - Automatic Generation, Verification, and Implementation of Security Protocols. In: Berry, G., Comon, H., Finkel, A. (eds.) CAV 2001. LNCS, vol. 2102, pp. 241–245. Springer, Heidelberg (2001)
175. Song, D.X., Berezin, S., Perrig, A.: Athena: a novel approach to efficient automatic security protocol analysis. Journal of Computer Security 9(1/2), 47–74 (2001)
176. Sprenger, C., Backes, M., Basin, D., Pfitzmann, B., Waidner, M.: Cryptographically sound theorem proving. In: CSFW 2006, pp. 153–166. IEEE, Los Alamitos (2006)

177. Swamy, N., Chen, J., Fournet, C., Strub, P.Y., Bharagavan, K., Yang, J.: Secure distributed programming with value-dependent types. In: Chakravarty, M.M.T., Hu, Z., Danvy, O. (eds.) ICFP 2011, pp. 266–278. ACM, New York (2011)
178. Tšahhirov, I., Laud, P.: Application of Dependency Graphs to Security Protocol Analysis. In: Barthe, G., Fournet, C. (eds.) TGC 2007. LNCS, vol. 4912, pp. 294–311. Springer, Heidelberg (2008)
179. Weidenbach, C.: Towards an Automatic Analysis of Security Protocols in First-Order Logic. In: Ganzinger, H. (ed.) CADE 1999. LNCS (LNAI), vol. 1632, pp. 314–328. Springer, Heidelberg (1999)
180. Woo, T.Y.C., Lam, S.S.: A semantic model for authentication protocols. In: IEEE Symposium on Security and Privacy, pp. 178–194. IEEE, Los Alamitos (1993)
181. Yao, A.C.: Theory and applications of trapdoor functions. In: FOCS 1982, pp. 80–91. IEEE, Los Alamitos (1982)

Analysing Routing Protocols:
Four Nodes Topologies Are Sufficient*

Véronique Cortier[1], Jan Degrieck[1,2], and Stéphanie Delaune[2]

[1] LORIA, CNRS, France
[2] LSV, ENS Cachan & CNRS & INRIA Saclay Île-de-France, France

Abstract. Routing protocols aim at establishing a route between nodes
on a network. Secured versions of routing protocols have been proposed
in order to provide more guarantees on the resulting routes. Formal methods have proved their usefulness when analysing standard security protocols such as confidentiality or authentication protocols. However, existing
results and tools do not apply to routing protocols. This is due in particular to the fact that all possible topologies (infinitely many) have to
be considered.

   In this paper, we propose a simple reduction result: when looking for
attacks on properties such as the validity of the route, it is sufficient to
consider topologies with only four nodes, resulting in a number of just
five distinct topologies to consider. As an application, we analyse the
SRP applied to DSR and the SDMSR protocols using the ProVerif tool.

1   Introduction

Routing protocols aim at establishing a route between distant nodes on a network. Attacking routing protocols is a first step towards mounting more sophisticated attacks. For example, forcing a route to visit a malicious node allows an
attacker to monitor and listen to the traffic, possibly blocking some messages.
Therefore, secured versions of routing protocols have been proposed to provide
more guarantees on the resulting routes, but they are often still subject to attacks. For example, the SRP protocol [26] is a generic construction for securing
protocols. However, applied to DSR [23], a standard routing protocol, it has been
shown to be flawed, allowing an attacker to modify the route, making the source
node to accept an invalid route [15]. This shows that the design of secure routing
protocols is difficult and error-prone.

   In the context of standard security protocols such as confidentiality or authentication protocols, formal methods have proved their usefulness for providing
security guarantees or detecting attacks. For example, a flaw has been discovered (see [5]) in the Single-Sign-On protocol used *e.g.* by Google Apps. It has

---

* The research leading to these results has received funding from the European
  Research Council under the European Union's Seventh Framework Programme
  (FP7/2007-2013) / ERC grant agreement no 258865, project ProSecure, and the
  ANR project JCJC VIP n° 11 JS02 006 01.

P. Degano and J.D. Guttman (Eds.): POST 2012, LNCS 7215, pp. 30–50, 2012.

been shown that a malicious application could very easily access to any other application (*e.g.* Gmail or Google Calendar) of their users. This flaw has been found when analyzing the protocol using formal methods, abstracting messages by a term algebra and using the AVISPA platform [6]. More generally, many decision procedures (*e.g.* [27,12]) have been proposed for automatically analyzing the security of protocols. Tools like AVISPA, ProVerif [13], or Scyther [18] have been developed and successfully applied to protocols, yielding discoveries of attacks or security proofs.

However, these results and tools do not apply to routing protocols. One of the main reasons is the fact that analysing routing protocols requires one to consider a different attacker model. Indeed, in contrast to standard security protocols where the attacker is assumed to control all the communications, an attacker for routing protocols is *localized, i.e.* it can control only a finite number of nodes (typically one or two). Since a node broadcasts its messages to all its neighbours, it is very easy for a malicious node to listen to the communication of its neighbours but it is not possible to listen beyond the neighbouring nodes. Therefore, the existence of an attack strongly depends on the network topology, that is, how nodes are connected and where malicious nodes are located.

Some dedicated techniques have been developed for formally analyzing routing protocols. For example, S. Nanz and C. Hankin [25] have proposed one of the first formal models for routing protocols and have shown how to automatically analyze a finite number of attack scenarios. For a general attacker, M. Arnaud *et al.* [7] have proposed an NP decision procedure for a finite number of sessions. Several case studies have also been conducted. For example, D. Benetti *et al.* [10] have analyzed the ARAN and endairA protocols with the AVISPA tool, considering a finite number of scenarios. G. Ács *et al.* [3] have developed a framework for analyzing the distance vector routing protocols SAODV and ARAN. However, these results are rather ad-hoc and no decision procedure has been implemented.

Our contribution. Instead of proposing a new decision procedure, we propose in this paper a simple reduction result: if there is an attack, then there is an attack on a small network topology with only four nodes. More precisely, we show that at most five distinct topologies (each with four nodes) need to be considered when looking for an attack. We therefore reduce the number of topologies to be considered from infinitely many to only five. Our reduction result holds for properties such as route validity and for a very general class of routing protocols. Indeed, we consider arbitrary cryptographic primitives (provided they can be expressed as terms) and arbitrary protocol transitions. For example, our model allows neighbourhood tests, recursive operations, and of course standard pattern-matching, encompassing the models proposed in [25,7,8].

The proof of our reduction result consists in two main steps. First, we show that if there is an attack, then the attack is preserved when adding all but one edge to the network topology, yielding a *quasi-complete graph*. Second, we show how to merge all the nodes having the same neighbourhood and honesty/dishonesty status. It is then sufficient to observe that merging quasi-complete graphs results into only five distinct topologies, each of them containing four nodes.

An interesting consequence of our reduction result is that it allows one to reuse techniques and tools developed for standard security protocols. Indeed, it is now possible to consider the five fixed topologies one by one and to analyse the protocol in each of the five cases using existing tools, provided of course that the protocol's primitives are supported by the tool. As an application, we analyse the SRP applied to DSR [23,26] and the SDMSR [20] protocols using the ProVerif tool, retrieving the existing attacks. Detailed proofs of our results can be found in [17].

Related work. Our result follows the spirit of [16] where it is shown that only two distinct identities need to be considered when studying confidentiality or authentication properties. To our knowledge, the only approach proposing a reduction result in the context of routing protocols is [4]. In this paper, the authors show how to reduce the number of network topologies that need to be considered, taking advantage of the symmetries. However, the total number of configurations is still infinite in the general case or really large even when considering a bounded number of nodes. For example, more than 30000 topologies need to be considered when the number of nodes is bounded by six. In contrast, our result reduces to only five topologies, even when considering attacks with arbitrarily many nodes.

2   Messages and Attacker Capabilities

For modeling messages, we consider an arbitrary term algebra and deduction system, which provides a lot of flexibility in terms on which cryptographic primitives can be modeled.

2.1   Messages

Messages are represented by terms where cryptographic primitives such as encryption, signature, and hash function, are represented by *function symbols*. More precisely, we consider a *signature* $(\mathcal{S}, \Sigma)$ made of a set of sorts $\mathcal{S}$ and a set of function symbols Σ together with arities of the form $ar(f) = s_1 \times \ldots \times s_k \to s$ where $f \in \Sigma$, and $s, s_1, \ldots, s_k \in \mathcal{S}$. We consider an infinite set of *variables* $\mathcal{X}$ and an infinite set of *names* $\mathcal{N}$ that typically represent nonces, session keys, or agent names. We assume that names and variables are given with sorts.

Regarding the sort system, we consider a special sort agent that only contains names and variables. These names represent the names of the agents, also called the nodes of the network. We assume a special sort term that subsumes all the other sorts and such that any term is of sort term. Terms are defined as names, variables, and function symbols applied to other terms. Of course function symbol application must respect sorts and arities. For $\mathcal{A} \subseteq \mathcal{X} \cup \mathcal{N}$, the set of terms built from $\mathcal{A}$ by applying function symbols in Σ is denoted by $\mathcal{T}(\Sigma, \mathcal{A})$. A term t is said to be a *ground* term if it does not contain any variable.

Example 1. A typical signature for representing the primitives used in routing protocols such as the SRP [26] protocol is the signature $(\mathcal{S}_{\mathsf{SRP}}, \Sigma_{\mathsf{SRP}})$ defined by $\mathcal{S}_{\mathsf{SRP}} = \{\mathsf{agent}, \mathsf{list}, \mathsf{term}\}$ and $\Sigma_{\mathsf{SRP}} = \{hmac, \langle\rangle, ::, \perp, shk, req, rep\}$, with the following arities:

- $hmac$: term $\times$ term $\rightarrow$ term,
- $\langle\rangle$: term $\times$ term $\rightarrow$ term,
- shk : agent $\times$ agent $\rightarrow$ term,
- $::$: agent $\times$ list $\rightarrow$ list,
- $\perp$: $\rightarrow$ list,
- req, rep : $\rightarrow$ term.

The symbol $::$ is the list constructor whereas $\perp$ is a constant representing an empty list. The constants req and rep are used to identify the request phase and the reply phase. The term $shk(A, B)$ $(= shk(B, A))$ represents a shared key between A and B. The term $hmac(m, k)$ represents the keyed hash message authentication code computed over message m with key k while $\langle\rangle$ is a pairing operator. We write $\langle t_1, t_2, t_3 \rangle$ for the term $\langle t_1, \langle t_2, t_3 \rangle \rangle$, and $[t_1; t_2; t_3]$ for $t_1 ::$ $(t_2 :: (t_3 :: \perp))$.

Substitutions are written $\sigma = \{x_1 \mapsto t_1, \ldots, x_n \mapsto t_n\}$ with $dom(\sigma) = \{x_1, \ldots, x_n\}$, and $img(\sigma) = \{t_1, \ldots, t_n\}$. We only consider *well-sorted* substitutions, that is substitutions for which x_i and t_i have the same sort. The substitution σ is *ground* if the t_i are ground. The application of a substitution σ to a term t is written $\sigma(t)$ or $t\sigma$. A *most general unifier* of two terms t and u is a substitution denoted by $mgu(t, u)$. We write $mgu(t, u) = \sharp$ when t and u are not unifiable.

2.2   Attacker Capabilities

The ability of the attacker is modeled by a deduction relation $\vdash \subseteq 2^{\mathsf{term}} \times \mathsf{term}$. The relation $\mathcal{I} \vdash v$ represents the fact that the term v is computable from the set of terms $\mathcal{I}$. Such a relation is defined through an inference system, *i.e.* a finite set of rules of the form $\dfrac{u_1 \ldots u_n}{u}$ where $u, u_1, \ldots, u_n \in \mathcal{T}(\Sigma, \mathcal{X})$. The deduction relation can be arbitrary in our model as long as the terms $u, u_1, \ldots u_n$ do not contain any names. An example of such a relation is provided below.

A term u is *deducible* from a set of terms $\mathcal{I}$, denoted by $\mathcal{I} \vdash u$, if there exists a proof, *i.e.* a tree such that the root is labelled with u and the leaves are labelled with $v \in \mathcal{I}$ and every intermediate node is an instance of one of the rules of the inference system.

Example 2. We can associate to the term algebra $(\mathcal{S}_{\mathsf{SRP}}, \Sigma_{\mathsf{SRP}})$ defined in Example 1, the following inference system.

$$\frac{y_1 \quad y_2}{\langle y_1, y_2 \rangle} \qquad \frac{\langle y_1, y_2 \rangle}{y_1} \qquad \frac{\langle y_1, y_2 \rangle}{y_2} \qquad \frac{x \quad z}{x :: z} \qquad \frac{x :: z}{x} \qquad \frac{x :: z}{z} \qquad \frac{y_1 \quad y_2}{hmac(y_1, y_2)}$$

The terms y_1, y_2 are variables of sort term, x is a variable of sort agent, whereas z is a variable of sort list. This inference system reflects the ability for the attacker to concatenate terms, to build lists, and to retrieve components of lists and pairs.

The last inference rule models the fact that an attacker can also compute a MAC when he knows the key (and the message to be MACed).

Let $\mathcal{I} = \{S, D, A_1, A_2, \bot, \langle req, S, D, id, [S], hmac(\langle req, S, D, id\rangle, shk(S, D))\rangle\}$ and $m = \langle req, S, D, id, [A_1; A_2; S], hmac(\langle req, S, D, id\rangle, shk(S, D))\rangle$ where S, D, A_1, and A_2 are names of sort agent. The term m typically represents a message that the attacker would like to send over the network while $\mathcal{I}$ represents its knowledge so far, typically having listened to the first step of the SRP protocol. Considering the inference system described above, we have that $\mathcal{I} \vdash m$.

2.3   Functions over Terms

In order to be as general as possible, we consider protocols that perform any operation on the terms they receive. We therefore consider *functions over terms*, that is, functions of the form $f : \mathcal{T}(\Sigma, \mathcal{N}) \times \ldots \times \mathcal{T}(\Sigma, \mathcal{N}) \to \mathcal{T}(\Sigma, \mathcal{N})$.

These functions can of course model standard applications of cryptographic operations. For example, the function $(x, y, z) \mapsto \{\langle x, y\rangle\}_z$ represent the function that concatenates the terms x and y and then encrypts it with z. They can also be used to model various operations on lists. For instance, we can define the reverse function that takes as input a list $[A_1, \ldots, A_n]$ and outputs the reversed list $[A_n, \ldots, A_1]$.

More interestingly, such functions encompass recursive operations and recursive tests. Typical examples can be found in the context of routing protocols, when nodes check for the validity of the route. For example, in the SMNDP protocol [20], a route from the source A_0 to the destination A_n is represented by a list $l_{route} = [A_1; \ldots; A_n]$. This list is accepted by the source node A_0 only if the received message is of the form:

$$[[\![\langle A_n, A_0, l_{route}\rangle]\!]_{sk(A_1)}; [\![\langle A_n, A_0, l_{route}\rangle]\!]_{sk(A_2)}; \ldots; [\![\langle A_n, A_0, l_{route}\rangle]\!]_{sk(A_n)}]$$

where $[\![\langle A_n, A_0, l_{route}]\!]_{sk(A_i)}$ is a signature performed by A_i. This test and many others (*e.g.* [21,15]) can be easily modelled using functions over terms. Clearly, not all functions over terms are meaningful to model protocols. In particular, some of them might not be executable. Actually, a precise definition of executability is not relevant for our result: our result holds for non executable functions as soon as they satisfy the properties stated in our Theorem 1.

3   Models for Protocols

Several calculi have been proposed to model security protocols (*e.g.* [2,1]). However, they are not well-adapted for routing protocols. For instance, in contrast to standard security protocols, the attacker is localized to some nodes and cannot control all the communications. The nodes, *i.e.* the processes, have to perform some specific actions that can not be easily modeled in such calculi, like recursive checks (checking a chain of signatures) or some sanity checks on the routes they receive, such as neighbourhood properties.

Actually, our calculus is inspired from CBS# [25] and generalize the calculus given in [7] by allowing processes to perform any operation on the terms they receive and considering an arbitrary signature for terms.

3.1 Syntax

The intended behavior of each node of the network can be modeled by a *process* defined by the grammar given below. Our calculus is parametrized by a set $\mathcal{P}$ of predicates and a set $\mathcal{F}$ of functions over terms, whose purpose is to represent the computations performed by the agents. We assume that these functions are total and deterministic. This means that a partial function will be modeled by returning a special constant *fail* when it is needed.

$$
\begin{array}{lll}
\Phi, \Phi_1, \Phi_2 := & & \text{Formula} \\
\quad p(u_1, \ldots, u_n) & \text{literal} & \text{with } p \in \mathcal{P} \\
\quad \Phi_1 \wedge \Phi_2 & \text{conjunction} &
\end{array}
$$

$$
\begin{array}{lll}
P, Q, R := & \text{Processes} & \\
\quad 0 & & \text{null process} \\
\quad \mathsf{out}(\mathsf{f}(u_1, \ldots, u_n)).P & & \text{emission} \\
\quad \mathsf{in}(u).P & & \text{reception} \\
\quad \text{if } \Phi \text{ then } P & & \text{conditional} \\
\quad P \mid Q & & \text{parallel composition} \\
\quad !P & & \text{replication} \\
\quad \mathsf{new}\ n.P & & \text{fresh name generation}
\end{array}
$$

where $u, u_1, \ldots, u_n$ are terms that may contain variables, n is a name, $\mathsf{f} \in \mathcal{F}$, and Φ is a formula.

Fig. 1. Syntax of processes

The process "$\mathsf{in}(u).P$" expects a message m of the form u and then behaves like $P\sigma$ where $\sigma = mgu(m, u)$. The process "$\mathsf{out}(\mathsf{f}(u_1, \ldots, u_n)).P$" computes the term $u = \mathsf{f}(u_1, \ldots, u_n)$, emits u, and then behaves like P. The purpose of $\mathsf{f}(u_1, \ldots, u_n)$ is to model any operation f on the terms $u_1, \ldots, u_n$ (the variables in $u_1, \ldots, u_n$ will be instantiated when the evaluation will take place). For instance, such a function f can be used to reverse a list, or to apply some cryptographic primitives on top of $u_1, \ldots, u_n$, or any combination of these operations. The process "if Φ then P" behaves like P when Φ is true and stops otherwise.

We assume that the predicates $p \in \mathcal{P}$ are given together with their semantics that may depend on the underlying graph G that models the topology of the network. Such a graph $G = (V, E)$ is given by a set of vertices $V \subseteq \{A \mid A \in \mathcal{N} \text{ of sort agent}\}$ and a set of edges $E \subseteq V \times V$. Since the purpose of this graph is to model the communication network, we consider topologies where E is a reflexive and symmetric relation. We consider two kinds of predicates: a set $\mathcal{P}_I$ of predicates whose semantics is independent of the graph, *i.e.* $[\![p(u_1, \ldots, u_k)]\!]_G =$

$[\![p(u_1, \ldots, u_k)]\!]_{G'}$ for any graphs G and G' and any ground terms $u_1, \ldots, u_k$; and a set $\mathcal{P}_D$ of predicates whose semantics is dependent on the graph. The semantics of a formula is then defined as expected. The purpose of $\mathcal{P}_D$ is to model neighbourhood checks that are typically performed in routing protocols.

Example 3. As an illustrative purpose, we consider the set $\mathcal{P}_{\mathsf{SRP}} = \mathcal{P}_I \cup \mathcal{P}_D$ where $\mathcal{P}_I = \{\mathsf{first}, \mathsf{last}\}$ and $\mathcal{P}_D = \{\mathsf{check}, \mathsf{checkl}\}$. The purpose of the predicates in $\mathcal{P}_I$ is to model some sanity checks that are performed by the source when it receives the path. The semantics of these predicates is independent of the graph and is defined as follows:

- $\mathsf{first}(A, l) = \mathsf{true}$ if and only if l is of sort list and its first element is A;
- $\mathsf{last}(A, l) = \mathsf{true}$ if and only if l is of sort list and its last element is A.

The purpose of the predicates in $\mathcal{P}_D$ is to model neighbourhood checks. Given a graph $G = (V, E)$, their semantics is defined as follows:

- $\mathsf{check}(A, B)$ checks for neighbourhood of two nodes, $[\![\mathsf{check}(A, B)]\!]_G = \mathsf{true}$ if and only if $(A, B) \in E$, with A, B of sort agent;
- $\mathsf{checkl}(C, l)$ checks for local neighbourhood of a node in a list, $[\![\mathsf{checkl}(C, l)]\!]_G = \mathsf{true}$ if and only if C is of sort agent, l is of sort list, and for any l' subterm of l, if $l' = A :: C :: l_1$, then $(A, C) \in E$; whereas if $l' = C :: B :: l_1$, then $(C, B) \in E$.

We write $fv(P)$ for the set of *free variables* that occur in P, *i.e.* the set of variables that are not in the scope of an input. We consider *ground processes*, *i.e.* processes P such that $fv(P) = \emptyset$, and *parametrized* processes, denoted $P(x_1, \ldots, x_n)$ where $x_1, \ldots, x_n$ are variables of sort agent, and such that $fv(P) \subseteq \{x_1, \ldots, x_n\}$. A *routing role* is a parametrized process that do not contain any name of sort agent. A *routing protocol* is then simply a set of routing roles.

3.2   Example: Modeling the SRP Protocol

We consider the secure routing protocol SRP applied on DSR introduced in [26], assuming that each node already knows his neighbours (running *e.g.* some neighbour discovery protocol). SRP is not a routing protocol by itself, it describes a generic way for securing source-routing protocols. We model here its application to the DSR protocol [23]. DSR is a protocol which is used when an agent S (the source) wants to communicate with another agent D (the destination), which is not his immediate neighbour. In an ad hoc network, messages can not be sent directly to the destination, but have to travel along a path of nodes.

To discover a route to the destination, the source constructs a request packet and broadcasts it to its neighbours. The request packet contains its name S, the name of the destination D, an identifier of the request id, a list containing the beginning of a route to D, and a hmac computed over the content of the request with a key $shk(S, D)$ shared by S and D. It then waits for an answer containing a route to D with a hmac matching this route, and checks that it is a plausible route by checking for instance that his neighbour in the route is indeed a neighbour of S in the network.

Consider the signature given in Example 1, the predicates $\mathcal{P}_{\mathsf{SRP}}$ introduced in Example 3, and the set $\mathcal{F}_{\mathsf{SRP}}$ of functions over terms that only contains the identity function (for sake of clarity, we omit it). Let id be a name, x_S, x_D be variables of sort agent, and x_L be a variable of sort list. The process executed by the agent x_S initiating the search of a route towards a node x_D is:

$$P_{\mathsf{src}}(x_S, x_D) = \mathsf{new}\ id.\mathsf{out}(u_1).\mathsf{in}(u_2).\mathsf{if}\ \Phi_S\ \mathsf{then}\ 0$$

where
$$\begin{cases} u_1 = \langle req, x_S, x_D, id, x_S :: \bot, hmac(\langle req, x_S, x_D, id\rangle, shk(x_S, x_D))\rangle \\ u_2 = \langle rep, x_D, x_S, id, x_L, hmac(\langle rep, x_D, x_S, id, x_L\rangle, shk(x_S, x_D))\rangle \\ \Phi_S = \mathsf{checkl}(x_S, x_L) \wedge \mathsf{first}(x_D, x_L) \wedge \mathsf{last}(x_S, x_L) \end{cases}$$

The names of the intermediate nodes are accumulated in the route request packet. Intermediate nodes relay the request over the network, except if they have already seen it. An intermediate node also checks that the received request is locally correct by verifying whether the head of the list in the request is one of its neighbours. Below, x_V, x_S, x_D and x_A are variables of sort agent whereas x_r is a variable of sort list and x_{id}, x_m are variables of sort term. The process executed by an intermediary node x_V when forwarding a request is as follows:

$$P_{\mathsf{request}}(x_V) = \mathsf{in}(w_1).\mathsf{if}\ \Phi_V\ \mathsf{then}\ \mathsf{out}(w_2).0$$

where
$$\begin{cases} w_1 = \langle req, x_S, x_D, x_{id}, x_A :: x_r, x_m\rangle \\ \Phi_V = \mathsf{check}(x_V, x_A) \\ w_2 = \langle req, x_S, x_D, x_{id}, x_V :: (x_A :: x_r), x_m\rangle \end{cases}$$

When the request reaches the destination D, it checks that the request has a correct hmac and that the first node in the route is one of his neighbours. Then, the destination D constructs a route reply, in particular it computes a new hmac over the route accumulated in the request packet with $shk(x_S, D)$, and sends the answer back over the network. The process executed by the destination node x_D is the following:

$$P_{\mathsf{dest}}(x_D) = \mathsf{in}(v_1).\mathsf{if}\ \Phi_D\ \mathsf{then}\ \mathsf{out}(v_2).0$$

where:

$$\begin{cases} v_1 = \langle req, x_S, x_D, x_{id}, x_A :: x_l, hmac(\langle req, x_S, x_D, x_{id}\rangle, shk(x_S, x_D))\rangle \\ \Phi_D = \mathsf{check}(x_D, x_A) \\ v_2 = \langle rep, x_D, x_S, x_{id}, l_{route}, hmac(\langle rep, x_D, x_S, x_{id}, l_{route}\rangle, shk(x_S, x_D))\rangle \\ l_{route} = x_D :: x_A :: x_l \end{cases}$$

Then, the reply travels along the route back to x_S. The intermediary nodes check that the route in the reply packet is locally correct (that is that the nodes before and after them in the list are their neighbours) before forwarding it. The process executed by an intermediary node x_V when forwarding a reply is the following:

$$P_{\mathsf{reply}}(x_V) = \mathsf{in}(w').\mathsf{if}\ \Phi'_V\ \mathsf{then}\ \mathsf{out}(w')$$

where $w' = \langle rep, x_D, x_S, x_{id}, x_r, x_m\rangle$, and $\Phi'_V = \mathsf{checkl}(x_V, x_r)$.

Example 4. In our model, the routing protocol SRP is defined by the following set of parametrized processes:

$$\{P_{\mathsf{src}}(x_S, x_D);\ P_{\mathsf{request}}(x_V);\ P_{\mathsf{reply}}(x_V);\ P_{\mathsf{dest}}(x_D)\}.$$

3.3   Configuration and Topology

Each process is located at a specified node of the network. Unlike the classical Dolev-Yao model [19], the intruder does not control the entire network but can only interact with its neighbours. More specifically, we assume that the *topology* of the network is represented by a tuple $\mathcal{T} = (G, \mathcal{M}, S, D)$ where:

- $G = (V, E)$ is an undirected graph with $V \subseteq \{A \in \mathcal{N} \mid A \text{ of sort agent}\}$, where an edge in the graph models the fact that two agents are neighbours. We only consider graphs such that $\{(A, A) \mid A \in V\} \subseteq E$ which means that an agent can receive a message sent by himself;
- $\mathcal{M}$ is a set of nodes that are controlled by the attacker. These nodes are called *malicious* whereas nodes *not in* $\mathcal{M}$ are called *honest*;
- S and D are two honest nodes that represent respectively the source and the destination for which we analyse the security of the routing protocol.

Note that our model is not restricted to a single malicious node. In particular, our results apply to the case of several compromised nodes that communicate (and therefore share their knowledge), using out-of-band resources or hidden channels (*e.g.* running other instances of the routing protocols).

A *configuration* of the network is a pair $(\mathcal{P}; \mathcal{I})$ where:

- $\mathcal{P}$ is a multiset of expressions of the form $\lfloor P \rfloor_A$ that represents the (ground) process P executed by the agent $A \in V$. We will write $\lfloor P \rfloor_A \cup \mathcal{P}$ instead of $\{\lfloor P \rfloor_A\} \cup \mathcal{P}$.
- $\mathcal{I}$ is a set of ground terms representing the messages seen by the malicious nodes as well as their initial knowledge.

Example 5. Continuing our modeling of SRP, a typical initial configuration for the SRP protocol is

$$K_0 = (\lfloor P_{\mathsf{src}}(S, D) \rfloor_S \mid \lfloor P_{\mathsf{dest}}(D) \rfloor_D; \mathcal{I}_0)$$

where both the source node S and the destination node D wish to communicate. A more realistic configuration would include intermediary nodes but this initial configuration is already sufficient to present an attack. We assume that the initial knowledge of the intruder is given by a possibly infinite set of terms $\mathcal{I}_0$ that typically contains the names of sort agent, the constants *req*, *rep*, and $\perp$, and the dishonest keys, *i.e.* those that belong to a malicious node.

(COMM) $(\{\lfloor in(u_j).P_j \rfloor_{A_j} \mid (A, A_j) \in E \wedge mgu(t, u_j) \neq \sharp\} \cup$
   $\lfloor out(f(t_1, \ldots, t_n)).P \rfloor_A \cup \mathcal{P}; \mathcal{I}) \rightarrow_{\mathcal{T}} (\{\lfloor P_j \sigma_j \rfloor_{A_j}\} \cup \lfloor P \rfloor_A \cup \mathcal{P}; \mathcal{I}')$

   where $\begin{cases} \sigma_j = mgu(t, u_j) \text{ where } t \text{ is the result of applying f on } t_1, \ldots, t_n \\ \mathcal{I}' = \mathcal{I} \cup \{t\} \text{ if } (A, I) \in E \text{ for some } I \in \mathcal{M} \text{ and } \mathcal{I}' = \mathcal{I} \text{ otherwise.} \end{cases}$

(IN) $(\lfloor in(u).P \rfloor_A \cup \mathcal{P}; \mathcal{I}) \rightarrow_{\mathcal{T}} (\lfloor P\sigma \rfloor_A \cup \mathcal{P}; \mathcal{I})$
   if $(A, I) \in E$ with $I \in \mathcal{M}$, $\mathcal{I} \vdash t$, and $\sigma = mgu(t, u)$

(THEN) $(\lfloor if\ \Phi\ then\ P \rfloor_A \cup \mathcal{P}; \mathcal{I}) \rightarrow_{\mathcal{T}} (\lfloor P \rfloor_A \cup \mathcal{P}; \mathcal{I})$ if $[\![\Phi]\!]_G = 1$

(PAR) $(\lfloor P_1 \mid P_2 \rfloor_A \cup \mathcal{P}; \mathcal{I}) \rightarrow_{\mathcal{T}} (\lfloor P_1 \rfloor_A \cup \lfloor P_2 \rfloor_A \cup \mathcal{P}; \mathcal{I})$

(REPL) $(\lfloor !P \rfloor_A \cup \mathcal{P}; \mathcal{I}) \rightarrow_{\mathcal{T}} (\lfloor P \rfloor_A \cup \lfloor !P \rfloor_A \cup \mathcal{P}; \mathcal{I})$

(NEW) $(\lfloor new\ m.P \rfloor_A \cup \mathcal{P}; \mathcal{I}) \rightarrow_{\mathcal{T}} (\lfloor P\{m \mapsto m'\} \rfloor_A \cup \mathcal{P}; \mathcal{I})$
   where m' is a fresh name

where $\mathcal{T} = (G, \mathcal{M}, S, D)$ and $G = (V, E)$.

Fig. 2. Transition system

A possible topology $\mathcal{T}_0 = (G_0, \mathcal{M}_0, S, D)$ is modeled by the graph G_0 below, where I is a malicious node, *i.e.* $\mathcal{M}_0 = \{I\}$ while A_1 and A_2 are two extra (honest) nodes.

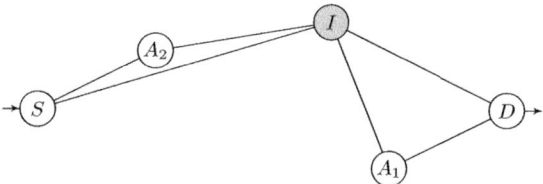

3.4   Execution Model

The communication system is formally defined by the rules of Figure 2. They are parametrized by the underlying topology $\mathcal{T}$.

The COMM rule allows nodes to communicate provided they are (directly) connected in the underlying graph. We do not assume that messages are necessarily delivered to the intended recipients. They may be lost. In particular, the exchange message is added to the knowledge of the attacker as soon as the agent emitting the message is a direct neighbour of a malicious node. This reflects the fact that a malicious node can listen to the communications of its neighbours since messages are typically broadcast to all neighbours. The IN rule allows a malicious node to send any message it can deduce to one of its neighbours. The other rules are standard.

The relation $\rightarrow_{\mathcal{T}}^*$ is the reflexive and transitive closure of $\rightarrow_{\mathcal{T}}$.

Example 6. Continuing the example developed in Section 3.2, the following sequence of transitions is enabled from the initial configuration K_0.

$$K_0 \rightarrow_{\mathcal{T}_0}^* \left(\lfloor \text{in}(u_2).\text{if } \Phi_S \text{ then } 0 \rfloor_S \cup \lfloor P_{\text{dest}}(D) \rfloor_D; \mathcal{I}_0 \cup \{u_1\} \right)$$

where $\begin{cases} u_1 = \langle req, S, D, id, S :: \bot, hmac(\langle req, S, D, id \rangle, shk(S, D)) \rangle \\ u_2 = \langle rep, D, S, id, x_L, hmac(\langle rep, D, S, id, x_L \rangle, shk(S, D)) \rangle \\ \Phi_S = \text{checkl}(S, x_L) \wedge \text{first}(D, x_L) \wedge \text{last}(S, x_L) \end{cases}$

During this transition, S broadcasts a request to find a route to D to its neighbours. The intruder I is a neighbour of S in $\mathcal{T}_0$, so he learns the request message. Assuming that the intruder knows the names of its neighbours, *i.e.* $A_1, A_2 \in \mathcal{I}_0$, he can then build the following fake message request:

$$m = \langle req, S, D, id, [A_1; A_2; S], hmac(\langle req, S, D, id \rangle, shk(S, D)) \rangle$$

and send it to D. Indeed, we have that $\mathcal{I}_0 \vdash m$ (see Example 2).

Since $(A_1, D) \in E$, D accepts this message and the resulting configuration of the transition is $\left(\lfloor \text{in}(u_2).\text{if } \Phi_S \text{ then } 0 \rfloor_S \cup \lfloor \text{out}(v_2\sigma).0 \rfloor_D; \mathcal{I}_0 \cup \{u_1\} \right)$ where:

$$v_2 = \langle rep, D, S, x_{id}, D :: x_A :: x_l, hmac(\langle rep, D, S, x_{id}, D :: x_A :: x_l \rangle, shk(S, D)) \rangle$$
$$\sigma = \{x_{id} \mapsto id, x_A \mapsto A_1, x_l \mapsto [A_2; S]\}.$$

3.5 Security Properties

Routing protocols aim at establishing a valid route between two nodes S and D, that is a route that represents an existing path from S to D in the graph representing the network topology. However, it is well-known that the presence of several colluding malicious nodes often yields straightforward attacks, the so-called wormhole attacks (*e.g.* [22,24]). Indeed, as soon as a malicious node is on the way of the request, he can behave as if he was a neighbour of another malicious node. This is a fact that our definition of security must tolerate, otherwise we cannot hope that any routing protocol will satisfy it. This observation leads to the following definition of *admissible path*.

Definition 1 (admissible path in $\mathcal{T}$). *Let $\mathcal{T} = (G, \mathcal{M}, S, D)$ be a topology with $G = (V, E)$. We say that a list $l = [A_1, \ldots, A_n]$ of agent names is an admissible path in $\mathcal{T}$ if for any $i \in \{1, \ldots, i-1\}$, $(A_i, A_{i+1}) \notin E$ implies that $A_i \in \mathcal{M}$ and $A_{i+1} \in \mathcal{M}$.*

Another option could be to consider a weaker attacker model, assuming that the attackers can not communicate using an out-of-band channel, and to consider a stronger security property requiring the path to be a real path in G. In such a setting, routing protocols are often vulnerable to hidden channel attacks (see *e.g.* [14]). In our setting, this type of attack would not be considered as an attack, as it is an instantiation of the so-called wormhole attack that consists, for two dishonest nodes, in making the network believe they are neighbors.

After having successfully executed a routing protocol, the source node typically stored the resulting received route. For the sake of simplicity, we assume that processes representing instances of routing protocols contain a process (typically a session of the source node) that contains a special action of the form $\mathsf{out}(end(l))$. Checking whether a routing protocol ensures the validity of accepted routes can be defined as a reachability property.

Definition 2 (attack on a configuration K in $\mathcal{T}$). *Let $\mathcal{T} = (G, \mathcal{M}, S, D)$ be a topology and K be a configuration. We say that K admits an attack in $\mathcal{T}$ if $K \to_{\mathcal{T}}^{*} (\lfloor \mathsf{out}(end(l)).P \rfloor_A \cup \mathcal{P}; \mathcal{I})$ for some $A, P, \mathcal{P}, \mathcal{I}$, and some term l that is not an admissible path in $\mathcal{T}$.*

Example 7. For the SRP protocol, we recover the attack mentioned in [15] with the topology given in Example 5, and from the initial configuration:

$$K_{\mathsf{init}} = \left(\lfloor P_0(S, D) \rfloor_S \mid \lfloor P_{\mathsf{dest}}(D) \rfloor_D; \mathcal{I}_0 \right)$$

where $P_0(x_S, x_D)$ is $P_{\mathsf{src}}(x_S, x_D)$ in which the null process 0 has been replaced by $\mathsf{out}(end(x_L)).0$.

Indeed, we have that:

$$
\begin{aligned}
K_{\mathsf{init}} \to_{\mathcal{T}_0}^{*} \ &(\lfloor \mathsf{in}(u_2).\mathsf{if}\ \Phi_S\ \mathsf{then}\ P \rfloor_S \cup \lfloor \mathsf{out}(m').0 \rfloor_D;\ \mathcal{I}) \\
\to_{\mathcal{T}_0} \ &(\lfloor \mathsf{in}(u_2).\mathsf{if}\ \Phi_S\ \mathsf{then}\ P \rfloor_S \cup \lfloor 0 \rfloor_D;\ \mathcal{I}') \\
\to_{\mathcal{T}_0} \ &(\lfloor \mathsf{out}(end([D; A_1; A_2; S])).0 \rfloor_S;\ \mathcal{I}')
\end{aligned}
$$

where:

$m' = \langle rep, D, S, id, [D; A_1; A_2; S], hmac(\langle rep, D, S, id, [D; A_1; A_2; S] \rangle, shk(S, D)) \rangle$
$\mathcal{I} = \mathcal{I}_0 \cup \{u_1\}$ with $u_1 = \langle req, S, D, id, S :: \bot, hmac(\langle req, S, D, id \rangle, shk(S, D)) \rangle$
$\mathcal{I}' = \mathcal{I}_0 \cup \{u_1\} \cup \{m'\}$.

The list $[D; A_1; A_2; S]$ is not an admissible path in $\mathcal{T}_0$. Indeed, $(A_1, A_2) \notin E_0$ whereas A_1 and A_2 are both honest nodes, *i.e.* not in $\mathcal{M}$.

4   Reduction Results

Our main contribution is a reduction result that allows one to analyse the security of a routing protocol considering only some specific and small topologies (typically the underlying graph will contain four nodes). Our reduction result is established in two main steps.

1. We show that the existence of an attack is preserved when adding edges to the graph, actually added all edges but one, yielding a *quasi-complete* topology (see Section 4.1).
2. We show how we can merge almost all nodes together, yielding a graph with only four nodes (see Section 4.2).

We finally conclude in Section 4.3 exhibiting five particular network topologies such that if there exists a network topology admitting an attack then there is an attack on one of the five exhibited topologies. This reduction result drastically reduces the search space (from infinitely many to only five network topologies). As a consequence, it is possible to analyse routing protocols using existing tools, *e.g.* the AVISPA platform [6] or the ProVerif tool [12], provided the protocols perform only actions supported by the tool.

4.1   From an Arbitrary Topology to a Quasi-Complete One

The main idea of our reduction result consists of projecting agents/nodes to the same node. However, we can only do that safely when the agents have the same status (honest/dishonest) and the same neighbourhood. The purpose of the first step (completing the graph) is to ensure that most of the nodes will have the same neighbourhood. This will ensure us to obtain a small graph after the merging step. Of course, we can not consider a complete graph since then any route would be valid thus there would not be any attack. The most complete topology on which an attack can be mounted is a *quasi-complete topology*.

Definition 3 (quasi-completion). *Let $\mathcal{T} = (G, \mathcal{M}, S, D)$ be a topology with $G = (V, E)$, and A, B be two nodes in V that are not both in $\mathcal{M}$, and such that $(A, B) \notin E$. The quasi-completion of $\mathcal{T}$ w.r.t. (A, B) is a topology $\mathcal{T}^+ = (G^+, \mathcal{M}, S, D)$ such that $G^+ = (V, E^+)$ with $E^+ = V \times V \smallsetminus \{(A, B); (B, A)\}$.*

Example 8. The quasi-completion of the topology $\mathcal{T}_0 = (G_0, \mathcal{M}_0, S, D)$ (defined in Example 5) w.r.t. (A_1, A_2) is the topology $\mathcal{T}_0^+ = (G_0^+, \mathcal{M}_0, S, D)$ described below. The only missing edge is (A_1, A_2).

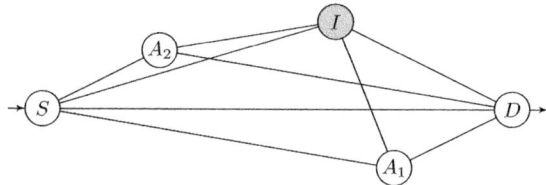

Note that the execution described in Example 7 is still an execution w.r.t. the topology $\mathcal{T}_0^+$ and this execution leads to an attack. This result holds for any protocol that uses completion-friendly predicates (see Proposition 1).

Definition 4 (completion-friendly). *A predicate p is completion-friendly if $[\![p(u_1, \ldots, u_k)]\!]_G = \mathsf{true}$ implies $[\![p(u_1, \ldots, u_k)]\!]_{G^+} = \mathsf{true}$ for any ground terms $u_1, \ldots, u_k$, and quasi-completion $\mathcal{T}^+ = (G^+, \mathcal{M}, S, D)$ of $\mathcal{T} = (G, \mathcal{M}, S, D)$.*

We say that a configuration (resp. a routing protocol) is completion-friendly if $\mathcal{P}_D$ (i.e. the predicates that are dependent of the graph) are completion-friendly.

Example 9. All the predicates that do not depend on the underlying graph are completion-friendly. The predicates check and checkl (see Example 3) that are those used in our running example are completion-friendly whereas their negation are not. This allows us to conclude that the routing protocol $\mathcal{P}_{\mathsf{SRP}}$ is completion-friendly.

Proposition 1. *Let $\mathcal{T} = (G, \mathcal{M}, S, D)$ be a topology and K be a configuration that is completion-friendly. If there is an attack on K in $\mathcal{T}$, then there exists an attack on K in $\mathcal{T}^+$ where $\mathcal{T}^+$ is a quasi-completion of $\mathcal{T}$. Moreover, $\mathcal{T}^+$ is a quasi-completion of $\mathcal{T}$ w.r.t. a pair (A_1, A_2) such that $A_1 \notin \mathcal{M}$ or $A_2 \notin \mathcal{M}$.*

4.2 Reducing the Size of the Topology

Let $\mathcal{T} = (G, \mathcal{M}, S, D)$ be a topology where $G = (V, E)$ with E a reflexive relation, and ρ be a renaming on the agent names (not necessarily a bijective one). We say that the renaming ρ

– *preserves neighbourhood of $\mathcal{T}$* if $\rho(A) = \rho(B)$ implies that
$$\{A' \in V \mid (A, A') \in E\} = \{B' \in V \mid (B, B') \in E\}$$
– *preserves honesty of $\mathcal{T}$* if $\rho(A) = \rho(B)$ implies that $A, B \in \mathcal{M}$ or $A, B \notin \mathcal{M}$.

Given a term u, we denote by $u\rho$ the term obtained by applying the renaming ρ on u. This notation is extended to set of terms, configurations, graphs, and topologies. In particular, given a graph $G = (V, E)$, we denote $G\rho$ the graph $(V\rho, E')$ such that $E' = \{(\rho(A), \rho(B)) \mid (A, B) \in E\}$.

Example 10. Going back to our running example, we may want to consider the identity renaming on agent names. Such a renaming preserves neighbourhood and honesty but it is not really interesting since it does not allow us to reduce the size of the topology, *i.e.* the number of vertices in the graph. A more interesting renaming that preserves neighbourhood and honesty of $\mathcal{T}_0^+$ is ρ defined as follows:
$$\rho(A_1) = A_1, \ \rho(A_2) = A_2, \ \rho(S) = \rho(D) = S, \ \text{and} \ \rho(I) = I$$

Note that ρ does not preserve neighbourhood of the topology $\mathcal{T}_0$ (thus the completion step is important). The topology $\mathcal{T}_0^+\rho$ is described below:

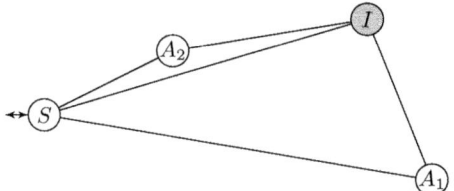

In order to safely merge nodes together, we need the predicates and the functions to be stable over renaming of names of sort **agent**.

Definition 5 (projection-friendly). *A predicate p is projection-friendly if $[\![p(u_1, \ldots, u_k)]\!]_G = \mathsf{true}$ implies $[\![p(u_1\rho, \ldots, u_k\rho)]\!]_{G\rho} = \mathsf{true}$ for any ground terms $u_1, \ldots, u_k$ and any renaming ρ that preserves neighbourhood and honesty.*

A function f over terms of arity k is projection-friendly if $\mathsf{f}(u_1\rho, \ldots, u_k\rho) = \mathsf{f}(u_1, \ldots, u_k)\rho$ for any ground terms $u_1, \ldots, u_k$ and any renaming ρ that preserves neighbourhood and honesty.

We say that a routing protocol (resp. a configuration) is projection-friendly if the predicates in $\mathcal{P}_I \cup \mathcal{P}_D$, and the functions in $\mathcal{F}$ are projection-friendly.

Example 11. The predicates **check** and **checkl** are projection-friendly since we consider renaming that preserves neighbourhood. In our running example, the set $\mathcal{F}_{\mathsf{SRP}}$ only contains the identity function. Clearly, this function is projection-preserving. More generally, all examples of functions provided in Section 2.3 are projection-friendly. Some predicates such as checking disequality constraints or verifying whether an agent name occurs twice in a list are not projection-friendly.

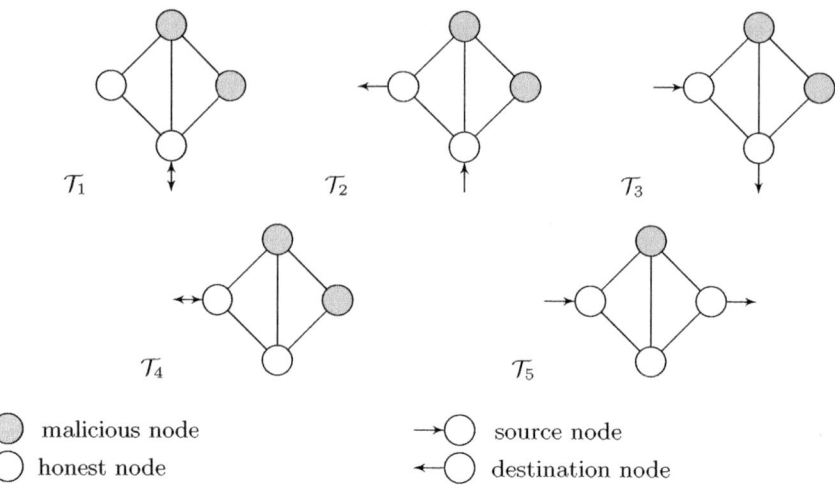

Fig. 3. Topologies $\mathcal{T}_1$, $\mathcal{T}_2$, $\mathcal{T}_3$, $\mathcal{T}_4$, and $\mathcal{T}_5$

Proposition 2. *Let $\mathcal{T}$ be a topology, K_0 be a configuration that is projection-friendly, and ρ be a renaming that preserves neighbourhood and honesty of $\mathcal{T}$. If there is an attack on K_0 in $\mathcal{T}$, then there exists an attack on K_0' in $\mathcal{T}'$ where K_0' and $\mathcal{T}'$ are obtained by applying ρ on K_0 and $\mathcal{T}$.*

4.3   Only Five Topologies Are Sufficient!

Relying on Proposition 1 and Proposition 2, we are now able to show that the existence of an attack on a routing protocol that is completion-friendly and projection-friendly can be reduced to the problem of deciding the existence of an attack for the five topologies given in Figure 3.

Our reduction result is even slightly stronger as we show that we can actually also reduce the initial knowledge of the attackers, considering only the keys associated to the four nodes appearing in the topologies defined in Figure 3. Typical initial knowledges for the attacker are defined as the union of some public information from any agent and private information from malicious agents. More precisely, we assume that such a knowledge is given by a *template* $\mathcal{I}_0$, *i.e.* a set of terms in $\mathcal{T}(\Sigma, \mathcal{N} \cup \mathcal{X}_V \cup \mathcal{X}_M)$ where $\mathcal{X}_V$ and $\mathcal{X}_M$ are two disjoint sets of variables of sort agent where $\mathcal{X}_V$ represents all the nodes while $\mathcal{X}_M$ represent the malicious nodes. Moreover, we assume that the only subterms of sort agent in $\mathcal{I}_0$ are the variables in $\mathcal{X}_V$ and $\mathcal{X}_M$ Then, given a set of nodes V and a set of malicious nodes $\mathcal{M}$, the *knowledge* Knowledge($\mathcal{I}_0, V, \mathcal{M}$) *derived from the template* $\mathcal{I}_0$ is obtained by considering all possible substitutions that preserve the honesty status:

$$\mathsf{Knowledge}(\mathcal{I}_0, V, \mathcal{M}) = \left\{ (t\sigma_V)\sigma_{\mathcal{M}} \middle| \begin{array}{l} t \in \mathcal{I}_0,\, dom(\sigma_V) = \mathcal{X}_V,\, img(\sigma_V) \subseteq V, \\ dom(\sigma_{\mathcal{M}}) = \mathcal{X}_{\mathcal{M}},\, \text{and}\, img(\sigma_{\mathcal{M}}) \subseteq \mathcal{M} \end{array} \right\}$$

Example 12. For instance, this allows us to express that the attackers know all the public keys, and all the private keys that belong to malicious nodes:

$$\mathcal{I}_0 = \{x_v, pk(x_v), sk(x_m), shk(x_v, x_m), shk(x_m, x_v)\}$$

with $x_v \in \mathcal{X}_V$, and $x_m \in \mathcal{X}_\mathcal{M}$.

Definition 6 (configuration valid for $\mathcal{P}_{\text{routing}}$ and P_0 w.r.t. $\mathcal{T}$ and $\mathcal{I}_0$).
Let $\mathcal{T} = (G, \mathcal{M}, S, D)$ be a topology where $G = (V, E)$, and $\mathcal{I}_0$ be a template representing the initial knowledge. A configuration $K = (\mathcal{P}, \mathcal{I})$ is valid for the routing protocol $\mathcal{P}_{\text{routing}}$ and the routing role P_0 w.r.t. $\mathcal{T}$ and $\mathcal{I}_0$ if

1. *$\mathcal{P} = \lfloor P_0(S, D) \rfloor_S \uplus \mathcal{P}'$ and for each $\lfloor P' \rfloor_{A_1} \in \mathcal{P}'$ there exists $P(x_1, \ldots, x_k) \in \mathcal{P}_{\text{routing}}$, and $A_2, \ldots, A_k \in V$ such that $P' = P(A_1, \ldots, A_k)$; and*
2. *the only process containing a special action of the form $\text{out}(\text{end}(l))$ is $P_0(S, D)$ witnessing the storage of a route by the source node S;*
3. *$\mathcal{I} = \text{Knowledge}(\mathcal{I}_0, V, \mathcal{M})$.*

The first condition says that we only consider configurations that are made up using $P_0(S, D)$ and roles of the protocol, and the agent who executes the process is located at the right place. Moreover, we check whether the security property holds when the source and the destination are honest. Note that, we consider the case where an honest source initiates a session with a malicious nodes ($P_{\text{src}}(S, I)$) can occur in the configuration). The second condition ensures that the process witnessing the route is the process $P_0(S, D)$.

Definition 7 (attack on $\mathcal{P}_{\text{routing}}$ and P_0 w.r.t. $\mathcal{I}_0$). *We say that there is an attack on the routing protocol $\mathcal{P}_{\text{routing}}$ and the routing role P_0 w.r.t. the template $\mathcal{I}_0$ if there exists a topology $\mathcal{T} = (G, \mathcal{M}, S, D)$ and a configuration K that is valid for $\mathcal{P}_{\text{routing}}$ and P_0 w.r.t. $\mathcal{T}$ and $\mathcal{I}_0$ such that K admits an attack in $\mathcal{T}$.*

If there is an attack, then there is an attack on one of the five topologies depicted in Figure 3.

Theorem 1. *Let $\mathcal{P}_{\text{routing}}$ be a routing protocol and P_0 be a routing role that are both completion-friendly and projection-friendly and $\mathcal{I}_0$ be a template.*
There is an attack on $\mathcal{P}_{\text{routing}}$ and P_0 w.r.t. $\mathcal{I}_0$ for some topology $\mathcal{T}$ if, and only if, there is an attack on $\mathcal{P}_{\text{routing}}$ and P_0 w.r.t. $\mathcal{I}_0$ for one of the topologies depicted in Figure 3.

The proof of Theorem 1 follows from the successive applications of graph completion (Proposition 1) and nodes projection (Proposition 2). Our result holds for an unbounded number of sessions since we consider arbitrarily many instances of the roles occurring in $\mathcal{P}_{\text{routing}}$, and it encompasses many families of routing protocols.

Corollary 1. *Let $\mathcal{P}_{\text{routing}}$ be a routing protocol and P_0 be a routing role that are both built using functions over terms defined in Section 2.3 and predicates defined in Example 3, and $\mathcal{I}_0$ be a template.*

There is an attack on $\mathcal{P}_{\text{routing}}$ and P_0 w.r.t. $\mathcal{I}_0$ for some topology $\mathcal{T}$ if, and only if, there is an attack on $\mathcal{P}_{\text{routing}}$ and P_0 w.r.t. $\mathcal{I}_0$ for one of the topologies depicted in Figure 3.

Interestingly, a more careful analysis of the proof shows that our reduction result strictly preserves the number of sessions: if there is an attack on an arbitrary topology with k sessions, then there is an attack with k sessions for one of the topologies of Figure 3. Therefore our result holds for a bounded number of sessions as well.

Example 13. Going back to our running example, the topology $\mathcal{T}_0$ on which an attack has been found does not correspond to one of the topologies presented in Figure 3. However, we can retrieve the attack by considering the topology $\mathcal{T}_1$.

The attack described in Example 7 is obtained considering the template $\mathcal{I}_0 = \{x_V\}$ with $x_V \in \mathcal{X}_V$ which corresponds to an attacker who knows the names of all the agents. The topology $\mathcal{T}_1$ (see the picture on the right) does not correspond exactly to the topology $\mathcal{T}_0^+\rho$, *i.e.* the one obtained after completion and projection of $\mathcal{T}_0$. Indeed, the node A_1 is assumed to be malicious in the topology $\mathcal{T}_1$, but not in $\mathcal{T}_0^+\rho$. Note that the attack still exists in presence of this additional malicious node.

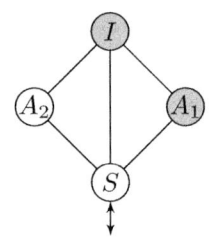

We consider the configuration $K'_{\text{init}} = (\lfloor P_0(S,S) \rfloor_S \mid \lfloor P_{\text{dest}}(S) \rfloor_S; \mathcal{I}')$ where $\mathcal{I}'_0 = \{A_1; A_2; I; S\}$. Since S is an honest node, this configuration is a valid configuration w.r.t. $\mathcal{T}$ and $\mathcal{I}_0$. We have that:

$$K'_{\text{init}} \to^*_{\mathcal{T}_1} (\lfloor \text{in}(u_2).\text{if } \varPhi_S \text{ then } P \rfloor_S \cup \lfloor \text{out}(m').0 \rfloor_S; \mathcal{I})$$
$$\to_{\mathcal{T}_1} (\lfloor \text{in}(u_2).\text{if } \varPhi_S \text{ then } P \rfloor_S \cup \lfloor 0 \rfloor_S; \mathcal{I}')$$
$$\to_{\mathcal{T}_1} (\lfloor \text{out}(end([S; A_1; A_2; S])).0 \rfloor_S; \mathcal{I}')$$

where $m' = \langle rep, S, S, id, l_{route}, hmac(\langle rep, S, S, id, l_{route} \rangle, shk(S,S)) \rangle$ and $l_{route} = [S; A_1; A_2; S]$. The list $[S; A_1; A_2; S]$ is not an admissible path in $\mathcal{T}_1$.

5   Case Studies Using ProVerif

In this section, relying on our reduction result, we propose an analysis of the SRP applied to DSR and the SDMSR protocols using the ProVerif tool [12].

5.1   Proverif

ProVerif constitutes a well-established automated protocol verifier based on Horn clauses resolution that allows for the verification of several security properties. The tool takes as input processes written in a syntax close to the one described in Section 3. It does not consider arbitrary functions over terms as we did, but it can handle many different cryptographic primitives, including shared and public key cryptography (encryption and signatures), hash functions, lists, ... It can handle an unbounded number of sessions of the protocol and an unbounded message space. This is possible thanks to some well-chosen approximations, which means that the tool can give false attacks. Actually, the tool may return three kinds of answer: either an attack is found (and ProVerif gives the attack trace), or no attack is found (but this does not mean that the protocol is secure), or else the protocol is proved secure.

It is interesting to notice that for the five topologies we have characterized, we can safely consider an attacker who listens all the communication channels. Moreover, we can easily encode neighbourhood checks, or the property to be an admissible path by defining predicates through Horn clauses. For instance, the predicate check(A, B) can be defined by enumerating all the existing links in the four-nodes topology under study.

5.2   Case Studies

As an application, we consider two source routing protocols. The first one is the protocol SRP applied on DSR that has been described in Section 3.2. We also studied the multipath routing protocol SDMSR introduced in [11] whose aim is to find several paths leading from the source S to the destination D.

We give below a brief description of the SDMSR protocol (a more detailed description can be found in [17]). First, the source constructs a request packet and broadcasts it to its neighbours.

$$\langle req, S, D, id, S :: [], [\![\langle req, S, D, id \rangle]\!]_{sk(S)} \rangle.$$

This packet contains in particular the beginning of a route to D, and a signature over the content of the request, computed with the private key $sk(S)$. The source then waits for a reply containing a route to D signed by one of his neighbours, and checks that this route is plausible. The names of the intermediate nodes are accumulated in the route request packet and the attached signature is checked by each intermediate node. When the request reaches the destination D via the node B, he performs some checks and constructs a route reply.

$$\langle rep, D, x_S, id, D, l_{route}, [\![\langle rep, D, S, id, l_{route} \rangle]\!]_{sk(D)} \rangle.$$

In particular it computes a signature over the route l_{route} accumulated in the request packet with its private key $sk(D)$. It then sends the reply back over the network. The reply travels along the route back to S, and the intermediate nodes check that the signature in the reply packet is correct, and that the route is plausible, before forwarding it. Each node V replaces the signature $[\![\langle rep, D, S, id, l_{route} \rangle]\!]_{sk(A)}$ computed by its neighbour by its own signature $[\![\langle rep, D, S, id, l_{route} \rangle]\!]_{sk(V)}$.

5.3   Results

We analyse these protocols considering the five different topologies that have been described in Section 4.3 and for an unbounded number of sessions. We analyse the configuration where each node of the topology plays an unbounded number of sessions of each role (each node can act as a source, a destination, or an intermediate node).

Note also that even if ProVerif is able to manipulate lists and predicates defined through Horn clauses, those predicates are quite powerful and ProVerif is not always able to handle them in a satisfactory way. Therefore, we did not model the sanity check $\mathsf{last}(S, x_L)$ that is normally performed by the source. But this did not introduce any false attack: the attacks that are reported by the ProVerif tool are still valid when considering this additional check.

	SRP applied on DSR	SDMSR
$\mathcal{T}_1$	**attack found**	**attack found**
$\mathcal{T}_2$	**attack found**	**attack found**
$\mathcal{T}_3$	no attack found	no attack found
$\mathcal{T}_4$	no attack found	no attack found
$\mathcal{T}_5$	no attack found	no attack found

We retrieve the attack on the protocol SRP applied to DSR, mentioned in Example 7. Actually, the SDMSR protocol is subject to the same kind of attack than SRP applied to DSR (see [9]). The running time of ProVerif was less than a few secondes for each topology. All the files for these experiments are available at: http://www.lsv.ens-cachan.fr/~{}delaune/RoutingProtocols.

6   Conclusion

When checking whether a routing protocol ensures that resulting routes are valid even in the presence of malicious nodes, we have shown a simple reduction result: there is an attack on an arbitrary topology if and only if there is an attack on one of five particular topologies, each of them having only four nodes. It is therefore possible to use standard verification tools for analysing routing protocols, provided they make use of primitives supported by the tools.

Our execution model of protocols is very general, encompassing many families of routing protocols, e.g. with recursive tests/operations and various kinds of neighbourhood checks. Our only restriction is the fact that tests should be stable under projection of nodes names, typically disallowing test of difference. Disequality tests are useful to discard a route that contains twice the same node, or for checking disequality of session ids to avoid answering twice the same request. Investigating how to extend our reduction result to some families of difference tests is left for future work. Also, the five topologies we obtain may seem unrealistic, for example because the source and the destination are neighbours. It seems feasible to refine our reduction result adding some topological constraints such as avoiding the source and the destination to be neighbours, possibly considering a larger (but still finite) number of nodes. A limitation of our work is the fact that it is limited to a single (crucial) property: the validity of the resulting route. Our reduction result certainly works for other properties. But understanding (and formalizing) which security properties are relevant for routing protocols is a difficult question. Another extension would be to model mobility during the execution of the protocol. This would allow us to consider changes in the network topology and to analyze the security of route updates. This requires to model an appropriate security property.

References

1. Abadi, M., Fournet, C.: Mobile values, new names, and secure communication. In: Proc. 28th Symposium on Principles of Programming Languages (POPL 2001), pp. 104–115. ACM Press (2001)
2. Abadi, M., Gordon, A.: A calculus for cryptographic protocols: The spi calculus. In: Proc. 4th Conference on Computer and Communications Security (CCS 1997), pp. 36–47. ACM Press (1997)
3. Ács, G., Buttyán, L., Vajda, I.: Provably secure on-demand source routing in mobile ad hoc networks. IEEE Trans. Mob. Comput. 5(11), 1533–1546 (2006)
4. Andel, T., Back, G., Yasinsac, A.: Automating the security analysis process of secure ad hoc routing protocols. Simulation Modelling Practice and Theory 19(9), 2032–2049 (2011)
5. Armando, A., Carbone, R., Compagna, L., Cuéllar, J., Tobarra, M.L.: Formal analysis of SAML 2.0 web browser single sign-on: breaking the SAML-based single sign-on for google apps. In: Proc. of the 6th ACM Workshop on Formal Methods in Security Engineering (FMSE 2008), pp. 1–10. ACM (2008)
6. Armando, A., Basin, D., Boichut, Y., Chevalier, Y., Compagna, L., Cuellar, J., Drielsma, P.H., Heám, P.C., Kouchnarenko, O., Mantovani, J., Mödersheim, S., von Oheimb, D., Rusinowitch, M., Santiago, J., Turuani, M., Viganò, L., Vigneron, L.: The AVISPA Tool for the Automated Validation of Internet Security Protocols and Applications. In: Etessami, K., Rajamani, S.K. (eds.) CAV 2005. LNCS, vol. 3576, pp. 281–285. Springer, Heidelberg (2005)
7. Arnaud, M., Cortier, V., Delaune, S.: Modeling and verifying ad hoc routing protocols. In: Proc. 23rd IEEE Computer Security Foundations Symposium (CSF 2010), pp. 59–74. IEEE Computer Society Press (July 2010)
8. Arnaud, M., Cortier, V., Delaune, S.: Deciding Security for Protocols with Recursive Tests. In: Bjørner, N., Sofronie-Stokkermans, V. (eds.) CADE 2011. LNCS (LNAI), vol. 6803, pp. 49–63. Springer, Heidelberg (2011)
9. Arnaud, M., Cortier, V., Delaune, S.: Modeling and verifying ad hoc routing protocols. Research Report LSV-11-24, Laboratoire Spécification et Vérification, ENS Cachan, France, 68 pages (December 2011)
10. Benetti, D., Merro, M., Viganò, L.: Model checking ad hoc network routing protocols: Aran vs. endaira. In: Proc. 8th IEEE International Conference on Software Engineering and Formal Methods (SEFM 2010), Pisa, Italy, pp. 191–202. IEEE Computer Society (2010)
11. Berton, S., Yin, H., Lin, C., Min, G.: Secure, disjoint, multipath source routing protocol(sdmsr) for mobile ad-hoc networks. In: Proc. 5th International Conference on Grid and Cooperative Computing, GCC 2006, pp. 387–394. IEEE Computer Society, Washington, DC (2006)
12. Blanchet, B.: An efficient cryptographic protocol verifier based on prolog rules. In: Proc., 14th Computer Security Foundations Workshop (CSFW 2001). IEEE Comp. Soc. Press (2001)

13. Blanchet, B.: An automatic security protocol verifier based on resolution theorem proving (invited tutorial). In: Proc. 20th International Conference on Automated Deduction, CADE 2005 (2005)
14. Burmester, M., de Medeiros, B.: On the security of route discovery in manets. IEEE Trans. Mob. Comput. 8(9), 1180–1188 (2009)
15. Buttyán, L., Vajda, I.: Towards Provable Security for Ad Hoc Routing Protocols. In: Proc. 2nd ACM Workshop on Security of Ad Hoc and Sensor Networks (SASN 2004), pp. 94–105. ACM, New York (2004)
16. Comon-Lundh, H., Cortier, V.: Security Properties: Two Agents Are Sufficient. In: Degano, P. (ed.) ESOP 2003. LNCS, vol. 2618, pp. 99–113. Springer, Heidelberg (2003)
17. Cortier, V., Degrieck, J., Delaune, S.: Analysing routing protocols: four nodes topologies are sufficient. Research Report LSV-11-25, Laboratoire Spécification et Vérification, ENS Cachan, France, 28 pages (December 2011)
18. Cremers, C.: The Scyther Tool: Verification, Falsification, and Analysis of Security Protocols. In: Gupta, A., Malik, S. (eds.) CAV 2008. LNCS, vol. 5123, pp. 414–418. Springer, Heidelberg (2008)
19. Dolev, D., Yao, A.C.: On the security of public key protocols. In: Proc. 22nd Symposium on Foundations of Computer Science (FCS 1981), pp. 350–357. IEEE Computer Society Press (1981)
20. Feng, T., Guo, X., Ma, J., Li, X.: UC-Secure Source Routing Protocol (2009)
21. Hu, Y.-C., Perrig, A., Johnson, D.: Ariadne: A Secure On-Demand Routing Protocol for Ad Hoc Networks. Wireless Networks 11, 21–38 (2005)
22. Hu, Y.-C., Perrig, A., Johnson, D.B.: Wormhole attacks in wireless networks. IEEE Journal on Selected Areas in Communications 24(2), 370–380 (2006)
23. Johnson, D.B., Maltz, D.A., Broch, J.: DSR: The dynamic source routing protocol for multi-hop wireless ad hoc networks. In: Perkins, C.E. (ed.) In Ad Hoc Networking, ch. 5, pp. 139–172. Addison-Wesley (2001)
24. Lazos, L., Poovendran, R., Meadows, C., Syverson, P., Chang, L.W.: Preventing wormhole attacks on wireless ad hoc networks: a graph theoretic approach. In: Wireless Communications and Networking Conference, vol. 2 (2005)
25. Nanz, S., Hankin, C.: A Framework for Security Analysis of Mobile Wireless Networks. Theoretical Computer Science 367(1), 203–227 (2006)
26. Papadimitratos, P., Haas, Z.: Secure routing for mobile ad hoc networks. In: Proc. SCS Communication Networks and Distributed Systems Modelling Simulation Conference, CNDS (2002)
27. Rusinowitch, M., Turuani, M.: Protocol insecurity with finite number of sessions is NP-complete. In: Proc. 14th Computer Security Foundations Workshop (CSFW 2001), pp. 174–190. IEEE Comp. Soc. Press (2001)

Parametric Verification of Address Space Separation

Jason Franklin, Sagar Chaki, Anupam Datta,
Jonathan M. McCune, and Amit Vasudevan

Carnegie Mellon University

Abstract. The address translation subsystem of operating systems, hypervisors, and virtual machine monitors must correctly enforce address space separation in the presence of adversaries. The size, and hierarchical nesting, of the data structures over which such systems operate raise challenges for automated model checking techniques to be fruitfully applied to them. We address this problem by developing a sound and complete parametric verification technique that achieves the best possible reduction in model size. Our results significantly generalize prior work on this topic, and bring interesting systems within the scope of analysis. We demonstrate the applicability of our approach by modeling shadow paging mechanisms of Xen version 3.0.3 and ShadowVisor, a research hypervisor developed for the x86 platform.

1 Introduction

A common use of protection mechanisms in systems software is to prevent one execution context from accessing memory regions allocated to a different context. For example, hypervisors, such as Xen [5], are designed to support memory separation not only among guest operating systems, but also between the guests and the hypervisor itself. Separation is achieved by an address translation subsystem that is self-contained and relatively small (around 7000 LOC in Xen version 3.0.3). Verifying security properties of such separation mechanisms is both: (i) important, due to their wide deployment in environments with malicious guests, e.g., the cloud; and (ii) challenging, due to their complexity. Addressing this challenge is the subject of our paper.

A careful examination of the source code for two hypervisors – Xen and ShadowVisor, a research hypervisor – reveals that a major source of complexity in separation mechanisms is the size, and hierarchical nesting, of the data-structures over which they operate. For example, Xen's address translation mechanism involves multi-level page tables where a level has up to 512 entries in a 3-level implementation, or up to 1024 entries in a 2-level implementation. The number of levels is further increased by optimizations, such as context caching (see Section 3 for a detailed description). Since the complexity of model checking grows exponentially with the size of these data-structures, verifying these separation mechanisms directly is intractable.

We address this problem by developing a parametric verification technique that is able to handle separation mechanisms operating over multi-level data structures of *arbitrary size* and with *arbitrary number of levels*. Specifically, we make the following contributions. First, we develop a parametric guarded command language ($PGCL^+$) for modeling hypervisors and adversaries. In particular, $PGCL^+$ supports: (i) nested parametric arrays to model data structures, such as multi-level page tables, where the parameters model the

P. Degano and J.D. Guttman (Eds.): POST 2012, LNCS 7215, pp. 51–68, 2012.

size of page tables at each level; and (ii) whole array operations to model an adversary who non-deterministically sets the values of data structures under its control.

In addition, the design of $PGCL^+$ is driven by the fact that our target separation mechanisms operate over tree-shaped data structures in a *row independent* and *hierarchically row uniform* manner. Consider a mechanism operating over a tree-shaped multi-level page table. Row independence means that the values in different rows of a page table are mutually independent. Hierarchical row uniformity implies that: (a) for each level i of the page table, the mechanism executes the same command on all rows at level i; (b) the command for a row at level i involves recursive operation over at most one page table at the next level $i + 1$; (c) the commands for distinct rows at level i never lead to operations over the same table at level $i + 1$. Both row independence and hierarchical uniformity are baked syntactically into $PGCL^+$ via restricted forms of commands and nested whole array operations.

Second, we propose a parametric specification formalism for expressing security policies of separation mechanisms modeled in $PGCL^+$. Our formalism is able to express both safety and liveness properties (via a new logic $PTSL^+$) that involve arbitrary nesting of quantifiers over multiple levels of the nested parametric arrays in $PGCL^+$.

Third, we prove a set of *small model theorems* that roughly state that for any system M expressible in $PGCL^+$, and any security property φ in our specification formalism, an instance of M with a data structure of arbitrary size satisfies φ iff the instance of M where the data structure has 1 element at every level satisfies φ. These theorems yield the best possible reduction – e.g., verifying security of a separation mechanism over an arbitrarily large page table is reduced to verifying the mechanism with just 1 page table entry at each level. This ameliorates the lack of scalability of verification due to data structure size. For brevity, we defer proofs to the full version [17].

Finally, we demonstrate the effectiveness of our approach by modeling, and verifying, shadow paging mechanisms of Xen version 3.0.3 and ShadowVisor, together with associated address separation properties. The models were created manually from the actual source code of these systems. In the case of ShadowVisor, our initial verification identified a previously unknown vulnerability. After fixing the vulnerability, we are able to verify the new model successfully.

The rest of the paper is organized as follows. Section 2 surveys related work. Section 3 presents an overview of address translation mechanisms and associated separation properties. Section 4 presents the parametric modeling language, the specification logic, as well as the small model theorems and the key ideas behind their proofs. Section 5 presents the case studies. Finally, Section 6 presents our conclusions.

2   Related Work

Parametric verification has been applied to a wide variety of problems [10, 11, 13, 15], notably to verify cache coherence protocols [9, 11, 12, 14, 19]. However, we are distinguished by the focus on security properties in the presence of an adversary (or, attacker). Existing formalisms for parameterized verification of data-independent systems either do not allow whole-array operations [23], or restrict them to a reset or copy operation that updates array elements to fixed values [24]. Neither case can model our adversary.

Pnueli et al [26], Arons et al., [4], and Fang et al. [16] investigate finite bounded-data systems, which support stratified arrays that map to Booleans, a notion similar to our hierarchical arrays. However, they consider a restricted logic that allows for safety properties and a limited form of liveness properties referred to as response properties. In contrast, we consider both safety and more expressive liveness properties that can include both next state and until operators in addition to the forall operator. Moreover, the cutoffs of their small model theorems are a function of the type signatures, number of quantified index variables, and other factors. When instantiated with the same types used in our language, their small model theorems have larger cutoffs than our own. By focusing on the specific case of address translation systems and address separation properties, we are able to arrive at smaller cutoffs.

This paper generalizes our prior work [18] from a single parametric array to a tree of parametric arrays of arbitrary depth. The generalization requires new conceptual and technical insights and brings interesting systems (such as multi-level paging and context caching as used in Xen) within the scope of analysis. The concept of hierarchical row uniformity did not arise in the previous work. Moreover, our language $PGCL^+$ supports a more general form of guarded commands. At a technical level, the proofs are more involved because of the generality of the language and the logic. In particular, the use of mutual recursion in the definition of the programming language necessitates the use of mutual induction in establishing several key lemmas.

Neumann et al. [25], Rushby [27], and Shapiro and Weber [28] propose verifying the design of secure systems by manually proving properties using a logic and without an explicit adversary model. A number of groups [20, 22, 29] have employed theorem proving to verify security properties of OS implementations. Barthe et al. [6] formalized an idealized model of a hypervisor in the Coq proof assistant and Alkassar et al. [1, 2] and Baumann et al. [7] annotated the C code of a hypervisor and utilized the VCC verifier to prove correctness properties. Our approach is based on automatic verification via model checking.

3   Address Space Translation and Separation

In this section, we give an overview of the systems we target, viz., address space translation schemes, and the properties we verify, viz., address separation.

3.1   Address Space Translation

Consider a system with memory sub-divided into pages. Each page has a base address (or address, for short). *Address space translation* maps source addresses to destination addresses. In the simplest setting, it is implemented by a single-level "page table" (PT). Each row of the PT is a pair (x, y) such that x is a source base address and y is its corresponding destination base address.

More sophisticated address translation schemes use multi-level PTs. A n-level PT is essentially a set of tables linked to form a tree of depth n. Specifically, each row of a table at level i contains either a destination address, or the starting address of a table at level $i + 1$. In addition to addresses, rows contain flags (e.g., to indicate if the

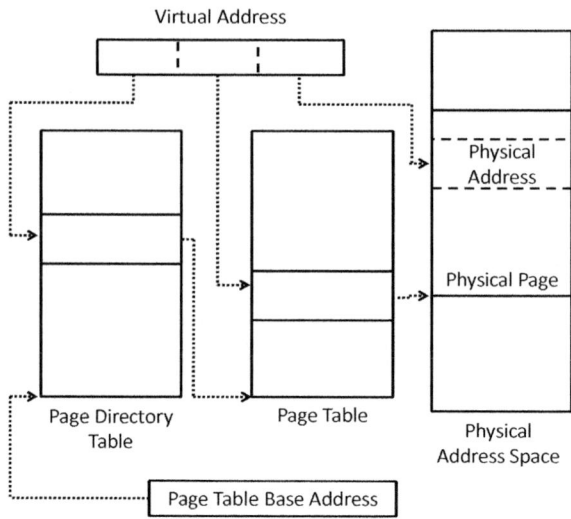

Fig. 1. Typical two-level page table structure

row contains a destination addresses or the address of another table). We now present a concrete example.

Example 1. Figure 1 shows a typical two-level address translation. A 2-level PT consists of a top level Page Directory Table (*PDT*) and a set of leaf PTs. A source address i is split into two parts, whose sizes are determined during the design of the PT. Let $i = (i_1, i_2)$. To compute the destination address corresponding to i, we first find the row (i_1, o_1) in the *PDT*. The entry o_1 contains an address a_1, a Page Size Extension flag *PSE*, and a present flag *PRESENT*. If *PRESENT* is unset, then there is no destination address corresponding to i. Otherwise, if *PSE* is set, then the destination address is a_1. Finally, if *PSE* is unset, we find the entry (i_2, a_2) in the table located at address a_1, and return a_2 as the destination address. Note the use of *PSE* and *PRESENT* to disambiguate between different types of rows. Also, note the dual use of the address field a_1 as either a destination address or a table address.

3.2   Address Space Separation

While the systems we target are address translation schemes, the broad class of properties we aim for is address separation. This is a crucial property – in essence requiring that disjoint source addresses spaces be mapped to disjoint destination address spaces. Our notion of address separation is conceptually similar to that used by Baumann et al. [7]. Formally, an address translation scheme M violates separation if it maps addresses a_1 and a_2 from two different source address spaces to the same destination address. For example, an OS's virtual memory manager enforces separation between the address spaces of the OS kernel and various processes. Address space separation is a safety property since its violation is exhibited by a finite execution.

The key technique, used by hypervisor address translation schemes, to ensure memory separation is "shadowing". For example, a separation kernel employs shadow paging to isolate critical memory regions from an untrusted guest OS. In essence, the kernel maintains its own trusted version of the guest's PT, called the shadow PT or sPT. The guest is allowed to modify its PT. However, the kernel interposes on such modifications and checks that the guest's modifications do not violate memory separation. If the check succeeds, the sPT is "synchronized" with the modified guest's PT.

Multi-level PTs are the canonical tree-shaped data-structures that motivates our work. In real systems, such PTs are used for various optimizations. One use is to translate large source address spaces without the overhead of one PT entry for each source base address. Another use is to implement context caching, a performance optimization – used by both Xen and VMWare – for shadow paging. Normally, every virtual address space (or, context) has its own PT, e.g., for a hypervisor, each process running on each guest OS has a separate context. Suppose that all context PTs are shadowed to a single sPT. When the context changes (e.g., when a new process is scheduled to run), the sPT is re-initialized from the PT of the new context. This hampers performance. Context caching avoids this problem by shadowing each context PT to a separate sPT. In essence, the sPT itself becomes a multi-level PT, where each row of the top-level PT points to a PT shadowing a distinct context.

Our goal is to verify address separation for address translation schemes that operate on multi-level PTs with arbitrary (but fixed) number of levels and arbitrary (but fixed) number of rows in each table, where each row has an arbitrary (but fixed) number of flags. These goals crucially influence the syntax and semantics of $PGCL^+$ and our specification formalism, and our technical results, which we present next.

4   Definitions of $PGCL^+$ and $PTSL^+$

In this section, we present our language $PGCL^+$ and our specification formalism for modeling programs and security properties, respectively.

4.1 $PGCL^+$ Syntax

All variables in $PGCL^+$ are Boolean. The language includes nested parametric arrays to a finite depth d. Each row of an array at depth d is a record with a single field F, a finite array of Booleans of size q_d. Each row of an array at depth z ($1 \leq z < d$) is a structure with two fields: F, a finite array of Booleans of size q_z, and P an array at depth $z+1$. Our results do not depend on the values of d and $\{q_z \mid 1 \leq z \leq d\}$, and hence hold for programs that manipulate arrays that are nested (as describe above) to arbitrary depth, and with Boolean arrays of arbitrary size at each level. Also, Boolean variables enable us to encode finite valued variables, and arrays, records, relations and functions over such variables.

Let 1 and 0 be, respectively, the representations of the truth values **true** and **false**. Let B be a set of Boolean variables, $i_1, \ldots, i_d$ be variables used to index into $P_1, \ldots, P_d$, respectively, and $n_1, \ldots, n_d$ be variables used to store the number of rows of $P_1, \ldots, P_d$,

Natural Numerals	K		
Boolean Variables	B		
Parametric Index Variables	$i_1, \ldots, i_d$		
Parameter Variables	$n_1, \ldots, n_d$		
Expressions	E	$::=$ $1 \mid 0 \mid * \mid B \mid E \vee E \mid E \wedge E \mid \neg E$	
Param. Expressions $(1 \leq z \leq d)$	$\widehat{E}_z$	$::=$ $E \mid P[i_1]\ldots P[i_z].F[K] \mid \widehat{E}_z \vee \widehat{E}_z \mid \widehat{E}_z \wedge \widehat{E}_z$ $\mid \neg \widehat{E}_z$	
Instantiated Guarded Commands	G	$::=$ $GC(K^d)$	
Guarded Commands	GC	$::=$ $E \ ? \ C_1 : C_1$	
		$\mid \ GC \parallel GC$	Parallel
Commands (depth $1 \leq z \leq d$)	C_z	$::=$ $B := E$ (if $z = 1$)	Assignment
		$\mid$ for i_z do $\widehat{E}_z$? $\widehat{C}_z : \widehat{C}_z$	Parametric for
		$\mid \ C_z ; C_z$	Sequencing
		$\mid$ skip	Skip
Param. Commands $(1 \leq z \leq d)$	$\widehat{C}_z$	$::=$ $P[i_1]\ldots P[i_z].F[K] := \widehat{E}_z$	Array assign
		$\mid \ \widehat{C}_z ; \widehat{C}_z$	Sequencing
		$\mid \ C_{z+1}$ (if $z < d$)	Nesting

Fig. 2. $PGCL^+$ Syntax, z denotes depth

respectively. The syntax of $PGCL^+$ is shown in Figure 2. $PGCL^+$ supports natural numbers, Boolean variables, propositional expressions over Boolean variables and F elements, guarded commands that update Boolean variables and F elements, and parallel composition of guarded commands. A skip command does nothing. A guarded command e ? c_1 : c_2 executes c_1 or c_2 depending on if e evaluates to true or false. We write e ? c to mean e ? c : skip. The parallel composition of two guarded commands executes by non-deterministically picking one of the commands to execute. The sequential composition of two commands executes the first command followed by the second command. Note that commands at depth $z + 1$ are nested within those at depth z.

Language Design. Values assigned to an element of an F array at depth z can depend only on: (i) other elements of the same F array; (ii) elements of parent F arrays along the nesting hierarchy (to ensure hierarchical row uniformity); and (iii) Boolean variables. Values assigned to Boolean variables depend on other Boolean variables only. This is crucial to ensure row-independence which is necessary for our small model theorems (cf. Sec. 4.5).

4.2   ShadowVisor Code in $PGCL^+$

We use ShadowVisor as a running example, and now describe its model in $PGCL^+$. ShadowVisor uses a 2-level PT scheme. The key unbounded data structures are the guest and shadow Page Directory Table (gPDT and sPDT) at the top level, and the guest and shadow Page Tables (gPTs and sPTs) at the lower level. Since each shadow table has the same size as the corresponding guest table, we model them together in the 2-level $PGCL^+$ parametric array.

```
shadow_page_fault ≡
  for i₁ do
    PDT[i₁].F[gPRESENT] ∧ PDT[i₁].F[gPSE]∧
    PDT[i₁].F[gADDR] < MEM_LIMIT − MPS_PDT ?
      PDT[i₁].F[sADDR] := PDT[i₁].F[gADDR];
    for i₂ do
      PDT[i₁].F[gPRESENT] ∧ PDT[i₁].PT[i₂].F[gPTE_PRESENT]∧
      PDT[i₁].PT[i₂].F[gPTE_ADDR] < MEM_LIMIT − MPS_PT ?
        PDT[i₁].PT[i₂].F[sPTE_ADDR] := PDT[i₁].PT[i₂].F[gPTE_ADDR];

shadow_invalidate_page ≡
  for i₁ do
    (PDT[i₁].F[sPRESENT] ∧ ¬PDT[i₁].F[gPRESENT])∨
    (PDT[i₁].F[sPRESENT] ∧ PDT[i₁].F[gPRESENT]∧
    (PDT[i₁].F[sPSE] ∨ PDT[i₁].F[gPSE])) ?
      PDT[i₁].F[sPDE] := 0;
  for i₁ do
    PDT[i₁].F[sPRESENT] ∧ PDT[i₁].F[gPRESENT]∧
    ¬PDT[i₁].F[gPSE] ∧ ¬PDT[i₁].F[sPSE] ?
      for i₂ do
        PDT[i₁].PT[i₂].F[sPTE] := 0;

  adversary ≡                          shadow_new_context ≡
    for i₁ do                            for i₁ do
      PDT[i₁].F[gPDE] := *;                 PDT[i₁].F[sPDE] := 0;
      for i₂ do
        PDT[i₁].PT[i₂].F[gPTE] := *;
```

Fig. 3. ShadowVisor model in $PGCL^+$

For simplicity, let PDT be the top-level array P. Elements $\text{PDT}[i_1].\text{F}[\text{gPRESENT}]$ and $\text{PDT}[i_1].\text{F}[\text{gPSE}]$ are the present and page size extension flags for the i_1-th gPD entry, while $\text{PDT}[i_1].\text{F}[\text{gADDR}]$ is the destination address contained in the i_1-th gPD entry. Elements sPRESENT, sPSE, and sADDR are defined analogously for sPD entries. Again for simplicity, let $\text{PDT}[i_1].\text{PT}$ be the array $\text{P}[i_1].\text{P}$. Elements gPTE_PRESENT and gPTE_ADDR of $\text{PDT}[i_1].\text{PT}[i_2].\text{F}$ are the present flag and destination address contained in the i_2-th entry of the PT pointed to by the i_1-th gPDT entry. Elements sPTE_PRESENT and sPTE_ADDR of $\text{PDT}[i_1].\text{PT}[i_2].\text{F}$ are similarly defined for the sPDT. Terms gPDE refers to the set of elements corresponding to a gPDT entry (i.e., gPRESENT, gPSE, and gADDR). Terms gPTE, sPDE and sPTE are defined similarly for the gPT, sPDT, and sPT, respectively.

Our ShadowVisor model (see Figure 3) is a parallel composition of four guarded commands shadow_page_fault, shadow_invalidate_page, shadow_new_context, and adversary. Command shadow_page_fault synchronizes sPDT and sPT with gPDT and gPT when the guest kernel: (i) loads a new gPT, or (ii) modifies or creates a gPT entry. To ensure separation, shadow_page_fault does not copy addresses from the gPT or gPDT that allow access to addresses at or above MEM_LIMIT. This requires two distinct checks depending on the level of the table since pages mapped in

$$\frac{\sigma^n = (\lceil k_1 \rceil, \ldots, \lceil k_d \rceil) \qquad \{\sigma\} \text{ gc } \{\sigma'\}}{\{\sigma\} \text{ gc}(k_1, \ldots, k_d) \{\sigma'\}} \text{Parameter Instantiation}$$

$$\frac{\{\sigma\} \text{ c } \{\sigma''\} \qquad \{\sigma''\} \text{ c}' \{\sigma'\}}{\{\sigma\} \text{ c}; \text{c}' \{\sigma'\}} \text{Sequential} \qquad\qquad \frac{}{\{\sigma\} \text{ skip } \{\sigma\}} \text{Skip}$$

$$\frac{\sigma_{1,z}^n = (1^{z-1}, N) \qquad \hat{e} ? \hat{c}_1 : \hat{c}_2 \in (\hat{E}_z ? \hat{C}_z : \hat{C}_z)[i_1 \mapsto 1] \ldots [i_{z-1} \mapsto 1]}{\forall y \in [1, N] \cdot \{\sigma \downarrow (1^{z-1}, y)\} \ (\hat{e} ? \hat{c}_1 : \hat{c}_2)[i_z \mapsto 1] \{\sigma' \downarrow (1^{z-1}, y)\}}{\{\sigma\} \text{ for } i_z \text{ do } \hat{e} ? \hat{c}_1 : \hat{c}_2 \{\sigma'\}} \text{Unroll}$$

$$\frac{\langle e, \sigma \rangle \rightarrow \mathbf{true} \wedge \{\sigma\} \text{ c}_1 \{\sigma'\} \ \bigvee \ \langle e, \sigma \rangle \rightarrow \mathbf{false} \wedge \{\sigma\} \text{ c}_2 \{\sigma'\}}{\{\sigma\} \text{ e } ? \text{ c}_1 : \text{c}_2 \{\sigma'\}} \text{GC}$$

$$\frac{\langle e, \sigma \rangle \rightarrow t}{\{\sigma\} \text{ b} := e \{\sigma[\sigma^B \mapsto \sigma^B[b \mapsto t]]\}} \text{Assign} \qquad \frac{\{\sigma\} \text{ gc } \{\sigma'\} \vee \{\sigma\} \text{ gc}' \{\sigma'\}}{\{\sigma\} \text{ gc } \| \text{ gc}' \{\sigma'\}} \text{Parallel}$$

$$\frac{\hat{e} \in \hat{E}_z \qquad \langle \hat{e}, \sigma \rangle \rightarrow t \qquad (\lceil k_1 \rceil, \ldots, \lceil k_z \rceil, \lceil r \rceil) \in Dom(\sigma_z^P)}{\{\sigma\} \text{ P}[k_1] \ldots \text{P}[k_z].\text{F}[r] := \hat{e} \{\sigma[\sigma^P \mapsto \sigma^P[\sigma_z^P \mapsto [\sigma_z^P[(\lceil k_1 \rceil, \ldots, \lceil k_z \rceil, \lceil r \rceil) \mapsto t]]]]\}} \text{P. Assign}$$

Fig. 4. Rules for commands

the PDT are of size MPS_PDT and pages mapped in the PT are of size MPS_PT. Command shadow_invalidate_page invalidates entries in the sPD and sPT (by setting to zero) when the corresponding guest entries are not present, the *PSE* bits are inconsistent, or if both structures are consistent and the guest OS invalidates a page. Command shadow_new_context initializes a new context by clearing all the entries of the sPD. Finally, command adversary models the attacker by arbitrarily modifying every gPD entry and every gPT entry.

For brevity, we write c to mean 1 ? c. Since all *PGCL*+ variables are Boolean, we write $x < C$ to mean the binary comparison between a finite valued variable x and a constant C.

4.3 *PGCL*+ Semantics

We now present the operational semantics of *PGCL*+ as a relation on stores. Let $\mathbb{B}$ be the truth values $\{\mathbf{true}, \mathbf{false}\}$. Let $\mathbb{N}$ denote the set of natural numbers. For two natural numbers j and k such that $j \leq k$, we write $[j, k]$ to mean the set of numbers in the closed range from j to k. For any numeral k we write $\lceil k \rceil$ to mean the natural number represented by k in standard arithmetic. Often, we write k to mean $\lceil k \rceil$ when the context disambiguates such usage.

We write $Dom(f)$ to mean the domain of a function f; (t, t') denotes the concatenation of tuples t and t'; $t_{i,j}$ is the subtuple of t from the ith to the jth elements, and t_i means $t_{i,i}$. Given a tuple of natural numbers $t = (t_1, \ldots, t_z)$, we write $\otimes(t)$ to denote the set of tuples $[1, t_1] \times \cdots \times [1, t_z]$. Recall that, for $1 \leq z \leq d$, q_z is the size of the array F at depth z. Then, a store σ is a tuple $(\sigma^B, \sigma^n, \sigma^P)$ such that:

- $\sigma^B : B \to \mathbb{B}$ maps Boolean variables to $\mathbb{B}$;
- $\sigma^n \in \mathbb{N}^d$ is a tuple of values of the parameter variables;
- σ^P is a tuple of functions defined as follows:

$$\forall z \in [1,d] \cdot \sigma_z^P : \otimes(\sigma_{1,z}^n, q_z) \to \mathbb{B}$$

We omit the superscript of σ when it is clear from the context. The rules for evaluating $PGCL^+$ expressions under stores are defined inductively over the structure of $PGCL^+$ expressions, and shown in Figure 5. To define the semantics of $PGCL^+$, we first present the notion of store projection.

$$\overline{\langle 1, \sigma \rangle \to \mathbf{true}} \qquad \overline{\langle 0, \sigma \rangle \to \mathbf{false}} \qquad \overline{\langle *, \sigma \rangle \to \mathbf{true}} \qquad \overline{\langle *, \sigma \rangle \to \mathbf{false}}$$

$$\frac{b \in dom(\sigma^B)}{\langle b, \sigma \rangle \to \sigma^B(b)} \qquad \frac{\langle e, \sigma \rangle \to t}{\langle \neg e, \sigma \rangle \to [\neg]t} \qquad \frac{(\lceil k_1 \rceil, \ldots, \lceil k_z \rceil, \lceil r \rceil) \in Dom(\sigma_z^P)}{\langle P[k_1] \ldots P[k_z].F[r], \sigma \rangle \to \sigma_z^P(\lceil k_1 \rceil, \ldots, \lceil k_z \rceil, \lceil r \rceil)}$$

$$\frac{\langle e, \sigma \rangle \to t \quad \langle e', \sigma \rangle \to t'}{\langle e \vee e', \sigma \rangle \to t[\vee]t'} \qquad \frac{\langle e, \sigma \rangle \to t \quad \langle e', \sigma \rangle \to t'}{\langle e \wedge e', \sigma \rangle \to t[\wedge]t'}$$

Fig. 5. Rules for expression evaluation. $[\wedge]$, $[\vee]$, and $[\neg]$ denote logical conjunction, disjunction, and negation, respectively.

We overload the $\mapsto$ operator as follows. For any function $f : X \to Y$, $x \in X$ and $y \in Y$, we write $f[x \mapsto y]$ to mean the function that is identical to f, except that x is mapped to y. $X[y \mapsto w]$ is a tuple that equals X, except that $(X[y \mapsto w])_y = w$. For any $PGCL^+$ expression or guarded command X, variable v, and expression e, we write $X[v \mapsto e]$ to mean the result of replacing all occurrences of v in X simultaneously with e. For any $z \in \mathbb{N}$, 1^z denotes the tuple of z 1's.

Definition 1 (Store Projection). *Let* $\sigma = (\sigma^B, \sigma^n, \sigma^P)$ *be any store and* $1 \leq z \leq d$. *For* $k = (k_1, \ldots, k_z) \in \otimes(\sigma_1^n, \ldots, \sigma_z^n)$ *we write* $\sigma \downarrow k$ *to mean the store* $(\sigma^B, \sigma^m, \sigma^Q)$ *such that:*

1. $\sigma^m = \sigma^n[1 \mapsto 1][2 \mapsto 1] \ldots [z \mapsto 1]$
2. $\forall y \in [1,z] \cdot \forall X \in Dom(\sigma_y^Q) \cdot \sigma_y^Q(X) = \sigma_y^P(X[1 \mapsto k_1][2 \mapsto k_2] \ldots [y \mapsto k_y])$
3. $\forall y \in [z+1,d] \cdot \forall X \in Dom(\sigma_y^Q) \cdot \sigma_y^Q(X) = \sigma_y^P(X[1 \mapsto k_1][2 \mapsto k_2] \ldots [z \mapsto k_z])$

Note: $\forall z \in [1,d] \cdot \forall k \in \otimes(\sigma_1^n, \ldots, \sigma_z^n) \cdot \sigma \downarrow k = (\sigma \downarrow k) \downarrow 1^z$.

Intuitively, $\sigma \downarrow k$ is constructed by retaining σ^B, changing the first z elements of σ^n to 1 and leaving the remaining elements unchanged, and projecting away all but the k_y-th row of the parametric array at depth y for $1 \leq y \leq z$. Note that since projection retains σ^B, it does not affect the evaluation of expressions that do not refer to elements of P.

Store Transformation. For any $PGCL^+$ command c and stores σ and σ', we write $\{\sigma\}$ c $\{\sigma'\}$ to mean that σ is transformed to σ' by the execution of c. We define $\{\sigma\}$ c $\{\sigma'\}$ via induction on the structure of c, as shown in Figure 4.

Basic Propositions	BP	$::=$	b , $b \in B$ $\mid \neg BP \mid BP \wedge BP$
Parametric Propositions	$PP(i_1, \ldots, i_z)$	$::=$	$\{P[i_1] \ldots P[i_z].F[r] \mid \lceil r \rceil \leq q_z\}$
			$\mid \neg PP(i_1, \ldots, i_z)$
			$\mid PP(i_1, \ldots, i_z) \wedge PP(i_1, \ldots, i_z)$
Universal State Formulas	USF	$::=$	BP
			$\mid \forall i_1 \ldots \forall i_z . PP(i_1, \ldots, i_z)$
			$\mid BP \wedge \forall i_1 \ldots \forall i_z . PP(i_1, \ldots, i_z)$
Existential State Formulas	ESF	$::=$	BP
			$\mid \text{Æ}_1 i_1 \ldots \text{Æ}_z i_z . PP(i_1, \ldots, i_z)$
			$\mid BP \wedge \text{Æ}_1 i_1 \ldots \text{Æ}_z i_z . PP(i_1, \ldots, i_z)$
Generic State Formulas	GSF	$::=$	USF $\mid$ ESF $\mid$ USF $\wedge$ ESF
$PTSL^+$ Path Formulas	TLPF	$::=$	TLF $\mid$ TLF $\wedge$ TLF $\mid$ TLF $\vee$ TLF
			$\mid \mathbf{X}$ TLF $\mid$ TLF $\mathbf{U}$ TLF
$PTSL^+$ Formulas	TLF	$::=$	USF $\mid \neg$USF $\mid$ TLF $\wedge$ TLF
			$\mid$ TLF $\vee$ TLF $\mid \mathbf{A}$ TLPF

Fig. 6. Syntax of $PTSL^+$ ($1 \leq z \leq d$). In ESF, Æ_y is $\forall$ or $\exists$, at least one Æ_y is $\exists$.

The "GC" rule states that σ is transformed to σ' by executing the guarded command $e ? c_1 : c_2$ if: (i) either the guard e evaluates to **true** under σ and σ is transformed to σ' by executing the command c_1; (ii) or e evaluates to **false** under σ and σ is transformed to σ' by executing c_2 .

The "Unroll" rules states that if c is a for loop, then $\{\sigma\}$ c $\{\sigma'\}$ if each row of σ' results by executing the loop body from the same row of σ. The nesting of for-loops complicates the proofs of our small model theorems. Indeed, we require to reason using mutual induction about loop bodies $(\widehat{E}_z ? \widehat{C}_z)$ and commands (C_z), starting with the loop bodies at the lowest level, and moving up to commands at the highest level.

4.4   Specification Formalism

We support both reachability properties and temporal logic specifications. Reachability properties are expressed via "state formulas". In addition, state formulas are also used to specify the initial condition under which the target system begins execution. The syntax of state formulas is defined in Figure 6. We support three types of state formulas – universal, existential, and generic. Specifically, universal formulas allow only nested universal quantification over P, existential formulas allow arbitrary quantifier nesting with at least one $\exists$, while generic formulas allow one of each.

Temporal logic specifications are expressed in $PTSL^+$, a new logic we propose in this paper. In essence, $PTSL^+$ is a subset of the temporal logic ACTL* [8] with USF as atomic propositions. The syntax of $PTSL^+$ is defined in Figure 6. The quantification nesting allowed in our specification logic allows expressive properties spanning multiple levels of P. This will be crucial for our case studies, as shown in Sec. 5.

ShadowVisor Security Properties in $PTSL^+$.   ShadowVisor begins execution with every entry of the sPDT and sPT set to not present. This initial condition is stated in the following USF state formula:

$$\varphi_{init} \triangleq \forall i_1, i_2. \quad \neg\text{PDT}[i_1].\text{F}[\text{sPRESENT}] \wedge \neg\text{PDT}[i_1].\text{PT}[i_2].\text{F}[\text{sPTE\_PRESENT}]$$

ShadowVisor's separation property states that the physical addresses accessible by the guest must be less than MEM_LIMIT. This requires two distinct conditions depending on the table since pages mapped in the PDT are of size MPS_PDT and pages mapped in the PT are of size MPS_PT. Given a PDT mapped page frame starting at address a, a guest OS can access from a to $a + \text{MPS\_PDT}$ and $a + \text{MPS\_PT}$ for a PT mapped page frame. Hence, to enforce separation, ShadowVisor must restrict the addresses in the shadow page directory to be less than MEM_LIMIT − MPS_PDT and page table to be less than MEM_LIMIT − MPS_PT. Note that we are making the reasonable assumption that MEM_LIMIT > MAX_PDT and MEM_LIMIT > MAX_PT to avoid underflow. This security property is stated in the following USF state formula:

$$\varphi_{sep} \triangleq \forall i_1, i_2. \quad \begin{aligned} &(\text{PDT}[i_1].\text{F}[\text{sPRESENT}] \wedge \text{PDT}[i_1].\text{F}[\text{sPSE}] \Rightarrow \\ &(\text{PDT}[i_1].\text{F}[\text{sADDR}] < \text{MEM\_LIMIT} - \text{MPS\_PDT})) \wedge \\ &(\text{PDT}[i_1].\text{F}[\text{sPRESENT}] \wedge \neg\text{PDT}[i_1].\text{F}[\text{sPSE}] \wedge \\ &\text{PDT}[i_1].\text{PT}[i_2].\text{F}[\text{sPTE\_PRESENT}] \Rightarrow \\ &(\text{PDT}[i_1].\text{PT}[i_2].\text{F}[\text{sADDR}] < \text{MEM\_LIMIT} - \text{MPT\_PT})) \end{aligned}$$

Semantics. We now present the semantics of our specification logic. We further overload the $\mapsto$ operator such that for any $PTSL^+$ formula π, variable x, and numeral m, we write $\pi[x \mapsto m]$ to mean the result of substituting all occurrences of x in π with m. We start with the notion of satisfaction of formulas by stores.

Definition 2. *The satisfaction of a formula π by a store σ (denoted $\sigma \models \pi$) is defined, by induction on the structure of π, as follows:*

- $\sigma \models b$ *iff* $\sigma^B(b) = $ **true**
- $\sigma \models P[k_1]\ldots P[k_z].F[r]$ *iff* $(\lceil k_1 \rceil, \ldots, \lceil k_z \rceil, \lceil r \rceil) \in Dom(\sigma_z^P)$ *and* $\sigma_z^P(\lceil k_1 \rceil, \ldots, \lceil k_z \rceil, \lceil r \rceil) = $ **true**
- $\sigma \models \neg\pi$ *iff* $\sigma \not\models \pi$
- $\sigma \models \pi_1 \wedge \pi_2$ *iff* $\sigma \models \pi_1$ *and* $\sigma \models \pi_2$
- $\sigma \models \pi_1 \vee \pi_2$ *iff* $\sigma \models \pi_1$ *or* $\sigma \models \pi_2$
- $\sigma \models \text{Æ}_1 i_1, \ldots, \text{Æ}_z i_z.\pi$ *iff* $\text{Æ}_1 k_1 \in [1, \sigma_1^n]\ldots\text{Æ}_z k_z \in [1, \sigma_z^n].\sigma \downarrow (k_1, \ldots, k_z) \models \pi[i_1 \mapsto 1]\ldots[i_z \mapsto 1]$

The definition of satisfaction of Boolean formulas and the logical operators are standard. Parametric formulas, denoted $P[k_1]\ldots P[k_z].F[r]$, are satisfied if and only if the indices $k_1, \ldots, k_z, r$ are in bounds, and the element at the specified location is **true**. Quantified formulas are satisfied by σ if and only if appropriate (depending on the quantifiers) projections of σ satisfy the formula obtained by substituting 1 for the quantified variables in π. We present the semantics of a $PGCL^+$ program as a *Kripke structure*.

Kripke Semantics. Let gc be any $PGCL^+$ guarded command and $k \in \mathbb{N}^d$. We denote the set of stores σ such that $\sigma^n = k$, as $Store(gc(k))$. Note that $Store(gc(k))$ is finite. Let *Init* be any formula and $AP = USF$ be the set of atomic propositions. Intuitively, a Kripke structure $M(gc(k), Init)$ over AP is induced by executing $gc(k)$ starting from any store $\sigma \in Store(gc(k))$ that satisfies *Init*.

Definition 3. *Let Init* $\in$ USF *be any formula. Formally, M*(gc(k),*Init*) *is a four tuple* $(S, I, \mathcal{T}, \mathcal{L})$, *where:*

- $S = Store(\text{gc}(k))$ *is a set of states;*
- $I = \{\sigma | \sigma \models Init\}$ *is a set of initial states;*
- $\mathcal{T} = \{(\sigma, \sigma') \mid \{\sigma\}\text{gc}(k)\{\sigma'\}\}$ *is a transition relation given by the operational semantics of PGCL$^+$; and*
- $\mathcal{L} : S \rightarrow 2^{AP}$ *is the function that labels each state with the set of propositions true in that state; formally,*

$$\forall \sigma \in S \cdot \mathcal{L}(\sigma) = \{\varphi \in AP \mid \sigma \models \varphi\}$$

If ϕ is a *PTSL$^+$* formula, then $M, \sigma \models \phi$ means that ϕ holds at state σ in the Kripke structure M. We use an inductive definition of $\models$ [8]. Informally, an atomic proposition π holds at σ iff $\sigma \models \pi$; **A** ϕ holds at σ if ϕ holds on all possible (infinite) paths starting from σ. TLPF formulas hold on paths. A TLF formula ϕ holds on a path Π iff it holds at the first state of Π; **X** ϕ holds on a path Π iff ϕ holds on the suffix of Π starting at second state of Π; ϕ_1 **U** ϕ_2 holds on Π if ϕ_1 holds on suffixes of Π until ϕ_2 begins to hold. The definitions for $\neg$, $\wedge$ and $\vee$ are standard.

Simulation. For Kripke structures M_1 and M_2, we write $M_1 \preceq M_2$ to mean that M_1 is simulated by M_2. We use the standard definition of simulation [8] (presented in the full version of our paper [17]). Since satisfaction of ACTL* formulas is preserved by simulation [8], and *PTSL$^+$* is a subset of ACTL*, we claim that *PTSL$^+$* formulas are also preserved by simulation.

4.5   Small Model Theorems

In this section, we present two small model theorems. Both theorems relate the behavior of a *PGCL$^+$* program when P has arbitrarily many rows to its behavior when P has a single row. First, a definition.

Definition 1 (Exhibits). *A Kripke structure M*(gc(k),*Init*) *exhibits a formula* φ *iff there is a reachable state* σ *of M*(gc(k),*Init*) *such that* $\sigma \models \varphi$.

The first theorem applies to safety properties.

Theorem 1 (Small Model Safety 1). *Let* gc(k) *be any instantiated guarded command. Let* $\varphi \in$ GSF *be any generic state formula, and Init* $\in$ USF *be any universal state formula. Then M*(gc(k),*Init*) *exhibits* φ *iff M*(gc(1^d),*Init*) *exhibits* φ.

The second theorem is more general, and relates Kripke structures via simulation.

Theorem 2 (Small Model Simulation). *Let* gc(k) *be any instantiated guarded command. Let Init* $\in$ GSF *be any generic state formula. Then M*(gc(k),*Init*) $\preceq$ *M*(gc(1^d),*Init*) *and M*(gc(1^d),*Init*) $\preceq$ *M*(gc(k),*Init*).

Since, simulation preserves *PTSL$^+$* specifications, we obtain the following immediate corrollary to Theorem 2.

Corollary 1 (Small Model Safety 2). *Let* $gc(k)$ *be any instantiated guarded command. Let* $\varphi \in$ USF *be any universal state formula, and Init* $\in$ GSF *be any generic state formula. Then* $M(gc(k), Init)$ *exhibits* φ *iff* $M(gc(1^d), Init)$ *exhibits* φ.

Note that Corollary 1 is the dual of Theorem 1 obtained by swapping the types of φ and *Init*. The proofs of Theorems 1 and 2 involve mutual induction over both the structure of commands, and the depth of the parametric array P. This is due to the recursive nature of $PGCL^+$, where commands at level z refer to paramaterized commands at level z, which in turn refer to commands at level $z + 1$. For brevity, we defer these proofs to the full version of our paper [17].

5 Case Studies

We present two case studies – ShadowVisor and Xen – to illustrate our approach. In addition to these two examples, we believe that our approach is, in general, applicable to all paging systems that are strictly hierarchical. This includes paging modes of x86 [21], and paging modes of ARM except for the super-pages [3] (due to the requirement that 16 adjacent entries must be identical).

5.1 ShadowVisor

Recall our model of ShadowVisor from Section 4.2 and the expression of ShadowVisor's initial condition and security properties as $PTSL^+$ formulas from Section 4.4. ShadowVisor's separation property states that the physical addresses accessible by the guest OS must be less than the lowest address of hypervisor protected memory, denoted MEM_LIMIT. This requires two distinct conditions depending on the table containing the mapping. Pages mapped in PDTs are of size MPS_PDT and pages mapped in PTs are of size MPS_PT. Given a page frame of size s with starting address a, a guest OS can access any address in the range $[a, a + s]$. Hence, subtracting the maximum page size prevents pages from overlapping the hypervisor's protected memory. Note that we are making the reasonable assumption that MEM_LIMIT > MPS_PDT and MEM_LIMIT > MPS_PT to avoid underflow.

In ShadowVisor's original shadow page fault handler (shown in shadow_page_fault_original), the conditionals allowed page directory and page table entries to start at addresses up to MEM_LIMIT. As a result, ShadowVisor running shadow_page_fault_original has a serious vulnerability where separation is violated by an adversary that non-deterministically chooses an address a such that $a + \text{MPS\_PDT} \geq \text{MEM\_LIMIT}$ or $a + \text{MPS\_PT} \geq \text{MEM\_LIMIT}$.

```
shadow_page_fault_original ≡
  for i₁ do
    PDT[i₁].F[gPRESENT] ∧ PDT[i₁].F[gPSE] ∧ PDT[i₁].F[gADDR] < MEM_LIMIT ?
      PDT[i₁].F[sADDR] := PDT[i₁].F[gADDR];
    for i₂ do
      PDT[i₁].F[gPRESENT] ∧ PDT[i₁].PT[i₂].F[gPTE_PRESENT]∧
      PDT[i₁].PT[i₂].F[gPTE_ADDR] < MEM_LIMIT ?
        PDT[i₁].PT[i₂].F[sPTE_ADDR] := PDT[i₁].PT[i₂].F[gPTE_ADDR];
```

Table 1. ShadowVisor verification with increasing PT size. * means out of 1GB memory limit; Vars, Clauses = # of CNF variables and clauses generated by CBMC.

PT-Size	Time(s)	Vars	Clauses
1	0.07	1816	3649
10	3.48	93503	199752
20	37.8	360275	775462
30	*	*	*

Verification of our initial model of ShadowVisor detected this vulnerability. The vulnerability exists in ShadowVisor's design and C source code implementation. We were able to fix the vulnerability by adding appropriate checks and verify that the resulting model is indeed secure. We present our verification of $PGCL^+$ models below.

Both the vulnerable and repaired ShadowVisor programs are expressible as a $PGCL^+$ program, the initial state is expressible in USF, and the negation of the address separation property is expressible in GSF. Therefore, Theorem 1 applies and we need only verify the system with one table at each depth with one entry per table (i.e., a parameter of (1,1)).

Effectiveness of Small Model Theorems. For a concrete evaluation of the effectiveness of our small model theorems, we verify ShadowVisor with increasing sizes of page tables at both levels. More specifically, we created models of ShadowVisor in C (note that a guarded command in $PGCL^+$ is expressible in C) for various PT sizes (the sizes at both PT levels were kept equal).

We verify two properties using CBMC[1], a state-of-the-art model checker for C:

Basis. The initial state of the system ensures separation;

Inductive step. If the system started in a state that ensures separation, executing any of the four guarded commands in the ShadowVisor model preserves separation.

By induction, this guarantees that ShadowVisor ensures separation perpetually. Our results are shown in Table 1. Note that verification for size 1 (which is sound and complete due to our small model theorem) is quick, while it blows up for even page tables of size 30 (an unrealistically small number, implying that brute-force verification of ShadowVisor is intractable). The tools and benchmarks for our experiments are available at https://www.cs.cmu.edu/~jfrankli/post12/vrfy-expr.tgz.

5.2 Xen

Next, we analyzed address separation in a model of the Xen hypervisor, built from the source code of Xen version 3.0.3. Xen manages multiple virtual machines (VMs), each running a guest OS instance with multiple processes (i.e., contexts). Xen maintains a separate sPT for each context, and uses context caching (cf. Sec. 3).

---

[1] www.cprover.org/cbmc

We model Xen's context cache using a nested parametric array of depth 4. At the top level, row $P_1[i_i]$ (denoted $VM[i_1]$ below) contains an entry for a particular VM's guest. At the next level, the array $P_1[i_1].P_2$ (denoted $VM[i_1].Ctx$ below) contains an entry for each context of the i_1-th guest. Next, the array $P_1[i_1].P_2[i_2].P_3$ (denoted $VM[i_1].Ctx[i_2].PDT$) represents the PDT of the i_2-th context of the i_1-th guest OS. Finally, the array $P_1[i_1].P_2[i_2].P_3[i_3].P_4$ (denoted $VM[i_1].Ctx[i_2].PDT[i_3].PT$) is the PT of the i_3-th page directory table entry of the i_2-th context of the i_1-th guest.

Our separation property requires that the destination addresses accessible by a guest OS are less than a pre-defined constant MEM_LIMIT. We consider a natural extension of this separation property for a context caching system with multiple VMs that states that all VMs and contexts should be separate from VMM protected memory. This security property is stated in the following USF formula:

$$
\begin{aligned}
\varphi_{sep} \triangleq \forall i_1, i_2, i_3, i_4. \\
(VM[i_1].Ctx[i_2].PDT[i_3].F[sPRESENT] \wedge \\
VM[i_1].Ctx[i_2].PDT[i_3].F[sPSE] \Rightarrow \\
(VM[i_1].Ctx[i_2].PDT[i_3].F[sADDR] < MEM\_LIMIT - MPS\_PDT)) \wedge \\
(VM[i_1].Ctx[i_2].PDT[i_3].F[sPRESENT] \wedge \\
\neg VM[i_1].Ctx[i_2].PDT[i_3].F[sPSE] \Rightarrow \\
(VM[i_1].Ctx[i_2].PDT[i_3].PT[i_4].F[sADDR] < MEM\_LIMIT - MPS\_PT))
\end{aligned}
$$

We model Xen as starting in an initial state where all entries of all of the shadow page directory tables and shadow page tables are marked as not present. This is expressed by the following USF formula:

$$
\begin{aligned}
Init \triangleq \forall i_1, i_2, i_3, i_4. \quad \neg VM[i_1].Ctx[i_2].PDT[i_3].F[sPRESENT] \wedge \\
\neg VM[i_1].Ctx[i_2].PDT[i_3].PT[i_4].F[sPRESENT]
\end{aligned}
$$

We define the Xen address translation system using context caching in $PGCL^+$ as follows:

```
XenAddressTrans  ≡        shadow_page_fault
                       ‖  shadow_invalidate_page
                       ‖  context_caching_new_context
                       ‖  Xen_adversary
```

The commands shadow_page_fault and shadow_invalidate_page generalize their counterparts for ShadowVisor over multiple VMs and contexts, and are omitted. The following $PGCL^+$ guarded command implements context_caching_new_context .

```
context_caching_new_context  ≡
  for i₁ do
    for i₂ do
      for i₃ do
        * ? VM[i₁].Ctx[i₂].PDT[i₃].F[sPDE] := 0;
```

Note that, to model VMs and process scheduling soundly, we assume non-deterministic context switching. Hence, we extend ShadowVisor's shadow_new_context to non-deterministically clear contexts.

Table 2. Xen verification with increasing PT size. * means out of 1GB memory limit; Vars, Clauses = # of CNF variables and clauses generated by CBMC.

PT-Size	Time(s)	Vars	Clauses
1	0.41	5726	13490
3	2.38	34192	80802
6	12.07	121206	286650
9	*	*	*

Finally, we consider an adversary model where the the attacker has control over an unbounded but finite number of VMs, each with a unbounded but finite number of contexts. This adversary is therefore expressed as follows:

```
Xen_adversary ≡
  for i₁ do
   for i₂ do
    for i₃ do
     VM[i₁].Ctx[i₂].PDT[i₃].F[gPDE] := *;
     for i₄ do
      VM[i₁].Ctx[i₂].PDT[i₃].PT[i₄].F[gPTE] := *;
```

Our Xen model is clearly expressible in $PGCL^+$, its initial state is expressible in USF, and the negation of the address separation property is expressible in GSF. Therefore, Theorem 1 applies and we need only verify the system with one table at each depth with one entry per table (i.e., a system parameter of (1,1,1,1)).

Effectiveness of Small Model Theorems. As in the case of ShadowVisor we verify the Xen model with increasing (but equal) sizes of page tables at both levels, and 2 VMs and 2 contexts per VM. We verify the same two properties as for ShadowVisor to inductively prove that Xen ensures separation perpetually. Our results are shown in Table 2. Note again that verification for size 1 (which is sound and complete due to our small model theorem) is quick, while it blows up for even page tables of size 9 (an unrealistically small number, implying that brute-force verification of Xen is also intractable).

6   Conclusion

Verifying separation properties of address translation mechanisms of operating systems, hypervisors, and virtual machine monitors in the presence of adversaries is an important challenge toward developing secure systems. A significant factor behind the complexity of this challenge is that the data structures over which the translation mechanisms operate have both unbounded size and unbounded nesting depth. We developed a parametric verification technique to address this challenge. Our approach involves a new modeling language and specification mechanism to model and verify such parametric systems. We applied this methodology to verify that the designs of two hypervisors – ShadowVisor and Xen – correctly enforce the expected security properties in the presence of adversaries. Extending our approach to operate directly on system implementations, and relaxing the restrictions of row independence and hierarchical row uniformity, are areas for further investigation.

References

1. Alkassar, E., Cohen, E., Hillebrand, M., Kovalev, M., Paul, W.: Verifying shadow page table algorithms. In: Proceedings of FMCAD (2010)
2. Alkassar, E., Hillebrand, M.A., Paul, W.J., Petrova, E.: Automated Verification of a Small Hypervisor. In: Leavens, G.T., O'Hearn, P., Rajamani, S.K. (eds.) VSTTE 2010. LNCS, vol. 6217, pp. 40–54. Springer, Heidelberg (2010)
3. ARM Holdings: ARM1176JZF-S technical reference manual. Revision r0p7 (2009)
4. Arons, T., Pnueli, A., Ruah, S., Xu, Y., Zuck, L.: Parameterized Verification with Automatically Computed Inductive Assertions. In: Berry, G., Comon, H., Finkel, A. (eds.) CAV 2001. LNCS, vol. 2102, pp. 221–234. Springer, Heidelberg (2001)
5. Barham, P., Dragovic, B., Fraser, K., Hand, S., Harris, T., Ho, A., Neugebauer, R., Pratt, I., Warfield, A.: Xen and the art of virtualization. In: Proceedings of SOSP (2003)
6. Barthe, G., Betarte, G., Campo, J.D., Luna, C.: Formally Verifying Isolation and Availability in an Idealized Model of Virtualization. In: Butler, M., Schulte, W. (eds.) FM 2011. LNCS, vol. 6664, pp. 231–245. Springer, Heidelberg (2011)
7. Baumann, C., Blasum, H., Bormer, T., Tverdyshev, S.: Proving memory separation in a microkernel by code level verification. In: Proc. of AMICS (2011)
8. Clarke, E.M., Grumberg, O., Peled, D.: Model Checking. MIT Press, Cambridge (2000)
9. Emerson, E.A., Kahlon, V.: Reducing Model Checking of the Many to the Few. In: McAllester, D. (ed.) CADE 2000. LNCS, vol. 1831, pp. 236–254. Springer, Heidelberg (2000)
10. Emerson, E.A., Kahlon, V.: Model Checking Large-Scale and Parameterized Resource Allocation Systems. In: Katoen, J.-P., Stevens, P. (eds.) TACAS 2002. LNCS, vol. 2280, pp. 251–265. Springer, Heidelberg (2002)
11. Emerson, E.A., Kahlon, V.: Exact and Efficient Verification of Parameterized Cache Coherence Protocols. In: Geist, D., Tronci, E. (eds.) CHARME 2003. LNCS, vol. 2860, pp. 247–262. Springer, Heidelberg (2003)
12. Emerson, E.A., Kahlon, V.: Model checking guarded protocols. In: Proceedings of LICS (2003)
13. Emerson, E.A., Kahlon, V.: Rapid Parameterized Model Checking of Snoopy Cache Coherence Protocols. In: Garavel, H., Hatcliff, J. (eds.) TACAS 2003. LNCS, vol. 2619, pp. 144–159. Springer, Heidelberg (2003)
14. Emerson, E.A., Namjoshi, K.S.: Automatic Verification of Parameterized Synchronous Systems (Extended Abstract). In: Alur, R., Henzinger, T.A. (eds.) CAV 1996. LNCS, vol. 1102, pp. 87–98. Springer, Heidelberg (1996)
15. Emerson, E.A., Namjoshi, K.S.: Verification of Parameterized Bus Arbitration Protocol. In: Vardi, M.Y. (ed.) CAV 1998. LNCS, vol. 1427, pp. 452–463. Springer, Heidelberg (1998)
16. Fang, Y., Piterman, N., Pnueli, A., Zuck, L.: Liveness with Invisible Ranking. In: Steffen, B., Levi, G. (eds.) VMCAI 2004. LNCS, vol. 2937, pp. 223–238. Springer, Heidelberg (2003)
17. Franklin, J., Chaki, S., Datta, A., McCune, J.M., Vasudevan, A.: Parametric verification of address space separation. Tech. Rep. CMU-CyLab-12-001, CMU (2012)
18. Franklin, J., Chaki, S., Datta, A., Seshadri, A.: Scalable parametric verification of secure systems: How to verify reference monitors without worrying about data structure size. In: Proceedings of IEEE S&P (2010)

19. German, S.M., Sistla, A.P.: Reasoning about systems with many processes. Journal of the ACM 39(3), 675–735 (1992)
20. Heitmeyer, C.L., Archer, M., Leonard, E.I., McLean, J.D.: Formal specification and verification of data separation in a separation kernel for an embedded system. In: Proceedings of ACM CCS (2006)
21. Intel Corporation: Intel 64 and IA-32 Intel architecture software developer's manual. Intel Publication nos. 253665–253669 (2008)
22. Klein, G., Elphinstone, K., Heiser, G., Andronick, J., Cock, D., Derrin, P., Elkaduwe, D., Engelhardt, K., Kolanski, R., Norrish, M., Sewell, T., Tuch, H., Winwood, S.: seL4: Formal verification of an os kernel. In: Proceedings of SOSP (2009)
23. Lazić, R., Newcomb, T., Roscoe, A.W.: On Model Checking Data-Independent Systems with Arrays with Whole-Array Operations. In: Abdallah, A.E., Jones, C.B., Sanders, J.W. (eds.) CSP 2004. LNCS, vol. 3525, pp. 275–291. Springer, Heidelberg (2005)
24. Lazić, R., Newcomb, T., Roscoe, A.: On model checking data-independent systems with arrays without reset. Theory and Practice of Logic Programming 4(5&6) (2004)
25. Neumann, P., Boyer, R., Feiertag, R., Levitt, K., Robinson, L.: A provably secure operating system: The system, its applications, and proofs. Tech. rep., SRI International (1980)
26. Pnueli, A., Ruah, S., Zuck, L.D.: Automatic Deductive Verification with Invisible Invariants. In: Margaria, T., Yi, W. (eds.) TACAS 2001. LNCS, vol. 2031, p. 82. Springer, Heidelberg (2001)
27. Rushby, J.: The design and verification of secure systems. In: Proceedings of SOSP (1981) (ACM OS Review 15(5))
28. Shapiro, J.S., Weber, S.: Verifying the eros confinement mechanism. In: Proceedings of IEEE S&P (2000)
29. Walker, B.J., Kemmerer, R.A., Popek, G.J.: Specification and verification of the UCLA Unix security kernel. CACM 23(2), 118–131 (1980)

Verification of Security Protocols with Lists: From Length One to Unbounded Length

Miriam Paiola and Bruno Blanchet

INRIA, École Normale Supérieure, CNRS, Paris
{paiola,blanchet}@di.ens.fr

Abstract. We present a novel, simple technique for proving secrecy properties for security protocols that manipulate lists of unbounded length, for an unbounded number of sessions. More specifically, our technique relies on the Horn clause approach used in the automatic verifier ProVerif: we show that if a protocol is proven secure by our technique with lists of length one, then it is secure for lists of unbounded length. Interestingly, this theorem relies on approximations made by our verification technique: in general, secrecy for lists of length one does not imply secrecy for lists of unbounded length. Our result can be used in particular to prove secrecy properties for group protocols with an unbounded number of participants and for some XML protocols (web services) with ProVerif.

1 Introduction

Security protocols are protocols that rely on cryptographic primitives such as encryption and signatures for securing communication between several parties. They aim at ensuring security properties such as secrecy or authentication. Historically, attacks were often found against protocols that were thought correct. Furthermore, security flaws cannot be detected by testing since they appear only in the presence of an attacker. The confidence in these protocols can then be increased by a formal analysis that proves the desired security properties. To ease formal verification, one often uses the symbolic, so-called Dolev-Yao model [8], which abstracts from the details of cryptographic primitives and considers messages as terms. In this work, we also rely on this model.

The formal verification of security protocols with fixed-size data structures has been extensively studied. However, the formal verification of protocols that manipulate more complex data structures, such as lists, has been less studied and presents additional difficulties: these complex data structures add another cause of undecidability.

In this work, we present a technique for proving secrecy properties for security protocols that manipulate lists of unbounded length. This technique is based on the Horn clause approach used in the automatic verifier ProVerif [1,4]. ProVerif is an automatic protocol verifier that takes as input a protocol, translates it into a representation in Horn clauses, and uses a resolution algorithm to determine

P. Degano and J.D. Guttman (Eds.): POST 2012, LNCS 7215, pp. 69–88, 2012.

whether a fact is derivable from the clauses. One can then infer security properties of the protocol. For instance, we use a fact $att(M)$ to mean that the attacker may have the message M. If $att(s)$ is not derivable from the clauses, then s is secret. The main goal of this approach is to prove security properties of protocols without bounding the number of sessions of the protocol.

Like other protocol verifiers, ProVerif can analyze protocols with lists if we fix the lengths of the lists a priori. However, if the protocol is verified only for some lengths, attacks may exist for other values. So our goal is to prove the protocols for lists of any length. To reach this goal, we extend the language of Horn clauses, introducing a new kind of clauses, generalized Horn clauses, to be able to represent lists of any length. We consider a class of protocols that manipulate list elements in a uniform way. Because of this uniformity, one might intuitively think that secrecy for lists of length one implies secrecy for lists of any length. We show that this intuition is not exactly true: in general, secrecy for lists of length one does not imply secrecy for lists of any length, as demonstrated in Sect. 4.2. However, we show that, for a certain class of Horn clauses, if secrecy is proved by our Horn clause technique for lists of length one, then secrecy also holds for lists of unbounded length. This result relies on the sound abstractions made by the translation into Horn clauses. Additionally, we provide an approximation algorithm that can transform generalized Horn clauses into clauses of the class on which our result holds. All facts derivable from the initial clauses are also derivable from the clauses generated by the approximation algorithm, so that we can prove secrecy on the latter clauses, and conclude secrecy for the initial clauses. Our result therefore provides an easy way of obtaining a strong security guarantee: we prove using ProVerif that $att(s)$ is not derivable from the clauses for lists of length one, and we can then immediately conclude that secrecy holds for lists of unbounded length, with an unbounded number of sessions.

Applications of our results include in particular proving secrecy properties for some group protocols that manipulate unbounded lists, with an unbounded number of participants. In this paper, we focus mainly on group protocols and illustrate our work on the Asokan-Ginzboorg protocol [2]. We prove secrecy of the session key exchanged in this protocol by verifying with ProVerif its version with lists of length one and the size of the group equal to one. Another possible application is the treatment of XML protocols such as web services, XML documents being modeled using possibly nested lists.

Related Work. The first approach considered for proving protocols with recursive data structures was interactive theorem proving: Paulson [17] and Bryans et al [5] study a recursive authentication protocol for an unbounded number of participants, using Isabelle/HOL for [17], and rank functions and PVS for [5]. However, this approach requires considerable human effort.

Meadows et al [15] used the NRL protocol analyzer (NPA), based on a combination of model checking and theorem-proving techniques, to verify the Group Domain of Interpretation (GDOI) protocol suite. NPA could not handle the infinite data structures required for modeling general group protocols, so a single key was used instead of a key hierarchy. Several problems including type flaw attacks were found in the protocol and fixed in later versions of GDOI. The early verification of the A.GDH-2 protocol using NPA [14] seems to have missed attacks [18], although the tool supports the Diffie-Hellman exponentiation [16].

Steel and Bundy [20] have used CORAL, a tool for finding counterexamples to incorrect inductive conjectures, to model protocols for group key agreement and group key management, without any restrictions on the scenario. They have discovered new attacks against several group protocols, but cannot prove that protocols are correct.

Kremer, Mercier, and Treinen [11] verify secrecy for group protocols with modular exponentiation and XOR, for any number of participants and an unbounded number of sessions, but only for a passive adversary (eavesdropper).

Several works consider the case of a bounded number of sessions. Pereira and Quisquater [18] discovered several attacks on the CLIQUES protocol suite [21], which extends the Diffie-Hellman key agreement method to support dynamic group operations (A-GDH). They converted the problem of the verification of security properties to the resolution of linear equation systems. In [19], they proved a first generic insecurity result for authentication protocols showing that it is impossible to design a correct authenticated group key agreement protocol based on the A-GDH. Truderung [22] showed a decidability result (in NEXPTIME) for secrecy in recursive protocols. This result was extended to a class of recursive protocols with XOR [13] in 3-NEXPTIME. Chridi et al [6,7] present an extension of the constraint-based approach in symbolic protocol verification to handle a class of protocols (Well-Tagged protocols with Autonomous keys) with unbounded lists in messages. They prove that the insecurity problem for Well-Tagged protocols with Autonomous keys is decidable for a bounded number of sessions.

We consider a class of protocols that includes the one of [6,7] but, instead of proving decidability for a bounded number of sessions, we provide a technique that can prove protocols for an unbounded number of sessions and any number of protocol participants, using abstractions.

Outline. The next section recalls the technique used by ProVerif. In Sect. 3, we formally define generalized Horn clauses, and their semantics by giving their translation into Horn clauses. Additionally, we introduce our running example and motivate the introduction of this new type of clauses. In Sect. 4, we show our main theorem: for a class of generalized Horn clauses, if $att(s)$ is not derivable for lists of length one, then it is also not derivable for lists of any length. In Sect. 5, we provide an approximation algorithm for transforming generalized Horn clauses into clauses that satisfy the hypothesis of our main theorem. The proofs can be found in the long version of the paper available at http://www.di.ens.fr/~paiola/publications/PaiolaBlanchetPOST12.html.

2   A Reminder on ProVerif

ProVerif translates the initial protocol into a set of Horn clauses. The syntax of these clauses is defined in Fig. 1. The patterns represent messages that are

$$
\begin{aligned}
p ::= && \text{patterns} \\
\quad x, y, z, v, w && \text{variable} \\
\quad a[p_1, \ldots, p_n] && \text{name} \\
\quad f(p_1, \ldots, p_n) && \text{constructor application}
\end{aligned}
$$

$$
F ::= \text{att}(p) \qquad \text{facts}
$$

$$
R ::= F_1 \wedge \cdots \wedge F_n \Rightarrow F \qquad \text{Horn clause}
$$

Fig. 1. Syntax of Horn clauses

exchanged between participants of the protocol. A variable can represent any pattern. Names represent atomic values, such as keys and nonces. Each participant can create new names. Instead of creating a fresh name at each run of the protocol, the created names are considered as functions of the messages previously received by the principal that creates it, represented by the pattern $a[p_1, \ldots, p_n]$. Hence names are distinguished only when they are created after receiving different messages. As shown in, e.g., [1], this is a sound approximation. When a name has no arguments, we write a instead of $a[\,]$. We use v, w, x, y, z for variables and other identifiers $a, b, c, e, L, pw, r, s, \ldots$ for names.

The fact $\text{att}(p)$ means that the attacker may have the pattern (message) p. A clause $F_1 \wedge \cdots \wedge F_n \Rightarrow F$ means that if all facts F_i are true then the conclusion F is also true. We use R for a clause, H for its hypothesis, and C for its conclusion. The hypothesis of a clause is considered as a multiset of facts. A clause with no hypothesis $\Rightarrow F$ is written simply F.

Cryptographic primitives are represented by functions and perfect cryptography is assumed. There are two kinds of functions: constructors and destructors. A constructor f is a function that explicitly appears in the patterns that represent messages and builds new patterns of the form $f(p_1, \ldots, p_n)$. Destructors manipulate patterns. A destructor g is defined by a set $def(g)$ of rewrite rules of the form $g(p_1, \ldots, p_n) \to p$ where $p_1, \ldots, p_n, p$ are patterns with only variables and constructors and the variables of p appear in $p_1, \ldots, p_n$. Using constructors and destructors, one can represent data structures and cryptographic operations. For instance, $senc(x, y)$ is the constructor that represents the symmetric key encryption of the message x under the key y. The corresponding destructor $sdec(x', y)$ returns the decryption of x' if x' is a message encrypted under y. The rewrite rule that defines $sdec$ is

$$
sdec(senc(x, y), y) \to x.
$$

A protocol is represented by three sets of Horn clauses:

1. initial knowledge of the attacker: we have a fact $\text{att}(p)$ for each p initially known by the attacker.
2. abilities of the attacker:
   - $\text{att}(a)$
   - for each constructor f of arity n:
     $\text{att}(x_1) \wedge \cdots \wedge \text{att}(x_n) \Rightarrow \text{att}(f(x_1, \ldots x_n))$

– for each destructor g,

  for each rule $g(p_1, \ldots, p_n) \to p$ in $def(g)$:

  $\mathrm{att}(p_1) \wedge \cdots \wedge \mathrm{att}(p_n) \Rightarrow \mathrm{att}(p)$

The first clause represents the ability of the attacker to create fresh names a: all fresh names that the adversary may create are represented by the single name a. The other clauses mean that if the attacker has some messages, then he can apply constructors and destructors to them.

3. the protocol itself: for each message p of the protocol sent by agent A, we create the clause $\mathrm{att}(p_1) \wedge \cdots \wedge \mathrm{att}(p_n) \Rightarrow \mathrm{att}(p)$, where $p_1, \ldots, p_n$ are patterns representing the messages received by A before sending message p. Indeed, if the attacker has $p_1, \ldots, p_n$, then it can send them to A and intercept A's reply p.

This representation of protocols by Horn clauses is approximate, in particular because Horn clauses that represent the protocol itself can be applied any number of times instead of exactly once per session. However, it is sound: if $\mathrm{att}(p)$ cannot be derived from the clauses, then the protocol preserves the secrecy of p. (This is proved by [1, Theorem 7.2.3] when the clauses are generated from a pi calculus model of the protocol.)

ProVerif determines whether $\mathrm{att}(p)$ is derivable from the clauses using resolution with free selection [3]: we combine pairs of clauses by resolution; the literals upon which we perform resolution are chosen by a selection function. Next, we define when a given fact is derivable from a given set of clauses.

Definition 1 (Subsumption). *We say that $R_1 = H_1 \Rightarrow C_1$ subsumes $R_2 = H_2 \Rightarrow C_2$, and we write $R_1 \sqsupseteq R_2$, if and only if there exists a substitution σ such that $\sigma C_1 = C_2$ and $\sigma H_1 \subseteq H_2$ (multiset inclusion).*

We say that R_1 subsumes R_2 when R_2 can be obtained by adding hypotheses to a particular instance of R_1. In this case, all facts that can be derived by R_2 can also be derived by R_1, so R_2 can be eliminated.

Definition 2 (Derivability). *Let F be a closed fact, that is, a fact without variable. Let $\mathcal{R}$ be a set of clauses. F is derivable from $\mathcal{R}$ if and only if there exists a derivation of F from $\mathcal{R}$, that is, a finite tree defined as follows:*

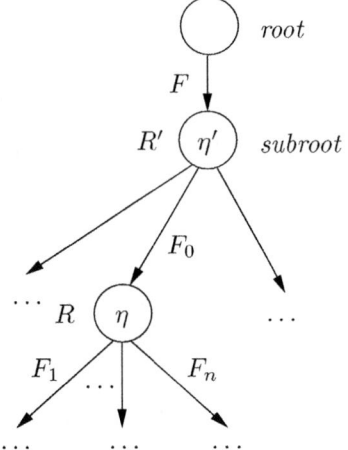

1. *Its nodes (except the root) are labeled by clauses $R \in \mathcal{R}$;*
2. *Its edges are labeled by closed facts;*
3. *If the tree contains a node labeled R with one incoming edge labeled by F_0 and n outgoing edges labeled by $F_1, \ldots, F_n$, then $R \sqsupseteq F_1 \wedge \cdots \wedge F_n \Rightarrow F_0$.*
4. *The root has one outgoing edge labeled by F. The unique son of the root is named the subroot.*

Fig. 2. Derivation of F

This definition is illustrated in Fig. 2. In a derivation, if there is a node labeled by R with one incoming edge labeled by F_0 and n outgoing edges $F_1, \ldots, F_n$ then F_0 can be derived by $F_1, \ldots, F_n$ by the clause R. Therefore there exists a derivation of F from $\mathcal{R}$ if and only if F can be derived from clauses in $\mathcal{R}$ (in classical logic).

3 Abstract Representation of Protocols by Generalized Horn Clauses

This section is devoted to the abstract representation of protocols by *generalized Horn clauses*. After introducing a running example and motivating our choices, we give the syntax and semantics of generalized Horn clauses.

3.1 Running Example

As a running example, we use a version of the Asokan-Ginzboorg protocol [2] for key agreement, also used in [7,20]. Let the set of players be $\{a_i, i = 1, \ldots, N\}$ for $N \geq 1$ and L be the leader. The protocol describes the establishment of a session key between the leader and the other N participants.

$$
\begin{aligned}
&(1) \ L \to ALL : \ (L, \{\!|e|\!\}_{pw}) \\
&(2) \ \ a_i \to L : \ \ (a_i, \{\!|(r_i, s_i)|\!\}_e) \\
&(3) \ \ L \to a_i : \ \ \{\!|(s_1, \ldots, s_N, s')|\!\}_{r_i} \\
&(4) \ \ a_i \to L : \ \ (a_i, \{\!|(s_i, h(s_1, \ldots, s_N, s'))|\!\}_K), \\
&\qquad\qquad\qquad \text{for some } i, \text{ where } K = f(s_1, \ldots, s_N, s')
\end{aligned}
$$

At the beginning, the participants share the knowledge of a password pw and of two $N + 1$-input hash functions f and h. (In this paper, we ignore dictionary attacks against pw and consider pw as a strong key.) First, the leader sends to all other participants his identity paired with a fresh key e encrypted with the password pw. Each participant a_i for $i \in \{1, \ldots, N\}$ decrypts $\{\!|e|\!\}_{pw}$ and then creates a fresh key r_i and a fresh nonce s_i which will be his contribution to the final session key. Then he sends $\{\!|(r_i, s_i)|\!\}_e$ paired with his identity. When L receives this message, he decrypts it and assumes that it has been created by a_i. After receiving all N messages, the leader creates his contribution s' to the final key and sends to each participant a_i for $i \in \{1, \ldots, N\}$ the list of all contributions encrypted with the key r_i that a_i previously sent. If step 3 is completed successfully, each participant can compute the session key $K = f(s_1, \ldots, s_N, s')$. In the end, the leader randomly picks one of the other players and asks him for step 4.

3.2 Need for Generalizing Horn Clauses

We would like to model the example protocol of Sect. 3.1 by Horn clauses and use ProVerif to verify it. Since we consider a parametric group size, we encounter several problems. First, we have to deal with lists whose length is not fixed but is the size N of the group, such as $s_1, \ldots, s_N$ in message 3 of the example. Next, we need conjunctions of N facts (and N is again not fixed) to represent that some agents receive one message from each group member. For example, when translating message 3 into Horn clauses, the leader L expects messages 2 of the form $(a_i, \{(v_i, w_i)\}_e)$ from each a_i. (The leader cannot verify the incoming values of r_i, s_i so they become variables v_i, w_i.) Then L replies with message 3 $\{(w_1, \ldots, w_N, s')\}_{v_i}$ where s' is a fresh name generated by L, modeled as a function of the previously received messages $s'[v_1, w_1, \ldots, v_N, w_N]$. The attacker can send the incoming messages and intercept L's reply, so we find the clause

$$
\begin{aligned}
&\mathrm{att}((a_1, senc((v_1, w_1), e))) \wedge \cdots \wedge \mathrm{att}((a_N, senc((v_N, w_N), e))) \Rightarrow \\
&\mathrm{att}(senc((w_1, \ldots, w_N, s'[v_1, w_1, \ldots, v_N, w_N]), v_i)).
\end{aligned} \tag{1}
$$

where $senc$ is the encryption function. We solve those two problems by adding two new constructs to the syntax of Horn clauses: $list(i \leq N, p_i)$ for the list of elements p_i with index i in the set $\{1, \ldots, N\}$, that is, $list(i \leq N, p_i)$ stands for $\langle p_1, \ldots, p_N \rangle$ (inspired by the $mpair$ construct of [7]) and $\bigwedge_{i_1 \leq N, \ldots, i_h \leq N} F$ for the conjunction of facts F with indices $i_1, \ldots, i_h$ in $\{1, \ldots, N\}$.

3.3 Syntax

This section formally defines the syntax and semantics of *generalized Horn clauses*.

$$
\begin{array}{lll}
p^G, s, t ::= & & \text{patterns} \\
\quad x_{i_1, \ldots, i_h} & & \text{variable } (h \geq 0) \\
\quad f(p_1^G, \ldots, p_l^G) & & \text{function application} \\
\quad a_i[p_1^G, \ldots, p_l^G] & & \text{indexed names} \\
\quad list(i \leq M, p^G) & & \text{list constructor} \\[4pt]
F^G ::= \bigwedge_{i_1 \leq M_1, \ldots, i_h \leq M_h} \mathrm{att}(p^G) & & \text{facts} \\[4pt]
R^G ::= F_1^G \wedge \cdots \wedge F_n^G \Rightarrow \mathrm{att}(p^G) & & \text{generalized Horn clause}
\end{array}
$$

Fig. 3. Syntax of our protocol representation

The syntax of these new clauses is defined in Fig. 3. The patterns p^G that represent messages are enriched with several new constructs. The variables may have indices $x_{i_1, \ldots, i_h}$. The pattern for function application $f(p_1^G, \ldots, p_l^G)$ includes not only constructor application but also names $a[p_1^G, \ldots, p_l^G]$ where a is a name without index. The indexed name $a_i[p_1^G, \ldots, p_l^G]$ represents a name created by the group member number i. We added a particular constructor $list(i \leq M, p^G)$ to represent lists of length M, where M is an unknown bound.

In the Asokan-Ginzboorg protocol, we can write, for example, at message 3: $senc((list(j \leq N, s_j), s'), r_i)$ for $senc((s_1, \ldots, s_N, s'), r_i)$. The last element s'

is not included in the list $list(j \leq N, s_j)$, to distinguish s' that has just been created by the leader from s_i with $i = 1, \ldots, N$ that has just been received by him: $s_1, \ldots, s_N$ are treated in a uniform way while s' is treated differently.

We extend facts to model the possibility of having a conjunction of facts depending on indices, so that the syntax for facts becomes $\bigwedge_{i_1 \leq M_1, \ldots, i_h \leq M_h} att(p^G)$. For example, intuitively, $\bigwedge_{i \leq M} att(p^G)$ represents $att(p^G\{i \mapsto 1\}) \wedge \cdots \wedge att(p^G\{i \mapsto M\})$, where $p^G\{i \mapsto i'\}$ denotes p^G in which i has been replaced with i'. The conjunction $\bigwedge_{i_1 \leq M_1, \ldots, i_h \leq M_h}$ with $h = 0$ is omitted: the fact is then simply $att(p^G)$.

The generalized Horn clause $F_1^G \wedge \cdots \wedge F_n^G \Rightarrow att(p^G)$ means that, if the facts $F_1^G, \ldots, F_n^G$ hold, then the fact $att(p^G)$ also holds. The conclusion of a clause does not contain a conjunction $\bigwedge_{i_1 \leq M_1, \ldots, i_h \leq M_h}$: we can simply leave the indices of $att(p^G)$ free to mean that $att(p^G)$ can be concluded for any value of these indices.

3.4   Representation of the Protocol

The representation of the abilities of the attacker includes the clauses given in Sect. 2. For our running example, $att(a_i)$ and $att(L)$ represent that the attacker initially knows a_i and L, and the clauses

$$att(a)$$

$$att(x) \wedge att(y) \Rightarrow att(senc(x, y)) \qquad att(senc(x, y)) \wedge att(y) \Rightarrow att(x)$$

$$att(x) \Rightarrow att(f(x)) \qquad\qquad att(x) \Rightarrow att(h(x))$$

$$att(x) \wedge att(y) \Rightarrow att((x, y)) \qquad att((x, y)) \Rightarrow att(x) \qquad att((x, y)) \Rightarrow att(y)$$

represent that the attacker can create fresh names, encrypt and decrypt messages, apply hash functions, compose and decompose pairs.

In addition, we have clauses for $list$, which generalize clauses for pairs:

$$\bigwedge_{i \leq M} att(x_i) \Rightarrow att(list(j \leq M, x_j)) \tag{2}$$

$$att(list(j \leq M, x_j)) \Rightarrow att(x_i) \tag{3}$$

Let us now give the clauses that represent the protocol itself. We suppose that each principal always plays the same role in the protocol; we could build a more complex model in which the same principal can play several roles by adding clauses. The leader L sends the first message $(L, \{\!|e|\!\}_{pw})$ and the attacker intercepts it, so we have the fact:

$$att((L, senc(e, pw))).$$

Each agent a_i with $i = 1, \ldots, N$ expects a message 1 of the form $(L, \{\!|y|\!\}_{pw})$. (a_i cannot verify the value of the key e, so it becomes a variable y.) Agent a_i replies with message 2: $(a_i, \{\!|(r_i, s_i)|\!\}_y)$, where the new names r_i and s_i are encoded as functions of the key y just received. If the attacker sends the first message

$(L, \{\!|y|\!\}_{pw})$ to a_i, a_i replies with $(a_i, \{\!|(r_i, s_i)|\!\}_y)$, and the attacker can intercept this reply, so we obtain the clause:

$$\text{att}((L, senc(y, pw))) \Rightarrow \text{att}((a_i, senc((r_i[y], s_i[y]), y))) \tag{4}$$

For the output of message 3, the leader replies with $\{\!|(w_1, \ldots, w_N, s')|\!\}_{v_i}$ where s' is a fresh name generated by L modeled as a function of the previously received messages $s'[v_1, w_1, \ldots, v_N, w_N]$: the clause (1) was already given in Sect. 3.2; we adapt it using $list$ and conjunctions over the set of participants:

$$\bigwedge_{j \leq N} \text{att}((a_j, senc((v_j, w_j), e))) \Rightarrow$$
$$\text{att}(senc((list(j \leq N, w_j), s'[list(j \leq N, (v_j, w_j))]), v_i)) \tag{5}$$

Finally, if a_i has received a message 1 of the form $(L, \{\!|y|\!\}_{pw})$ and a message 3 of the form $\{\!|(z_1, \ldots, z_N, z')|\!\}_{r_i[y]}$, encoded as $\{\!|(list(j \leq N, z_j), z')|\!\}_{r_i[y]},$[1] then a_i computes the session key $K = f((list(j \leq N, z_j), z'))$ and one a_i sends to the leader message 4: $(a_i, \{\!|(s_i[y], h((list(j \leq N, z_j), z')))|\!\}_K)$.

$$\text{att}((L, senc(y, pw))) \wedge \text{att}(senc((list(j \leq N, z_j), z'), r_i[y])) \Rightarrow$$
$$\text{att}((a_i, senc((s_i[y], h((list(j \leq N, z_j), z'))), K))) \tag{6}$$
$$\text{where } K = f((list(j \leq N, z_j), z'))$$

We want to prove the secrecy of the session key K. However, this key depends on data received by protocol participants, so we cannot simply test the derivability of $\text{att}(K)$. We can use the following trick: to test the secrecy of the key K that participant a_i has, we consider that a_i sends the encryption $\{\!|s''|\!\}_K$ of a secret s'' under K. If K is secret, the adversary will not be able to decrypt the message, so s'' will remain secret. Therefore, we add the clause

$$\text{att}(senc((list(j \leq N, z_j), z'), r_i[y])) \Rightarrow$$
$$\text{att}(senc(s'', f((list(j \leq N, z_j), z'))))$$

to model the output of $\{\!|s''|\!\}_K$, and we test the derivability of $\text{att}(s'')$. We have also used a similar clause to prove the secrecy of the key K that L has.

3.5   Type System for the New Clauses

In Fig. 4, we define a simple type system for the generalized Horn clauses. The goal of this type system is to guarantee that all variables use indices that vary

---

[1] In the protocol, the participant a_i can check whether the component z_i of the list is his own contribution $s_i[y]$, but cannot check the other components. Our representation of lists does not allow us to model such a test: in fact, we cannot substitute a_i directly because, in the construct for lists $list(j \leq N, z_j)$, all elements z_j need to have the same form. Moreover, we have built examples of protocols with such tests, for which our result does not hold: intuitively, the test breaks the uniform treatment of the elements of lists, so proving secrecy by the Horn clause technique for lists of length one does not imply secrecy for lists of unbounded length. We shall prove secrecy without the test on z_i; this implies a fortiori secrecy with this test, because the clause without test subsumes the one with the test. In general, removing these tests may obviously lead to false attacks.

$$\frac{i : [1, M] \in \Gamma}{\Gamma \vdash i : [1, M]} \text{(EnvIndex)} \qquad \frac{x_{\_} : [1, M_1] \times \cdots \times [1, M_h] \in \Gamma}{\Gamma \vdash x_{\_} : [1, M_1] \times \cdots \times [1, M_h]} \text{(EnvVar)}$$

$$\frac{\Gamma \vdash x_{\_} : [1, M_1] \times \cdots \times [1, M_h] \quad \Gamma \vdash i_1 : [1, M_1] \ldots \Gamma \vdash i_h : [1, M_h]}{\Gamma \vdash x_{i_1, \ldots, i_h}} \text{(Var)}$$

$$\frac{\Gamma \vdash p_1^G \ldots \Gamma \vdash p_h^G}{\Gamma \vdash f(p_1^G, \ldots, p_h^G)} \text{(Fun)}$$

$$\frac{\Gamma \vdash p_1^G \ldots \Gamma \vdash p_h^G \quad \Gamma \vdash i : [1, N]}{\Gamma \vdash a_i[p_1^G, \ldots, p_h^G]} \text{(Name)} \qquad \frac{\Gamma, i : [1, M] \vdash p^G}{\Gamma \vdash list(i \leq M, p^G)} \text{(List)}$$

$$\frac{\Gamma, i_1 : [1, M_1], \ldots, i_h : [1, M_h] \vdash p^G}{\Gamma \vdash \bigwedge_{i_1 \leq M_1, \ldots, i_h \leq M_h} att(p^G)} \text{(Fact)}$$

$$\frac{\Gamma \vdash F_1^G \ldots \Gamma \vdash F_n^G \quad \Gamma \vdash F^G}{\Gamma \vdash F_1^G \wedge \cdots \wedge F_n^G \Rightarrow F^G} \text{(Clause)}$$

Fig. 4. Type system for generalized Horn clauses

in the appropriate interval. We shall see in Sect. 4 that this type system is also very helpful in order to establish our main result.

Definition 3. *An index i is bound if:*

- *it appears as an index of a conjunction defining a fact, so, for instance, in the fact $\bigwedge_{i_1 \leq M_1, \ldots, i_h \leq M_h} att(p^G)$, $i_1, \ldots, i_h$ are bound in $att(p^G)$.*
- *it appears as an index for a list constructor, that is, in the pattern $list(i \leq M, p^G)$, i is bound in p^G.*

Indices that are not bound are free.

For simplicity, we suppose that the bound indices of clauses have pairwise distinct names, and names distinct from the names of free indices. This can easily be guaranteed by renaming the bound indices if needed.

In the type system, the type environment Γ is a list of type declarations:

- $i : [1, M]$ means that i is of type $[1, M]$, that is, intuitively, the value of index i can vary between 1 and the value of the bound M.
- $x_{\_} : [1, M_1] \times \cdots \times [1, M_h]$ means that the variable x expects indices of types $[1, M_1], \ldots, [1, M_h]$.

The type system defines the judgments:

- $\Gamma \vdash i : [1, M]$, which means that i has type $[1, M]$ in environment Γ, by rule (EnvIndex);
- $\Gamma \vdash x_{\_} : [1, M_1] \times \cdots \times [1, M_h]$, which means that x expects indices of types $[1, M_1], \ldots, [1, M_h]$ according to environment Γ, by rule (EnvVar);
- $\Gamma \vdash p^G$, $\Gamma \vdash F^G$, $\Gamma \vdash R^G$, which mean that p^G, F^G, R^G, respectively, are well typed in environment Γ.

Most type rules are straightforward. For instance, the rule (Var) means that $x_{i_1,\ldots,i_h}$ is well typed when the types expected by x for its indices match the types of $i_1, \ldots, i_h$. The rule (Name) deserves an additional explanation: we have no information in Γ to set the type of the index of name a, and hence the index of a can have any type. A priori, it is obviously expected that the index of a certain name a always has the same type. However, the additional freedom given by the type rule will be useful in the rest of the paper: the transformations of Sect. 5 can create clauses in which the same name a has indices of different types. The formal meaning of such clauses can be defined by assuming that the name a exists for indices up to the value of the largest bound.

It is easy to verify that the clauses of Sect. 3.4 are well typed in our type system. Clause (2) is well typed in the environment $x_\_ : [1, M]$, (3) in the environment $x_\_ : [1, M], i : [1, M]$, and the other clauses in the environment in which all free indices have type $[1, N]$ and the variables expect indices of type $[1, N]$.

3.6   Translation from Generalized Horn Clauses to Horn Clauses

A generalized Horn clause represents several Horn clauses: for each value of the bounds M and of the free indices i that occur in a generalized Horn clause R^G, R^G corresponds to a certain Horn clause. This section formally defines this correspondence.

$$
\begin{array}{lll}
\overline{p} ::= & & \text{patterns} \\
\quad x_{\overline{i}_1,\ldots,\overline{i}_h} & & \text{variable} \\
\quad a_{\overline{i}}[\overline{p}_1,\ldots,\overline{p}_h] & & \text{name} \\
\quad f(\overline{p}_1,\ldots,\overline{p}_h) & & \text{constructor application} \\
\quad \langle \overline{p}_1,\ldots,\overline{p}_h \rangle & & \text{list} \\
\\
\overline{F} ::= \mathsf{att}(\overline{p}) & & \text{facts} \\
\\
\overline{R} ::= \overline{F}_1 \wedge \ldots \wedge \overline{F}_n \Rightarrow \overline{F} & & \text{Horn clauses}
\end{array}
$$

Fig. 5. Syntax of Horn clauses

The syntax of Horn clauses obtained by translation of generalized Horn clauses is given in Fig. 5. This syntax is similar to that of initial Horn clauses (Fig. 1) except that variables and names can now have indices $\overline{i}$, which are integer values, and that we include a pattern $\langle \overline{p}_1,\ldots,\overline{p}_h \rangle$ for representing lists (which will be generated by translation of *list*).

Definition 4. *Given a generalized Horn clause R^G well typed in Γ, an environment T for R^G is a function that associates to each bound M a fixed integer M^T and to each free index i that appears in R^G, an index $i^T \in \{1, \ldots, M^T\}$, if $\Gamma \vdash i : [1, M]$.*

Given an environment T and values $\overline{i}_1, \ldots, \overline{i}_h$, we write $T[i_1 \mapsto \overline{i}_1, \ldots, i_h \mapsto \overline{i}_h]$ for the environment that associates to indices i_1, $\ldots$, i_h the values $\overline{i}_1$, $\ldots$, $\overline{i}_h$ respectively and that maps all other indices as in T.

Given an environment T, a generalized Horn clause R^G is translated into the standard Horn clause R^{GT} defined next. We denote respectively $p^{GT}, F^{GT}, \ldots$ the translation of $p^G, F^G, \ldots$ using the environment T.

The translation of a pattern p^G is defined as follows:

- $(x_{i_1,\ldots,i_h})^T = x_{i_1^T,\ldots,i_h^T}$.
- $f(p_1^G,\ldots,p_l^G)^T = f(p_1^{GT},\ldots,p_l^{GT})$.
- $a_i[p_1^G,\ldots,p_l^G]^T = a_{i^T}[p_1^{GT},\ldots,p_l^{GT}]$.
- $list(i \leq M, p^G)^T = \langle p^{GT[i\mapsto 1]},\ldots,p^{GT[i\mapsto M^T]}\rangle$.

The translation of *list* is a list; we stress that this translation uses a list symbol $\langle\ldots\rangle$ different from the tuple symbol $(\ldots)$: *list* is the only construct that can introduce the list symbol $\langle\ldots\rangle$. This is important to make sure that confusions between tuples that may occur in the protocol and *list* do not occur for particular list lengths. In the implementation of the protocol, one must also make sure to use distinct encodings for *list* and for tuples.

The translation of a fact $F^G = \bigwedge_{i_1 \leq M_1,\ldots,i_h \leq M_h} \mathrm{att}(p^G)$ is

$$F^{GT} = \mathrm{att}(p_1) \wedge \ldots \wedge \mathrm{att}(p_k)$$

where $\{p_1,\ldots,p_k\} = \{p^{GT'} \mid T' = T[i_1 \mapsto \bar{\imath}_1,\ldots,i_h \mapsto \bar{\imath}_h]$ where $\bar{\imath}_j \in \{1,\ldots,M_j^T\}$ for all j in $\{1,\ldots,h\}\}$, and $(F_1^G \wedge \cdots \wedge F_n^G)^T = F_1^{GT} \wedge \cdots \wedge F_n^{GT}$.

Finally, we define the translation of the generalized Horn clause $R^G = H^G \Rightarrow \mathrm{att}(p^G)$ as $R^{GT} = H^{GT} \Rightarrow \mathrm{att}(p^{GT})$.

For instance, the translation of the clause (5) in the environment $T = \{N \mapsto 1, i \mapsto 1\}$ is $\mathrm{att}((a_1, senc((v_1, w_1), e))) \Rightarrow \mathrm{att}(senc(((\langle w_1\rangle, s'[\langle(v_1, w_1)\rangle]), v_1))$.

When $\mathcal{R}^G$ is a set of generalized Horn clauses, we define $\mathcal{R}^{GT} = \{R^{GT} \mid R^G \in \mathcal{R}^G,\ T$ is an environment for $R^G\}$. In terms of abstract interpretation, the sets of generalized Horn clauses ordered by inclusion constitute the abstract domain, the sets of Horn clauses ordered by inclusion the concrete domain, and $\mathcal{R}^{GT}$ is the concretization of $\mathcal{R}^G$. The set $\mathcal{R}^{G\mathcal{T}}$ includes clauses translated for any values of the bounds. In our running example, for instance, this allows one to consider several sessions of the protocol that have different group sizes N, and interactions between such sessions.

4   From Any Length to Length One

In this section, we define a mapping from lists of any length to lists of length one, and show that derivability for lists of any length implies derivability for lists of length one, for a particular class of Horn clauses.

4.1   Main Result

Given a generalized Horn clause R^G, there exists only one environment T for R^G such that all bounds are equal to 1. Hence by now we use R^{G1} for the only possible translation of R^G when all bounds are 1. We define $\mathcal{R}^{G1} = \{R^{G1} \mid R^G \in \mathcal{R}^G\}$.

Next, we define a translation from clauses in which bounds can have any value, following the syntax of Fig. 5, to clauses in which the bounds are fixed to 1:

$$
\mathbb{I}(\overline{p}) = \begin{cases} \underbrace{\{x_{1,\ldots,1}\}}_{h} & \text{if } \overline{p} = x_{\overline{i}_1,\ldots,\overline{i}_h} \\ \{f(p'_1,\ldots,p'_h) \mid p'_1 \in \mathbb{I}(\overline{p}_1),\ldots,p'_h \in \mathbb{I}(\overline{p}_h)\} & \text{if } \overline{p} = f(\overline{p}_1,\ldots,\overline{p}_h) \\ \{a_1[p'_1,\ldots,p'_h] \mid p'_1 \in \mathbb{I}(\overline{p}_1),\ldots,p'_h \in \mathbb{I}(\overline{p}_h)\} & \text{if } \overline{p} = a_{\overline{i}}[\overline{p}_1,\ldots,\overline{p}_h] \\ \{\langle p \rangle \mid p \in \mathbb{I}(\overline{p}_1) \cup \cdots \cup \mathbb{I}(\overline{p}_h)\} & \text{if } \overline{p} = \langle \overline{p}_1,\ldots,\overline{p}_h \rangle \end{cases}
$$

This translation maps all indices of variables and names to 1. The translation of a list is a list with one element, containing the translation of any element of the initial list. Several choices are possible for the translation of a list; $\mathbb{I}(\overline{p})$ returns the set of all possible patterns.

Given a fact $\overline{F} = \text{att}(\overline{p})$, its translation when the bounds are fixed to 1 is $\mathbb{I}(\text{att}(\overline{p})) = \{\text{att}(p) \mid p \in \mathbb{I}(\overline{p})\}$ Given a conjunction of facts $\overline{F}_1 \wedge \cdots \wedge \overline{F}_h$, its translation when the bounds are fixed to 1 is $\mathbb{I}(\overline{F}_1 \wedge \cdots \wedge \overline{F}_h) = \mathbb{I}(\overline{F}_1) \cup \cdots \cup \mathbb{I}(\overline{F}_h)$.

We say that a term or fact is *linear* when it contains at most one occurrence of each variable $x_{\_}$ (with any indices, so it cannot contain x_i and x_j for instance). Finally, we can state the main theorem of our paper:

Theorem 1. *Let $\mathcal{R}^G$ be a set of generalized Horn clauses such that, for each clause $R^G \in \mathcal{R}^G$, R^G is well typed, that is, there exists Γ such that $\Gamma \vdash R^G$, with the following conditions:*

1. *the free indices of R^G have pairwise distinct types in Γ;*
2. *the conclusion of R^G is linear and the bound indices in the conclusion of R^G have pairwise distinct bounds, and bounds different from the bounds of free indices of R^G in Γ.*

For all facts $\overline{F}$, if $\overline{F}$ is derivable from $\mathcal{R}^{GT}$, then for all $F \in \mathbb{I}(\overline{F})$, F is derivable from $\mathcal{R}^{G1}$.

If we show that, for some $F \in \mathbb{I}(\overline{F})$, F is not derivable from $\mathcal{R}^{G1}$, then using this theorem, $\overline{F}$ is not derivable from $\mathcal{R}^{GT}$. Suppose that we want to show that s is secret in a protocol represented by the clauses $\mathcal{R}^G$. We show using for instance ProVerif that $\text{att}(s)$ is not derivable from $\mathcal{R}^{G1}$, that is, we prove secrecy when the bounds are all fixed to 1. By Theorem 1, we conclude that $\text{att}(s)$ is not derivable from $\mathcal{R}^{GT}$, so we obtain secrecy for any bounds.

Unfortunately, this theorem does not apply to all Horn clauses: Hypotheses 1 and 2 have to be satisfied. The clauses of our running example do not satisfy these hypotheses. We shall see in Sect. 5 how to transform the clauses so that they satisfy the required hypotheses.

4.2 Examples

To illustrate why the hypotheses of the theorem are necessary, we provide examples for which the theorem does not hold because some hypotheses are not satisfied. Consider the following protocol:

(1) $A \to B : \{(a, a)\}_k$
(2) $B \to A : (\{(b, b)\}_k, \{s\}_{f(a,b)})$
(3) $A \to C : \langle \{(a_1, a_1')\}_k, \ldots, \{(a_N, a_N')\}_k \rangle$
(4) $C \to A : \langle \langle f(a_1, a_1'), \ldots, f(a_1, a_N') \rangle, \ldots, \langle f(a_N, a_1'), \ldots, f(a_N, a_N') \rangle \rangle$

At the beginning, the participants A, B, C share a key k. A first sends to B a fresh nonce a paired with itself and encrypted under k. When B receives it, he creates a fresh nonce b, computes the hash $f(a, b)$ and sends the pair $(\{(b, b)\}_k, \{s\}_{f(a,b)})$, where s is some secret. A can then decrypt $\{(b, b)\}_k$, obtain b, compute $f(a, b)$, decrypt $\{s\}_{f(a,b)}$, and obtain s, but an adversary should be unable to compute s. In the second part of the protocol (Messages 3 and 4), A sends to C a list of N fresh pairs (a_i, a_i') encrypted with k and C replies with the matrix of the hashes $f(a_i, a_j')$.

Now, if an attacker sends $\langle \{(a, a)\}_k, \{(b, b)\}_k \rangle$ to C as Message 3, he obtains $f(a, b)$ by decomposition of the list $\langle \langle f(a, a), f(a, b) \rangle, \langle f(b, a), f(b, b) \rangle \rangle$ and can now decrypt $\{s\}_{f(a,b)}$ and obtain the secret s.

However, if we consider only lists of one element, there is no attack: the last message consists of $\langle \langle f(a, a') \rangle \rangle$ if Message 3 was $\{(a, a')\}_k$, so the adversary would need to have $\{(a, b)\}_k$ in order to obtain $f(a, b)$.

The generalized Horn clause for Message 4 is:

$$\text{att}(list(i' \leq N, senc((x_{i'}, y_{i'}), k))) \Rightarrow \text{att}(list(i \leq N, list(j \leq N, f(x_j, y_i))))$$

In this clause, the Hypothesis 2 of Theorem 1 is not satisfied, because the bound indices i and j have the same bound N. If we translate this clause for lists of one element, we obtain

$$\text{att}(\langle senc((x_1, y_1), k) \rangle) \Rightarrow \text{att}(\langle \langle f(x_1, y_1) \rangle \rangle)$$

and with this clause (and other clauses representing this protocol), $\text{att}(s)$ is not derivable because $\text{att}(f(a, b))$ is not derivable, while with lists of length two, as we previously showed, there is an attack: $\text{att}(s)$ is derivable. This example confirms that bound indices in the conclusion must have pairwise distinct bounds.

Similarly, we can define a group protocol between a participant B, a leader L, and N group members A_i:

(1) $L \to B : \{(a, a)\}_p$
(2) $B \to L : (\{(b, b)\}_p, \{s\}_{f(a,b)})$
(3) $L \to A_i : \langle \{(a_1, a_1')\}_p, \ldots, \{(a_N, a_N')\}_p \rangle$
(4) $A_i \to L : \langle f(a_1, a_i'), \ldots, f(a_N, a_i') \rangle$

In this case, the generalized Horn clause for Message 4 is:

$$\text{att}(list(i' \leq N, senc((x_{i'}, y_{i'}), p))) \Rightarrow \text{att}(list(j \leq N, f(x_j, y_i)))$$

where again the Hypothesis 2 of Theorem 1 is not satisfied: the bound index j has the same bound N as the free index i, because they index the same variable $x\_$. As above, att(s) is derivable from the clauses for lists of length 2 but not for lists of length one. There are similar examples regarding Hypothesis 1, for instance with the clause

$$\text{att}(list(i' \leq N, senc((x_{i'}, y_{i'}), p))) \Rightarrow \text{att}(f(x_j, y_i))$$

in which the free indices i and j have the same type $[1, N]$, but it is more difficult to find a concrete protocol that would generate such a clause. (Typically, the protocol participants are indexed by a single index i, so clauses often have a single free index.)

Next, we consider a different kind of example: for the following protocol, the set of Horn clauses satisfies the hypothesis of Theorem 1, so we can apply the theorem. However, the protocol preserves secrecy for lists of length one but not for lists of unbounded length. This illustrates that the approximations made in the translation to Horn clauses are key for our theorem to hold: att(s) is derivable from the clauses, even for lists of length one. Let A and B be the two participants of the protocol that share a key k. Let h be a hash function.

(1) $A \rightarrow B : \{e\}_k, (b_1, b_2), \{s\}_{h(\{b_1\}_e, \{b_2\}_e)}$
(2) $B \rightarrow A : \langle x_1, \ldots, x_M \rangle$
(3) $A \rightarrow B : \langle \{x_1\}_e, \ldots, \{x_M\}_e \rangle$

A chooses a fresh key e and two random nonces b_1, b_2, and sends to B the message $\{e\}_k, (b_1, b_2), \{s\}_{h(\{b_1\}_e, \{b_2\}_e)}$ where s is a secret. B obtains e by decryption, computes the key $h(\{b_1\}_e, \{b_2\}_e)$, and obtains s by decrypting with this key. Later, B sends a list $\langle x_1, \ldots, x_M \rangle$ and A returns that list with all components encrypted under e. Clearly, if we consider this protocol for lists of length $M \geq 2$, there is an attack: the attacker can send to A the list $\langle b_1, b_2, \ldots \rangle$ and he obtains at Message 3 the list $\langle \{b_1\}_e, \{b_2\}_e, \{\ldots\}_e \rangle$. He can then compute the hash $h(\{b_1\}_e, \{b_2\}_e)$ and decrypt $\{s\}_{h(\{b_1\}_e, \{b_2\}_e)}$ to obtain the secret s. However, if we translate this protocol to lists of length one, we do not find the attack: the attacker can only ask for $\langle \{b_1\}_e \rangle$ or $\langle \{b_2\}_e \rangle$, but cannot obtain both. For this point to hold, it is important that the participants do not repeat the Messages 2-3 more than once for each session.

ProVerif finds an attack against this protocol (which is a false attack for lists of length one): the abstraction done with the representation by Horn clauses in fact allows the participants to repeat their messages more than once. The translation of the protocol into clauses for lists of length one contains:

A sends the first message:
$$\text{att}((senc(e, k), (b_1, b_2), senc(s, h(senc(b_1, e), senc(b_2, e))))) \tag{7}$$

A receives message 2 and sends message 3:
$$\text{att}(\langle x \rangle) \Rightarrow \text{att}(\langle senc(x, e) \rangle) \tag{8}$$

plus clauses for tuples, encryption, and the hash function h, where $\langle \cdot \rangle$ is a unary function such that att($\langle x \rangle$) $\Rightarrow$ att(x) and att(x) $\Rightarrow$ att($\langle x \rangle$). Now, if we query for the secrecy of s, ProVerif will find the attack: $att(s)$ is derivable from these clauses. Indeed, we get b_1 and b_2 from (7), then obtain $senc(b_1, e)$ and $senc(b_2, e)$ by two applications of (8) (note that we apply this clause twice for the same e, while the corresponding action can in fact be applied only once in the protocol itself), then compute $h(senc(b_1, e), senc(b_2, e))$, and finally obtain s by decrypting $senc(s, h(senc(b_1, e), senc(b_2, e)))$.

4.3   Proof of Theorem 1

This section sketches the proof of Theorem 1. Lemmas and details of the proof can be found in the long version of the paper. The proof proceeds by building a derivation of F from $\mathcal{R}^{G1}$, from a derivation of $\overline{F}$ from $\mathcal{R}^{GT}$, by induction on this derivation. Informally, the derivation of F from $\mathcal{R}^{G1}$ is obtained by applying $\mathbb{I}$ to the derivation of $\overline{F}$ from $\mathcal{R}^{GT}$. If $\overline{F}$ is derived by $R^{GT} = H^{GT} \Rightarrow C^{GT}$, $\overline{F}$ is an instance of C^{GT} by a substitution σ: $\overline{F} = \sigma C^{GT}$; we show that any $F \in \mathbb{I}(\overline{F})$ is an instance of C^{G1} by a substitution σ' obtained from σ: $F = \sigma' C^{G1}$. Hence, in order to derive F using $R^{G1} = H^{G1} \Rightarrow C^{G1}$, we need to derive $\sigma' H^{G1}$ from $\mathcal{R}^{G1}$, knowing a derivation of σH^{GT} from $\mathcal{R}^{GT}$. Informally, to show that this is possible, we prove that $\sigma' H^{G1} \subseteq \mathbb{I}(\sigma H^{GT})$ and conclude by induction.

5   An Approximation Algorithm

In Sect. 3.4, we gave the representation of the Asokan-Ginzboorg protocol with generalized Horn clauses. However, some of them do not satisfy the hypotheses of Theorem 1. For example, the clause (6) does not have a linear conclusion and the same bound appears twice in the conclusion.

5.1   Approximation Algorithm

Here we give an algorithm for transforming generalized Horn clauses into clauses that satisfy the hypothesis of Theorem 1. We suppose that the initial set of clauses $\mathcal{R}^G$ satisfies:

Hypothesis 1. *For each clause $R^G \in \mathcal{R}^G$, R^G is well-typed, that is, there exists Γ such that $\Gamma \vdash R^G$, and each variable has indices of pairwise distinct types, that is, if $\Gamma \vdash x\_ : [1, N_1] \times \ldots, \times [1, N_h]$, then $N_1, \ldots, N_h$ are pairwise distinct.*

This hypothesis on the initial clauses is often satisfied in practice. In particular, it is satisfied by our running example, and it should generally be satisfied by group protocols. Indeed, the variables typically have only one index (the number of the group member).

Given a clause R^G well typed in Γ, the approximation algorithm performs the following three steps, until it reaches a fixpoint:

1. Suppose $R^G = H^G \Rightarrow att(p^G)$, where H^G contains a free index i such that $\Gamma \vdash i : [1, N]$ and p^G contains a bound index j with bound N, or R^G contains two free indices i, j such that $\Gamma \vdash i : [1, N]$ and $\Gamma \vdash j : [1, N]$.

The algorithm chooses a fresh variable $y_- = \rho x_-$ for each variable x_- that occurs in R^G with index i, and replaces all occurrences of variables x_- that have index i with ρx_- (the indices remain the same).

The obtained clause can then be typed in an environment Γ' equal to Γ except that $\Gamma' \vdash i : [1, M]$ for some fresh bound M and that $\Gamma' \vdash y_- : [1, M_1] \times \cdots \times [1, M_h]$ if $y_- = \rho x_-$, $\Gamma \vdash x_- : [1, N_1] \times \cdots \times [1, N_h]$, and for each $k = 1, \ldots, h$, $M_k = N_k$ if $N_k \neq N$ and $M_k = M$ if $N_k = N$. The indices i and j then have different types in the obtained clause.

2. Suppose $R^G = H_1^G \wedge H_2^G \Rightarrow \text{att}(p^G)$, where p^G contains a pattern $list(i \leq N, p_1^G)$ as well as a pattern $list(j \leq N, p_2^G)$ or a free index j such that $\Gamma \vdash j : [1, N]$, H_1^G contains all hypotheses of R^G in which the bound N appears or a free index of type $[1, N]$ appears, and H_2^G contains the other hypotheses of R^G.

The algorithm chooses a fresh bound M and replaces R^G with

$$H_1^G \wedge H_1'^G \wedge H_2^G \Rightarrow \text{att}(p'^G)$$

where:

- ρ is a substitution that replaces each variable x_- of H_1^G and p_1^G such that $\Gamma \vdash x_- : [1, N_1] \times \cdots \times [1, N_h]$ with $N_k = N$ for some $k \in \{1, \ldots, h\}$ with a fresh variable y_- (the indices remain the same); the obtained clause will be typed in an environment Γ' obtained from Γ by adding $\Gamma' \vdash y_- : [1, M_1] \times \cdots \times [1, M_h]$ where, for each $k = 1, \ldots, h$, $M_k = N_k$ if $N_k \neq N$ and $M_k = M$ if $N_k = N$;
- $H_1'^G$ is obtained from ρH_1^G by replacing the bound N with M;
- p'^G is obtained from p^G by replacing $list(i \leq N, p_1^G)$ with $list(i \leq M, p_1'^G)$, where $p_1'^G$ is p_1^G in which all occurrences of variables x_- that have index i have been replaced with ρx_-.

3. Suppose $R^G = H_1^G \wedge H_2^G \Rightarrow \text{att}(p^G)$ where p^G contains at least two occurrences of a variable x_-, H_1^G contains all hypotheses of R^G in which x_- appears, and H_2^G contains the other hypotheses of R^G.

The algorithm chooses a fresh variable y_- and replaces R^G with

$$H_1^G \wedge H_1'^G \wedge H_2^G \Rightarrow \text{att}(p'^G)$$

where $H_1'^G$ is obtained from H_1^G by replacing each occurence of x_- with y_- (the indices remain the same), and p'^G is obtained from p^G by replacing one occurrence of x_- with y_-.

Step 1 is applied first, until it cannot be applied. Then step 2 is applied, until there are no list constructors that match the condition. Step 2 may already rename some variables that occur more than once in the conclusion of the clause. Then, when a fixpoint is reached with step 2, we start applying step 3, until no variable occurs more than once in the conclusion. Step 1 ensures that free indices have pairwise distinct types and that free indices of the hypothesis have types distinct from those of bound indices in the conclusion. Step 2 ensures that the bound indices in the conclusion have pairwise distinct bounds and bounds distinct from the bounds of free indices in the conclusion. Step 3 ensures that the conclusion is linear.

This algorithm is similar to the algorithm that transforms any Horn clauses into Horn clauses of the class $\mathcal{H}_1$ [10]. Both algorithms ensure the linearity of the conclusion in the same way (step 3). Step 2 uses an idea similar to step 3 to guarantee that the types of the indices are distinct.

We illustrate this algorithm on an example below. The next theorem shows its correctness. Its proof can be found in the long version of the paper.

Theorem 2. *Let $\mathcal{R}^G$ be a set of clauses that satisfies Hypothesis 1. The approximation algorithm terminates on $\mathcal{R}^G$ and the final set of clauses $\mathcal{R}'^G$ satisfies the hypothesis of Theorem 1. Moreover, for any fact F, if F is derivable from $\mathcal{R}^{GT}$, then F is also derivable from $\mathcal{R}'^{GT}$.*

5.2   Examples

We apply the approximation algorithm to our running example. For instance, let us transform the clause (6):

$$\text{att}((L, senc(y, pw))) \wedge \text{att}(senc((list(j \leq N, z_j), z'), r_i[y]))$$
$$\Rightarrow \text{att}((a_i, senc((s_i[y], h((list(j \leq N, z_j), z'))), f((list(j \leq N, z_j), z')))))$$

First, as there are two list constructors with the same bound N in the conclusion, we apply step 2 of the algorithm: we rename the bound and variables of one of the two occurrences of $list(j \leq N, z_j)$ in the conclusion, so we obtain:

$$\text{att}((L, senc(y, pw))) \wedge$$
$$\text{att}(senc((list(j \leq N, z_j), z'), r_i[y])) \wedge \text{att}(senc((list(j \leq M, x_j), z'), r_i[y]))$$
$$\Rightarrow \text{att}((a_i, senc((s_i[y], h((list(j \leq N, z_j), z'))), f((list(j \leq M, x_j), z')))))$$

Next, as variable z' appears twice in the conclusion, we apply step 3 and obtain:

$$\text{att}((L, senc(y, pw))) \wedge$$
$$\text{att}(senc((list(j \leq N, z_j), z'), r_i[y])) \wedge \text{att}(senc((list(j \leq M, x_j), z'), r_i[y]))$$
$$\text{att}(senc((list(j \leq N, z_j), x'), r_i[y])) \wedge \text{att}(senc((list(j \leq M, x_j), x'), r_i[y]))$$
$$\Rightarrow \text{att}((a_i, senc((s_i[y], h((list(j \leq N, z_j), z'))), f((list(j \leq M, x_j), x')))))$$

Finally, this clause satisfies the hypothesis of Theorem 1. All clauses $\mathcal{R}^G$ given in Sect. 3.4, which represent our running example, can be transformed in a similar way, yielding clauses $\mathcal{R}'^G$. We have then shown that $\text{att}(s)$ is not derivable from $\mathcal{R}'^{G1}$, using ProVerif with the input file given at http://www.di.ens.fr/~paiola/publications/PaiolaBlanchetPOST12.html. By Theorem 1, we conclude that $\text{att}(s)$ is not derivable from $\mathcal{R}'^{GT}$, so by Theorem 2, $\text{att}(s)$ is not derivable from $\mathcal{R}^{GT}$. Therefore, the Azokan-Ginzboorg protocol preserves the secrecy of s, that is, it preserves the secrecy of the key K that a_i has. We have shown in a similar way that it preserves the secrecy of the key K that L has.

We have also considered a basic XML encryption [9] protocol. It is a very simple protocol between two principals A and B that share an encryption key

k and a MAC key k'. In order to encrypt a list $\langle a_1, \ldots, a_M \rangle$ using the encrypt-then-MAC scheme, one encrypts each component of the list, and computes a MAC of the list of ciphertexts:

$$A \to B : (\langle \{a_1\}_k, \ldots, \{a_M\}_k \rangle, mac(k', \langle sha1(\{a_1\}_k), \ldots, sha1(\{a_M\}_k) \rangle)).$$

We have used ProVerif to show that $att(a_1)$ is not derivable from the set of Horn clauses for the protocol with lists of length one. Therefore, this protocol preserves the secrecy of each a_j, for $j = 1, \ldots, M$.

6   Conclusions and Future Work

We have proposed a new type of clauses, generalized Horn clauses, useful to represent protocols that manipulate lists of unbounded length, as well as group protocols with an unbounded number of participants. We have shown that, for a subclass of generalized Horn clauses, if secrecy is proved by the Horn clause technique for lists of length one, then we have secrecy for lists of any length. We have also provided an approximation algorithm that transforms a set of generalized Horn clauses for satisfying the hypothesis of our main theorem. Using these results, one can prove secrecy for lists of any length for some group protocols, as we did for the Azokan-Ginzboorg protocol, and for simple XML protocols.

Future work includes supporting more general data structures and protocols, including more realistic XML protocols (web services). This will probably require a new extension of Horn clauses and of the resolution algorithm, since these protocols may not fit in a class for which secrecy for lists of any length can be proved from underivability for lists of length one. In particular, as we mentioned in Sect. 3.4, our technique does not support equality tests on certain components of lists, because in the representation of unbounded lists, all elements need to have the same form. We plan to support such tests in the future. Moreover, some group protocols (e.g. A.GDH-2) use the Diffie-Hellman key agreement, which we cannot handle yet. We believe that it could be handled by combining our result with [12].

ProVerif supports a variant of the applied pi calculus for modeling protocols. However, our result models group protocols with generalized Horn clauses. We plan to extend the input language of ProVerif to model group protocols, and to translate it automatically to generalized Horn clauses.

Finally, we plan to consider other security properties, such as authentication, perhaps using lists of length two instead of one.

Acknowledgments. This work was partly supported by the ANR project ProSe (decision number ANR-2010-VERS-004-01).

References

1. Abadi, M., Blanchet, B.: Analyzing Security Protocols with Secrecy Types and Logic Programs. Journal of the ACM 52(1), 102–146 (2005)

2. Asokan, N., Ginzboorg, P.: Key agreement in ad hoc networks. Computer Communications 23(17), 1627–1637 (2000)
3. Bachmair, L., Ganzinger, H.: Resolution theorem proving. In: Handbook of Automated Reasoning, vol. 1, ch. 2, pp. 19–100. North Holland (2001)
4. Blanchet, B.: Using Horn clauses for analyzing security protocols. In: Cortier, V., Kremer, S. (eds.) Formal Models and Techniques for Analyzing Security Protocols. Cryptology and Information Security Series, vol. 5, pp. 86–111. IOS Press, Amsterdam (2011)
5. Bryans, J., Schneider, S.: CSP, PVS and recursive authentication protocol. In: DIMACS Workshop on Formal Verification of Security Protocols (1997)
6. Chridi, N., Turuani, M., Rusinowitch, M.: Constraints-based Verification of Parameterized Cryptographic Protocols. Research Report RR-6712, INRIA (2008), http://hal.inria.fr/inria-00336539/en/
7. Chridi, N., Turuani, M., Rusinowitch, M.: Decidable analysis for a class of cryptographic group protocols with unbounded lists. In: CSF 2009, pp. 277–289. IEEE, Los Alamitos (2009)
8. Dolev, D., Yao, A.C.: On the security of public key protocols. IEEE Transactions on Information Theory IT-29(12), 198–208 (1983)
9. Eastlake, D., Reagle, J.: XML encryption syntax and processing. W3C Candidate Recommendation (2002), http://www.w3.org/TR/2002/CR-xmlenc-core-20020802/
10. Goubault-Larrecq, J.: Une fois qu'on n'a pas trouvé de preuve, comment le faire comprendre à un assistant de preuve? In: JFLA 2004, pp. 1–20. INRIA (2004)
11. Kremer, S., Mercier, A., Treinen, R.: Proving Group Protocols Secure Against Eavesdroppers. In: Armando, A., Baumgartner, P., Dowek, G. (eds.) IJCAR 2008. LNCS (LNAI), vol. 5195, pp. 116–131. Springer, Heidelberg (2008)
12. Küsters, R., Truderung, T.: Using ProVerif to analyze protocols with Diffie-Hellman exponentiation. In: CSF 2009, pp. 157–171. IEEE, Los Alamitos (2009)
13. Küsters, R., Truderung, T.: On the Automatic Analysis of Recursive Security Protocols with XOR. In: Thomas, W., Weil, P. (eds.) STACS 2007. LNCS, vol. 4393, pp. 646–657. Springer, Heidelberg (2007)
14. Meadows, C.: Extending formal cryptographic protocol analysis techniques for group protocols and low-level cryptographic primitives. In: WITS 2000 (2000)
15. Meadows, C., Syverson, P., Cervesato, I.: Formal specification and analysis of the Group Domain of Interpretation protocol using NPATRL and the NRL protocol analyzer. Journal of Computer Security 12(6), 893–931 (2004)
16. Meadows, C., Narendran, P.: A unification algorithm for the group Diffie-Hellman protocol. In: WITS 2002 (2002)
17. Paulson, L.C.: Mechanized proofs for a recursive authentication protocol. In: CSFW 1997, pp. 84–95. IEEE, Los Alamitos (1997)
18. Pereira, O., Quisquater, J.J.: Some attacks upon authenticated group key agreement protocols. Journal of Computer Security 11(4), 555–580 (2003)
19. Pereira, O., Quisquater, J.J.: Generic insecurity of cliques-type authenticated group key agreement protocols. In: CSFW 2004, pp. 16–19. IEEE, Los Alamitos (2004)
20. Steel, G., Bundy, A.: Attacking group protocols by refuting incorrect inductive conjectures. Journal of Automated Reasoning 36(1-2), 149–176 (2006)
21. Steiner, M., Tsudik, G., Waidner, M.: CLIQUES: A new approach to group key agreement. In: ICDCS 1998, pp. 380–387. IEEE, Los Alamitos (1998)
22. Truderung, T.: Selecting Theories and Recursive Protocols. In: Abadi, M., de Alfaro, L. (eds.) CONCUR 2005. LNCS, vol. 3653, pp. 217–232. Springer, Heidelberg (2005)

Privacy Supporting Cloud Computing: ConfiChair, a Case Study*

Myrto Arapinis, Sergiu Bursuc, and Mark Ryan

School of Computer Science, University of Birmingham
{m.d.arapinis,s.bursuc,m.d.ryan}@cs.bham.ac.uk

Abstract. Cloud computing means entrusting data to information systems that are managed by external parties on remote servers, in the "cloud", raising new privacy and confidentiality concerns. We propose a general technique for designing cloud services that allows the cloud to see only encrypted data, while still allowing it to perform data-dependent computations. The technique is based on key translations and mixes in web browsers.

We focus on the particular cloud computing application of conference management. We identify the specific security and privacy risks that existing systems like EasyChair and EDAS pose, and address them with a protocol underlying ConfiChair, a novel cloud-based conference management system that offers strong security and privacy guarantees.

In ConfiChair, authors, reviewers, and the conference chair interact through their browsers with the cloud, to perform the usual tasks of uploading and downloading papers and reviews. In contrast with current systems, in ConfiChair the cloud provider does not have access to the content of papers and reviews and the scores given by reviewers, and moreover is unable to link authors with reviewers of their paper.

We express the ConfiChair protocol and its properties in the language of ProVerif, and prove that it does provide the intended properties.

1 Introduction

Cloud computing means entrusting data to information systems that are managed by external parties on remote servers, "in the cloud." Cloud-based storage (such as Dropbox), on-line documents (such as Google docs), and customer-relationship management systems (such as salesforce.com) are familiar examples. Cloud computing raises privacy and confidentiality concerns because the service provider has access to all the data, and could accidentally or deliberately disclose it.

Cloud-based conference management systems such as EasyChair or the Editor's Assistant (EDAS) represent a particularly interesting example [29]. For example, EasyChair currently hosts more than 3000 conferences per year, and therefore contains a vast quantity of sensitive data about the authoring and reviewing performance of tens of thousands of researchers world-wide. This data is

---

* This is a short version of the paper. A longer version is available on our web pages.

P. Degano and J.D. Guttman (Eds.): POST 2012, LNCS 7215, pp. 89–108, 2012.
© Springer-Verlag Berlin Heidelberg 2012

in the possession of the EasyChair administrators, and could be accidentally or deliberately disclosed. A conference chair that is thinking of hosting her conference on a cloud-based conference system therefore faces a dilemma: if she uses the system, she adds to this mountain of data and the risks associated with it; if she doesn't use the system, she deprives herself of the advantages of a readily-available, well-engineered system that already has user accounts for the majority of participants in her conference (authors, PC members, and reviewers).

Note that the data confidentiality issue concerns the cloud conference system administrator (who administrates the system for all conferences), not the conference chair (who is concerned with a single conference). The conference system administrator has access to all the data on the system, across thousands of conferences and tens of thousands of authors and reviewers. An individual conference chair, on the other hand, has access to the data only for the particular conference of which she is chair. Moreover, an author or reviewer that chooses to participate in the conference can be assumed to be willing to trust the chair (for if he didn't, he would not participate); but there is no reason to assume that he trusts or even knows the conference management system provider.

In this paper, we identify a set of confidentiality requirements for conference management and propose ConfiChair, a cloud-based conference management protocol that supports them. The confidentiality guarantees ensure that no-one has access to conference data, beyond the access that is explicitly granted to them by their participation in the conference. In particular, this is true about the cloud provider and managers. ConfiChair is loosely modelled on EasyChair or EDAS, but with the additional security guarantees. We describe a protocol in which authors, reviewers and the conference chair interact through their web browsers with the cloud-based management system, to perform the usual tasks of uploading and downloading papers and reviews. The cloud is responsible for fine-grained routing of information, in order to ensure that the right agents are equipped with the right data to perform their task. It is also responsible for enforcing access control, for example concerning conflicts of interest and to ensure that a reviewer doesn't see other reviews of a paper before writing her own. However, all the sensitive data is seen by the cloud only in encrypted form.

For brevity, we use the term "cloud" to include all roles that are not an explicit part of the conference management; that includes the conference management system administrator, the cloud service provider, the network administrator, etc. The security properties that our system provides may be summarised as follows.

- **Secrecy of papers, reviews and scores.** The cloud does not have access to the content of papers or reviews, or the numerical scores given by reviewers to papers.
- **Unlinkability of author-reviewer.** The cloud *does* have access to the names of authors and the names of reviewers. This access is required in order to route information correctly, to enforce access control, and to allow a logged-in researcher to see all his data in a unified way. However, the cloud does not have the ability to tell if a particular author was reviewed

by a particular reviewer. In particular, for each encryption of each review or score held by the cloud, either the cloud does not know which author it applies to, or does not know which reviewer submitted it.

Summary of contribution

1. We identify a set of requirements for cloud-based conference management systems, notably privacy requirements such as secrecy and unlinkability.
2. We propose ConfiChair, a conference management protocol that provides the usual functionalities while offering strong privacy guaranties.
3. We show the usability of ConfiChair by providing a prototype implementation. We demonstrate that using ConfiChair is as easy and useful as using EasyChair, except for the requirement of two copy-paste operations (one performed by authors, one performed by reviewers).
4. We formalise the required privacy properties and automatically prove them with ProVerif.

Applicability of the ideas. Cloud-based services are being adopted widely throughout business. The following examples raise similar security concerns to those of conference management:

- Customer relationship management systems (such as salesforce.com);
- Cloud-hosted recruitment process services, in which applicants, referees, recruiters and employers interact to process job applications;
- Cloud-based finance and accounting services;
- Social networks, in which users share posts and status updates without wishing that data to be mined by the cloud provider for profiling purposes.

We believe our technique of browser-based key translation and mixnets is readily applicable to these examples too.

2   Description of the Problem and Related Work

Our problem is determined by three conflicting sets of requirements, namely functionality, privacy and usability. As we show below, there is much existing work related to our paper, but it can not be used to solve our problem either because of its complexity, or because of its different perspectives on privacy, or because it does not achieve the required balance between privacy and functionality.

2.1   Desired Properties and Threat Model

Functional requirements. As previously mentioned, we use the term "cloud" to refer to the cloud service provider, conference management system and its administrators, and the network. The responsibilities of the cloud are:

- To collect and store data relevant to the conference, including names of reviewers and authors, papers, reviews and scores.
- To enforce access control in respect of conflicts of interest and ensuring that reviewers see other reviews of a paper only after they have submitted their own.
- To manage the information flow of the conference: from authors, to conference chair, to reviewers and back.
- To notify the authors of the acceptance decision about their papers.

Privacy requirements. We require that the cloud does not know

- the content of submitted papers,
- the content of submitted reviews,
- the scores attributed to submitted papers.

Further, when data is necessarily known to the cloud in order that it can fulfil the functional requirements, we require what we call *unlinkability* property: the cloud is unable to link

- authors to reviewers of their papers

Threat model. It is reasonable to trust the cloud to execute the specified functional requirements. Indeed, an incorrect functionality would be detected in the long run and the users would simply move into another cloud. On the other hand, the cloud may try to violate privacy without affecting functionality, in a way that cannot readily be detected. ConfiChair is designed to remove this possibility. Obviously, there are inherent limitations on any protocol's ability to achieve this. For instance, if the cloud provider was invited to participate as a PC member or a chair, then he necessarily would have access to privileged information. Consequently, the privacy requirements are expected to hold in our threat model only for conferences in which the cloud provider does not participate, except as provider of the cloud service or as author of a paper.

We assume that users are running uncorrupted browsers on malware-free machines. The HTML, Java, and Javascript code that they download is also assumed to be obtained from a trustworthy source and properly authenticated (*e.g.* by digital signatures).

Usability requirements. The system should be as easy to use as present day conference management systems, such as EasyChair, iChair, OpenConf or HotCRP. The cost of security should not be unreasonable waiting time (e.g. for encryption, data download), or software installation on the client-side (e.g. a browser should be sufficient), or complex key management (e.g. public key infrastructure), etc. We discuss more about usability in section 4 which describes our prototype implementation.

2.2   Related Work

Generic solutions. Much work has been done that highlights the confidentiality and security risks that are inherent in cloud computing (e.g., [12] includes an overview), and there is now a conference series devoted to that topic [17]. Although the issue is well-known, the solutions described are mostly based on legislative and procedural approaches. Some generic technological solutions have appeared in the literature. The first one uses trusted hardware tokens [30], in which some trusted hardware performs the computations (such as key translations) that involve sensitive data. Solutions based on trusted hardware tokens may work, but appear to have significant scalability issues, and require much more research. Other papers advise designing cloud services to avoid having to store private data, and include measures to limit privacy loss [25].

Fully-homomorphic encryption (FHE) has been suggested as another generic solution to cloud-computing security. FHE is the idea that data processing can be done through the encryption, and has recently been shown to be possible in theory [19]. However, the range of functionality that can be provided through the encryption is not completely general. For example, one cannot extract from a list the items satisfying a given predicate, but one can return a list of encrypted truth values that indicate the items that satisfy the predicate, which is less useful. It is not clear to what extent FHE could alleviate the requirement to perform the browser-side computations of ConfiChair. Moreover, FHE is currently woefully inefficient in practice, and can only be considered usable in very specialised circumstances.

Data confidentiality and access control. Many works consider the problem of restricting the access of data in the cloud to authorised users only. For example, attribute-based encryption [6,4] allows fine-grained control over what groups of users are allowed to decrypt a piece of data. A different example is work that aims to identify functionally encryptable data, i.e. data that can be encrypted while preserving the functionality of a system [27]. Such systems, and others, aim to guarantee that the cloud, or unauthorised third parties, do not access sensitive data. Our problem requires a different perspective: how to design systems that allow the cloud, i.e. the intruder, to handle sensitive data, but at the same time ensure that sensitive data value links between them are not revealed.

Unlinkability. In many applications it is important that links between participants, data, or transactions are kept hidden. In RFID-based systems [14] or in privacy enhancing identity management systems [16] for example, an important requirement is that two transactions of a same agent should not be linkable in order to prevent users from being tracked or profiled. Another exemplar application that requires unlinkability is electronic voting: a voter must not be linked to the vote that he has cast [18]. Moreover, like scores or identities in our case study, a vote is at the same time functional (to be counted) and sensitive (to be private). Voting systems achieve unlinkability by relying either on mix nets [22,21], or on restricted versions of homomorphic encryption that allow the addition of plaintexts [3,5]. Our proposed protocol also relies on mixing, showing how that idea can be adapted to new application areas.

Other systems identify applications where the cloud can be provided with "fake" data without affecting functionality [20]. In that case, privacy of "real" data may be preserved, without the cloud being able to detect the substitution. That is a stronger property than what we aim for, and at the same time the solution proposed in [20] is restricted to very specific applications. In particular, a conference management system can not function correctly with "fake" data provided to the cloud.

Conference management. There has been work exposing particular issues with conference management systems, related to data secrecy, integrity and access control [23,28]. These are also important concerns, but that are quite orthogonal to ours, where we are interested in system design for ensuring unlinkability properties. More importantly, none of these works considers our threat model, where the attacker is the cloud.

3   The Protocol

3.1   Description

The protocol is informally described in Figures 1-3 on the following pages. Some details, such as different tags for messages in each phase of the conference, are left out, but the detailed formal definition is given in an appendix of the long version. The main idea of the protocol is to use a symmetric key K_{Conf} that is shared among the members of the programme committee. This key will be used to encrypt sensitive data before uploading it to the cloud. However, the cloud needs access to some sensitive data, like the reviewers of a paper, in order to implement the functional requirements of the protocol. To reveal that data to the cloud, without compromising privacy, our protocol makes use of the fact that different types of data are needed by the cloud at different phases of the conference. Thus, in transitioning from one phase to another, the conference chair can hide the links between authors and reviewers. He does so by performing a random mix on the data he needs to send to the cloud before moving to the next phase. Each conference has a public key, that authors use to encrypt symmetric keys, that in turn serve to encrypt papers.

Notation. As we just explained, the privacy of participants relies on the chair performing random mixes of the data he sends to the cloud. This is specified in Figures 1-3 by representing the databases $\mathrm{DB}^r_{\mathrm{Keys}}$, $\mathrm{DB}^r_{\mathrm{notf}}$ as randomised permutations (denoted by by $\leftarrow_{\mathcal{R}}$) of sets.

In the description of the ConfiChair protocol in Figures 1-3, we haven't included a biding phase. Although this phase is of great practical importance, it is conceptually similar to reviewing and discussion phases, and can be handled in a similar way. Indeed, provding a biding phase in a way that would preserve the users' privacy would also rely on the chair performing a reencryption mix on the papers before sending them to the reviewers through the cloud.

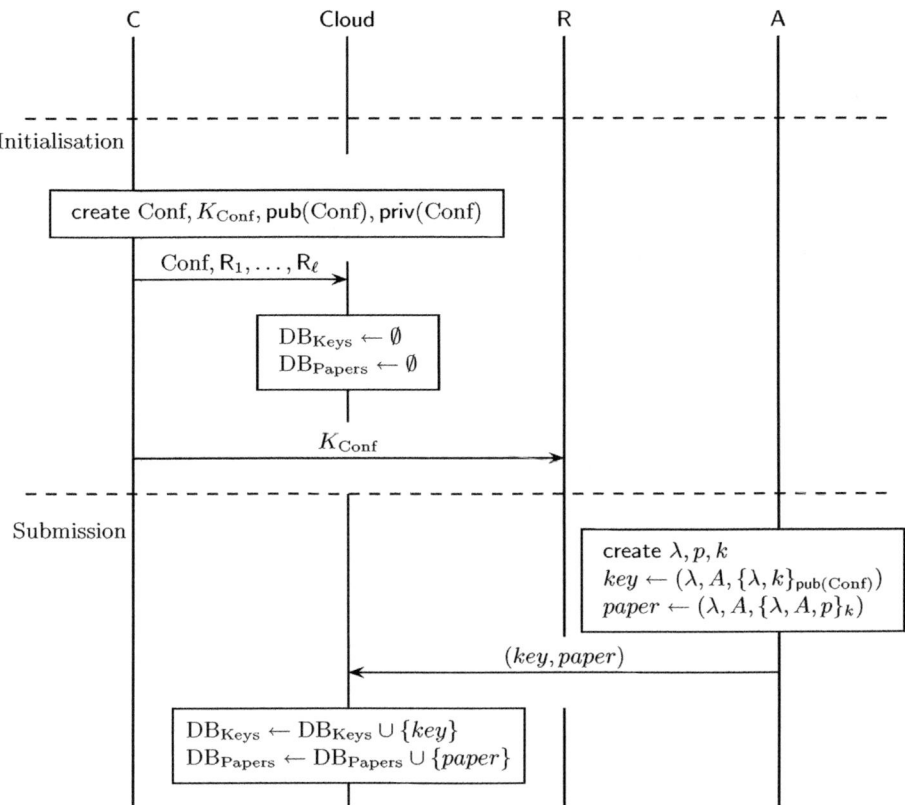

Fig. 1. ConfiChair: initialisation and submission phases

Initialisation. The conference chair C generates the symmetric key K_{Conf}, a public key pub(Conf) and a corresponding private key priv(Conf). The symmetric key is then shared among the reviewers in a way that does not reveal it to the cloud (see section 3.2). Then C requests from the cloud the creation of the conference named Conf, sending along the names of the chosen reviewers $R_1, \ldots, R_\ell$ for the programme committee.

Submission. An author A creates a paper p and a symmetric key k. He uploads to the cloud p encrypted with k and k encrypted with pub(Conf). An identifier λ is used to refer to this encrypted submission. The first role of the key k is to provide a symmetric key for the encryption of papers. The second role of k will be to encrypt the reviews assigned to p, for the notification that will be sent through the cloud back to the author. The cloud creates two corresponding databases: one with encrypted submission keys and one with encrypted papers.

Fig. 1. ConfiChair: initialisation and submission phases

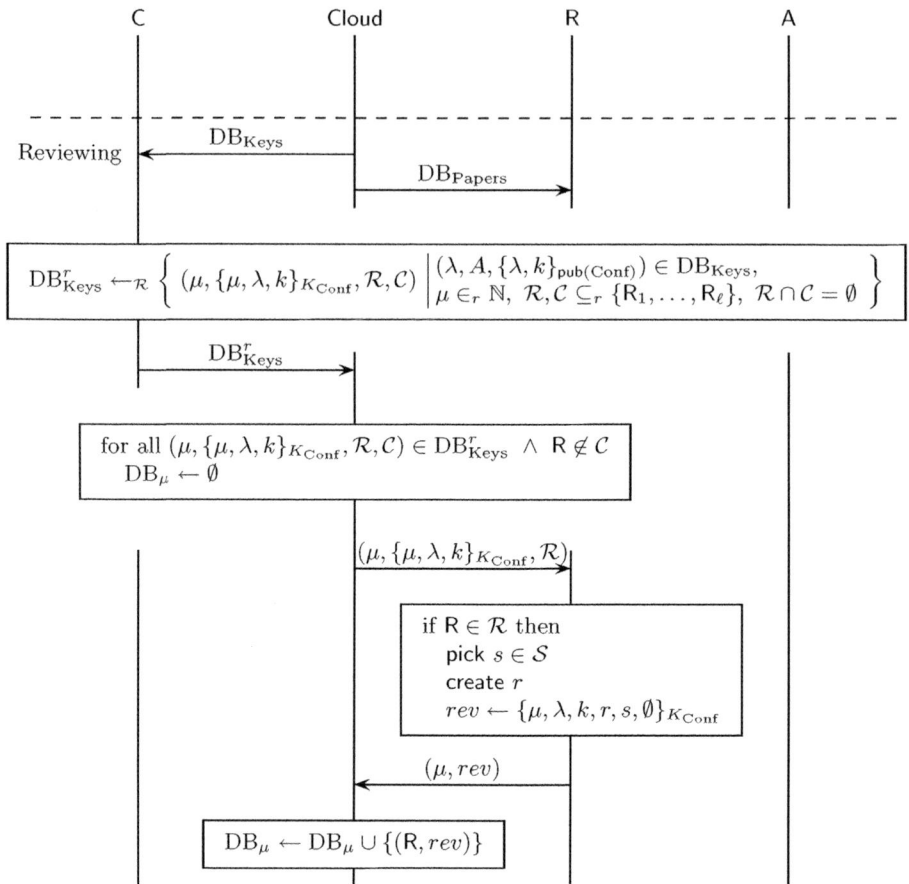

Reviewing. The chair downloads the database with encrypted keys, decrypts them using the private key priv(Conf) of the conference and encrypts them back with the shared symmetric key K_{Conf}. A new identifier μ is introduced for each paper. C also assigns the reviewers $\mathcal{R}$ to review the paper corresponding to μ, and declares the conflicts $\mathcal{C}$ restricting the set of reviewers that are allowed to see the data concerning μ. Finally, he mixes the elements in $\text{DB}^r_{\text{Keys}}$ before sending it to the cloud. The cloud filters the submissions according to these choices and sends them to reviewers.

The reviewers download the database with papers and can decrypt papers. For the papers they have been assigned to review ($R \in \mathcal{R}$), they upload reviews and scores in encrypted form back to the cloud. Note that the cloud is told to what identifier μ this encrypted review refers to. This allows the cloud to manage the data flow, without being able to link μ with λ, and hence the reviewer with the author.

Fig. 2. ConfiChair: reviewing phase

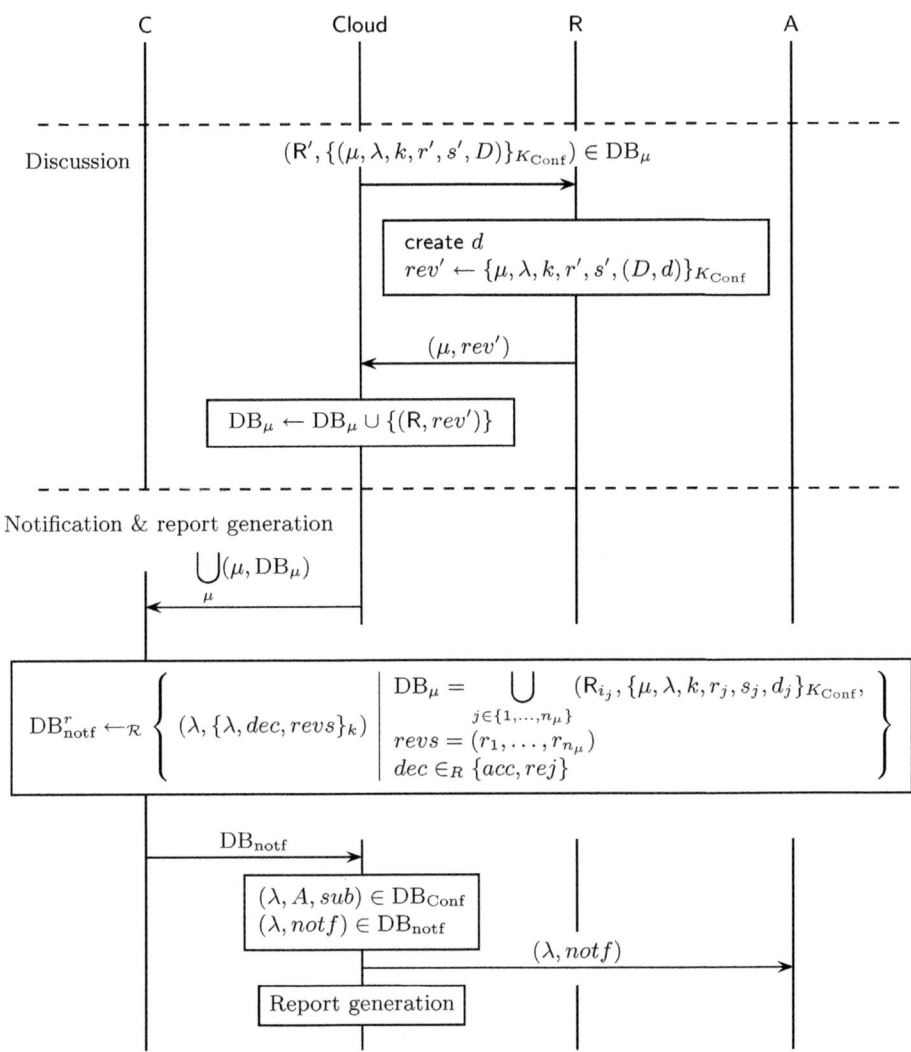

Fig. 3. ConfiChair: discussion and notification phases

Discussion. The reviews of each paper are submitted to the programme committee members (except for the conflicting reviewers) for discussion. Each reviewer can read a submitted review and the ongoing discussion D and add a comment d to it.

Notification. For each paper, the chair of the conference creates a notification including the decision and the reviews. This notification is encrypted with the author's symmetric key k (chosen at submission). The encrypted notification along with the submission identifier λ is uploaded to the cloud, allowing it to manage the information flow without compromising the privacy of the authors.

3.2   Discussion

Distribution of the reviewing symmetric key. The privacy properties of our protocol rely on the sharing of a symmetric key K_{Conf} among the members of the programme committee in such a way that the cloud does not get hold of K_{Conf}. Here we suggest a few possible solutions in the context of our application, reflecting different trade-offs between security and usability. Our protocol is independent of which of the three solutions is adopted:

(1) Public keys. Each reviewer may be expected to have a public key. Then, the symmetric key can be encrypted with each of the chosen reviewer's public key and uploaded to the cloud. The distribution can be made more flexible and efficient by relying on key distribution protocols like [10]. An important issue in this setting is the authentication of public keys of reviewers invited to participate in the conference. This may be done either relying on a hierarchical certification model such as *PKI* or, what is more probable in the case of conference management, on a distributed web of trust, such as that of *PGP*.

(2) Token. In this solution, each reviewer generates a symmetric key k_{R} and uploads $\{k_{\text{R}}\}_{\text{pub(Conf)}}$ to the cloud. Then, the chair sends $\{K_{\text{Conf}}\}_{k_{\text{R}}}$ to the reviewer using a channel that is outside the control of the cloud. He does this by checking the reviewer's authenticated email address and sends $\{K_{\text{Conf}}\}_{k_{\text{R}}}$ to that address. The reviewer then decrypts this token to obtain K_{Conf}. In this case, even if the cloud has access later to a reviewer's email, it cannot compromise the privacy properties that our protocol ensures.

(3) Email. If we assume that email infrastructure is not in the control of the cloud service provider that hosts ConfiChair (as is most probably the case in conference management), the key K_{Conf} could be sent to reviewers directly by email. In that case, if the email of a reviewer is compromised later on, its privacy for the conference Conf is also compromised. Note that it is only the key K_{Conf} that must be sent by email, all the rest of the protocol being executed in the cloud.

Computation in the cloud. We stress that non-trivial computation takes place in the cloud, namely routing of messages, and optionally collection of statistics. It is essential for usability and take-up of the proposed system that these computations are done by the cloud. The difficulties in designing the protocol thus lie in releasing the necessary information for the cloud to perform these operations without compromising the users of our system's privacy. In particular, the link between the sender of a message (*e.g.* the author of a paper) and the end receiver of this message (*e.g.* the reviewer of this paper) should remain private and this although it is the cloud that is responsible for routing messages.

Optionally, the protocol can be extended to allow the cloud to collect statistics or other anonymised data about the conference, its authors, papers, and reviewers. This can be achieved by adding code which extracts this information during the manipulations performed by the chair's browser. For example, along with the computation of $\text{DB}^r_{\text{notf}}$ in Figure 3.1, the chair could also compute the average score $as_\mu = (s_1 + \cdots + s_{n_\mu})/n_\mu$ for each paper and return the vector $(as_\mu)_\mu$ to the cloud. (Such optional features must be carefully designed to avoid weakening the security properties, and are not considered in our formal model in Secrion 5.)

Efficiency and usability. It may seem that there is a considerable amount of work to be done by the chair, especially in the transition between phases. As we discuss in the next section, this does not have to be evident to the chair. Our experiments with our prototype show that the browser can transparently execute the protocol.

4   Implementation

The ideal implementation of our protocol would look and feel very similar to existing cloud-based conference management systems such as OpenConf, EDAS and EasyChair, and should require no additional software beyond a web browser.

We constructed a prototype implementation [26], in order to discover any potential problems with a practical implementation and to find how much time and memory such a system may require, both on server-side and on client-side.

Overview. We implemented the ConfiChair prototype so that only a browser is necessary for participating as an author, a reviewer, or a chair. Overall, our prototype of ConfiChair feels very similar to current web-based management systems. A user of the system can perform his usual tasks by simply clicking a few buttons.

For example, to submit a paper an author logs to his ConfiChair account, selects the link for the conference to which he wants to submit, clicks the *new submission* button, selects the PDF file of his paper and clicks the *submit* button to complete his submission. All the key generation and the secure storing, as well as the encryption dictated by our protocol is transparently performed by the browser. The only aspect not currently performed by the browser is the retrieval of the conference public-key pub(Conf); this key must be manually input by the author (by copy-paste from the call for papers for example).

Similarily, the chair of a conference wanting to create a ConfiChair page for his conference Conf, loggins to his ConfiChair account and clicks the *create new conference* button. His browser will transparently, generate and securely store the keys K_{Conf}, pub(Conf), and priv(Conf).

Performance. The system is expected to handle hundreds of papers without overhead on the chair. In particular, browser-side re-encryption and mixing while transitioning between phases should not take more than a few minutes. From that perspective, the results of our experiments with the prototype implementation are promising. They are presented in a figure of the long version. The time taken for transitioning to the review stage is about 25s for 500 papers. The times for the other two transitions are about 70s and 350s.

Transparency of key management. To hide the complexity of the encryption keys from the user, these are managed and retrieved by the browser transparently when logging to ConfiChair. The login procedure implemented relies on each user having an identity id and a secret password psw_{id} from which the browser derives two keys: the ConfiChair account key $\mathsf{Kdf}_1(psw_{id})$ to authenticate the user to the the cloud provider, and a second key $\mathsf{Kdf}_2(psw_{id})$ used to encrypt the key purse of the user. This key purse contains the set of keys generated by the browser in previous accesses to the ConfiChair system, for example submission keys if the user has used ConfiChair as an author in the past, or conference keys if he has used it as a programme committee member.

When submitting a paper, the author's browser generates a symmetric key k which it uses to automatically encrypt the paper before sending it to the cloud. This key k is in turn added to the key purse of the user, which is uploaded encrypted with $\mathsf{Kdf}_2(psw_{authorid})$ to the cloud. To the submitter, this does not look like anything other than a normal file upload. Similarly, when the chair moves the conference to the review stage, it appears to be just like clicking on a normal link, since the chair's browser has already retrieved from the cloud the chair's key purse, and decrypted it with $\mathsf{Kdf}_2(psw_{chairid})$, and can then transparently decrypt and reencrypt the submissions according to the protocol.

In this way, the only key that needs to be securely backed up by a user id is his ConfiChair password psw_{id}. All the other keys are stored in encrypted form in the cloud, and retrieved when needed by his browser.

Currently, the authors need to copy and paste from the call for papers the public key of the conference $\mathsf{pub}(\mathsf{Conf})$ to which they want to submit, and the reviewers need to copy and paste from their email the shared-key of the conference $K(\mathsf{Conf})$ for which they are reviewers.

5   Formal Model and Verification

(This section has been shortened for the proceedings version of the paper. We recommend the full version on our web pages for more details of the verification.)

It is difficult to ascertain whether or not a cryptographic protocol satisfies its security requirements. Numerous deployed protocols have subsequently been found to be flawed, *e.g.* the Needham-Schroeder public-key protocol [24], the public-key Kerberos protocol [13], the PKCS#11 API [11], or the BAC protocol in e-Passports [15]. In this section, we formally show that ConfiChair does satisfy the announced security properties. The formal verification of the protocol has been done automatically using the ProVerif tool [7,9]. The ProVerif specification of the ConfiChair protocol is available online [26]. The verification requires a rigorous description of the protocol in the ProVerif calculus as well as formal definitions of the desired properties, each discussed in detail in the following section.

5.1   The Process Calculus

The ProVerif calculus [7,9] is a language for modelling distributed systems and their interactions. It is a dialect of the applied pi calculus [2]. In this section, we briefly review the basic ideas and concepts of the ProVerif calculus.

Terms. The calculus assumes an infinite set of *names*, $a, b, c, \ldots$, an infinite set of *variables*, $x, y, z, \ldots$ and a finite *signature* Σ, that is, a finite set of *function symbols* each with an associated arity. Function symbols are divided in two categories, namely *constructors* and *destructors*. Constructors are used for building messages from other messages, while destructors are used for analysing messages and obtaining parts of the messages they are applied to. Names and variables are messages. A new message M may be built by applying a constructor $f \in \Sigma$, to names, variables and other messages, $M_1, \ldots, M_n$, and denoted as usual $f(M_1, \ldots, M_n)$. A term evaluation D is built by applying any function symbol $g \in \Sigma$ (constructor or destructor) to variables, messages or term evaluations, $D_1, \ldots, D_n$, denoted $g(D_1, \ldots, D_n)$. The semantics of a destructor g of arity n is given by a finite set of rewrite rules of the form $g(M_1, \ldots, M_n) \to M_0$, where $M_0, M_1, \ldots, M_n$ are messages that only contain constructors and variables. Constructors and destructors are used to model cryptographic primitives such as *shared-key* or *public-key encryption*. The ProVerif calculus uses tuples of messages $(M_1, \ldots, M_n)$, keeping the obvious projection rules implicit.

In the following, and for the purpose of modelling the ConfiChair protocol presented in section 3, we will consider the signature

$$\Sigma = \{\mathsf{senc}_{/3}, \mathsf{sdec}_{/2}, \mathsf{pub}_{/1}, \mathsf{aenc}_{/3}, \mathsf{adec}_{/2}, \mathsf{subm}_{/0},$$
$$\mathsf{initrv}_{/0}, \mathsf{revw}_{/0}, \mathsf{dsc}_{/0}, \mathsf{ntf}_{/0}, \mathsf{one}_{/0}, \mathsf{two}_{/0}\}$$

where senc (*resp.* aenc) is a constructor of arity 3 that models the randomised shared-key (*resp.* randomised public-key) encryption primitive, sdec (*resp.* adec) is the corresponding destructor of arity 2, and pub is a constructor of arity 1 that models the public key associated to the private key given in argument. The signature also contains the constants initrv, revw, dsc, and ntf corresponding to the tags used to label messages originating from different phases of the protocol; and the constants one and two representing the possible scores for papers. The semantics of the two destructors is given by the two following rules

$$\mathsf{sdec}(x, \mathsf{senc}(x, y, z)) \to z$$
$$\mathsf{adec}(x, \mathsf{aenc}(\mathsf{pub}(x), y, z)) \to z$$

We model the probabilistic shared-key encryption of the message m with the key k by $\mathsf{senc}(k, r, m)$, where the r is fresh for every encryption; and the probabilistic public-key encryption of the message m with the pubic key corresponding to the secret key k by $\mathsf{aenc}(\mathsf{pub}(k), r, m)$.

We will write $D \Downarrow M$ if the term evaluation D can be reduced to the message M by applying some destructor rules. For example, if we consider the following term evaluation E and message N

$$E = \mathsf{senc}(k, r, \mathsf{sdec}(k', \mathsf{senc}(k', r', s)))$$
$$N = \mathsf{senc}(k, r, s),$$

by application of the first rewrite rule given above, we have $E \Downarrow N$.

Processes. Processes are built according to the grammar given below, where M is a message, D is a term evaluation, n is a name, and c is a channel name.

$P, Q, R ::=$	processes
0	null process
$P \mid Q$	parallel composition
$!P$	replication
new $n; P$	name restriction
let $M = D$ in P else Q	term evaluation
$\mathsf{in}(c, M); P$	message input
$\mathsf{out}(c, M); P$	message output

Replication handles the creation of an unbounded number of instances of a process. The process let $M = D$ in P else Q tries to evaluate D and matches the result with M; if this succeeds, then the variables in M are instantiated accordingly and P is executed; otherwise Q is executed. We will omit the else branch of a let when the process Q is 0. Names that are introduced by a new construct are *bound* in the subsequent process, and they represent the creation of fresh data. Variables that are introduced in the term M of an input or of a let construct are *bound* in the subsequent process, and they represent the reception or computation of fresh data. Names and variables that are not bound are called *free*. We denote by $\mathsf{fn}(P)$, respectively $\mathsf{fv}(P)$, the free names, respectively free variables, that occur in P.

Notation. A process definition P will sometimes be denoted by $P(\vec{v})$, where $\vec{v}$ is a vector of free variables that occur in P and that can be seen as parameters for the process P. Then we will abbreviate the process let $\vec{v} = \vec{w}$ in P simply by $P(\vec{w})$, and we will say that $P(\vec{w})$ is an instance of $P(\vec{v})$.

Example 1. The process A models the authors' part of the ConfiChair protocol.

$$A \quad\quad\quad\quad\quad \overset{\text{def}}{=} \text{new } ida; !A'(ida)$$
$$A'(xida) \quad\quad\quad\quad \overset{\text{def}}{=} \text{new } p; \text{ new } k; \ A''(xida, p, k)$$
$$A''(yida, yp, yk) \overset{\text{def}}{=} \text{new } l; \text{ new } r1; \text{ new } r2;$$
$$\mathsf{in}(cpbk, xpbk);$$
$$\text{let } k\_subm = (l, ida, \mathsf{aenc}(xpbk, r1, (\mathsf{subm}, l, k))) \text{ in } ($$
$$\text{let } p\_subm = (l, ida, \mathsf{senc}(k, r2, (l, ida, pap))) \text{ in } ($$
$$\mathsf{out}(c, (k\_subm, p\_subm));$$
$$\mathsf{in}(c, xn)))$$

An author with identity *ida* can submit many times to many different conferences ($!A'(ida)$). For each submission he generates the paper p and the submission key k, he chooses the conference he wants to submit to, fetches the corresponding public (in($cpbk, xpbk$)), and generates the identifier l (corresponding to the λ in the diagrams of Section 3). He then builds the submission message ((k_subm, p_subm)) as described in the diagrams of Section 3, and sends his submission to the cloud on the public channel c. He finally waits for the notification (in(c, xn)).

Altogether, the ConfiChair protocol can be fully modelled by the process

$$CC \stackrel{\text{def}}{=} \text{new } cshk; \text{ new } cpbk; \; (!C \mid !R \mid !A)$$

The subprocesses C, R, and A model the behaviour of a conference chair, a reviewer, and an author respectively. A is fully detailed above, and C and R are detailed in an appendix of the long version. We consider a general system CC with an unbounded number of chairs, reviewers, and authors. In CC, $cshk$ is the private channel (discussed in the first paragraph of Section 3.2) on which the shared-keys of conferences are sent to reviewers. The channel $cpbk$ is an authenticated channel from which the authors can access the public key of a conference in order to submit a paper. Although this channel is restricted to model that the public keys of conferences should be authenticated, the chair also publishes on the public channel c the public key of his conference, for anyone including the attacker to submit papers to it.

Semantics. Details of the semantics of the process language are given in the long version. Two processes are said to be observationally equivalent if their behaviour is identical in all contexts. We express secrecy and unlinkability as the observational equivalence of two processes.

5.2   Properties and Analysis

In this work, we prove using the ProVerif tool, that the ConfiChair protocol satisfies the intended secrecy and unlinkability properties informally described in section 2.1. The purpose of this section is to formally define these properties, and to show how they can be automatically verified with ProVerif. We define both secrecy and unlinkability properties as equivalences between processes adapting the classical approach of [31,1,18] to our context.

To express security properties we will need to consider particular authors and reviewers in interaction with the rest of the system. For this we consider a hole in the process CC, where we can plug any process, *i.e.* we let:

$$CC[\_] \stackrel{\text{def}}{=} \text{new } cshk; \text{ new } cpbk; \; (!C \mid !R \mid !A \mid \_)$$

To express authors and reviewers who submit some specific data (of which the privacy will be tested), we consider the processes:

- $A_{pap}(ida, p, k)$ - for an author whose identity is *ida* and that behaves like a regular author, with the single difference that amongst other submissions, he also submits the paper p with the corresponding submission-key k.

- $R_{sc}(idr, sc)$ - for a reviewer whose identity is idr and that behaves like a regular reviewer, with the single difference that amongst other reviews, he also reviews a paper to which it attributes the score sc.
- $R_{rev}(idr, k, rev)$ - for a reviewer whose identity is idr and that behaves like a regular reviewer, with the single difference that amongst other reviews, he also reviews the paper corresponding to the submission-key k, and writes the review rev.

The formal definition of these processes is detailed in an appendix of the long version of this paper.

Secrecy properties. To formalise the considered secrecy properties, we rely on the notion of strong secrecy defined in [8].

Paper secrecy. We say that a conference management protocol satisfies strong secrecy of papers if, even if the cloud initially knows p_1 and p_2, the cloud cannot make a distinction between an execution of the protocol where an author submitted the paper p_1 and an execution where he has submitted the paper p_2.

To formally capture this, we construct from $CC[\_]$ two processes: in the first one the hole is filled with an author that submits the publicly known (*i.e.* free) paper p_1, and in the second one the hole is filled with that author submitting the publicly known (*i.e.* free) paper p_2. We verify using ProVerif that these two processes are observationally equivalent:

$$CC[\text{new } ida; \text{ new } k; A_{pap}(ida, p_1, k)] \approx CC[\text{new } ida; \text{ new } k; A_{pap}(ida, p_2, k)]$$

Score secrecy. Similarly, in order to verify the strong secrecy of scores, we build from $CC[\_]$ one process in which the hole is filled with a reviewer that attributes one to some paper, and one process in which the hole is filled with the reviewer attributing two to it.

$$CC[\text{new } idr; R_{sc}(idr, \text{one})] \approx CC[\text{new } idr; R_{sc}(idr, \text{two})]$$

Review secrecy. The definition of secrecy of reviews is a bit more subtle. Reviews are sent to the authors at the notification phase, and the attacker could very well have submitted a paper. He would then rightfully obtain the review to his paper. So the property we want to formalise is that an attacker doesn't get to see the reviews of other authors' papers. In other words, review secrecy holds if, even if the cloud initially knows rev_1 and rev_2, the cloud cannot distinguish an execution of the protocol where a reviewer to a paper not submitted by the attacker writes the review rev_1 from an execution where the reviewer writes the review rev_2.

To capture this, we construct from $CC[\_]$ two processes. In the first one, the hole is filled with an honest author that submits a paper p with the corresponding submission-key k and a reviewer reviewing this paper and writing the publicly known (*i.e.* free) review rev_1. In the second one, an honest author that submits a paper p with the corresponding submission-key k and a reviewer reviewing this paper and writing the publicly known (*i.e.* free) review rev_2. For review secrecy to hold, the following equivalence must hold:

$$CC \begin{bmatrix} \text{new } ida; \text{new } p; \text{new } k; \text{new } idr; \\ (A_{pap}(ida, p, k) \mid \\ R_{rev}(idr, k, rev_1)) \end{bmatrix} \approx CC \begin{bmatrix} \text{new } ida; \text{new } p; \text{new } k; \text{new } idr; \\ (A_{pap}(ida, p, k) \mid \\ R_{rev}(idr, k, rev_2)) \end{bmatrix}$$

Analysis. We used the ProVerif tool to prove that the equivalences described above hold, and thus that as announced ConfiChair does provide secrecy of papers, scores and reviews. The ProVerif source code for each of these equivalences is available online [26].

Author-reviewer unlinkability. This property aims to guarantee that the links between a given author and the reviewers of his papers remain hidden from the cloud. To formalise it one could ask whether two processes are in observational equivalence: one in which ida's paper is reviewed by a reviewer idr_1, and another in which ida's paper is reviewed by a reviewer idr_2.

However, similarly to privacy in electronic voting [18], definitions of unlinkability are a bit more tricky. Since the identities of the authors that submit papers are revealed to the cloud at submission time, and the identities of the reviewers are published when the review is submitted, unlinkability can not be ensured when there is a single reviewer, or a single author.

In order to give robust definitions of unlinkability we need to consider conferences with at least two reviewers and at least two authors submitting papers to it that are being reviewed by these reviewers. It is the chair's task to ensure that this is indeed the case. Accordingly, there is in the formal model a processes C_{ar} that ensures that at each stage of the conference at least two authors and two reviewers have executed their role. The detailed definition of C_{ar} is given in an appendix of the long version of this paper.

We prove that there is no observable difference between the case where reviewer idr_1 reviews ida_1's paper and reviewer idr_2 reviews ida_2's paper (left-hand-side process), and the case where reviewer idr_2 reviews ida_1's paper and reviewer idr_1 reviews ida_2's paper (right-hand-side process):

$$CC \begin{bmatrix} \text{new } p_1; \text{new } p_2; \text{new } k_1; \text{new } k_2; \\ \text{new } rev_1; \text{new } rev_2 \\ C_{ar}(k_1, k_2, idr_1, idr_2) \mid \\ A_{pap}(ida_1, p_1, k_1) \mid \\ A_{pap}(ida_2, p_2, k_2) \mid \\ R_{rev}(idr_1, k_1, rev_1) \mid \\ R_{rev}(idr_2, k_2, rev_2) \end{bmatrix} \approx CC \begin{bmatrix} \text{new } p_1; \text{new } p_2; \text{new } k_1; \text{new } k_2; \\ \text{new } rev_1; \text{new } rev_2 \\ C_{ar}(k_1, k_2, idr_2, idr_1) \mid \\ A_{pap}(ida_1, p_1, k_1) \mid \\ A_{pap}(ida_2, p_2, k_2) \mid \\ R_{rev}(idr_1, k_2, rev_1) \mid \\ R_{rev}(idr_2, k_1, rev_2) \end{bmatrix}$$

Analysis. We used the ProVerif tool to prove that the equivalence described above hold, and thus that as announced ConfiChair does provide author-reviewer unlinkability. The ProVerif source code for this equivalence is available online [26].

6   Conclusion

The accumulation of sensitive data on servers around the world is a major problem for society, and will be considerably exacerbated by the anticipated take-up of cloud-computing technology. The fact that confidential data about the authoring and reviewing performance of tens of thousands of researchers across thousands of conferences is stored by well-known cloud-based systems serves to show how widespread and ubiquitous the problem is [29].

We have introduced a general technique that can be used to address this problem in a wide variety of circumstances, namely, the technique of translating between keys and mixing data in a trustworthy browser. We have proposed ConfiChair, a conference management system that uses this technique to obtain strong privacy properties while having all the advantages of cloud computing. In ConfiChair, the cloud sees sensitive data only in encrypted form, with no single person holding all the encryption keys (our protocol uses a different key for each conference). The conference chair's browser decrypts data with one key and encrypts it with possibly another one, while mixing and re-randomising to ensure unlinkability properties.

We are able to state and prove strong secrecy and unlinkability properties for ConfiChair. The protocol still enables the cloud provider to route information to the necessary chairs, reviewers and authors, to enforce access control, and optionally to perform statistics collection. We have demonstrated that the cryptography and key management can be handled by a regular web browser [26] (specifically, we used LiveConnect). We plan to continue developing our prototype into a complete system.

An important design decision in ConfiChair is the fact that a single key K_{Conf} is used to encrypt all the information for the conference Conf. Stronger secrecy properties could be obtained if a different key were used for different subsets of reviewers and papers, but this would be at the cost of simplicity. Using a single key per conference seems to strike a good balance between usability and security. Finer-grained access control is implemented (as on current systems) by the cloud, e.g. for managing the conflicts of interest.

In further work, we intend to apply the ideas to work with other cloud-computing applications (such as those mentioned in the introduction), and to provide a framework for expressing secrecy and unlinkability properties in a more systematic way.

Acknowledgments. Thanks to Joshua Phillips for much help with the implementation and typesetting. We also gratefully acknowledge financial support from EPSRC via the projects *Trust Domains* (TS/I002529/1) and *Trustworthy Voting Systems* (EP/G02684X/1).

References

1. Abadi, M.: Security protocols and their properties. In: Foundations of Secure Computation. NATO Science Series, pp. 39–60. IOS Press (2000)
2. Abadi, M., Fournet, C.: Mobile values, new names, and secure communication. In: Proceedings of the 28th ACM Symposium on Principles of Programming Languages (POPL 2001), pp. 104–115 (January 2001)
3. Adida, B.: Helios: Web-based open-audit voting. In: van Oorschot, P.C. (ed.) USENIX Security Symposium, pp. 335–348. USENIX Association (2008)
4. Baden, R., Bender, A., Spring, N., Bhattacharjee, B., Starin, D.: Persona: an online social network with user-defined privacy. In: Rodriguez, P., Biersack, E.W., Papagiannaki, K., Rizzo, L. (eds.) SIGCOMM, pp. 135–146. ACM (2009)
5. Baudron, O., Fouque, P.-A., Pointcheval, D., Stern, J., Poupard, G.: Practical multi-candidate election system. In: PODC, pp. 274–283 (2001)
6. Bethencourt, J., Sahai, A., Waters, B.: Ciphertext-policy attribute-based encryption. In: IEEE Symposium on Security and Privacy, pp. 321–334. IEEE Computer Society (2007)
7. Blanchet, B.: An efficient cryptographic protocol verifier based on Prolog rules. In: Computer Security Foundations Workshop, CSFW 2001 (2001)
8. Blanchet, B.: Automatic proof of strong secrecy for security protocols. In: IEEE Symposium on Security and Privacy, pp. 86–100 (2004)
9. Blanchet, B., Abadi, M., Fournet, C.: Automated verification of selected equivalences for security protocols. Journal of Logic and Algebraic Programming (2007)
10. Boneh, D., Gentry, C., Waters, B.: Collusion Resistant Broadcast Encryption with Short Ciphertexts and Private Keys. In: Shoup, V. (ed.) CRYPTO 2005. LNCS, vol. 3621, pp. 258–275. Springer, Heidelberg (2005)
11. Bortolozzo, M., Centenaro, M., Focardi, R., Steel, G.: Attacking and fixing PKCS#11 security tokens. In: ACM Conference on Computer and Communications Security, pp. 260–269 (2010)
12. Buyya, R., Yeo, C.S., Venugopal, S., Broberg, J., Brandic, I.: Cloud computing and emerging IT platforms: Vision, hype, and reality for delivering computing as the 5th utility. Future Generation Computer Systems 25(6), 599–616 (2009)
13. Cervesato, I., Jaggard, A.D., Scedrov, A., Tsay, J.-K., Walstad, C.: Breaking and fixing public-key kerberos. Inf. Comput. 206, 402–424 (2008)
14. Chatmon, C., van Le, T., Burmester, T.: Secure anonymous RFID authentication protocols. Technical Report TR-060112, Florida Stat University, Department of Computer Science (2006)
15. Chothia, T., Smirnov, V.: A Traceability Attack against e-Passports. In: Sion, R. (ed.) FC 2010. LNCS, vol. 6052, pp. 20–34. Springer, Heidelberg (2010)
16. Clauß, S., Kesdogan, D., Kölsch, T., Pimenidis, L., Schiffner, S., Steinbrecher, S.: Privacy enhancing identity management: Protection against re-identification and profiling. In: Proceedings of the 2005 ACM Workshop on Digital Identity Management (2005)
17. Cloud Security Alliance. Secure Cloud (2010), http://www.cloudsecurityalliance.org/sc2010.html
18. Delaune, S., Kremer, S., Ryan, M.D.: Verifying privacy-type properties of electronic voting protocols. Journal of Computer Security 17(4), 435–487 (2009)
19. Gentry, C.: Fully homomorphic encryption using ideal lattices. In: 41st ACM Symposium on Theory of Computing, STOC (2009)

20. Guha, S., Tang, K., Francis, P.: NOYB: Privacy in online social networks. In: Proceedings of the First ACM SIGCOMM Workshop on Online Social Networks (2008)
21. Jakobsson, M., Juels, A., Rivest, R.L.: Making mix nets robust for electronic voting by randomized partial checking. In: Boneh, D. (ed.) USENIX Security Symposium, pp. 339–353. USENIX (2002)
22. Juels, A., Catalano, D., Jakobsson, M.: Coercion-resistant electronic elections. In: Atluri, V., di Vimercati, S.D.C., Dingledine, R. (eds.) WPES, pp. 61–70. ACM (2005)
23. Lo, S.-W., Phan, R.C.-W., Goi, B.-M.: On the Security of a Popular Web Submission and Review Software (WSaR) for Cryptology Conferences. In: Kim, S., Yung, M., Lee, H.-W. (eds.) WISA 2007. LNCS, vol. 4867, pp. 245–265. Springer, Heidelberg (2008)
24. Lowe, G.: An attack on the Needham-Schroeder public-key authentication protocol. Information Processing Letters 56(3), 131–133 (1996)
25. Pearson, S., Shen, Y., Mowbray, M.: A Privacy Manager for Cloud Computing. In: Jaatun, M.G., Zhao, G., Rong, C. (eds.) CloudCom 2009. LNCS, vol. 5931, pp. 90–106. Springer, Heidelberg (2009)
26. Phillips, J., Roberts, M.: ConfiChair - prototype privacy-supporting conference management system, https://confichair.markryan.eu
27. Puttaswamy, K.P.N., Kruegel, C., Zhao, B.Y.: Silverline: Toward data confidentiality in third-party clouds. Technical Report 08, University of California Santa Barbara (2010)
28. Qunoo, H., Ryan, M.: Modelling Dynamic Access Control Policies for Web-Based Collaborative Systems. In: Foresti, S., Jajodia, S. (eds.) Data and Applications Security and Privacy XXIV. LNCS, vol. 6166, pp. 295–302. Springer, Heidelberg (2010)
29. Ryan, M.D.: Cloud computing privacy concerns on our doorstep. Communications of the ACM 54(1), 36–38 (2011)
30. Sadeghi, A.-R., Schneider, T., Winandy, M.: Token-Based Cloud Computing. In: Acquisti, A., Smith, S.W., Sadeghi, A.-R. (eds.) TRUST 2010. LNCS, vol. 6101, pp. 417–429. Springer, Heidelberg (2010)
31. Schneider, S., Sidiropoulos, A.: CSP and Anonymity. In: Martella, G., Kurth, H., Montolivo, E., Bertino, E. (eds.) ESORICS 1996. LNCS, vol. 1146, pp. 198–218. Springer, Heidelberg (1996)

A Formal Analysis of the Norwegian E-voting Protocol*

Véronique Cortier and Cyrille Wiedling

LORIA - CNRS, Nancy, France

Abstract. Norway has used e-voting in its last political election in September 2011, with more than 25 000 voters using the e-voting option. The underlying protocol is a new protocol designed by the ERGO group, involving several actors (a bulletin box but also a receipt generator, a decryption service, and an auditor). Of course, trusting the correctness and security of e-voting protocols is crucial in that context. Formal definitions of properties such as privacy, coercion-resistance or verifiability have been recently proposed, based on equivalence properties.

In this paper, we propose a formal analysis of the protocol used in Norway, w.r.t. privacy, considering several corruption scenarios. Part of this study has conducted using the ProVerif tool, on a simplified model.

Keywords: e-voting, privacy, formal methods.

1 Introduction

Electronic voting protocols promise a convenient, efficient and reliable way for collecting and tallying the votes, avoiding for example usual human errors when counting. It is used or have been used for political elections in several countries like e.g. USA, Estonia, Switzerland and recently Norway, at least in trials. However, the recent history has shown that these systems are highly vulnerable to attacks. For example, the Diebold machines as well as the electronic machines used in India have been attacked [13,24]. Consequently, the use of electronic voting raises many ethical and political issues. For example, the German Federal Constitutional Court decided on 3 March 2009 that electronic voting used for the last 10 years was unconstitutional [1].

There is therefore a pressing need for a rigorous analysis of the security of e-voting protocols. A first step towards the security analysis of e-voting protocols consists in precisely defining security w.r.t. e-voting. Formal definitions have been proposed for several key properties such as privacy, receipt-freeness, coercion resistance, or verifiability, most of them in terms of equivalence-based properties (see e.g. [12,17]). It is however difficult to formally analyse e-voting protocols for two main reasons. First there are very few tools that can check

---

* The research leading to these results has received funding from the European Research Council under the European Union's Seventh Framework Programme (FP7/2007-2013) / ERC grant agreement no 258865, project ProSecure.

P. Degano and J.D. Guttman (Eds.): POST 2012, LNCS 7215, pp. 109–128, 2012.

equivalence properties: ProVerif [5,6] is probably the only one but it does not really work in the context of e-voting (because it tries to show a stronger notion of equivalence, which is not fulfilled when checking for ballot secrecy). Some other very recent (yet preliminary) tools have been proposed such as Datep [8] or AKiSs [7]. However, the cryptographic primitives used in e-voting are rather complex and non standard and are typically not supported by existing tools.

In this paper, we study the protocol used in last September for political elections in Norway [2]. E-voting was proposed as trials in several municipalities and more than 25 000 voters did use e-voting to actually cast their vote. The protocol is publicly available [15] that has four main components: a Bulletin Box, a Decryption Service, and a Receipt Generator and an Auditor which aim at watching the Bulletin Box recording the votes. The resulting protocol is therefore complex, e.g. using El Gamal encryption in a non standard way. In [15], Gjøsteen describes the protocol and discusses its security. To our knowledge, there does not exist any security proof, even for the crucial property of vote privacy.

Our contribution. We conduct a formal analysis of the Norwegian protocol w.r.t. privacy. Our first contribution is the proposition of a formal model of the protocol in applied-pi calculus [3]. One particularity of the protocol is to distribute public keys $\mathsf{pk}(a_1)$, $\mathsf{pk}(a_2)$, and $\mathsf{pk}(a_3)$ for the three authorities, such that the corresponding private keys a_1, a_2, and a_3 verify the relation $a_1 + a_2 = a_3$, allowing one component (here the Bulletin Box) to re-encrypt messages. The protocol also makes use of signature, of zero-knowledge proofs, of blinding functions and coding functions. We have therefore proposed a new equational theory reflecting the unusual behavior of the primitives.

Our second contribution is a formal security proof of privacy, in the presence of arbitrarily many dishonest voters. Given the complexity of the equational theory (with e.g. four associative and commutative symbols), the resulting processes can clearly not be analyzed with existing tools, even ProVerif. We therefore proved privacy (expressed as an equivalence property) by hand. The proof happens to be quite technical. Its first step is rather standard and consists in guessing a relation such that the two initial processes and all their possible evolutions are in relation. The second step is more involved: it requires to prove equivalent an infinite number of frames, the frames representing all possible attacker knowledge. Indeed, unlike most previously analyzed protocols, the Norwegian protocol emits receipts for the voters, potentially providing extra information to the attacker. Proving static equivalence is also made difficult due to our equational theory (e.g. four associative and commutative symbols).

Our third contribution is an analysis of the protocol for further corruption scenarios, using the ProVerif tool in a simplified model (therefore possibly losing attacks). In conclusion, we did not find any attack, except when the bulletin box and the receipt generator or the decryption service alone (if no shuffling is made) are corrupted. These attacks are probably not surprising but we found interesting to make them explicit.

Related Work. [15] provides a discussion on the security of the Norwegian protocol but no security proof. We do not know any other study related to this protocol. Several other e-voting protocols have been studying using formal methods. The FOO [14], Okamoto [23] and Lee *et al.* [21] voting protocols have been analysed in [12]. Similarly, Helios has been recently proved secure both in a formal [10] and a computational [4] model. However, all these protocols were significantly simpler to analyse. The more complex Civitas protocol was analyzed in [18]. In contrast, the Norwegian protocol is both complex and fully deployed. There are also been studies of hybrid protocols (not fully electronic), such as Scantegrity [20] or ThreeBallot [19].

We informally describe the protocol in Section 2. The applied-pi calculus is briefly defined in Section 3. We then provide a formal modeling of the protocol in Section 4 and formally state and prove the privacy properties satisfied by the protocol in Section 5. The results obtained with ProVerif are described in Section 6. Concluding remarks can be found in Section 7. All the proofs are provided in a research report [11].

2 Norwegian E-voting Protocol

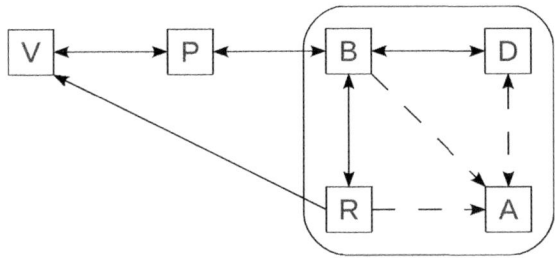

Norwegian protocol features several players including four players representing the electronic poll's infrastructure : a ballot box (B), a receipt generator (R), a decryption service (D) and an auditor (A). Each voter (V) can log in using a computer (P) in order to submit his vote. Channels between computers (voters) and the ballot box are considered as authenticated channel, channels between infrastructure's player are untappable channels and channel between voters and receipt generator is a unidirectional out-of-band channel. (Example of SMS is given in [15].) The protocol can be divided in three phases : the setting phase, the submission phase, where voters submit their votes, and the counting phase, where ballots are counted and auditor verifies the correctness of the election.

2.1 Setting Phase

Before the election, private keys a_1, a_2, and a_3 (such that $a_1 + a_2 = a_3$) are distributed over, respectively D, B, and R, while the corresponding public keys are made publicly available. The receipt generator R is assumed to have a signing key id_R which corresponding verification key is distributed to P. The voters are

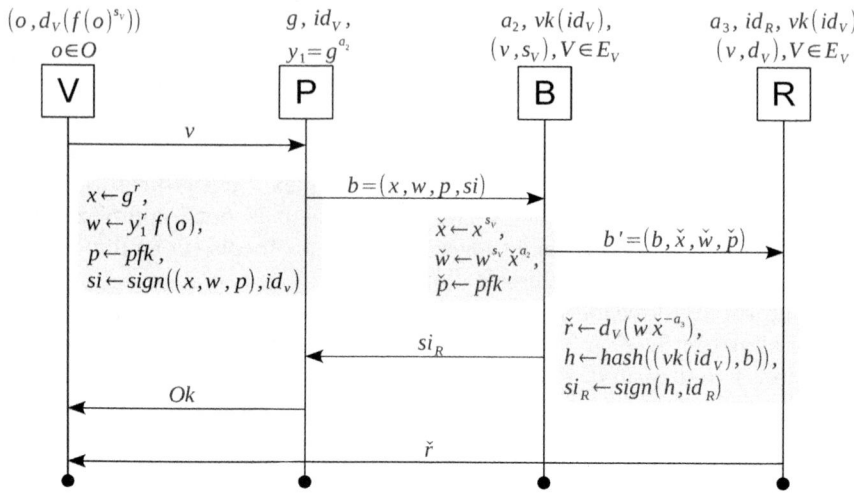

Fig. 1. Submission of one vote

also assume to each have a signing key id_V with the corresponding verification key distributed to B. The bulletin board B is provided with a table $V \mapsto s_V$ with a blinding factor s_V for each voter V. The receipt generator R is given a table $V \mapsto d_V$ with a permutation function d_V for each voter V. Finally, each voter V is assumed to received by post a table where, for each voting option o corresponds a precomputed receipt code $d_V(f(o)^{s_V})$ where f is some encoding function for voting options.

2.2   Submission Phase

The submission phase is depicted in Figure 1. We detail below the expected behavior of each participant.

Voter (V). Each voter tells his computer what voting option o to submit and allows it to sign the corresponding ballot on his behalf. Then, he has to wait for an acceptance message coming from the computer and a receipt $\check{r}$ sent by the receipt generator through the out-of-band channel. Using the receipt, he verifies that the correct vote was submitted, that is, he checks that $\check{r} = d_V(f(o)^{s_V})$ by verifying that the receipt code $\check{r}$ indeed appears in the line associated to o.

Computer (P). Voter's computer encrypts voter's ballot with the public key y_1 using standard El Gamal encryption. The resulting ballot is $(g^r, y^r f(o))$. P also proves that the resulting ciphertext corresponds to the correct vote, by computing a standard signature proof of knowledge *pfk*. How *pfk* is computed exactly can be found in [15]. P also signs the ballot with id_V and sends it to the ballot box. It then waits for a confirmation si_R coming from the latter, which is a hash of the initial encrypted ballot, signed by the receipt generator. After checking this signature, the computer notifies the voter that his vote has been taken into account.

Bulletin Box (B). Receiving an encrypted and signed ballot b from a computer, the ballot box checks first the correctness of signatures and proofs before re-encrypting with a_2 and blinding with s_V the original encrypted ballot, also generating a proof pfk', showing that its computation is correct. B then sends the new modified ballot b' to the receipt generator. Once the ballot box receives a message si_R from the receipt generator, it simply checks that the receipt generator's signature is valid, and sends it to the computer.

Receipt generator (R). When receiving an encrypted ballot $b' = (b, \check{x}, \check{w}, \check{p})$ from the ballot box, the receipt generator first checks signature and proofs (from the computer and the ballot box). If the checks are successful, it generates:

- a receipt code $\check{r} = d_V(\check{w}\check{x}^{a_3})$ sent by out-of-band channel directly to the voter. Intuitively, the receipt generator decrypts the (blinded) ballot, applying the permutation function d_V associated to the voter. This gives assurance to the voter that the correct vote was submitted to the bulletin board.
- a signature on a hash of the original encrypted ballot for the ballot box. Once transmitted by the bulletin board, it allows the computer to inform the voter that his vote has been accepted.

2.3 Counting Phase

Once the ballot box is closed, the counting phase begins (Figure 2). The ballot box selects the encrypted votes $x_1, \ldots, x_k$ which need to be decrypted (if a voter is re-voting, all the submitted ballots are in the memory of the ballot box and only the last ballot should be sent) and sends them to the decryption service. The whole content of the ballot box $b_1, \ldots, b_n$ $(n \geq k)$ is revealed to the auditor, including previous votes from re-voting voters. The receipt generator sends to the auditor the list of hashes of ballots it has seen during the submission phase. The decryption service decrypts the incoming ciphertexts $x_1, \ldots, x_k$ received from the ballot box and mix the results before outputting them $\mathsf{dec}(x_{\sigma(1)}, a_1), \ldots, \mathsf{dec}(x_{\sigma(k)}, a_1)$ where σ denotes the permutation obtained by shuffling the votes. It also provides the auditor with a proof pfk showing that the input ciphertexts and the outcoming decryption indeed match. Using the ballot box content and the list of hashes from the receipt generator, the auditor verifies that no ballots have been inserted or lost and computes his own list of encrypted ballots which should be counted. He compares this list with the one received from the decryption service and verifies the proof given by the latter.

3 Applied Pi Calculus

We use the framework of the applied-pi calculus [3] for formally describing the Norwegian protocol. To help with readability, the definitions of the applied-pi calculus are briefly recalled here.

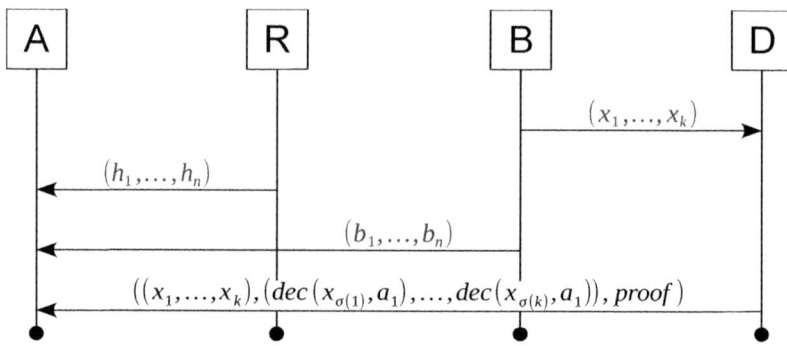

Fig. 2. Counting phase

3.1   Terms

As usual, messages are represented by *terms* built upon an infinite set of *names* $\mathcal{N}$ (for communication channels or atomic data), a set of *variables* $\mathcal{X}$ and a *signature* Σ consisting of a finite set of *function symbols* (to represent cryptographic primitives). A function symbol f is assumed to be given with its arity $ar(f)$. Then the set of terms $T(\Sigma, \mathcal{X}, \mathcal{N})$ is formally defined by the grammar :

$$t, t_1, t_2, \ldots ::=$$

$$\begin{array}{ll} x & x \in \mathcal{X} \\ n & n \in \mathcal{N} \\ f(t_1, \ldots, t_n) & f \in \Sigma, n = ar(f) \end{array}$$

We write $\{^{M_1}/_{x_1}, \ldots, ^{M_n}/_{x_n}\}$ for the *substitution* that replaces the variables x_i with the terms M_i. $N\sigma$ refers to the result of applying substitution σ to the free variables of term N. A term is called *ground* when it does not contain variables.

In order to represent the properties of the primitives, the signature Σ is equipped with an *equational theory* E that is a set of equations which hold on terms built from the signature. We denote $=_E$ the smallest equivalence relation induced by E, closed under application of function symbols, substitution of terms for variables and bijective renaming of names. We write $M =_E N$ when the equation $M = N$ is in the theory E.

Example 1. A standard signature for representing encryption is $\Sigma = \{\mathsf{dec}, \mathsf{penc}\}$ where penc represents encryption while dec is decryption. Decryption is modeled by the theory E_{enc}, defined by the equation $\mathsf{dec}(\mathsf{penc}(x, r, \mathsf{pk}(k)), k) = x$.

3.2   Processes

Processes and *extended processes* are defined in Figure 3. The process 0 represents the null process that does nothing. $P \mid Q$ denotes the parallel composition of P with Q while $!P$ denotes the unbounded replication of P (*i.e.* the unbounded parallel composition of P with itself). $\nu n.P$ creates a fresh name n and the behaves like P. if ϕ then P else Q behaves like P if ϕ holds and like Q otherwise.

$P, Q, R ::=$	(plain) processes
0	null process
$P \mid Q$	parallel composition
$!P$	replication
$\nu\, n.P$	name restriction
if ϕ then P else Q	conditional
$u(x).P$	message input
$\overline{u}\langle M \rangle.P$	message output
$A, B, C ::=$	extended processes
P	plain process
$A \mid B$	parallel composition
$\nu\, n.A$	name restriction
$\nu\, x.A$	variable restriction
$\{M/x\}$	active substitution

Fig. 3. Syntax for processes

$u(x).P$ inputs some message in the variable x on channel u and then behaves like P while $\overline{u}\langle M \rangle.P$ outputs M on channel u and then behaves like P. We write $\nu\, \tilde{u}$ for the (possibly empty) series of pairwise-distinct binders $\nu\, u_1. \cdots .\nu\, u_n$. The active substitution $\{M/x\}$ can replace the variable x for the term M in every process it comes into contact with and this behaviour can be controlled by restriction, in particular, the process $\nu\, x\, (\{M/x\} \mid P)$ corresponds exactly to let $x = M$ in P. As in [10], we slightly extend the applied-pi calculus by letting conditional branches now depend on formulae $\phi, \psi ::= M = N \mid M \neq N \mid \phi \wedge \psi$. If M and N are ground, we define $[\![M = N]\!]$ to be true if $M =_E N$ and false otherwise. The semantics of $[\![\ ]\!]$ is then extended to formulae as expected.

The *scope* of names and variables are delimited by binders $u(x)$ and $\nu\,(u)$. Sets of bound names, bound variables, free names and free variables are respectively written $\mathrm{bn}(A)$, $\mathrm{bv}(A)$, $\mathrm{fn}(A)$ and $\mathrm{fv}(A)$. Occasionally, we write $\mathrm{fn}(M)$ (respectively $\mathrm{fv}(M)$) for the set of names (respectively variables) which appear in term M. An extended process is *closed* if all its variables are either bound or defined by an active substitution.

An *context* $C[\_]$ is an extended process with a hole instead of an extended process. We obtain $C[A]$ as the result of filling $C[\_]$'s hole with the extended process A. An *evaluation context* is a context whose hole is not in the scope of a replication, a conditional, an input or an output. A context $C[\_]$ closes A when $C[A]$ is closed.

A *frame* is an extended process built up from the null process 0 and active substitutions composed by parallel composition and restriction. The *domain* of a frame φ, denoted $\mathrm{dom}(\varphi)$ is the set of variables for which φ contains an active substitution $\{M/x\}$ such that x is not under restriction. Every extended process A can be mapped to a frame $\varphi(A)$ by replacing every plain process in A with 0.

Par-0	$A \equiv A \mid 0$	
Par-A	$A \mid (B \mid C) \equiv (A \mid B) \mid C$	
Par-C	$A \mid B \equiv B \mid A$	
Repl	$!P \equiv P \mid !P$	
New-0	$\nu\, n.0 \equiv 0$	
New-C	$\nu\, u.\nu\, w.A \equiv \nu\, w.\nu\, u.A$	
New-Par	$A \mid \nu\, u.B \equiv \nu\, u.(A \mid B)$	if $u \notin \mathrm{fv}(A) \cup \mathrm{fn}(A)$
Alias	$\nu\, x.\{M/x\} \equiv 0$	
Subst	$\{M/x\} \mid A \equiv \{M/x\} \mid A\{M/x\}$	
Rewrite	$\{M/x\} \equiv \{N/x\}$	if $M =_E N$

Fig. 4. Structural equivalence

3.3   Operational Semantics

The operational semantics of processes in the applied pi calculus is defined by three relations : *structural equivalence* ($\equiv$), *internal reduction* ($\rightarrow$) and *labelled reduction* ($\xrightarrow{\alpha}$). *Structural equivalence* is defined in Figure 4. It is closed by α-conversion of both bound names and bound variables, and closed under application of evaluation contexts. The *internal reductions* and *labelled reductions* are defined in Figure 5. They are closed under structural equivalence and application of evaluation contexts. Internal reductions represent evaluation of condition and internal communication between processes. Labelled reductions represent communications with the environment.

3.4   Equivalences

Privacy properties are often stated as equivalence relations [12]. Intuitively, if a protocol preserves ballot secrecy, an attacker should not be able to distinguish between a scenario where a voter votes 0 from a scenario where the voter votes 1. *Static equivalence* formally expresses indistinguishability of sequences of terms.

Definition 1 (Static equivalence). *Two closed frames φ and ψ are statically equivalent, denoted $\varphi \approx_s \psi$, if $dom(\varphi) = dom(\psi)$ and there exists a set of names $\tilde{n}$ and substitutions σ, τ such that $\varphi \equiv \nu\,\tilde{n}.\sigma$ and $\psi \equiv \nu\,\tilde{n}.\tau$ and for all terms M, N such that $\tilde{n} \cap (fn(M) \cup fn(N)) = \emptyset$, we have $M\sigma =_E N\sigma$ holds if and only if $M\tau =_E N\tau$ holds. Two closed extended processes A, B are statically equivalent, written $A \approx_s B$, if their frames are statically equivalent; that is, $\varphi(A) \approx_s \varphi(B)$.*

Example 2. Consider the signature and equational theory E_{enc} defined in Example 1. Let $\varphi_1 = \nu\, k.\sigma_1$ and $\varphi_2 = \nu\, k.\sigma_2$ where $\sigma_1 = \{\mathsf{penc}(s_1,r_1,\mathsf{pk}(k))/x_1,\ \mathsf{pk}(k)/x_2\}$, $\sigma_2 = \{\mathsf{penc}(s_2,r_2,\mathsf{pk}(k))/x_1,\ \mathsf{pk}(k)/x_2\}$ and s_1, s_2, k are names. We have that $\varphi_1 \not\approx_s \varphi_2$. Indeed, we $\mathsf{penc}(s_1,r_1,x_2)\sigma_1 =_E x_1\sigma_1$ but $\mathsf{penc}(s_1,r_1,x_2)\sigma_2 \neq_E x_1\sigma_2$. However, we have that $\nu\, k, r_1.\sigma_1 \approx_s \nu\, k, r_2.\sigma_2$.

(COMM) $\bar{c}\langle x\rangle.P \mid c(x).Q \rightarrow P \mid Q$

(THEN)   if ϕ then P else $Q \rightarrow P$ if $[\![\phi]\!] = $ true

(ELSE)   if ϕ then P else $Q \rightarrow Q$ otherwise

(IN) $$c(x).P \xrightarrow{c(M)} P\{M/x\}$$

(OUT-ATOM) $$\bar{c}\langle u\rangle.P \xrightarrow{\bar{c}\langle u\rangle} P$$

(OPEN-ATOM) $$\frac{A \xrightarrow{\bar{c}\langle u\rangle} A' \quad u \neq c}{\nu u.A \xrightarrow{\nu u.\bar{c}\langle u\rangle} A'}$$

(SCOPE) $$\frac{A \xrightarrow{\alpha} A' \quad u \text{ does not occur in } \alpha}{\nu u.A \xrightarrow{\alpha} \nu u.A'}$$

(PAR) $$\frac{A \xrightarrow{\alpha} A' \quad \mathrm{bv}(\alpha) \cap \mathrm{fv}(B) = \mathrm{bn}(\alpha) \cap \mathrm{fn}(B) = \emptyset}{A \mid B \xrightarrow{\alpha} A' \mid B}$$

(STRUCT) $$\frac{A \equiv B \quad B \xrightarrow{\alpha} B' \quad B' \equiv A'}{A \xrightarrow{\alpha} A'}$$

where α is a *label* of the form $c(M)$, $\bar{c}\langle u\rangle$, or $\nu u.\bar{c}\langle u\rangle$ such that u is either a channel name or a variable of base type.

Fig. 5. Semantics for processes

Observational equivalence is the active counterpart of static equivalence, where the attacker can actively interact with the processes. The definition of observational equivalence requires to reason about all contexts (*i.e.* all adversaries), which renders the proofs difficult. Since observational equivalence has been shown to coincide [3,22] with labelled bisimilarity, we adopt the later in this paper.

Definition 2 (Labelled bisimilarity). *Labelled bisimilarity ($\approx_l$) is the largest symmetric relation $\mathcal{R}$ on closed extended processes such that $A\mathcal{R}B$ implies:*

1. *$A \approx_s B$;*
2. *if $A \rightarrow A'$, then $B \rightarrow^* B'$ and $A'\mathcal{R}B'$ for some B';*
3. *if $A \xrightarrow{\alpha} A'$ such that $fv(\alpha) \subseteq dom(A)$ and $bn(\alpha) \cap fn(B) = \emptyset$, then $B \rightarrow^* \xrightarrow{\alpha} \rightarrow^* B'$ and $A'\mathcal{R}B'$ for some B'.*

Examples of labelled bisimilar processes will be provided in Section 5.

4   Modelling the Protocol in Applied-Pi Calculus

We now provide a formal specification of the protocol, using the framework of the applied-pi calculus, defined in the previous section. The first step consists in modeling the cryptographic primitives used by the protocol.

4.1 Equational Theory

We adopt the following signature to capture the cryptographic primitives used by the protocol.

$$\Sigma_{sign} = \{\mathsf{Ok}, \mathsf{fst}, \mathsf{hash}, \mathsf{p}, \mathsf{pk}, \mathsf{s}, \mathsf{snd}, \mathsf{vk}, \mathsf{blind}, \mathsf{d}, \mathsf{dec}, +, *, \circ, \diamond, \mathsf{pair},$$
$$\mathsf{renc}, \mathsf{sign}, \mathsf{unblind}, \mathsf{checkpfk}_1, \mathsf{checkpfk}_2, \mathsf{checksign}, \mathsf{penc}, \mathsf{pfk}_1, \mathsf{pfk}_2\}$$

with function Ok is a constant; $\mathsf{fst}, \mathsf{hash}, \mathsf{p}, \mathsf{pk}, \mathsf{s}, \mathsf{snd}, \mathsf{vk}$ are unary functions; blind, $\mathsf{d}, \mathsf{dec}, +, *, \circ, \diamond, \mathsf{pair}, \mathsf{renc}, \mathsf{sign}, \mathsf{unblind}$ are binary functions; $\mathsf{checkpfk}_1, \mathsf{checkpfk}_2$, $\mathsf{checksign}, \mathsf{penc}$ are ternary functions and $\mathsf{pfk}_1, \mathsf{pfk}_2$ are quaternary functions.

The term $\mathsf{pk}(K)$ denotes the public key corresponding to the secret key K in asymmetric encryption. Terms $\mathsf{s}(I)$, $\mathsf{p}(I)$, and $\mathsf{vk}(I)$ are respectively the blinding factor, the parameter and the verification key associated to a secret id I. The specific coding function used by the receipt generator for a voter with secret id I, applied to a message M is represented by $\mathsf{d}(\mathsf{p}(I), M)$. It corresponds to the function $d_I(M)$ explained in Section 2.2. The term $\mathsf{blind}(M, N)$ the message M blinded by N. Unblinded such a blinded term P, using the same blinding factor N is denoted by $\mathsf{unblind}(P, N)$. The term $\mathsf{penc}(M, N, P)$ refers to the encryption of plaintext M using random nonce N and public key P. The term $M \circ N$ denotes the homomorphic combination of ciphertexts M and M' and the corresponding operation on plaintexts is written $P \diamond Q$ and $R * S$ on nonces. The decryption of ciphertext C using secret key K is denoted $\mathsf{dec}(C, K)$. The term $\mathsf{renc}(M, K)$ is the re-encryption of the ciphertext M using a secret key K and leads to another ciphertext of the same plaintext with the same nonce but a different public key. The operation between secret keys is denoted by $K + L$. The term $\mathsf{sign}(M, N)$ refers to the signature of the message M using secret id N. The term $\mathsf{pfk}_1(M, N, P, Q)$ represents a proof of knowledge that proves that Q is a ciphertext on the plaintext P using nonce N. The term $\mathsf{pfk}_2(M, N, P, Q)$ denotes another proof of knowledge proving that Q is either a re-encryption or a masking of a term P using a secret key or nonce N. We introduce tuples using pairings and, for convenience, $\mathsf{pair}(M_1, \mathsf{pair}(\ldots, \mathsf{pair}(M_{n-1}, M_n)))$ is abbreviated as $(M_1, \ldots, M_n)$ and $\mathsf{fst}(\mathsf{snd}^{i-1}(M))$ is denoted Π_i with $i \in \mathbb{N}$.

The properties of the primitives are then modelled by equipping the signature with an equational theory E that asserts functions $+, *, \circ$ and $\diamond$ are commutative and associative, and includes the equations defined in Figure 6. The three first equations are quite standard. Equation (4) allows to decrypt a blinded ciphertext in order to get the corresponding blinded plaintext. Equation (5) models the homomorphic combination of ciphertexts. Equation (6) represents the re-encryption of a ciphertext. The operation of unblinding is described through Equation (7). Equations (8), (9) and (10) allows respectively the verification of signatures and proofs of knowledge for pfk_1 and pfk_2 proofs.

4.2 Norwegian Protocol Process Specification

The description of the processes representing the actors of the protocol makes use of auxiliary checks that are defined in Figure 7. We did not model re-voting

$$\text{fst}(\text{pair}(x, y)) = x \tag{1}$$

$$\text{snd}(\text{pair}(x, y)) = y \tag{2}$$

$$\text{dec}(\text{penc}(x_{plain}, x_{rand}, \text{pk}(x_{sk})), x_{sk}) = x_{plain} \tag{3}$$

$$\text{dec}(\text{blind}(\text{penc}(x_{plain}, x_{rand}, \text{pk}(x_{sk})), x_{blind}), x_{sk}) = \text{blind}(x_{plain}, x_{blind}) \tag{4}$$

$$\text{penc}(x_{pl}, x_{rand}, x_{pub}) \circ \text{penc}(y_{pl}, y_{rand}, x_{pub}) =$$
$$\text{penc}(x_{pl} \diamond y_{pl}, x_{rand} * y_{rand}, x_{pub}) \tag{5}$$

$$\text{renc}(\text{penc}(x_{plain}, x_{rand}, \text{pk}(x_{sk})), y_{sk}) =$$
$$\text{penc}(x_{plain}, x_{rand}, \text{pk}(x_{sk} + y_{sk})) \tag{6}$$

$$\text{unblind}(\text{blind}(x_{plain}, x_{blind}), x_{blind}) = x_{plain} \tag{7}$$

$$\text{checksign}(x_{plain}, \text{vk}(x_{id}), \text{sign}(x_{plain}, x_{id})) = \text{Ok} \tag{8}$$

$$\text{checkpfk}_1(\text{vk}(x_{id}), \text{ball}, \text{pfk}_1(x_{id}, x_{rand}, x_{plain}, \text{ball})) = \text{Ok}$$
$$\text{where ball} = \text{penc}(x_{plain}, x_{rand}, x_{pub}) \tag{9}$$

$$\text{checkpfk}_2(\text{vk}(x_{id}), \text{ball}, \text{pfk}_2(\text{vk}(x_{id}), x_{bk}, x_{plain}, \text{ball})) = \text{Ok}$$
$$\text{where ball} = \text{renc}(x_{plain}, x_{bk}) \text{ or ball} = \text{blind}(x_{plain}, x_{bk}) \tag{10}$$

Fig. 6. Equations for encryption, blinding, signature and proof of knowledge

since it is explicitely and strongly discouraged in [15], as it may allow an attacker to swap two votes (the initial casted one and its revoted one).

The voting process V represents both the voter and his computer. It is parametrized by a free variable x_{vote} representing voter's vote and free names c_{auth}, c_{RV} which denote the channel shared with the voter and, respectively, the ballot box and the receipt generator. g_1 is a variable representing the public key of the election, id is the secret id of the voter and idp_R is a variable representing the verification key of the receipt generator. Note that messages sent over c_{auth} and c_{RV} are also sent on the public channel c_{out} to the adversary, to simulate authenticated but not confidential channels.

$$\phi_b(idp_i, x) = [(\Pi_1(x), \Pi_2(x), \Pi_3(x)) = x$$
$$\wedge \text{checksign}((\Pi_1(x), \Pi_2(x)), \text{vk}(id_i), \Pi_3(x)) = \text{Ok}$$
$$\wedge \text{ checkpfk}_1(idp_i, \Pi_1(x), \Pi_2(x)) = \text{Ok}]$$

$$\phi_s(idp_R, x, y) = [\text{checksign}(x, idp_R, y) = \text{Ok}]$$

$$\phi_v(idp_R, id_i, x, y, v, z) = [\text{checksign}(x, idp_R, y) = \text{Ok} \ \wedge \ \text{d}(\text{p}(id_i), \text{blind}(v, \text{s}(id_i))) = z]$$

$$(\forall k = 1..3, \ x_i^k = \Pi_k(\Pi_1(x)), \ \forall k = 4..7, \ x_i^k = \Pi_{k-2}(x))$$
$$\phi_r(idp_i, x) = [(x_i^1, x_i^2, x_i^3) = \Pi_1(x) \wedge (\Pi_1(x), x_i^4, x_i^5, x_i^6, x_i^7) = x$$
$$\wedge \ \text{checksign}((x_i^1, x_i^2), idp_i, x_i^3) = \text{Ok} \wedge \text{checkpfk}_1(idp_i, x_i^1, x_i^2) = \text{Ok}$$
$$\wedge \ \text{checkpfk}_2(idp_i, x_i^4, x_i^5) = \text{Ok} \wedge \text{checkpfk}_2(idp_i, x_i^6, x_i^7) = \text{Ok}]$$

Fig. 7. Auxiliary checks performed by the participants to the protocol

$V(c_{auth}, c_{out}, c_{RV}, g_1, id, idp_R, x_{vote}) = \nu\, t$.
    let $e = \mathsf{penc}(x_{vote}, t, g_1)$ in
    let $p = \mathsf{pfk}_1(id, t, x_{vote}, e)$ in
    let $si = \mathsf{sign}((e, p), id)$ in
    $\overline{c_{out}}\langle(e, p, si)\rangle$.
    $\overline{c_{auth}}\langle(e, p, si)\rangle$.   % encrypted ballot sent to B
    $c_{RV}(x)$. $c_{auth}(y)$.
    $\overline{c_{out}}\langle x\rangle$. $\overline{c_{out}}\langle y\rangle$.
    let $hv = \mathsf{hash}((\mathsf{vk}(id), e, p, si))$ in   % recomputes what should
                                            be sent by R
    if $\phi_{\mathsf{v}}(idp_R, id, h, x, x_{vote}, y)$ then $\overline{c_{auth}}\langle\mathsf{Ok}\rangle$ % checks validity

Process B_n corresponds to the ballot box, ready to listen to n voters. The ballots are coming from authenticated channels $c_1, \ldots, c_n$ and the ballot box can send messages to the receipt generator, the decryption service and the auditor through secure channels c_{BR}, c_{BD} and c_{BA}. The parameters of the ballot box are keys : g_1, g_3 (public) and a_2 (secret); public ids of voters $idp_1, \ldots, idp_n$ (*i.e.* verification keys) and corresponding blinding factors $s_1, \ldots, s_n$. (Step $c(sy_1)$ is a technical synchronisation, it does not appear in the real specification.)

$B_n(c_{BR}, c_{BD}, g_1, a_2, g_3, idp_R, c_1, idp_1, s_1, \ldots, c_n, idp_n, s_n) =$
    $\ldots$. $c_i(x_i)$.
    if $\phi_{\mathsf{b}}(idp_i, x_i)$ then   % checks validity of ballot
    let $e_i = \mathsf{renc}(\varPi_1(x_i), a_2)$ in
    let $pfk_i^e = \mathsf{pfk}_2(idp_i, a_2, \varPi_1(x_i), e_i)$ in
    let $b_i = \mathsf{blind}(e_i, s_i)$ in
    let $pfk_i^b = \mathsf{pfk}_2(idp_i, s_i, e_i, b_i)$ in   % computes re-encrypted masked
                                              ballot and corresponding proofs.
    $\overline{c_{BR}}\langle(x_i, e_i, pfk_i^e, b_i, pfk_i^b)\rangle.c_{BR}(y_i)$.   % message sent to R
    let $hb_i = \mathsf{hash}((\mathsf{vk}(id_i), \varPi_1(x_i), \varPi_2(x_i), \varPi_3(x_i)))$ in
    if $\phi_{\mathsf{s}}(idp_R, hb_i, y_i)$ then   % checks validity of confirmation
    $\overline{c_i}\langle y_i\rangle$. $c_i(sy_i)$ $\ldots$ % transmit confirmation to the voter
    $\overline{c_n}\langle y_n\rangle$. $c_n(sy_n)$.
    $\overline{c_{BD}}\langle\varPi_1(x_1)\rangle$. $\ldots$. $\overline{c_{BD}}\langle\varPi_1(x_n)\rangle$.   % output encrypted votes to the
                                            Decryption Service
    $\overline{c_{BA}}\langle x_1\rangle$. $\ldots$. $\overline{c_{BA}}\langle x_n\rangle$ % output the content to the Auditor

Receipt generator's process is denoted by R_n. It deals with the ballot box and the auditor through secure channels c_{BR} and c_{RA} and directly with voters through out-of-band channels $c_{RV_1}, \ldots, c_{RV_n}$. It is parametrized with keys: g_1, g_2 (public) and a_3 (secret); the public ids of voters and corresponding receipt coding functions parametrized by $pr_1, \ldots, pr_n$.

$R_n(c_{BR}, g_1, g_2, a_3, id_R, c_{RV_1}, idp_1, pr_1, \ldots, c_{RV_n}, idp_n, pr_n) =$
    $\ldots$. $c_{BR}(x_i)$.
    let $x_i^k = \varPi_k(\varPi_1(x_i))$, $k = 1..3$ in

let $x_i^k = \Pi_{k-2}(x_i), \ k = 4...7$ in
if $\phi_r(idp_i, x_i)$ then   % checks ballot box's computations
let $hbr_i = \mathsf{hash}((idp_i, x_i^1, x_i^2, x_i^3))$ in
let $hbpr_i = \mathsf{hash}((idp_i, x_i^1, x_i^2))$ in
let $r_i = \mathsf{d}(pr_i, \mathsf{dec}(x_i^6, a_3))$ in   % computes the receipt code for V
let $sig_i = \mathsf{sign}(hbr_i, id_R)$ in   % computes confirmation for B
$\overline{c_{RV_i}}\langle r_i \rangle \ . \ \overline{c_{BR}}\langle sig_i \rangle \ . \ ...$
$\overline{c_{RV_n}}\langle r_n \rangle \ . \ \overline{c_{BR}}\langle sig_n \rangle \ . \ ...$
$\overline{c_{RA}}\langle(idp_1, hbpr_1, hbr_1)\rangle \ . \ ... \ . \ \overline{c_{RA}}\langle(idp_n, hbpr_n, hbr_n)\rangle$
                                                                 % output content to the Auditor

The decryption service is represented by process D_n. Communicating securely with the ballot box and the auditor through channels c_{BD} and c_{DA}, it also outputs results through public channel c_{out}. In order to decrypt ballots, it needs to know the secret key a_1. We model two processes, one including a swap between the two first votes, to model the shuffling which is necessary to ensure ballot secrecy.

$D_n(c_{BD}, c_{DA}, c_{out}, a_1) =$
  $c_{BD}(x_1) \ . \ ... \ . \ c_{BD}(x_n) \ .$
  $\overline{c_{DA}}\langle\mathsf{hash}((x_1, ..., x_n))\rangle \ . \ c_{DA}(x) \ .$ % creating hash of ciphertexts and
                                                                 waiting for auditor's approval
  let $dec_k = \mathsf{dec}(x_k, a_1), \ k = 1..n$ in   % decryption of ciphertexts
  $\overline{c_{out}}\langle dec_1 \rangle \ . \ ... \ . \ \overline{c_{out}}\langle dec_n \rangle$ % publication of results

$\overline{D_n}(c_{BD}, c_{DA}, c_{out}, a_1) =$
  $c_{BD}(x_1) \ . \ ... \ . \ c_{BD}(x_n) \ .$
  $\overline{c_{DA}}\langle\mathsf{hash}((x_1, ..., x_n))\rangle \ . \ c_{DA}(x) \ .$
  let $dec_1 = \mathsf{dec}(x_2, a_1)$ in   % the swap between the two first
  let $dec_2 = \mathsf{dec}(x_1, a_1)$ in   votes is modelled here
  let $dec_k = \mathsf{dec}(x_k, a_1), \ k = 3..n$ in
  $\overline{c_{out}}\langle dec_1 \rangle \ . \ ... \ . \ \overline{c_{out}}\langle dec_n \rangle$

Finally, the auditor process, AD_n, communicates with the other infrastructure players using secure channels c_{BA}, c_{RA} and c_{DA}. It knows public ids of voters.

$AD_n(c_{BA}, c_{RA}, c_{DA}, idp_1, ..., idp_n) =$
  $c_{DA}(h_d) \ .$ % input of contents of B, R and D
  $c_{BA}(x_1) \ . \ ... \ . \ c_{BA}(x_n) \ . \ c_{RA}(h_1) \ . \ ... \ . \ c_{RA}(h_1) \ .$
  let $hba_i = \mathsf{hash}((\Pi_1(x_i), \Pi_2(x_i), \Pi_3(x_i)))$ in
  let $hbpa_i = \mathsf{hash}((\Pi_1(x_i), \Pi_2(x_i)))$ in
  let $ha = \mathsf{hash}((\Pi_1(x_1), ..., \Pi_n(x_n)))$ in
  if $\phi_a(x_1, h_1, idp_1, ..., x_n, h_n, idp_n, h, h_d)$ then $\overline{c_{DA}}\langle Ok \rangle$ else 0
                                                                 % checks and approval sent to D.

where $\phi_a(x_1, h_1, idp_1, ..., x_n, h_n, idp_n, h, h_d) = [(\Pi_1(x_i), \Pi_2(x_i), \Pi_3(x_i)) = x_i$
  $\wedge (\Pi_1(h_i), \Pi_2(h_i), \Pi_3(h_i)) = h_i \wedge \ \Pi_2(h_i) = hbp_i \wedge \Pi_3(h_i) = hb_i \wedge h_d = h$
  $\wedge \ \mathsf{checksign}((\Pi_1(x_i), \Pi_2(x_i)), idp_i, \Pi_3(x_i)) = Ok]$

The interaction of all the players is simply modeled by considering all the processes in parallel, with the correct instantiation and restriction of the parameters. In what follows, the restricted name a_1, a_2, a_3 model secret keys used in the protocol and public keys $\mathsf{pk}(a_1)$, $\mathsf{pk}(a_2)$ and $\mathsf{pk}(a_3)$ are added in the process frame. The restricted name c_1, c_2 and c_{RV_1}, c_{RV_2} model authentic channels between honest voters and, respectively, the ballot box and the receipt generator. The restricted name id_1, id_2, id_R represent secret ids of honest voters and receipt generator, the corresponding public id's are added in the process's frame.

Then the setting of the authorities is modeled by $A_n\,[\_]$ where n is the number of voters and the hole is the voter place. $A_n\,[\_]$ is the analogue of $\overline{A}_n\,[\_]$ with the Decryption service swapping the two first votes (its use will be clearer in the next section, when defining vote privacy).

$$\tilde{n} = (a_1, a_2, id_1, id_2, id_R, c_1, c_2, c_{RV_1}, c_{RV_2}, c_{BR}, c_{BD}, c_{BA}, c_{RA}, c_{DA})$$
$$\Gamma = \{^{\mathsf{pk}(a_1)}/_{g_1}, ^{\mathsf{pk}(a_2)}/_{g_2}, ^{\mathsf{pk}(a_3)}/_{g_3}, ^{\mathsf{vk}(id_1)}/_{idp_1}, \ldots, ^{\mathsf{vk}(id_n)}/_{idp_n}, ^{\mathsf{vk}(id_R)}/_{idp_R}\}$$
$$A_n\,[\_] = \nu\,\tilde{n}\,.(\text{let } a_3 = a_1 + a_2 \text{ in } [\_|B_n\{^{\mathsf{s}(id_1)}/_{s_1}, \cdots ^{\mathsf{s}(id_n)}/_{s_n}\}$$
$$|R_n\{^{\mathsf{p}(id_1)}/_{pr_1}, \cdots ^{\mathsf{p}(id_n)}/_{pr_n}\}|D_n|AD_n|\Gamma])$$
$$\overline{A}_n\,[\_] = \nu\,\tilde{n}\,.(\text{let } a_3 = a_1 + a_2 \text{ in } [\_|B_n\{^{\mathsf{s}(id_1)}/_{s_1}, \cdots ^{\mathsf{s}(id_n)}/_{s_n}\}$$
$$|R_n\{^{\mathsf{p}(id_1)}/_{pr_1}, \cdots ^{\mathsf{p}(id_n)}/_{pr_n}\}|\overline{D}_n|AD_n|\Gamma])$$

The frame Γ represents the initial knowledge of the attacker: it has access to the public keys of the authorities and the verification keys of the voters. Moreover, since only the two first voters are assumed to be honest, only their two secret ids are restricted (in $\tilde{n}$). The attacker has therefore access to the secret ids of all the other voters. Parameters of subprocesses are left implicit except for $s_1, \ldots, s_n$ for the ballot box and $pr_1, \ldots, pr_n$ for the receipt generator which are respectively replaced by $\mathsf{s}(id_1), \ldots, \mathsf{s}(id_n)$, the blinding factors, and $\mathsf{p}(id_1), \ldots, \mathsf{p}(id_n)$, used to distinguish the coding dunction associated to a voter.

5   Formal Analysis of Ballot Secrecy

Our analysis shows that the Norwegian e-voting protocol preserves ballot secrecy, even when all but two voters are corrupted, provided that the other components are honest. We also identified several cases of corruption that are subject to attacks. Though not surprising, these cases were not previously mentioned in the literature.

5.1   Ballot Secrecy with Corrupted Voters

Ballot secrecy has been formalized in terms of equivalence by Delaune, Kremer, and Ryan in [12]. A protocol with voting process $V(v, id)$ and authority process A preserves *ballot secrecy* if an attacker cannot distinguish when votes are swapped, *i.e.* it cannot distinguish when a voter a_1 votes v_1 and a_2 votes v_2 from the case where a_1 votes v_2 and a_2 votes v_1. This is formally specified by:

$$\nu\tilde{n}.(A \mid V\{^{v_2}/_x, ^{a_1}/_y\} \mid V\{^{v_1}/_x, ^{a_2}/_y\}) \approx_l \nu\tilde{n}.(A \mid V\{^{v_1}/_x, ^{a_1}/_y\} \mid V\{^{v_2}/_x, ^{a_2}/_y\})$$

We are able to show that the Norwegian protocol preserves ballot secrecy, even all but two voters are corrupted.

Theorem 1. *Let n be the number of voters. The Norwegian e-voting protocol process specification satisfies ballot secrecy with the auditing process, even with $n - 2$ voters are corrupted, provided that the other components are honest.*

$$A_n[V\{{}^{c_1}/_{c_{auth}}, {}^{c_{RV_1}}/_{c_{RV}}\}\sigma \mid V\{{}^{c_2}/_{c_{auth}}, {}^{c_{RV_2}}/_{c_{RV}}\}\tau]$$
$$\approx_l \overline{A}_n[V\{{}^{c_1}/_{c_{auth}}, {}^{c_{RV_1}}/_{c_{RV}}\}\tau | V\{{}^{c_2}/_{c_{auth}}, {}^{c_{RV_2}}/_{c_{RV}}\}\sigma]$$

where $\sigma = \{{}^{v_1}/_{x_{vote}}\}$ and $\tau = \{{}^{v_2}/_{x_{vote}}\}$.

We can also show ballot secrecy, without an auditor. This means that the auditor does not contribute to ballot secrecy in case the administrative components are honest (which was expected). Formally, we define $A'_n[\_]$ and $\overline{A}_n[\_]'$ to be the analog of $A_n[\_]$ and $\overline{A}_n[\_]$, removing the auditor.

Theorem 2. *Let n be the number of voters. The Norwegian e-voting protocol process specification satisfies ballot secrecy without the auditing process, even with $n - 2$ voters are corrupted, provided that the other components are honest.*

$$A'_n[V\{{}^{c_1}/_{c_{auth}}, {}^{c_{RV_1}}/_{c_{RV}}\}\sigma \mid V\{{}^{c_2}/_{c_{auth}}, {}^{c_{RV_2}}/_{c_{RV}}\}\tau]$$
$$\approx_l \overline{A'}_n[V\{{}^{c_1}/_{c_{auth}}, {}^{c_{RV_1}}/_{c_{RV}}\}\tau | V\{{}^{c_2}/_{c_{auth}}, {}^{c_{RV_2}}/_{c_{RV}}\}\sigma]$$

where $\sigma = \{{}^{v_1}/_{x_{vote}}\}$ and $\tau = \{{}^{v_2}/_{x_{vote}}\}$.

The proof of Theorems 1 and 2 works in two main steps. First we guess a relation $\mathcal{R}$ such that for any two processes P, Q in relation ($P\mathcal{R}Q$) any move of P can be matched by a move of Q such that the resulting processes remain in relation. This amounts to characterize all possible successors of $A_n[V\{{}^{c_1}/_{c_{auth}}, {}^{c_{RV_1}}/_{c_{RV}}\}\sigma \mid V\{{}^{c_2}/_{c_{auth}}, {}^{c_{RV_2}}/_{c_{RV}}\}\tau]$ and $\overline{A}_n[V\{{}^{c_1}/_{c_{auth}}, {}^{c_{RV_1}}/_{c_{RV}}\}\tau | V\{{}^{c_2}/_{c_{auth}}, {}^{c_{RV_2}}/_{c_{RV}}\}\sigma]$. We show in particular that whenever the attacker sends a term N that is accepted by the ballot box for a voter with secret id id, then N is necessarily an id - *valid ballot* for the following definition.

Definition 3. *Let $id \in \{id_1, \ldots, id_n\}$. A term N is said to be a id - valid ballot if $\phi_b(id, N) = \mathsf{true}$, equivalently :*

$$\begin{cases} N = (N_1, N_2, N_3) \\ \mathsf{checksign}((N_1, N_2), \mathsf{vk}(id), N_3) =_E \mathsf{Ok} \\ \mathsf{checkpfk}_1(\mathsf{vk}(id), N_1, N_2) =_E \mathsf{Ok} \end{cases}.$$

The second and most involved step of the proof consists in showing that the sequences of messages observed by the attacker remain in static equivalence. This requires to prove an infinite number of static equivalences. Let us introduce some notations.

$$\theta_{sub} = \{{}^{\mathsf{pk}(a_1)}/{}_{g_1}\}|\{{}^{\mathsf{pk}(a_2)}/{}_{g_2}\}|\{{}^{\mathsf{pk}(a_3)}/{}_{g_3}\}|\{{}^{\mathsf{vk}(id_R)}/{}_{idp_R}\}|\{{}^{ball_1}/{}_{b_1}\}|\{{}^{ballo_2}/{}_{b_2}\}|$$

$$\{\{{}^{\mathsf{vk}(id_i)}/{}_{idp_i}\}|\ i=1..n\}|\{\{{}^{\mathsf{d}(\mathsf{p}(id_i),\mathsf{dec}(\mathsf{blind}(\mathsf{renc}(\Pi_1(x_i),a_2),\mathsf{s}(id_i)),a_3))}/{}_{y_i}\}|$$

$$\{{}^{\mathsf{sign}(\mathsf{hash}((\mathsf{vk}(id_i),x_i)),id_R)}/{}_{z_i}\}|\ i=1..n\}$$

$$\Sigma_L = \{{}^{v_1}/{}_{x_{vote}^1}, {}^{v_2}/{}_{x_{vote}^2}\}$$

$$\Sigma_R = \{{}^{v_2}/{}_{x_{vote}^1}, {}^{v_1}/{}_{x_{vote}^2}\}$$

$$\theta_{ct} = \{{}^{\mathsf{dec}(\Pi_1(x_1),a_1)}/{}_{result_1}, {}^{\mathsf{dec}(\Pi_1(x_2),a_1)}/{}_{result_2}, {}^{\mathsf{dec}(\Pi_1(x_i),a_1)}/{}_{result_i}|i=3..n\}$$

$$\overline{\theta}_{ct} = \{{}^{\mathsf{dec}(\Pi_1(x_2),a_1)}/{}_{result_1}, {}^{\mathsf{dec}(\Pi_1(x_1),a_1)}/{}_{result_2}, {}^{\mathsf{dec}(\Pi_1(x_i),a_1)}/{}_{result_i}|i=3..n\}$$

where $ball_1$ and $ball_2$ are the terms sent by the two honest voters.

The frame θ_{sub} represents the messages sent over the (public) network during the submission phase. Σ_L represents the scenario where voter 1 votes v_1 and voter 2 votes v_2 while Σ_L represents the opposite scenario. θ_{ct} and $\overline{\theta}_{ct}$ represent the results published by the decryption service.

All voters with secret id id_i with $i \geq 3$ are corrupted. Therefore, the attacker can submit any deducible term as a ballot, that is any term that can be represented by N_i with $\mathsf{fv}(N_i) \subseteq \mathsf{dom}(\theta_{sub})\backslash\{y_j, z_j\}_{j \geq i}$ (*i.e.* a recipe that can only re-use previously received messages). We are able to show that whenever the message submitted by the attacker is accepted by the ballot box, then $N_i\theta_{sub}\Sigma$ is necessarily an id_i-valid ballots for $\Sigma \in \{\Sigma_L, \Sigma_R\}$.

A key result of our proof is that the final frames are in static equivalence, for any behavior of the corrupted users (reflected in the N_i).

Proposition 1. *Let $N_i\theta_{sub}\Sigma$ be id_i-valid ballots for $\Sigma \in \{\Sigma_L, \Sigma_R\}$ and $i \in \{3,\ldots,n\}$, we have: $\nu\tilde{n}.(\theta_{sub}|\theta_{ct})\sigma_{\tilde{N}}\Sigma_L \approx_s \nu\tilde{n}.(\theta_{sub}|\overline{\theta}_{ct})\sigma_{\tilde{N}}\Sigma_R$, where $\sigma_{\tilde{N}} = \{{}^{ball_1}/{}_{x_1}, {}^{ball_2}/{}_{x_2}, {}^{N_j}/{}_{x_j}|\ j \in \{3,\ldots,n\}\}$.*

5.2   Attacks

Our two previous results of ballot secrecy hold provided all the administrative components (bulletin box, receipt generator, decryption service, and auditor) behave honestly. However, in order to enforce the level of trust, the voting system should remain secure even if some administrative components are corrupted. We describe two cases of corruption where ballot secrecy is no longer guaranteed.

Dishonest decryption service. The decryption service is a very sensitive component since it has access to the decryption key a_1 of the public key used for the election. Therefore, a corrupted decryption service can very easily decrypt all encrypted ballots and thus learns the votes as soon as he has access to the communication between the voters and the bulletin box (these communications being conducted on the *public* Internet network). Even if we did not find any explicit mention of this, we believe that the designers of the protocol implicitly assume that a corrupted decryption would not be able to control (some of) the communication over the Internet. It should also be noted that a corrupted decryption service could learn the votes even *without access to Internet* if the bulletin box does not shuffle the ballots before sending them. Whether or not shuflling is performed is not completely clear in [15].

Dishonest bulletin box and receipt generator. Clearly, if the bulletin box and the receipt generator collude, they can compute $a_1 = a_3 - a_2$ and they can then decrypt all incoming encrypted ballots. More interestingly, a corrupted receipt generator does not need the full cooperation of the bulletin box for breaking ballot secrecy. Indeed, assume that the receipt generator has access, for some voter V, to the blinding factor s_V used by the bulletin to blind the ballot. Recall that the receipt generator retrieves $f(o)^{s_V}$ when generating the receipt codes (by computing $\tilde{w}\tilde{x}^{-a_3}$). Therefore, the receipt generator can compute $f(o')^{s_V}$ for any possible voting option o'. Comparing with the obtained values with $f(o)^{s_V}$ it would easily deduce the chosen option o. Of course, the more blinding factors the receipt generator can get, the more voters it can attack. Therefore, the security of the protocol strongly relies on the security of the blinding factors which generation and distribution are left unspecified in the documentation. The bulletin box can also perform a similar attack, provided it can learn some coding function d_V and additionally, provided that it has access to the SMS sent by the receipt generator, which is probably a too strong corruption scenario.

6   Further Corruption Cases Using ProVerif

In order to study further corruption cases, we have used ProVerif, the only tool that can analyse equivalence properties in the context of security protocols. Of course, we needed to simplify the equational theory since ProVerif does not handle associative and commutative (AC) symbols and our theory needs four of them. So we have considered the theory E' defined by the equations of Figure 6, except equation (5) that represents homomorphic combination of ciphertexts and we have replaced AC symbols $+$ and $*$ by free function symbols f and g. Using this simplified theory, it is clear that we can miss some attacks, but testing corruption assumptions is still relevant even if the attacker is a bit weaker than in our first study.

As ProVerif is designed to prove equivalences between processes that differ only by terms, we need to use another tool, ProSwapper [16], to model the shuffle done by the decryption service. More precisely, we actually used their algorithm to compute directly a shuffle in our ProVerif specification.

The results are displayed in Table 1 and 2 and have been obtained with a standard (old) laptop[1]. In these tables, ✓ indicates that ballot secrecy is satisfied, × shows that there is an attack, and - indicates that ProVerif was not able to conclude. No indication of times means that we do not proceed to a test in ProVerif but, as we already knew that there was an attack. In particular, all the attacks described in Section 5.2 are displayed in the tables.

---

[1] 2.00 Ghz processor with 2 GB of RAM Memory.

Table 1. Results and computation times for the protocol without auditor

Corr. Players \ Corr. Voters	0	1	2	5	10
None	✓ 0.4"	✓ 0.9"	✓ 2.4"	✓ 16.1"	✓ 20'59"
Ballot Box (B)			-- >1h		
Receipt Generator (R)	✓ 1.1"	✓ 2.4"	✓ 5.7"	✓ 1'15"	✓ 39'30"
Decryption Service (D)	× 0.2"		×		
B + R	× 0.3"		×		
D+B, D+R, D+R+B			×		

Table 2. Results and computation times for the protocol with auditor

Corr. Players \ Corr. Voters	0	1	2	3	4
None	✓ 0.6"	✓ 1,8"	✓ 4.1"	✓ 27.7"	✓ 11'1"
Ballot Box (B)			-- >1h		
Receipt Generator (R)	✓ 1.1"	✓ 1.9"	✓ 5.9"	✓ 29.1"	✓ 10'33"
Auditor (A)	✓ 0.4"	✓ 1.9"	✓ 2.6"	✓ 5.8"	✓ 12.1"
R + A	✓ 0.6"	✓ 1.9"	✓ 5.5"	✓ 14.5"	✓ 34.4"
B+R, B+R+A, D D + any other combination			×		

Our case study with ProVerif indicates that ballot secrecy is still preserved even when the Receipt Generator is corrupted (as well as several voters), at least in the simplified theory. Unfortunately, ProVerif was not able to conclude in the case the Ballot Box is corrupted.

7   Discussion

We have proposed the first formal proof that the e-voting protocol recently used in Norway indeed satisfies ballot secrecy, even when all but two voters are corrupted and even without the auditor. As expected, ballot secrecy is no longer guaranteed if both the bulletin box and the receipt generator are corrupted. Slightly more surprisingly, the protocol is not secure either if the decryption service is corrupted, as discussed in Section 5.2. More cases of corruption need to be studied, in particular when the bulletin board alone is corrupted, we leave this as future work. In addition, it remains to study other security properties such as coercion-resistance or verifiability. Instead of doing additional (long and technical) proofs, a further step consists in developing a procedure for automatically checking for equivalences. Of course, this is a difficult problem. A first decision procedure has been proposed in [9] but is limited to subterm convergent theories. An implementation has recently been proposed [8] but it does not support such a complex equational theory. An alternative step would be to develop a sound procedure that over-approximate the relation, losing completeness in the spirit of ProVerif [5] but tailored to privacy properties.

We would like to emphasize that the security proofs have been conducted in a symbolic thus abstract model. This provides a first level of certification, ruling out "logical" attacks. However, a full computational proof should be developed. Our symbolic proof can been seen as a first step, identifying the set of messages an attacker can observe when interacting with the protocol. There is however still a long way to go for a computational proof. In particular, it remains to identify which the security assumptions are needed.

It is also important to note that the security of the protocol strongly relies on the way initial secrets are pre-distributed. For example, three private decryption keys a_1, a_2, a_3 (such that $a_1 + a_2 = a_3$) need to be securely distributed among (respectively) the bulletin board, the receipt generator and the decryptor. Also, a table $(id, s(id))$ containing the blinding factor for each voter needs to be securely distributed to bulletin board and a table (id, d_{id}) containing a permutation for each voter needs to be securely distributed to the receipt generator. Moreover, anyone with access with both the codes mailed to the voters and to the SMS emitted by the receipt generator would immediately learn the values of all the votes. We did not find in the documentation how and by who all these secret values were distributed. It should certainly be clarified as it could be a weak point of the system.

References

1. http://www.dw-world.de/dw/article/0,,4069101,00.html
2. Web page of the norwegian government on the deployment of e-voting, http://www.regjeringen.no/en/dep/krd/ prosjekter/e-vote-2011-project.html
3. Abadi, M., Fournet, C.: Mobile values, new names, and secure communication. In: 28th ACM Symposium on Principles of Programming Languages, POPL 2001 (2001)
4. Bernhard, D., Cortier, V., Pereira, O., Smyth, B., Warinschi, B.: Adapting Helios for Provable Ballot Privacy. In: Atluri, V., Diaz, C. (eds.) ESORICS 2011. LNCS, vol. 6879, pp. 335–354. Springer, Heidelberg (2011)
5. Blanchet, B.: An automatic security protocol verifier based on resolution theorem proving (invited tutorial). In: 20th International Conference on Automated Deduction (CADE-20), Tallinn, Estonia (July 2005)
6. Blanchet, B., Abadi, M., Fournet, C.: Automated verification of selected equivalences for security protocols. In: 20th IEEE Symposium on Logic in Computer Science (LICS 2005), pp. 331–340. IEEE Computer Society (June 2005)

7. Chadha, R., Ciobâcă, Ş., Kremer, S.: Automated Verification of Equivalence Properties of Cryptographic Protocols. In: 21th European Symposium on Programming (ESOP 2012). LNCS, Springer, Heidelberg (to appear, 2012)
8. Cheval, V., Comon-Lundh, H., Delaune, S.: Trace equivalence decision: Negative tests and non-determinism. In: 18th ACM Conference on Computer and Communications Security (CCS 2011). ACM Press (October 2011)
9. Cortier, V., Delaune, S.: A method for proving observational equivalence. In: 22nd Computer Security Foundations Symposium (CSF 2009). IEEE Computer Society (2009)
10. Cortier, V., Smyth, B.: Attacking and fixing Helios: An analysis of ballot secrecy. In: 24th Computer Security Foundations Symposium (CSF 2011). IEEE Computer Society (2011)
11. Cortier, V., Wiedling, C.: A formal analysis of the Norwegian e-voting protocol. Technical Report RR-7781, INRIA (November 2011)
12. Delaune, S., Kremer, S., Ryan, M.D.: Verifying privacy-type properties of electronic voting protocols. Journal of Computer Security 17(4), 435–487 (2009)
13. Feldman, A.J., Halderman, J.A., Felten, E.W.: Security analysis of the diebold accuvote-ts voting machine (2006), http://itpolicy.princeton.edu/voting/
14. Fujioka, A., Okamoto, T., Ohta, K.: A Practical Secret Voting Scheme for Large Scale Elections. In: Zheng, Y., Seberry, J. (eds.) AUSCRYPT 1992. LNCS, vol. 718, pp. 244–251. Springer, Heidelberg (1993)
15. Gjøsteen, K.: Analysis of an internet voting protocol. Cryptology ePrint Archive, Report 2010/380 (2010), http://eprint.iacr.org/
16. Klus, P., Smyth, B., Ryan, M.D.: ProSwapper: Improved equivalence verifier for ProVerif (2010), http://www.bensmyth.com/proswapper.php
17. Kremer, S., Ryan, M., Smyth, B.: Election Verifiability in Electronic Voting Protocols. In: Gritzalis, D., Preneel, B., Theoharidou, M. (eds.) ESORICS 2010. LNCS, vol. 6345, pp. 389–404. Springer, Heidelberg (2010)
18. Küsters, R., Truderung, T.: An Epistemic Approach to Coercion-Resistance for Electronic Voting Protocols. In: IEEE Symposium on Security and Privacy (S&P 2009), pp. 251–266. IEEE Computer Society (2009)
19. Küsters, R., Truderung, T., Vogt, A.: A Game-Based Definition of Coercion-Resistance and its Applications. In: 23nd IEEE Computer Security Foundations Symposium (CSF 2010). IEEE Computer Society (2010)
20. Küsters, R., Truderung, T., Vogt, A.: Proving Coercion-Resistance of Scantegrity II. In: Soriano, M., Qing, S., López, J. (eds.) ICICS 2010. LNCS, vol. 6476, pp. 281–295. Springer, Heidelberg (2010)
21. Lee, B., Boyd, C., Dawson, E., Kim, K., Yang, J., Yoo, S.: Providing Receipt-Freeness in Mixnet-Based Voting Protocols. In: Lim, J.-I., Lee, D.-H. (eds.) ICISC 2003. LNCS, vol. 2971, pp. 245–258. Springer, Heidelberg (2004)
22. Liu, J.: A Proof of Coincidence of Labeled Bisimilarity and Observational Equivalence in Applied Pi Calculus (2011), http://lcs.ios.ac.cn/~jliu/papers/LiuJia0608.pdf
23. Okamoto, T.: Receipt-Free Electronic Voting Schemes for Large Scale Elections. In: Christianson, B., Lomas, M. (eds.) Security Protocols 1997. LNCS, vol. 1361, pp. 25–35. Springer, Heidelberg (1998)
24. Wolchok, S., Wustrow, E., Halderman, J.A., Prasad, H.K., Kankipati, A., Sakhamuri, S.K., Yagati, V., Gonggrijp, R.: Security analysis of india's electronic voting machines. In: 17th ACM Conference on Computer and Communications Security, CCS 2010 (2010)

Provably Repairing the ISO/IEC 9798 Standard for Entity Authentication

David Basin, Cas Cremers, and Simon Meier

Institute of Information Security
ETH Zurich, Switzerland

Abstract. We formally analyze the family of entity authentication protocols defined by the ISO/IEC 9798 standard and find numerous weaknesses, both old and new, including some that violate even the most basic authentication guarantees. We analyse the cause of these weaknesses, propose repaired versions of the protocols, and provide automated, machine-checked proofs of the correctness of the resulting protocols. From an engineering perspective, we propose two design principles for security protocols that suffice to prevent all the weaknesses. Moreover, we show how modern verification tools can be used for falsification and certified verification of security standards. The relevance of our findings and recommendations has been acknowledged by the responsible ISO working group and an updated version of the standard will be released.

Introduction

Entity authentication is a core building block for security in networked systems. In its simplest form, entity authentication boils down to establishing that a party's claimed identity corresponds to its real identity. In practice, stronger guarantees are usually required, such as mutual authentication, agreement among the participating parties on the identities of their peers, or authentication of transmitted data [27, 32].

The ISO (International Organization for Standardization) and IEC (International Electrotechnical Commission) jointly provide standards for Information Technology. Their standard 9798 specifies a family of entity authentication protocols. This standard is mandated by numerous other standards that require entity authentication as a building block. Examples include the Guidelines on Algorithms Usage and Key Management [13] by the European Committee for Banking Standards and the ITU-T multimedia standard H.235 [24].

Analysis of previous versions of the ISO/IEC 9798 standard has led to the discovery of several weaknesses [3, 8, 12]. The standard has been revised several times to address weaknesses and ambiguities, with the latest updates stemming from 2010. One may therefore expect that such a mature and pervasive standard is "bullet-proof" and that the protocols satisfy strong, practically relevant, authentication properties.

On request by CRYPTREC, the Cryptography Research and Evaluation Committee set up by the Japanese Government, we formally analyzed the most recent

P. Degano and J.D. Guttman (Eds.): POST 2012, LNCS 7215, pp. 129–148, 2012.
© Springer-Verlag Berlin Heidelberg 2012

versions of the protocols specified in parts 1–4 of the ISO/IEC 9798 standard using the SCYTHER tool [9]. To our surprise, we not only found that several previously reported weaknesses are still present in the standard, but we also found new weaknesses. In particular, many of the protocols guarantee only weak authentication properties and, under some circumstances, even no authentication at all. For the majority of implementations of the standard where only weak authentication is required, these weaknesses will not lead to security breaches. However, our findings clearly show that the guarantees provided by the protocols are much weaker than might be expected. Moreover, in some cases, additional assumptions are required to ensure even the weakest possible form of authentication.

We analyze the shortcomings in the protocols' design and propose repairs. We justify the correctness of our fixes by providing machine-checked proofs of the repaired protocols. These proofs imply the absence of logical errors: the repaired protocols provide strong authentication properties in a Dolev-Yao model, even when multiple protocols from the standard are run in parallel using the same key infrastructure. Consequently, under the assumption of perfect cryptography, the repaired protocols guarantee strong authentication.

To generate the correctness proofs, we first extend the SCYTHER-PROOF tool [31] to handle bidirectional keys. We then use the tool to generate proof scripts that are checked independently by the Isabelle/HOL theorem prover. As input, SCYTHER-PROOF takes a description of a protocol and its properties and produces a proof in higher-order logic of the protocol's correctness. Both the generation of proof scripts and their verification by Isabelle/HOL are completely automatic.

From an engineering perspective, we observe that applying existing principles for constructing cryptographic protocols such as those of Abadi and Needham [2] would not have prevented most of the discovered weaknesses. We therefore additionally propose two design principles in the spirit of [2] whose application would have prevented all of the weaknesses.

Based on our analysis, the ISO/IEC working group responsible for the 9798 standard will release an updated version of the standard, incorporating our proposed fixes.

Summary of Contributions. First, we find previously unreported weaknesses in the most recent version of the ISO/IEC 9798 standard. Second, we repair this practically relevant standard, and provide machine-checked proofs of the correctness of the repairs. Third, we propose two principles for engineering cryptographic protocols in the spirit of [2] that would have prevented the weaknesses. Fourth, our work highlights how modern security protocol analysis tools can be used for falsification and machine-checked verification of security standards.

Organization. In Section 1, we describe the ISO/IEC 9798 standard. In Section 2, we model the protocols and analyze them, discovering numerous weaknesses. In Section 3, we analyze the sources of these weaknesses and present two design principles that eliminate them. In Section 4, we explain how we automatically generate machine-checked correctness proofs for these repaired protocols. We describe related work in Section 5 and conclude in Section 6.

1 The ISO/IEC 9798 Standard

1.1 Overview

We give a brief overview of the standard, which specifies a family of entity authentication protocols. We consider here the first four parts of the standard. Part 1 is general and provides background for the other parts. The protocols are divided into three groups. Protocols using symmetric encryption are described in Part 2, those using digital signatures are described in Part 3, and those using cryptographic check functions such as MACs are described in Part 4.

Because the standard has been revised, we also take into account the most recent technical corrigenda and amendments. Our analysis covers the protocols specified by the following documents. For the first part of the standard, we cover ISO/IEC 9798-1:2010 [21]. For the second part, we cover ISO/IEC 9798-2:2008 [18] and Corrigendum 1 from 2010 [22]. For the third part, we cover ISO/IEC 9798-3:1998 [16], the corrigendum from 2009 [19], and the amendment from 2010 [23]. Finally, for the fourth part, our analysis covers ISO/IEC 9798-4:1999 [17] and the corrigendum from 2009 [20].

Table 1 lists the 17 associated protocols. For each cryptographic mechanism, there are unilateral and bilateral authentication variants. The number of messages and passes differs among the protocols as well as the communication structure. Some of the protocols also use a trusted third party (TTP).

Note that there is no consistent protocol naming scheme shared by the different parts of the ISO/IEC 9798 standard. The symmetric-key based protocols are referred to in [18] as "mechanism 1", "mechanism 2", etc., whereas the protocols in [16, 20, 23] are referred to by their informal name, e.g., "One-pass unilateral authentication". In this paper we will refer to protocols consistently by combining the document identifier, e.g., "9798-2" with a number n to identify the n-th protocol in that document. For protocols proposed in an amendment, we continue the numbering from the base document. Hence we refer to the first protocol in [23] as "9798-3-6". The resulting identifiers are listed in Table 1.

Most of the protocols are parameterized by the following elements:

- All text fields included in the protocol specification are optional and their purpose is application-dependent.
- Many fields used to ensure uniqueness or freshness may be implemented either by random numbers, sequence numbers, or timestamps.
- Some protocols specify alternative message contents.
- Some identifier fields may be dropped, depending on implementation details.

1.2 Notation

We write $X \,\|\, Y$ to denote the concatenation of the bit strings X and Y. We write $\{\!| X |\!\}_k^{\mathsf{enc}}$ to denote the encryption of X with the symmetric key k and $\{\!| X |\!\}_k^{\mathsf{sign}}$ to denote the digital signature of X with the signature key k. The application of a cryptographic check function f, keyed with key k, to a message m, is denoted by $f_k(m)$.

Table 1. Protocols specified by Parts 1-4 of the standard

Protocol	Description
Part 2: Symmetric-key Cryptography	
9798-2-1	One-pass unilateral authentication
9798-2-2	Two-pass unilateral authentication
9798-2-3	Two-pass mutual authentication
9798-2-4	Three-pass mutual authentication
9798-2-5	Four-pass with TTP
9798-2-6	Five-pass with TTP
Part 3: Digital Signatures	
9798-3-1	One-pass unilateral authentication
9798-3-2	Two-pass unilateral authentication
9798-3-3	Two-pass mutual authentication
9798-3-4	Three-pass mutual authentication
9798-3-5	Two-pass parallel mutual authentication
9798-3-6	Five-pass mutual authentication with TTP, initiated by A
9798-3-7	Five-pass mutual authentication with TTP, initiated by B
Part 4: Cryptographic Check Functions	
9798-4-1	One-pass unilateral authentication
9798-4-2	Two-pass unilateral authentication
9798-4-3	Two-pass mutual authentication
9798-4-4	Three-pass mutual authentication

In the standard, TVP denotes a Time-Variant Parameter, which may be a sequence number, a random value, or a timestamp. TN denotes a time stamp or sequence number. I_X denotes the identity of agent X. $Text_n$ refers to a text field. These fields are always optional and their use is not specified within the standard. We write K_{AB} to denote the long-term symmetric key shared by A and B. If the key is directional, we assume that A uses K_{AB} to communicate with B and that B uses K_{BA}. By convention, we use lower case strings for fresh session keys, like kab.

1.3   Protocol Examples

Example 1: 9798-4-3. The 9798-4-3 protocol is a two-pass mutual authentication protocol based on cryptographic check functions, e. g., message authentication codes. Its design, depicted in Figure 1, is similar to two related protocols based on symmetric key encryption (9798-2-3) and digital signatures (9798-3-3).

The initiator starts in role A and sends a message that consists of a time stamp or sequence number TN_A, concatenated with an optional text field and a cryptographic check value. This check value is computed by applying a cryptographic check function to the key shared between A and B and a string consisting of

$$1.\ A \to B : TN_A \parallel Text_2 \parallel f_{K_{AB}}(TN_A \parallel I_B \parallel Text_1)$$
$$2.\ B \to A : TN_B \parallel Text_4 \parallel f_{K_{AB}}(TN_B \parallel I_A \parallel Text_3)$$

Fig. 1. The 9798-4-3 two-pass mutual authentication protocol using a cryptographic check function

$$Token_{PA} = Text_4 \parallel \{\!\!\{ TVP_A \parallel kab \parallel I_B \parallel Text_3 \}\!\!\}^{enc}_{K_{AP}} \parallel \{\!\!\{ TN_P \parallel kab \parallel I_A \parallel Text_2 \}\!\!\}^{enc}_{K_{BP}}$$
$$Token_{AB} = Text_6 \parallel \{\!\!\{ TN_P \parallel kab \parallel I_A \parallel Text_2 \}\!\!\}^{enc}_{K_{BP}} \parallel \{\!\!\{ TN_A \parallel I_B \parallel Text_5 \}\!\!\}^{enc}_{kab}$$
$$Token_{BA} = Text_8 \parallel \{\!\!\{ TN_B \parallel I_A \parallel Text_7 \}\!\!\}^{enc}_{kab}$$

$$1.\ A \to P : TVP_A \parallel I_B \parallel Text_1$$
$$2.\ P \to A : Token_{PA}$$
$$3.\ A \to B : Token_{AB}$$
$$4.\ B \to A : Token_{BA}$$

Fig. 2. The 9798-2-5 four pass protocol with TTP using symmetric encryption

TN_A, B's identity, and optionally a text field $Text_1$. When B receives this message he computes the cryptographic check himself and compares the result with the received check value. He then computes the response message in a similar way and sends it to A, who checks it.

Example 2: 9798-2-5. Figure 2 depicts the 9798-2-5 protocol, which is based on symmetric-key encryption and uses a Trusted Third Party. A first generates a time-variant parameter TVP_A (which must be non-repeating), and sends it with B's identity I_B and optionally a text field to the trusted party P. P then generates a fresh session key kab and computes $Token_{PA}$, which essentially consists of two encrypted copies of the key, using the long-term shared keys between P and A, and P and B, respectively. Upon receiving $Token_{PA}$, A decrypts the first part to retrieve the session key, and uses the second part to construct $Token_{AB}$. Finally, B retrieves the session key from this message and sends his authentication message $Token_{BA}$ to A.

1.4 Optional Fields and Variants

There are variants for each protocol listed in Table 1. Each protocol contains *text fields*, whose purpose is not specified, and which may be omitted, giving rise to another protocol variant. As can be seen in the previous examples, some of these text fields are plaintext, whereas others are within the scope of cryptographic operations (i. e., signed, encrypted, or cryptographically checked). Note that the standard does not provide a rationale for choosing among these options.

In setups where symmetric keys are used, it is common that if Alice wants to communicate with Bob, she will use their shared key, which is the same key that Bob would use to communicate with Alice. Such keys are called *bidirectional*. Alternatively one can use *unidirectional* keys where each pair of agents shares two symmetric keys, one for each direction. In this case $K_{\text{Alice,Bob}}$ and $K_{\text{Bob,Alice}}$ are different. For some protocols that employ symmetric keys, the standard specifies that if unidirectional keys are used, some identity fields may be omitted from the encrypted (or checked) payload. This yields another variant.

The two protocols 9798-3-6 and 9798-3-7 both provide two options for the tokens included in their messages, giving rise to further variants. Note that in Section 4 we verify corrected versions of all 17 protocols in Table 1, taking all variants into account.

1.5 Threat Model and Security Properties

The ISO/IEC 9798 standard neither specifies a threat model nor defines the security properties that the protocols should satisfy. Instead, the introduction of ISO/IEC 9798-1 simply states that the protocols should satisfy mutual or unilateral authentication. Furthermore, the following attacks are mentioned as being relevant: man-in-the-middle attacks, replay attacks, reflection attacks, and forced delay attacks. We note that the standard does not explicitly claim that any of the protocols are resilient against the above attacks.

2 Protocol Analysis

We use two different analysis tools. In this section, we use the SCYTHER tool [9] to find attacks on the ISO/IEC 9798 protocols. In Section 4, we will use the related SCYTHER-PROOF tool [31] to generate machine-checked proofs of the corrected versions.

SCYTHER performs an automatic analysis of security protocols in a Dolev-Yao style model, for an unbounded number of instances. It is very efficient at both verification and falsification, in particular for authentication protocols such as those considered here. Using SCYTHER, we performed protocol analysis with respect to different forms of authentication. We explain these forms below when discussing particular protocols.

Our analysis reveals that the majority of the protocols in the standard ensure weak entity authentication. However, we also found attacks on five protocols and two protocol variants. These attacks fall into the following categories: role-mixup attacks, type flaw attacks, multiple-role TTP attacks, and reflection attacks. In all cases, when an agent finishes his role of the protocol, the protocol has not been executed as expected, which can lead the agent to proceed on false assumptions about the state of the other involved agents.

In Table 2 we list the attacks we found using SCYTHER. The rows list the protocols, the properties violated, and any additional assumptions required for the attacks. We have omitted in the table all attacks that are necessarily entailed by the attacks listed. For example, since 9798-2-5 does not satisfy aliveness from B's perspective, it also does not satisfy any stronger properties such as (weak) agreement. We now describe the classes of attacks in more detail.

Table 2. Overview of attacks found

Protocol	Violated property	Assumptions
9798-2-3	A Agreement(B,TNB,Text3)	
9798-2-3	B Agreement(A,TNA,Text1)	
9798-2-3-udkey	A Agreement(B,TNB,Text3)	
9798-2-3-udkey	B Agreement(A,TNA,Text1)	
9798-2-5	A Alive	Alice-talks-to-Alice
9798-2-5	B Alive	
9798-2-6	A Alive	
9798-2-6	B Alive	
9798-3-3	A Agreement(B,TNB,Text3)	
9798-3-3	B Agreement(A,TNA,Text1)	
9798-3-7-1	A Agreement(B,Ra,Rb,Text8)	Type-flaw
9798-4-3	A Agreement(B,TNb,Text3)	
9798-4-3	B Agreement(A,TNa,Text1)	
9798-4-3-udkey	A Agreement(B,TNb,Text3)	
9798-4-3-udkey	B Agreement(A,TNa,Text1)	

2.1 Role-Mixup Attacks

Some protocols are vulnerable to a *role-mixup attack* in which an agent's assumptions on another agent's role are wrong. Many relevant forms of strong authentication, such as *agreement* [27], matching conversations [4] or synchronisation [10], require that when Alice finishes her role apparently with Bob, then Alice and Bob not only agree on the exchanged data, but additionally Alice can be sure that Bob was performing in the intended role. Protocols vulnerable to role-mixup attacks violate these strong authentication properties.

Figure 3 on the following page shows an example of a role-mixup attack on the 9798-4-3 protocol from Figure 1. Agents perform actions such as sending and receiving messages, resulting in message transmissions represented by horizontal arrows. Actions are executed within threads, represented by vertical lines. The box at the top of each thread denotes the parameters involved in the thread's creation. Claims of security properties are denoted by hexagons and a crossed-out hexagon denotes that the claimed property is violated.

In this attack, the adversary uses a message from Alice in role A (thread 1) to trick Alice in role B (thread 3) into thinking that Bob is executing role A and is trying to initiate a session with her. However, Bob (thread 2) is only replying to a message provided to him by the adversary, and is executing role B. The adversary thereby tricks Alice into thinking that Bob is in a different state than he actually is.

Additionally, when the optional text fields $Text_1$ and $Text_3$ are used, the role-mixup attack also violates the agreement property with respect to these fields: Alice will end the protocol believing that the optional field data she receives from Bob was intended as Text1, whereas Bob actually sent this data in the

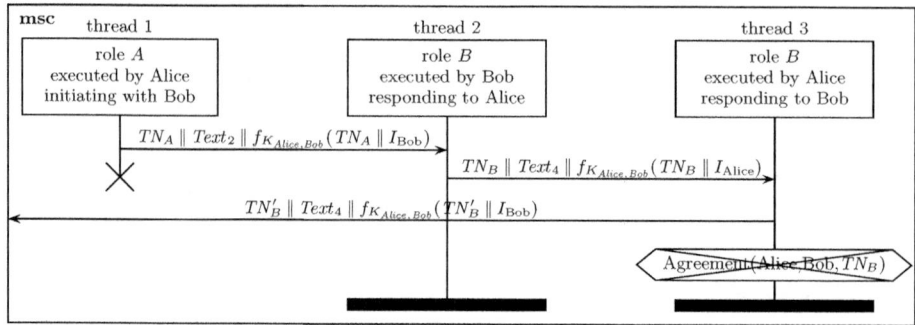

Fig. 3. Role-mixup attack on 9798-4-3: when Alice finishes thread 3 she wrongly assumes that Bob was performing the A role

Text3 field. Depending on the use of these fields, this can constitute a serious security problem. Note that exploiting these attacks, as well as the other attacks described below, does not require "breaking" cryptography. Rather, the adversary exploits similarities among messages and the willingness of agents to engage in the protocol.

Summarizing, we found role-mixup attacks on the following protocols: 9798-2-3 with bi- or unidirectional keys, 9798-2-5, 9798-3-3, and 9798-4-3 with bi- or unidirectional keys.

2.2   Type Flaw Attacks

Some protocol implementations are vulnerable to *type flaw attacks* where data of one type is parsed as data of another type. Consider, for example, an implementation where agent names are encoded into bit-fields of length n, which is also the length of the bit-fields representing nonces. It may then happen that an agent who expects to receive a nonce (any fresh random value that it has not seen before), therefore accepts a bit string that was intended to represent an agent name.

SCYTHER finds such an attack on the 9798-3-7 protocol, also referred to as "Five pass authentication (initiated by B)" [23, p. 4]. In the attack, both (agent) Alice and (trusted party) Terence mistakenly accept the bit string corresponding to the agent name "Alice" as a nonce.

2.3   Attacks Involving TTPs That Perform Multiple Roles

Another class of attacks occurs when parties can perform both the role of the trusted third party and another role. This scenario is not currently excluded by the standard.

In Figure 4 we show an attack on 9798-2-5, from Figure 2. The attack closely follows a regular protocol execution. In particular, threads 1 and 3 perform the

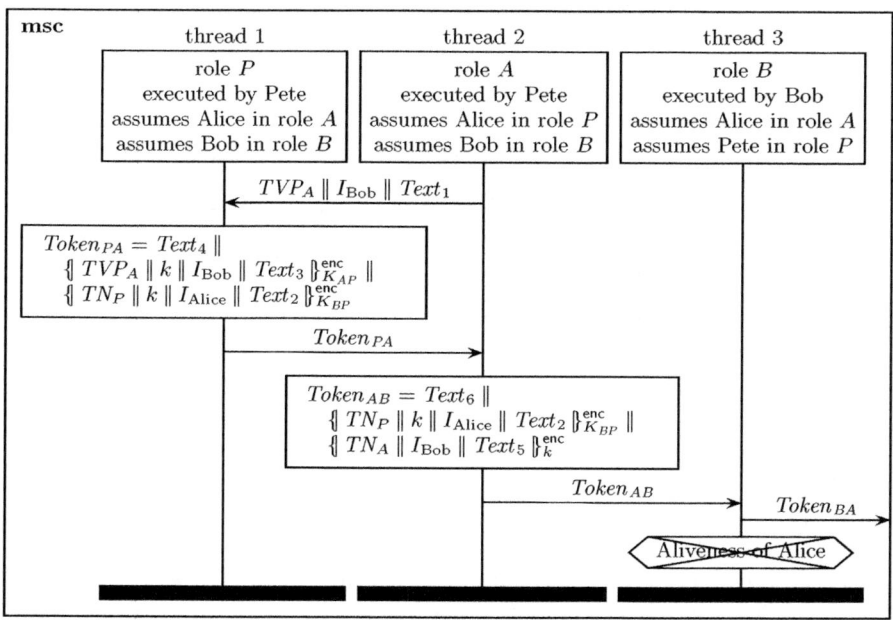

Fig. 4. Attack on the 9798-2-5 protocol where the trusted third party Pete performs both the P role and the A role. The assumptions of thread 1 and 3 agree. Bob wrongly concludes that Alice is alive.

protocol as expected. The problem is thread 2. Threads 1 and 3 assume that the participating agents are Alice (in the A role), Bob (in the B role), and Pete (in the P role). From their point of view, Alice should be executing thread 2. Instead, thread 2 is executed by Pete, under the assumption that Alice is performing the P role. Thread 2 receives only a single message in the attack, which is $Token_{PA}$. Because the long-term keys are symmetric, thread 2 cannot determine from the part of the message encrypted with K_{AP} that thread 1 has different assumptions. Thread 2 just forwards the other encrypted message part blindly to thread 3, as it does not expect to be able to decrypt it. Finally, thread 3 cannot detect the confusion between Alice and Pete, because the information in $Token_{AB}$ that was added by thread 2 only includes Bob's name.

Summarizing, we found attacks involving TTPs that perform multiple roles on the 9798-2-5 and 9798-2-6 protocol.

2.4   Reflection Attacks

Reflection attacks occur when agents may start sessions communicating with the same identity, a so-called *Alice-talks-to-Alice* scenario. The feasibility and relevance of this scenario depends on the application and its internal checks.

If an Alice-talks-to-Alice scenario is possible, some protocols are vulnerable to reflection attacks. The Message Sequence Chart in Figure 5 shows an example for

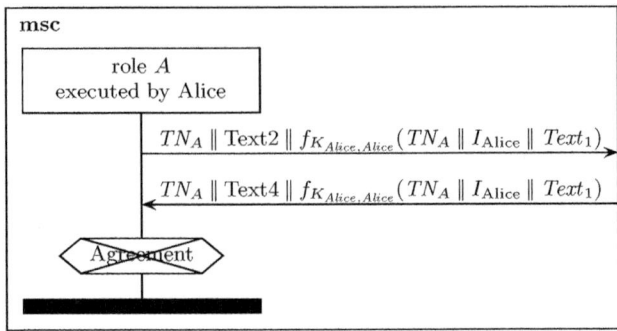

Fig. 5. Reflection attack on 9798-4-3

the 9798-4-3 protocol from Figure 1. In this attack, the adversary (not depicted) reflects the time stamp (or nonce) and cryptographic check value from the message sent by Alice back to the same thread, while prepending the message Text4. This attack violates one of the main requirements explicitly stated in the ISO/IEC 9798-1 introduction, namely absence of reflection attacks.

Summarizing, we found reflection attacks on the following protocols: 9798-2-3 with bi- or unidirectional keys, 9798-2-5, 9798-3-3, and 9798-4-3 with bi- or unidirectional keys.

3   Repairing the Protocols

3.1   Root Causes of the Problems

We identify two shortcomings in the design of the protocols, which together account for all of the weaknesses detected.

1) Cryptographic Message Elements May Be Accepted at Wrong Positions. In both the reflection and role mixup attacks, the messages that are received in a particular step of a role were not intended to be received at that position. By design, the protocol messages are all similar in structure, making it impossible to determine at which point in the protocols the messages were intended to be received.

As a concrete example, consider the reflection attack in Figure 5. Here, the message sent in the protocol's first step can be accepted in the second step, even though this is not part of the intended message flow.

2) Underspecification of the Involved Identities and their Roles. As noted, the symmetric-key based protocols with a TTP, 9798-2-5 and 9798-2-6, do not explicitly state that entities performing the TTP role cannot perform other roles. Hence it is consistent with the standard for Alice to perform both the role of the TTP as well as role A or B. In these cases, the aliveness of the partner cannot be guaranteed, as explained in Section 2.3. The source of this problem is that one cannot infer from each message which identity is associated to which role.

For example, consider the first encrypted component from the third message in the 9798-2-5 protocol with bidirectional keys, in Figure 2.

$$\{\!\!\| \ TN_P \ \| \ kab \ \| \ I_A \ \| \ Text_2 \ \|\!\!\}^{\mathrm{enc}}_{K_{BP}}$$

This message implicitly includes the identities of the three involved agents: the identity of the agent performing the A role is explicitly included in the encryption, and the shared long-term key K_{BP} implicitly associates the message to the key shared between the agent performing the B and P roles. However, because the key is bidirectional, the recipient cannot determine which of the two agents (say, Bob and Pete) sharing the key performed which role: either Bob performed the B role and Pete the P role, or vice versa. Our attack exploits exactly this ambiguity.

3.2 Associated Design Principles

To remedy these problems, we propose two principles for designing security protocols. These principles are in the spirit of Abadi and Needham's eleven principles for prudent engineering practice for cryptographic protocols [2].

Our first principle concerns tagging.

> **Principle: positional tagging.** Cryptographic message components should contain information that uniquely identifies their origin. In particular, the information should identify the protocol, the protocol variant, the message number, and the particular position within the message, from which the component was sent.

This is similar in spirit to Abadi and Needham's Principle 1, which states that *"Every message should say what it means: the interpretation of the message should depend only on its content. It should be possible to write down a straightforward English sentence describing the content — though if there is a suitable formalism available that is good too."* Our principle does not depend on the meaning of the message as intended by the protocol's designer. Instead, it is based solely on the structure of the protocol messages and their acceptance conditions.

Note that we consider protocols with optional fields to consist of multiple protocol variants. Thus, a message component where fields are omitted, should contain information to uniquely determine which fields were omitted.

Our second principle is a stricter version of Abadi and Needham's Principle 3.

> **Principle: inclusion of identities and their roles.** Each cryptographic message component should include information about the identities of all the agents involved in the protocol run and their roles, unless there is a compelling reason to do otherwise.

A compelling reason to leave out identity information might be that *identity hiding* is a requirement, i. e., Alice wants to hide that she is communicating with

Bob. However, such requirements can usually be met by suitably encrypting identity information.

Contrast this principle with the Abadi and Needham's Principle 3: *"If the identity of a principal is essential to the meaning of a message, it is prudent to mention the principal's name explicitly in the message."* The original principle is only invoked when the identity is essential. Instead, we propose to always include information on all the identities as well as their roles. This principle would have prevented attacks on many protocols, including the attacks on the 9798-2-5 and 9798-2-6 protocols, as well as the Needham-Schroeder protocol [26].

For protocols with a fixed number of roles, this principle can be implemented by including an ordered sequence of the identities involved in each cryptographic message component, such that the role of an agent can be inferred from its position in the sequence.

3.3   Proposed Modifications to the Standard

All the previously mentioned attacks on the ISO/IEC 9798 can be prevented by applying the previous two principles. Specifically, we propose three modifications to the ISO standard, shown in Figure 6. The first two directly follow from the principles and the third modification restricts the use of two protocols in the standard. Afterwards we give an example of a repaired protocol.

Note that in this section we only give informal arguments why our modifications prevent the attacks. In Section 4, we provide machine-checked proofs that this is the case.

Ensuring That Cryptographic Data Cannot Be Accepted at the Wrong Point. We factor the first principle (positional tagging) into two parts and propose two corresponding amendments to the standard. First, we explicitly include in each cryptographic message component constants that uniquely identify the protocol, the message number, and the position within the message. Second, we ensure that protocol variants can be uniquely determined from the messages.

In our first amendment, shown in Figure 6, we implement unique protocol identifiers by using an existing part of the standard: the object identifier from Annex B of the standard, which specifies an encoding of a unique protocol identifier. We also introduce a unique identifier for the position of the cryptographic component within the protocol.

Amendment 1 prevents all reflection attacks because messages sent in one step will no longer be accepted in another step. Furthermore, it prevents all role mixup attacks, because the unique constants in the messages uniquely determine the sending role. The final part of Amendment 1, stating that cryptographic keys should not be used by other protocols, provides distinctness of cryptographic messages with respect to any other protocols.

Our second amendment, also shown in Figure 6, ensures that the protocol variant (determined by the omission of optional fields) can be uniquely determined from the messages. We implement this by requiring that the recipient of a message can uniquely determine which optional fields, if any, were omitted.

Amendment 1:
The cryptographic data (encryptions, signatures, cryptographic check values) used at different places in the protocols must not be interchangeable. This may be enforced by including in each encryption/signature/CCF value the following two elements:

1. The object identifier as specified in Annex B [23, p. 6], in particular identifying the ISO standard, the part number, and the authentication mechanism.
2. For protocols that contain more than one cryptographic data element, each encryption must contain a constant that uniquely identifies the position of the element within the protocol.

The recipient of a message must verify that the object identifier and the position identifiers are as expected. The cryptographic keys used by implementations of the ISO/IEC 9798 protocols must be distinct from the keys used by other protocols.

Amendment 2:
When optional fields, such as optional identities or optional text fields, are not used then they must be set to empty. In particular, the message encoding must ensure that the concatenation of a field and an empty optional field is uniquely parsed as a concatenation. This can be achieved by implementing optional fields as variable-length fields. If the optional field is not used, the length of the field is set to zero.

Amendment 3:
Entities that perform the role of the TTP in the 9798-2-5 and 9798-2-6 protocols must not perform the A or B role.

Fig. 6. Proposed amendments to the ISO/IEC 9798 standard

To see why protocols with omitted optional fields must be considered as protocol variants, consider the following example: Consider a protocol in which a message contains the sequence $X \parallel I_A \parallel Text$, where I_A is an identity field that may be dropped (e. g., with unidirectional keys) and $Text$ is an optional text field. Then, it may be the case that in one protocol variant, an agent expects a message of the form $X \parallel I_A$, whereas the other implementation expects a message of the form $X \parallel Text$. The interaction between the two interpretations can result in attacks. For example, the text field is used to insert a false agent identity, or an agent identity is wrongly assumed to be the content of the text field.

If we follow the second amendment in the above example, the expected messages correspond to $X \parallel I_A \parallel \perp$ and $X \parallel \perp \parallel Text$, respectively, where $\perp$ denotes the zero-length field. Because the ISO/IEC 9798 standard requires that concatenated fields can be uniquely decomposed into their constituent parts, misinterpretation of the fields is no longer possible.

Together, Amendments 1 and 2 implement our first principle.

Addressing Underspecification of the Role Played by Agents. Almost all the protocols in the ISO/IEC 9798 standard already adhere to our second principle: unique identification of the involved parties and their roles. However, all protocols in the standard conform to Abadi and Needham's third principle because the messages uniquely determine the identities of all involved parties.

1. $A \rightarrow B : TN_A \parallel Text_2 \parallel f_{K_{AB}}(\text{"}\mathbf{9798\text{-}4\text{-}3\ ccf1}\text{"} \parallel TN_A \parallel I_B \parallel \perp)$
2. $B \rightarrow A : TN_B \parallel Text_4 \parallel f_{K_{AB}}(\text{"}\mathbf{9798\text{-}4\text{-}3\ ccf2}\text{"} \parallel TN_B \parallel I_A \parallel Text_3)$

Fig. 7. Repaired version of the 9798-4-3 protocol with omitted $Text_1$ field

There are only two protocols in the standard that conform to Abadi and Needham's principle but not to our second principle: 9798-2-5 and 9798-2-6. For example, the messages of the 9798-2-5 protocol identify all parties involved by their association to the long-term keys. However they do not conform to our second principle because the roles of the involved identities cannot be uniquely determined from the messages. This is the underlying reason why, as currently specified, the 9798-2-5 and 9798-2-6 protocols do not guarantee the aliveness of the partner, as shown in Section 2.3.

This problem can be solved by applying our principle, i.e., including the identities of all three participants in each message, so that their roles can be uniquely determined. This is an acceptable solution and we have formally verified it using the method of Section 4. However, from our analysis with SCYTHER, we observe that the attacks require that the Trusted Third Party also performs other roles (A or B). Under the assumption that in actual applications a TTP will, by definition, not perform the A or B role, the protocols already provide strong authentication. Thus, an alternative solution is to leave the protocols unchanged and make this restriction explicit. This results in more streamlined protocols and also requires minimal changes to the standard. This is the proposal made in Amendment 3 in Figure 6. We have also verified this solution as described in Section 4.

Repaired Protocols. Applying our principles and proposed amendments to the standard, we obtain repaired versions of the protocols. As an example, we show the repaired version of the 9798-4-3 protocol with bidirectional keys in Figure 7. In this example, the $Text_1$ field is not used, and is therefore replaced by $\perp$. Each use of a cryptographic primitive (in this case the cryptographic check function) includes a constant that uniquely identifies the protocol (9798-4-3) as well as the position within the protocol specification (`ccf1` and `ccf2`).

4   Proving the Correctness of the Repaired Protocols

The principles and amendments proposed in the previous section are motivated by our analysis of the attacks and the protocol features that enable them. Consequently, the principles and amendments are designed to eliminate these undesired behaviors. Such principles are useful guides for protocol designers but their application does not strictly provide any security guarantees. In order to ensure that the repaired protocols actually have the intended strong authentication properties, we provide machine-checked correctness proofs.

We use a version of the SCYTHER-PROOF tool proposed in [31] to generate proofs of these properties. Given a description of a protocol and its security properties, the tool generates a proof script that is afterwards automatically checked by the Isabelle/HOL theorem prover [33]. If the prover succeeds, then the protocol is verified with respect to a symbolic, Dolev-Yao model. To verify our repaired protocols, we extended the tool with support for bidirectional symmetric long-term keys.

The proofs generated by SCYTHER-PROOF are based on a security protocol verification theory that provides a sound way to perform finite case distinctions on the possible sources of messages that are known to the intruder, in the context of a given protocol. The generated proofs use these case distinctions to show that the assumptions of a security property imply its conclusions, as explained in Example 1. The theorems constituting this verification theory are formally derived in Isabelle/HOL from the formalization of a symbolic, Dolev-Yao model.

The tool searches for the proofs with the fewest number of such case distinctions. For example, in the proofs of our repaired protocols, two such case distinctions are required on average to prove a security property. Therefore, the generated proof scripts (available from [1]) are amenable to human inspection and understanding. To simplify the task of understanding how the proofs work and, hence, why the protocol is correct, the tool also generates proof outlines. These consist of a representation of the security property proven and a tree of case distinctions constituting the proof.

For each repaired protocol, we prove that it satisfies non-injective agreement on all data items within the scope of cryptographic operators in the presence of a Dolev-Yao intruder. Moreover, we prove that this holds even when all the protocols from the standard are executed in parallel using the same key infrastructure, provided that the set of bidirectional keys is disjoint from the set of unidirectional keys. As the content of text fields is underspecified in the standard, we assume that the intruder chooses their content immediately before they are sent. We model timestamps and sequence numbers by random numbers that are chosen at the beginning of a role and are public.

Example 1. Figure 8 on the next page specifies our model of the repaired 9798-4-3 protocol with bidirectional keys in the input language of the SCYTHER-PROOF tool. The leak_A and the leak_B steps model that the timestamps (represented here as randomly generated numbers) are publicly known by leaking them to the intruder. We model that the contents of the text_1 and text_2 fields is chosen by the intruder by defining them as variables that receive their content from the network, and therefore from the intruder. We model the cryptographic check function by the hash function h.

Figure 9 on the following page shows the proof outline for non-injective agreement for the A-role of this protocol, which is automatically generated by our tool. We have taken minor liberties here in its presentation to improve readability. In the figure, #i is a symbolic variable denoting some thread i and A#i is the value of the A-variable in the thread i. Lines 3-9 state the security property: for all threads #i that execute the A-role and have executed its Step 2 with uncompromised (honest) agents A#i and B#i, there exists some thread #j that

```
———————————————— Repaired version of 9798-4-3 ——————————
protocol isoiec_9798_4_3_bdkey_repaired
{
  leak_A. A -> : TNa
  leak_B. B -> : TNb

  text_1.   -> A: Text1, Text2
       1. A -> B: A, B, TNa, Text2, Text1, h(('CCF', k[A,B]), ('isoiec_9798_4_3_ccf_1',
                  TNa, B, Text1))
  text_2.   -> B: Text3, Text4
       2. B -> A: B, A, TNb, Text4, Text3, h(('CCF', k[A,B]), ('isoiec_9798_4_3_ccf_2',
                  TNb, A, Text3))
}
properties (of isoiec_9798_4_3_bdkey_repaired)
  A_non_injective_agreement: niagree(A_2[A,B,TNb,Text3] -> B_2[A,B,TNb,Text3], {A, B})
  B_non_injective_agreement: niagree(B_1[A,B,TNa,Text1] -> A_1[A,B,TNa,Text1], {A, B})
```

Fig. 8. Example input provided to the SCYTHER-PROOF tool

```
1   property (of isoiec_9798_4_3_bdkey_repaired)
2     A_non_injective_agreement:
3     "All #i.
4       role(#i) = isoiec_9798_4_3_bdkey_repaired_A &
5       step(#i, isoiec_9798_4_3_bdkey_repaired_A_2) &
6       uncompromised( A#i, B#i )
7       ==> (Ex #j. role(#j) = isoiec_9798_4_3_bdkey_repaired_B &
8                   step(#j, isoiec_9798_4_3_bdkey_repaired_B_2) &
9                   (A#j, B#j, TNb#j, Text3#j) = (A#i, B#i, TNb#i, Text3#i)) "
10  sources( h(('CCF', k[A#i,B#i]), ('isoiec_9798_4_3_ccf_2', TNb#i, A#i, Text3#i)) )
11    case fake
12    contradicts secrecy of k[A#i,B#i]
13  next
14    case (isoiec_9798_4_3_bdkey_B_2_repaired_hash #k)
15    tautology
16  qed
```

Fig. 9. Example proof outline automatically produced by the SCYTHER-PROOF tool

executed Step 2 of the B-role and thread #j agrees with thread #i on the values of A, B, TNb, and Text3.

The proof proceeds by observing that thread #i executed Step 2 of the A-role. Therefore, thread #i received the hash in line 10 from the network, which implies that the intruder knows this hash. For our protocol, a case distinction on the sources of this hash results in two cases: (1) the intruder could have constructed (faked) this hash by himself or (2) the intruder could have learned this hash from some thread #k that sent it in Step 2 of the B-role. There are no other cases because all other hashes have different tags. Case 1 is contradictory because the intruder does not know the long-term key shared between the two uncompromised agents A#i and B#i. In Case 2, the security property holds because we can instantiate thread #j in the conclusion with thread #k. Thread #k executed Step 2 of the B-role and agrees with thread #i on all desired values because they are included in the hash.   □

We verify the parallel composition of all repaired protocols of the ISO/IEC 9798 standard as follows. Given the disjoint encryption theorem [14], it is sufficient to verify only the parallel composition of protocols that use the same cryptographic primitive and the same keys. We verify the properties of each protocol when composed in parallel with all other protocols that use the same cryptographic primitive and the same keys. Note that in the corresponding proofs, the case distinctions on the source of messages known to the intruder range over the roles of each protocol in the protocol group. Despite the substantial increase in the scope of these case distinctions, the proof structure of the composed protocols is the same as for the individual protocols, as all additional cases are always trivially discharged due to the tagging: cryptographic components received by a thread of one protocol contain tags that do not match with the tags in messages produced by roles from other protocols.

Our extension of the SCYTHER-PROOF tool as well as the protocol models (including the property specifications) can be downloaded at [1]. Using a Core 2 Duo 2.20GHz laptop with 2GB RAM, the full proof script generation requires less than 20 seconds, and Isabelle's proof checking requires less than three hours.

5 Related Work

Previous Analyses of the ISO/IEC 9798 Protocols. Chen and Mitchell [8] reported attacks based on parsing ambiguities on protocols from several standards. They identify two types of ambiguities in parsing strings involving concatenation: (1) recipients wrongly parse an encrypted string after decryption, or (2) recipients wrongly assume that a different combination of data fields was input to the digital signature or MAC that they are verifying. They show that such errors lead to attacks, and propose modifications to the standards. Their analysis resulted in a technical corrigendum to the ISO/IEC 9798 standard [19,20,22].

Some of the protocols have been used as case studies for security protocol analysis tools. In [12], the Casper/FDR tool is used to discover weaknesses in six protocols from the ISO/IEC 9798 standard. The attacks discovered are similar to our reflection and role-mixup attacks. They additionally report so-called multiplicity attacks, but these are prevented by following the specification of the time-variant parameters in Part 1 of the standard. Contrary to our findings, their analysis reports "no attack" on the 9798-2-5 and 9798-2-6 protocols as they do not consider type-flaw attacks. A role-mixup attack on the 9798-3-3 protocol was also discovered by the SATMC tool [3]. Neither of these two works suggested how to eliminate the detected weaknesses.

In [11], the authors verify the three-pass mutual authentication protocols that use symmetric encryption and digital signatures, i. e., 9798-2-4 and 9798-3-4. Their findings are consistent with our results.

Related Protocols. The SASL authentication mechanism from RFC 3163 [34] claims to be based on Part 3 of the ISO/IEC 9798 standard. However, the SASL protocol is designed differently than the ISO/IEC protocols and is vulnerable to a man-in-the-middle attack similar to Lowe's well-known attack on the Needham-Schroeder public-key protocol. Currently, the SASL protocol is not recommended for use (as noted in the RFC). The SASL protocol only provides authentication in the presence of an eavesdropping adversary, which can also be achieved using only plaintext messages.

In the academic literature on key exchange protocols, one finds references to a Diffie-Hellman-based key exchange protocol known as "ISO 9798-3". This protocol seems to be due to [7, p. 464-465], where a protocol is given that is similar in structure to the three-pass mutual authentication ISO/IEC 9798 protocol based on digital signatures, where each random value n is replaced by ephemeral public keys of the form g^x. However, in the actual ISO/IEC 9798 standard, no key exchange protocols are defined, and no protocols use Diffie-Hellman exponentiation.

6 Conclusions

Our findings show that great care must be taken when using current implementations of the ISO/IEC 9798 standard. Under the assumption that trusted third parties do not play other roles, the protocols guarantee a weak form of authentication, namely, aliveness. However, many of the protocols do not satisfy any stronger authentication properties, which are needed in realistic applications. For example, when using these protocols one cannot assume that when a text field is encrypted with a key and was apparently sent by Bob, that Bob indeed sent it, or that he was performing the intended role. In contrast, our repaired versions satisfy strong authentication properties and hence ensure not only aliveness but also agreement on the participating agents, their roles, the values of time-variant parameters, and the message fields that are cryptographically protected.

Based on our analysis of the standard's weaknesses, we have proposed amendments and provided machine-checked proofs of their correctness. Our proofs guarantee the absence of these weaknesses even in the case that all protocols from the standard are run in parallel using the same key infrastructure. The working group responsible for the ISO/IEC 9798 standard will release an updated version of the standard based on our analysis and proposed fixes.

Formal methods are slowly starting to have an impact in standardization bodies, e. g., [5, 6, 15, 25, 29, 30]. We expect this trend to continue as governments and other organizations increasingly push for the use of formal methods for the development and evaluation of critical standards. For example, ISO/IEC JTC 1/SC 27 started the project "Verification of cryptographic protocols (ISO/IEC 29128)" in 2007 which is developing standards for certifying cryptographic protocols, where the highest evaluation levels require the use of formal, machine checked correctness proofs [28].

We believe that the approach we have taken here to analyze and provably repair the ISO/IEC 9798 standard can play an important role in future standardization efforts. Our approach supports standardization committees with both falsification, for analysis in the early phases of standardization, and verification, providing objective and verifiable security guarantees in the end phases.

References

1. Models and proofs of the repaired ISO/IEC 9798 protocols and source code of Scyther-Proof (May 2011),
   http://www.infsec.ethz.ch/research/software#ESPL
2. Abadi, M., Needham, R.: Prudent engineering practice for cryptographic protocols. IEEE Transactions on Software Engineering 22(1), 6–15 (1996)
3. Armando, A., Compagna, L.: SAT-based model-checking for security protocols analysis. Int. J. Inf. Sec. 7(1), 3–32 (2008)
4. Bellare, M., Rogaway, P.: Entity Authentication and Key Distribution. In: Stinson, D.R. (ed.) CRYPTO 1993. LNCS, vol. 773, pp. 232–249. Springer, Heidelberg (1994)
5. Bhargavan, K., Fournet, C., Corin, R., Zalinescu, E.: Cryptographically verified implementations for TLS. In: ACM Conference on Computer and Communications Security, pp. 459–468. ACM (2008)
6. Bhargavan, K., Fournet, C., Gordon, A.D., Swamy, N.: Verified implementations of the information card federated identity-management protocol. In: ASIACCS, pp. 123–135. ACM (2008)
7. Canetti, R., Krawczyk, H.: Analysis of Key-Exchange Protocols and Their Use for Building Secure Channels. In: Pfitzmann, B. (ed.) EUROCRYPT 2001. LNCS, vol. 2045, pp. 453–474. Springer, Heidelberg (2001)
8. Chen, L., Mitchell, C.J.: Parsing ambiguities in authentication and key establishment protocols. Int. J. Electron. Secur. Digit. Forensic 3, 82–94 (2010)
9. Cremers, C.J.F.: The Scyther Tool: Verification, Falsification, and Analysis of Security Protocols. In: Gupta, A., Malik, S. (eds.) CAV 2008. LNCS, vol. 5123, pp. 414–418. Springer, Heidelberg (2008),
   http://people.inf.ethz.ch/cremersc/scyther/
10. Cremers, C., Mauw, S., de Vink, E.: Injective synchronisation: an extension of the authentication hierarchy. Theoretical Computer Science, 139–161 (2006)
11. Datta, A., Derek, A., Mitchell, J., Pavlovic, D.: Abstraction and refinement in protocol derivation. In: Proc. 17th IEEE Computer Security Foundations Workshop (CSFW), pp. 30–45. IEEE Comp. Soc. (June 2004)
12. Donovan, B., Norris, P., Lowe, G.: Analyzing a library of security protocols using Casper and FDR. In: Proc. of the Workshop on Formal Methods and Security Protocols (1999)
13. European Payments Council. Guidelines on algorithms usage and key management. Technical report, EPC342-08 Version 1.1 (2009)
14. Guttman, J.D., Thayer, F.J.: Protocol independence through disjoint encryption. In: CSFW, pp. 24–34 (2000)
15. He, C., Sundararajan, M., Datta, A., Derek, A., Mitchell, J.C.: A modular correctness proof of IEEE 802.11i and TLS. In: Proc. of the 12th ACM Conference on Computer and Communications Security, CCS 2005, pp. 2–15. ACM, New York (2005)
16. International Organization for Standardization, Genève, Switzerland. ISO/IEC 9798-3:1998, Information technology – Security techniques – Entity Authentication – Part 3: Mechanisms using digital signature techniques, 2nd edn. (1998)
17. International Organization for Standardization, Genève, Switzerland. ISO/IEC 9798-4:1999, Information technology – Security techniques – Entity Authentication – Part 3: Mechanisms using a cryptographic check function, 2nd edn. (1999)

18. International Organization for Standardization, Genève, Switzerland. ISO/IEC 9798-2:2008, Information technology – Security techniques – Entity Authentication – Part 2: Mechanisms using symmetric encipherment algorithms, 3rd edn. (2008)
19. International Organization for Standardization, Genève, Switzerland. ISO/IEC 9798-3:1998/Cor.1:2009, Information technology – Security techniques – Entity Authentication – Part 3: Mechanisms using digital signature techniques. Technical Corrigendum 1 (2009)
20. International Organization for Standardization, Genève, Switzerland. ISO/IEC 9798-4:1999/Cor.1:2009, Information technology – Security techniques – Entity Authentication – Part 3: Mechanisms using a cryptographic check function. Technical Corrigendum 1 (2009)
21. International Organization for Standardization, Genève, Switzerland. ISO/IEC 9798-1:2010, Information technology – Security techniques – Entity Authentication – Part 1: General, 3rd edn. (2010)
22. International Organization for Standardization, Genève, Switzerland. ISO/IEC 9798-2:2008/Cor.1:2010, Information technology – Security techniques – Entity Authentication – Part 2: Mechanisms using symmetric encipherment algorithms. Technical Corrigendum 1 (2010)
23. International Organization for Standardization, Genève, Switzerland. ISO/IEC 9798-3:1998/Amd.1:2010, Information technology – Security techniques – Entity Authentication – Part 3: Mechanisms using digital signature techniques. Amendment 1 (2010)
24. ITU-T. Recommendation H.235 - Security and encryption for H-series (H.323 and other H.245-based) multimedia terminals (2003)
25. Kuhlman, D., Moriarty, R., Braskich, T., Emeott, S., Tripunitara, M.: A correctness proof of a mesh security architecture. In: Proc. of the 2008 21st IEEE Computer Security Foundations Symposium, pp. 315–330. IEEE Computer Society (2008)
26. Lowe, G.: Breaking and Fixing the Needham-Schroeder Public-Key Protocol Using FDR. In: Margaria, T., Steffen, B. (eds.) TACAS 1996. LNCS, vol. 1055, pp. 147–166. Springer, Heidelberg (1996)
27. Lowe, G.: A hierarchy of authentication specifications. In: Proc. 10th IEEE Computer Security Foundations Workshop (CSFW), pp. 31–44. IEEE (1997)
28. Matsuo, S., Miyazaki, K., Otsuka, A., Basin, D.: How to Evaluate the Security of Real-Life Cryptographic Protocols? - the Cases of ISO/IEC 29128 and CRYPTREC. In: Sion, R., Curtmola, R., Dietrich, S., Kiayias, A., Miret, J.M., Sako, K., Sebé, F. (eds.) FC 2010 Workshops. LNCS, vol. 6054, pp. 182–194. Springer, Heidelberg (2010)
29. Meadows, C.: Analysis of the Internet Key Exchange protocol using the NRL Protocol Analyzer. In: IEEE Symposium on Security and Privacy, pp. 216–231 (1999)
30. Meadows, C., Syverson, P.F., Cervesato, I.: Formal specification and analysis of the Group Domain Of Interpretation Protocol using NPATRL and the NRL Protocol Analyzer. Journal of Computer Security 12(6), 893–931 (2004)
31. Meier, S., Cremers, C.J.F., Basin, D.A.: Strong invariants for the efficient construction of machine-checked protocol security proofs. In: CSF, pp. 231–245. IEEE Computer Society (2010)
32. Menezes, A., Oorschot, P.V., Vanstone, S.: Handbook of Applied Cryptography, 5th edn. CRC Press, Inc. (2001)
33. Nipkow, T., Paulson, L.C., Wenzel, M.T.: Isabelle/HOL - A Proof Assistant for Higher-Order Logic. LNCS, vol. 2283, p. 218. Springer, Heidelberg (2002)
34. Zuccherato, R., Nystrom, M.: RFC 3163: ISO/IEC 9798-3 Authentication SASL Mechanism (2001), http://www.rfc-editor.org/info/rfc3163

Security Proof with Dishonest Keys[*]

Hubert Comon-Lundh[1], Véronique Cortier[2], and Guillaume Scerri[1,2]

[1] LSV, ENS Cachan & CNRS & INRIA, France
[2] LORIA, CNRS, France

Abstract. Symbolic and computational models are the two families of
models for rigorously analysing security protocols. Symbolic models are
abstract but offer a high level of automation while computational models
are more precise but security proof can be tedious. Since the seminal work
of Abadi and Rogaway, a new direction of research aims at reconciling
the two views and many *soundness results* establish that symbolic models
are actually sound w.r.t. computational models.

This is however not true for the prominent case of encryption. Indeed,
all existing soundness results assume that the adversary only uses honestly generated keys. While this assumption is acceptable in the case of
asymmetric encryption, it is clearly unrealistic for symmetric encryption.
In this paper, we provide with several examples of attacks that do not
show-up in the classical Dolev-Yao model, and that do not break the
IND-CPA nor INT-CTXT properties of the encryption scheme.

Our main contribution is to show the first soundness result for symmetric encryption and arbitrary adversaries. We consider arbitrary indistinguishability properties and an unbounded number of sessions.

This result relies on an extension of the symbolic model, while keeping standard security assumptions: IND-CPA and IND-CTXT for the
encryption scheme.

1 Introduction

Formal proofs of security aim at increasing our confidence in the security protocols. The first formal proofs/attacks go back to the early eighties (for instance
[DY81]). Such proofs require a formal model for the concurrent execution of processes in a hostile environment (for instance [AG99, AF01]). As a consequence,
the security proof only proves something about a formal model. That is why
we were faced to paradoxical situations, in which a protocol is proved to be secure and later an attack is found. This is the case for the Bull authentication
protocol [RS98], or the Needham-Schroeder-Lowe protocol [War03, BHO09]. In
such cases, the proof is simply carried in a model that differs from the model in
which the attack is mounted. There are much more examples, since the security
proofs always assume some restrictions on the attacker's capabilities, ruling out

---

[*] The research leading to these results has received funding from the European
Research Council under the European Union's Seventh Framework Programme
(FP7/2007-2013) / ERC grant agreement no 258865, project ProSecure.

P. Degano and J.D. Guttman (Eds.): POST 2012, LNCS 7215, pp. 149–168, 2012.
© Springer-Verlag Berlin Heidelberg 2012

some side-channel attacks. The examples show however that we need to specify as precisely as possible the scope of the proofs, i.e., the security assumptions.

This is one of the main goals of the work that started ten years ago on computational soundness [AR00, BPW03]: what is the scope of formal proofs in a Dolev-Yao style model ? This is important, because the automatic (or checkable) proofs are much easier in a Dolev-Yao, called *symbolic* hereafter, model, in which messages are abstract terms and the attacker is any formal process that can intercept and send new messages that can be forged from the available ones.

Numerous results have been obtained in this direction, but we will only focus on the case of symmetric encryption. If we assume only two primitives: symmetric encryption and pairing, to what extent is the symbolic model accounting for attacks performed by a probabilistic polynomial time attacker ? The first result [AR00] investigates the case of a passive attacker, who cannot send fake messages, but only observes the messages in transit. Its goal is to distinguish between two message sequences, finding a test that yields 1 on a sequence and yields 0 on the other sequence (for a significant subset of the sample space). The authors show for instance that, if the encryption scheme is IND-CPA, is "which key-preserving" (two encrypted messages with the same key are indistinguishable from two messages encrypted with different keys) and hides the length, then the symbolic indistinguishability implies the computational indistinguishability. In short, in that case, the symbolic model accounts for the probabilistic polynomial time attacks on the implementations of the messages.

To our knowledge, only two further works extend this result: first M. Backes *et al* in [BP04] and two of us in [CLC08a]. Both works try to consider an active attacker, thus allowing an interaction of the attacker with the protocol. Both works require additional assumptions: INT-CTXT for the encryption scheme, no dynamic corruption of keys, no key cycles,... The main difference between the two results lies in the security properties that are considered: while [BP04] considers trace properties, [CLC08a] considers equivalence properties. Therefore the proof methods are quite different.

We wish however to insist on another issue: in [CLC08a], the encryption keys are assumed to be authentic. In other words, if the attacker forges a key, then this key must be generated using the key generation algorithm. This is a strong assumption, that is hard to ensure in practice. For a public key cryptosystem, we can imagine that the public keys are certified by a key-issuing authority and that this authority is trusted. But in the case of symmetric encryption, there are many examples in which a participant generates himself a session key. This limitation and its consequences are discussed at length in [CC11].

Concerning [BP04], the case of dishonest keys is not mentioned explicitly, while the proof assumes that there is no such key: the paper implicitly assumes that all keys are generated using the key generation algorithm.

On the other hand, the problem of dishonest keys is important: the cryptographic assumptions, such as IND-CPA, INT-CTXT, IND-CCA,... rely on a sampling of the keys. This does not say anything on any particular key: there could be a key for which all the properties fail and such a key could be chosen by the attacker. As we show in section 2, there are many situations in which we can mount an attack, even when the encryption scheme has all the desired properties.

The main source of examples of formal security proofs of protocols using symmetric key encryption (not assuming that keys are always honest) is CRYP-TOVERIF [Bla08]. These proofs show, as an intermediate step, that the keys used for encryption by a honest agent for a honest agent are honestly generated. In this way, the security properties of the encryption scheme are only applied to ciphertexts using a randomly generated key. This works for many protocols, but cannot work for a soundness result since there are protocols that are secure, while at some point a honest agent may use a fake key (sent by the attacker) for encrypting a message sent to a honest participant.

The issue of dishonest keys is also considered in [KT09]. Here, the authors identify sufficient conditions on protocols such that dishonest keys are provably harmless. These conditions are satisfied by a large family of key exchange protocols. These conditions may however be too strong. For example, the protocol we analyse at the end of this paper does not meet their conditions, while we can prove it secure using our framework.

In this paper, we propose a solution to the dishonest keys problem, adding capabilities to the symbolic attacker. We try to capture the ability to forge a key, that has an arbitrary behavior (choosen by the attacker), *on messages that have been sent so far*. Roughly, the attacker may forge a particular key k, such that given any pair of known messages (m_1, m_2), the encryption (resp. decryption) of m_1 with k yields m_2. As we show in an example in section 2, the attacker must also get any encryption/decryption of a message that uses a fake key.

This model is formalized in section 3, building on the applied π-calculus of [AF01]. We then show in section 5 that this model is computationally sound, without assuming of course that keys are honestly generated. More precisely, we prove, in the case of simple processes, that, if two processes P, Q are observationally equivalent, then their implementations $[\![P]\!]$, $[\![Q]\!]$ are computationally indistinguishable, provided that the encryption scheme is IND-CPA and INT-CTXT. In other words, as in [CLC08a] we (also) cover equivalence properties. This soundness proof is similar to the proof of [CLC08a]: we prove a tree soundness result and a trace mapping. There are some significant technical differences, that will be pointed out. Also, a gap in the final proof of [CLC08a] is fixed here, considering a new indistinguishability game.

Finally, we show that our soundness result does not give too much power to the symbolic attacker: we give a computationally secure process in our extended model, in which the attacker may send fake keys that are then used for decryption.

2   Motivation : Some Examples of Insufficiency of Current Models

Standard cryptographic assumptions do not provide any guarantee for keys that are not generated using the key generation algorithm. In particular, the IND-CPA and IND-CTXT properties do not exclude the case where some keys have particular properties. We provide below several examples of protocols whose security is broken due to the behavior of dishonestly generated keys. For the sake of clarity, we provide with an informal specification of the protocols and we consider attacks that consist of some agent reaching an undesired **bad** state. These examples could be easily turned into examples with confidentiality or authenticity properties. For simplicity, we also omit the randomness used for encryption.

A first fact about dishonest keys is that decrypting honest cyphertexts with dishonest keys does not necessary fail and may, on the contrary, result into plaintext that can be exploited by an attacker.

Example 1. Assume k_{AB} is a secret key shared between A and B.

$$A \rightarrow \langle c, \{c\}_{k_{AB}} \rangle \qquad \begin{aligned} B &\leftarrow \langle z, \{\{b\}_z\}_{k_{AB}} \rangle \\ B &\rightarrow \textbf{bad} \end{aligned}$$

B waits for a key z and a message looking like $\{\{b\}_z\}_{k_{AB}}$ and goes in a bad state. For all usual formal models, B can not reach the bad sate. On the other hand, it is computationally feasible for an adversary to forge a key k such that $\mathcal{D}(c, k) = b$ ($\mathcal{D}(c, k)$ is the decryption of c with k), in that case B goes in the bad state receiving $\langle k, \{c\}_{k_{AB}} \rangle$.

This example can easily be generalized to the case where the decryption of several ciphertexts with some dishonest key yields exploitable results.

Example 2. Assume k_{AB} is a secret key shared between A and B.

$$A \rightarrow \langle \langle c, \{c\}_{k_{AB}} \rangle, \langle d, \{d\}_{k_{AB}} \rangle \rangle \qquad \begin{aligned} B &\leftarrow \langle k, \langle \{\{b\}_k\}_{k_{AB}}, \{\{b'\}_k\}_{k_{AB}} \rangle \rangle \\ B &\rightarrow \textbf{bad} \end{aligned}$$

The standard cryptographic assumptions do not prevent the adversary from forging a key k such that $\mathcal{D}(c, k) = b$ and $\mathcal{D}(d, k) = b'$ simultaneously.

The two previous examples seem to rely on the fact that the adversary knows the (honest) cyphertexts that are decrypted. This is actually not needed to mount attacks.

Example 3. Assume k_{AB} is a secret key shared between A and B and s be a secret known only to A.

$$A \rightarrow \{s\}_{k_{AB}} \qquad \begin{aligned} B &\leftarrow \langle k, \{\{b\}_k\}_{k_{AB}} \rangle \\ B &\rightarrow \textbf{bad} \end{aligned}$$

In the computational setting the adversary could forge a key k such that, if s is randomly chosen , $\mathcal{D}(s, k) = b$ with a non negligible probability. Receiving $k, \{s\}_{k_{AB}}$, B would reach the bad state with non negligible probability.

Another important behavior of dishonest keys is the fact that attempting to decrypt a message with a dishonest key may actually reveal the message.

Example 4. Consider the following protocol where s is secret.

$$A \to \{s\}_{k_{AB}} \qquad \begin{array}{l} B \leftarrow \langle k, \{\{z\}_k\}_{k_{AB}} \rangle \\ B \to \mathbf{ok} \end{array}$$

The agent B simply tries to decrypt the message received under k_{AB} and outputs **ok** if he succeeds. In any usual formal model, s stays secret.

Let us consider a key k_i such that k_i decrypts s if and only if the i-th bit of s is with a 0. Sending $k_i, \{s\}_{k_{AB}}$ to a copy of B the adversary learns the $i - th$ bit of s and is then able to learn s entirely.

The previous examples exhibit problematic behaviors when decrypting with a dishonest key. Similar issues occur when encrypting with a dishonest key. The next example shows that the adversary may use dishonest keys to build equalities between cyphertexts.

Example 5. Assume k_{AB} is a secret key shared by A and B.

$$\begin{array}{l} A \to \{a\}_{k_{AB}} \\ A \leftarrow k \\ A \to \{\{s\}_k, \{a\}_{k_{AB}}\}_{k_{AB}} \end{array} \qquad \begin{array}{l} B \leftarrow \{x, x\}_{k_{AB}} \\ B \to \mathbf{bad} \end{array}$$

As previously, nothing prevents the adversary from building a key k such that for a random s, $\{s\}_k^r = \{a\}_{k_{AB}}$ with non negligible probability. Using that key, it is possible to drive B in the bad state.

More generally, $\{x\}_k$ may be an arbitrary function of (x, r) and the previous knowledge of the adversary.

Example 6. Assume k_{AB} is a secret key shared by A and B, s is a secret nonce known to A and s' is a nonce (not necessarily secret).

$$\begin{array}{l} A \leftarrow k \\ A \to \{\{\langle s, s' \rangle\}_k\}_{k_{AB}} \end{array} \qquad \begin{array}{l} B \leftarrow \langle k', \{\{\langle s, s \rangle\}_{k'}\}_{k_{AB}} \rangle \\ B \to \mathbf{bad} \end{array}$$

The adversary could forge k, k' such that $\mathcal{D}(\{\langle x, y \rangle\}_k^r, k') = \langle x, x \rangle$ (when x and y are of equal length) which allows B to go in the bad state.

One could think that the collisions induced by a dishonest key k are determined by the message under encryption/decryption and the knowledge of the adversary *at the moment* he forged k. The last example shows that it is actually not the case.

Example 7. Assume that k_{AB} is a secret ket shared by A and B and that s is initially secret.

$$\begin{array}{l} A \leftarrow \langle k_0, k_1, k_2 \rangle \\ A \to \langle \{k_0\}_{k_{AB}}, \{k_1\}_{k_{AB}}, \{k_2\}_{k_{AB}} \\ A \to \{\langle A, A \rangle\}_{k_{AB}} \\ A \to s \\ A \leftarrow \{\langle x, s \rangle\}_{k_{AB}} \\ A \to \mathbf{bad} \end{array} \qquad \begin{array}{l} B \leftarrow \langle \{k\}_{k_{AB}}, \{t\}_{k_{AB}} \rangle \\ B \to \{\{t\}_k\}_{k_{AB}} \end{array}$$

Running B an arbitrary (polynomial) number of times yields a computational attack. Consider the three following keys :

- k_0 such that $\{\langle i, n \rangle\}_{k_0} = \langle i + 1, n \rangle$
- k_1 such that $\{\langle i, n \rangle\}_{k_1} = \langle i - 1, n \rangle$
- k_2 such that $\{\langle i, n \rangle\}_{k_2} = \langle i, n' \rangle$ where n' is the same bitstring as n apart from the i-th bit which is flipped.

With these keys, we can use role B to transform any cyphertext $\{\langle m_1, m_2 \rangle\}_{k_{AB}}$ into $\{\langle x, s \rangle\}_{k_{AB}}$.

Let us summarize the lessons provided by these examples. Clearly, existing symbolic models are unsound. There are three main options for establishing soundness: either re-enforcing the security assumptions of the primitives, or identifying sufficient conditions for recovering soundness, or relaxing the symbolic models. In this paper, we have opted for the third option. Examples 1, 2, and 3 show that we need to let the adversary adds equations when decrypting or encrypting with a dishonest key. Examples 5 and 6 show that these equations may depend on the knowledge of the attacker when he add them. Example 4 demonstrates that any message under decryption/encryption with a dishonest key should be added to the adversary knowledge. Example 7 shows that we have to delay the commitment on the properties of the dishonest key until the state, at which the encryption/decryption with that key is used.

Let us note that in some examples we try to decrypt a honest nonce which should be forbidden by tagging but it is easy to patch these examples by replacing the honest nonces by honest encryptions.

3   Model

Our model is an adaptation of the applied pi-calculus [AF01], enriched with a syntax that allows the attacker to create new equalities between terms, corresponding to equalities permitted by the IND-CCA and the IND-CTXT properties, as illustrated in the previous section.

3.1   Syntax and Deduction

Messages are represented by terms build upon a set $\mathcal{V}$ of variables, a set $\mathcal{N}ames$ of names and the signature $\mathcal{F} = \{\{\_\}\_ , \langle\_, \_\rangle, \text{dec}(\_, \_), \pi_1(\_), \pi_2(\_)\}$. As usual, the term $\{s\}_k^r$ represents the encryption of s with the key k and the randomness r, $\langle u, v \rangle$ represents the concatenation of u and v, while $\text{dec}(\_, \_)$, $\pi_1(\_)$, $\pi_2(\_)$ represent respectively the decryption and the left and right projections of a concatenation. We may write $\langle x, y, z \rangle$ for $\langle\langle x, y \rangle, z \rangle$. The set of ground terms (i.e. terms without variables) is denoted by $T(\mathcal{F})$. We divide the set $\mathcal{N}ames$ into three (infinite) subsets: $\mathcal{K}_1$ for honest keys, $\mathcal{K}_2$ for dishonest keys, and $\mathcal{N}$ for the nonces. The set $\mathcal{V}$ is divided into $\mathcal{V}_1 = \{x_1, x_2, \cdots\}$ and $\mathcal{V}_2 = \{y_1, y_2, \cdots\}$ that will be respectively used to store terms and equations.

We assume given a length function $l : T(\mathcal{F}) \mapsto H$ from ground terms to a set H that measures the symbolic length of a term. An example of a length function will be given in the Section 4.2.

We write $\{x_1 \mapsto u_1, \ldots, x_n \mapsto u_n\}$ for the substitution that maps x_i to u_i. The substitution is *ground* when every term u_i is ground. The application of a substitution σ to a term u is denoted $u\sigma$. The signature $\mathcal{F}$ is equipped with an equational theory, that is closed under application of function symbols, substitution of terms for variables. We write $M =_E N$ when the equation $M = N$ is in the theory E. We may omit the subscript E when it is clear from the context. In this paper, we will consider in particular the theory E_0 defined by the following (infinite, yet recursive) set of equations.

$$\text{dec}(\{x\}_k^z, k) = x \quad \text{for } k \in \mathcal{K}_1 \cup \mathcal{K}_2 \qquad \pi_1(\langle x, y \rangle) = x \qquad \pi_2(\langle x, y \rangle) = y$$

E_0 will then be enriched by the equalities created by the adversary.

The current knowledge of an adversary is represented by a *frame* $\phi = \nu\bar{n} \cdot \sigma$ where σ is a ground substitution that represents the messages accessible to the adversary while $\bar{n}$ denotes the private names (that the adversary does not know initially). From its knowledge ϕ, an attacker can then deduce any term that it can build from the terms in σ and applying function symbols and public names.

Definition 1 (deductibility). *A ground term s is deducible from $\phi = \nu\bar{n} \cdot \sigma$ and an equation set E (we write $\phi \vdash_E s$) if there exists a public term (i.e. not containing names from $\bar{n}$) R such that $R\sigma =_E s$.*

Example 8. Let $\phi = \nu n_1, n_2, n_3, r_1, r_2, r_3 \cdot \sigma$ with $\sigma = \{x_1 \mapsto \{n_1\}_{k_1}^{r_1}, x_2 \mapsto \langle\{n_2\}_{n_1}^{r_2}, \{n_3\}_{n_2}^{r_3}\rangle\}$. Then $\phi \vdash_{E_0} n_3$. The corresponding public term is : $R = \text{dec}(\pi_2(x_2), \text{dec}(\pi_1(x_2), \text{dec}(x_1, k_1)))$.

As in [CLC08b], we first extend the applied pi-calculus with predicates that represent the tests that an adversary can perform. We consider four predicates: $M(u)$ states whether a term u is valid (i.e. will have a computational interpretation); $EQ(u, v)$ checks whether two terms are equal; $P_{\text{samekey}}(u, v)$ checks whether u and v are two cyphertexts using the same key; and $EL(u, v)$ checks whether two terms have the same length. A formula, as defined in Figure 1, is a Boolean combination of these atomic formulas.

The processes are then defined as usual (in Figure 1) with the addition of two new constructors (*eq* and *neq*) that allow to generate new equalities or disequalities between terms. These constructions may appear in attackers processes, but not in the protocols.

The behaviour of a process depends on the equational theory. We therefore consider *localized process* E, X_w, X_c, P where E is a set of ground equations and disequations, that have already been added by the adversary, X_w and X_c are sets of variables and P is a process. The adversary will be allowed to add equations in E "on-the-fly" depending on what he learns. More precisely, when we need to evaluate a test, that involves dishonest keys, the attackers enters a "ADD" mode in which he has to commit to the (non)-validity of equalities containing

$\Phi_1, \Phi_2 ::=$	Formula
$\mathrm{EQ}(s,t), \mathrm{M}(s), \mathrm{P_{samekey}}(s,t), \mathrm{EL}(s,t)$	predicate application
$\Phi_1 \wedge \Phi_2$	conjunction
$\Phi_1 \vee \Phi_2$	disjunction
$\neg \Phi_1$	negation

$P, Q, R ::=$	Processes
$c(x) \cdot P, \bar{c}(s) \cdot P$	input, output on channel c
$eq(s,t) \cdot P, neq(s,t) \cdot P$	equation, disequation
$\mathbf{0}$	null process
$P \| Q$	parallel composition
$!P$	replication
$(\nu \alpha)P$	restriction
if Φ then P else Q	conditional

$A, B ::=$	Extended processes
P	process
$A \| B$	parallel composition
$(\nu \alpha)A$	restriction
$\{x \mapsto s\}$	substitution

For simplicity reasons we will often write if Φ then P else $\overline{c_{out}}(\bot)$ as $[\Phi]P$.

Fig. 1. Syntax of Formula and Processes

such keys. In this mode, the frame of P records, using the variables in X_w, the equalities that need a commitment. It also records, using the variables X_c, the equalities on which he committed since he entered the "ADD" mode. When leaving the mode, committed (dis)-equalities have been flushed in E.

Example 9. Let us consider the protocols of the Examples 4 and 5. For the sake of conciseness, we do not describe the role of A. We instead directly enrich the initial frame with the message emitted by A. We also make use of a pattern-matching notation like in ProVerif [Bla05]. For example, $c(\langle a, \{y\}_{k_{ab}} \rangle).\bar{c}(y)$ denotes the process $c(x).[(\pi_1(x) = a) \wedge M(\mathrm{dec}(\pi_2(x), k_{ab}))].\bar{c}(\mathrm{dec}(\pi_2(x), k_{ab}))$.

The process modeling the protocol described in Example 4 is:

$$P_4 = (\nu k, r, k_{AB})\{x \mapsto \{s\}_{k_{AB}}^r\} \| !c_{in}(\langle z_1, \{z_2\}_{k_{AB}} \rangle).[M(\mathrm{dec}(z_2, z_1))]\overline{c_{out}}(\mathbf{ok})$$

where $s = \{n\}_k^r$. Similarly, the process modeling Example 5 is:

$$P_5 = (\nu k, r, r_1, r_2, r_3, k_{AB})\{x_1 \mapsto \{a\}_{k_{AB}}^{r_2}, x_2 \mapsto k, x_3 \mapsto \{\{s\}_k^{r_1}, \{a\}_{k_{AB}}^{r_3}\}_{k_{AB}}^{r_2}\}$$
$$\| c_{in}(\{z_1, z_2\}_{k_{AB}}).[\mathrm{EQ}(z_1, z_2)]\overline{c_{out}}(\mathbf{bad})$$

where $s = \{n\}_k^r$.

3.2 Operational Semantics

Our operational semantics is inspired by the applied π-calculus. For localized processes of the form E, X_w, X_c, A, terms are interpreted in $T/E \cup E_0$. $E \cup E_0$

$$E, X_w, X_c, A\|\mathbf{0} \equiv E, X_w, X_c, A$$
$$E, X_w, X_c, A\|B \equiv E, X_w, X_c, B\|A$$
$$E, X_w, X_c, (A\|B)\|C \equiv E, X_w, X_c, A\|(B\|C)$$
$$E, X_w, X_c, (\nu\alpha)(\nu\beta)A \equiv E, X_w, X_c, (\nu\beta)(\nu\alpha)A$$
$$E, X_w, X_c, (\nu\alpha)(A\|B) \equiv E, X_w, X_c, A\|(\nu\alpha)B \qquad \text{if } \alpha \notin \mathrm{fn}(A) \cup \mathrm{fv}(A)$$
$$E, X_w, X_c, (\nu x)\{x \mapsto s\} \equiv E, X_w, X_c, \mathbf{0}$$
$$E, X_w, X_c, (\nu\alpha)\mathbf{0} \equiv E, X_w, X_c, \mathbf{0}$$
$$E, X_w, X_c, !P \equiv E, X_w, X_c, P\|!P$$
$$E, X_w, X_c, \{x \mapsto s\}\|A \equiv E, X_w, X_c, \{x \mapsto s\}\|A\{x \mapsto s\}$$
$$E, X_w, X_c, \{x \mapsto s\} \equiv E, X_w, X_c, \{x \mapsto t\} \qquad \text{if } s =_E t$$
$$E, \emptyset, X_c, P \equiv E, \emptyset, \emptyset, P$$

Fig. 2. Structural equivalence

is completed into a convergent rewriting system, that minimizes the number of destructors in a term. $t{\downarrow}_E$ will denote the normal form of the term t w.r.t. such a rewrite system. More generally, in what follows, when we refer to E, we will implicitly assume $E \cup E_0$.

Structural equivalence is very similar to applied π-calculus and is defined in Figure 2.

We first define the semantics of the four predicates as follows.

- $E \vDash M(s)$ if, for all subterms t of s, $t{\downarrow}_E$ does not contain destructors or variables and uses only keys in key position.
- $E \vDash \mathrm{EQ}(s,t)$ if $E \vDash M(s) \wedge M(t)$ and $s{\downarrow}_E = t{\downarrow}_E$.
- $E \vDash P_{\mathrm{samekey}}(s,t)$ if $E \vDash M(s) \wedge M(t)$ and $\exists k, u, v, r, r'$ such that $E \vDash \mathrm{EQ}(s, \{u\}_k^r) \wedge \mathrm{EQ}(t, \{v\}_k^{r'})$
- $E \vDash \mathrm{EL}(s,t)$ if $E \vDash M(s) \wedge M(t)$ and $l(s) = l(t)$.

The semantics of formulas is then defined as expected.

We are now ready to define how an attacker can add new equalities between terms. A first condition is that equalities should be *well-formed* in the sense that they should not contradict previously added equalities and they should involve either dishonest encryption or dishonest decryption.

Definition 2. *Let s and t be two ground terms such that $l(s) = l(t)$ and t is without destructors. An equation $s = t$ is well formed with respect to an equation set E, a set of expected equations Y and a frame ϕ (written $\mathrm{wf}_{Y,\phi}^E(s = t)$) if*

- $E \nvDash (s = t)$
- *if $(v \neq w) \in E$, $E \cup \{s = t\} \nvDash v = w$*
- $E \cup \{s = t\} \nvDash n = n'$ *with n, n' names and $n \neq n'$*
- $E \cup \{s = t\} \nvDash \{u\}_k^r = \{u'\}_{k'}^{r'}$ *with $k, k' \in \mathcal{K}_1$ and $k \neq k'$ or $r \neq r'$*
- $E \cup \{s = t\} \nvDash u = v$ *when u is a pair and v is not a pair or when u is a ciphertext and v is a private name.*

and the equation satisfies of one of the two following sets of conditions:

1. $s = \{u\}_k^r$ *with* $k \in \mathcal{K}_2$ *and* $\langle u, k, r, t, \mathrm{enc} \rangle \in Y$
2. $\phi, u \vdash t$
3. u *is in normal form for* E *and without destructors*

   i $s = \mathrm{dec}(u, k)$ *with* $k \in \mathcal{K}_2$ *and* $\langle u, k\,\mathrm{dec} \rangle \in Y$ *and* $(\mathrm{dec}(u, k) = *) \notin E$
   ii $\phi, u \vdash t$ *or* $t = \bot$
   iii u *is in normal form for* E, *without destructors, and* u *is either a public nonce or an encryption.*

Similarly, a disequation $(s \neq t)$ *is well formed, denoted* $\mathrm{wf}^E_{X, \phi}(s \neq t)$ *if* s *is also without destructors and*

   — $s = \{u\}_k^r$ *with* $k \in \mathcal{K}_2$ *and* $\langle u, k, r, t, \mathrm{enc} \rangle \in X$
   — $E \cup E_0 \nvdash s = t$

We define $\mathrm{wf}^E_\phi(e)$ *to hold if there exists* X *such that* $\mathrm{wf}^E_{X, \phi}(e)$ *holds.*

Intuitively, an adversary can add an equation of the form $\{u\}_k^r = t$ or $\mathrm{dec}(u, k) = t$ only if t deducible from ϕ, u since dishonest encryption and decryption must be function of the current knowledge ϕ and their input u.

After receiving a message, an agent typically checks the validity of some condition. This test may pass or fail, depending on the value of dishonest encryptions and decryptions performed during the test. As illustrated in Example 4, this may provide the adversary with an additional knowledge, which we define now:

Definition 3. *Let* E *be a set of ground equations,* φ *and* X *be two frames, and* Φ *be a formula. The* additional knowledge *induced by the condition* Φ *w.r.t.* E *and* X, *written* $K^E_{X, \varphi}(\Phi)$ *is the union of the two following sets :*
the set of all $\langle s, k, \mathrm{dec} \rangle$ *s.t.*

   — *There exists a literal* $\mathrm{M}(u)$ *in* Φ *such that* $\mathrm{dec}(s, t) \in St(u)$ *with* $E \vDash \mathrm{M}(s)$, $t{\downarrow}_E = k$ *and* $k \in \mathcal{K}_2$.
   — $E \nvDash \mathrm{M}(\mathrm{dec}(s, k))$ *(to ensure that the condition is not trivially true, in which case the adversary does not learn anything)*
   — $\forall y' \in \mathcal{V}_2, \forall s' =_E s, \{y' \mapsto \langle s', k, \mathrm{dec} \rangle\} \notin X$ *(avoiding redundancy)*

and the set of all $\langle s, k, r, v, \mathrm{enc} \rangle$ *s.t.*

   — *there exists a literal* $\mathrm{EQ}(t, u)$ *in* Φ *such that* $E \vDash \mathrm{M}(t) \wedge \mathrm{M}(u)$ *and* $t{\downarrow}_E = C[t_1, \cdots, t_n], u{\downarrow}_E = C[u_1, \cdots, u_n]$
   — *for all* $i \in \{1, \cdots, n\}$ *there exist* s_i *and* $k_i \in \mathcal{K}_2$ *such that*
     • *either* $t_i = \{s_i\}_{k_i}^{r_i}$ *and* $\mathrm{wf}^E_\varphi(t_i = u_i)$. *In that case we let* $v_i = u_i$.
     • *or* $u_i = \{s_i\}_{k_i}^{r_i}$ *and* $\mathrm{wf}^E_\varphi(u_i = t_i)$. *In that case we let* $v_i = t_i$.
   — $\exists i \in \{1 \cdots n\}$ *such that* $s_i = s, k_i = k, r_i = r, v_i = v$ *(we chose a pair of terms)*
   — $\forall y' \in \mathcal{V}_2, \{y' \mapsto \langle s, k, r, v, \mathrm{enc} \rangle\} \notin X$ *(to avoid redundancy)*.

Example 10. Back to Example 4 , $K^\emptyset_{\emptyset, (\nu s, r, k_{AB})\{x \mapsto \{s\}_{k_{AB}}^r\}}(\mathrm{M}(\mathrm{dec}(s, k)))$. Indeed, the only literal in the condition is $\mathrm{M}(\mathrm{dec}(s, k))$, and the knowledge set is empty, therefore $K^\emptyset_{\emptyset, (\nu s, r, k_{AB})\{x \mapsto \{s\}_{k_{AB}}^r\}}(\mathrm{M}(\mathrm{dec}(s, k))) = \langle s, k, \mathrm{dec} \rangle$.

$$\frac{\tilde{y} \text{ are the next } \#K^E_{\phi(P)_{|X_w},\phi(P)\backslash(X_w\cup X_c)}(t_\Phi(P)) \text{ free variables in } \mathcal{V}_2}{E,X_w,X_c,P \xrightarrow{\varepsilon} E,X_w\cup\{\tilde{y}\},X_c,P\|\{\tilde{y}\mapsto K^E_{X_w}(Pt_\Phi(P))\}} \text{ R-Add}$$

$$\frac{\text{wf}^E_{\phi(z),\phi\backslash(X_w\cup X_c)}(s=t) \qquad z\in X_w}{E,X_w,X_c,eq(s,t).P\|\phi \xrightarrow{\tau} E\cup\{s=t\},X_w\backslash z,X_c\cup\{z\},P\|\phi} \text{ R-Eq}$$

$$\frac{\text{wf}^E_{\phi(z),\phi\backslash(X_w\cup X_c)}(s\neq t) \qquad z\in X_w}{E,X_w,X_c,neq(s,t).P\|\phi \xrightarrow{\tau} E\cup\{s\neq t\},X_w\backslash z,X_c\cup\{z\},P\|\phi} \text{ R-Neq}$$

$$\frac{}{E,\emptyset,\emptyset,c(x).P\|\bar{c}(t).Q \xrightarrow{\tau} E,\emptyset,\emptyset,P\|Q\|\{x\mapsto t\}} \text{ R-Com}$$

$$\frac{E\cup E_0 \vDash \Phi}{E,\emptyset,\emptyset,\text{if } \Phi \text{ then } P \text{ else } Q \xrightarrow{\tau} E,\emptyset,\emptyset,P} \text{ R-Cond1}$$

$$\frac{E\cup E_0 \nvDash \Phi}{E,\emptyset,\emptyset,\text{if } \Phi \text{ then } P \text{ else } Q \xrightarrow{\tau} E,\emptyset,\emptyset,Q} \text{ R-Cond2}$$

$\phi(P)$ denotes the maximal frame which can be extracted from process P. If $X = \{x_1,\cdots,x_n\}$ is a set of terms (ordered), then $\{\tilde{y}\mapsto X\}$ denotes the frame $\{y_1\mapsto x_1,\cdots,y_n\mapsto x_n\}$. $\phi\backslash X$ stands for $\phi_{|\mathcal{V}\backslash X}$. $t_\Phi(P)$ is set of conditions that occurs in head in P, that is $t_\Phi(P) = \{\Phi_1,\ldots,\Phi_n\}$ if $P \equiv \nu\tilde{n}[\Phi_1]P_1\|\cdots\|[\Phi_n]P_n\|Q$ where n is maximal.

Fig. 3. Reduction semantics

The reduction semantics is defined in Figure 3. The rules R-Com, R-Cond1, R-Cond2 are the standard communication and conditional rules. Note that these rules require the sets X_w and X_c to be empty. The validity of a condition Φ may depend on the behavior of dishonest encryption/decryption performed when evaluating the condition. The R-Add rule adds to the frame the knowledge induced by the conditions that are about to be evaluated, making it available to the attacker. Simultaneously, R-Add adds in X_w the variables referring to all the equations that need to be decided before evaluating the conditions. It is then necessary to apply the rules R-Eq and R-Neq until X_w is empty, in order to decide whether each possible equality involving a dishonest encryption/decryption should be set at true or false.

The R-Add rule should be applied before evaluating a condition (i.e. before applying R-Cond1, R-Cond2). Therefore, we define $\rightarrow^*$ as the smallest transitive relation containing $\equiv$, $(\xrightarrow{\tau},\xrightarrow{\varepsilon})$ and closed by application of contexts.

We will write, if $t\#\tilde{n} : P \xrightarrow{c(t)} Q$ if $P \rightarrow^* E,X_w,X_c,(\nu\tilde{n})c(x).P'\|Q'$, and $E,X_w,X_c,(\nu\tilde{n})P'\|Q'\|\{x\mapsto t\} \xrightarrow{\varepsilon}\rightarrow^* Q$

We also write, if $t\#\tilde{n} : P \xrightarrow{\bar{c}(t)} Q$ if $P \rightarrow^* E,X_w,X_c,(\nu\tilde{n})\bar{c}(t).P'\|Q'$, and $E,X_w,X_c,(\nu\tilde{n})P'\|Q'\|\{x\mapsto t\} \xrightarrow{\varepsilon}\rightarrow^* Q$

We also write $E,X_w,X_c,P \xrightarrow{(n)eq(s,t)} E\cup\{s=t\},X'_w,X'_c,Q$ if we have $E,X_w,X_c,P\|(n)eq(s,t) \rightarrow^* E\cup\{s(\neq)=t\},X'_w,X'_c,Q$

3.3   Examples

We show how the computational attacks described in Section 2 are now reflected in our symbolic model.

For attacking the process P_4, we consider the following (symbolic) adversary:

$$A_4 = \overline{c_{in}}(\langle k, x \rangle).eq(\text{dec}(\pi_2(y_1)), n).\overline{c}(\pi_2(y_1))$$

With rule R-COM and some structural congruences, $\emptyset, \emptyset, \emptyset, A_4 \| P_4$ reduces to $\emptyset, \emptyset, \emptyset, Q_1$ where Q_1 is:

$$(\nu s, r, k_{AB})\{x \mapsto \{s\}^r_{k_{AB}}\} \| [\text{M}(\text{dec}(s, k))] \overline{c_{out}}(\mathbf{ok})$$
$$\| eq(\text{dec}(\pi_2(y_1)), n).\overline{c}(\pi_2(y_1)) \| \{z \mapsto \langle k, \{s\}^r_{k_{AB}} \rangle\}$$

As explained in Example 10, $K^{\emptyset}_{\emptyset, (\nu s, r, k_{AB})\{x \mapsto \{s\}^r_{k_{AB}}\}}(\text{M}(\text{dec}(s, k))) = \langle s, k, \text{dec}\rangle$. Applying R-ADD we get that $\emptyset, \emptyset, \emptyset, Q_1$ reduces to $\emptyset, \{y_1\}, \emptyset, Q_2$ where Q_2 is:

$$(\nu s, r, k_{AB})\{x \mapsto \{s\}^r_{k_{AB}}\} \| [\text{M}(\text{dec}(s, k))] \overline{c_{out}}(\mathbf{ok})$$
$$\| eq(\text{dec}(\pi_2(y_1)), n).\overline{c}(\pi_2(y_1)) \| \{z \mapsto \langle k, \{s\}^r_{k_{AB}} \rangle\} \| \{y_1 \mapsto \langle \text{dec}, s, k \rangle\}$$

With rule R-EQ and some structural congruences, as $\text{dec}(s, k) = n$ is well formed, we obtain $\{\text{dec}(s, k) = n\}, \emptyset, \{y_1\}, Q_3$ where Q_3 is:

$$(\nu s, r, k_{AB})\{x \mapsto \{s\}^r_{k_{AB}}\} \| [\text{M}(\text{dec}(s, k))] \overline{c_{out}}(\mathbf{ok})$$
$$\| \overline{c}(s) \| \{z \mapsto \langle k, \{s\}^r_{k_{AB}} \rangle\} \| \{y_1 \mapsto \langle \text{dec}, s, k \rangle\}$$

With rule R-COND1 and some structural equivalence, we have $\{\text{dec}(s, k) = n\}, \emptyset, \emptyset, Q_4$ where Q_4 is :

$$(\nu s, r, k_{AB})\{x \mapsto \{s\}^r_{k_{AB}}\} \| \{z \mapsto \langle k, \{s\}^r_{k_{AB}} \rangle\} \| \{y_1 \mapsto \langle \text{dec}, s, k \rangle\}$$
$$\| \overline{c_{out}}(\mathbf{ok}) \| \overline{c}(s)$$

The adversary is now able to emit s on channel c and, even if it was not necessary to learn s, the process P_4 has progressed to his last state, which would not have been possible with another symbolic model.

Let now show how we also capture the computational attack described for Example 5. The adversary is as follows :

$$A_5 = \overline{c_{in}}(x_3).eq(\{\pi_1(y_1)\}^{\pi_3(y_1)}_{\pi_2(y_1)}, x_1)$$

The localized process $\emptyset, \emptyset, \emptyset, P_5 \| A_5$ reduces in some steps to $\emptyset, \{y_1\}, \emptyset, Q_1$ where Q_1 is

$$(\nu s, r, r_1, r_2, k_{AB})\{x_1 \mapsto \{a\}^r_{k_{AB}}, x_2 \mapsto k, x_3 \mapsto \{\{s\}^{r_1}_k, \{a\}^r_{k_{AB}}\}^{r_2}_{k_{AB}}\}$$
$$\| \{z \mapsto \{\{s\}^{r_1}_k, \{a\}^r_{k_{AB}}\}^{r_2}_{k_{AB}}\} \| \{y_1 \mapsto \langle s, k, r_1, \{a\}^r_{k_{AB}}, \text{enc}\rangle\}$$
$$\| [\text{EQ}(\{s\}^{r_1}_k, \{a\}^r_{k_{AB}}] \overline{c_{out}}(\mathbf{bad}) \| eq(\{s\}^{r_1}_k, \{a\}^r_{k_{AB}})$$

$$\emptyset, \{y_1\}, \emptyset, Q_1 \xrightarrow{eq(\{s\}_k^{r_1}, \{a\}_{k_{AB}}^r, \varepsilon, \tau, \varepsilon)} \{\{s\}_k^{r_1} = \{a\}_{k_{AB}}^r\}, \emptyset, \emptyset, Q_2 \text{ where } Q_2 \text{ is :}$$

$$(\nu s, r, r_1, r_2, k_{AB})\{x_1 \mapsto \{a\}_{k_{AB}}^r, x_2 \mapsto k, x_3 \mapsto \{\{s\}_k^{r_1}, \{a\}_{k_{AB}}^r\}_{k_{AB}}^{r_2}\}$$

$$\|\{z \mapsto \{\{s\}_k^{r_1}, \{a\}_{k_{AB}}^r\}_{k_{AB}}^{r_2}\} \| \{y_1 \mapsto \langle s, k, r_1, \{a\}_{k_{AB}}^r, \text{enc} \rangle\}$$

$$\|\overline{c_{out}}(\mathbf{bad})$$

where P_5 is in the bad state we wanted to avoid.

3.4 Observational Equivalence

We recall the classical definition of observational equivalence, stating that there is no context (or adversary) yielding an emission on a channel c in one experiment, and no emission on c in the other experiment:

Definition 4 (observational equivalence). *An evaluation context is a process* $C = (\nu\bar{a})([\cdot]\|P)$ *where* P *is a process. We write* $C[Q]$ *for* $(\nu\bar{a})(Q\|P)$. *A context (resp. process) is called* closed *if* $\text{fv}(C) \cap \mathcal{V}_1 = \emptyset$. *Let us note that we do not forbid free names.*

The observational equivalence relation $\sim_o$ *is the largest equivalence relation on completed processes such that* $A \sim_o B$ *implies :*

- *If, for some evaluation context* C, *term* s *and process* A', $A \xrightarrow{*} C[\bar{c}(s) \cdot A']$, *then for some context* C', *term* s' *and process* B', $B \xrightarrow{*} C'[\bar{c}(s') \cdot B']$
- *If* $A \xrightarrow{*} A'$, *then for some* B', $B \xrightarrow{*} B'$ *and* $A' \sim_o B'$
- *For any closed evaluation context* C, $C[A] \sim_o C[B]$

In the proof, we also rely on static equivalence, in order to model the indistinguishability of two sequences of term for the adversary. Two frames ϕ, ϕ' are statically equivalent if, for any public term sequence $s_1, \ldots, s_k$ and any predicate p, $E \models p(s_1, \ldots, s_k)\phi$ iff $E \models p(s_1, \ldots, s_k)\phi'$.

4 Computational Interpretation

We only need a small fragment of our calculus in order to describe the vast majority of protocols. These are called *simple processes* and are built as described in Section 4.1. We then provide their computational interpretation in Section 4.2.

4.1 Simple Processes

Definition 5. *A simple condition with respect to a set of terms* S *is a conjunction of atomic formulas of one of the following forms :*

- $M(s)$ *where* s *contains only destructors, names and variables*
- $EQ(s_1, s_2)$ *where each* s_i *is of one of the two following forms :*
  - s_i *contains only destructors, names and variables*

- s_i *is a subterm of the a term in* S.
  We also exclude the case in which s_1 *and* s_2 *are two subterms of the frame.*

Let $\bar{x}$ be a sequence of variable in $\mathcal{V}_1$, i a name called *pid* (the process identifier), and $\bar{n}$ a sequence of names, S be a set of terms such that $\mathrm{fv}(S) \subseteq \bar{x}$ and $\mathrm{fn}(S) \subseteq \bar{n}$. We define recursively *basic processes* $\mathcal{B}(i, \bar{n}, \bar{x}, S)$ as follows.

- $\mathbf{0} \in \mathcal{B}(i, \bar{n}, \bar{x}, S)$
- If $B \in \mathcal{B}(i, \bar{n}, \bar{x}, S \cup \{s\})$, $s \in \mathcal{T}(\bar{n}, \bar{x})$, Φ is a simple condition with respect to S such that $\mathrm{fn}(\Phi) \subseteq \bar{n}$ and $\mathrm{fv}(\Phi) \subseteq \bar{x}$, then :

$$[\Phi \wedge \mathrm{M}(s)]\overline{c_{out}}(s).B \qquad \in \mathcal{B}(i, \bar{n}, \bar{x}, S)$$

  If Φ is true, the the process checks if s is well formed and sends it out.
- If $B \in \mathcal{B}(i, \bar{n}, \bar{x}, x, S)$ and $x \notin \bar{x}$ then

$$c_{in}(x) \cdot [\mathrm{EQ}(\pi_1(x), i)]B \qquad \in \mathcal{B}(i, \bar{n}, \bar{x}, S)$$

The process checks that it was the intended recipient of the message and processes it.

Basic processes are sequences of inputs and tests followed by an output. Else branches must be trivial. Basic processes are used to build *simple processes*.

Definition 6. *A* simple process *is obtained by composing and replicating basic processes, hiding some names and variables. Formally it is a process of the following form :*

$$(\nu\bar{n})[(\nu\bar{x}_1, \bar{n}_1 B_1 \| \sigma_1) \| \cdots \| (\nu\bar{x}_k, \bar{n}_k B_k \| \sigma_k) \|$$
$$!(\nu\bar{z}_1, l_1, \bar{m}_1 \overline{c_{out}}(\langle 1, l_1 \rangle)B_1') \| \cdots \| !(\nu\bar{z}_n, l_n, \bar{m}_n \overline{c_{out}}(\langle n, l_n \rangle)B_n')]$$

with $B_j \in \mathcal{B}(i_j, \bar{n} \uplus \bar{n}_j, \bar{x}_j, \emptyset)$, $\mathrm{dom}(\sigma_j) \subseteq \bar{x}_j$, $B_j' \in \mathcal{B}(l_j, \bar{n} \uplus \bar{m}_j, \bar{z}_j, \{l_j\})$. *Let us note that each replicated process outputs its pid in order to let the adversary communicate with it.*

We also assume that for every subterm $\{t\}_k^v$ *occurring in a process,* v *is a name which occur only in this term and is restricted. We allow several occurrences of the term* $\{t\}_k^v$. *This ensures that the randomness of an encryption is re-used somewhere else.*

In what follows, we also assume that no key cycle is generated by the process. This can be ensured by defining a key hierarchy.

4.2   Computational Model

As in [CLC08b] each simple process is interpreted as a network of Communicating Turing Machine (CTM), and we can relate each state of a process to a state of the corresponding Turing Machine. We assume that each Turing Machine has an independent random tape. We denote by τ the set of random tapes of the machines under consideration. The attacker controls the network: it is a CTM equipped with an additional control tape, that contains the CTM's id that will be used for the next communication. It may perform an internal transition, or a *send* (resp. *receive*) action, that copies the contents of its sending (resp.the designated CTM sending) tape to the designated CTM receiving (resp. its receiving) tape. In addition, it may perform a *new* action, creating a new copy of a machine implementing the replicated process specified on the control tape. We only give the implementation hypotheses here.

The implementation of the symmetric encryption is a joint IND-CPA and INT-CTXT symmetric encryption scheme. Let $\mathcal{K}$ be the key generation algorithm, $\mathcal{E}$ the encryption algorithm an $\mathcal{D}$ the decryption algorithm. All honest keys are drawn using $\mathcal{K}$ and, for any key k, message m, and randomness r, $\mathcal{D}(\mathcal{E}(m,k,r),k) = m$.

We assume that pairing is non ambiguous and that there are four different tags, one for the pairs, one for the encryptions, one for the keys and one for the honest nonces; every bitstring starts with the tag corresponding to the last constructor used to build it. Dishonest messages need not to be properly tagged. We assume that the symbolic length function l is such that two terms have the same length if and only if the corresponding bitstrings have the same length. It is easy to build such a function for example if the length of the nonces are proportional to the security parameter η, the computational length of pair is $|v\|w| = |v|+|w|+a.\eta$ for some a and the length of the encryption is $|\mathcal{E}(m,k,r)| = |m| + b.\eta$ for some b.

We also need to give the implementation of the predicates used by the simple processes : $[\![M]\!]$ is the set of bitstring which are different from $\perp$, and $[\![EQ]\!]$ is the set pairs of non $\perp$ identical bitstrings.

Let us note that for simple processes, the computation of the network answer to a request is always in polynomial time. This ensures that if the attacker is a PPT (with an oracle for the process), then running it with the process as oracle is still in polynomial time. We write $[\![P]\!]_\eta^\tau$ for the implementation of the simple process P with security parameter η and randomness τ. We will often write A_τ for the attacker using the random tape specified by τ.

5 Main Result

We show two main results. First, any computational trace is now reflected by a symbolic one, even in the presence of an attacker that dishonestly generates its keys. This allows to transfer all trace-based properties. Second, we show that we can also transfer equivalence-based properties, showing that observational equivalence implies computational indistinguishability.

5.1 Results

Let us start by defining the sequence of the messages exchanged between P and $\mathcal{A}$, and what it means for such a trace to be fully abstracted in the process P.

Note that, given τ and η, the behaviour of $\mathcal{A}$ interacting with P, denoted by $[\![P]\!]_\eta^\tau \| \mathcal{A}_\tau$, is deterministic.

Definition 7. *Given τ, let (γ_i) be the sequence of configurations preceding a send action in the deterministic computation of $\mathcal{A}_\tau$ interacting with $[\![P]\!]_\eta^\tau$. The execution sequence of $\mathcal{A}_\tau \| [\![P]\!]_\eta^\tau$ is the sequence $\gamma_1, L_1 \xrightarrow{m_1} \gamma_2, L_2 \cdots \xrightarrow{m_n} \gamma_n, L_n$ where m_i is the content of the sending tape in γ_i, $L_i = L_{i-1} \cdot m_{i-1} \cdot R_i$ and R_i is the sequence of contents of the receiving tape along the computation from γ_{i-1} to γ_i $(L_1 = R_1)$.*

Let us now define *symbolic traces* of a process P as the sequence of terms exchanged with the adversary:

Definition 8. $s = \alpha_1. \cdots . \alpha_n$ *is a trace of P if $\emptyset, \emptyset, \emptyset, P \xrightarrow{\alpha_1} E^1, X_w^1, X_c^1, P_1 \xrightarrow{\alpha_2} \cdots \xrightarrow{\alpha_n} E^n, X_w^n, X_c^n, P_n$ and for all $i \le n$ if $\alpha_i = c_{in}(t_i)$, then $P_{i-1} = P' \| \phi$ with ϕ a frame and $\phi \vdash_{E_{i-1}} t_i$.*

The full abstraction property states that a computational execution is the interpretation of some symbolic trace:

Definition 9 (Full abstraction). *Let $\gamma_1, L_1 \xrightarrow{m_1} \gamma_2, L_2 \cdots \xrightarrow{m_n} \gamma_n, L_n$ be an execution, s be a trace of P. Let us write $s = \alpha_1. \cdots . \alpha_m$. Let $\alpha_{n_1} \cdots \alpha_{n_k}$ be the subsequence of s which are inputs.*

s fully abstracts $\gamma_1, L_1 \xrightarrow{m_1} \gamma_2, L_2 \cdots \xrightarrow{m_n} \gamma_n, L_n$ if $k = n$ and $\forall j \le n$

- *$\alpha_{n_j} = c_{in}(t_j)$ and $[\![t_j]\!]_\eta^\tau = m_j$*
- *If $P \xrightarrow{\alpha_1. \cdots . \alpha_{n_{j+1}-1}} E^j, X_c^j, X_w^j, Q^j \| \phi^j$ with Q^j not containing active substitutions, then*
  - *$[\![Q^j]\!]_\eta^\tau = \gamma_j$*
  - *$[\![\phi_j \cap \{x \mapsto t | t \in \mathcal{T}, x \in \mathcal{V}_1\}]\!]_\eta^\tau = L_j$*
  - *$\forall (s = t) \in E^j, [\![s]\!]_\eta^\tau = [\![t]\!]_\eta^\tau$*
  - *$\forall (s \ne t) \in E^j, [\![s]\!]_\eta^\tau \ne [\![t]\!]_\eta^\tau$*

A computational trace Γ is fully abstracted *if there exists a trace s of the process P which fully abstracts Γ.*

We are now able to give our full abstraction theorem :

Theorem 1. *Let P be a simple process without key cycles. For every PPT $\mathcal{A}$, for every security parameter η, the sequence $\mathrm{Messages}(P, \eta, \tau)$ is fully abstracted with overwhelming probability (over τ).*

This result ensures that it is sufficient to prove trace properties in our model for them to hold in the computational model. Our second result is the computational soundness of observational equivalence.

Theorem 2. *Let P and Q be two simple processes without key cycles, such that $P \sim_o Q$. Then $[\![P]\!] \approx [\![Q]\!]$.*

This second result allows us to prove any indistinguishability property in our model instead of proving it in a computational setting.

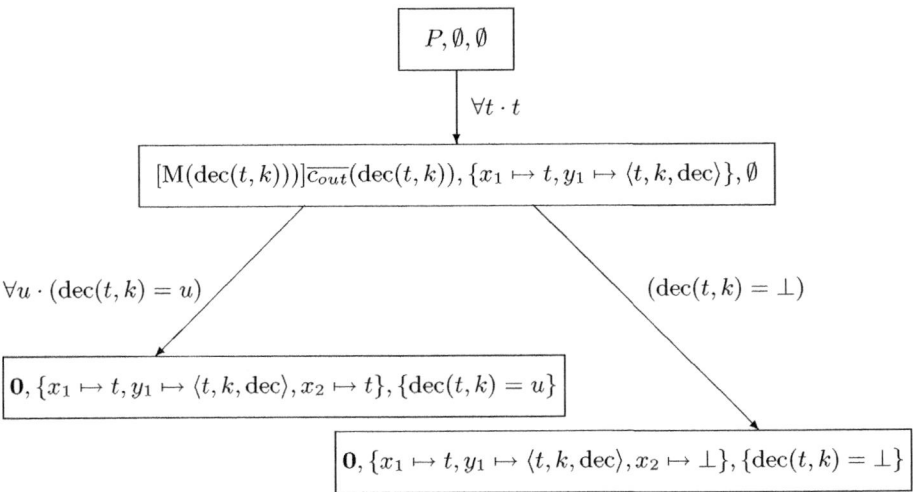

The edge labelled by $\forall t \cdot t$ is in fact a multiple edge representing the edges t for all t. As well the edge $\forall u \cdot (\text{dec}(t, k) = u)$ is a multiple edge representing the edge for all u.

Fig. 4. Process execution tree corresponding to the process $P = c_{in}(x) \cdot$ if $\text{M}(\text{dec}(x, k))$ then $\overline{c_{out}}(x)$ else $\overline{c_{out}}(\perp)$ with k dishonest

5.2   Sketch of Proof

The main tool of the proof of Theorem 2 is the use of execution trees. The execution tree of a process is the set of traces of a process organized in a tree. An example is provided in Figure 4. An execution tree is not necessarily the execution tree of a process. This generalization allows to consider transformations on process trees, which would not have being possible directly on processes.

The proof then proceeds in the following steps.

1. We show that the observational equivalence of processes transfers to equivalence of process execution trees.
2. We then replace all honest encryptions in a process tree by encryption of zeros, showing that the trees are symbolically equivalent.
3. If two trees are equivalent, then their computational interpretation are indistinguishable.
4. The only result left to prove is that a process is computationally indistinguishable from its process tree. As all the traces are listed in the tree, this amounts in proving Theorem 1. For this, we need to classify the cases in which the full abstraction fails, and we then add these failure cases in the execution trees (this is the originality of our approach with respect to [CLC08b]) and prove that these cases can not be found with a non negligible probability by the adversary given the computational hypotheses.

6   Application

We show how our framework can be used to show the computational security
for protocols, even in the case where the attacker can create interesting equalities between ciphertexts using dishonest keys. This section also demonstrates
that our symbolic model does not over-approximate too much the behavior of
computational attackers: our model is fine enough to complete security proof.

6.1   Specification of the Protocol

We describe below a protocol that is designed in such a way that honest participants may indeed use dishonest keys, making the security proof more challenging.
The protocols aims at securely transmitting s_{AB} from B to A. We will use N as
a shortcut for $\{N'\}_{k_N}^{r_N}$ where k_N is a secret key known only to $\mathbf{A}$. We actually
simply need N to be of type cyphertext to make our example more interesting.

$$\mathbf{A} \longrightarrow \mathbf{B}\ k_1, \{\{\{k_2\}_{k_3}\}_{k_1}, N\}_{k_{AB}}$$
$$\mathbf{B} \longrightarrow \mathbf{A}\ \{\{k_2\}_{k_3}, N\}_{k_{AB}}$$
$$\mathbf{A} \longrightarrow \mathbf{B}\ \{N, k_3\}_{k_{AB}}$$
$$\mathbf{B} \longrightarrow \mathbf{A}\ \{s_{AB}\}_{k_2}$$

k_{AB} is a long term shared key between A and B, the keys k_1, k_2, and k_3 are
fresh and N is a fresh "session" nonce.

We first specify this protocol in the applied π-calculus, using a syntax with
pattern matching for simplicity reasons. The interpretation is that the protocol
checks with M and EQ all the constraints given by the pattern matching. For the
sake of clarity, we omit the verifications of process session identifiers. But it would
be easy to transform our process into a simple process. Instead of restricting all
the names used in N, we simply write (νN) as a shortcut for $(\nu N', k_N, r_N)$.

$$P_A = (\nu k_1, k_2, k_3, N, r_1, r_2, r_3, r_4)\overline{c_{out}}(\langle k_1, \{\{\{k_2\}_{k_3}^{r_1}\}_{k_1}^{r_2}, N\}_{k_{AB}}^{r_3}\rangle).$$
$$c_{in}(\{\{k_2\}_{k_3}^{r_1}, N\}_{k_{AB}}^{-}).\overline{c_{out}}(\{N, k_3\}_{k_{AB}}^{r_4})$$
$$P_B = (\nu r_5, r_6)c_{in}(\langle x_1, \{\{x\}_{x_1}^{-}, x_N\}_{k_{AB}}^{-}\rangle).\overline{c_{out}}(\{x, x_N\}_{k_{AB}}^{r_5}).$$
$$c_{in}(\{x_N, x_3\}_{k_{AB}}^{-}).[\mathrm{M}(\mathrm{dec}(x, x_3))]\overline{c_{out}}(\{s_{AB}\}_{\mathrm{dec}(x,x_3)}^{r_6})$$

The process we consider is $(\nu k_{AB}, s_{AB})!P_B \| !P_A$ and the security property we
want to prove is as follows. For every $\mathcal{A}$ PPT with an oracle :

$$\mathrm{Pr}(\mathcal{A}\|[(\nu k_{AB}, s_{AB})!P_B\|!P_A] \to s_{AB}) = \mathrm{negl}(\eta)$$

where for a PPT M, $M \leftarrow m$ stands for M accepts writing m on its output
tape.

This *a priori* not straightforward since introducing dishonest keys allows the
attacker to tamper with the normal behavior of the protocol. For example, the
adversary can learn any instance of N and can obtain as output $\{u, k_3^l\}_{k_{AB}}$ where
u is any deducible term, with k_3^l an instance of k_3. Indeed, once the attacker
knows $\{N, k_3\}_{k_{AB}}$, it can forward it to B together with a dishonest key, that is

sending $k_1^*, \{N, k_3\}_{k_{AB}}$. As explained in Example 4, attempting to decrypt with the dishonest key k_1^* potentially reveals N to the attacker. Then for any deducible message u, the attacker can forge a dishonest key k_2^* such that $\text{dec}(N, k_2^*) = u$, which allows the attacker to obtain $\{u, k_3^l\}_{k_{AB}}$ from B.

6.2   Security

Despite the behaviors described in the preceding section, the protocol is secure and we are able to prove it. Applying Theorem 1, it is sufficient to prove weak secrecy in our symbolic model, that is, it is sufficient to prove the following proposition.

Proposition 1. *The process* $(\nu k_{AB}, s_{AB})!P_B \| !P_A \| c_{in}(x).[x = s_{AB}].\overline{c_{error}}$ *never emits on channel* c_{error}.

The process $c_{in}(x).[x = s_{AB}].\overline{c_{error}}$ serves as a witness, checking whether the intruder is able to emit s_{AB}. The idea of the proof is that the second component of the pair is only transmitted,so dishonnest keys will not help learning something about it, and the k_3 stays secret, which ensures that k_2 also stays secret. This is formally proved by computing on over-approximation of the messages learned by the attacker.

7   Conclusion

We designed a symbolic model, for which the observational equivalence is sound, even when the attacker may forge his own keys. We believe that it is the first result on computational soundness considering dishonest keys.

We assumed in this work that the processes do not contain non-trivial conditional branching and no nested replications, but it should not be very hard to extend our results to these cases.

Another issue, that might be the subject of future work, concerns the automatisation of the proofs of observational equivalence, in this new model. It is likely that deducibility constraint solving can be extended to ground equational theories, which is what we need.

A full version of this paper, including the proofs, is available on the Cryptology ePrint Archive at http://eprint.iacr.org/2012/008.

References

[AF01]   Abadi, M., Fournet, C.: Mobile values, new names, and secure communication. In: Principles of Programming Languages (POPL 2001), pp. 104–115 (2001)

[AG99]   Abadi, M., Gordon, A.D.: A calculus for cryptographic protocols: the spi calculus. Information and Computation 148(1) (1999)

[AR00]   Abadi, M., Rogaway, P.: Reconciling Two Views of Cryptography: the Computational Soundness of Formal Encryption. In: Watanabe, O., Hagiya, M., Ito, T., van Leeuwen, J., Mosses, P.D. (eds.) TCS 2000. LNCS, vol. 1872, pp. 3–22. Springer, Heidelberg (2000)

[BHO09]   Bana, G., Hasebe, K., Okada, M.: Computational Semantics for First-Order Logical Analysis of Cryptographic Protocols. In: Cortier, V., Kirchner, C., Okada, M., Sakurada, H. (eds.) Formal to Practical Security. LNCS, vol. 5458, pp. 33–56. Springer, Heidelberg (2009)

[Bla05]   Blanchet, B.: An automatic security protocol verifier based on resolution theorem proving (invited tutorial). In: 20th International Conference on Automated Deduction (CADE-20), Tallinn, Estonia (July 2005)

[Bla08]   Blanchet, B.: A computationally sound mechanized prover for security protocols. IEEE Trans. on Dependable and Secure Computing 5(4), 193–207 (2008); Special issue IEEE Symposium on Security and Privacy (2006)

[BP04]   Backes, M., Pfitzmann, B.: Symmetric encryption in a simulatable dolev-yao style cryptographic library. In: Proc. IEEE Computer Security Foundations Workshop (2004)

[BPW03]   Backes, M., Pfitzmann, B., Waidner, M.: A composable cryptographic library with nested operations. In: Proc. 10th ACM Concerence on Computer and Communications Security, CCS 2003 (2003)

[CC11]   Comon-Lundh, H., Cortier, V.: How to prove security of communication protocols? A discussion on the soundness of formal models w.r.t. computational ones. In: 28th Annual Symposium on Theoretical Aspects of Computer Science (STACS 2011). LIPIcs, vol. 9, pp. 29–44 (2011)

[CLC08a] Comon-Lundh, H., Cortier, V.: Computational soundness of observational equivalence. In: ACM Conf. Computer and Communication Security, CCS 2008 (2008)

[CLC08b] Comon-Lundh, H., Cortier, V.: Computational soundness of observational equivalence. Research Report RR-6508, INRIA (2008)

[DY81]   Dolev, D., Yao, A.C.: On the security of public key protocols. In: Proc. IEEE Symp. on Foundations of Computer Science, pp. 350–357 (1981)

[KT09]   Küsters, R., Tuengerthal, M.: Computational Soundness for Key Exchange Protocols with Symmetric Encryption. In: 16th ACM Conference on Computer and Communications Security (CCS 2009), pp. 91–100 (2009)

[RS98]   Ryan, P., Schneider, S.: An attack on a recursive authentication protocol: a cautionary tale. Information Processing Letters 65, 7–10 (1998)

[War03]   Warinschi, B.: A computational analysis of the needham-schroeder(-lowe) protocol. In: 16th Computer Science Foundation Workshop (CSFW 2003), pp. 248–262 (2003)

Reduction of Equational Theories for Verification of Trace Equivalence: Re-encryption, Associativity and Commutativity*

Myrto Arapinis, Sergiu Bursuc, and Mark D. Ryan

School of Computer Science, University of Birmingham**
{m.d.arapinis,s.bursuc,m.d.ryan}@cs.bham.ac.uk

Abstract. Verification of trace equivalence is difficult to automate in general because it requires relating two infinite sets of traces. The problem becomes even more complex when algebraic properties of cryptographic primitives are taken in account in the formal model. For example, no verification tool or technique can currently handle automatically a realistic model of re-encryption or associative-commutative operators.

In this setting, we propose a general technique for reducing the set of traces that have to be analyzed to a set of local traces. A local trace restricts the way in which some function symbols are used, and this allows us to perform a second reduction, by showing that some algebraic properties can be safely ignored in local traces.

In particular, local traces for re-encryption will contain only a bounded number of re-encryptions for any given ciphertext, leading to a sound elimination of equations that model re-encryption. For associativity and commutativity, local traces will determine a canonical use of the associative-commutative operator, where reasoning modulo AC is no stronger than reasoning without AC.

We illustrate these results by considering a non-disjoint combination of equational theories for the verification of vote privacy in Prêt à Voter. ProVerif can not handle the input theory as it is, but it does terminate with success on the theory obtained using our reduction result.

1 Introduction

Equivalence of formal processes, typically under the form of observational equivalence or trace equivalence, is fundamental in modeling security properties related to privacy. Some examples are strong secrecy [7], resistance against guessing attacks [14], authentication [3], unlinkability and anonymity [4], etc. Process equivalence can also be used to verify that a system implementation

---

* A long version of the paper and the ProVerif code are available online.
** We gratefully acknowledge financial support from EPSRC via the projects *Trust Domains* (TS/I002529/1) and *Trustworthy Voting Systems* (EP/G02684X/1).

P. Degano and J.D. Guttman (Eds.): POST 2012, LNCS 7215, pp. 169–188, 2012.
© Springer-Verlag Berlin Heidelberg 2012

conforms to a given system specification [3]. Another example is ballot secrecy in electronic voting [20], which is of particular relevance for this paper.

In order to not miss attacks, and sometimes even to be able to execute the protocols, the formal model has to take into account relevant algebraic properties of cryptographic primitives that are used [17]. The integration of algebraic properties in models and tools for automated verification of reachability properties, like secrecy, has been quite successful. However, only few results are known for verification of process equivalence. They are in general restricted to a bounded number of sessions and a basic Dolev-Yao theory [22,29,9,10], and do not go further than subterm-convergent theories [5,15], where the right-hand side of each equation is either a constant or a subterm of the left-hand side. ProVerif can handle an unbounded number of sessions and a broad class of equational theories [8], but may not terminate and may discover false attacks. None of the above-mentioned techniques can handle associative-commutative properties, like those of XOR, abelian groups, Diffie-Hellman, etc.

The starting point of our work is a case study that can not be handled by ProVerif, namely analysis of vote privacy in Prêt à Voter (PaV) [28]. Privacy in many electronic voting systems, not only in PaV, is based on a re-encryption mixnet, whose role is to break the link between ballots that are cast and ballots that are decrypted. A realistic model for such protocols has to contain not only equations that model re-encryption, but also at least equations for the associative-commutative properties of the underlying group and for the zero-knowledge proofs output by the mixnet. However, ProVerif does not terminate for PaV even when only the single re-encryption equation $\mathsf{renc}(\mathsf{enc}(x, y, z), z') = \mathsf{enc}(x, y, f(z, z'))$ is considered along with the standard Dolev-Yao theory for public-key encryption.

Our contributions. We show how, in general, trace equivalence modulo a non-disjoint combination $\mathcal{E} \cup \mathcal{E}_{\mathsf{renc}} \cup \mathsf{AC}$, can be reduced to trace equivalence modulo $\mathcal{E}'$ - a slightly augmented version of $\mathcal{E}$. If $\mathcal{E}$ is subterm-convergent, then $\mathcal{E}'$ is subterm-convergent as well. In particular, ProVerif terminates with success for $\mathcal{E}'_{\mathsf{PaV}}$ - the result of applying our reduction to the combination of theories suggested above. The main idea in the construction of $\mathcal{E}'$ is to anticipate in advance the maximal number of re-encryptions that are necessary to apply for any given ciphertext. We only prove the soundness of the given reduction in this paper. This means that our reduction may fail to prove that some processes are equivalent, but the value of the proposed approach is shown by our ability to carry an automated proof of privacy for PaV. This is a first automated proof of trace equivalence for protocols relying on re-encryption and AC symbols.

Related work. The idea of bounding the number of application of rewrite rules is similar to the finite variant property [13] and has already been helpful to make ProVerif work modulo XOR [25]. Less like [13], and more like [25], our bound is not intrinsic to the theory, but comes from a restriction on the class of protocols. Another similarity with [25] is in our way of removing AC, but we will show that there is a fundamental difference when one considers equivalence properties. The reduction of [25], and also the one for Diffie-Hellman in [24], have also been proven to be complete. On the other hand, these reductions are restricted to reachability properties, and do not cover equivalence properties. Furthermore, they consider a representation of protocols in terms of Horn clauses, which limits the aplicability of their results to ProVerif (or other tools based on Horn clauses) and is less general than the applied pi-calculus [2], that we use. [27,26] also consider abstractions of Diffie-Hellman and show that they are sound for reachability properties. Diffie-Hellman has some similarities with re-encryption, but the interaction of re-encryption with encryption is making it significantly different.

If results for process equivalence are limited to subterm-convergent theories [22,29,9,10,5,15], results for static equivalence go further than that. [1] shows decidability in presence of blind signatures and homomorphic encryption (without AC), and there is also a tool available [6]. Furthermore, the theory and implementation of [11] cover also trapdoor bit-commitment and malleable encryption. Malleable encryption is similar to re-encryption, but it is not associative-commutative: the value of the random can be changed, but it does not depend on its previous value. There are also results showing that algorithms for static equivalence can be combined for disjoint theories [16], and that a function symbol can be eliminated from the theory if it respects a hierarchy of sorts [23]. Our theory is a non-disjoint combination of encryption, re-encryption and other cryptographic primitives. Furthermore, [23] can not be applied to separate re-encryption from encryption, because a strict hierarchy of sorts can not be established due to the presence of the equation $\mathsf{renc}(\mathsf{enc}(x, y, z), z') = \mathsf{enc}(x, y, f(z, z'))$.

2   Preliminaries

2.1   Terms and Equational Theories

We start with an infinite set of constants $\mathcal{N}$, called names, and an infinite set of variables $\mathcal{X}$. Given a finite signature $\mathcal{F}$, $\mathcal{N}' \subseteq \mathcal{N}$ and $\mathcal{X}' \subseteq \mathcal{X}$, we denote by $\mathcal{T}(\mathcal{F}, \mathcal{N}', \mathcal{X}')$ the set of terms obtained by recursively applying symbols from $\mathcal{F}$ to elements from $\mathcal{N}' \cup \mathcal{X}'$. Terms will be denoted by $u, v, s, t, \ldots$, variables by $x, y, z, \ldots$, and names by $n, m, r, \ldots$ We let $\mathcal{F}_0$ be the set of constants in $\mathcal{F}$.

For a term t, we will denote by $\mathsf{var}(t)$ the set of its variables, by $\mathsf{st}(t)$ the set of its subterms and by $\mathsf{sig}(t)$ the set of function symbols that occur in t. We say that a term is ground if $\mathsf{var}(t) = \emptyset$. A *term context* $\mathsf{C}[\_]$ is a term that has a special symbol $\_$, called hole, in place of a subterm. The application of $\mathsf{C}[\_]$ to a term t is the term $\mathsf{C}[t]$, i.e. the result of replacing the hole with t.

Given three terms t, u, v, we denote by $t\{u \mapsto v\}$ the term obtained from t by replacing every occurence of u with v. A *replacement* ρ is a partial function from terms to terms: if $\rho = \{u_1 \mapsto v_1, \ldots, u_n \mapsto v_n\}$, we have $\mathsf{dom}(\rho) = \{u_1, \ldots, u_n\}$ and $\mathsf{ran}(\rho) = \{v_1, \ldots, v_n\}$. We assume that $u_1, \ldots, u_n$ are ordered such that $u_i \in \mathsf{st}(u_j) \implies j < i$. Then, for any term t, the application of ρ to t is $t\rho = t\{u_1 \mapsto v_1\} \ldots \{u_n \mapsto v_n\}$.

A *substitution* σ is a replacement with $\mathsf{dom}(\sigma) \subseteq \mathcal{X}$. Substitutions will be denoted by $\sigma, \theta, \tau \ldots$, whereas replacements will be denoted by (annotations of) ρ.

The composition of two substitutions σ and θ is a substitution $\sigma \circ \theta$ defined by the set $\{x \mapsto (x\sigma)\theta \mid x \in \mathsf{dom}(\sigma)\} \cup \{x \mapsto x\theta \mid x \in \mathsf{dom}(\theta) \smallsetminus \mathsf{dom}(\sigma)\}$. Given a substitution σ, if the composition $\sigma \circ \ldots \circ \sigma$ has a finite least fix point we denote it by σ^*, i.e. we have $\sigma^* = \sigma \circ \ldots \circ \sigma$ and $\sigma^* \circ \sigma = \sigma^*$. Note that, if the variables in $\mathsf{dom}(\sigma)$ can be ordered as $x_1, \ldots, x_n$ such that $i < j \implies x_j \notin \mathsf{var}(x_i\sigma)$, then σ^* exists. The restriction of a substitution σ to a set $\mathcal{V} \subseteq \mathsf{dom}(\sigma)$ is denoted by $\sigma|_{\mathcal{V}}$.

An equational theory is given by a pair $\mathcal{E} = (\mathcal{R}, \mathsf{AC}_\mathcal{S})$, where $\mathsf{AC}_\mathcal{S}$ is a set of equations modeling the associativity and commutativity of symbols in $\mathcal{S} \subseteq \mathcal{F}$ and $\mathcal{R}$ is a rewrite system convergent modulo $\mathsf{AC}_\mathcal{S}$. The rules of $\mathcal{R}$ are written as $l \to r$, with $l, r \in \mathcal{T}(\mathcal{F}, \mathcal{X})$ and $\mathsf{var}(r) \subseteq \mathsf{var}(l)$. Given a rewrite system $\mathcal{R}$, there is a rewriting step (resp. rewriting step modulo $\mathsf{AC}_\mathcal{S}$) from u to v if $u = \mathsf{C}[w]$, $w = l\sigma$ (resp. $w =_{\mathsf{AC}_\mathcal{S}} l\sigma$) and $v = \mathsf{C}[r\sigma]$, for some context C, rewrite rule $l \to r \in \mathcal{R}$ and substitution σ. The term w is called a redex. The normal form of a term t with respect to $\mathcal{R}$ (resp. modulo $\mathsf{AC}_\mathcal{S}$) will be denoted by $t{\downarrow}$ (resp. $t{\downarrow}_{\mathsf{AC}}$), or by $t{\downarrow}_\mathcal{R}$ (resp. $t{\downarrow}_{\mathcal{R},\mathsf{AC}}$) when $\mathcal{R}$ is not clear from the context. Then, we have by definition $u =_\mathcal{E} v$ if and only if $u{\downarrow}_{\mathcal{R},\mathsf{AC}} =_{\mathsf{AC}} v{\downarrow}_{\mathcal{R},\mathsf{AC}}$. The existence of a rewriting step (resp. modulo AC) from u to v will be denoted by $u \to v$ (resp. $u \to_{\mathsf{AC}} v$). Relying on the convergence of $\mathcal{R}$, we can restrict ourselves to bottom-up rewriting steps, i.e. all the strict subterms of a redex are in normal form. For two terms u, v, we write $u = v$ to denote their syntactic equality, $u =_\mathcal{E} v$ to denote their equality modulo $\mathcal{E}$, and $u =_{\mathsf{AC}} v$ to denote their equality modulo $\mathsf{AC}_\mathcal{S}$.

An equational theory $(\mathcal{R}, \emptyset)$ is subterm-convergent if for every rule $l \to r \in \mathcal{R}$, we have $r \in \mathsf{st}(l) \cup \mathcal{F}_0$. To avoid confusion, when the equational theory is not clear from the context, we annotate all our symbols by the theory to which they refer to.

Example 1. The classical Dolev-Yao theory for public-key encryption is modeled by the signature $\mathcal{F}_{\mathsf{DY}} = \{\mathsf{enc}, \mathsf{dec}, \mathsf{pub}, \langle, \rangle, \pi_1, \pi_2\}$ and the subterm-convergent equational theory $\mathcal{E}_{\mathsf{DY}} = (\mathcal{R}_{\mathsf{DY}}, \emptyset)$, where

$$\mathcal{R}_{\mathsf{DY}} = \{\, \mathsf{dec}(\mathsf{enc}(x, \mathsf{pub}(y)), z), y) \to x, \; \pi_1(\langle x, y \rangle) = x, \; \pi_2(\langle x, y \rangle) = y \,\}$$

The re-encryption property of public-key encryption schemes like El-Gamal can be modeled by the signature $\mathcal{F}_{\mathsf{renc}} = \{\mathsf{enc}, \mathsf{renc}, f\}$ and the equational theory $\mathcal{E}_{\mathsf{renc}} = (\mathcal{R}_{\mathsf{renc}}, \mathsf{AC}_f)$, where

$$\mathcal{R}_{\mathsf{renc}} = \begin{cases} \mathsf{renc}(\mathsf{enc}(x, y, z), z') \to \mathsf{enc}(x, y, f(z, z')) \\ \mathsf{renc}(\mathsf{renc}(x, z), z') \to \mathsf{renc}(x, f(z, z')) \end{cases}$$

2.2   Processes and Operational Semantics

To model communication channels we consider a distinct set of constants Ch such that $\mathsf{Ch} \cap (\mathcal{N} \cup \mathcal{F}) = \emptyset$. Elements of Ch are called channel names and will be typically denoted by $a, b, c, \ldots$ Processes of our calculus are defined by the following grammar [2]:

$A, B := 0$	plain processes		$P, Q :=$	processes
$A \mid B$	$\bar{c}\langle u \rangle.A$	$c(x).A$ $\quad \nu n.A$	A	$\nu x.P$ $\quad \nu n.P$
$!A$	if $u = v$ then A else B		$P \mid Q$	$\{x \mapsto u\}$

A name n that occurs in a process P is bound if it occurs under a νn, otherwise it is free. A variable x that occurs in P is bound if it occurs under a νx or under a $c(x)$, otherwise it is free. We will denote by $\mathsf{bn}(P), \mathsf{bv}(P), \mathsf{bv}(P)$, resp. $\mathsf{fv}(P)$ the bound names (including channel names), free names, bound variables and resp. free variables of P. By α-conversion of bound names and variables we will always assume that $\mathsf{bn}(P) \cap \mathsf{fn}(P) = \emptyset, \mathsf{bv}(P) \cap \mathsf{fv}(P) = \emptyset$, and there are no two distinct binders for the same name or the same variable. We denote by P^α the process obtained by substituting every bound name and variable in P with a fresh one. A process P is *closed* if any variable in P is either bound or occurs in a subprocess of the form $\{x \mapsto u\}$. A *process context* $\mathsf{C}[\_]$ is a process that has a special symbol $\_$, called hole, in the place of a sub-process. The application of $\mathsf{C}[\_]$ to a process P is $\mathsf{C}[P]$, i.e. the result of replacing the hole with P. An *evaluation context* is a process context whose hole is not in the scope of a replication, a conditional, an input, or an output. We let $\mathsf{sp}(P) = \{Q \mid \exists \mathsf{C}[\_]. \ P = \mathsf{C}[Q]\}$ be the set of sub-processes, $\mathsf{st}(P)$ be the set of terms (and their subterms) and $\mathsf{sig}(P) = \mathsf{sig}(\mathsf{st}(P))$ be the set of function symbols that occur in P.

Structural equivalence is the smallest equivalence relation $\equiv$ on processes that is closed under the application of evaluation contexts and the application of the following equations:

$$P \mid 0 \equiv P; \quad \nu u.0 \equiv 0; \quad !P \equiv P^\alpha \mid !P; \quad P \mid Q \equiv Q \mid P; \quad \nu u.\nu w.P \equiv \nu w.\nu u.P$$
$$P \mid (Q \mid R) \equiv (P \mid Q) \mid R; \quad P \mid \nu u.Q \equiv \nu u.(P \mid Q), \text{ if } u \notin \mathsf{fn}(P) \cup \mathsf{fv}(P)$$

A *frame* ϕ is a (static) process of the form $\nu \tilde{n}.\nu \tilde{x}.\sigma$, where $\tilde{n}$ is a sequence of names in $\mathcal{N}$, $\tilde{x}$ is a sequence of variables and σ is a substitution such that σ^* exists. We have $\mathsf{bn}(\phi) = \tilde{n}$ and $\mathsf{dom}(\phi) = \mathsf{dom}(\sigma) \smallsetminus \tilde{x}$. The set of *recipes* for ϕ is defined as $\mathfrak{R}(\phi) = \mathcal{T}(\mathcal{F}, \mathcal{N} \smallsetminus \mathsf{bn}(\phi), \mathsf{dom}(\phi))$. Recipes will sometimes be denoted by $\zeta, \chi, \dots$ For a term u (in particular, u can be a recipe), we define the application of the frame $\phi = \nu \tilde{n}.\nu \tilde{x}.\sigma$ to u as the application of σ^* to u, i.e. we let $u[\phi] = u\sigma^*$. For a frame $\phi = \nu \tilde{n}.\nu \tilde{x}.\sigma$ and a substitution θ, we let $\phi \cup \theta = \nu \tilde{n}.\nu \tilde{x}.(\sigma \cup \theta)$.

For a process P, we let $\mathsf{fr}(P)$ be the frame associated to P, defined as $\mathsf{fr}(P) = \nu \tilde{n}.\nu \tilde{x}.\sigma$, where $\tilde{n} = \mathsf{bn}(P) \cap \mathcal{N}$, $\tilde{x} = \mathsf{bv}(P)$ and σ is the substitution obtained by the union of all the sub-processes of P of the form $\{x \mapsto u\}$. Our transition relation will ensure that all variable x has a single occurence as $\{x \mapsto u\}$ in P, thus σ is well-defined. Furthermore, for all processes P, it will be the case that the variables in $\mathsf{dom}(\sigma)$ can be ordered as $x_1, \dots, x_n$ such that $i < j \implies x_j \notin \mathsf{var}(x_i\sigma)$. Therefore, σ^* always exists and $\mathsf{fr}(P)$ is indeed a frame.

Labeled reduction is a relation between closed processes defined by the following rules, modulo structural equivalence: for any evaluation context $\mathsf{C}[\_]$ with $\phi_{\mathsf{C}} = \mathsf{fr}(\mathsf{C}[\_])$,

COMM	$\mathsf{C}[\bar{c}\langle u\rangle.A \mid c(x).B] \xrightarrow{\tau} \mathsf{C}[\nu x.(A \mid B \mid \{x \mapsto u\})]$	
THEN	$\mathsf{C}[\text{if } u = v \text{ then } A \text{ else } B] \xrightarrow{\tau} \mathsf{C}[A]$	if $u[\phi_{\mathsf{C}}] =_\mathcal{E} v[\phi_{\mathsf{C}}]$
ELSE	$\mathsf{C}[\text{if } u = v \text{ then } A \text{ else } B] \xrightarrow{\tau} \mathsf{C}[B]$	if $u[\phi_{\mathsf{C}}] \neq_\mathcal{E} v[\phi_{\mathsf{C}}]$
IN	$\mathsf{C}[c(x).A] \xrightarrow{c(\zeta)} \mathsf{C}[\nu x.(A \mid \{x \mapsto \zeta\})]$	if $c \notin \mathsf{bn}(\mathsf{C}[\_]) \ \& \ \zeta \in \mathfrak{R}(\phi_{\mathsf{C}})$
OUT	$\mathsf{C}[\bar{c}\langle u\rangle.A] \xrightarrow{\nu x.\bar{c}\langle x\rangle} \mathsf{C}[A \mid \{x \mapsto u\}]$	if $c \notin \mathsf{bn}(\mathsf{C}[\_]) \ \& \ x \notin \mathsf{var}(\mathsf{C}[\bar{c}\langle u\rangle.A])$

The semantics is very similar to the one in [2], with superficial differences that help in our proofs. The most notable difference is that we never apply the frame to the process, but only use the frame where it makes a difference, i.e. in tests. Similarly, equational reasoning is not part of structural equivalence, but is only used in tests. A *trace* is a sequence of labeled reductions $P_1 \xrightarrow{\alpha_1} P_2 \xrightarrow{\alpha_2} \ldots \xrightarrow{\alpha_n} P_n$. We will denote such a trace by $P_1 \xrightarrow{w} P_n$, where $w = \alpha_1 \ldots \alpha_n$. We let $\mathsf{obs}(w)$ be the sequence of labels obtained by erasing all occurence of τ in w.

Example 2. Consider the theory $\mathcal{E} = \mathcal{E}_{\mathsf{DY}} \cup \mathcal{E}_{\mathsf{renc}}$ from Example 1, and
$P = \nu k.\bar{c}\langle \mathsf{enc}(a, \mathsf{pub}(k), r)\rangle.c(x).\bar{c}\langle\langle x, x\rangle\rangle.c(y).\mathsf{if}\ x \neq \mathsf{enc}(a, \mathsf{pub}(k), r)\ \&$
$\quad y \neq \mathsf{enc}(a, \mathsf{pub}(k), r)\ \&\ \mathsf{dec}(x, k) = \mathsf{dec}(y, k)\ \mathsf{then}\ \bar{c}\langle \mathsf{dec}(y, k)\rangle$
We have $P \xrightarrow{\nu z_1.\bar{c}\langle z_1 \rangle} \xrightarrow{c(\mathsf{renc}(z_1, n_1))} \xrightarrow{\nu z_2.\bar{c}\langle z_2 \rangle} \xrightarrow{c(\mathsf{renc}(\pi_1(z_2), n_2))} \xrightarrow{\tau} P_0$, where

$$P_0 \equiv \nu k.\nu x.\nu y.(\bar{c}\langle \mathsf{dec}(y, k)\rangle \mid \{z_1 \mapsto \mathsf{enc}(a, \mathsf{pub}(k), r)\} \mid \{x \mapsto \mathsf{renc}(z_1, n_1)\} \mid$$
$$\{z_2 \mapsto \langle x, x\rangle\} \mid \{y \mapsto \mathsf{renc}(\pi_1(z_2), n_2)\})$$

and $y[\mathsf{fr}(P_0)] = \mathsf{renc}(\pi_1(\langle \mathsf{renc}(z_1[\phi], n_1), x[\phi]\rangle), n_2) =_{\mathcal{E}} \mathsf{enc}(a, \mathsf{pub}(k), f(f(r, n_1), n_2))$. Furthermore, $P_0 \xrightarrow{\nu z_3.\bar{c}\langle z_3 \rangle} P_1$ for some process $P_1 = \nu k.\nu x.\nu y.\mathsf{fr}(P_1)$ such that $\mathsf{fr}(P_1) = \mathsf{fr}(P_0) \cup \{z_3 \mapsto \mathsf{dec}(y, k)\}$. Then, we have $z_3[\mathsf{fr}(P_1)] =_{\mathcal{E}} a$.

2.3   Trace Equivalence and Secrecy

Definition 1 (static equivalence). *We say that two frames ϕ, ψ are in static equivalence modulo an equational theory $\mathcal{E}$, denoted by $\phi \overset{s}{\sim} \psi$, if $\mathsf{dom}(\phi) = \mathsf{dom}(\psi)$ and $\forall \zeta_1, \zeta_2 \in \Re(\phi) \cap \Re(\psi)$. $\zeta_1[\phi] =_{\mathcal{E}} \zeta_2[\phi] \Leftrightarrow \zeta_1[\psi] =_{\mathcal{E}} \zeta_2[\psi]$*

When $\mathcal{E}$ is not clear from the context, we use the notation $\phi \overset{s}{\sim}_{\mathcal{E}} \psi$. We say that two traces $P \xrightarrow{w_1} P'$ and $Q \xrightarrow{w_2} Q'$ are in static equivalence if $\mathsf{obs}(w_1) = \mathsf{obs}(w_2)$ and $\mathsf{fr}(P') \overset{s}{\sim} \mathsf{fr}(Q')$.

Definition 2 (trace equivalence). *We say that two plain processes P, Q are in trace equivalence, denoted by $P \sim Q$, if for every trace $P \xrightarrow{w_1} P'$, there exists a trace $Q \xrightarrow{w_2} Q'$ such that $\mathsf{obs}(w_1) = \mathsf{obs}(w_2)$ and $\mathsf{fr}(P') \overset{s}{\sim} \mathsf{fr}(Q')$. Moreover, each trace of Q must have a corresponding statically equivalent trace of P.*

Example 3. Continuing example 2, let us consider the process $Q = P\{a \mapsto b\}$ and let $P \xrightarrow{w_1} P_1$ be the exhibited trace. Then, we have $P \not\sim Q$, because

- for $z_3, a \in \Re(\mathsf{fr}(P_1))$, we have $z_3[\mathsf{fr}(P_1)] =_{\mathcal{E}} a[\mathsf{fr}(P_1)]$
- for every corresponding trace $Q \xrightarrow{w_2} Q_1$ with $\mathsf{obs}(w_1) = \mathsf{obs}(w_2)$, we have $z_3[\mathsf{fr}(Q_1)] \neq_{\mathcal{E}} a[\mathsf{fr}(Q_1)]$, and thus $\mathsf{fr}(P_1) \overset{s}{\not\sim} \mathsf{fr}(Q_1)$. In fact, we have $z_3[\mathsf{fr}(Q_1)] =_{\mathcal{E}} b[\mathsf{fr}(Q_1)]$.

Definition 3 (intruder knowledge and secrecy). *Let $\mathcal{E}$ be an equational theory. For a frame ϕ, we let $\mathcal{I}(\phi, \mathcal{E}) = \{u \mid \exists \zeta \in \Re(\phi).\ \zeta[\phi] =_{\mathcal{E}} u\}$. For all processes P, we let $\mathcal{I}(P, \mathcal{E}) = \{u \mid \exists Q, w.\ P \xrightarrow{w} Q\ \&\ u \in \mathcal{I}(\mathsf{fr}(Q), \mathcal{E})\}$ and $\mathcal{S}(P, \mathcal{E}) = \mathsf{bn}(P) \setminus \mathcal{I}(P, \mathcal{E})$.*

3   Motivation and Statement of the Reduction Result

3.1   Starting Point: The Case Study

In this paper and in the corresponding ProVerif code, we only perform the analysis of PaV for the case of two eligible voters idA, idB and two candidates a, b. This is mainly for simplicity of presentation, but also because we believe that a result like the one in [12] could be translated to privacy properties.

In addition to El-Gamal encryption and re-encryption, modeled by $\mathcal{E}_{\mathsf{DY}}$ and $\mathcal{E}_{\mathsf{renc}}$ from example 1, PaV relies on zero-knowledge proofs to provide universal verifiability of the election result. We have to model these proofs in our analysis, to ensure that we do not miss any attacks on privacy that may be made possible by the additional information that is published. In particular, PaV relies on mixnet proofs and on proofs of correct decryption, that we model by the signature $\mathcal{F}_{\mathsf{ver}} = \{\mathsf{mixPf}/6, \mathsf{checkMix}/5, \mathsf{decPf}/3, \mathsf{checkDec}/4, \mathsf{ok}/0\}$ and the equational theories $\mathcal{E}_{\mathsf{decP}} = (\mathcal{R}_{\mathsf{decP}}, \emptyset)$, $\mathcal{E}_{\mathsf{mixP}} = (\mathcal{R}_{\mathsf{mixP}}, \emptyset)$, where:

$$\mathcal{R}_{\mathsf{decP}} = \left\{ \begin{array}{r} \mathsf{checkDec}(\mathsf{decPf}(\mathsf{enc}(x, \mathsf{pub}(y), z), x, y), \\ \mathsf{enc}(x, \mathsf{pub}(y), z), x, \mathsf{pub}(y)) \to \mathsf{ok} \end{array} \right.$$

$$\mathcal{R}_{\mathsf{mixP}} = \left\{ \begin{array}{r} \mathsf{checkMix}(\mathsf{mixPf}(x, y, \mathsf{renc}(x, z_x), \mathsf{renc}(y, z_y), z_x, z_y), \\ x, y, \mathsf{renc}(x, z_x), \mathsf{renc}(y, z_y)) \to \mathsf{ok} \\ \mathsf{checkMix}(\mathsf{mixPf}(x, y, \mathsf{renc}(y, z_y), \mathsf{renc}(x, z_x), z_y, z_x), \\ x, y, \mathsf{renc}(y, z_y), \mathsf{renc}(x, z_x)) \to \mathsf{ok} \end{array} \right.$$

The main idea of PaV is that an election authority A creates ballots that contain the names of the candidates in a random order on the left-hand side and their corresponding encryption in the same order on the right-hand side. This allows the voter to mark a vote for the desired candidate and scan only the encrypted part of the ballot, the right-hand side, to be posted on the bulletin board. Because the random order of candidates in the ballot and the decryption key are assumed to be secret, this ensures vote privacy, and even coercion-resistance, if care is taken to destroy the left-hand side. We use the following equational theory to model the actions of the voter during voting: $\mathcal{F}_{\mathsf{vote}} = \{\mathsf{vote}, \langle, \rangle\}$ and $\mathcal{E}_{\mathsf{vote}} = \{\mathcal{R}_{\mathsf{vote}}, \emptyset\}$, where $\mathcal{R}_{\mathsf{vote}} = \{\mathsf{vote}(\langle x, y \rangle, \langle x_e, y_e \rangle), x) \to x_e, \mathsf{vote}(\langle x, y \rangle, \langle x_e, y_e \rangle), y) \to y_e\}$.

After the encrypted votes get to the bulletin board, the design of PaV is similar to other voting systems like JCJ/Civitas or Helios: ballots are anonymized by a re-encryption mixnet and decrypted by the holders of the secret key. Putting it all together, the equational theory and the process that model PaV are given by $\mathcal{E}_{\mathsf{PaV}}$ and P_{PaV} in figure 1. V is the process for a voter, A is the process for the election authority that constructs the ballots, B is the process for the public bulletin board, M is the process for a mix server and T is the process for a trustee holding the decryption key.

In process M, we have $\{i, j\} = \{1, 2\}$ and $\mathsf{mixProof} = \mathsf{mixPf}(x_1, x_2, \mathsf{renc}(\pi_i(x_{\mathsf{ballots}}), n_1), \mathsf{renc}(\pi_j(x_{\mathsf{ballots}}), n_2), n_1, n_2)$. In process T, we have $\mathsf{decP}_i = \mathsf{decPf}(\pi_i(x_{\mathsf{ballots}}), \mathsf{dec}(\pi_i(x_{\mathsf{ballots}}), \mathsf{sk}), \mathsf{sk})$, for all $i \in \{1, 2\}$. The channel c_{printer} is

$$\mathcal{E}_{\mathsf{PaV}} = \mathcal{E}_{\mathsf{DY}} \cup \mathcal{E}_{\mathsf{renc}} \cup \mathcal{E}_{\mathsf{decP}} \cup \mathcal{E}_{\mathsf{mixP}} \cup \mathcal{E}_{\mathsf{vote}}$$
$$P_{\mathsf{PaV}} = \nu\mathsf{sk}.\nu c_{\mathsf{printer}}.\nu c_{\mathsf{ver}}.\nu c_{\mathsf{trustee}}.\ (\mathsf{V}(\mathsf{idA}, v_1)\ |\ \mathsf{V}(\mathsf{idB}, v_2)\ |\ \mathsf{A}\ |\ \mathsf{B}\ |\ \mathsf{M}\ |\ \mathsf{T})$$

$$\mathsf{A} = \nu c_{\mathsf{auth}}.(\overline{c_{\mathsf{auth}}}\langle a, b\rangle\ |\ \overline{c_{\mathsf{auth}}}\langle b, a\rangle\ |\ c_{\mathsf{auth}}(x_{\mathsf{can}}).\nu r_1.\nu r_2.$$
$$\overline{c_{\mathsf{printer}}}\langle x_{\mathsf{can}}, \langle \mathsf{enc}(\pi_1(x_{\mathsf{can}}), \mathsf{pub}(\mathsf{sk}), r_1), \mathsf{enc}(\pi_2(x_{\mathsf{can}}), \mathsf{pub}(\mathsf{sk}), r_2)\rangle\rangle$$
$$\mathsf{V}(\mathsf{id}, v) = c_{\mathsf{printer}}(x_{\mathsf{ballot}}).\overline{c_{\mathsf{scanner}}}\langle \mathsf{id}, \mathsf{vote}(x_{\mathsf{ballot}}, v)\rangle.\overline{c_{\mathsf{ver}}}\langle \mathsf{id}, \mathsf{vote}(x_{\mathsf{ballot}}, v)\rangle$$
$$\mathsf{B} = c_{\mathsf{scanner}}(\mathsf{ballot}_1).c_{\mathsf{scanner}}(\mathsf{ballot}_2).\overline{c_{\mathsf{mix}}}\langle \mathsf{ballot}_1, \mathsf{ballot}_2\rangle$$
$$\mathsf{M} = c_{\mathsf{ver}}(y).c_{\mathsf{ver}}(z).c_{\mathsf{mix}}(x_{\mathsf{ballots}}).\mathsf{if}\ \langle\pi_1(y), \pi_1(z), \langle\pi_2(y), \pi_2(z)\rangle\rangle = \langle\mathsf{idA}, \mathsf{idB}, x_{\mathsf{ballots}}\rangle$$
$$\mathsf{then}\ \nu n_1.\nu n_2.\overline{c_{\mathsf{trustee}}}\langle\mathsf{renc}(\pi_i(x_{\mathsf{ballots}}), n_1), \mathsf{renc}(\pi_j(x_{\mathsf{ballots}}), n_2)\rangle.$$
$$\overline{c_{\mathsf{board}}}\langle\mathsf{renc}(\pi_i(x_{\mathsf{ballots}}), n_1), \mathsf{renc}(\pi_j(x_{\mathsf{ballots}}), n_2), \mathsf{mixProof}\rangle$$
$$\mathsf{T} = \overline{c_{\mathsf{board}}}\langle\mathsf{pub}(\mathsf{sk})\rangle.c_{\mathsf{trustee}}(x_{\mathsf{ballots}}).\overline{c_{\mathsf{board}}}\langle\pi_1(x_{\mathsf{ballots}}), \mathsf{dec}(\pi_1(x_{\mathsf{ballots}}), \mathsf{sk}), \mathsf{decP}_1\rangle.$$
$$\overline{c_{\mathsf{board}}}\langle\pi_2(x_{\mathsf{ballots}}), \mathsf{dec}(\pi_2(x_{\mathsf{ballots}}), \mathsf{sk}), \mathsf{decP}_2\rangle$$

Fig. 1. Formal model of Prêt à Voter

where V gets the ballots - it is private because the order of candidates should be kept secret. c_{ver} is a private channel whose role is to enforce eligibility: exactly the ballots of idA and idB go into the mix. Without this, the intruder could mount an attack against the privacy of idA by replacing the ballot of idB with a copy of the ballot of idA in one of the public channels c_{scanner} or c_{mix}, as in e.g. [19]. The channel c_{trustee} has to be private to ensure that the ballots that are decrypted are indeed the ones that are mixed, and are not supplied by the intruder. Note that the channels c_{scanner}, c_{board} and c_{mix} are public, and all information that goes on private channels is also published on c_{board}.

To verify that P_{PaV} satisfies vote-privacy we check that $P_{\mathsf{PaV}}\{v_1 \mapsto a\}\{v_2 \mapsto b\} \sim_{\mathcal{E}_{\mathsf{PaV}}} P_{\mathsf{PaV}}\{v_1 \mapsto b\}\{v_2 \mapsto a\}$ [20]. The motivation of our work is that, when given as input this task (even without AC_f, $\mathcal{E}_{\mathsf{mixP}}$ and $\mathcal{E}_{\mathsf{decP}}$), ProVerif does not terminate. The non-termination is certainly due to $\mathcal{E}_{\mathsf{renc}}$, because $\mathcal{E}_{\mathsf{DY}} \cup \mathcal{E}_{\mathsf{decP}} \cup \mathcal{E}_{\mathsf{mixP}} \cup \mathcal{E}_{\mathsf{vote}}$ is a subterm-convergent theory and is easily handled by ProVerif.

3.2   General Setting for the Reduction

For a term t and process P, we let:
$\mathsf{re}(t) = \{u \in \mathsf{st}(t)\ |\ \mathsf{top}(u) \in \{\mathsf{enc}, \mathsf{renc}\}\}$; $\mathsf{re}(P) = \{u \in \mathsf{st}(P)\ |\ \mathsf{top}(u) \in \{\mathsf{enc}, \mathsf{renc}\}\}$
$\mathsf{ran}(t) = v$, if $t = \mathsf{enc}(t_1, t_2, v) \vee t = \mathsf{renc}(t_1, v)$; $\mathsf{ran}(P) = \{\mathsf{ran}(u)\ |\ u \in \mathsf{re}(P)\}$

Assumptions about the equational theory. In general, we consider a signature $\mathcal{F}$ such that $\{\mathsf{enc}, \mathsf{renc}, f\} \subseteq \mathcal{F}$ and a class of equational theories InpTh such that for all $\mathcal{E} \in \mathsf{InpTh}$, we have $\mathcal{E} = \mathcal{E}' \cup \mathcal{E}_{\mathsf{renc}}$, for some equational theory $\mathcal{E}' = (\mathcal{R}', \emptyset)$. We assume furthermore that for each rule $l \to r \in \mathcal{R}'$:

(ae$_1$) $\mathsf{top}(l) \notin \{\mathsf{enc}, \mathsf{renc}\}$ and $f \notin \mathsf{sig}(l)$	(ae$_3$) for all $t, t' \in \mathsf{re}(l)$, we have:
(ae$_2$) $\mathsf{sig}(r) \cap \{\mathsf{renc}, \mathsf{enc}, f\} = \emptyset$	$\cdot\ \mathsf{ran}(t) \in \mathsf{var}(l) \smallsetminus \mathsf{var}(r)$
	$\cdot\ \mathsf{ran}(t) = \mathsf{ran}(t') \implies t = t'$

It is easy to see that $\mathcal{E}_{\mathsf{PaV}}$ satisfies (ae$_1$)-(ae$_3$).

Assumptions about the class of processes. We define the weak symbols of $\mathcal{E} = (\mathcal{R}, \mathsf{AC}_f)$ by $\mathsf{W}(\mathcal{E}) = \{g \in \mathcal{F} \mid l \to r \in \mathcal{R} \ \& \ g \in \mathsf{sig}(l) \implies r \in \mathcal{F}_0\}$. For example, we have $\mathsf{W}(\mathcal{E}_{\mathsf{PaV}}) = \mathcal{F}_{\mathsf{ver}} \cup \{f\}$. For all term u, we define:

$$\mathsf{st}_p(u) = \{t \in \mathsf{st}(u) \mid u = \mathsf{C}[t] \implies \exists \mathsf{C}_1, \mathsf{C}_2. \ \mathsf{C}[\_] = \mathsf{C}_1[\mathsf{C}_2[\_]] \ \& $$
$$(\mathsf{top}(\mathsf{C}_2) \in \mathsf{W}(\mathcal{E}) \vee \mathsf{C}_2 = \mathsf{renc}(t_1, \mathsf{C}_2'[\_]) \vee \mathsf{C}_2 = \mathsf{enc}(t_1, t_2, \mathsf{C}_2'[\_]))\}$$

Intuitively, $\mathsf{st}_p(t)$ are the subterms of t whose every occurence is "protected" by a weak symbol or by $\{\mathsf{enc}, \mathsf{renc}\}$. For example, $\mathsf{st}_p(\langle a, c, \mathsf{renc}(b, c), \mathsf{renc}(b, d)\rangle) = \{d\}$. We assume the following properties about every process P that we consider:

(ap_1) $f \notin \mathsf{sig}(P)$	(ap_3) $\cdot$ $u, u' \in \mathsf{re}(P)$ & $\mathsf{ran}(u) = \mathsf{ran}(u') \implies u = u'$
(ap_2) $\mathsf{ran}(P) \subseteq \mathsf{bn}(P)$	$\cdot$ $t \in \mathsf{ran}(P)$ & $u \in \mathsf{st}(P)$ & $t \in \mathsf{st}(u) \implies t \in \mathsf{st}_p(u)$
	(ap_4) $!Q \in \mathsf{sp}(P) \implies \{\mathsf{renc}, \mathsf{enc}\} \cap \mathsf{sig}(Q) = \emptyset$

The main goal of assumptions $(\mathsf{ap}_2),(\mathsf{ap}_3)$ is to ensure that the elements of $\mathsf{ran}(P)$ are kept secret by the process. It is easy to see that P_{PaV} satisfies (ap_1)-(ap_4).

The reduced theory. Given an input theory $\mathcal{E} = (\mathcal{R}' \cup \mathcal{R}_{\mathsf{renc}}, \mathsf{AC}_f) \in \mathsf{InpTh}$, let $\mathcal{R}_{\mathsf{renc}}^{-1}$ be the inverse of $\mathcal{R}_{\mathsf{renc}}$, that is: $\mathcal{R}_{\mathsf{renc}}^{-1} = \begin{cases} \mathsf{enc}(x, y, f(z, z')) \to \mathsf{renc}(\mathsf{enc}(x, y, z), z') \\ \mathsf{renc}(x, f(z, z')) \to \mathsf{renc}(\mathsf{renc}(x, z), z') \end{cases}$

Note that $\mathcal{R}_{\mathsf{renc}}^{-1}$ is convergent modulo AC. Given a term t, we let $\mathsf{var}_f(t) = \{s \in \mathsf{var}(t) \mid \mathsf{enc}(u, v, s) \in \mathsf{st}(t) \vee \mathsf{renc}(u, s) \in \mathsf{st}(t)\}$. Then, for all $m \geq 1$, an (f, m)-substitution for t is a substitution σ such that $\mathsf{dom}(\sigma) \subseteq \mathsf{var}_f(t)$ and $\forall x \in \mathsf{dom}(\sigma). \ x\sigma = f(\ldots f(x_0, x_1) \ldots, x_k)$, where $1 \leq k \leq m \ \& \ x_0, \ldots, x_k \notin \mathsf{var}(t) \ \& \ \forall x' \neq x. x_0, \ldots, x_k \notin \mathsf{var}(x'\sigma)$. We denote by $\Theta_{f,m}(t)$ the set of (f, m)-substitutions for t. Now, we consider a particular case of narrowing [21] with respect to $\mathcal{R}_{\mathsf{renc}}^{-1}$ to define a set of variants [13] of a term: $\mathcal{V}_m^{\mathsf{renc}}(t) = \{(t\sigma)\downarrow_{\mathcal{R}_{\mathsf{renc}}^{-1}} \mid \sigma \in \Theta_{f,m}(t)\}$.

Example 4. We have $\mathcal{V}_2^{\mathsf{renc}}(\mathsf{enc}(a, b, x)) = \{\mathsf{enc}(a, b, x), \mathsf{renc}(\mathsf{enc}(a, b, x_0), x_1), \mathsf{renc}(\mathsf{renc}(\mathsf{enc}(a, b, x_0), x_1), x_2)\}$ and $\mathcal{V}_2^{\mathsf{renc}}(\mathsf{renc}(a, x)) = \{\mathsf{renc}(a, x), \mathsf{renc}(\mathsf{renc}(a, x_0), x_1), \mathsf{renc}(\mathsf{renc}(\mathsf{renc}(a, x_0), x_1), x_2)\}$

Finally, we can define the reduced theory that corresponds to $\mathcal{E}$ and m:

$$\mathcal{E}_m = (\mathcal{R}_m, \emptyset) \qquad\qquad \mathcal{R}_m = \{l' \to r \mid \exists l \to r \in \mathcal{R}'. \ l' \in \mathcal{V}_m^{\mathsf{renc}}(l)\}$$

We let OutTh be the set of all reduced theories that correspond to some $\mathcal{E} \in \mathsf{InpTh}$ and some $m \geq 1$.

Example 5. Let us consider the theory $\mathcal{E}_{\mathsf{PaV}}$ and $m = 1$. We have $\mathcal{E}_{\mathsf{PaV},m} = (\mathcal{E}_{\mathsf{PaV}} \smallsetminus \mathcal{E}_{\mathsf{renc}}) \cup (\mathcal{S}, \emptyset)$, where

$$\mathcal{S} = \begin{cases} \mathsf{dec}(\mathsf{renc}(\mathsf{enc}(x, \mathsf{pub}(y), z_0), z_1), y) \to x \\ \mathsf{checkDec}(\mathsf{decPf}(\mathsf{renc}(\mathsf{enc}(x, \mathsf{pub}(y), z_0), z_1), x, y), \\ \quad \mathsf{renc}(\mathsf{enc}(x, \mathsf{pub}(y), z_0), z_1), x, \mathsf{pub}(y)) \to \mathsf{ok} \\ \mathsf{checkMix}(\mathsf{mixPf}(x, x, \mathsf{renc}(\mathsf{renc}(x, z_x^0), z_x^1), \mathsf{renc}(y, z_y), f(z_x^0, z_x^1), z_y), \\ \quad x, y, \mathsf{renc}(\mathsf{renc}(x, z_x^0), z_x^1), \mathsf{renc}(y, z_y)) \to \mathsf{ok} \\ \text{plus rules for checkMix corresponding to other permutations and} \\ \text{to substitutions } \{z_y \mapsto f(z_y^0, z_y^1)\} \text{ and } \{z_x \mapsto f(z_x^0, z_x^1), z_y \mapsto f(z_y^0, z_y^1)\} \end{cases}$$

Lemma 1. *For all* $\mathcal{E} = \mathcal{E}' \cup \mathcal{E}_{\text{renc}} \in \mathsf{InpTh}$ *such that* $\mathcal{E}'$ *is subterm-convergent,* $\mathcal{E}_m$ *is subterm-convergent.*

We let $\mathsf{ran}_r(P) = \{t \mid \mathsf{renc}(u,t) \in \mathsf{st}(P)\}$. Our main result is a reduction of trace equivalence modulo any $\mathcal{E} \in \mathsf{InpTh}$ to trace equivalence modulo $\mathcal{E}_m \in \mathsf{OutTh}$, for a well-chosen m:

Theorem 1 (Main theorem). *For all processes* P, Q *that satisfy* (ap$_1$)-(ap$_4$) *let* $m = 2 * \max(|\mathsf{ran}_r(P)|, |\mathsf{ran}_r(Q)|) + 1$. *Then, for all equational theory* $\mathcal{E} \in \mathsf{InpTh}$, *we have*

$$P \sim_{\mathcal{E}_m} Q \implies P \sim_{\mathcal{E}} Q$$

where $\mathcal{E}_m \in \mathsf{OutTh}$ *is the reduced theory that corresponds to* $\mathcal{E}$ *and* m.

4   Reduction of the Set of Traces

As a first step in the proof of theorem 1, we introduce a restricted notion of trace equivalence, $P \simeq Q$, that depends only on so-called local traces of P and Q. We show that $P \sim_{\mathcal{E}_m} Q \implies P \simeq_{\mathcal{E}_m} Q$ and $P \simeq_{\mathcal{E}} Q \implies P \sim_{\mathcal{E}} Q$.

4.1   Occurence Order for a Frame

In the following, we assume that for all frame ϕ we are given a partial order $\prec$ on variables in $\mathsf{var}(\phi)$. For all P, Q such that $P \xrightarrow{w} Q$, we associate such an order $\prec$ to $\mathsf{fr}(Q)$: for all $x, y \in \mathsf{var}(\mathsf{fr}(Q))$ we have $x \prec y$ iff $w = w_1 w_2$ and there is a P_1 such that $P \xrightarrow{w_1} P_1 \xrightarrow{w_2} Q$, $x \in \mathsf{var}(\phi(P_1))$ and $y \notin \mathsf{var}(\mathsf{fr}(P_1))$. We let $x \preceq y$ if $x \prec y \lor x = y$. The orders $\prec$ and $\preceq$ are extended to sets of variables from $\mathsf{var}(\phi)$ by: $S_1 \preceq S_2 \Leftrightarrow \forall x \in S_1 \exists y \in S_2.x \preceq y$ and $S_1 \prec S_2 \Leftrightarrow S_1 \preceq S_2 \,\&\, \exists y \in S_2 \forall x \in S_1.x \prec y$. Finally, we extend $\prec$ (and $\preceq$) to a preorder on terms in $\mathcal{T}(\mathcal{F}, \mathcal{N}, \mathsf{var}(\phi))$ by letting $u \prec v \Leftrightarrow \mathsf{var}(u) \prec \mathsf{var}(v)$ (and $u \preceq v \Leftrightarrow \mathsf{var}(u) \preceq \mathsf{var}(v)$).

Example 6. Let $P = \bar{c}\langle a\rangle.\bar{c}\langle b\rangle.\bar{c}\langle\mathsf{renc}(a,b)\rangle$. Then, we have

$$P \xrightarrow{\nu x_1.\bar{c}\langle x_1\rangle,\ \nu x_2.\bar{c}\langle x_2\rangle,\ \nu x_3.\bar{c}\langle x_3\rangle} \{x_1 \mapsto a\} \mid \{x_2 \mapsto b\} \mid \{x_3 \mapsto \mathsf{renc}(a,b)\} = Q$$

and $x_1 \prec x_2 \preceq \mathsf{renc}(x_1, x_2) \prec x_3$ and $\mathsf{renc}(x_1, x_2)[\mathsf{fr}(Q)] = x_3[\mathsf{fr}(Q)]$.

For the trace $P \xrightarrow{w} P_1$ of example 2, we have $z_1 \preceq \mathsf{renc}(z_1, n_1) \prec x \prec z_2 \preceq \mathsf{renc}(\pi_2(z_2), n_2) \prec y$.

4.2   Local Traces in General

The definitions and results from this section stand for any equational theory $\mathcal{E}$, with no restriction on $\mathcal{E}$ and no restriction on the class of processes.

In the following, we consider given a *locality function* $\mathcal{L}$, that associates to each frame ϕ a subset of its recipes, i.e. $\mathcal{L}(\phi) \subseteq \Re(\phi)$.

Definition 4 (local static equivalence). *Let $\mathcal{L}$ be a locality function. We say that two frames ϕ, ψ are in $\mathcal{L}$-local static equivalence, denoted by $\phi \overset{s}{\simeq} \psi$, if $\mathsf{dom}(\phi) = \mathsf{dom}(\psi)$ and $\forall \zeta_1, \zeta_2 \in \mathcal{L}(\phi) \cap \mathcal{L}(\psi)$. $\zeta_1[\phi] =_{\varepsilon} \zeta_2[\phi] \Leftrightarrow \zeta_1[\psi] =_{\varepsilon} \zeta_2[\psi]$.*

When $\mathcal{L}$ or $\mathcal{E}$ is not clear from the context, we use the notation $\phi \overset{s}{\simeq}_{\mathcal{L}, \mathcal{E}} \psi$. We say that two traces $P \xrightarrow{w_1} P'$ and $Q \xrightarrow{w_2} Q'$ are in $\mathcal{L}$-local static equivalence if $\mathsf{obs}(w_1) = \mathsf{obs}(w_2)$ and $\mathsf{fr}(P') \overset{s}{\simeq}_{\mathcal{L}} \mathsf{fr}(Q')$. For a sequence of labels w, we let $\mathsf{inp}(w)$ be the set of recipes that occur as inputs in w, i.e. $\mathsf{inp}(w) = \{\zeta \mid \exists w_1, w_2, c.\ w = w_1 \mathsf{c}(\zeta) w_2\}$. A trace $P \xrightarrow{w} Q$ is $\mathcal{L}$-local if $\mathsf{inp}(w) \subseteq \mathcal{L}(\mathsf{fr}(Q))$.

Definition 5 (local trace equivalence). *Let $\mathcal{L}$ be a locality function. We say that two processes P, Q are in $\mathcal{L}$-local trace equivalence, denoted by $P \simeq Q$, if for all $\mathcal{L}$-local trace $P \xrightarrow{w_1} P'$ there exists a $\mathcal{L}$-local trace $Q \xrightarrow{w_2} Q'$ such that $\mathsf{obs}(w_1) = \mathsf{obs}(w_2)$ and $\mathsf{fr}(P') \overset{s}{\simeq} \mathsf{fr}(Q')$. Moreover, for all $\mathcal{L}$-local trace of Q there must exist a corresponding $\mathcal{L}$-local statically equivalent $\mathcal{L}$-local trace of P.*

When $\mathcal{L}$ is not clear from the context, we use the notation $P \simeq_{\mathcal{L}, \mathcal{E}} Q$.

The idea of $\mathcal{L}$-locality is to restrict the set of traces that have to be considered. A locality function is especially useful if it admits a *normalization function* that assigns to each recipe an equivalent local recipe:

Definition 6 (Normalization function). *Given two locality functions $\mathcal{L}_1, \mathcal{L}_2$ and a frame ϕ, a normalization function from $\mathcal{L}_1$ to $\mathcal{L}_2$ associates to each recipe $\zeta \in \mathcal{L}_1(\phi)$ an equivalent $\mathcal{L}_2$-local recipe $\mathsf{N}(\zeta)$ that is smaller wrt $\preceq$ than ζ, i.e. we have $\forall \zeta \in \mathcal{L}_1(\phi)$. $\mathsf{N}(\zeta) \in \mathcal{L}_2(\phi)$ & $\mathsf{N}(\zeta)[\phi] =_{\varepsilon} \zeta[\phi]$ & $\mathsf{N}(\zeta) \preceq \zeta$.*
We denote by $\mathsf{norm}_{\mathcal{L}_1, \mathcal{L}_2}(\phi)$ the set of normalization functions from $\mathcal{L}_1$ to $\mathcal{L}_2$ for ϕ. When $\mathcal{L}_1 = \mathfrak{R}$, we may use the notation $\mathsf{norm}_{\mathcal{L}_2}(\phi)$ for this set.

We say that a frame ϕ is *issued from a ($\mathcal{L}$-local) trace* if there is a process P and a ($\mathcal{L}$-local) trace $P \xrightarrow{w} P'$ such that $\phi = \mathsf{fr}(P')$. The following two propositions show under which conditions trace equivalence and local trace equivalence coincide.

Proposition 1. *Let $\mathcal{L}$ be a locality function such that, for all frames ϕ, ψ that are issued from two statically equivalent traces, we have $\mathcal{L}(\phi) = \mathcal{L}(\psi)$. Then, for all plain processes P, Q, we have $P \sim Q \implies P \simeq_{\mathcal{L}} Q$.*

Proposition 2. *Let $\mathcal{L}$ be a locality function such that, for all frames ϕ, ψ that are issued from two $\mathcal{L}$-statically equivalent and $\mathcal{L}$-local traces, there exists a normalization function $\mathsf{N} \in \mathsf{norm}_{\mathcal{L}}(\phi) \cap \mathsf{norm}_{\mathcal{L}}(\psi)$. Then, for all processes P, Q, we have $P \simeq_{\mathcal{L}} Q \implies P \sim Q$.*

To ease the construction of a normalization function for a locality function $\mathcal{L}_2$, we can introduce an intermediary locality function $\mathcal{L}_1$, with $\mathcal{L}_2(\phi) \subseteq \mathcal{L}_1(\phi) \subseteq \mathfrak{R}(\phi)$, and provide two normalization functions: one from $\mathfrak{R}$ to $\mathcal{L}_1$, and one from $\mathcal{L}_1$ to $\mathcal{L}_2$. This is the role of the following corollary:

Corollary 1. *Let $\mathcal{L}_1, \mathcal{L}_2$ be two locality functions such that,*

- *for all frames ϕ, ψ that are issued from two $\mathcal{L}_2$-statically equivalent and $\mathcal{L}_2$-local traces, there exists a normalization function $\mathsf{N}_2 \in \mathsf{norm}_{\mathcal{L}_1, \mathcal{L}_2}(\phi) \cap \mathsf{norm}_{\mathcal{L}_1, \mathcal{L}_2}(\psi)$.*
- *for all frames ϕ, ψ that are issued from two $\mathcal{L}_1$-statically equivalent and $\mathcal{L}_1$-local traces, there exists a normalization function $\mathsf{N}_1 \in \mathsf{norm}_{\Re, \mathcal{L}_1}(\phi) \cap \mathsf{norm}_{\Re, \mathcal{L}_1}(\psi)$.*
- *for all frames ϕ, ψ that are issued from two statically equivalent traces, we have $\mathcal{L}_1(\phi) = \mathcal{L}_1(\psi)$*

Then, for all processes P, Q, we have $P \simeq_{\mathcal{L}_2} Q \implies P \simeq_{\mathcal{L}_1} Q \implies P \sim Q$

4.3   Local Traces for Re-encryption

We define a locality function $\mathcal{L}_{\mathsf{renc}}$ that will allow us to infer a bound on the number of re-encryptions applied to any given ciphertext. The main idea of $\mathcal{L}_{\mathsf{renc}}$ is to disalow nested applications of the function renc in recipes. In spite of this strong restriction, $\mathcal{L}_{\mathsf{renc}}$ will admit a normalization function, because nested applications of renc can be replaced with equivalent terms that are somehow smaller, e.g. $\mathsf{renc}(\pi_1(\langle \mathsf{renc}(\zeta_1, \zeta_2), \chi \rangle, \zeta_3)$ can be replaced with $\mathsf{renc}(\zeta_1, f(\zeta_2, \zeta_3))$.

Let ϕ be a frame and $\prec$ be an occurence order on recipes associated to ϕ. For two recipes $\zeta_1, \zeta_2 \in \Re(\phi)$, we define

$$\zeta_1 \ll \zeta_2 \Leftrightarrow \zeta_2 = \mathsf{renc}(\chi_1, \chi_2) \ \& \ \zeta_1[\phi] =_{\mathcal{E}} \chi_1[\phi] \ \& \ (\zeta_1 \in \mathsf{st}(\chi_1) \ \vee \ \zeta_1 \prec \chi_1)$$

Intuitively, we have $\zeta_1 \ll \zeta_2$ if ζ_2 is a re-encryption of ζ_1. The role of the intermediary recipe χ_1 in the definition of $\ll$ is to take into account the case where ζ_2 is not a direct re-encryption of ζ_1, but there exists a context inbetween ζ_2 and ζ_1 that may dissapear by rewriting. This context may be entirely contained in χ_1, and then we have $\zeta_1 \in \mathsf{st}(\chi_1)$, or it may descent into the substitution part of $\chi_1[\phi]$, and then we have $\zeta_1 \prec \chi_1$ (note that we require $\prec$, and not simply $\preceq$).

Example 7. Let us consider the trace $P \xrightarrow{w} P_1$ of example 2. Let $\phi = \mathsf{fr}(P_1)$ and $\prec$ be the corresponding occurence order. Then, we have $\mathsf{renc}(z_1, n_1) \ll \mathsf{renc}(\pi_2(z_2), n_2)$, because $\pi_2(z_2)[\phi] = \pi_2(\langle x[\phi], x[\phi] \rangle) =_{\mathcal{E}} x[\phi] = \mathsf{renc}(z_1, n_1)[\phi]$ and $\mathsf{renc}(z_1, n_1) \prec x \prec z_2 \preceq \pi_2(z_2)$.

Now, given a frame ϕ, we can define the sets of recipes $\mathsf{RR}(\phi)$ and respectively $\mathsf{RE}(\phi)$ that represent a nested application of re-encryptions and respectively the re-encryption of an encryption. Local traces will avoid the use of such recipes. Formally, we have:
$\mathsf{RR}(\phi) = \{\zeta_0 \in \Re(\phi) \mid \exists \zeta_1 \in \Re(\phi). \ \zeta_1 \ll \zeta_0 \ \& \ \mathsf{top}(\zeta_1) = \mathsf{renc}\}$
$\mathsf{RE}(\phi) = \{\zeta_0 \in \Re(\phi) \mid \exists \zeta_1 \in \Re(\phi). \ \zeta_1 \ll \zeta_0 \ \& \ \mathsf{top}(\zeta_1) = \mathsf{enc}\}$

Definition 7 (Locality function $\mathcal{L}_{\mathsf{renc}}$). *For all frame ϕ, we let*

$$\mathcal{L}_{\mathsf{renc}}(\phi) = \{\zeta \in \Re(\phi) \mid \mathsf{st}(\zeta) \cap (\mathsf{RR}(\phi) \cup \mathsf{RE}(\phi)) = \emptyset\}$$

Example 8. Continuing example 7, we have $\mathsf{renc}(\pi_2(z_2), n_2) \notin \mathcal{L}_{\mathsf{renc}}(\phi)$, because $\mathsf{renc}(z_1, n_1) \ll \mathsf{renc}(\pi_2(z_2), n_2)$ and $\mathsf{top}(\mathsf{renc}(z_1, n_1)) = \mathsf{renc}$.

Lemma 2. *For all equational theory $\mathcal{E}$ and all frames ϕ, ψ that are issued from two statically equivalent traces, we have $\mathcal{L}_{\mathsf{renc}}(\phi) = \mathcal{L}_{\mathsf{renc}}(\psi)$.*

Lemma 3 (Normalization function $\mathsf{N}_{\mathsf{renc}}$). *Consider the locality function $\mathcal{L}_{\mathsf{renc}}$ and an equational theory $\mathcal{E} \in \mathsf{InpTh}$. For all frames ϕ, ψ that are issued from two $\mathcal{L}_{\mathsf{renc}}$-statically equivalent and $\mathcal{L}_{\mathsf{renc}}$-local traces, there exists a normalization function $\mathsf{N}_{\mathsf{renc}} \subseteq \mathsf{norm}_{\mathcal{L}_{\mathsf{renc}}}(\phi) \cap \mathsf{norm}_{\mathcal{L}_{\mathsf{renc}}}(\psi)$.*

We prove lemma 3 by replacing every recipe $\mathsf{renc}(\zeta_0, \chi_0) \in \mathsf{st}(\zeta) \cap (\mathsf{RR}(\phi) \cup \mathsf{RR}(\psi))$, such that $\mathsf{renc}(\zeta_1, \chi_1) \ll \mathsf{renc}(\zeta_0, \chi_0)$, with $\mathsf{renc}(\zeta_1, f(\chi_0, \chi_1))$. We rely on $\phi \overset{s}{\simeq} \psi$ and on a well-chosen ordering of replacements to ensure that their application is consistent in both frames. None of assumptions (ae$_1$)-(ae$_3$) or (ap$_1$)-(ap$_4$) are used in the proof.

Example 9. Continuing example 8, we have $\mathsf{N}_{\mathsf{renc}}(\mathsf{renc}(\pi_2(z_2), n_2)) = \mathsf{renc}(z_1, f(n_1, n_2))$. Indeed, we have $\mathsf{renc}(z_1, f(n_1, n_2)) \in \mathcal{L}_{\mathsf{renc}}(\phi)$, $\mathsf{renc}(z_1, f(n_1, n_2))[\phi] = \mathsf{renc}(\pi_2(z_2), n_2)[\phi]$ and $\mathsf{renc}(z_1, f(n_1, n_2)) \prec \mathsf{renc}(\pi_2(z_2), n_2)$.

4.4   Local Traces for Associativity-Commutativity

We define a locality function $\mathcal{L}_f$ that will ensure a canonical use of the AC symbol f: the nested application of f-symbols always follows the same pattern and arguments of f always respect a well-chosen order.

We consider multi-hole term contexts: $\mathsf{C}[\_, \ldots, \_]_n$ is a context with n holes, and the subscript n will be dropped when n is clear from the context. For all $n \geq 1$, we let C_f^n be the n-hole context $f(\ldots f(f(\_, \_), \_) \cdots, \_)$.

Definition 8. *Assume that t is a term such that $t = \mathsf{C}[t_1, \ldots, t_n]$, with $\mathsf{sig}(\mathsf{C}) = \{f\}$ and $\mathsf{top}(t_1) \neq f, \ldots, \mathsf{top}(t_n) \neq f$. Then, we define $\mathsf{Fact}_f(t) = (t_1, \ldots, t_n)$ and $\mathsf{C}_f(t) = \mathsf{C}[\_, \ldots, \_]$. Sometimes we use the notation $\mathsf{Fact}_f(t)$ to also denote the set $\{t_1, \ldots, t_n\}$.*

For example, $\mathsf{C}_f(f(f(a, b), f(a, b))) = f(f(\_, \_), f(\_, \_))$ and $\mathsf{Fact}_f(f(f(a, b), f(a, b))) = (a, b, a, b)$.

Let ϕ be a frame and $\prec$ be the associated occurence ordering. We consider any total extension of $\prec$, denoted by $\prec_f$, that is compatible with the subterm ordering, i.e. $u \in \mathsf{st}(v) \setminus \{v\} \implies u \prec_f v$. For all $\zeta \in \Re(\phi)$, we define $\mathsf{min}_f^\phi(\zeta)$ to be the minimal wrt $\prec_f$ recipe that is equivalent to ζ in ϕ, i.e. we have $\mathsf{min}_f^\phi(\zeta)[\phi] =_{\mathcal{E}} \zeta[\phi]$ and $\forall \zeta' \in \Re(\phi). \ \zeta'[\phi] =_{\mathcal{E}} \zeta[\phi] \implies \mathsf{min}_f^\phi(\zeta) \prec_f \zeta'$.

Now, given a frame ϕ, we can define the set of terms $\mathsf{GF}(\phi)$ that will determine the restricted use of the symbol f:

$$\mathsf{GF}(\phi) = \{t \mid \mathsf{Fact}_f(t) = (t_1, \ldots, t_n) \implies \mathsf{C}_f(t) = \mathsf{C}_f^n \ \& \ \exists \zeta_1, \ldots, \zeta_n \in \Re(\phi).$$
$$\zeta_1[\phi]\!\downarrow = t_1, \ldots, \zeta_n[\phi]\!\downarrow = t_n \ \& \ \mathsf{min}_f^\phi(\zeta_1) \preceq_f \cdots \preceq_f \mathsf{min}_f^\phi(\zeta_n)\}$$

Intuitively, $\mathsf{GF}(\phi)$ requires that its members are in canonical form wrt associativity of f, via $\mathsf{C}_f(t) = \mathsf{C}_f^n$, and in canonical form wrt commutativity of f, via

$\min_f^\phi(\zeta_1) \preceq_f \dots \preceq_f \min_f^\phi(\zeta_n)$. Recall that, for all term u, $u\downarrow$ represents the normalization of u wrt to $\mathcal{R}$ only, not considering AC_f:

Definition 9 (Locality function $\mathcal{L}_f$). *For all frame ϕ, we let*

$$\mathcal{L}_f(\phi) = \{\zeta \in \Re(\phi) \mid \forall \zeta' \in \mathsf{st}(\zeta).\ \zeta'[\phi]\downarrow \in \mathsf{GF}(\phi)\}$$

One may wonder why, in the definition of $\mathsf{GF}(\phi)$, we compare the minimal recipes $\min_f^\phi(\zeta_i)$ and not simply the terms t_i, like in [25], or the recipes ζ_i. We do not compare the terms t_i, because they may contain information that is irrelevant to observations that can be made in a frame, in particular they may contain secret names. We want to abstract away from such details, especially since we want to relate two frames that may well be distinct on their non-observable parts. Furthermore, we do not compare the recipes ζ_i because that would not be sufficient to eliminate AC properties in a $\mathcal{L}_f$-local trace: we may have $\zeta_1 \prec_f \zeta_2$, $\chi_1 \prec_f \chi_2$, $f(\zeta_1[\phi]\downarrow, \zeta_2[\phi]\downarrow) =_{\mathsf{AC}} f(\chi_1[\phi]\downarrow, \chi_2[\phi\downarrow])$ and $f(\zeta_1[\phi]\downarrow, \zeta_2[\phi]\downarrow) \neq f(\chi_1[\phi]\downarrow, \chi_2[\phi]\downarrow)$. On the other hand, comparing $\min_f^\phi(\zeta_i)$ ensures an ordering on equivalence classes, and not merely an ordering on recipes.

Example 10. Consider the frames $\phi = \nu a.\nu b.\ \{x_1 \mapsto a, x_2 \mapsto b, x_3 \mapsto \langle b, a \rangle\}$ and $\psi = \nu a.\nu b.\ \{x_1 \mapsto b, x_2 \mapsto a, x_3 \mapsto \langle a, b \rangle\}$, such that $x_1 \prec x_2 \prec x_3$. Then, $\min_f^\phi(\pi_1(x_3)) = x_1$ and $\min_f^\phi(\pi_2(x_3)) = x_2$. The recipes $f(x_1, f(x_1, x_1)), f(x_2, x_1)$ and $f(\pi_1(x_3), \pi_2(x_3))$ are not in $\mathcal{L}_f(\phi)$ and not in $\mathcal{L}_f(\psi)$.

In example 9, if we assume $n_2 \prec_f n_1$, the recipe $\mathsf{renc}(z_1, f(n_1, n_2))$ is in $\mathcal{L}_{\mathsf{renc}}(\phi) \smallsetminus \mathcal{L}_f(\phi)$.

Definition 10 (Locality function $\mathcal{L}_{\mathsf{rf}}$). *For all frame ϕ, we let*

$$\mathcal{L}_{\mathsf{rf}}(\phi) = \mathcal{L}_{\mathsf{renc}}(\phi) \cap \mathcal{L}_f(\phi)$$

The following lemma is crucial in defining a normalization function for $\mathcal{L}_f$, because it will allow us to obtain recipes of terms in $\mathsf{Fact}_f(\zeta[\phi]\downarrow)$, that we can re-arrange to transform a non-local recipe into a local one:

Lemma 4. *Let P, Q be processes such that $P \xrightarrow{w} Q$ and let $\phi = \mathsf{fr}(Q)$. Then, for all recipe $\zeta \in \Re(\phi)$ such that $\zeta[\phi]\downarrow = f(t_1, t_2)$ there exist $f(\zeta_1, \zeta_2) \in \Re(\phi)$ such that*

- $f(\zeta_1, \zeta_2) \in \mathsf{st}(\zeta)$ *or* $f(\zeta_1, \zeta_2) \in \mathsf{st}(\mathsf{inp}(w))$ & $f(\zeta_1, \zeta_2) \prec \zeta$
- *and* $f(\zeta_1, \zeta_2)[\phi]\downarrow = f(t_1, t_2)$

Note that $f(\zeta_1, \zeta_2) \in \Re(\phi) \Leftrightarrow \{\zeta_1, \zeta_2\} \subseteq \Re(\phi)$. The proof of lemma 4 relies on assumptions $(\mathsf{ae}_2),(\mathsf{ae}_3)$ and (ap_1) to deduce that, whenever $f(t_1, t_2)$ is deducible in a trace, it must be the case that both t_1 and t_2 are deducible.

Lemma 5. *For all equational theory $\mathcal{E} = (\mathcal{R}, \emptyset) \in \mathsf{OutTh}$ and all frames ϕ, ψ that are issued from two statically equivalent traces, we have $\mathcal{L}_f(\phi) = \mathcal{L}_f(\psi)$.*

The proof of lemma 5 is eased by the absence of AC symbols, and it relies on lemma 4 and $\phi \overset{s}{\sim} \psi$ to transfer the $\mathcal{L}_f$-locality of a recipe from ϕ to ψ.

Lemma 6 (Normalization function N_f). *Consider the locality functions $\mathcal{L}_{\text{renc}}, \mathcal{L}_{\text{rf}}$ and an equational theory $\mathcal{E} \in \text{InpTh}$. For all frames ϕ, ψ that are issued from two $\mathcal{L}_{\text{rf}}$-statically equivalent and $\mathcal{L}_{\text{rf}}$-local traces, there exists a normalization function $N_f \subseteq \text{norm}_{\mathcal{L}_{\text{renc}}, \mathcal{L}_{\text{rf}}}(\phi) \cap \text{norm}_{\mathcal{L}_{\text{renc}}, \mathcal{L}_{\text{rf}}}(\psi)$.*

We prove lemma 6 by replacing all $\zeta' \in \text{st}(\zeta)$ such that $\zeta'[\phi]\!\downarrow \notin \text{GF}(\phi)$ and $\text{Fact}_f(\zeta'[\phi]\!\downarrow) = (t_1, \ldots, t_n)$ with an equivalent ζ'' such that $\zeta''[\phi]\!\downarrow \in \text{GF}(\phi)$, to obtain an $\mathcal{L}_f$-local recipe. To construct ζ'', we start with a sequence of recipes $\zeta_1, \ldots, \zeta_n$ such that $\zeta_1[\phi]\!\downarrow = t_1, \ldots, \zeta_n[\phi]\!\downarrow = t_n$, whose existence is ensured by lemma 4. Then, we consider $\zeta'' = C_f^n[\zeta_{i_1}, \ldots, \zeta_{i_n}]$, where $\zeta_{i_1}, \ldots, \zeta_{i_n}$ is a reordering of $\zeta_1, \ldots, \zeta_n$ such that $\min_f^\phi(\zeta_{i_1}) \prec_f \ldots \prec_f \min_f^\phi(\zeta_{i_n})$. We rely on $\phi \overset{s}{\simeq} \psi$ to ensure that these replacements are consistent in both frames ϕ and ψ.

Example 11. Continuing example 10, we have $N_f(f(x_1, f(x_1, x_1)) = f(f(x_1, x_1), x_1), N_f(f(x_2, x_1)) = f(x_1, x_2)$ and $N_f(f(\pi_1(x_3), \pi_2(x_3))) = f(x_1, x_2)$.

4.5 Main Results of This Section

From proposition 1, lemma 2 and lemma 5, we have

Corollary 2. *Consider the locality function $\mathcal{L}_{\text{rf}}$ and any equational theory $\mathcal{E}_m \in \text{OutTh}$. Then, for all plain processes P, Q, we have $P \sim Q \implies P \simeq_{\mathcal{L}_{\text{rf}}} Q$.*

From corollary 1 (applied to $\mathcal{L}_{\text{renc}}$ and $\mathcal{L}_{\text{rf}}$) and lemmas 6, 3 and 2, we have:

Corollary 3. *Consider the locality function $\mathcal{L}_{\text{rf}}$ and any equational theory $\mathcal{E} \in \text{InpTh}$. Then, for all plain processes P, Q, we have $P \simeq_{\mathcal{L}_{\text{rf}}} Q \implies P \sim Q$.*

To bridge the gap between $P \sim_{\mathcal{E}_m} Q$ and $P \sim_{\mathcal{E}} Q$ it is sufficient now to show that $P \simeq_{\mathcal{L}_{\text{rf}}, \mathcal{E}_m} Q \implies P \simeq_{\mathcal{L}_{\text{rf}}, \mathcal{E}} Q$. This is the subject of the next section.

5 Reduction of Equational Theories

In this section, we use $\mathcal{R}$ for a rewrite system corresponding to a theory in InpTh, and $\mathcal{R}_m$ for a corresponding rewrite system of a theory in OutTh. Lemma 7 simplifies reasoning modulo AC, by showing that AC_f does not interfere with rewriting. The proof relies on assumption (ae_1), in particular on the fact that f does not occur on the left-hand side of rewrite rules:

Lemma 7. *For any equational theory $\mathcal{E} \in \text{InpTh}$ and for all terms u, v, we have $u \rightarrow_{\text{AC}}^* v$ if and only if $u \rightarrow^* v'$, for some term v' such that $v' =_{\text{AC}} v$.*

Lemma 8 simplifies reasoning modulo re-encryption, by showing that nonces from the protocol always stay secret:

Lemma 8. *For all process P that satisfies (ap_1)-(ap_4) and all equational theory $\mathcal{E}$ that satisfies (ae_1)-(ae_3), we have $\text{ran}(P) \subseteq \mathcal{S}(P, \mathcal{E})$.*

The proof relies on assumptions (ap_2) and (ap_3), to ensure that elements of $\mathrm{ran}(P)$ are handled in a restricted way. Then, assumption (ae_3) and the definitions of $\mathsf{st}_p, \mathsf{W}(\mathcal{E})$ ensure that this indeed guarantees secrecy.

We will show that $\mathcal{L}_{\mathsf{rf}}$-local traces have a bounded *re-encryption depth*. To define it, we must identify the chain of re-encryptions that have been applied to obtain a given ciphertext. This chain will be the limit of recursively identifying *re-encryption witnesses*:

Definition 11 (Re-encryption witness). *Assume* $u \to_{\mathcal{R}}^* v$. *Then, for all term* $t \in \mathsf{st}(v)$ *with* $\mathsf{top}(t{\downarrow}) \in \{\mathsf{enc}, \mathsf{renc}\}$, *a re-encryption witness for* t *in* u *is a term* $\mathsf{rw}_u(t) \in \mathsf{st}(u)$, *such that* $\mathsf{rw}_u(t) \to_{\mathcal{R}}^* t{\downarrow}$ *and* $\mathsf{top}(\mathsf{rw}_u(t)) \in \{\mathsf{enc}, \mathsf{renc}\}$.

For intuition, note that $u = \mathsf{C}'[\mathsf{rw}_u(t)] \to_{\mathcal{R}}^* \mathsf{C}[t] = v$, for some contexts C and C'.

Example 12. Let $u = \pi_1(\langle \mathsf{renc}(\pi_1(\langle \mathsf{enc}(a, b, r_1), c \rangle), r_2), c \rangle)$. We have $u \to v_1 \to^*$ v_2 where $v_1 = \pi_1(\langle \mathsf{renc}(\mathsf{enc}(a, b, r_1), r_2), c \rangle)$ and $v_2 = \mathsf{enc}(a, b, f(r_1, r_2))$. Then, for $t = \mathsf{enc}(a, b, r_1) \in \mathsf{st}(v_1)$, we have $\mathsf{rw}_u(t) = t$. For $t = \mathsf{enc}(a, b, f(r_1, r_2)) \in \mathsf{st}(v_2)$, we have $\mathsf{rw}_{v_1}(t) = \mathsf{renc}(\mathsf{enc}(a, b, r_1), r_2)$ and $\mathsf{rw}_u(t) = \mathsf{renc}(\pi_1(\langle \mathsf{enc}(a, b, r_1), c \rangle), r_2)$.

Lemma 9. *Assume* $u \to_{\mathcal{R}}^* v$. *Then, for all term* $t \in \mathsf{st}(v)$ *with* $\mathsf{top}(t{\downarrow}) \in \{\mathsf{enc}, \mathsf{renc}\}$, *there always exists a re-encryption witness* $\mathsf{rw}_u(t)$.

In particular, the previous lemma shows that for all term t with $\mathsf{top}(t{\downarrow}) \in \{\mathsf{enc}, \mathsf{renc}\}$ there exists a re-encryption witness of $t{\downarrow}$ in t, that is $\mathsf{rw}_t(t{\downarrow})$.

Definition 12 (Re-encryption depth). *For all term* t, *we define its re-encryption depth* $\mathsf{rd}(t)$ *as follows:*

- $\mathsf{rd}(t) = 0$, *if* $\mathsf{top}(t{\downarrow}_{\mathcal{R}}) \notin \{\mathsf{enc}, \mathsf{renc}\}$
- $\mathsf{rd}(t) = 1$, *if* $\mathsf{top}(t{\downarrow}_{\mathcal{R}}) = \mathsf{enc}$ *and* $\mathsf{top}(\mathsf{rw}_t(t{\downarrow})) = \mathsf{enc}$
- $\mathsf{rd}(t) = \mathsf{rd}(t') + 1$, *if* $\mathsf{top}(t{\downarrow}_{\mathcal{R}}) \in \{\mathsf{enc}, \mathsf{renc}\}$ *and* $\mathsf{rw}_t(t{\downarrow}) = \mathsf{renc}(t', t'')$

Example 13. We have $\mathsf{rd}(\mathsf{renc}(\pi_1(\langle \mathsf{renc}(\mathsf{enc}(a, b, r_1), r_2), \mathsf{renc}(a, r_0) \rangle), r_3)) = 3$. Continuing example 12, we have $\mathsf{rd}(u) = 2$.

Next we show that for all term u with a re-encryption depth bounded by m, its normal form modulo $\mathcal{R}_m$ is the normal form modulo $\mathcal{R}_m$ of its re-encryption witness modulo $\mathcal{R}$:

Lemma 10. *Let* u *be a term such that, for all* $t \in \mathsf{st}(u)$, $\mathsf{rd}(t) \leq m + 1$. *Then, for all term* v *such that* $u \to_{\mathcal{R}}^* v$ *following a bottom-up rewriting sequence, we have* $u \to_{\mathcal{R}_m}^* v\rho$ *where*

$$\rho = \{t \mapsto \mathsf{rw}_u(t){\downarrow}_{\mathcal{R}_m} \mid t \in \mathsf{st}(v) \ \& \ \mathsf{top}(t) \in \{\mathsf{enc}, \mathsf{renc}\} \ \& \ t = t{\downarrow}_{\mathcal{R}}\}$$

Example 14. Consider the terms $u = \mathsf{renc}(\pi_1 \langle \mathsf{enc}(a, \mathsf{pub}(k), r_1), a \rangle, r_2)$ and $u_1 = \mathsf{dec}(u, k)$. Then, $\mathsf{rw}_u(u{\downarrow}_{\mathcal{R}}) = u$, and we obviously have $u{\downarrow}_{\mathcal{R}_m} = (u{\downarrow}_{\mathcal{R}})\rho = \mathsf{rw}_u(u{\downarrow}_{\mathcal{R}}){\downarrow}_{\mathcal{R}_m} = \mathsf{renc}(\mathsf{enc}(a, \mathsf{pub}(k), r_1), r_2)$. On the other hand, we have $u_1 \to_{\mathcal{R}_m} \mathsf{dec}(u{\downarrow}_{\mathcal{R}_m}, k) \to_{\mathcal{R}_m} a = u_1{\downarrow}_{\mathcal{R}} = u_1{\downarrow}_{\mathcal{R}}\rho$, where we have used the rule $\mathsf{dec}(\mathsf{renc}(\mathsf{enc}(x, \mathsf{pub}(y), z_0), z_1), y) \to x$ for the last rewriting step.

The following lemma bridges the gap backwards, from $\rightarrow^*_{\mathcal{R}_m}$ to $\rightarrow^*_{\mathcal{R}}$, and is an easy consequence of assumption (ae$_3$):

Lemma 11. *For all terms u, v such that $u \rightarrow^*_{\mathcal{R}_m} v$, we have $u \rightarrow^*_{\mathcal{R}} v$.*

Relying on (ap$_2$)-(ap$_4$) and lemma 8, we can show that for all trace $P \xrightarrow{w} Q$ and all nonce $t \in \mathrm{ran}(P)$, there exists a unique term $\mathrm{ciph}(t)$ such that $t = \mathrm{ran}(\mathrm{ciph}(t))$ and $\mathrm{ciph}(t) = u[\mathrm{fr}(Q)]$, for some term $u \in \mathrm{st}(P) \cup \mathcal{L}_{\mathrm{rf}}(\mathrm{fr}(Q))$.

Lemma 12. *Let $P \xrightarrow{w}_{\mathcal{R}} Q$ be a $\mathcal{L}_{\mathrm{rf}}$-local trace and $\phi = \mathrm{fr}(Q)$. Let T be a term in $\mathrm{st}(P) \cup \mathcal{L}_{\mathrm{rf}}(\mathrm{fr}(Q))$. Then, for all $t \in \mathrm{st}(T[\phi])$, we have:*

(a) $\mathrm{rd}(t) \leq 2 * |\mathrm{ran}_r(P)| + 2$
(b) $\mathrm{rd}(t) > 1 \implies \mathsf{Fact}_f(\mathrm{ran}(t{\downarrow})) \cap \mathrm{ran}(P) \neq \emptyset$
(c) $\mathrm{rw}_t(t{\downarrow}) = \mathrm{renc}(u, v) \implies$
   $-$ *either $v \in \mathrm{ran}(P)$ and $\mathrm{renc}(u, v) = \mathrm{ciph}(v)$*
   $-$ *or else $\mathsf{Fact}_f(v{\downarrow}) \cap \mathrm{ran}(P) = \emptyset$ and*
       $\bullet$ *either $\mathrm{top}(u{\downarrow}) \notin \{\mathrm{enc}, \mathrm{renc}\}$*
       $\bullet$ *or else $\exists t' \in \mathrm{ran}(P). \; \mathrm{rw}_u(u{\downarrow}) = \mathrm{ciph}(t')$*

The point (a) is obviously useful because it bounds the re-encryption depth of all term t that occurs in $\mathcal{L}_{\mathrm{rf}}$-local traces. It is proved by considering any chain of re-encryption witnesses starting from $\mathrm{rw}_t(t{\downarrow})$ and showing that each re-encryption performed by the environment (i.e. in recipes) must be followed by a re-encryption performed in P. Because $\mathrm{ciph}(t)$ is unique for all $t \in \mathrm{ran}_r(P)$, we can deduce from assumption (ap$_4$) that the total number of re-encryptions performed by P for every single ciphertext is bounded by $|\mathrm{ran}_r(P)|$, thus we deduce a bound of $2 * |\mathrm{ran}_r(P)| + 1$ for the length of any re-encryption chain. The points (b) and (c) will be useful to show that equalities of terms with positive re-encryption depth transfer to equalities of their respective re-encryption witnesses. In conjunction with lemma 10, this will allow us to transfer equalities modulo $\mathcal{E}$ to equalities modulo $\mathcal{E}_m$.

Finally, we prove a lemma showing that equivalence classes of $\mathcal{E}$ and $\mathcal{E}_m$ are the same in local traces:

Lemma 13. *Let $\mathcal{E} \in \mathsf{InpTh}$ and $P \xrightarrow{w}_{\mathcal{E}} Q$ be a $\mathcal{L}^{\mathcal{E}}_{\mathrm{rf}}$-local trace. Let $\phi = \mathrm{fr}(Q)$, $m = 2 * |\mathrm{ran}_r(P)| + 1$ and $\mathcal{E}_m \in \mathsf{OutTh}$ be the reduced theory that corresponds to $\mathcal{E}$ and m. Then,*

A. *for all terms $u_1, u_2 \in \mathrm{st}(P) \cup \mathcal{L}_{\mathrm{rf}}(\mathrm{fr}(Q))$, we have $u_1[\phi] =_{\mathcal{E}} u_2[\phi] \implies u_1[\phi] =_{\mathcal{E}_m} u_2[\phi]$*
B. *for all terms u_1, u_2, we have $u_1[\phi] =_{\mathcal{E}_m} u_2[\phi] \implies u_1[\phi] =_{\mathcal{E}} u_2[\phi]$*

To prove A, we first eliminate the AC equations, relying on lemma 7, the point (c) of lemma 12, lemma 8 and the definition of $\mathcal{L}_f$. This gives us $u_1[\phi] =_{\mathcal{E}} u_2[\phi] \implies u_1[\phi]{\downarrow}_{\mathcal{R}} = u_2[\phi]{\downarrow}_{\mathcal{R}}$. To complete the reduction, we first use the point (a) of lemma 12 and lemma 10 to show that $u_1[\phi]{\downarrow}_{\mathcal{R}_m} = u_1[\phi]{\downarrow}_{\mathcal{R}}\rho_1$ and $u_2[\phi]{\downarrow}_{\mathcal{R}_m} = u_2[\phi]{\downarrow}_{\mathcal{R}}\rho_2$, for some replacements ρ_1, ρ_2. Then, we use the points (b),(c) of lemma 12 to show that we must have $\rho_1 = \rho_2$. Therefore, we have $u_1[\phi]{\downarrow}_{\mathcal{R}} = u_2[\phi]{\downarrow}_{\mathcal{R}} \implies u_1[\phi]{\downarrow}_{\mathcal{R}_m} = u_2[\phi]{\downarrow}_{\mathcal{R}_m}$. As a consequence of lemma 13, we have:

Proposition 3. *Consider given the locality function $\mathcal{L}_{rf}$ and $\mathcal{E} \in$ InpTh. Then, for all plain processes P, Q, we have $P \simeq_{\mathcal{E}_m} Q \Leftrightarrow P \simeq_{\mathcal{E}} Q$, where $m = 2 *$ $\max(|\mathrm{ran}_r(P)|, |\mathrm{ran}_r(Q)|) + 1$.*

We conclude the proof of theorem 1 as a consequence of corollary 2, proposition 3 and corollary 3.

Application to vote privacy in Prêt à Voter. We have $\mathcal{E}_{\mathsf{PaV}} = (\mathcal{R}_{\mathsf{PaV}}, \mathsf{AC}_f)$, with $\mathcal{R}_{\mathsf{PaV}} = \mathcal{R}_{\mathsf{DY}} \cup \mathcal{R}_{\mathsf{renc}} \cup \mathcal{R}_{\mathsf{decP}} \cup \mathcal{R}_{\mathsf{mixP}} \cup \mathcal{R}_{\mathsf{vote}}$. Each of these five rewrite systems is AC-convergent, and so is the system $\mathcal{R}_{\mathsf{PaV}} \setminus \mathcal{R}_{\mathsf{mixP}}$. However, $\mathcal{R}_{\mathsf{PaV}}$ is not AC-confluent (and therefore not AC-convergent) due to critical pairs between rules in $\mathcal{R}_{\mathsf{renc}}$ and rules in $\mathcal{R}_{\mathsf{mixP}}$. The system $\mathcal{R}_{\mathsf{PaV}}$ can be made AC-convergent by completion, but this introduces other problems, notably violation of conditions (ae_1)-(ae_3) and the addition of a significant number of new rules, that may pose problems for ProVerif. That is why our current analisys does not cover the mixnet proofs in $\mathcal{R}_{\mathsf{mixP}}$ - we leave it as a subject for future work.

Note that $|\mathrm{ran}_r(P_{\mathsf{PaV}}\{v_1 \mapsto a\}\{v_2 \mapsto b\})| = |\mathrm{ran}_r(P_{\mathsf{PaV}}\{v_1 \mapsto b\}\{v_2 \mapsto a\})| = 2$, corresponding to the re-encryption of ballots from idA and idB, and we deduce a bound $m = 5$ in the application of Theorem 1. Therefore, from Theorem 1 and the result returned by the ProVerif code available online, we conclude

Corollary 4. *Prêt à Voter (without mixnet proofs) satisfies vote privacy for two eligible voters and two candidates.*

6   Conclusion and Future Work

Note that proposition 3 shows that abstracting $\mathcal{E}$ with $\mathcal{E}_m$ is not only sound, but also complete in local traces. This means that, to derive the completeness of our reduction for the full set of traces, we only have to extend lemma 5 to theories in InpTh and lemma 3 to theories in OutTh. In conjunction with lemma 1 and [5,15,10], this would lead to a first decision procedure for trace equivalence outside the class of subterm-convergent systems.

To be really faithul to algebraic properties of ElGamal re-encryption, AC_f should probably be extended to AG_f, unless e.g. it is computationally sound to consider only AC_f [18].

It would be nice to see how some of our restrictions can be lifted, in particular the quite strong restrictions on the occurence of the AC symbol in the protocol and in the theory. The restriction not to have re-encryptions in replicated processes, (ap_4), looks natural for the reduction that we have in mind, but is it really necessary in order to be able to handle re-encryption automatically?

Observational equivalence is stronger than trace equivalence, but it is unclear whether it is more appropriate for definitions of security. In any case, our reduction could also be used for verification of observational equivalence, and we would have to consider a notion of local trees instead of local traces for the correctness proof.

This paper shows that there exists an interesting relation between restrictions of the set of traces and restrictions of the equational theory. We have exhibited this relation only for two particular algebraic properties, and it would be interesting to see how it can be formulated in general.

References

1. Abadi, M., Cortier, V.: Deciding knowledge in security protocols under equational theories. Theoretical Computer Science 367(1-2), 2–32 (2006)
2. Abadi, M., Fournet, C.: Mobile values, new names, and secure communication. In: Proceedings of the 28th ACM Symposium on Principles of Programming Languages (POPL 2001), pp. 104–115 (January 2001)
3. Abadi, M., Gordon, A.D.: A calculus for cryptographic protocols: the spi calculus. Information and Computation 148(1) (1999)
4. Arapinis, M., Chothia, T., Ritter, E., Ryan, M.: Analysing unlinkability and anonymity using the applied pi calculus. In: CSF, pp. 107–121. IEEE Computer Society (2010)
5. Baudet, M.: Deciding security of protocols against off-line guessing attacks. In: Proceedings of the 12th ACM Conference on Computer and Communications Security (CCS 2005), Alexandria, Virginia, USA, pp. 16–25. ACM Press (November 2005)
6. Baudet, M., Cortier, V., Delaune, S.: YAPA: A Generic Tool for Computing Intruder Knowledge. In: Treinen, R. (ed.) RTA 2009. LNCS, vol. 5595, pp. 148–163. Springer, Heidelberg (2009)
7. Blanchet, B.: Automatic proof of strong secrecy for security protocols. In: IEEE Symposium on Security and Privacy, pp. 86–100 (2004)
8. Blanchet, B., Abadi, M., Fournet, C.: Automated verification of selected equivalences for security protocols. Journal of Logic and Algebraic Programming 75(1), 3–51 (2008)
9. Cheval, V., Comon-Lundh, H., Delaune, S.: Automating Security Analysis: Symbolic Equivalence of Constraint Systems. In: Giesl, J., Hähnle, R. (eds.) IJCAR 2010. LNCS, vol. 6173, pp. 412–426. Springer, Heidelberg (2010)
10. Cheval, V., Comon-Lundh, H., Delaune, S.: Trace equivalence decision: Negative tests and non-determinism. In: Proceedings of the 18th ACM Conference on Computer and Communications Security (CCS 2011), Chicago, Illinois, USA. ACM Press (October 2011)
11. Ciobâcă, Ş., Delaune, S., Kremer, S.: Computing knowledge in security protocols under convergent equational theories. Journal of Automated Reasoning (2011)
12. Comon-Lundh, H., Cortier, V.: Security Properties: Two Agents Are Sufficient. In: Degano, P. (ed.) ESOP 2003. LNCS, vol. 2618, pp. 99–113. Springer, Heidelberg (2003)
13. Comon-Lundh, H., Delaune, S.: The Finite Variant Property: How to Get Rid of Some Algebraic Properties. In: Giesl, J. (ed.) RTA 2005. LNCS, vol. 3467, pp. 294–307. Springer, Heidelberg (2005)
14. Corin, R., Doumen, J., Etalle, S.: Analysing password protocol security against off-line dictionary attacks. Electr. Notes Theor. Comput. Sci. 121, 47–63 (2005)
15. Cortier, V., Delaune, S.: A method for proving observational equivalence. In: Proceedings of the 22nd IEEE Computer Security Foundations Symposium (CSF 2009), Port Jefferson, NY, USA, pp. 266–276. IEEE Computer Society Press (July 2009)

16. Cortier, V., Delaune, S.: Decidability and combination results for two notions of knowledge in security protocols. Journal of Automated Reasoning (2011)
17. Cortier, V., Delaune, S., Lafourcade, P.: A survey of algebraic properties used in cryptographic protocols. Journal of Computer Security 14(1), 1–43 (2006)
18. Cortier, V., Kremer, S., Warinschi, B.: A survey of symbolic methods in computational analysis of cryptographic systems. Journal of Automated Reasoning 46(3-4), 225–259 (2010)
19. Cortier, V., Smyth, B.: Attacking and fixing helios: An analysis of ballot secrecy. In: Proc. of the 24th IEEE Computer Security Foundations Symposium, pp. 297–311 (2011)
20. Delaune, S., Kremer, S., Ryan, M.D.: Verifying privacy-type properties of electronic voting protocols. Journal of Computer Security 17(4), 435–487 (2009)
21. Dershowitz, N., Jouannaud, J.-P.: Rewrite systems. In: van Leeuwen, J. (ed.) Handbook of Theoretical Computer Science, vol. B, pp. 243–309. North-Holland (1990)
22. Durante, L., Sisto, R., Valenzano, A.: Automatic testing equivalence verification of spi calculus specifications. ACM Trans. Softw. Eng. Methodol. 12(2), 222–284 (2003)
23. Kremer, S., Mercier, A., Treinen, R.: Reducing equational theories for the decision of static equivalence. Journal of Automated Reasoning (2011)
24. Küsters, R., Truderung, T.: Using proverif to analyze protocols with Diffie-Hellman exponentiation. In: CSF, pp. 157–171. IEEE Computer Society (2009)
25. Küsters, R., Truderung, T.: Reducing protocol analysis with XOR to the XOR-free case in the horn theory based approach. J. Autom. Reasoning 46(3-4), 325–352 (2011)
26. Lynch, C., Meadows, C.: Sound Approximations to Diffie-Hellman Using Rewrite Rules. In: López, J., Qing, S., Okamoto, E. (eds.) ICICS 2004. LNCS, vol. 3269, pp. 262–277. Springer, Heidelberg (2004)
27. Mödersheim, S.: Diffie-Hellman without difficulty. In: FAST (2011)
28. Ryan, P.Y.A., Schneider, S.A.: Prêt à Voter with Re-encryption Mixes. In: Gollmann, D., Meier, J., Sabelfeld, A. (eds.) ESORICS 2006. LNCS, vol. 4189, pp. 313–326. Springer, Heidelberg (2006)
29. Tiu, A., Dawson, J.E.: Automating open bisimulation checking for the spi calculus. In: Proc. of the 23rd IEEE Computer Security Foundations Symposium, pp. 307–321 (2010)

Towards Unconditional Soundness: Computationally Complete Symbolic Attacker

Gergei Bana[1,*] and Hubert Comon-Lundh[2,**]

[1] NTT Communication Science Laboratories, Atsugi, Kanagawa, Japan
gergei.bana@lab.ntt.co.jp
[2] CNRS, INRIA Project SecSi and LSV, ENS Cachan, France
comon@lsv.ens-cachan.fr

Abstract. We consider the question of the adequacy of symbolic models versus computational models for the verification of security protocols. We neither try to include properties in the symbolic model that reflect the properties of the computational primitives nor add computational requirements that enforce the soundness of the symbolic model. We propose in this paper a different approach: everything is possible in the symbolic model, unless it contradicts a computational assumption. In this way, we obtain unconditional soundness almost by construction. And we do not need to assume the absence of dynamic corruption or the absence of key-cycles, which are examples of hypotheses that are always used in related works. We set the basic framework, for arbitrary cryptographic primitives and arbitrary protocols, however for trace security properties only.

1 Introduction

The automatic analysis of security protocols has been quite successful since 1990, yielding several tools [10,17,23]. However, when the outcome of one of these provers is "the protocol is secure", it must be understood as "secure in our model". Nothing guarantees that the necessary abstractions are relevant to actual implementations. For instance, consider the Needham-Schroder-Lowe protocol [20]. It has been proved secure by all the above-mentioned provers. However, there are several attacks, for instance when the encryption scheme does not guarantee the ciphertext integrity [26] or when the pairing is associative [21] or when some random number could be confused with some pairings [8].

For this reason, it is important to investigate what exactly the assumptions are, on the cryptographic primitives' implementations, that guarantee the faithfulness of the abstraction. (It is called *soundness* in the literature).

There are a lot of works providing some soundness results, typically the works initiated by Backes et al [5,3,6] and Abadi et al [1,15,13]. They essentially prove that a given symbolic model is fully abstract with respect to a computational one, assuming some properties of the security primitives. This guarantees that the security proofs that have been completed in the abstract model are also valid in a computational model.

---

* Partially supported by FCT project ComFormCrypt PTDC/EIA-CCO/113033/2009.
** Partially supported by the ANR project ProSe.

P. Degano and J.D. Guttman (Eds.): POST 2012, LNCS 7215, pp. 189–208, 2012.

However, these works require a very large set of assumptions, that are not always emphasized. For instance in [7] the complete list of assumptions for public-keys is listed; it is a long list of strong hypotheses, that are not fullfilled by most actual protocols. [13] make even less realistic assumptions, in order to get a stronger soundness result (which includes more security properties). All these results typically assume that no key cycles can ever be created, that bitstrings can be parsed in deterministic polynomial time into terms, that there is no dynamic corruption, that keys are certified, etc. These assumptions, as well as reasons why they are not realistic enough is discussed in [14]. Furthermore, each primitive requires a new soundness proof and each combination of primitives also requires a new soundness proof, unless much stronger properties are assumed [12]. Currently, it seems more realistic to use CRYPTOVERIF [11], completing the proofs directly in the computational model, than using a soundness result [2]. Is it really impossible to avoid manipulating computation times, probabilities, bitstring lengths... ?

In this paper, we advocate a new way of performing proofs in a symbolic, abstract, model, while keeping strong, computational guarantees establishing a general soundness result, but without establishing many specific soundness results for specific properties of primitives. Such properties can later be proven and added.

The idea is to design a symbolic setting, in which any adversarial action is possible, unless it contradicts some axiom expressing a property that must be satisfied under standard computational assumptions. In other words, computational properties, such as IND-CCA, can be (symbolically) axiomatized and added to the system in order to limit the possible adversarial moves. We do not require the axiomatization to be complete. The idea is to only list properties that we know for certain about the implementation, and allow any symbolic move consistent with those properties. In this way, either we find an attack, in which case there is at least one possible set of primitives satisfying the assumed properties and for which the security goal is violated, or the axioms were sufficient to ensure the security of the protocol, in which case any implementation fulfilling these axioms will ensure the security.

This approach has several advantages:

1. Though the proofs are performed in a symbolic setting, they are computationally valid.
2. Thanks to our result (Theorem 2), adding a new cryptographic primitive only requires to design an axiomatization of this primitive and prove it sound due to the cryptographic assumptions: the additional soundness proof is short and modular; it focuses on designated properties instead of considering whole execution models.
3. We may be able prove the security of protocols with weaker assumptions on the primitives. For instance, if we prove the security using only axioms that are sound for IND-CPA encryption, then IND-CPA will be a sufficient hypothesis for security.
4. In each security proof, all assumptions are clearly and formally stated as axioms.
5. In case an attack is found, it may be sufficient to add an axiom (expressing stronger hypotheses on the computational implementation of the primtives) ruling out the attack, then try proving again.
6. We may consider any cryptographic primitive, including XOR for instance (for which there are strong limitations of the computational soundness approach [4,25]). Dynamic corruption, key cycles, etc. are not a priori discarded.

Related works. The most closely related works are probably those that consider a proof system that is sound w.r.t. the computational semantics, such as [16,8]. Though these works are related, as far as the computational semantics of the logic is concerned, the overal strategy is completely different. We do not try to design a proof system working directly in the computational model: we only use first-order logic and standard inference rules in the symbolic model. Our approach is more inspired by circumscription [19], however circumscribing what is *not* possible. In other words, we do not design inference rules, we modify the transition system instead. This is similar in spirit to [24], in which any property of the hash function, that is not explicitly forbidden by some axiom, is considered as valid.

Contents of the paper. In this paper, we only state the framework of the method, prove a general soundness theorem in the case of trace properties, and prove soundness of an example axiom expressing secrecy of an IND-CCA encryption.

More precisely, protocols are identified to a formal transition system in the same spirit as CoSP [7]: we do not commit to a very particular way of specifying such a transition system. The possible transitions are, roughly, defined by a formula, that guards the transition by constraining the input message, a state move and a message that is sent out when the guard is satisfied. Such transitions can be interpreted in different models: symbolic models, in which the messages are terms and the guards are interpreted in a Herbrand model, or computational models, in which messages are bitstrings. In the symbolic models, we constrain the input messages to be *deducible* from the previous outputs and the public information. Such a deducibility condition is formalised using a deducibility predicate, whose interpretation is not fixed. This is a main difference with classical protocol verification: the attacker capabilities are not fixed, but rather they parametrize the model. Actually, we consider any attacker capability, that does not contradict the (computationally sound) axioms. On the computational side, the attacker is any probabilistic polynomial time Turing machine: the deduction capabilities are given by any such machine. These models are explained in the sections 2.2, 2.3, 2.5.

Next, we need to speficy the axioms and the (trace) security properties. We consider any first-order formula, that is built on the predicate symbols, that are used in the guards, as well as the deducibility predicate symbol. We need such general formulas, since we need to constrain the symbolic models of the deducibility relations, i.e., the symbolic attacker capabilities, according to the computational assumptions on the primitives. Typically, we may consider an axiom of the form: "if a plaintext can be deduced (resp. computed) from a ciphertext and a set of messages ϕ, then the decryption key has been sent out or else the plaintext can be deduced (resp. computed) from ϕ", that reflects some property of the encryption scheme. The meanings of these axioms/security properties become clear when we define a computational interpretation of such formulas, which we provide in the section 2.6.

The Section 3 is devoted to the main result, which states a general trace-mapping soundness property: independently of the primitives and their specific characteristics, if there is a computational attack, then there is a symbolic attack. Once more, the symbolic attacker has any capability, that is consistent with the axioms. So, this result, though subtle and not at all trivial to prove, is not surprising. The whole system was actually carefully designed with this aim in mind.

We also show in the Section 4 some axiom examples, that are proven sound under some standard cryptographic properties. We do not aim however at covering a large set of axioms. Further axioms will be added to a library each time they are required for the proof of a case study.

This paper aims at opening a new research direction: it seems very appealing and promising. We need however to investigate several case studies. As a "proof of concept", we have designed a complete set of axioms and proved the NSL protocol in our framework (available from the first-author's web page or upon request). This sufficient set of axioms shows also that some hypotheses of earlier works are not necessary (at least for weak secrecy and authentication).

2 Symbolic and Computational Models

2.1 Terms and Frames

Terms are built out of a set of function symbols $\mathcal{F}$ that contains an unbounded set of names $\mathcal{N}$ and an unbounded set of handles $\mathcal{H}$. Let $\mathcal{X}$ be an unbounded set of variables. Names and handles are zero arity function symbols. We will use names to denote items honestly generated by agents, while handles will denote inputs of the adversary. A ground term is a term without variables. *Frames* are sequences of terms together with name binders: a frame ϕ can be written $(\nu \bar{n}).p_1 \mapsto t_1, \ldots, p_n \mapsto t_n$ where $p_1, \ldots p_n$ are place holders that do not occur in $t_1, \ldots, t_n$ and $\bar{n}$ is a sequence of names. $\mathsf{fn}(\phi)$, the *free names* of ϕ are names occurring in some t_i and not in $\bar{n}$. The *variables* of ϕ are the variables of $t_1, \ldots, t_n$.

Example 1. We typically use a randomized public-key encryption symbol: $\{m\}^r_{eK_Q}$ is intended to represent the encryption of the plaintext m with the public-key of the principal Q, with a random seed r. More generally, we consider the example when there is a set of constructors $\mathcal{F}_c = \{\{\_\}^\__\_, \langle \_, \_ \rangle, e_\_, d_\_, K_\_\}$, and a set of destructors $\mathcal{F}_d = \{dec(\_, \_), \pi_1(\_), \pi_2(\_)\}$, and $\mathcal{F} = \mathcal{F}_c \cup \mathcal{F}_d \cup \mathcal{N} \cup \mathcal{H}$.

2.2 Formulas

Let $\mathcal{P}$ be a set of predicate symbols over tems. $\mathcal{P}$ is assumed to contain the equality $=$ (which is interpreted as a congruence), used as $t_1 = t_2$, and a predicate $\vdash$, which takes as arguments an n-tuple of terms on its left and a term on its right (and which is intended to model the computation capabilities), that is, written as $t_1, \ldots, t_n \vdash t$. (More precisely, it is an infinite sequence of predicates, with arguments $n + 1$.)

We are not interested in any specific symbolic interpretation of these predicate symbols. We wish to consider *any* possible symbolic interpretation, that satisfies some requirements; the aim is to allow anything that is not forbidden by explicit assumptions.

Example 2. $\forall x, \forall y.(\{x\}^s_{eK_Q} = \{y\}^{s'}_{eK_Q} \to x = y)$ is such a formula, the validity of which follows from the uniqueness of decryption.

Let $\mathcal{M}$ denote then any first-order structure that interprets the function and predicate symbols of the logic. We only assume that $=$ is interpreted in $\mathcal{M}$ as the equality in the underlying domain $D_{\mathcal{M}}$. The relation in $\mathcal{M}$ (that is, a relation for elements in $D_{\mathcal{M}}$), interpreting the deducibility predicate $\vdash$ is denoted as $\vdash_{\mathcal{M}}$.

Given an assigment σ of elements in $D_{\mathcal{M}}$ to the free variables of term t, we write $[\![t]\!]_{\mathcal{M}}^{\sigma}$ for the interpretation of t in $\mathcal{M}$ ($[\![\_]\!]_{\mathcal{M}}^{\sigma}$ is the unique extension of σ into a homomorphism of $\mathcal{F}$-algebras).

For any first order structure $\mathcal{M}$ over the functions $\mathcal{F}$ and predicates $\mathcal{P}$, given a first order formula θ and an assignment σ of elements in the domain of $\mathcal{M}$ to the free variables of θ, the satisfaction relation $\mathcal{M}, \sigma \models \theta$ is defined as usual in first-order logic.

Example 3. Consider the public-key encryption setting of example 1. We may use unary predicate symbols to restrict sets of data. Assume for instance that W is supposed to represent the set of agent names, and M is supposed to represent well formed terms (that are equal to a term built with symbols in $\mathcal{F}_c$).

$$W(\pi_1(dec(h, db))) \wedge M(\pi_2(dec(h, db)))$$

is a formula, that expresses that the handle h can be decrypted and projected into two components, one of which is an agent name.

2.3 Protocols

We do not stick to any particular syntax for the definition of protocols. We only assume that it defines a transition system as follows. Q is a set of *control states*, together with a finite set of free variables.

Definition 1. *A* protocol *is a recursive (actually PTIME) set of tuples*

$$(q(\overline{n}), q'(\overline{n} \cdot \overline{n'}), \langle x_1, \ldots, x_k \rangle, x, \psi, s)$$

where $q, q' \in Q$, $x_1, \ldots, x_k, x$ are variables $\overline{n}, \overline{n'}$ are finite sequences of names, ψ is a first order formula over the set of predicate symbols $\mathcal{P}$ and function symbols $\mathcal{F}$ and the names $\overline{n} \cup \overline{n'}$, whose free variables are in $\{x_1, \ldots, x_n, x\}$ and s is a term whose free variables are in $\{x_1, \ldots, x_n, x\}$.

For example, ψ can be a formula such as $dec(x, k) = n$, that checks that the current input is a ciphertext whose plaintext is a previously generated nonce n: ψ guards the transition. s is the output message, when the transition succeeds. The intended meaning of these rules is that a transition from the sate q to the state q' is possible, given the previous inputs $x_1, \ldots, x_n$ and the new input x, if the formula ψ is satisfied. In such a case, the names $\overline{n'}$ are generated and the message s is sent.

Such a formalism is quite general; we only assume here (for simplicity) a single, public, communication channel. Typically, applied π-calculus processes can be translated into such transition rules, that are similar to the CoSP framework of [7].

Example 4. Consider a single session of the NSL protocol. The states consist of pairs of the local states of each of the processes for A and B. Instead of listing the transitions as tuples, we write $\psi : q(\overline{n}) \xrightarrow{s} q'(\overline{n})$ and they are diplayed in the figure 1. In this version of the protocol, the responder is willing to communicate with anybody, hence only checks $W(\pi_1(dec(y, dK_B)))$; the intended meaning of W is a set of agent names. If

$$T :$$

$$q_0^A(n, r, r'') \qquad \xrightarrow{\{\langle A,n \rangle\}_e^r K_B} \qquad q_1^A(n, r, r'')$$

$$\left.\begin{array}{l} \pi_1(dec(x, dK_A)) = B \\ \wedge\ \pi_1(\pi_2(dec(x, dK_A))) = n \end{array}\right\} : q_1^A(n, r, r'') \qquad \xrightarrow{\{\pi_2(\pi_2(dec(x, dK_A)))\}_e^{r''} K_B} \qquad q_2^A(n, r, r'')$$

$$\left.\begin{array}{l} W(\pi_1(dec(y, dK_B))) \\ \wedge\ M(\pi_2(dec(y, dK_B))) \end{array}\right\} : q_0^B(n', r') \qquad \xrightarrow{\{\langle B,\langle \pi_2(dec(y,dK_B)),n' \rangle\rangle\}_e^{r'} K_{\pi_1(dec(y,dK_B))}} \qquad q_1^B(n', r')$$

$$dec(z, dK_B)) = n' : \qquad q_1^B(n', r') \qquad \longrightarrow \qquad q_2^B(n', r')$$

Fig. 1. The 3 transitions of 1 session of NSL

we wish to describe an unbounded number of sessions, we need to record in the control state the states of every (opened) *A*-session and (opened) *B*-session. This yields an infinite, yet recursive, set of transition rules.

Definition 2. A symbolic state *of the network consists of:*

- *a control state $q \in Q$ together with a sequence of names (that have been generated so far) $n_1, \ldots, n_k$*
- *a sequence constants called* handles $h_1, \ldots, h_n$ *(recording the attacker's inputs)*
- *a ground frame ϕ (the agents outputs)*
- *a set of formulas Θ (the conditions that have to be satisfied in order to reach the state).*

A *symbolic transition sequence* of a protocol Π is a sequence

$$(q_0(\overline{n_0}), \emptyset, \phi_0, \emptyset) \to \ldots \to (q_m(\overline{n_m}), \langle h_1, \ldots, h_m \rangle, \phi_m, \Theta_m)$$

if, for every $m - 1 \geq i \geq 0$, there is a transition rule

$$(q_i(\overline{\alpha_i}), q_{i+1}(\overline{\alpha_{i+1}}), \langle x_1, \ldots, x_i \rangle, x, \psi, s)$$

such that $\overline{n} = \overline{\alpha_{i+1}} \setminus \overline{\alpha_i}$, $\phi_{i+1} = (\nu\overline{n}).(\phi_i \cdot p \mapsto s\rho_i\sigma_{i+1})$, $\overline{n_{i+1}} = \overline{n_i} \uplus \overline{n}$, $\Theta_{i+1} = \Theta_i \cup \{\phi_i \vdash h_{i+1}, \psi\rho_i\sigma_{i+1}\}$ where $\sigma_i = \{x_1 \mapsto h_1, \ldots, x_i \mapsto h_i\}$ and ρ_i is a renaming of the sequence $\overline{\alpha_i}$ into the sequence $\overline{n_i}$. We assume a renaming that ensures the freshness of the names $\overline{n}$: $\overline{n} \cap \overline{n_i} = \emptyset$.

Definition 3. *Given an interpretation $\mathcal{M}$, a transition sequence of Π*

$$(q_0(\overline{n_0}), \emptyset, \phi_0, \emptyset) \to \ldots \to (q_m(\overline{n_m}), \langle h_1, \ldots, h_m \rangle, \phi_m, \Theta_m)$$

is valid w.r.t. $\mathcal{M}$ *if, for every $m - 1 \geq i \geq 0$,*

$$\mathcal{M} \models \Theta_{i+1}$$

Example 5. We show the beginning of a possible branch in the symbolic execution of NSL.

$$(q_0, \emptyset, \phi_0, \emptyset) \quad (q_1, H_1, \phi_1, \Theta_1) \quad (q_2, H_2, \phi_2, \Theta_2) \quad (q_3, H_3, \phi_3, \Theta_3) \quad (q_4, H_4, \phi_4, \Theta_4)$$

Where $\overline{n} = n, r, r'', n', r'$, $q_0 = (q_0^A, q_0^B)(\overline{n})$, and $q_1 = (q_1^A, q_0^B)(\overline{n})$, $q_2 = (q_1^A, q_1^B)(\overline{n})$, and $q_3 = (q_2^A, q_1^B)(\overline{n})$ and $q_4 = (q_2^A, q_2^B)(\overline{n})$. In other words, we interleave the actions of A and B, as in an expected execution and assume that the two processes were first activated (if not, we could introduce two transitions activating the processes).

- $\phi_0 = \nu_{K_A K_B A B}(p_0 \mapsto (A, B, eK_A, eK_B))$,
  $\Theta_0 = \emptyset$
- $H_1 = \langle h_1 \rangle$,
  ϕ_1 extends ϕ_0 with $p_1 \mapsto \{\langle A, n \rangle\}_{eK_B}^r$,
  $\Theta_1 = \{\phi_0 \vdash h_1\}$
- $H_2 = \langle h_1, h_2 \rangle$,
  ϕ_2 extends ϕ_1 with $p_2 \mapsto \{\langle B, \langle \pi_2 (dec(h_2, dK_B)), n' \rangle \rangle\}_{eK_{\pi_1(dec(h_2, dK_B))}}^{r'}$,
  $\Theta_2 = \Theta_1 \cup \{\phi_1 \vdash h_2, M(\pi_2 (dec(h_2, dK_B))), W(\pi_1 (dec(h_2, dK_B)))\}$
- $H_3 = \langle h_1, h_2, h_3 \rangle$,
  ϕ_3 extends ϕ_2 with $p_3 \mapsto \{\pi_2 (\pi_2 (dec(h_3, dK_A)))\}_{eK_B}^{r''}$,
  $\Theta_3 = \Theta_2 \cup \{\phi_2 \vdash h_3, \pi_1 (\pi_2 (dec(h_3, dK_A))) = n, \pi_1 (dec(h_3, dK_A)) = B\}$,
- $H_4 = \langle h_1, h_2, h_3, h_4 \rangle$, $\phi_4 = \phi_3$,
  $\Theta_4 = \Theta_3 \cup \{\phi_3 \vdash h_4, dec(h_4, dK_B)) = n'\}$,

Let $\mathcal{M}$ be a model in which $\pi_1 (dec(h_2, dK_B)) = A$ and

$$h_2 =_{\mathcal{M}} \{\langle A, n \rangle\}_{eK_B}^r, \qquad h_3 =_{\mathcal{M}} \{\langle B, \langle n, n' \rangle \rangle\}_{eK_A}^{r'}, \qquad h_4 =_{\mathcal{M}} \{n'\}_{eK_B}^{r''},$$

and $\vdash_{\mathcal{M}}$ is simply the classical Dolev-Yao deduction relation. Then the execution sequence is valid w.r.t. $\mathcal{M}$, and this corresponds to the correct execution of the NSL protocol between A and B.

There are however other models in which this transition sequence is valid. For instance let $\mathcal{M}'$ be such that $h_2 =_{\mathcal{M}'} n$ and $\phi_1 \vdash_{\mathcal{M}'} n$ and $n =_{\mathcal{M}'} \{\langle A, n \rangle\}_{eK_B}^r$, (and h_3, h_4 as above). We get again a valid transition sequence w.r.t. $\mathcal{M}'$. Though, in what follows, we will discard such sequences, thanks to some axioms.

Example 6. Consider again the transitions of the example 5. Now consider a model $\mathcal{M}$ in which $n_0, \{B, n, n'\}_{eK_A}^r \vdash_{\mathcal{M}} \{B, n_0, n'\}_{eK_A}^r$ for an honestly generated nonce n_0 that can be chosen by the attacker: the transition sequence of the previous example is also valid w.r.t. this model. This will yield an attack, using a malleability property of the encryption scheme, as in [26]. Discarding such attacks requires some properties of the encryption scheme (for instance IND-CCA). It can be ruled out by a non-malleability axiom (the discussion of which is out of the scope of this paper, but included in the NSL proof referred to in the introduction).

From these examples, we see that unexpected attacks can be found when some assumption is not explicitly stated as an axiom to limit adversarial capabilities.

2.4   Axioms and Security Properties

For simplicity, we only consider reachability security properties. The extension to any trace property should not be very difficult: it suffices to record some values along the trace. Security properties (and, later, axioms) are first-order formulas that may contain state-dependent predicates and/or predicates that get fixed interpretation. As in the previous sections, $\mathcal{M}$ is an arbitrary first-order structure and σ is an assignment of the free variables to elements of $D_{\mathcal{M}}$.

First, we add atomic formulas $\hat{\phi}, s_1, \ldots, s_n \vdash t$, where $\hat{\phi}$ is just part of the syntax of this predicate (not an input of the predicate), which aims at ranging over frames (when interpretating the predicate) and is evaluated in every state. For $t_1, \ldots, t_m$ closed terms, $\mathcal{M}, \sigma, \langle t_1, \ldots, t_m \rangle, \overline{n} \models \hat{\phi}, s_1, \ldots, s_n \vdash t$ iff $\mathcal{M}, \sigma \models s_1, \ldots, s_n, t_1, \ldots, t_m \vdash t$.

In addition, we consider the following atomic formulas, whose evaluation only depends on the state, independently of the first-order structure $\mathcal{M}$.

- RandGen(s) (s is a ground term) expresses that s has been randomly generated:
  $\mathcal{M}, \sigma, \langle t_1, \ldots, t_m \rangle, (n_1, \ldots, n_k) \models$ RandGen(s)   iff $s \in \{n_1, \ldots, n_k\}$
- $t \sqsubseteq \hat{\phi}$ (t is a ground term) expresses that t is a subterm of the messages sent so far:
  $\mathcal{M}, \sigma, \langle t_1, \ldots, t_m \rangle, \overline{n} \models t \sqsubseteq \hat{\phi}$ iff t is a subterm of some t_i.
- We also may use the derived predicate (as an abbreviation):

$$\mathsf{fresh}(x, \hat{\phi}) = \mathsf{RandGen}(x) \wedge x \not\sqsubseteq \hat{\phi}$$

$\sqsubseteq$ and RandGen() are *interpreted predicates* since their interpretation does not depend on $\mathcal{M}$. Bound variables that appear within an interpreted predicate are called *constrained variables*. As in other works on constrained logics (see for instance [18]), such variables are used to schematize several first-order formulas and are replaced with ground terms built on $\mathcal{F}$. Therefore, the interpretation of axioms and security properties that may involve interpreted predicates, is modified, only in case of a quantification on a constrained variable x, in which case x is replaced by any (or some, for existential quantification) ground term:

If x is a constrained variable (that is, θ has an interpreted predicate and x appears in it), then,

$$\mathcal{M}, \sigma, \langle t_1, \ldots, t_n \rangle, (n_1, \ldots, n_k) \models \forall x.\theta$$

iff, for every ground term t,

$$\mathcal{M}, \sigma, \langle t_1, \ldots, t_n \rangle, (n_1, \ldots, n_k) \models \theta\{x \mapsto t\}$$

We have a similar definition for existential quantifications of such variables. All other cases follow the classical definition of the first-order satisfaction relation.[1] This yields a satisfaction relation $\mathcal{M}, \sigma, \langle t_1, \ldots, t_m \rangle, \overline{n} \models \theta$, and thus of $\mathcal{M}, \sigma, \phi, \overline{n} \models \theta$ with ϕ

---

[1] It would in fact be possible to avoid the notion of constrained variables if we defined $D_{\mathcal{M}}$ to be a free $\mathcal{F}$-algebra, and $=$ a congruence relation on it (as opposed to the equality of $D_{\mathcal{M}}$), and later parts of the paper could be adjusted accordingly. However, since constrained variables are more convenient for automatic verification, the authors decided to present the theory utilizing them.

having the terms $\langle t_1, \ldots, t_m \rangle$. When θ has no free variable, we may omit σ. Similarly, if θ does not contain atomic formulas that depend on ϕ (resp. $\overline{n}$), we may omit these components: we get back to the satisfaction relation of section 2.2.

We define now the satisfaction relation in a state:

$$\mathcal{M}, (q, \langle h_1, \ldots, h_m \rangle, \overline{n}, \phi_m, \Theta) \models \theta \quad \text{iff} \quad \mathcal{M}, \phi_m, \overline{n} \models \theta.$$

Definition 4. *A symbolic interpretation and a protocol* satisfy the security property θ, *written as*

$$\mathcal{M}, \Pi \models \theta,$$

if for any sequence of transitions that is executable in $\mathcal{M}$ and that yields the state $(q_m, \langle h_1, \ldots, h_m \rangle, \overline{n_m}, \phi_m, \Theta_m)$,

$$\mathcal{M}, (q_m, \langle h_1, \ldots, h_m \rangle, \overline{n_m}, \phi_m, \Theta_m) \models \theta.$$

Example 7. Concerning security properties, consider the NSL protocol. We may state the confidentiality of n:

$$\neg \hat{\phi} \vdash n$$

Consider now an authenticity property. We modify slightly the states of the transition system, including a commitment on the nonce on which the parties are supposed to agree. We let c_i be a special function symbol, that takes as arguments A, B, n_1, n_2: who commits, for who and the corresponding nonces. $c_i(A, B, n_1, \pi_2(\pi_2(dec(x, dK_B))))$ is sent at the end by the initiator. For the responder, there is a similar commitment: at the end of the protocol, B emits $c_r(\pi_1(dec(x, dK_B)), B, \pi_2(dec(y, dK_B), n_2))$. We state as axioms that c_i, c_r cannot help the attacker and cannot be forged. For instance: $\forall x, y, z, w. \hat{\phi}, c_i(x, y, z, w) \not\vdash z, w$ and $\forall x, y, z, w. \hat{\phi} \vdash c_i(x, y, z, w) \rightarrow c_i(x, y, z, w) \sqsubseteq \hat{\phi}$. The agreement property (on n) may then be stated (for instance) as:

$$\forall x, y, z, w. c_r(x, y, z, w)) \sqsubseteq \hat{\phi} \rightarrow \exists x' z' w' (c_i(x', y, z', w') \sqsubseteq \hat{\phi} \wedge x = x' \wedge z = z' \wedge w = w')$$

That is: x's view of z, w is the same as y's view of z, w.

With such a definition, for any security property and any protocol there will (almost) always be an interpretation for which the property is violated. Hence we restrict the class of symbolic interpretations, ruling out the interpretation whose all computational counterparts would violate some security assumption on the primitives. More precisely, we consider a set of *axioms* $\mathcal{A}$, which is a set of first-order formulas in the same format as the security properties. We restrict our attention to symbolic interpretations that satisfy $\mathcal{A}$.

Example 8.   – For instance we could include in $\mathcal{A}$ a formula

$$\mathsf{fresh}(k, \hat{\phi}) \rightarrow \neg(\hat{\phi} \vdash k)$$

that states that an attacker cannot guess (except with negligible probability) a randomly generated name. Adding such an axiom in $\mathcal{A}$ rules out symbolic interpretations in which this deduction is possible.

– If the computational implementation is such (e.g. they are tagged), we may include,

$$\forall x, y, z, A, r. \langle x, y \rangle \neq \{z\}_{K_A}^r$$

stating that pairs and ciphertexts cannot be confused.

We will see more examples in Section 4.

We may assume w.l.o.g that the axioms and security properties are just (universally quantified) clauses.

2.5   Computational Interpretation

The computational interpretations are just a special case of interpretation of our formulas, when they do not depend on the state of the transition system. We define them again here, since we wish to introduce some additional notions. Also, the computational executions of the protocols rely on a concrete adversary, given by a Turing machine, while in general, the interpretation of functions and predicates need not to be computable.

We consider a familly computational algebras, parametrized by a security parameter η, in which each function symbol is interpreted as a polynomially computable function on bitstrings (that may return an error message). Given then a sample τ of names (for every name n, its interpretation is a bitstring $\tau(n)$), every ground term t is interpreted as a bitstring $[\![t]\!]_\tau$ in such a way that $[\![\_]\!]_\tau$ is a homomorphism of $\mathcal{F}$-algebras. More generally, if σ is an assignment of the variables of t to bitstrings $[\![t]\!]_\tau^\sigma$ is the (unique) extension of τ (on names) and σ (on variables) as a homomorphism of $\mathcal{F}$-algebras.

Similarly, all predicate symbols are interpreted as polynomially computable functions on bitstrings. The equality predicate is interpreted as a strict equality on bitsrings: $\tau \models^c t_1 = t_2$ if $[\![t_1]\!]_\tau$ is not an error, $[\![t_2]\!]_\tau$ is not an error and $[\![t_1]\!]_\tau = [\![t_2]\!]_\tau$.

This interpretation is extended to arbitrary closed formulas whose atomic formulas do not depend on the state. This yields the satisfaction relation $\tau \models^c \theta$. We will define later the computational interpretation of arbitrary formulas in a given state.

We now define computational executions.

Definition 5. *Given a set of transition rules, a* computational state *consists of*

– *A symbolic state s (that is itself a tuple $q(\overline{n}, \overline{h}, \phi, \Theta)$)*
– *a sequence of bitstrings $\langle b_1, \ldots, b_m \rangle$ (the attacker's outputs)*
– *A sequence $\langle b_1', \ldots, b_n' \rangle$ of bitstrings (the agents outputs)*
– *The configuration γ of the attacker.*

Definition 6. *Given a PPT interactive Turing machine $\mathcal{M}$ and a sample τ, a sequence of transitions*

$$(s_0, \emptyset, \boldsymbol{b_0'}, \gamma_0) \to \ldots \to (s_m, \langle b_1, \ldots, b_m \rangle, \langle b_1', \ldots, b_m' \rangle, \gamma_m)$$

is (computationally) valid w.r.t. $\mathcal{M}$ and τ *if*

– *$s_0 \to \cdots \to s_m$ is a transition sequence of the protocol*
– *for every $i = 0, \ldots m - 1$, $s_i = (q_i(\overline{n_i}), \overline{h}_i, \phi_i, \Theta_i)$, $\phi_{i+1} = (\nu\overline{n}).\phi_i \cdot u_i$, $[\![u_i]\!]_\tau = b_{i+1}'$*

- *for every $i = 0, ..., m - 1$, there is a configuration γ_i' of the machine $\mathcal{M}$ such that $\gamma_i \vdash_M^* \gamma_i' \vdash_M^* \gamma_{i+1}$ and γ_i' is in a sending state, the sending tape containing b_{i+1}, γ_{i+1} is in a receiving state, the receiving tape containing b_{i+1}'*
- *for every $i = 0, ..., m - 1$, $\tau, \{x_1 \mapsto b_1, ..., x \mapsto b_{i+1}\} \models^c \Theta_{i+1}$.*

Intuitively, b_0' is the attacker's initial knowledge and we simply replaced symbolic deductions/symbolic models of the section 2.3 with computations/computational models.

2.6   Computational Validity of Security Properties and Axioms

We already considered the computational satisfaction of formulas, except for formulas that depend on the states. Given a PT Turing machine $\mathcal{A}$, we define then

$$\mathcal{A}, \tau \models^c t_1, ..., t_n \vdash t \quad \text{iff} \quad \mathcal{A}(\llbracket t_1 \rrbracket_\tau, ..., \llbracket t_n \rrbracket_\tau) = \llbracket t \rrbracket_\tau$$

The difficulty now is that we do not want to define $\mathcal{A}, \tau \models^c \hat{\phi} \vdash t_1 \rightarrow \hat{\phi} \vdash t_2$ as $\mathcal{A}, \tau \models \hat{\phi} \vdash t_2$ or $\mathcal{A}, \tau \not\models \hat{\phi} \vdash t_1$. In order to understand this, consider for instance the formula

$$\theta : \quad \forall_{t,K,R}(\hat{\phi}, \{t\}_{eK}^R \vdash t \rightarrow \{t\}_{eK}^R \sqsubseteq \hat{\phi} \vee dK \sqsubseteq \hat{\phi} \vee \hat{\phi} \vdash t)$$

We want (intuitively) IND-CCA encryption schemes to satisfy this formula. However, consider an instance of this axiom in which $\hat{\phi}$ is the pair $\phi = \nu n_1 n_2 . \langle n_1, n_2 \rangle$, and t is n_1. Now, let $\mathcal{A}$ be a machine which, on input $\llbracket \langle n_1, n_2 \rangle \rrbracket_\tau, \llbracket \{n_1\}_{eK}^r \rrbracket_\tau$ returns n_1 and, on input $\llbracket \langle n_1, n_2 \rangle \rrbracket_\tau$ only, returns $\llbracket n_2 \rrbracket_\tau$. For every τ, $\mathcal{A}, \tau \not\models^c \theta$. Hence, whatever security is provided by the encryption scheme, there is an attack on the property.

This paradox comes from the deterministic interpretation of the deducibility relation: while, symbolically, it is a relation, it must be a function in the computational setting since we cannot consider non-deterministic machines. The intended interpretation therefore involves several machines: roughly, for any machine that can compute $\llbracket t \rrbracket_\tau$ from $\llbracket \phi \rrbracket_\tau, \llbracket \{t\}_{eK}^r \rrbracket_\tau$, either there is a machine that can compute $\llbracket t \rrbracket_\tau$ from $\llbracket \phi \rrbracket_\tau$ or else the actual frame contains either dK or $\{t\}_{eK}^r$. These two machines need of course to be independent of τ. This is the definition that we formalize now for arbitrary security properties.

Let $\mathcal{M}$ be an interactive PPT Turing machine with a special challenge control state q_c. We may regard this machine as an attacker, who moves to the state q_c when (s)he thinks that (s)he is ready to break the security property.

In what follows, S is any (polynomial time) non-negligible set of interpretations of names, and $S_\top$ is the set of all name interpretations. $\mathcal{M}, \Pi \models^c \theta$ iff $\mathcal{M}, \Pi, S_\top \models^c \theta$ and $\Pi \models^c \theta$ if $\mathcal{M}, \Pi \models^c \theta$ for every $\mathcal{M}$ with q_c.

We introduce machines that compute witnesses for the unconstrainted quantified variables.

- $\mathcal{M}, \Pi, S \models^c \exists x.\theta$ iff there is a PT machine $\mathcal{A}_x$ such that $\mathcal{M}, \Pi, S, \mathcal{A}_x \models^c \theta$
- $\mathcal{M}, \Pi, S, \mathcal{A}_{x_1}, ..., \mathcal{A}_{x_n} \models^c \forall x.\theta$ iff for any probabilistic polynomial time machine $\mathcal{A}_x$, $\mathcal{M}, \Pi, S, \mathcal{A}_{x_1}, ..., \mathcal{A}_{x_n}, \mathcal{A}_x \models^c \theta$

If x is a constrained variable, the interpretation of $\forall x.\theta$ is analogous to the symbolic case: $\mathcal{M}, \Pi, S, \mathcal{A}_{x_1}, \ldots, \mathcal{A}_{x_n} \models^c \forall x.\theta$ if and only if for every ground term t, the satisfaction $\mathcal{M}, \Pi, S, \mathcal{A}_{x_1}, \ldots, \mathcal{A}_{x_n} \models^c \theta\{x \mapsto t\}$ holds (and similarly for existential quantification). If σ is a sequence of machines, one for each free variable x of θ,

- $\mathcal{M}, \Pi, S, \sigma \models^c \theta_1 \wedge \theta_2$ iff $\mathcal{M}, \Pi, S, \sigma \models^c \theta_1$ and $\mathcal{M}, \Pi, S, \sigma \models^c \theta_2$.
- $\mathcal{M}, \Pi, S, \sigma \models^c \theta_1 \vee \theta_2$ iff there are sets $S_1 \cup S_2 = S$ such that $\mathcal{M}, \Pi, S_1, \sigma \models^c \theta_1$ and $\mathcal{M}, \Pi, S_2, \sigma \models^c \theta_2$.
- $\mathcal{M}, \Pi, S, \sigma \models^c \theta_1 \to \theta_2$ iff for any $S' \subseteq S$ non-negligible, $\mathcal{M}, \Pi, S', \sigma \models^c \theta_1$ implies $\mathcal{M}, \Pi, S', \sigma \models^c \theta_2$
- $\mathcal{M}, \Pi, S, \sigma \models^c \neg\theta$ iff for any S', if $\mathcal{M}, \Pi, S', \sigma \models^c \theta$, then $S \cap S'$ is negligible
- in the case of an atomic formula $P(t_1, \ldots, t_n)$ where $P \notin \{\vdash, \sqsubseteq, \mathsf{RandGen}()\}$, $\mathcal{M}, \Pi, S, \sigma \models^c P(t_1, \ldots, t_n)$ if there is an overwhelming subset S' of S such that the following holds. For any $\tau \in S'$, consider the unique valid computation (if there is one) of Π with respect to $\mathcal{M}, \tau$ that yields a configuration of $\mathcal{M}$, which is in the control state q_c with a bitstring b on the output tape. Let $q(\overline{n})$ be the control state reached at this point and c be the restriction of τ to $\overline{n}$. Let $b_x = \mathcal{A}_x(b, c)$ for every $\mathcal{A}_x \in \sigma$, and α be the sequence of assignments $x \mapsto b_x$. Then $(\llbracket t_1 \rrbracket_\tau^\alpha, \ldots, \llbracket t_n \rrbracket_\tau^\alpha) \in \llbracket P \rrbracket$.
- For the deducibility predicate, $\mathcal{M}, \Pi, S, \sigma \models^c \hat{\phi}, t_1, \ldots, t_n \vdash t$ if for all non-negligible $S' \subseteq S$, there is a non-negligible $S'' \subseteq S'$ such that there is a PT Turing machine $\mathcal{A}_D$ such that, for all $\tau \in S''$, the unique valid computation (if there is one) of Π with respect to $\mathcal{M}, \tau$ that yields a configuration of $\mathcal{M}$, which is in the control state q_c with a bitstring b on the output tape, an actual frame ϕ_m and such that, letting $b_x = \mathcal{A}_x(b, \overline{c})$ where $\overline{c} = \tau(\overline{n})$ for the names $\overline{n}$ in the current state, for every $\mathcal{A}_x \in \sigma$, and α be the sequence of assignments $x \mapsto b_x$, $\mathcal{A}_D(\llbracket \phi_m \rrbracket_\tau, \llbracket t_1 \rrbracket_\tau^\alpha, \ldots, \llbracket t_n \rrbracket_\tau^\alpha, b) = \llbracket t \rrbracket_\tau^\alpha$.
- $\mathcal{M}, \Pi, S, \sigma \models^c t_1, \ldots, t_n \vdash t$ is defined exactly as above, however removing ϕ.
- If P is an interpreted predicate, $\mathcal{M}, \Pi, S, \sigma \models P(t_1, \ldots, t_n)$ iff there is an overwhelming subset $S' \subseteq S$ such that, for any $\tau \in S'$, the unique valid computation of Π with respect to $\mathcal{M}, \tau$ that yields a computational state $(q(\overline{n}, \overline{h}, \phi, \Theta), \overline{b}, \overline{b'}, \gamma)$ in the control state q_c such that $P(t_1, \ldots, t_n)$ is true in $q(\overline{n}, \overline{h}, \phi, \Theta)$. (Remember that the evaluation of such predicates do not depend on the model).

$\mathcal{M}, \Pi \models^{nnp} \theta$ (read "$\mathcal{M}, \Pi$ satisfies θ with non negligible probability") if there is a non-negligible set S and a PPT machine $\mathcal{A}$ such that $\mathcal{A}(n_1, \ldots, n_k, b_1, \ldots, b_k)$ returns 1 iff there is a $\tau \in S$ such that, for all i, $\tau(n_i) = b_i$ and $\mathcal{M}, \Pi, S \models^c \theta$.

Lemma 1. *If* $\mathcal{M}, \Pi, S, \sigma \models^c \theta$ *and* $S' \subseteq S$, *then we also have* $\mathcal{M}, \Pi, S', \sigma \models^c \theta$.

Proof. We proceed by induction on θ. Since $\mathcal{M}, \Pi$ are fixed, we sometimes omit these components.

- If θ is an atomic formula $P(t_1, \ldots, t_n)$ and $P \notin \{\vdash, \mathsf{fresh}(), \sqsubseteq\}$, then, by definition, there is an overwhelming subset $S_1 \subseteq S$ such that, for any $\tau \in S_1$, $(\llbracket t_1 \rrbracket_\tau^\alpha, \ldots, \llbracket t_n \rrbracket_\tau^\alpha) \in \llbracket P \rrbracket$. If $S' \subseteq S$, we choose $S_1' = S' \cap S_1$. It is an overwhelming subset of S' and, for any $\tau \in S_1'$, $(\llbracket t_1 \rrbracket_\tau^\alpha, \ldots, \llbracket t_n \rrbracket_\tau^\alpha) \in \llbracket P \rrbracket$.

- If θ is a formula $\hat{\phi}, t_1, \ldots, t_n \vdash t$, then for any non negligible $S_1 \subseteq S$, there is a non-negligible $S_2 \subseteq S_1$ and there is a machine $\mathcal{A}$, such that, for any $\tau \in S_2$, $\mathcal{A}(\llbracket \phi \rrbracket_\tau, \llbracket t_1 \rrbracket_\tau^\alpha, \ldots, \llbracket t_n \rrbracket_\tau^\alpha) = \llbracket t \rrbracket_\tau^\alpha$. If $S' \subseteq S$ is non negligible, then any non-negligible $S_1' \subseteq S'$ is also a non-negligible $S_1' \subseteq S$, hence the result.
- Other atomic formulas with $=$ and $\sqsubseteq$ are rather trivial.
- If $\theta = \neg\theta_1$, $\mathcal{M}, \Pi, S, \sigma \models^c \theta$ iff for any $S_1 \subseteq S$ such that $\mathcal{M}, \Pi, S_1, \sigma \models^c \theta_1$, $S_1 \cap S$ is negligible. In that case, for any $S' \subseteq S$, $S' \cap S_1$ is also negligible, hence the result (we do not use here the induction hypothesis).
- If $\theta = \theta_1 \vee \theta_2$, $S, \sigma \models^c \theta_1 \vee \theta_2$ implies $S = S_1 \cup S_2$ and $S_1, \sigma \models^c \theta_1, S_2, \sigma \models^c \theta_2$. If $S' \subseteq S$, then $S_1' = S_1 \cap S' \subseteq S_1$ and $S_2' = S_2 \cap S' \subseteq S_2$, hence, by induction hypothesis, $S_1', \sigma \models^c \theta_1$ and $S_2', \sigma \models^c \theta_2$. It follows that $(S' =)S_1' \cup S_2' \models^c \theta_1 \vee \theta_2$
- If $\theta = \theta_1 \wedge \theta_2$, we simply use the induction hypothesis for θ_1 and θ_2, with the same $S' \subseteq S$.
- If $\theta = \exists x.\theta_1$, then we use the induction hypothesis with the same S, S' (and a different σ). Similarly for universal quantification.

3   Computational Soundness

We assume here that, in any formula, the negations appear only in front of an atomic formula.

Theorem 1. *Let Π be a protocol, $s_1 \to \ldots \to s_m$ be a symbolic transition sequence of Π and $\mathcal{M}$ be a probabilistic polynomial time interactive Turing machine. If there is a non-negligible set of coins S such that, for any $\tau \in S$, there is a sequence of transitions $(s_0, \boldsymbol{b_0}, \boldsymbol{b_0'}, \gamma_0) \to \cdots \to (s_m, \boldsymbol{b_m}, \boldsymbol{b_m'}, \gamma_m)$ that is computationally valid w.r.t. $\mathcal{M}, \tau$ and γ_m is in the challenge state q_c, then for any formula θ, $\mathcal{M}, \Pi, S \models^c \theta$ implies there is a symbolic model $\mathcal{S}$ such that $s_0 \to \cdots \to s_m$ is a valid symbolic execution w.r.t. $\mathcal{S}$ and $\mathcal{S} \models \theta$.*

Proof. We assume in this proof that there are only two predicate symbols: $=$ and $\vdash$. The extension to other predicate symbols is straightforward.

For any term t with free variables $x_1, \ldots, x_n$ and machines $\mathcal{A}_{x_1}, \ldots, \mathcal{A}_{x_n}$, and any sample $\tau \in S$, let $\llbracket t \rrbracket_{\tau, \sigma}$ be the computational interpetation of t, in which each variable x_i is interepreted according to $\sigma(\tau)(x_i) = \mathcal{A}_{x_i}(b_\tau, \tau(\boldsymbol{n}))$ if b_τ is the bitstring on the output tape of γ_m, and $\boldsymbol{n}$ is the set of names in the state s_m, for the execution corresponding to τ.

Given a a decreasing chain of non-negligible sets of coins $S \supseteq S_1 \supseteq S_2 \supseteq \ldots$, we define a first-order structure $\mathcal{M}_{S_1 \supseteq S_2 \supseteq \ldots}$ as follows. The domain of $\mathcal{M}_{S_1 \supseteq S_2 \supseteq \ldots}$ is the set of terms built on the function symbols, the names and the additional constants $\mathcal{A}$ for any PT machine $\mathcal{A}$. The interpretation of the predicate symbols is given, for any assignment σ of the variables $x_1, \ldots, x_n$ to machines $\mathcal{A}_{x_1}, \ldots, \mathcal{A}_{x_n}$ by:

- $\mathcal{M}_{S_1 \supseteq S_2 \supseteq \ldots}, \sigma \models t = u$ iff there is an i such that $\forall \tau \in S_i$, $\llbracket t \rrbracket_{\tau, \sigma(\tau)} = \llbracket u \rrbracket_{\tau, \sigma(\tau)}$
- $\mathcal{M}_{S_1 \supseteq S_2 \supseteq \ldots}, \sigma \models t_1, \ldots, t_n \vdash t$ iff there is a PT algorithm $\mathcal{A}$, an i such that $\forall \tau \in S'$, $\mathcal{A}(\llbracket t_1 \rrbracket_{\tau, \sigma(\tau)}, \ldots, \llbracket t_n \rrbracket_{\tau, \sigma(\tau)}) = \llbracket t \rrbracket_{\tau, \sigma}(\tau)$.

Let

$$\mathcal{M}_S = \mathcal{M}_{S \supseteq S \supseteq ...}$$

Remark 1. Notice, that the definition is such that for $S_1 \supseteq S_2 \supseteq ...$ and $S_1' \supseteq S_2' \supseteq ...$, if for some $m \in \mathbb{N}$, $S_i' = S_i$ for all $i > m$, then $\mathcal{M}_{S_1 \supseteq S_2 \supseteq...}, \sigma \models \theta$ if and only if $\mathcal{M}_{S_1' \supseteq S_2' \supseteq...}, \sigma \models \theta$. This is rather trivially true for θ atomic formula, and hence true for any formula.

Let θ be a formula with free variables $x_1, \ldots, x_n$ such that only atomic formulas are negated. We prove, by induction on θ that, if on a non-negligible set of coins S, $\mathcal{M}, \Pi, S, \sigma \models^c \theta$, then for any decreasing chain of non-negligible subsets $S \supseteq S_1 \supseteq S_2 \supseteq ....$, there is a decreasing chain of non-negligible subsets $S_1' \supseteq S_2' \supseteq ....$ such that $S_i' \subseteq S_i$ for all $i = 1, 2, ...$, and for any decreasing chain of non-negligible subsets $S_1'' \supseteq S_2'' \supseteq ....$ with $S_i'' \subseteq S_i'$ for all $i = 1, 2, ...$, $\mathcal{M}_{S_1'' \supseteq S_2'' \supseteq....}, \sigma \models \theta$.

- Suppose $\theta \equiv t = u$. We know from Lemma 1 that $\mathcal{M}, \Pi, S, \sigma \models^c \theta$ implies $\mathcal{M}, \Pi, S', \sigma \models^c \theta$ for any subset $S' \subseteq S$. Hence, given any decreasing chain of non-negligible subsets $S \supseteq S_1 \supseteq S_2 \supseteq ....$, it suffices to choose $S_i' = S_i$ for every i:
- If $\theta \equiv t \neq u$ and $S \supseteq S_1 \supseteq S_2 \supseteq ....$ is any decreasing sequence of non-negligible sets, let $S_i' = S_i$ for every i. For any decreasing sequence of non-negligible sets $S_i'' \subseteq S_i'$, for all i, since $S_i'', \sigma \models^c t \neq u$ by lemma 1, $\{\tau \in S_i'' : [\![t]\!]_{\tau,\sigma} = [\![u]\!]_{\tau,\sigma}$ is negligible. Hence there is at least one $\tau \in S_i''$ such that $[\![t]\!]_{\tau,\sigma} \neq [\![u]\!]_{\tau,\sigma}$. Hence $\mathcal{M}_{S_1'' \supseteq S_2'' \supseteq....}, \sigma \not\models t = u$.
- For $\theta \equiv t_1, ..., t_n \vdash t$, again given any decreasing chain of non-negligible subsets $S \supseteq S_1 \supseteq S_2 \supseteq ....$, it suffices to choose $S_i' = S_i$.
- If $\theta \equiv \hat{\phi}, u_1, \ldots, u_k \vdash t$, we may replace $\hat{\phi}$ with the frame ϕ_m of the symbolic state s_m (this is because for any $\tau \in S$, we reach the same symbolic state s_m), hence we are back to the previous case.
- If $\theta \equiv t_1, ..., t_n \not\vdash t$, given any decreasing chain of non-negligible subsets $S \supseteq S_1 \supseteq S_2 \supseteq ....$, it suffices to choose $S_i' = S_i$, as $\mathcal{M}, \Pi, S', \sigma \models^c t_1, ..., t_n \vdash t$ is not true on any non-negligible S'.
- If $\theta \equiv \hat{\phi}, t_1, \ldots, t_n \not\vdash t$, as before, we may replace $\hat{\phi}$ with the frame in s_m and we are back to the previous case.
- If $\theta \equiv \theta_1 \vee \theta_2$, then $S, \sigma \models^c \theta$ means that there are S' and S'' such that $S' \cup S'' = S$ and $S', \sigma \models^c \theta_1$ and $S'', \sigma \models^c \theta_2$. At least one of the two sets S', S'' is non-negligible. Take any decreasing chain of non-negligible subsets $S \supseteq S_1 \supseteq S_2 \supseteq .....$ Then either $S' \cap S_1 \supseteq S' \cap S_2 \supseteq ....$ is a non-negligible chain, or $S'' \cap S_1 \supseteq S'' \cap S_2 \supseteq ....$ is a non-negligible chain. (Because if both are negligible from a certain point on, then there is an i such that $S' \cap S_i$ and $S'' \cap S_i$ are both negligible, but that contradicts that their union, S_i is not negligible.) Suppose the first. Notice, that the first is a chain in S'. Then, by the induction hypothesis for θ_1, there is a chain $S \supseteq S' \supseteq S_1' \supseteq S_2' \supseteq ...$ such that $S_i' \subseteq S' \cap S_i$ and for any non-negligible decreasing chain $S_1'' \supseteq S_2'' \supseteq ...$ with $S_i'' \subseteq S_i'$, $\mathcal{M}_{S_1'' \supseteq S_2'' \supseteq...}, \sigma \models \theta_1$. Then $\mathcal{M}_{S_1'' \supseteq S_2'' \supseteq...}, \sigma \models \theta$. So the same $S_1' \supseteq S_2' \supseteq ...$ works for θ.
- If $\theta \equiv \theta_1 \wedge \theta_2$, by definition, $S, \sigma \models^c \theta_1$ and $S, \sigma \models^c \theta_2$. By induction hypothesis for θ_1, given any decreasing chain of non-negligible subsets $S \supseteq S_1 \supseteq$

$S_2 \supseteq \ldots$, there is a chain $S \supseteq S'_{11} \supseteq S'_{12} \supseteq \ldots$ with $S'_{1i} \subseteq S_i$, such that, for any non-negligible decreasing chain $S''_1 \supseteq S''_2 \supseteq \ldots$ with $S''_i \subseteq S'_{1i}$ for all i, $\mathcal{M}_{S''_1 \supseteq S''_2 \supseteq \ldots}, \sigma \models \theta_1$. By induction hypothesis for θ_2, there is a chain $S \supseteq S'_{21} \supseteq S'_{22} \supseteq \ldots$ with $S'_{2i} \subseteq S'_{1i}$ such that, for any non-negligible decreasing chain $S''_1 \supseteq S''_2 \supseteq \ldots$ with $S''_i \subseteq S'_{2i}$ for all i, $\mathcal{M}_{S''_1 \supseteq S''_2 \supseteq \ldots}, \sigma \models \theta_2$. Since $S'_{2i} \subseteq S'_{1i}$, by the choice of S'_{1i}, we also have that for any non-negligible decreasing chain $S''_1 \supseteq S''_2 \supseteq \ldots$ with $S''_i \subseteq S'_{2i}$ for all i, $\mathcal{M}_{S''_1 \supseteq S''_2 \supseteq \ldots}, \sigma \models \theta_1$. Hence, for any non-negligible decreasing chain $S''_1 \supseteq S''_2 \supseteq \ldots$ with $S''_i \subseteq S'_{2i}$ for all i, $\mathcal{M}_{S''_1 \supseteq S''_2 \supseteq \ldots}, \sigma \models \theta_1 \wedge \theta_2$. Thus, taking $S'_i = S'_{2i}$ works.

- If $\theta \equiv \exists x.\theta_1$, then there is an $\mathcal{A}_x$, for which we have that $S, \mathcal{A}_{x_1}, \ldots, \mathcal{A}_{x_k}, \mathcal{A}_x \models^c \theta$. By induction hypothesis, for a chain $S \supseteq S_1 \supseteq S_2 \supseteq \ldots$, there is a chain $S'_1 \supseteq S'_2 \supseteq \ldots$ with $S'_i \subseteq S_i$, such that, for any non-negligible $S''_i \subseteq S'_i$, $\mathcal{M}_{S''_1 \supseteq S''_2 \supseteq \ldots}, \sigma, x \mapsto \mathcal{A}_x \models \theta_1$. But then this implies $\mathcal{M}_{S''_1 \supseteq S''_2 \supseteq \ldots}, \sigma \models \exists x.\theta_1$. So the same $S'_1 \supseteq S'_2 \supseteq \ldots$ works.

- If $\theta \equiv \forall x \theta_1$, then for all $\mathcal{A}_x$, $S, \mathcal{A}_{x_1}, \ldots, \mathcal{A}_{x_k} \mathcal{A}_x \models^c \theta_1$. Let's fix $S \supseteq S_1 \supseteq S_2 \supseteq \ldots$. Enumerate all possible algorithms for $\mathcal{A}_x$: $\mathcal{A}_1$, $\mathcal{A}_2, \ldots$ First we show that for $\mathcal{A}_1$, $S, \mathcal{A}_{x_1}, \ldots, \mathcal{A}_{x_k} \mathcal{A}_1 \models^c \theta_1$ holds. By induction hypothesis, there is a chain $S'_{11} \supseteq S'_{12} \supseteq S'_{13} \supseteq \ldots$ with $S'_{1i} \subseteq S_i$, such that, for any non-negligible $S''_1 \supseteq S''_2 \supseteq \ldots$, if $S''_i \subseteq S'_{1i}$ for all i, then $\mathcal{M}_{S''_1 \supseteq S''_2 \supseteq \ldots}, \sigma, x \mapsto \mathcal{A}_1 \models \theta_1$. Take now $\mathcal{A}_2$. Then $S, \mathcal{A}_{x_1}, \ldots, \mathcal{A}_{x_k} \mathcal{A}_2 \models^c \theta_1$ holds. By the induction hypothesis, there is a chain $S'_{21} \supseteq S'_{22} \supseteq \ldots$ with $S'_{2i} \subseteq S'_{1i}$, such that, for any non-negligible chain $S''_1 \supseteq S''_2 \supseteq \ldots$ such that $S''_i \subseteq S'_{2i}$ for all i, $\mathcal{M}_{S''_1 \supseteq S''_2 \supseteq \ldots}, \sigma, x \mapsto \mathcal{A}_2 \models \theta_1$. But, because of Remark 1, it is also true, that for the chain $S'_{11} \supseteq S'_{22} \supseteq S'_{23} \supseteq \ldots$, for any non-negligible $S''_1 \supseteq S''_2 \supseteq \ldots$, with $S''_1 \subseteq S'_{11}$, and $S''_i \subseteq S'_{2i}$ for $i = 2, 3 \ldots$, $\mathcal{M}_{S''_1 \supseteq S''_2 \supseteq \ldots}, \sigma, x \mapsto \mathcal{A}_2 \models \theta_1$, as it does not matter what the first set is. Furthermore, since $S'_{2i} \subseteq S'_{1i}$ holds, we also have $\mathcal{M}_{S''_1 \supseteq S''_2 \supseteq \ldots}, \sigma, x \mapsto \mathcal{A}_1 \models \theta_1$. Continuing in this manner, we get a chain $S'_{11} \supseteq S'_{22} \supseteq S'_{33} \supseteq \ldots$. Then, take any chain $S''_1 \supseteq S''_2 \supseteq \ldots$, with $S''_i \subseteq S'_{ii}$. Clearly, because of the construction, $S''_i \subseteq S'_{1i}$ also holds (as $S'_{ii} \subseteq S'_{1i}$. Hence we have $\mathcal{M}_{S''_1 \supseteq S''_2 \supseteq \ldots}, \sigma, x \mapsto \mathcal{A}_1 \models \theta_1$. Further, since $S''_i \subseteq S'_{2i}$ for $i = 2, 3 \ldots$, and $S''_1 \subseteq S'_{11}$, we also have $\mathcal{M}_{S''_1 \supseteq S''_2 \supseteq \ldots}, \sigma, x \mapsto \mathcal{A}_2 \models \theta_1$. And so on, we have for all n, $\mathcal{M}_{S''_1 \supseteq S''_2 \supseteq \ldots}, \sigma, x \mapsto \mathcal{A}_n \models \theta_1$. Now, if v is any term in the domain of our models, $\mathcal{M}_{S''_1 \supseteq S''_2 \supseteq \ldots}, \sigma, x \mapsto v \models \theta_1$. Indeed, let v' be the term v, in which any $\mathcal{A}_i$ occurring in v is replaced with a variable x_i and σ' be $x_i \mapsto \mathcal{A}_i$. The algorithm, that computes, for every $\tau \in S$, $[\![v']\!]_{\tau, \sigma'}$ can be constructed from the $\mathcal{A}_i$ and is PT. Hence there is an index n such that, for any $\tau \in S$, $\mathcal{A}_n$ outputs $[\![v']\!]_{\tau, \sigma'}$. Therefore, we also have $\mathcal{M}_{S'_1 \supseteq S'_2 \supseteq \ldots}, \sigma \models \forall x \theta_1$, and that is what we wanted to prove. □

The above result can be applied to a formula θ that is the conjunction of

- the intermediate conditions (that are part of the symbolic states) Θ
- finitely many computationally valid axioms A
- a formula that expresses the existence of an attack. NotSec.

Then it can be read as follows: if there is a computational attack, corresponding to a symbolic trace $s_1 \to \cdots \to s_m$, then this symbolic trace is valid in a model, which is also a model of A and NotSec.

Consider then a symbolic procedure, that discards only symbolic states, in which $\Theta \wedge A$ is inconsistent. Then the symbolic procedure will not miss any attack. More precisely, we get:

Theorem 2. *For a bounded number of sessions, if there is a computational attack, there is also a symbolic attack.*

In other words, if the protocol is symbolically secure, then it is also computationally secure.

It might be true for an undbounded number of sessions as well, but we need the boundedness assumption if we wish to derive the theorem from the theorem 1: The trick is, that in the bounded case, if there is a computational attack, there is also a computational attack corresponding to a fixed sequence of symbolic states. This is simply because the bounded number of sessions ensures that there are only finitely many possible sequences, and if there is a computational attack, that is, the property expressing the attack is satisfied on some non-negligible set, then it must be satisfied non-negligibly on one of the possible sequences.

4 Examples of Axioms

4.1 Examples of Axioms That Are Computationally Valid

- Increasing capabilities: $\hat{\phi} \vdash y \rightarrow \hat{\phi}, x \vdash y$
- Function of derivable items: $\hat{\phi} \vdash t_1 \wedge \hat{\phi} \vdash t_2 \wedge \dots \wedge \hat{\phi} \vdash t_n \rightarrow \hat{\phi} \vdash f(t_1, t_2, \dots, t_n)$
- Self derivability: $\hat{\phi}, t \vdash t$

The validity of these axioms is straightforward. We also include the following:

No telepathy: $\mathsf{fresh}(x, \hat{\phi}) \rightarrow \hat{\phi} \not\vdash x$

whose computational soundness follows from the polynomial bound on the machines that interpret the deducibility relation on the one hand and the exponential number of interpretations of any names, on the other hand.

4.2 Secrecy Axiom

The intuitive meaning of the following axiom is that the adversary cannot derive the plaintext of a freshly generated encryption, unless its decryption key has been sent out, or the plaintext could be derived earlier.

Proposition 1. *If the encryption scheme is IND-CCA2, then the following axiom*

$$\theta = \forall_{tKR} \left(\mathsf{RandGen}(K) \wedge \mathsf{fresh}(R, \hat{\phi}) \wedge \hat{\phi}, \{t\}_{eK}^R \vdash t \longrightarrow dK \sqsubseteq \hat{\phi} \vee \hat{\phi} \vdash t \right)$$

is computationally valid.

Proof. Suppose that it is not computationally valid. That is, there is a computational structure $(\mathcal{M}, \Pi, S)$, with $\mathcal{M}, \Pi, S \not\models \theta$. There are PPT machines $\mathcal{A} = (\mathcal{A}_t, \mathcal{A}_K, \mathcal{A}_R)$ such that $\mathcal{M}, \Pi, S, \mathcal{A} \not\models \mathsf{fresh}(R, \hat{\phi}) \wedge \hat{\phi}, \{t\}_{eK}^R \vdash t \longrightarrow dK \sqsubseteq \hat{\phi} \vee \hat{\phi} \vdash t$. Therefore, there is a $S_1 \subseteq S$ non-negligible such that $\mathcal{M}, \Pi, S_1, \mathcal{A} \models \mathsf{fresh}(R, \hat{\phi}) \wedge \hat{\phi}, \{t\}_{eK}^R \vdash t$ and $\mathcal{M}, \Pi, S_1, \mathcal{A} \not\models dK \sqsubseteq \hat{\phi} \vee \hat{\phi} \vdash t$. We claim that the second implies that there is a non-negligible subset S_2 of S_1 such that $\mathcal{M}, \Pi, S_2, \mathcal{A} \models \neg(dK \sqsubseteq \hat{\phi})$ and $\mathcal{M}, \Pi, S_2, \mathcal{A} \not\models \hat{\phi} \vdash t$. To see this, consider the following:

- Take $S_2 = S_1 \backslash \{\tau \mid$ the computation of $\mathcal{A}$ on τ yields a state q such that $q \models dK \sqsubseteq \hat{\phi}\}$. Clearly, $\mathcal{M}, \Pi, S_2, \mathcal{A} \models \neg(dK \sqsubseteq \hat{\phi})$, and $\mathcal{M}, \Pi, S_1 \backslash S_2, \mathcal{A} \models dK \sqsubseteq \hat{\phi}$
- Since $\mathcal{M}, \Pi, S_1 \backslash S_2, \mathcal{A} \models dK \sqsubseteq \hat{\phi}$, we have $\mathcal{M}, \Pi, S_2, \mathcal{A} \not\models \hat{\phi} \vdash t$, because otherwise we would have $\mathcal{M}, \Pi, S_1, \mathcal{A} \models dK \sqsubseteq \hat{\phi} \vee \hat{\phi} \vdash t$ contradicting $\mathcal{M}, \Pi, S_1, \mathcal{A} \not\models dK \sqsubseteq \hat{\phi} \vee \hat{\phi} \vdash t$.

Since $\mathcal{M}, \Pi, S_2, \mathcal{A} \not\models \hat{\phi} \vdash t$, by the definition of the computational semantics of the derivability predicate, there is a subset S_4 of S_2 such that on all subsets of S_4, there is no PT algorithm that computes the interpretation of t from the computational frame. Then it is straightforward to check that $\mathcal{M}, \Pi, S_4, \mathcal{A} \models \neg(\hat{\phi} \vdash t)$:

- Suppose it is not true, that is, $\mathcal{M}, \Pi, S_4, \mathcal{A} \not\models \neg(\hat{\phi} \vdash t)$.
- Then there is an $S_5 \subseteq S_4$ such that $\mathcal{M}, \Pi, S_4, \mathcal{A} \models \hat{\phi} \vdash t$.
- That implies that S_5 has a subset on which there is an algorithm that computes the interpretation t from the computational frame, a contradiction.

Since $S_4 \subseteq S_2$, we also have that $\mathcal{M}, \Pi, S_4, \mathcal{A} \models \neg(dK \sqsubseteq \hat{\phi})$, and since $S_4 \subseteq S_1$, we also have $\mathcal{M}, \Pi, S_4, \mathcal{A} \models \mathsf{fresh}(R, \hat{\phi}) \wedge \hat{\phi}, \{t\}_{eK}^R \vdash t$. That is, $\mathcal{M}, \Pi, S_4, \mathcal{A} \models \hat{\phi}, \{t\}_{eK}^R \vdash t$ and $\mathcal{M}, \Pi, S_4, \mathcal{A} \models \mathsf{fresh}(R, \hat{\phi})$ and $\mathcal{M}, \Pi, S_4, \mathcal{A} \models \neg(dK \sqsubseteq \hat{\phi})$ and $\mathcal{M}, \Pi, S_4, \mathcal{A} \models \neg(\hat{\phi} \vdash t)$. We have to create an adversary $\mathcal{A}_{\mathrm{CCA2}}$ that wins the CCA2 game. Let $x = \{t\}_{eK}^R$.

Since $\mathcal{M}, \Pi, S_4, \mathcal{A} \models \hat{\phi}, \{t\}_{eK}^R \vdash t$ holds, there is an $S_5 \subseteq S_4$ and an algorithm $\mathcal{C}$ that computes the interpretation of t from the interpretation of $\hat{\phi}$ and $\{t\}_{eK}^R$ on S_5. Clearly, $\mathcal{M}, \Pi, S_5, \mathcal{A} \models \mathsf{fresh}(R, \hat{\phi})$ and $\mathcal{M}, \Pi, S_5, \mathcal{A} \models \neg(dK \sqsubseteq \hat{\phi})$ and $\mathcal{M}, \Pi, S_5, \mathcal{A} \models \neg(\hat{\phi} \vdash t)$. It may be the case that the S_5 we have chosen depends on evaluations of τ that are determined after $\mathcal{M}$ reaches the challenge state q_c. However, clearly, if we include all possible future evaluations, the set that we receive this way, S' will still be such that there is an algorithm $\mathcal{C}$ that computes the interpretation of t from the frame at the challenge state q_c and $\{t\}_{eK}^R$ on S'. Moreover, it is easy to see that $\mathcal{M}, \Pi, S', \mathcal{A} \models \mathsf{fresh}(R, \hat{\phi})$ and $\mathcal{M}, \Pi, S', \mathcal{A} \models \neg(dK \sqsubseteq \hat{\phi})$ and $\mathcal{M}, \Pi, S', \mathcal{A} \models \neg(\hat{\phi} \vdash t)$ because these properties that depend only on conditions in the challenge stated, and not later ones.

Since $\mathcal{M}, \Pi, S', \mathcal{A} \models dK \not\sqsubseteq \hat{\phi}$, the decryption key has never been sent.

We show that we can construct an algorithm $\mathcal{A}_{\mathrm{CCA2}}$ that breaks CCA2 security.

Let $\mathcal{A}_\Pi$ mean the protocol adversary.

- $\mathcal{A}_{\mathrm{CCA2}}$ generates computational keys that $\mathcal{A}_\Pi$ uses, except for the one corresponding to K.

- The encryption oracle generates a random bit b.
- The encryption oracle generates a computational key and publishes its public part. $\mathcal{A}_{\text{CCA2}}$ encrypts with this key for encryptions with K, except for t.
- $\mathcal{A}_{\text{CCA2}}$ simulates both the agents and $\mathcal{A}_\Pi$: It computes all messages that the agents output according to their algorithm, and computes all messages that $\mathcal{A}_\Pi$ outputs according to its algorithm. This way it builds up ϕ and the bit strings corresponding to them as well as the equations.
- Whenever a decryption with dK has to be computed, there are two possibilities:
  - If the ciphertext was created by $\mathcal{A}_{\text{CCA2}}$ using the encryption algorithm, then it knows the plaintext, so it can use it without decryption.
  - If the ciphertext was created in some other way, the decryption oracle is used. This can be freely done until x occurs.
- When $\mathcal{A}$ reaches the challenge state q_c, using $\mathcal{A}_t$, $\mathcal{A}_{\text{CCA2}}$ computes the bit string for t, and submits it to the encryption oracle as well as a random bit string that has the same length as the plaintext.
- According to our definition of satisfaction the computation by $\mathcal{C}$ is based on the frame at the challenge state. We had $\mathcal{M}, \Pi, S', \mathcal{A} \models \text{fresh}(R, \hat{\phi})$, which means that R is independent of the items in ϕ. Further, since we included all future random choices in S', R is also independent of S'. Hence having it encrypted by the encryption oracle will not lose any information as long as the oracle encrypts the correct bit.
- The encryption oracle encrypts the interpretation of t if $b = 0$, and encrypts the random bit string if $b = 1$. It gives the result c back to $\mathcal{A}_{\text{CCA2}}$.
- Run $\mathcal{C}$ on the bit string c returned by the oracle and on the bit strings of $\phi_\mathbf{n}$.
- If
  - $\mathcal{A}_{\text{CCA2}}$ receives the value for t back using c and if the execution is in S', then $\mathcal{A}_{\text{CCA2}}$ returns $b_{\mathcal{A}_{\text{CCA2}}} = 0$.
  - Otherwise $\mathcal{A}_{\text{CCA2}}$ throws a fair coin and stores $b_{\mathcal{A}_{\text{CCA2}}} = 0$ or $b_{\mathcal{A}_{\text{CCA2}}} = 1$ with probability $1/2$.
- We have $\mathbf{Prob}\{b_{\mathcal{A}_{\text{CCA2}}} = b \mid S' \wedge b = 0\}$ (the conditional probability of $b_{\mathcal{A}_{\text{CCA2}}} = b$ given S' and $b = 0$) is negligibly different from 1 because in this case the oracle encrypts the correct string, and $\mathcal{C}$'s computations are employed on the correct bit string, and so it gives the interpretation of t. Note, we also use here that S' and the interpretation of R do not correlate.
- On the other hand, observe that $\mathbf{Prob}\{b_{\mathcal{A}_{\text{CCA2}}} = b \mid S' \wedge b = 1\} - 1/2$ is negligible. The reason is that when $b = 1$, the encryption oracle computes something that has nothing to do with the protocol and t. So the probability of computing t with or without the encryption in this case, is the same. But, remember, we had that $\mathcal{M}, \Pi, S', \mathcal{A} \models \hat{\phi} \nvdash t$. This means that t cannot be computed without the encryption anywhere and therefore the adversary's computation on the fake encryption cannot give good result by more than negligible probability. So the adversary will end up throwing a coin in this case.
- Putting the previous two points together, we have $\mathbf{Prob}\{b_{\mathcal{A}_{\text{CCA2}}} = b \mid S'\} - \frac{1}{2}$ is non-negligible. Then, since outside S', $\mathcal{A}_{\text{CCA2}}$ throws a coin, $\mathbf{Prob}\{b_{\mathcal{A}_{\text{CCA2}}} = b\} - \frac{1}{2}$ is non-negligible, which means CCA2 security is broken. $\square$

5 Conclusions

We have shown a technique to define symbolic adversaries that are at least as strong as computational adversaries. The basic idea is that, instead of listing all manipulations the symbolic adversary is allowed to do, we allow the symbolic adversary to do anything unless it contradicts some axioms, which are derived from the limitations of the computational adversary. In a rather involved theorem, we showed that at least when only bounded number of protocol sessions are allowed, to any computational attack there is a corresponding symbolic attack. Further, we have shown a few axioms that arise from the limitations of computational adversaries, and which are to limit the symbolic adversary. Besides some rather trivially valid axioms, we showed the validity of a "secrecy axiom", that relies on IND-CCA2 security.

From our method, we can derive a verification procedure, simulating the (symbolic) protocol rules, and checking at each computation step the consistency of the formulas expressing that transitions are enabled, together with the axioms and the negation of the security properties. In order to automate this process we mainly need a (hopefully efficient) procedure checking the consistency of such a set of constrained formulas. This is future work. We are however optimistic, because the examples of axioms that we considered yield a saturated set of constrained formulas (as defined in [22]). On the other hand, as shown in [9], the consistency of ground clauses, together with a saturated set of clauses, can be performed in polynomial time.

We carried out a proof of a two sessions NSL, showing what are the minimal assumptions that guarantee its correctness, but we need to design an automated tool, in order to carry out further experiments. Also extensions of the results to indistinguishability properties could be investigated.

References

1. Abadi, M., Rogaway, P.: Reconciling Two Views of Cryptography: the Computational Soundness of Formal Encryption. In: Watanabe, O., Hagiya, M., Ito, T., van Leeuwen, J., Mosses, P.D. (eds.) TCS 2000. LNCS, vol. 1872, pp. 3–22. Springer, Heidelberg (2000)
2. Abadi, M., Blanchet, B., Comon-Lundh, H.: Models and Proofs of Protocol Security: A Progress Report. In: Bouajjani, A., Maler, O. (eds.) CAV 2009. LNCS, vol. 5643, pp. 35–49. Springer, Heidelberg (2009)
3. Backes, M., Pfitzmann, B.: Symmetric encryption in a simulatable dolev-yao style cryptographic library. In: Proc. IEEE Computer Security Foundations Workshop (2004)
4. Backes, M., Pfitzmann, B.: Limits of the Cryptographic Realization of Dolev-Yao-Style XOR. In: di Vimercati, S.d.C., Syverson, P.F., Gollmann, D. (eds.) ESORICS 2005. LNCS, vol. 3679, pp. 178–196. Springer, Heidelberg (2005)
5. Backes, M., Pfitzmann, B., Waidner, M.: A composable cryptographic library with nested operations. In: Proc. 10th ACM Concerence on Computer and Communications Security, CCS 2003 (2003)
6. Backes, M., Pfitzmann, B., Waidner, M.: The reactive simulatability (rsim) framework for asynchronous systems. Information and Computation 205(12) (2007)
7. Backes, M., Hofheinz, D., Unruh, D.: Cosp: A general framework for computational soundness proofs. In: ACM CCS 2009, pp. 66–78 (November 2009); Preprint on IACR ePrint 2009/080

8. Bana, G., Hasebe, K., Okada, M.: Secrecy-oriented first-order logical analysis of cryptographic protocols (2010), http://eprint.iacr.org/2010/080
9. Basin, D., Ganzinger, H.: Automated complexity analysis based on ordered resolution. Journal of the Association of Computing Machinery 48(1), 70–109 (2001)
10. Blanchet, B.: An automatic security protocol verifier based on resolution theorem proving (invited tutorial). In: 20th International Conference on Automated Deduction (CADE-20), Tallinn, Estonia (July 2005)
11. Blanchet, B.: A computationally sound mechanized prover for security protocols. IEEE Transactions on Dependable and Secure Computing 5(4), 193–207 (2008); Special issue IEEE Symposium on Security and Privacy (2006)
12. Canetti, R., Rabin, T.: Universal Composition with Joint State. In: Boneh, D. (ed.) CRYPTO 2003. LNCS, vol. 2729, pp. 265–281. Springer, Heidelberg (2003)
13. Comon-Lundh, H., Cortier, V.: Computational soundness of observational equivalence. In: Proc. ACM Conf. Computer and Communication Security, CCS (2008)
14. Comon-Lundh, H., Cortier, V.: How to prove security of communication protocols? a discussion on the soundness of formal models w.r.t. computational ones. In: Dürr, C., Schwentick, T. (eds.) Proceedings of the 28th Annual Symposium on Theoretical Aspects of Computer Science (STACS 2011), Dortmund, Germany. Leibniz International Proceedings in Informatics, vol. 9, pp. 29–44. Leibniz-Zentrum für Informatik (March 2011)
15. Cortier, V., Warinschi, B.: Computationally Sound, Automated Proofs for Security Protocols. In: Sagiv, M. (ed.) ESOP 2005. LNCS, vol. 3444, pp. 157–171. Springer, Heidelberg (2005)
16. Datta, A., Derek, A., Mitchell, J.C., Turuani, M.: Probabilistic Polynomial-Time Semantics for a Protocol Security Logic. In: Caires, L., Italiano, G.F., Monteiro, L., Palamidessi, C., Yung, M. (eds.) ICALP 2005. LNCS, vol. 3580, pp. 16–29. Springer, Heidelberg (2005)
17. Armando, A., Basin, D., Boichut, Y., Chevalier, Y., Compagna, L., Cuellar, J., Drielsma, P.H., Heám, P.C., Kouchnarenko, O., Mantovani, J., Mödersheim, S., von Oheimb, D., Rusinowitch, M., Santiago, J., Turuani, M., Viganò, L., Vigneron, L.: The AVISPA Tool for the Automated Validation of Internet Security Protocols and Applications. In: Etessami, K., Rajamani, S.K. (eds.) CAV 2005. LNCS, vol. 3576, pp. 281–285. Springer, Heidelberg (2005)
18. Ganzinger, H., Nieuwenhuis, R.: Constraints and Theorem Proving. In: Comon, H., Marché, C., Treinen, R. (eds.) CCL 1999. LNCS, vol. 2002, pp. 159–201. Springer, Heidelberg (2001)
19. Lifschitz, V.: Closed-world databases and circumscription. Artif. Intell. 27(2), 229–235 (1985)
20. Lowe, G.: Breaking and Fixing the Needham-Schroeder Public-Key Protocol Using FDR. In: Margaria, T., Steffen, B. (eds.) TACAS 1996. LNCS, vol. 1055, pp. 147–166. Springer, Heidelberg (1996)
21. Millen, J., Shmatikov, V.: Constraint solving for bounded-process cryptographic protocol analysis. In: Proc. 8th ACM Conference on Computer and Communications Security (2001)
22. Nieuwenhuis, R., Rubio, A.: Paramodulation-based theorem proving. In: Handbook of Automated Reasoning, pp. 371–443. Elsevier and MIT Press (2001)
23. Ryan, P., Schneider, S., Goldsmith, M., Lowe, G., Roscoe, B.: The Modelling and Analysis of Security Protocols. Addison Wesley (2000)
24. Unruh, D.: Computational soundness of hash functions. Presented at the 6th Workshop on Formal and Computational Cryptography (FCC) (July 2010)
25. Unruh, D.: The impossibility of computationally sound xor (July 2010); Preprint on IACR ePrint 2010/389
26. Warinschi, B.: A computational analysis of the needham-schroeder protocol. In: 16th Computer Security Foundation Workshop (CSFW), pp. 248–262. IEEE (2003)

Verified Indifferentiable Hashing
into Elliptic Curves

Gilles Barthe[1], Benjamin Grégoire[2], Sylvain Heraud[2],
Federico Olmedo[1], and Santiago Zanella Béguelin[1]

[1] IMDEA Software Institute, Madrid, Spain
{Gilles.Barthe,Federico.Olmedo,Santiago.Zanella}@imdea.org
[2] INRIA Sophia Antipolis-Méditerranée, France
{Benjamin.Gregoire,Sylvain.Heraud}@inria.fr

Abstract. Many cryptographic systems based on elliptic curves are proven secure in the Random Oracle Model, assuming there exist probabilistic functions that map elements in some domain (e.g. bitstrings) onto uniformly and independently distributed points in a curve. When implementing such systems, and in order for the proof to carry over to the implementation, those mappings must be instantiated with concrete constructions whose behavior does not deviate significantly from random oracles. In contrast to other approaches to public-key cryptography, where candidates to instantiate random oracles have been known for some time, the first generic construction for hashing into ordinary elliptic curves indifferentiable from a random oracle was put forward only recently by Brier et al. We present a machine-checked proof of this construction. The proof is based on an extension of the CertiCrypt framework with logics and mechanized tools for reasoning about approximate forms of observational equivalence, and integrates mathematical libraries of group theory and elliptic curves.

1   Introduction

Following an established trend [18], the prevailing methodology for building secure cryptosystems is to conduct a rigorous analysis that proves security under standard hypotheses. Sometimes this analysis is performed assuming that some components of the system have an ideal behavior. However, ideal functionalities are difficult or even impossible to realize, leading to situations where provably secure systems have no secure implementation. An alternative methodology is to devise systems based on constructions that do not deviate significantly from ideal ones, and to account for these deviations in the security analysis. Statistical distance is a natural notion for quantifying the deviation between idealized functionalities and their implementations.

Verifiable security [3,4] is an emerging approach that advocates the use of interactive proof assistants and automated provers to establish the security of cryptographic systems. It improves on the guarantees of provable security by delivering fully machine-checked and independently verifiable proofs. The CertiCrypt framework, built on top of the Coq proof assistant, is one prominent tool that realizes verifiable security by using standard techniques from programming languages and program verification. CertiCrypt is built around the central notion of observational equivalence of probabilistic programs, which unfortunately cannot model accurately other weaker, quantitative,

P. Degano and J.D. Guttman (Eds.): POST 2012, LNCS 7215, pp. 209–228, 2012.

forms of equivalence. As a result, CertiCrypt cannot be used as it is to reason about the statistical distance of distributions generated by probabilistic programs. More generally, the development of quantitative notions of equivalence is quite recent and rather limited; see Section 7 for an account of related work.

One main contribution of this article is the formalization of several quantitative notions of program equivalence and logics for reasoning about them. More specifically, we extend CertiCrypt with the notion of statistical distance and develop a logic to upper bound the distance between distributions generated by probabilistic programs. Moreover, we introduce approximate and conditional variants of observational equivalence and develop equational theories for reasoning about them.

In a landmark article, Maurer et al. [23] introduce the concept of indifferentiability to justify rigorously the substitution of an idealized component in a cryptographic system by a concrete implementation. In a subsequent article, Coron et al. [13] argue that a secure hash function should be indifferentiable from a random oracle, i.e. a perfectly random function. Although the random oracle model has been under fierce criticism [10] and the indifferentiability framework turns out to be weaker than initially believed [16, 25], it is generally accepted that proofs in these models provide some evidence that a system is secure. Not coincidentally, all finalists in the ongoing NIST Cryptographic Hash Algorithm competition have been proved indifferentiable from a random oracle.

Elliptic curve cryptography allows to build efficient public-key cryptographic systems with comparatively short keys and as such is an attractive solution for resource-constrained applications. In contrast to other approaches to public-key cryptography, where candidates to instantiate random oracles have been known for some time, adequate constructions for hashing into ordinary elliptic curves have remained elusive. In 2010, Brier et al. [9] proposed the first generic construction indifferentiable from a random oracle into elliptic curves. This construction is of practical significance since it allows to securely implement elliptic curve cryptosystems. We present a machine-checked and independently verifiable proof of the security of this construction. The proof involves the various notions of equivalence we develop in this paper and is thus an excellent testbed for evaluating the applicability of our methods. Additionally, the proof builds on several large developments (including Théry's formalization of elliptic curves [30] and Gonthier et al. formalization of finite groups [19]) and demonstrates that CertiCrypt blends well with large and complex mathematical libraries, and is apt to support proofs involving advanced algebraic and number-theoretical reasoning.

Organization of the paper. The remainder of the paper is structured as follows. Section 2 provides a brief introduction to CertiCrypt. Section 3 introduces the notion of statistical distance between probabilistic programs and describes programming language techniques to bound it, whereas Sect. 4 defines weak forms of observational equivalence and their associated reasoning principles. Section 5 presents a machine-checked proof of the indifferentiability of a generalization of Brier et al.'s construction from a random oracle into an abelian finite group; its application to elliptic curves is discussed in Sect. 6. We survey prior art and conclude in Sections 7 and 8.

2   An Overview of CertiCrypt

This section provides a brief description of the CertiCrypt framework. We refer the
reader to [4] for further details.

2.1   Representation of Distributions

CertiCrypt adopts the monadic representation of distributions proposed by Audebaud
and Paulin in [2]. A distribution over a set A is represented as a monotonic, continuous
and linear function of type

$$\mathcal{D}(A) \stackrel{\text{def}}{=} (A \to [0, 1]) \to [0, 1]$$

where $[0, 1]$ denotes the unit interval. Intuitively, an element of type $\mathcal{D}(A)$ models the
expectation operator of a sub-probability distribution over A. Thus, the probability that
a distribution $\mu : \mathcal{D}(A)$ assigns to an event $X \subseteq A$ can be computed by measuring its
characteristic function $\mathbb{1}_X$, i.e. $\Pr[\mu : X] \stackrel{\text{def}}{=} \mu(\mathbb{1}_X)$.

2.2   Programming Model

We model games as probabilistic imperative programs with procedure calls. The set of
commands $\mathcal{C}$ is defined inductively by the clauses:

$$
\begin{array}{lll}
\mathcal{C} ::= & \text{skip} & \text{nop} \\
\mid & \mathcal{V} \leftarrow \mathcal{E} & \text{deterministic assignment} \\
\mid & \mathcal{V} \stackrel{\$}{\leftarrow} \mathcal{D}\mathcal{E} & \text{random assignment} \\
\mid & \text{if } \mathcal{E} \text{ then } \mathcal{C} \text{ else } \mathcal{C} & \text{conditional} \\
\mid & \text{while } \mathcal{E} \text{ do } \mathcal{C} & \text{while loop} \\
\mid & \mathcal{V} \leftarrow \mathcal{P}(\mathcal{E}, \dots, \mathcal{E}) & \text{procedure call} \\
\mid & \mathcal{C}; \mathcal{C} & \text{sequence}
\end{array}
$$

where $\mathcal{V}$ is a set of variables tagged with their scope (either local or global), $\mathcal{E}$ is a set
of deterministic expressions, and $\mathcal{D}\mathcal{E}$ is a set of expressions that denote distributions
from which values can be sampled in random assignments. In the remainder, we let
true $\oplus_\delta$ false denote the Bernoulli distribution with success probability δ, so that the
instruction $x \stackrel{\$}{\leftarrow}$ true $\oplus_\delta$ false assigns true to x with probability δ, and we denote by
$x \stackrel{\$}{\leftarrow} A$ the instruction that assigns to x a value uniformly chosen from a finite set A.

A program (or game) consists of a command c and an environment E that maps procedure identifiers to their declaration, specifying its formal parameters, its body, and a
return expression that is evaluated upon exit. (Although procedures are single-exit, we
often write games using explicit return expressions for the sake of readability.) Declarations are subject to well-formedness and well-typedness conditions; these conditions
are enforced using the underlying dependent type system of Coq. Procedures corresponding to adversaries are modelled as procedures with unknown code.

Program states (or memories) are dependently typed functions that map a variable of
type T to a value in its interpretation $[\![T]\!]$; we let $\mathcal{M}$ denote the set of states. Expressions

have a deterministic semantics: an expression e of type T is interpreted as a function $[\![e]\!] : \mathcal{M} \to [\![T]\!]$. The semantics of a command c in an environment E relates an initial memory to a probability sub-distribution over final memories: $[\![c, E]\!] : \mathcal{M} \to \mathcal{D}(\mathcal{M})$. We often omit the environment when it is irrelevant.

By specializing the above definition of probability $\Pr[\mu : X]$ to programs, we have that the probability $\Pr[G, m : X]$ of an event X in a game G and an initial memory m is given by $[\![G]\!]\, m\, \mathbb{1}_X$. The probability of termination of a game G starting in an initial memory m is given by $\Pr[G, m : \mathrm{true}]$. We say that a game is *lossless* if it terminates with probability 1 independently from the initial memory.

In order to reason about program complexity and define the class of probabilistic polynomial-time computations, the semantics of programs is indexed by a security parameter (a natural number) and instrumented to compute the time and memory cost of evaluating a command, given the time and memory cost of each construction in the expression language. We chose not to make this parameterization explicit to avoid cluttering the presentation.

2.3   Reasoning Tools

CertiCrypt provides several tools for reasoning about games. One main tool is a probabilistic relational Hoare logic. Its judgments are of the form $\models G_1 \sim G_2 : \Psi \Rightarrow \Phi$, where G_1 and G_2 are games, and Ψ and Φ are relations over states. We represent relations as first-order formulae over tagged program variables; we use the tags $\langle 1 \rangle$ and $\langle 2 \rangle$ to distinguish between the value of a variable or formula in the left and right-hand side program, respectively.

Formally, a judgment $\models G_1 \sim G_2 : \Psi \Rightarrow \Phi$ is valid, iff for all memories m_1 and m_2 such that $m_1 \Psi m_2$, we have that $([\![G_1]\!]\, m_1)\, \mathcal{L}(\Phi)\, ([\![G_2]\!]\, m_2)$, where $\mathcal{L}(\Phi)$ denotes the lifting of Φ to distributions. Relational Hoare logic can be used to prove claims about the probability of events in games by using, for instance, the following rule:

$$\frac{m_1 \Psi m_2 \qquad \models G_1 \sim G_2 : \Psi \Rightarrow \Phi \qquad \Phi \implies (A\langle 1 \rangle \implies B\langle 2 \rangle)}{\Pr[G_1, m_1 : A] \leq \Pr[G_2, m_2 : B]}$$

Observational equivalence is defined by specializing the judgments to relations Ψ and Φ corresponding to the equality relation on subsets of program variables. Formally, let X be a set of variables, $m_1, m_2 \in \mathcal{M}$ and $f_1, f_2 : \mathcal{M} \to [0, 1]$. We define

$$m_1 =_X m_2 \stackrel{\mathrm{def}}{=} \forall x \in X.\, m_1(x) = m_2(x)$$
$$f_1 =_X f_2 \stackrel{\mathrm{def}}{=} \forall m_1\, m_2.\, m_1 =_X m_2 \implies f_1(m_1) = f_2(m_2)$$

Then, two games G_1 and G_2 are observationally equivalent w.r.t. an input set of variables I and an output set of variables O, written $\models G_1 \simeq_O^I G_2$, iff $\models G_1 \sim G_2 : =_I \Rightarrow =_O$. Equivalently, $\models G_1 \simeq_O^I G_2$ iff for all memories $m_1, m_2 \in \mathcal{M}$ and functions $f_1, f_2 : \mathcal{M} \to [0, 1]$,

$$m_1 =_I m_2 \wedge f_1 =_O f_2 \implies [\![G_1]\!]\, m_1\, f_1 = [\![G_2]\!]\, m_2\, f_2$$

Observational equivalence is amenable to automation. CertiCrypt provides mechanized tactics based on dependency analyses to perform common program transformations and to prove that two programs are observationally equivalent (note that observational equivalence is only a partial equivalence relation). The mechanized transformations include dead code elimination, call inlining, inter- and intra-procedural code motion and expression propagation.

We sometimes use a standard Hoare logic for reasoning about single programs. Its judgments are of the form $\{P\}\ G\ \{Q\}$, where G is a game and P and Q are predicates on states. Formally, a judgment $\{P\}\ G\ \{Q\}$ is valid iff for every memory $m \in \mathcal{M}$ and function $f : \mathcal{M} \to [0, 1]$,

$$P\ m \wedge (\forall m.\ Q\ m \implies f(m) = 0) \implies [\![G]\!]\ m\ f = 0$$

This logic is subsumed by the relational Hoare logic,

$$\models \{P\}\ G\ \{Q\} \iff \models G \sim \mathsf{skip} : P\langle 1 \rangle \Rightarrow Q\langle 1 \rangle.$$

3   Statistical Distance

Statistical distance quantifies the largest difference between the probability that two distributions assign to the same event. We refer to [28] for an in-depth presentation of statistical distance and its properties. Formally, the statistical distance $\Delta(\mu_1, \mu_2)$ between two distributions μ_1 and μ_2 over a set A is defined as:

$$\Delta(\mu_1, \mu_2) \stackrel{\text{def}}{=} \sup_{f:A \to [0,1]} |\mu_1\ f - \mu_2\ f|$$

One important property of statistical distance that we frequently use in proofs is its invariance under function application, i.e. for any function $F : \mathcal{D}(A) \to \mathcal{D}(B)$ and distributions μ_1, μ_2 over A, $\Delta(F(\mu_1), F(\mu_2)) \leq \Delta(\mu_1, \mu_2)$.

Remark. In the traditional definition of statistical distance, f ranges only over Boolean-valued functions. Our definition is more convenient for reasoning about our monadic formalization of distributions. We have proved in Coq that the two definitions coincide for discrete distributions.

3.1   A Logic for Bounding Statistical Distance

Statistical distance admits a natural extension to programs; we define the statistical distance between two programs G_1 and G_2 as follows:

$$\Delta(G_1, G_2) \stackrel{\text{def}}{=} \max_{m,f} |[\![G_1]\!]\ m\ f - [\![G_2]\!]\ m\ f|$$

Or, fixing an initial memory m,

$$\Delta_m(G_1, G_2) \stackrel{\text{def}}{=} \max_f |[\![G_1]\!]\ m\ f - [\![G_2]\!]\ m\ f|$$

We define a logic that allows to upper bound $\Delta_m(G_1, G_2)$ by a function of the memory m; the logic deals with judgments of the form $(\!|G_1, G_2|\!) \preceq g$, where

$$(\!|G_1, G_2|\!) \preceq g \stackrel{\text{def}}{=} \forall m.\ \Delta_m(G_1, G_2) \leq g\ m \equiv \forall m\ f.\ |[\![G_1]\!]\ m\ f - [\![G_2]\!]\ m\ f| \leq g\ m$$

$$\overline{(\!|skip, skip|\!) \preceq \lambda m.\, 0}^{[Skip]} \qquad \overline{(\!|x \leftarrow e, x \leftarrow e|\!) \preceq \lambda m.\, 0}^{[Ass]}$$

$$\frac{\forall m.\, \Delta\left([\![\mu_1]\!]\, m, [\![\mu_2]\!]\, m\right) \leq g\, m}{(\!|x \xleftarrow{\$} \mu_1, x \xleftarrow{\$} \mu_2|\!) \preceq g}[Rnd] \qquad \frac{(\!|c_1, c_2|\!) \preceq g \qquad (\!|c_1', c_2'|\!) \preceq g'}{(\!|c_1; c_1', c_2; c_2'|\!) \preceq \lambda m. [\![c_1]\!]\, m\, g' + g\, m}[Seq]$$

$$\frac{(\!|c_1, c_1'|\!) \preceq g_1 \qquad (\!|c_2, c_2'|\!) \preceq g_2}{(\!|if\ b\ then\ c_1\ else\ c_2, if\ b\ then\ c_1'\ else\ c_2'|\!) \preceq \lambda m.\ if\ [\![b]\!]\, m\ then\ g_1\, m\ else\ g_2\, m}[Cond]$$

$$\frac{(\!|c_1, c_2|\!) \preceq g \quad g_0(m) = 0 \quad g_{n+1}(m) = if\ [\![b]\!]\, m\ then\ [\![c_1]\!]\, m\, g_n + g(m)\ else\ 0}{(\!|while\ b\ do\ c_1, while\ b\ do\ c_2|\!) \preceq \sup(\lambda n.\ g_n)}[Whl]$$

$$\frac{(\!|E_1(p), E_2(p)|\!) \preceq g \quad g =_X g \quad \forall x.\, x \in X \Rightarrow global(x)}{(\!|y \leftarrow p(x), y \leftarrow p(x)|\!) \preceq g}[Call]$$

Fig. 1. Logic to bound the statistical distance between two probabilistic programs

Figure 1 presents the main rules of the logic; for readability, rules are stated for pairs of commands rather than pairs of programs, and assume that this pair of programs are executed in two fixed environments E_1 and E_2 respectively.

To prove the soundness, for instance, of the rule for sequential composition, we introduce an intermediate program $c_1; c_2'$ (where c_1 is executed in environment E_1 and c_2' in environment E_2) and prove that the distance between $[\![c_1; c_2']\!]\, m$ and $[\![c_1; c_1']\!]\, m$ is bounded by $[\![c_1]\!]\, m\, g'$, while the distance between $[\![c_1; c_2']\!]\, m$ and $[\![c_2; c_2']\!]\, m$ is bounded by $g\, m$. The rule for loops relies on the characterization of the semantics of a while loop as the least upper bound of its n-th unrolling $[while\ e\ do\ c]_n$, and on the auxiliary rule

$$\frac{(\!|[while\ b\ do\ c_1]_n, [while\ b\ do\ c_2]_n|\!) \preceq g_n}{(\!|while\ b\ do\ c_1, while\ b\ do\ c_2|\!) \preceq \sup(\lambda n.\ g_n)}$$

While the rules in Figure 1 are sufficient to reason about closed programs, they do not allow to reason about games in the presence of adversaries. We enhance the logic with a rule that allows to bound the statistical distance between calls to an adversary $\mathcal{A}$ executed in two different environments E_1 and E_2, i.e. it allows to draw conclusions of the form $(\!|\mathcal{A}, \mathcal{A}|\!) \preceq g$.[1] In its simplest formulation, the rule assumes that oracles are instrumented with a counter that keeps track of the number of queries made, and that the statistical distance between the distributions induced by a call to an oracle $x \leftarrow \mathcal{O}(\vec{e})$ in E_1 and E_2 is upper bounded by a constant ϵ, i.e. $(\!|\mathcal{O}, \mathcal{O}|\!) \preceq \epsilon$. In this case, the statistical distance between calls to the adversary $\mathcal{A}$ in E_1 and E_2 is upper bounded by $q \cdot \epsilon$, where q is an upper bound on the number of oracle calls made by the adversary.

For the application presented in Section 5, we need to formalize a more powerful rule, in which the statistical distance between two oracle calls can depend on the program state. Moreover, we allow the counter to be any integer expression, and only require that it does not decrease across oracle calls.

---

[1] For the sake of readability, we write $(\!|\mathcal{A}, \mathcal{A}|\!) \preceq g$ instead of $(\!|x \leftarrow \mathcal{A}(\vec{e}), x \leftarrow \mathcal{A}(\vec{e})|\!) \preceq g$, and likewise for oracles.

Lemma 1 (Adversary rule). *Let $\mathcal{A}$ be an adversary and let* cntr *be an integer expression whose variables cannot be written by $\mathcal{A}$. Let $h : \mathbb{N} \to [0, 1]$ and define*

$$\bar{h}_{\mathsf{cntr}}(m, m') \stackrel{def}{=} \min\left(1, \sum_{i=[\![\mathsf{cntr}]\!]m}^{[\![\mathsf{cntr}]\!]m'-1} h(i)\right)$$

Assume that for every oracle $\mathcal{O}$,

$$(\![\mathcal{O}, \mathcal{O}]\!) \preceq \lambda m.\ [\![E_1(\mathcal{O})]\!]\ m\ (\lambda m'.\ \bar{h}_{\mathsf{cntr}}(m, m'))$$

and $\{\mathsf{cntr} = i\}\ E_1(\mathcal{O})\ \{i \leq \mathsf{cntr}\}$. Then,

$$(\![\mathcal{A}, \mathcal{A}]\!) \preceq \lambda m.\ [\![E_1(\mathcal{A})]\!]\ m\ (\lambda m'.\ \bar{h}_{\mathsf{cntr}}(m, m'))$$

3.2   Reasoning about Failure Events

Transitions based on failure events allow to transform a game into another game that is semantically equivalent unless some *failure* condition is triggered. The main tool to justify such transitions is the following lemma.

Lemma 2 (Fundamental Lemma). *Consider two games G_1, G_2 and let A, B, and F be events. If $\Pr[G_1 : A \wedge \neg F] = \Pr[G_2 : B \wedge \neg F]$, then*

$$|\Pr[G_1 : A] - \Pr[G_2 : B]| \leq \max\{\Pr[G_1 : F], \Pr[G_2 : F]\}$$

Note also that if, for instance, game G_2 is lossless, then $\Pr[G_1 : F] \leq \Pr[G_2 : F]$.

When $A = B$ and $F = \mathbf{bad}$ for some Boolean variable $\mathbf{bad}$, the hypothesis of the lemma can be automatically established by inspecting the code of both games: it holds if their code differs only after program points setting $\mathbf{bad}$ to true and $\mathbf{bad}$ is never reset to false. As a corollary, if two games G_1, G_2 satisfy this syntactic criterion and e.g. G_2 is lossless, $(\![G_1, G_2]\!) \preceq \lambda m.\ \Pr[G_2, m : \mathbf{bad}]$.

4   Weak Equivalences

In this section we introduce quantitative notions of program equivalence and equational theories to reason about them.

4.1   Approximate Observational Equivalence

Approximate observational equivalence generalizes observational equivalence between two games by allowing that their output distributions differ up to some quantity ϵ. Informally, two games G_1 and G_2 are ϵ-observationally equivalent w.r.t. an input set of variables I and an output set of variables O iff for every pair of memories m_1, m_2 coinciding on I,

$$\Delta(([\![G_1]\!]\ m_1)/=_O, ([\![G_2]\!]m_2)/=_O) \leq \epsilon,$$

where for a distribution μ over a set A and an equivalence relation R on A, we let μ/R denote the quotient distribution of μ over A/R. For the purpose of formalization, it is more convenient to rely on the following alternative characterization that does not use quotient distributions, in part because the underlying language of Coq does not support quotient types.

Definition 1. *Two games* G_1 *and* G_2 *are* ϵ-*observationally equivalent w.r.t. an input set of variables* I *and an output set of variables* O, *written* $\models G_1 \simeq_O^I G_2 \preceq \epsilon$, *iff for all memories* $m_1, m_2 \in \mathcal{M}$ *and functions* $f_1, f_2 : \mathcal{M} \to [0, 1]$

$$m_1 =_I m_2 \wedge f_1 =_O f_2 \implies |[\![G_1]\!] \, m_1 \, f_1 - [\![G_2]\!] \, m_2 \, f_2| \leq \epsilon$$

Figure 2 provides an excerpt of an equational theory for approximate observational equivalence; further and more general rules appear in the formal development. Most rules generalize observational equivalence in the expected way. For instance, the rule for random assignment considers the case of uniformly sampling over two finite sets A and B: in case $A = B$, one obtains $\epsilon = 0$.

$$\frac{\models c_1 \simeq_O^I c_2 \preceq \epsilon_1 \quad \models c_2 \simeq_O^I c_3 \preceq \epsilon_2}{\models c_1 \simeq_O^I c_3 \preceq \epsilon_1 + \epsilon_2} \qquad \frac{\models c_1 \simeq_{O'}^{I'} c_2 \preceq \epsilon' \quad I' \subseteq I \quad O \subseteq O' \quad \epsilon' \leq \epsilon}{\models c_1 \simeq_O^I c_2 \preceq \epsilon}$$

$$\frac{\models c_1 \simeq_{O'}^I c_2 \preceq \epsilon_1 \quad \models c_1' \simeq_O^{O'} c_2' \preceq \epsilon_2}{\models c_1; c_1' \simeq_O^I c_2; c_2' \preceq \epsilon_1 + \epsilon_2}$$

$$\frac{\models c_1 \simeq_O^I c_1' \preceq \epsilon \quad \models c_2 \simeq_O^I c_2' \preceq \epsilon \quad \forall m, m'. \, I \, m \, m' \implies [\![b]\!] \, m = [\![b']\!] \, m'}{\models \text{if } b \text{ then } c_1 \text{ else } c_2 \simeq_O^I \text{ if } b' \text{ then } c_1' \text{ else } c_2' \preceq \epsilon}$$

$$\frac{\epsilon = \#(A \cap B)|\frac{1}{\#A} - \frac{1}{\#B}| + \max\left\{\frac{\#(A \backslash B)}{\#A}, \frac{\#(B \backslash A)}{\#B}\right\}}{\models x \xleftarrow{\$} A \simeq_{I \cup \{x\}}^I x \xleftarrow{\$} B \preceq \epsilon}$$

Fig. 2. Selected rules for reasoning about approximate observational equivalence

4.2   A Conditional Variant

The application we describe in Section 5 requires reasoning about conditional approximate observational equivalence, a generalization of approximate observational equivalence. We define for each distribution μ and event P the conditional distribution $\mu \mid_P$ as

$$\mu \mid_P \stackrel{\text{def}}{=} \lambda f. \, \mu \left(\lambda a. \frac{f(a) \, \mathbb{1}_P(a)}{\mu \, \mathbb{1}_P}\right)$$

Intuitively, $\mu \mid_P \mathbb{1}_Q$ yields the conditional probability of Q given P.

Definition 2. *A game* G_1 *conditioned on predicate* P_1 *is* ϵ-*observationally equivalent to a game* G_2 *conditioned on* P_2 *w.r.t. an input set of variables* I *and an output set of variables* O, *written* $\models [G_1]_{P_1} \simeq_O^I [G_2]_{P_2} \preceq \epsilon$, *iff for any* $m_1, m_2 \in \mathcal{M}$ *and* $f_1, f_2 : \mathcal{M} \to [0, 1]$,

$$m_1 =_I m_2 \wedge f_1 =_O f_2 \implies |([\![G_1]\!] \, m_1)|_{P_1} \, f_1 - ([\![G_2]\!] \, m_2)|_{P_2} \, f_2| \leq \epsilon$$

Conditional approximate observational equivalence subsumes classic approximate observational equivalence, which can be recovered by taking $P_1 = P_2 = \text{true}$.

5 Indifferentiability

In this section we present an application of the techniques introduced above to prove the security of cryptographic constructions in the indifferentiability framework of Maurer et al. [23]. In particular, we consider the notion of indifferentiability from a random oracle. A random oracle is an ideal primitive that maps elements in some domain into uniformly and independently distributed values in a finite set; queries are answered consistently so that identical queries are given the same answer. A proof conducted in the random oracle model for a function $h : A \to B$ assumes that h is made publicly available to all parties.

Definition 3 (Indifferentiability). *A procedure* $\mathcal{F}$ *that has access to a random oracle* $h : \{0, 1\}^* \to A$ *is said to be* $(t_S, t_D, q_1, q_2, \epsilon)$-*indifferentiable from a random oracle* $\mathcal{H} : \{0, 1\}^* \to B$ *if there exists a simulator* S *with oracle access to* $\mathcal{H}$ *and executing within time* t_S *such that any distinguisher* $\mathcal{D}$ *running within time* t_D *and making at most* q_1 *queries to an oracle* $\mathcal{O}_1$ *and* q_2 *queries to an oracle* $\mathcal{O}_2$ *has at most probability* ϵ *of distinguishing a scenario where* $\mathcal{O}_1$ *is implemented as* $\mathcal{F}$ *and* $\mathcal{O}_2$ *as* h *from a scenario where* $\mathcal{O}_1$ *is implemented as* H *and* $\mathcal{O}_2$ *as* S *instead. Put in terms of games,*

Game $G : \mathbf{L} \leftarrow$ nil; $b \leftarrow \mathcal{D}(\,)$	**Game** $G' : \mathbf{L} \leftarrow$ nil; $b \leftarrow \mathcal{D}(\,)$
Oracle $\mathcal{O}_1(x)$: return $\mathcal{F}(x)$ **Oracle** $\mathcal{O}_2(x)$: if $x \notin \text{dom}(\mathbf{L})$ then $\quad y \xleftarrow{\$} A; \mathbf{L}(x) \leftarrow y$ return $\mathbf{L}(x)$	**Oracle** $\mathcal{O}_1(x)$: if $x \notin \text{dom}(\mathbf{L})$ then $\quad y \xleftarrow{\$} B; \mathbf{L}(x) \leftarrow y$ return $\mathbf{L}(x)$ **Oracle** $\mathcal{O}_2(x)$: return $\mathcal{S}(x)$

$$|\Pr[G : b = \text{true}] - \Pr[G' : b = \text{true}]| \leq \epsilon$$

Random oracles into elliptic curves over finite fields are typically built from a random oracle h on the underlying field and a deterministic encoding f that maps elements of the field into the elliptic curve. Examples of such encodings include Icart function [21] and the Shallue-Woestijne-Ulas (SWU) algorithm [27]. In general, and in particular for the aforementioned mappings, the function f is not surjective and only covers a fraction of points in the curve. Hence, the naive definition of a hash function H as $f \circ h$ would not cover the whole curve, contradicting the assumption that H behaves as a random oracle. In a recent paper, Brier et al. [9] show how to build hash functions into elliptic curves that are indifferentiable from a random oracle from a particular class of encodings, including both SWU and Icart encodings.

We prove the indifferentiability of the construction put forward by Brier et al. in the formal framework of CertiCrypt. The proof introduces two intermediate constructions and is structured in three steps:

1. We first prove that any efficiently invertible encoding f can be turned into a *weak encoding* (Theorem 1);
2. We then show an efficient construction to transform any weak encoding f into an *admissible encoding* (Theorem 2);
3. Finally, we prove that any admissible encoding can be turned into a hash function indifferentiable from a random oracle (Theorem 3).

Moreover, we show in Sect. 6 that Icart encoding is efficiently invertible and thus yields a hash function indifferentiable from a random oracle when plugged in into the above construction. We recall the alternative definitions of weak and admissible encoding from [22]. Note that these do not match the definitions in [9], but, in comparison, are better behaved: e.g. admissible encodings as we define them are closed under functional composition and cartesian product.

Definition 4 (Weak encoding). *A function* $f : S \to R$ *is an* (α, ϵ)-*weak encoding if it is computable in polynomial-time and there exists a probabilistic polynomial-time algorithm* $\mathcal{I}_f : R \to S_\perp$ *such that*

1. $\{\mathsf{true}\}\ r \xleftarrow{\$} R;\ s \leftarrow \mathcal{I}_f(r)\ \{s = \perp \lor f(s) = r\}$
2. $\models [r \xleftarrow{\$} R;\ s \leftarrow \mathcal{I}_f(r)]_{s \neq \perp} \simeq^\emptyset_{\{s\}} [s \xleftarrow{\$} S] \preceq \epsilon$
3. $\Pr[r \xleftarrow{\$} R;\ s \leftarrow \mathcal{I}_f(r) : s = \perp] \leq 1 - \alpha^{-1}$

Definition 5 (Admissible encoding). *A function* $f : S \to R$ *is an* ϵ-*admissible encoding if it is computable in polynomial-time and there exists a probabilistic polynomial-time algorithm* $\mathcal{I}_f : R \to S_\perp$ *such that*

1. $\{\mathsf{true}\}\ r \xleftarrow{\$} R;\ s \leftarrow \mathcal{I}_f(r)\ \{s = \perp \lor f(s) = r\}$
2. $\models r \xleftarrow{\$} R;\ s \leftarrow \mathcal{I}_f(r) \simeq^\emptyset_{\{s\}} s \xleftarrow{\$} S \preceq \epsilon$

Brier et al. [9] prove that if $\mathbb{G}$ is a finite cyclic group of order N with generator g, a function into $\mathbb{G}$ indifferentiable from a random oracle can be built from any polynomially invertible function $f : A \to \mathbb{G}$ and hash functions $h_1 : \{0,1\}^\star \to A$ and $h_2 : \{0,1\}^* \to \mathbb{Z}_N$ as follows:

$$H(m) \stackrel{\text{def}}{=} f(h_1(m)) \otimes g^{h_2(m)} \tag{1}$$

Intuitively, the term $g^{h_2(m)}$ behaves as a one-time pad and ensures that H covers all points in the group even if f covers only a fraction. Our proof generalizes this construction to finitely generated abelian groups.

We begin by showing that any efficiently invertible encoding is a weak encoding.

Theorem 1. *Let* $f : S \to R$ *be a function computable in polynomial-time such that for any* $r \in R$, $\#f^{-1}(r) \leq B$. *Assume there exists a polynomial-time algorithm* $\mathcal{I}$ *that given* $r \in R$ *outputs the set* $f^{-1}(r)$. *Then,* f *is an* $(\alpha, 0)$-*weak encoding, with* $\alpha = B \, \#R/\#S$.

Proof. Using $\mathcal{I}$, we build a partial inverter $\mathcal{I}_f : R \to S_\perp$ of f that satisfies the properties in Definition 4:

$$\mathcal{I}_f(r) : X \leftarrow \mathcal{I}(r); \; b \xleftarrow{\$} \text{true} \oplus_{\#X/B} \text{false};$$
$$\text{if } b = \text{true then } s \xleftarrow{\$} X; \text{ return } s \text{ else return } \perp$$

First observe that $\mathcal{I}_f(r)$ fails with probability $1 - \#f^{-1}(r)/B$ or else returns an element uniformly chosen from the set of pre-images of r, and thus satisfies the first property trivially. In addition, for any $x \in S$ we have

$$\Pr\left[r \xleftarrow{\$} R; \; s \leftarrow \mathcal{I}_f(r) : s = x\right] = \frac{1}{B \# R}$$
$$\Pr\left[r \xleftarrow{\$} R; \; s \leftarrow \mathcal{I}_f(r) : s \neq \perp\right] = \frac{1}{\#R} \sum_{r \in R} \frac{\#f^{-1}(r)}{B} = \frac{\#S}{B \# R}$$

Hence, for a uniformly chosen r, the probability of $\mathcal{I}_f(r)$ failing is exactly $1 - \alpha^{-1}$, and the probability of returning any particular value in S conditioned to not failing is uniform. $\qquad\qquad\square$

We show next how to construct an admissible encoding from a weak-encoding into a finite abelian group. Recall that every finite abelian group $\mathbb{G}$ is isomorphic to a product of cyclic groups[2]

$$\mathbb{G} \simeq \mathbb{Z}_{n_1} \times \cdots \times \mathbb{Z}_{n_k}$$

If we fix generators g_i for each $\mathbb{Z}_{n_i}$, then any $x \in \mathbb{G}$ admits a unique representation as a vector $(g_1^{z_1}, \ldots, g_k^{z_k})$. We use log to denote the operator that returns the canonical representation $\vec{z} = (z_1, \ldots, z_k)$ for any $x \in \mathbb{G}$.

Theorem 2. *Let $\mathbb{G} \simeq \mathbb{Z}_{n_1} \times \cdots \times \mathbb{Z}_{n_k}$ be a finite abelian group and let g_i be a generator of $\mathbb{Z}_{n_i}$ for $i = 1 \ldots k$. Assume that $f : A \to \mathbb{G}$ is an (α, ϵ)-weak encoding. Then, for any polynomially bounded T, the function*

$$F \qquad\qquad : A \times \mathbb{Z}_{n_1} \times \cdots \times \mathbb{Z}_{n_k} \to \mathbb{G}$$
$$F(a, z_1, \ldots, z_k) = f(a) \otimes g_1^{z_1} \otimes \cdots \otimes g_k^{z_k}$$

is an ϵ'-admissible encoding into $\mathbb{G}$, with $\epsilon' = \epsilon + \left(1 - \alpha^{-1}\right)^{T+1}$.

Proof. Since f is a weak encoding, there exists a polynomial-time computable inverter $\mathcal{I}_f$ of f satisfying the conditions in Definition 4. Let $T \in \mathbb{N}$ be polynomially bounded. Using $\mathcal{I}_f$, we build a partial inverter $\mathcal{I}_F$ of F that satisfies the properties in Definition 5:

$$\mathcal{I}_F(r) : i \leftarrow 0; \; a \leftarrow \perp;$$
$$\text{while } (i \leq T \wedge a = \perp) \text{ do}$$
$$\vec{z} \xleftarrow{\$} \mathbb{Z}_{n_1} \times \cdots \times \mathbb{Z}_{n_k};$$
$$x \leftarrow r \otimes g_1^{-z_1} \otimes \cdots \otimes g_k^{-z_k};$$
$$a \leftarrow \mathcal{I}_f(x); \; i \leftarrow i + 1$$
$$\text{end};$$
$$\text{if } a \neq \perp \text{ then return } (a, \vec{z}) \text{ else return } \perp$$

---

[2] The decomposition can be made unique by fixing additional conditions on $n_1 \ldots n_k$.

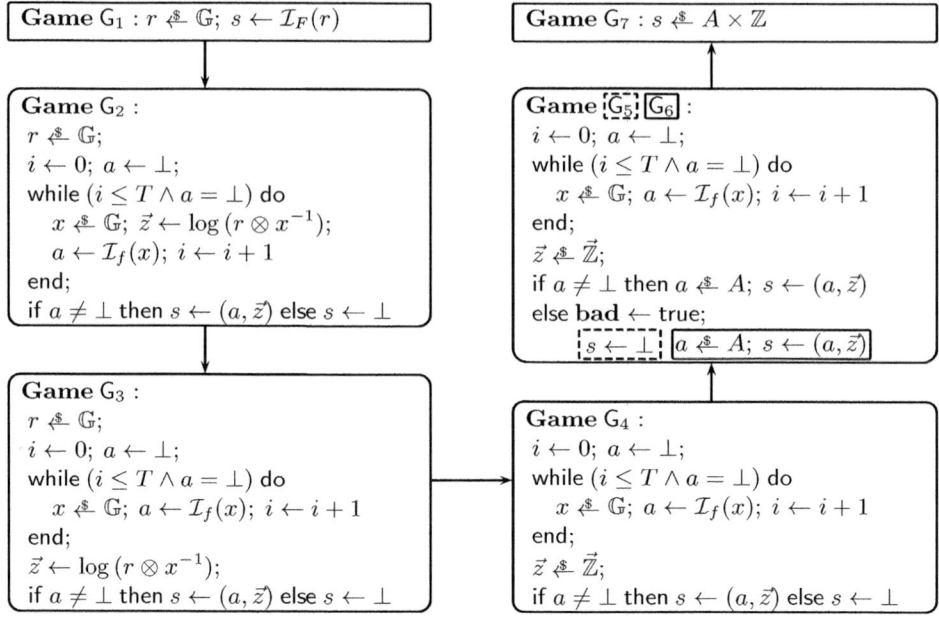

Fig. 3. Sequence of games used in Theorem 2

The partial inverter $\mathcal{I}_F$ runs in time $t_{\mathcal{I}_F} = (T + 1)\, t_{\mathcal{I}_f}$, where $t_{\mathcal{I}_f}$ is a bound on the running time of $\mathcal{I}_f$. Hence, $\mathcal{I}_F$ is polynomial-time for any polynomially bounded T.

For the sake of readability in the following we use $\vec{\mathbb{Z}}$ to denote $\mathbb{Z}_{n_1} \times \cdots \times \mathbb{Z}_{n_k}$ and $\vec{g}^{\vec{z}}$ to denote $g_1^{z_1} \otimes \cdots \otimes g_k^{z_k}$. We prove that

$$\models r \xleftarrow{\$} \mathbb{G};\; s \leftarrow \mathcal{I}_F(r) \simeq^{\emptyset}_{\{s\}} s \xleftarrow{\$} A \times \vec{\mathbb{Z}} \preceq \epsilon'$$

using the sequence of games $G_1, \ldots, G_7$ shown in Figure 3, the mechanized program transformations of CertiCrypt, and the proof rules for observational and approximate observational equivalence. We briefly describe the proof below.

We obtain game G_2 by first inlining the call to $\mathcal{I}_F$ in the initial game and then applying the following algebraic equivalence to transform the body of the while loop:

$$\models \vec{z} \xleftarrow{\$} \vec{\mathbb{Z}};\; x \leftarrow r \otimes \vec{g}^{-\vec{z}} \simeq^{\{r\}}_{\{r,x,z\}} x \xleftarrow{\$} \mathbb{G};\; \vec{z} \leftarrow \log\left(r \otimes x^{-1}\right)$$

We obtain game G_3 by moving the assignment to $\vec{z}$ outside the loop in game G_2. This transformation is semantics-preserving because $\vec{z}$ is never used inside the loop and the value that it has when exiting the loop only depends on the value of x in the last iteration. Formally, this is proven by unfolding the first iteration of the loop and establishing that the relation

$$=_{\{i,x,a,r\}} \wedge (\vec{z} = \log\left(r \otimes x^{-1}\right))\langle 1 \rangle$$

is a relational invariant between the loop in G_2 and the loop resulting from removing the assignment to $\vec{z}$. By appending $\vec{z} \leftarrow \log\left(r \otimes x^{-1}\right)$ to the latter loop, we recover equivalence on $\vec{z}$.

Since r is no longer used inside the loop, we can postpone its definition after the loop, and use the following algebraic equivalence to sample $\vec{z}$ instead of r:

$$\models r \stackrel{\$}{\leftarrow} \mathbb{G}; \ \vec{z} \leftarrow \log\left(r \otimes x^{-1}\right) \simeq^{\{x\}}_{\{r,x,z\}} \vec{z} \stackrel{\$}{\leftarrow} \vec{\mathbb{Z}}; \ r \leftarrow x \otimes \vec{g}^{\vec{z}}$$

We obtain G_4 by additionally removing the assignment to r, which is now dead code.

For the next step in the proof we use the fact that f is a weak encoding and therefore the distribution of a after a call $a \leftarrow \mathcal{I}_f(x)$ conditioned to $a \neq \bot$ is ϵ-away from the uniform distribution. This allows us to resample the value of a after the loop, provided $a \neq \bot$, incurring a penalty ϵ on the statistical distance of the distribution of s between G_4 and G_5. To prove this formally, let b be the condition of the loop and c its body. Observe that the semantics of the loop coincides with the semantics of its $(T+1)$-unrolling $[\text{while } b \text{ do } c]_{T+1}$. We show by induction on T that for any $[0,1]$-valued functions f, g s.t. $f =_{\{a'\}} g$,

$$m_1 =_{\{a,i\}} m_2 \ \wedge \ m_1(a) = \bot \implies |[\![c_1]\!] \, m_1 \, f' - [\![c_2]\!] \, m_2 \, g'| \leq \epsilon$$

where

$$
\begin{aligned}
c_1 &= [\text{while } b \text{ do } c]_{T+1}; \ \text{if } a \neq \bot \text{ then } a' \leftarrow a \\
c_2 &= [\text{while } b \text{ do } c]_{T+1}; \ \text{if } a \neq \bot \text{ then } a' \stackrel{\$}{\leftarrow} A \\
f'(m) &= \text{if } m(a) \neq \bot \text{ then } f(m) \text{ else } 0 \\
g'(m) &= \text{if } m(a) \neq \bot \text{ then } g(m) \text{ else } 0
\end{aligned}
$$

and use this to conclude the ϵ-approximate equivalence of G_4 and G_5.

Since G_5 and G_6 are syntactically equivalent except for code appearing after the flag **bad** is set, we apply the corollary of the Fundamental Lemma in Section 3.2 to obtain the bound

$$(\!(G_5, G_6)\!) \preceq \Pr\left[G_5 : \textbf{bad}\right]$$

Since the probability of failure of $\mathcal{I}_f$ on a uniformly chosen input is upper bounded by $1 - \alpha^{-1}$, we can show by induction on T that

$$\Pr\left[G_5 : \textbf{bad}\right] \leq \left(1 - \alpha^{-1}\right)^{T+1},$$

from which we conclude $\models G_5 \simeq^{\emptyset}_{\{s\}} G_6 \preceq \left(1 - \alpha^{-1}\right)^{T+1}$.

By coalescing the branches in the conditional at the end of G_6 and removing dead code, we prove that the game is observational equivalent w.r.t a and $\vec{z}$ to the game $a \stackrel{\$}{\leftarrow} A; \ \vec{z} \stackrel{\$}{\leftarrow} \vec{\mathbb{Z}}; \ s \leftarrow (a, z)$, which is trivially equivalent to G_7.

By composing the above results, we conclude

$$\models G_1 \simeq^{\emptyset}_{\{s\}} G_7 \preceq \epsilon + \left(1 - \alpha^{-1}\right)^{T+1} \tag{2}$$

We must also show that $s = \bot \ \vee \ F(s) = r$ is a post-condition of G_1. As G_1 and G_3 are observationally equivalent with respect to s and r, it is sufficient to establish the validity of the post-condition for G_3. We show that $a \neq \bot \Rightarrow x = f(a)$ is an invariant of the loop. When the loop finishes, either $a = \bot$ and in this case $s = \bot$, or $a \neq \bot$ and we have $F(s) = f(a) \otimes \vec{g}^{\vec{z}} = x \otimes r \otimes x^{-1} = r$. $\qquad \square$

Finally, we show that the composition of an admissible encoding $f : S \to R$ and a random oracle into S is indifferentiable from a random oracle into R.

Theorem 3. *Let $f : S \to R$ be an ϵ-admissible encoding with inverter algorithm $\mathcal{I}_f$ and let $h : \{0,1\}^* \to S$ be a random oracle. Then, $f \circ h$ is $(t_S, t_D, q_1, q_2, \epsilon')$-indifferentiable from a random oracle into R, where $t_S = q_1 \, t_{\mathcal{I}_f}$ and $\epsilon' = 2(q_1 + q_2)\epsilon$.*

Before moving to the proof of Theorem 3, we prove the following useful result.

Lemma 3. *Let $f : S \to R$ be an ϵ-admissible encoding with inverter algorithm $\mathcal{I}_f$. Then*

$$\models s \xleftarrow{\$} S; \ r \leftarrow f(s) \simeq^{\emptyset}_{\{r,s\}} r \xleftarrow{\$} R; \ s \leftarrow \mathcal{I}_f(r) \preceq 2\epsilon$$

Proof. Define

$$
\begin{aligned}
c_i &\stackrel{\text{def}}{=} s \xleftarrow{\$} S; \ r \leftarrow f(s) \\
c_f &\stackrel{\text{def}}{=} r \xleftarrow{\$} R; \ s \leftarrow \mathcal{I}_f(r) \\
c_1 &\stackrel{\text{def}}{=} c_i; \ \text{if } s = \bot \text{ then } r \xleftarrow{\$} R \text{ else } r \leftarrow f(s) \\
c_2 &\stackrel{\text{def}}{=} c_f; \ \text{if } s = \bot \text{ then } \mathbf{bad} \leftarrow \text{true}; \ r \xleftarrow{\$} R \text{ else } r \leftarrow f(s) \\
c_3 &\stackrel{\text{def}}{=} c_f; \ \text{if } s = \bot \text{ then } \mathbf{bad} \leftarrow \text{true else } r \leftarrow f(s)
\end{aligned}
$$

Since the first branch of the conditional in c_1 is never executed, we have:

$$\models c_i \simeq^{\emptyset}_{\{r,s\}} c_1$$

Due to the second property of Definition 5, the distributions of s after executing c_i and c_f are ϵ-away. Using the rules for approximate observational equivalence, we obtain

$$\models c_1 \simeq^{\emptyset}_{\{r,s\}} c_2 \preceq \epsilon$$

The corollary to the Fundamental Lemma in Section 3.2 implies that $(\!|c_2, c_3|\!) \preceq \Pr\left[c_2 : \mathbf{bad}\right]$. Moreover,

$$\Pr\left[c_2 : \mathbf{bad}\right] = 1 - \Pr\left[c_f : s \neq \bot\right] = \Pr\left[s \xleftarrow{\$} S : s \neq \bot\right] - \Pr\left[c_f : s \neq \bot\right] \leq \epsilon$$

where the last inequality holds again because of the second property of Definition 5. Since the final values of r and s in programs c_2 and c_3 are independent of the initial memory, we have

$$\models c_2 \simeq^{\emptyset}_{\{r,s\}} c_3 \preceq \epsilon$$

Because $\mathcal{I}_f$ is a partial inverter for f, the else branch of the conditional in c_3 has no effect and can be removed, and thus $\models c_3 \simeq^{\emptyset}_{\{r,s\}} c_f$. We conclude by transitivity of approximate observational equivalence. $\qquad\square$

Proof (of Theorem 3). Let $\mathcal{D}$ be a distinguisher against the indifferentiability of $f \circ h$ making at most q_1 queries to $\mathcal{O}_1$ and at most q_2 queries to $\mathcal{O}_2$. We exhibit a simulator $\mathcal{S}$ that uses a random oracle into R to simulate h and show that $\mathcal{D}$ cannot distinguish a game G where $\mathcal{O}_1$ and $\mathcal{O}_2$ are implemented by $f \circ h$ and h respectively from a game G$'$ where they are implemented by $\mathcal{S}$ and a random oracle into R instead. An overview

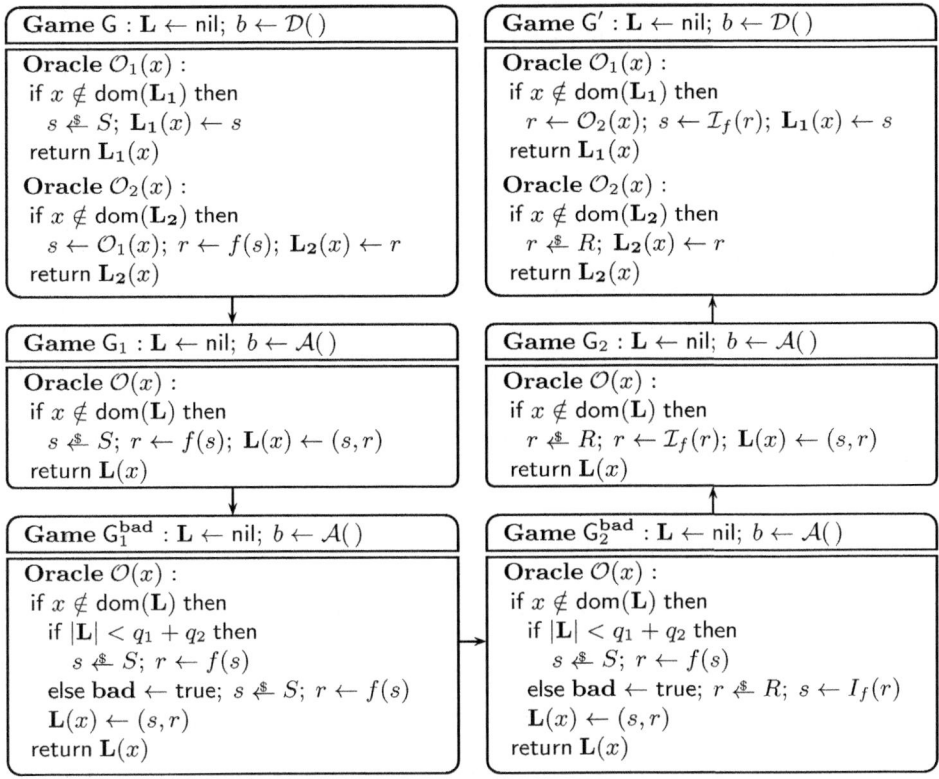

Fig. 4. Games used in the proof of Theorem 3

of the proof, including these two games and the definition of the simulator is shown in Figure 4.

Our goal is to prove

$$|\Pr[G : b = \text{true}] - \Pr[G' : b = \text{true}]| \le 2(q_1 + q_2)\epsilon \qquad (3)$$

The crux of the proof is an application of Lemma 1. In order to apply it, we need first to transform the initial games to replace oracles $\mathcal{O}_1$ and $\mathcal{O}_2$ by a single joint oracle that simultaneously returns the responses of both. Using $\mathcal{D}$, we construct an adversary $\mathcal{A}$ with access to a single joint oracle, such that games G and G' are equivalent to games G_1 and G_2 in the figure. Adversary $\mathcal{A}$ simply calls the distinguisher $\mathcal{D}$ and forwards the value it returns; it simulates $\mathcal{O}_1$ and $\mathcal{O}_2$ by using its own oracle $\mathcal{O}$.

We assume without loss of generality the equivalence between games G and G_1, and G' and G_2, respectively. This is identical to the assumption in [9] that the distinguisher always makes the same queries to both its oracles. Games G_1 and G_2 satisfy the equalities:

$$\Pr[G : b = \text{true}] = \Pr[G_1 : b = \text{true}] \qquad \Pr[G' : b = \text{true}] = \Pr[G_2 : b = \text{true}]$$

Furthermore, since D makes at most q_1 queries to O_1 and q_2 queries to oracle O_2, A makes at most $q = q_1 + q_2$ queries to its oracle.

We next transform the implementation of oracle O in games G_1 and G_2 to enforce the bound $q_1 + q_2$ on the total number of queries. After the allotted number of queries is exhausted, oracle O behaves the same way in the two games. This ensures that further queries will not make the statistical distance between the two games grow and paves the way to applying Lemma 1. This transformation preserves observational equivalence because we know that A will not make more queries than allowed. One way of justifying this is using the syntactic criterion for Lemma 2: we annotate the games with a flag **bad** that is set to true at points where the implementations of the oracle O in the games differ and obtain

$$\Pr\left[G_1^{\mathbf{bad}} : b = \text{true} \wedge \neg\mathbf{bad}\right] = \Pr\left[G_2^{\mathbf{bad}} : b = \text{true} \wedge \neg\mathbf{bad}\right]$$

But since $\mathbf{bad} \implies q < |\mathbf{L}|$ is an invariant and $|\mathbf{L}| \leq q$ is a post-condition of both games,

$$\Pr\left[G_1^{\mathbf{bad}} : b = \text{true}\right] = \Pr\left[G_2^{\mathbf{bad}} : b = \text{true}\right]$$

We can now apply Lemma 1 to the games G_2 and $G_2^{\mathbf{bad}}$, defining $\text{cntr} = |\mathbf{L}|$ and $h(i) = \text{if } i < q \text{ then } 2\epsilon \text{ else } 0$. The second hypothesis of the lemma, i.e that a call to $E_2(O)$ cannot decrease $|\mathbf{L}|$, is immediate. We can assume that $2q\epsilon < 1$ (otherwise the theorem is trivially true). Then,

$$\sum_{i=[\![\text{cntr}]\!]m}^{[\![\text{cntr}]\!]m'-1} h(i) \leq 2q\epsilon < 1, \qquad \text{and} \qquad \bar{h}_{\text{cntr}}(m, m') = \sum_{i=[\![\text{cntr}]\!]m}^{[\![\text{cntr}]\!]m'-1} h(i)$$

We are only left to prove that

$$(\!|E_2(O), E_2^{\mathbf{bad}}(O)|\!) \preceq \lambda m.\, [\![E_2(O)]\!]\, m\, (\lambda m'.\, \bar{h}_{\text{cntr}}(m, m'))$$

Doing a case analysis on the conditions $x \in \text{dom}(\mathbf{L})$ and $|\mathbf{L}| < q$ yields four cases; three of them yield a null distance and are immediate. The remaining case, where $x \notin \text{dom}(\mathbf{L})$ and $|\mathbf{L}| < q$, yields a distance 2ϵ and follows from Lemma 3. We finally obtain $(\!|G_2, G_2^{\mathbf{bad}}|\!) \preceq 2(q_1+q_2)\epsilon$, which combined with the previous results implies the desired inequality. □

6   Application to Elliptic Curves

This section discuss the application of the proof presented in the previous section to hashing into elliptic curves.

Let $\mathbb{F}_{p^m}$ be a finite field of cardinal p^m, with $p > 3$ prime. An elliptic curve over $\mathbb{F}_{p^m}$ is defined by the equation $Y^2 = X^3 + aX + b$ where the parameters a, b are elements of $\mathbb{F}_{p^m}$ such that $4a^3 + 27b^2 \neq 0$ (the curve must be non-singular). The set of points of such a curve, which we denote $\mathbb{E}_{a,b}$, can be construed as a finite abelian group with the *point at infinite O* as the identity element. Furthermore, it can be shown that the group $\mathbb{E}_{a,b}$ is either cyclic or a product of two cyclic groups.

Hence, applying the results from the previous section, any polynomially invertible function into a $\mathbb{E}_{a,b}$ can be transformed into a hash function that is indifferentiable from a random oracle. In particular, this holds for Icart encoding, as we show next.

For $p^m \equiv 2 \pmod{3}$, Icart function $f_{a,b} : \mathbb{F}_{p^m} \to \mathbb{E}_{a,b}$ is defined as:

$$f_{a,b}(u) \stackrel{\text{def}}{=} \begin{cases} (x, ux + v) & \text{if } u \neq 0 \\ ((-b)^{\frac{1}{3}}, 0) & \text{if } u = 0 \wedge a = 0 \\ O & \text{if } u = 0 \wedge a \neq 0 \end{cases} \tag{4}$$

$$\text{where} \qquad x = \left(v^2 - b - \frac{u^6}{27} \right)^{\frac{1}{3}} + \frac{u^2}{3} \qquad v = \frac{3a - u^4}{6u}$$

As a side remark, observe that the original definition only deals with the case $a \neq 0$; the definition for the case $a = 0$ was suggested to us by Thomas Icart in a private communication.

The set of pre-images of a point in the curve under Icart function can be computed efficiently by solving for the roots of polynomials over $\mathbb{F}_{p^m}$ of degree at most 4—any point in the curve has at most 4 pre-images:

$$f_{a,b}^{-1}(O) \stackrel{\text{def}}{=} \begin{cases} \{0\} & \text{if } a \neq 0 \\ \emptyset & \text{if } a = 0 \end{cases} \qquad f_{a,b}^{-1}(X, Y) \stackrel{\text{def}}{=} \begin{cases} \{u | u^3 - 6uX + 6Y = 0\} & \text{if } a = 0 \\ \{u | u^4 - 6u^2X + 6uY = 3a\} & \text{if } a \neq 0 \end{cases}$$

This can be done using any efficient algorithm for factoring polynomials over finite fields, e.g. Berlekamp's algorithm. Thus, Icart encoding is polynomially invertible.

Formalization. To apply our generic proof of indifferentiability to Icart function, we proceeded as follows:

1. We integrated Théry's formalization of elliptic curves [30] in our framework, and showed that the set of points of the elliptic curve $\mathbb{E}_{a,b}$ can be construed as a finite cyclic group, as defined in SSREFLECT standard library [19];
2. We defined Icart function, and showed that it generates points in the curve $\mathbb{E}_{a,b}$. This required showing the existence of cubic roots in the field $\mathbb{F}_{p^m}$ (the cubic root of $x \in \mathbb{F}_{p^m}$ is the element $x^{(2p^m-1)/3}$);
3. We defined the inverse of Icart function, for which we need to assume an efficient method for factoring polynomials of degree 4 over the underlying field, as no existing Coq library readily provides the necessary background;
4. We applied Theorem 1 to show that Icart function is an $(\alpha, 0)$-weak encoding, where $\alpha = 4N/p^m$ where N is the order of $\mathbb{E}_{a,b}$;
5. We applied Theorem 2 to show that for any polynomially bounded T, the function $F : \mathbb{F}_{p^m} \times \mathbb{Z}_N$, defined as $F(u, z) = f_{a,b}(u) + g^z$, where g is a generator of $\mathbb{Z}_N$, is an ϵ-admissible encoding, where $\epsilon = (1 - \alpha^{-1})^{T+1}$;
6. We finally applied Theorem 3 to show that if F is composed with a random oracle into $\mathbb{F}_{p^m} \times \mathbb{Z}_N$ (equivalently, a random oracle into $\mathbb{F}_{p^m}$ and a random oracle into $\mathbb{Z}_N$), the resulting construction is $(t_S, t_D, q_1, q_2, 2(q_1 + q_2)\epsilon)$-indifferentiable from a random oracle into $\mathbb{E}_{a,b}$, where $t_S = q_1 \, t_{\mathcal{I}_F} = q_1 \, (T + 1) \, t_{f^{-1}}$ and $t_{f^{-1}}$ is an upper bound on the time needed to compute the pre-image of a point under Icart function, i.e. to solve a polynomial of degree 4 in $\mathbb{F}_{p^m}$.

7   Related Work

Weak Equivalences. The impossibility to achieve perfect security has motivated several proposals for weaker, quantitative, definitions of security. Prominent examples include notions of confidentiality based on information theory [11, 12, 24, 29]. More recently, Dwork [14] has suggested differential privacy as an alternative notion that quantifies the privacy guaranteed by confidential data analysis. All of these definitions can be construed as quantitative hyperproperties [12], and readily extend to relational properties that are closely related to statistical distance.

Approximate observational equivalence is also closely related to weak notions of bisimulations [26]. Barthe et al. [6] generalize approximate observational equivalence to an approximate relational Hoare logic and report on an extension of the CertiCrypt framework for reasoning about differential privacy. The validity of judgments in this logic is based on a notion of approximate lifting of a relation that is closely related to the notion used in [26].

Hashing into Elliptic Curves. A number of highly relevant cryptographic constructions, including identity based schemes [8] and password based key exchange protocols [7], require hashing into elliptic curves. Indeed, there have been a number of proposals for such hash functions, see for instance [17, 21, 27]. Recently, Farashahi et al. [15] developed powerful techniques to show the indifferentiability of hash function constructions based on deterministic encodings. Their results improve on [9], in the sense that they apply to a larger class of encodings, including encodings to hyperelliptic curves, and that they provide tighter bounds for encodings that are covered by both methods.

Formalization and Verification of Elliptic Curves. To our best knowledge, our work provides the first machine-checked proof of security for a cryptographic primitive based on elliptic curves. There are, however, previous works on the formalization of elliptic curves: Hurd, Gordon and Fox [20] report on the verification in HOL of the group laws and an application to the functional correctness of ElGamal encryption. Théry and Hanrot [30] use Coq to formalize the group laws, and show how the formalization of elliptic curves can be used to build efficient reflective tactics for testing primality.

8   Conclusion

This paper reports on a machine-checked proof of a recent construction to build hash functions that are indifferentiable from a random oracle into an elliptic curve. The example is singular among other examples that have been formalized using CertiCrypt, because it involves complex reasoning about algebraic geometry and requires the formalization of new weak forms of program equivalence.

The formalization establishes the ability of CertiCrypt to integrate smoothly with existing libraries of complex mathematics. Overall, the formalization consists of over 65,000 lines of Coq (without counting components reused from the standard libraries of Coq and SSReflect), which break down as follows: 45,000 lines corresponding to the original CertiCrypt framework, 3,500 lines of extensions to CertiCrypt, 7,000 lines written originally for our application to indifferentiability, and 10,000 lines of a slightly adapted version of Théry [30] elliptic curve library.

Our work paves the way for further developments. We are interested in leveraging our earlier formalization of zero-knowledge protocols [5] to statistical zero-knowledge, and to use the result as a back-end for a certifying ZK compiler, in the style of [1]. We also intend to pursue the machine-checked formalization of indifferentiability proofs, and in particular to show that the finalists of NIST SHA-3 competition are indifferentiable from a random oracle. Finally, it would be of interest to enhance EasyCrypt [3], an automated front-end that generates verifiable security proofs in CertiCrypt, so that it can manipulate the notions of equivalence considered in this paper (and in [6]).

Acknowledgments. This work was partially funded by European Projects FP7-256980 NESSoS and FP7-229599 AMAROUT, Spanish project TIN2009-14599 DESAFIOS 10, Madrid Regional project S2009TIC-1465 PROMETIDOS and French project ANR SESUR-012 SCALP.

References

1. Almeida, J.B., Bangerter, E., Barbosa, M., Krenn, S., Sadeghi, A.-R., Schneider, T.: A Certifying Compiler for Zero-Knowledge Proofs of Knowledge Based on Σ-Protocols. In: Gritzalis, D., Preneel, B., Theoharidou, M. (eds.) ESORICS 2010. LNCS, vol. 6345, pp. 151–167. Springer, Heidelberg (2010)
2. Audebaud, P., Paulin-Mohring, C.: Proofs of randomized algorithms in Coq. Sci. Comput. Program. 74(8), 568–589 (2009)
3. Barthe, G., Grégoire, B., Heraud, S., Zanella Béguelin, S.: Computer-Aided Security Proofs for the Working Cryptographer. In: Rogaway, P. (ed.) CRYPTO 2011. LNCS, vol. 6841, pp. 71–90. Springer, Heidelberg (2011)
4. Barthe, G., Grégoire, B., Zanella Béguelin, S.: Formal certification of code-based cryptographic proofs. In: 36th ACM SIGPLAN-SIGACT Symposium on Principles of Programming Languages, POPL 2009, pp. 90–101. ACM, New York (2009)
5. Barthe, G., Hedin, D., Zanella Béguelin, S., Grégoire, B., Heraud, S.: A machine-checked formalization of Sigma-protocols. In: 23rd IEEE Computer Security Foundations Symposium, CSF 2010, pp. 246–260. IEEE Computer Society, Los Alamitos (2010)
6. Barthe, G., Köpf, B., Olmedo, F., Zanella Béguelin, S.: Probabilistic reasoning for differential privacy. In: 39th ACM SIGPLAN-SIGACT Symposium on Principles of Programming Languages, POPL 2012. ACM (2012)
7. Bellovin, S., Merritt, M.: Encrypted key exchange: password-based protocols secure against dictionary attacks. In: 13th IEEE Symposium on Security and Privacy, S&P 1992, pp. 72–84. IEEE Computer Society, Los Alamitos (1992)
8. Boneh, D., Lynn, B., Shacham, H.: Short signatures from the Weil pairing. Journal of Cryptology 17, 297–319 (2004)
9. Brier, E., Coron, J.-S., Icart, T., Madore, D., Randriam, H., Tibouchi, M.: Efficient Indifferentiable Hashing into Ordinary Elliptic Curves. In: Rabin, T. (ed.) CRYPTO 2010. LNCS, vol. 6223, pp. 237–254. Springer, Heidelberg (2010)
10. Canetti, R., Goldreich, O., Halevi, S.: The random oracle methodology, revisited. J. ACM 51(4), 557–594 (2004)
11. Clark, D., Hunt, S., Malacaria, P.: A static analysis for quantifying information flow in a simple imperative language. Journal of Computer Security 15(3), 321–371 (2007)

12. Clarkson, M.R., Schneider, F.B.: Hyperproperties. Journal of Computer Security 18(6), 1157–1210 (2010)
13. Coron, J.-S., Dodis, Y., Malinaud, C., Puniya, P.: Merkle-Damgård Revisited: How to Construct a Hash Function. In: Shoup, V. (ed.) CRYPTO 2005. LNCS, vol. 3621, pp. 430–448. Springer, Heidelberg (2005)
14. Dwork, C.: Differential Privacy. In: Bugliesi, M., Preneel, B., Sassone, V., Wegener, I. (eds.) ICALP 2006. LNCS, vol. 4052, pp. 1–12. Springer, Heidelberg (2006)
15. Farashahi, R.R., Fouque, P.A., Shparlinski, I., Tibouchi, M., Voloch, J.F.: Indifferentiable deterministic hashing to elliptic and hyperelliptic curves. Mathematics of Computation (2011)
16. Fleischmann, E., Gorski, M., Lucks, S.: Some Observations on Indifferentiability. In: Steinfeld, R., Hawkes, P. (eds.) ACISP 2010. LNCS, vol. 6168, pp. 117–134. Springer, Heidelberg (2010)
17. Fouque, P.-A., Tibouchi, M.: Deterministic Encoding and Hashing to Odd Hyperelliptic Curves. In: Joye, M., Miyaji, A., Otsuka, A. (eds.) Pairing 2010. LNCS, vol. 6487, pp. 265–277. Springer, Heidelberg (2010)
18. Goldwasser, S., Micali, S.: Probabilistic encryption. J. Comput. Syst. Sci. 28(2), 270–299 (1984)
19. Gonthier, G., Mahboubi, A., Rideau, L., Tassi, E., Théry, L.: A Modular Formalisation of Finite Group Theory. In: Schneider, K., Brandt, J. (eds.) TPHOLs 2007. LNCS, vol. 4732, pp. 86–101. Springer, Heidelberg (2007)
20. Hurd, J., Gordon, M., Fox, A.: Formalized elliptic curve cryptography. In: High Confidence Software and Systems, HCSS 2006 (2006)
21. Icart, T.: How to Hash into Elliptic Curves. In: Halevi, S. (ed.) CRYPTO 2009. LNCS, vol. 5677, pp. 303–316. Springer, Heidelberg (2009)
22. Icart, T.: Algorithms Mapping into Elliptic Curves and Applications. Ph.D. thesis, Université du Luxembourg (2010)
23. Maurer, U.M., Renner, R.S., Holenstein, C.: Indifferentiability, Impossibility Results on Reductions, and Applications to the Random Oracle Methodology. In: Naor, M. (ed.) TCC 2004. LNCS, vol. 2951, pp. 21–39. Springer, Heidelberg (2004)
24. Pierro, A.D., Hankin, C., Wiklicky, H.: Approximate non-interference. Journal of Computer Security 12(1), 37–82 (2004)
25. Ristenpart, T., Shacham, H., Shrimpton, T.: Careful with Composition: Limitations of the Indifferentiability Framework. In: Paterson, K.G. (ed.) EUROCRYPT 2011. LNCS, vol. 6632, pp. 487–506. Springer, Heidelberg (2011)
26. Segala, R., Turrini, A.: Approximated computationally bounded simulation relations for probabilistic automata. In: 20th IEEE Computer Security Foundations Symposium, CSF 2007, pp. 140–156 (2007)
27. Shallue, A., van de Woestijne, C.E.: Construction of Rational Points on Elliptic Curves over Finite Fields. In: Hess, F., Pauli, S., Pohst, M. (eds.) ANTS 2006. LNCS, vol. 4076, pp. 510–524. Springer, Heidelberg (2006)
28. Shoup, V.: A Computational Introduction to Number Theory and Algebra, 2nd edn. Cambridge University Press (2009)
29. Smith, G.: On the Foundations of Quantitative Information Flow. In: de Alfaro, L. (ed.) FOSSACS 2009. LNCS, vol. 5504, pp. 288–302. Springer, Heidelberg (2009)
30. Théry, L., Hanrot, G.: Primality Proving with Elliptic Curves. In: Schneider, K., Brandt, J. (eds.) TPHOLs 2007. LNCS, vol. 4732, pp. 319–333. Springer, Heidelberg (2007)

Provable De-anonymization of Large Datasets with Sparse Dimensions

Anupam Datta, Divya Sharma, and Arunesh Sinha

Carnegie Mellon University
{danupam,divyasharma,aruneshs}@cmu.edu

Abstract. There is a significant body of empirical work on statistical de-anonymization attacks against databases containing micro-data about individuals, e.g., their preferences, movie ratings, or transaction data. Our goal is to analytically explain why such attacks work. Specifically, we analyze a variant of the Narayanan-Shmatikov algorithm that was used to effectively de-anonymize the Netflix database of movie ratings. We prove theorems characterizing mathematical properties of the database and the auxiliary information available to the adversary that enable two classes of privacy attacks. In the first attack, the adversary successfully identifies the individual about whom she possesses auxiliary information (an *isolation attack*). In the second attack, the adversary learns additional information about the individual, although she may not be able to uniquely identify him (an *information amplification attack*). We demonstrate the applicability of the analytical results by empirically verifying that the mathematical properties assumed of the database are actually true for a significant fraction of the records in the Netflix movie ratings database, which contains ratings from about 500,000 users.

Keywords: Privacy, database, de-anonymization.

1   Introduction

In recent years, there has been a steady increase in the number of publicly released databases containing micro-data about individuals, e.g., their preferences, movie ratings, or transaction data. There are a number of reasons for this phenomena, for example, enabling useful tasks such as improving recommendation systems [8] and providing transparency about the activities of government agencies, such as the justice system [1].

At the same time, these databases raise privacy concerns because they contain personal information about individuals that they may not want to share with the whole world. In order to alleviate these concerns, various techniques have been proposed to "anonymize" databases before releasing them. These anonymization techniques have been developed in response to specific classes of attacks observed in practice. It is now well known that just removing obvious identifiers, such as names, social security numbers and IP addresses, is not sufficient for anonymization—an adversary can use auxiliary information acquired from

P. Degano and J.D. Guttman (Eds.): POST 2012, LNCS 7215, pp. 229–248, 2012.

other sources to de-anonymize individual data records by computing database joins. Examples of attacks of this form include de-anonymizing records in a hospital discharge database and AOL search logs [2, 16]. More recently, a class of statistical de-anonymization attacks have been presented that work on high-dimensional micro-data and the applicability of the attack has been *empirically* demonstrated on the publicly available Netflix movie ratings database; the attacks work even when the released data has been perturbed and the auxiliary information available to the adversary is noisy [11].

Our goal is to *analytically* explain why such attacks work. Specifically, we analyze a variant of the Narayanan-Shmatikov weighted algorithm that was used to effectively de-anonymize the Netflix database of movie ratings. Roughly, this algorithm takes as input noisy auxiliary information about an individual (e.g., movie ratings) and a database, and outputs the record in the database that has the highest score on the common attributes. The score is a weighted sum of the similarity of individual attributes where rare attributes are assigned higher weights. We prove theorems characterizing mathematical properties of the database and the noisy auxiliary information available to the adversary that enable two classes of privacy attacks. In the first attack, the adversary successfully identifies the individual about whom she possesses auxiliary information (an *isolation attack*), i.e., the algorithm outputs the correct record. In the second attack, the adversary learns additional information about the individual, although she may not be able to uniquely identify him (an *information amplification attack*), i.e., the algorithm outputs a record of a 'similar' individual. We empirically verify that the mathematical properties assumed of the database are actually true for a significant fraction of the records in the Netflix movie ratings database, which contains ratings from about 500,000 users, even when the auxiliary information is noisy. Thus, our theorems formally explain why these attacks work on the Netflix database.

The analytical and empirical study led to several insights about the nature of de-anonymization attacks. First, it provides a technical characterization of an observation due to Narayanan and Shmatikov [12] that *"any information that distinguishes one person from another can be used to re-identify anonymous data"*. This intuition is reflected in the weighted scoring algorithm: rare attributes directly correspond to distinguishing attributes because, by definition, a record's non-null value for a rare attribute means that that record is different from the many records that have null value for the rare attribute. In addition, the weighted linear combination is combining different distinguishing attributes into a single metric that distinguishes the records better than the individual attributes. While the effectiveness of this idea has been empirically demonstrated [11], to the best of our knowledge our theorem about the isolation attack is the first analytical characterization of this idea. (Note that while Narayanan and Shmatikov present analytical results about a simpler unweighted algorithm, they do not analyze the weighted algorithm that was actually used in the empirical study.)

Second, we formulate and prove the theorem about the information amplification attack under the following assumption: *records which agree on distinguishing (rare) attributes must be similar overall.* This assumption is justified by the observation that people with similar tastes, e.g., in rare movies are likely to also share similar opinions on other movies. It is important to note that this assumption may not hold for all databases, but our empirical results demonstrate that it holds for the Netflix database.

Third, in formulating our theorems, a guiding consideration was that the *assumptions should be empirically verifiable* on a released database even if we do not know what distribution the database was drawn from. We conduct experiments to verify the assumptions on the Netflix database. We find that the assumptions for both the theorems for the weighted algorithm are true for a significant fraction of the records. In particular, the assumptions required for the isolation attack hold for 90% of the records when the perturbation in the auxiliary information is less than 10%. As expected, the percentage of records for which the assumption holds decreases as the perturbation is increased, and increases as the number of attributes in the auxiliary information is increased. For the information amplification attack, we verify that if auxiliary information aux_y about a target record y is not too perturbed ($< 10\%$) and a significant fraction of the attributes in aux_y (> 0.75) are rare, then for a significant fraction of target records (> 0.90), if any record r is similar (similarity value > 0.75) to aux_y, then r is also similar (similarity value > 0.65) to y. Also, as the fraction of rare attributes in auxiliary information increases and the threshold for similarity between auxiliary information and the output record increases, the similarity between the target record and the output record increases.

Finally, we comment on the relation of our results to prior work on *quasi-identifers*. Observing that de-anonymization attacks are possible even when obviously identifying information (such as names and social security numbers) is removed from micro-data databases, Samarati and Sweeney [13, 15] introduced the concept of quasi-identifers—attributes that could be used to re-identify individuals by linking with another source. An important challenge that this line of work does not address (see also [9,10,17]) is *how to identify quasi-identifiers.* As mentioned earlier, our formalization captures the intuition that any attribute can be a quasi-identifier—the rarer the attribute, the greater is its contribution towards distinguishing an individual. Thus, one might view our results as providing a semantic characterization of database properties and auxiliary information that *provably* enable de-anonymization by linking in this more general setting. Note that in our characterization, the analog of a quasi-identifier (the property that enables linking attacks) is not just a property of the database; it also depends on the adversary's auxiliary information.

The rest of the paper is organized as follows. Section 2 describes related work. Section 3 presents preliminary definitions. Section 4 presents an analysis of the simpler generic (unweighted) algorithm for de-anonymization [11]. Section 5 presents the main technical results of the paper—the analysis of isolation and information amplification attacks using the weighted algorithm. Section 6 presents empirical results demonstrating that the analytical results apply to the Netflix database. Finally, Section 7 presents conclusions and directions for future work.

2   Related Work

Dwork and Naor [5] prove a fundamental tradeoff between utility and a strong form of privacy property (due to Dalenius [4]) capturing the intuition that nothing about an individual should be learnable from the database that cannot be learned without access to the database. They prove that it is not possible to satisfy this definition if the database is to have any utility assuming that the adversary has *arbitrary* auxiliary information. In contrast, in our work we seek to characterize a restricted class of auxiliary information (which adversaries may realistically possess) and database perturbation techniques (employed in practice to release micro-data) for which de-anonymization attacks provably work. The starting point of our analysis is the formal model proposed by Narayanan and Shmatikov, which they used to analyze a simpler algorithm [11] (see also [3]). In the original paper by Narayanan and Shmatikov [11], two algorithms have been proposed- generic and weighted scoring algorithms. The first algorithm (generic scoring algorithm) is analyzed, however, it is not used in the actual attack. In our work, we analyze a minor variant of the weighted scoring algorithm, used in the attack on Netflix database by Narayanan and Shmatikov. We present an alternative definition of the similarity metric (as mentioned in Section 3), a different notion of "eccentricity" (as described in Section 5) and prove theorems characterizing both the isolation and information amplification attacks using the weighted algorithm that was only empirically evaluated in their paper. In addition, we empirically validate that the assumptions hold on the Netflix database.

Boreale et al [3] present an alternative approach to analyzing de-anonymization attacks. Specifically, the authors model the process of de-anonymization of a database using an Information Hiding System (IHS) whose input includes identified records, output includes observable information (e.g., perturbed attributes), and the conditional probability matrix models the process of acquiring auxiliary information. They prove theorems characterizing information leakage using a sparsity assumption about rows in the database (which roughly captures the idea that no two records in the database are similar except with low probability) and assuming that the auxiliary information includes attributes sampled uniformly at random. In contrast, we use an assumption about sparsity of columns (rare attributes) and leverage knowledge of rare attributes in the auxiliary information to provide an analysis of the weighted algorithm of Narayanan and Shmatikov, which as also remarked by Boreale et al., allows more effective de-anonymization.

In a separate attack, ratings from an "anonymized" database released by another recommender service, Movielens, were linked to individuals by using movies publicly mentioned by users online [7]. We use a similar scoring methodology as

was proposed by Narayanan and Shmatikov [11] and Frankowski et al [7], however the algorithms we analyze allow for information to be perturbed, unlike the
attack on the MovieLens database.

Differential privacy is useful for releasing privacy-preserving statistics [5, 6].
However, the focus of this work is on databases containing microdata.

3   Definitions

In this section, we describe notation used throughout the paper and present definitions of the asymmetric similarity metric and perturbed auxiliary information.

Let D_0 denote the original database containing individuals' records (which
have not been anonymized). An 'anonymized' version of this database is released
as D with n rows and c columns. D is obtained by running an anonymization
algorithm on the original database D_0. Each row in the database corresponds to
a different individual's record and each column corresponds to an attribute. Let
$r(i)$ denote the value of ith column for the row corresponding to record $r \in D$.
The target record (i.e., the record the adversary is looking for), denoted by y,
is assumed to be always present in the released database D. The set of non-null
values of any record r is denoted by $supp(r)$; similarly, the set of non-null values
in any column i is denoted by $supp(i)$.

In order to compare the values of any two records in the database, we define
a similarity metric S.

Definition 1 (Asymmetric Similarity Metric). *Similarity of record r when
compared against record y is defined as:*

$$S(y, r) \triangleq \sum_{i \in supp(y)} \frac{T(y(i), r(i))}{|supp(y)|} \qquad (1)$$

where

$$T(y(i), r(i)) \triangleq 1 - \frac{|y(i) - r(i)|}{p} \qquad (2)$$

and p is the maximum possible difference between values of the column i.

Here, $T(y(i), r(i))$ is defined as a scaled measure of difference between two records
y and r when compared on the ith attribute. The value of each column is scaled
by p (the range of values for the column), so that the value for $T(.,.)$ lies in the
interval $[0, 1]$.

In contrast, Narayanan and Shmatikov use a symmetric similarity measure
Sim that compares two records on the union of the non-null attributes in the
two records [11]. Observe that when $S(y, r)$ is high, r reveals information about
the attributes of y. However, even if $S(y, r)$ is high, $Sim(y, r)$ could be low if r
has a large number of a non-null attributes that do not overlap with non-null
attributes in y. Thus, we believe that S is a better measure to use in the design
and analysis of de-anonymization attacks than Sim.

Definition 2 ((m, γ)-perturbed auxiliary information). *Auxiliary information about record $y \in D$, denoted by aux_y, contains perturbed values of m non-null attributes sampled from attributes in record y. aux_y is defined to be (m, γ)-perturbed if $\forall i \in supp(aux_y).T(y(i), aux_y(i)) \geq 1 - \gamma$ where $0 \leq \gamma \leq 1$.*

Note that the definition above abstracts away from whether the perturbation is in the released database or in the auxiliary information by noting that the relevant property is a lower bound on the attribute-wise similarity between the auxiliary information and the target record. The structure of aux_y is similar to that of a record in the database, with m columns ($|supp(aux_y)| = m$).

4   Analysis of Generic Scoring Algorithm

In this section, we analyze and obtain provable bounds for the generic scoring algorithm proposed by Narayanan and Shmatikov. The generic algorithm considers all the attributes in the auxiliary information as equally important for re-identification. Our theorem uses the asymmetric similarity metric defined in Section 3 and gives a lower bound on the similarity of the record output by the algorithm with the target record y. However, this algorithm might not de-anonymize records effectively as the effect of perturbation in even a single attribute of the auxiliary information would lower the overall score [11]. We include this analysis for completeness.

The scoring function used by the generic scoring algorithm is defined below.

Definition 3 ($Score_g$). *$Score_g(aux_y, r)$ of a record $r \in D$ w.r.t. auxiliary information aux_y about target record y is defined as:*

$$Score_g(aux_y, r) = min_{i \in supp(aux_y)} T(aux_y(i), r(i)) \tag{3}$$

The Narayanan-Shmatikov generic scoring algorithm is described in Algorithm 1.

Algorithm 1. Generic Scoring Algorithm

- Fix a target record y
- aux_y is (m, γ)-perturbed auxiliary information about target record y
- Compute $Score_g(aux_y, r)$ for every record r in the dataset
- Form a matching set of records that satisfy:

$$M = \{r \in D : Score_g(aux_y, r) \geq 1 - \gamma\} \tag{4}$$

- Output a randomly chosen record from the matching set.

We prove a lower bound on the similarity of the record output by the algorithm with the target record, assuming that the auxiliary information is (m, γ) perturbed. The full proof is included in the appendix.

Theorem 1. *Let y denote the target record from given database D. Let aux_y denote (m, γ)-perturbed auxiliary information, uniformly sampled from the attributes in record y. Let $\epsilon > 0$. Then with probability $\geq 1 - g$, a record o can be found in the dataset such that the value of $S(y, o)$ is greater than $1 - 2\gamma - \epsilon$, where $g = e^{-2*\epsilon^2*m}$.*

5 Analysis of Weighted Scoring Algorithm

In this section, we analyze a variant of the weighted scoring algorithm proposed by Narayanan and Shmatikov. The weighted scoring algorithm gives higher weight to 'rare' attributes in the auxiliary information. We present the algorithm and two theorems characterizing the effectiveness of the algorithm for isolation and information amplification attacks. Specifically, we prove that if the score of a record is significantly higher than the scores of other records, then the record can be isolated using the weighted scoring algorithm. We also prove a theorem that quantifies the probability and degree of an information amplification attack assuming that (a) a fraction of the attributes in perturbed auxiliary information is rare; and (b) if people agree on several rare attributes, then with high probability they are also similar on other attributes.

We begin by presenting definitions that are used in the description of the algorithm and its analysis.

Definition 4 (Weight of an attribute). *The weight of an attribute i is denoted by w_i and is defined as $w_i = \frac{1}{\log_2 |supp(i)|}$[1].*

We denote the scaled sum of weights of attributes in aux_y by $M = \frac{\sum_{i \in supp(aux_y)} w_i}{|supp(aux_y)|}$ where aux_y refers to the perturbed auxiliary information corresponding to the target record y. Next, we formalize the notion of rarity of an attribute.

Definition 5 (t-rare attribute). *An attribute is said to be t-rare if $w_i = \frac{1}{\log_2 |supp(i)|} \geq t$ where t is a threshold value and $0 < t \leq 1$.*

Definition 6 ((δ, t)-rare auxiliary information). *Auxiliary information about record $y \in D$, denoted by aux_y, is said to be (δ, t)-rare if the fraction of t-rare attributes in auxiliary information aux_y, denoted by δ_{aux_y} equals δ where $0 < \delta, t \leq 1$.*

Definition 7 ($Score_w$). *$Score_w(aux_y, r)$ of a record $r \in D$ w.r.t. auxiliary information aux_y about target record y is defined as:*

$$Score_w(aux_y, r) = \sum_{i \in supp(aux_y)} \frac{w_i * T(aux_y(i), r(i))}{m} \tag{5}$$

---

[1] We assume that $|supp(i)| > 2$; for the Netflix dataset we have $\min_i |supp(i)| = 3$.

Definition 8 (Eccentricity). *We define eccentricity* e *as*

$$e(aux_y, D) = \max_{r \in D}(Score_w(aux_y, r)) - \max_{2, r \in D}(Score_w(aux_y, r)) \qquad (6)$$

where $r \in D$, y *is the target record and* aux_y *refers to the perturbed auxiliary information obtained from target record* y. $\max_{r \in D}(Score_w(aux_y, r))$ *and* $\max_{2, r \in D}(Score_w(aux_y, r))$ *refer to the highest and second highest value, respectively, of* $Score_w(aux_y, r)$ *taken over the scores of all the records* r *in* D.

Eccentricity is a measure of how far apart the highest scoring record is from the second highest score when a scoring algorithm is employed. The eccentricity measure would be useful in eliminating false positives in the result output by the algorithm, as described in Algorithm 2.

Algorithm 2. Weighted Scoring Algorithm

 – Fix a target record y
 – aux_y is (m, γ)-perturbed auxiliary information about target record y
 – Compute $Score_w(aux, r)$ for every record r in the dataset
 – Output the record with the highest score if $e(aux_y, D) > T$, where T is a preset threshold[2], else output NULL. Let o denote the record output by the algorithm.

Isolation Attack. In the first attack, an adversary with some auxiliary information successfully isolates an individual from a database. We prove that for a given target record y, if auxiliary information aux_y is (m, γ)-perturbed and if the score of the record o output by the algorithm differs from the second-highest score by a certain threshold, then $o = y$. The intuition behind the assumption in this theorem is that if a record is significantly different from other records on attributes present in auxiliary information, then the record can be isolated using the weighted scoring algorithm.

The proof proceeds as follows: by using the assumption that aux_y is (m, γ)-perturbed, we derive a lower bound for the score of target record y when compared with aux_y. We prove the main result in the theorem by contradiction. We assume that the maximum possible value of the scoring function when computed over all records in the database is not equal to the score of the target record y. We show that this assumption leads to the conclusion that the maximum possible score is greater than M, which is not possible since M equals the value of the scoring function assuming that every attribute in aux_y matches completely with the attributes in the record being compared against.

Theorem 2. *Let* y *denote the target record from given database* D. *Let* aux_y *denote* (m, γ)-*perturbed auxiliary information about record* y. *If the eccentricity measure* $e(aux_y, D) > \gamma M$ *where* $M = \dfrac{\sum_{i \in supp(aux_y)} w_i}{|supp(aux_y)|}$ *is the scaled sum of weights of attributes in* aux_y, *then*

1. $\max_{r \in D}(Score_w(aux_y, r)) = Score_w(aux_y, y)$.
2. *Additionally, if only one record has maximum score value* $= Score_w(aux_y, y)$, *then the record returned by the algorithm o is the same as target record y.*

Proof. By definition of Similarity metric $S(.,.)$, for any record $r \in D$ and given target record y, $S(y, r) = \sum_{i \in supp(y)} \frac{T(y(i), r(i))}{k}$, where $k = |supp(y)|$.

Also, by definition of $Score_w(.,.)$,

$$Score_w(aux_y, r) = \frac{\sum_{i \in supp(aux_y)} w_i * T(aux_y(i), r(i))}{m} \tag{7}$$

where $w_i = \frac{1}{\log_2 |supp(i)|}$. Given the assumption $\forall i \in supp(aux_y).T(y(i), aux_y(i)) \geq 1 - \gamma$, we can use equation 7, to conclude that

$$Score_w(aux_y, y) = \frac{\sum_{i \in supp(aux_y)} w_i * T(aux_y(i), y(i))}{m}$$

$$= \frac{\sum_{i \in supp(aux_y)} w_i * T(y(i), aux_y(i))}{m}$$

$$\geq \frac{\sum_{i \in supp(aux_y)} (1 - \gamma) w_i}{m} \geq (1 - \gamma) * \frac{\sum_i w_i}{m} = (1 - \gamma) * M$$

since $T(y(i), aux_y(i)) = T(aux_y(i), y(i))$ by definition.

We prove the result in our theorem by contradiction. We assume that

$$\max_{r \in D}(Score_w(aux_y, r)) \neq Score_w(aux_y, y) \tag{8}$$

Observe that

$$\max_{r \in D}(Score_w(aux_y, r)) > Score_w(aux_y, y) \text{ (from equation 8)} \tag{9}$$

If $\max_{r \in D}(Score_w(aux_y, r))$, is greater than $Score_w(aux_y, y)$ then

$$\max_{2, r \in D}(Score_w(aux_y, r)) \geq Score_w(aux_y, y) \tag{10}$$

since $\max_{2, r \in D}(Score_w(aux_y, r))$ is the second highest value of all scores.

Further, it is assumed that $e(aux_y, D) > \gamma M$, therefore,

$$\max_{r \in D}(Score_w(aux_y, r)) > \gamma M + \max_{2, r \in D}(Score_w(aux_y, r))$$

$$> \gamma M + Score_w(aux_y, y) > \gamma M + (1 - \gamma) * M = M$$

which is not possible since M is the maximum possible score for any record r in the database as shown below

$$Score_w(aux_y, r) = \frac{\sum_{i \in supp(aux_y)} w_i}{m} * T(aux_y(i), r(i))$$

$$\max_{r \in D}(Score_w(aux_y, r)) \leq \frac{\sum_{i \in supp(aux_y)} w_i}{m} \leq M$$

since $\max(T(.,.)) = 1$.

Therefore, our assumption is wrong and we conclude that

$$\max_{r \in D}(Score_w(aux_y, r)) = Score_w(aux_y, y)$$

Also, since we assumed that target record y is always part of the released database D, therefore, if there is only one record with the maximum score and $Score_w(aux_y, y)$ is same as the maximum score then the the record with maximum score has to be y, which is returned by the algorithm. Hence proved.

Information Amplification Attack. In the second attack, although an adversary may not be able to uniquely isolate a record, she can still obtain additional information about the randomly chosen target record y under certain assumptions about the database. The intuition that if people agree on several rare attributes, then with high probability they are similar on other attributes, guided us to define a function f_D for database D. We use f_D to measure the overall similarity of the target record y and r by an indirect comparison of the rare attributes of y and the record r. The comparison is indirect because we use aux_y as a proxy for y and compare the rare attributes of aux_y with r. To capture the intuition that the agreement must happen on rare attributes the function f_D depends on the fraction of rare attributes in aux_y (η_1). To capture the intuition that there should be agreement on the rare attributes, f_D also depends on a lower bound (η_2) for $S(aux_y, r)$. In addition, to capture the fraction of target records (η_3) for which the overall similarity of the target record y and r is given by f_D we also include η_3 as a parameter for f_D. We define two parameterized sets before formalizing this intuition in Property 1.

Definition 9 (D_{m,η_1}). D_{m,η_1} *is the subset of the records of a database D that have no less than m non-null attributes and at least η_1 of those attributes are t-rare.*

We denote the above set as D_{m,η_1}, ignoring the parameter t for notational ease.

Definition 10 (Aux_{y,m,η_1}). Aux_{y,m,η_1} *is the set of all (m, γ)-perturbed and (η_1, t)-rare sets of auxiliary information about record y.*

Again, we ignore some parameters in Aux_{y,m,η_1} for the sake of notational ease. We assume that for the given database D there exists a function f_D with $Range(f_D) \subseteq [0, 1]$ and the following property:

Property 1. *Choose any m and η_1. Let y be chosen uniformly at random from D_{m,η_1}. Let aux_y be chosen uniformly at random from Aux_{y,m,η_1}. Then*

$$\forall \eta_2, \eta_3, r. \, (S(aux_y, r) \geq \eta_2) \rightarrow Pr[S(y, r) \geq f_D(\eta_1, \eta_2, \eta_3)] \geq \eta_3$$

where $r \in D$. The probability is over the random choices made in choosing y.

We state the theorem below.

Theorem 3. *Let t and γ be in $(0,1)$. Fix any $l_1 \in (0,1)$. Let y denote the target record chosen uniformly at random from D_{m,l_1}. Let aux_y denote a (m, γ)-perturbed and (l_1, t)-rare auxiliary information about record y chosen uniformly at random from Aux_{y,m,l_1}. Additionally, we assume the existence of function $f_D(.,.,.)$ that satisfies Property 1. Then $Pr[S(y,o) \geq f_D(l_1, l_2, \eta_3)] > \eta_3$, where $l_2 = \frac{\left(\sum_{i \in supp(aux_y)} w_i\right)^2}{\sum_{i \in supp(aux_y)} (w_i)^2} \frac{(1-\gamma)^2}{m}$, o is the record output by the Weighted Algorithm and the probability is taken over the random choices made in choosing y.*

The proof proceeds as follows:

1. We derive a relationship between $S(aux_y, r)$ and $Score_w(aux_y, r)$ by using the Cauchy-Schwarz inequality [14] for any record r.
2. By using the assumption that aux_y is (m, γ)-perturbed, we derive a lower bound for $Score_w(aux_y, o)$. Using this and the last step we obtain a lower bound for $S(aux_y, o)$.
3. By using this bound in conjunction with the function f_D stated above, we give a probabilistic guarantee about $S(y, o)$.

Proof. Let $x_i(y,r) = T(y(i), r(i))$ for any record $r \in D$. Therefore, $S(y,r) = \sum_i \frac{x_i(y,r)}{k}$, where $k = |supp(y)|$. Also,

$$Score_w(aux_y, r) = \frac{\sum_{i \in supp(aux_y)} w_i * T(aux_y(i), r(i))}{m}$$
$$= \frac{\sum_{i \in supp(aux_y)} w_i * x_i(aux_y, r)}{m}$$

We prove the first part of the proof by Cauchy Schwarz inequality,

$$\left(\sum_i A_i B_i\right)^2 < \sum_i A_i^2 \sum_i B_i^2$$

Therefore

$$\left(\sum_{i \in supp(aux_y)} w_i * x_i(aux_y, r)\right)^2 < \left(\sum_{i \in supp(aux_y)} w_i^2\right)\left(\sum_{i \in supp(aux_y)} x_i(aux_y, r)^2\right)$$

Since $0 \leq T(aux_y(i), r(i)) \leq 1$

$$\left(\sum_{i \in supp(aux_y)} x_i(aux_y, r)^2\right) \leq \left(\sum_{i \in supp(aux_y)} x_i(aux_y, r)\right)$$

Therefore,

$$\left(\sum_{i \in supp(aux_y)} w_i * x_i(aux_y, r)\right)^2 < \left(\sum_{i \in supp(aux_y)} (w_i)^2\right)\left(\sum_{i \in supp(aux_y)} x_i(aux_y, r)\right)$$

By definition of $Score_w(aux_y, r)$ and $S(aux_y, r)$ we get

$$(m * Score_w(aux_y, r))^2 < (\sum_{i \in supp(aux_y)} (w_i)^2) S(aux_y, r) m$$

$$S(aux_y, r) > \frac{(m * Score_w(aux_y, r))^2}{m \left(\sum_{i \in supp(aux_y)} (w_i)^2\right)} = \frac{m * (Score_w(aux_y, r))^2}{\sum_{i \in supp(aux_y)} (w_i)^2}$$

For the second step of the proof we use the assumption $\forall i \in supp(aux_y).T(y(i), aux_y(i)) \geq 1 - \gamma$. We can use the definition of $Score_w(.,.)$ (equation 7), to conclude that

$$
\begin{aligned}
Score_w(aux_y, y) &= \frac{\sum_{i \in supp(aux_y)} w_i * T(aux_y(i), y(i))}{m} \\
&= \frac{\sum_{i \in supp(aux_y)} w_i * T(y(i), aux_y(i))}{m} \\
&\geq \frac{\sum_{i \in supp(aux_y)} (1 - \gamma) w_i}{m} \\
&\geq (1 - \gamma) * \frac{\sum_i w_i}{m} \geq (1 - \gamma) * M
\end{aligned}
$$

since $T(y(i), aux_y(i)) = T(aux_y(i), y(i))$ by definition.

Also since o has the max score $Score_w(aux_y, o) \geq Score_w(aux_y, y)$ and hence

$$
\begin{aligned}
Score_w(aux_y, o) &\geq \frac{\sum_{i \in supp(aux_y)} w_i * T(aux_y(i), y(i))}{m} \\
&\geq (1 - \gamma) \frac{\sum_{i \in supp(aux_y)} w_i}{m} \geq (1 - \gamma) M
\end{aligned}
$$

Substituting in equation derived for $S(aux_y, o)$ above,

$$S(aux_y, o) > \frac{m(Score_w(aux_y, o))^2}{(\sum_{i \in supp(aux_y)} w_i^2)} > \frac{m((1 - \gamma) M)^2}{(\sum_{i \in supp(aux_y)} w_i^2)} > \frac{(\sum_{i \in supp(aux_y)} w_i)^2}{\sum_{i \in supp(aux_y)} (w_i)^2} \frac{(1 - \gamma)^2}{m}$$

Thus, $S(aux_y, o) > l_2$.

Finally for the last part of the proof, we use the assumption that y was chosen uniformly at random from D_{m,l_1}, aux_y was chosen uniformly at random from Aux_{y,m,l_i} and the result above that $S(aux_y, o) > l_2$ to invoke Property 1 and claim the following:

$$Pr[S(y, o) \geq f_D(l_1, l_2, \eta_3)] \geq \eta_3$$

To summarize, we use a function f_D parametrized by a database D in formulating and proving the theorem about the information amplification attack. The idea here is that the theorem provides bounds on the information amplification attack for 'any' database D for which there exists an f_D such that the assumptions in the above stated theorem holds. Note that the bounds will be good (i.e., the information amplification attack is effective) if η_3 is close to 1 (i.e., the attack succeeds with high probability) and the value of f_D is also close to 1 (i.e., the target record is very similar to the record output by the algorithm) given (a) the fraction of rare attributes in the auxiliary information (l_1) and (b) the similarity between the auxiliary information and the record output by the algorithm (l_2). We demonstrate in the next section that the function f_D computed for the Netflix database enables us to claim that with high probability, the output of the Weighted Algorithm run on the Netflix database will be similar to the target record.

6   Empirical Results

For empirically testing the assumptions in our theorems, we use the 'anonymized' Netflix database with $480,189$ users and $17,770$ movies, also used by Narayanan and Shmatikov. We run the modified Narayanan-Shmatikov weighted scoring algorithm as described in Section 5. Note that when we use m attributes in auxiliary information, we filter out records that have less than m attributes. Additionally, when we have the condition that δ_{aux_y} is a fixed fraction, this leads to more records being filtered out as the criteria is not met for these records. The percentage values claimed in all our results are percentage of records that are not filtered out. The following table shows the fraction of records that get filtered out for different values of m and t.

Table 1. Percentage of records that get filtered out, when $t= 0.07, 0.075$

m	t	Percentage of records	m	t	Percentage of records
8	0.07	28.4	8	0.075	38.4
10	0.07	31.3	10	0.075	41.4
20	0.07	46.6	20	0.075	56.9

We list some of our key findings and explain these in detail.

1. Isolation Attack

   - We verify the percentage of records in the database for which both the assumptions in Theorem 2 presented in Section 5 hold true, over the Netflix database. Our empirical analysis verifies that the assumptions hold true for majority of records.
   - We also test the assumptions for varying levels of perturbation in aux_y.
   - Additionally we compute the percentage of records for which the eccentricity assumption holds when we vary threshold for rarity of an attribute, t and number of attributes in aux_y, m.
   - As compared to the attack demonstrated by Narayanan and Shmatikov [11], we do not use dates for analysis. However, we consider perturbation in ratings in aux_y, as opposed to exact ratings being present in aux_y.

2. Information Amplification Attack
   - We develop an algorithm that computes the value of f_D for different values of the parameters γ, η_1, η_2 and η_3 for any database D and auxiliary information aux_y.
   - Our results show that for the Netflix database the function f_D is monotonically increasing in η_1, η_2 and tends to 1 as η_1, η_2 increases. Then the weighted scoring algorithm output will be quite similar to the target record for Netflix database, hence the Narayanan-Shmatikov weighted scoring algorithm was successful in finding attacks.

6.1   Isolation Attack

Verifying assumptions for varying levels of perturbation in aux_y. For the first result based on the isolation attack, we plot the fraction of records for which the eccentricity assumption holds, against the value of perturbation in auxiliary information aux_y, where fraction of rare attributes in aux_y (δ_{aux_y}) = 0.75. These results have been obtained by averaging the results from a sample of 10, 000 records randomly chosen with replacement. We obtain results for varying levels of perturbation in auxiliary information, $\gamma = 0.07, 0.1, 0.15, 0.2$. The results are shown and plotted in Figure 1. In this figure, we consider an attribute as rare if the column corresponding to the movie has weight ≥ 0.07 ($t = 0.07$) which implies that any column with less than $\sim 19, 972$ entries will be defined as rare.

   We conclude that when perturbation in aux_y is less than 10%, then the score of the best-match record exceeds the second-best score by a value greater than our theoretic threshold ($= \gamma * M$) for a significant fraction of the records (> 0.90), which implies that $> 90\%$ of the records can be successfully isolated. Also, we observe that as perturbation in auxiliary information (γ) increases, the number of records for which the assumption holds decreases. One factor causing this decrease could be that an increase in γM implies that the best match record would need to be different from the second highest score by a much higher value than when γ is lower, which may not always be true. However, we note that even with 20% perturbation, the assumption holds for $> 10\%$ of the records when the auxiliary information set contains 10 attributes. There are approximately 500000 users in the database; without considering the records that get filtered out, the attack still affects more than 34,000 users, which is quite significant.

   Additionally in Figure 1, we also vary the number of attributes m in the auxiliary information aux_y; specifically we run the algorithm for $m = 10, 20$. We observe that as the number of attributes in auxiliary information set increases, the fraction of target records for which the eccentricity assumption holds and thus fraction of target records which can be isolated from a database, increases.

Verifying assumptions for unperturbed aux_y. We compute the fraction of records that are isolated for $m = 8, \gamma = 0, \delta_{aux_y} = 0.75$. Since the perturbation γ in aux_y is 0, the score of the best-match record exceeds the second-best score by γM trivially. So for $> 99\%$ of the records that have greater than 8 attributes and

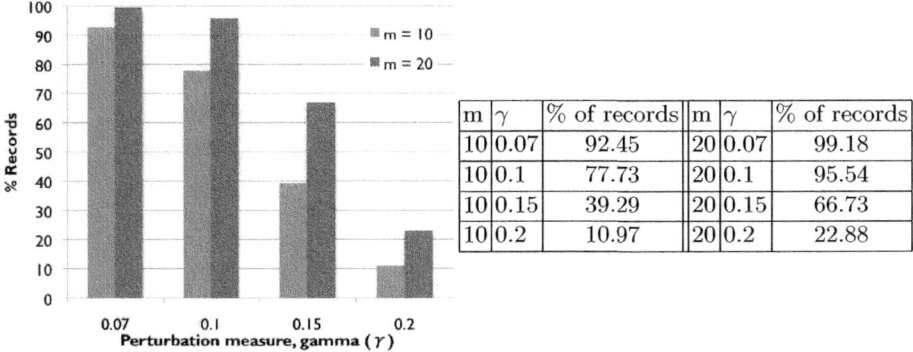

m	γ	% of records	m	γ	% of records
10	0.07	92.45	20	0.07	99.18
10	0.1	77.73	20	0.1	95.54
10	0.15	39.29	20	0.15	66.73
10	0.2	10.97	20	0.2	22.88

Fig. 1. Percentage of records for which eccentricity assumption holds when $t = 0.07$

more than 6 rare attributes and 2 non-rare attributes, there is only one record with the highest score and all these target records can be isolated. However, if we do not filter out records that have less than 8 attributes we get the result that 72% of all the records can be isolated when threshold for rarity of an attribute, $t = 0.07$ and 61% of all the records can be isolated when $t = 0.075$. This conclusion is not as good as the results obtained by Narayanan and Shmatikov, as they de-identified 84% of the records in the database with exact ratings and no dates at all. However, our results are computed using the generalized variant of the weighted scoring algorithm and not the heuristically tuned algorithm that Narayanan and Shmatikov actually use in the experiments. Our guarantees are supported by the theorems in Section 5, however as the authors themselves point out, the specifically tuned parameters in their algorithm might not work for another database.

Additionally in Figure 2, we plot the fraction of records for which eccentricity assumption holds when we consider an attribute as rare if the weight of the column i corresponding to the attribute has $w_i \geq 0.075$ ($t = 0.075$) which implies that any column with less than $\sim 10,000$ entries will be defined as rare. We plot the results for $m = 20$. In Figure 2, overall less attributes are considered as rare as compared to Figure 1.

6.2 Information Amplification Attack

Computing $f_D(\eta_1, \eta_2, \eta_3)$. We compute $f_D(.,.,.)$ using the routine shown in Algorithm 3. In the given code we would ideally want to take n as large as possible, but, that is not feasible. Hence we take n as 50 and then run the code 60 times and take the average value of f_D over the 60 runs as the final computed value. This is not the exact value of f_D, but is a good estimate.

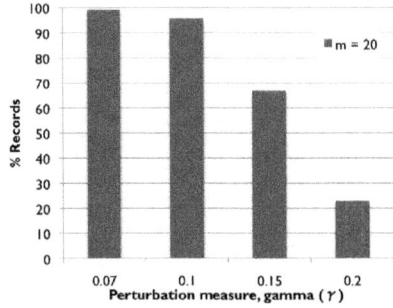

m	γ	% of records
20	0.07	99.22
20	0.1	96.49
20	0.15	74
20	0.2	29.84

Fig. 2. Percentage of records for which eccentricity assumption holds when $t = 0.075$

Algorithm 3. Calculation of f_D

Require: m, t, γ
  for $\eta_1 : \{0.7, 0.8, .., 1.0\}$ **do**
    for $\eta_2 : \{0.5, 0.6, .., 1.0\}$ **do**
      for $i : \{1, 2, .., n\}$ **do**
        Choose y uniformly at random from D_{m,η_1}
        Choose aux_y uniformly at random from Aux_{y,m,η_1}
        $k_i = \min_{r \ \mid \ S(aux_y, r) \geq \eta_2} S(y, r)$
      end for
      $f_D(\eta_1, \eta_2, \eta_3) = \eta_3$ percentile of $k_1, .., k_n$
    end for
  end for

Value of $f_D(\eta_1, \eta_2, \eta_3)$ for varying levels of perturbation in aux_y and η_3. We plot the value of $f_D(\eta_1, \eta_2, \eta_3)$ by varying values of η_3, i.e. the probability of a record y having greater than $f_D(\eta_1, \eta_2, \eta_3)$ similarity with r given $\delta_{aux_y} = \eta_1$ and $S(aux_y, r) \geq \eta_2$. We obtain results for varying levels of perturbation in auxiliary information, $\gamma = 0.07, 0.1$, keeping the number of attributes in aux_y, $m = 10$. The results are plotted in Figures 3, 4. In each of these figures, we plot the value of $f_D(\eta_1, \eta_2, \eta_3)$ when $\eta_1 = \{0.7, 0.8, 0.9, 1.0\}$ and $\eta_2 = \{0.5, 0.6, 0.7, 0.8, 0.9, 1.0\}$. Figures 3, 4 show the value of $f_D(\eta_1, \eta_2, \eta_3)$ when $(\eta_3 = 0.9, \gamma = 0.07)$ and $(\eta_3 = 0.9, \gamma = 0.1)$ respectively. We conclude that, keeping γ, η_1, η_2 constant, the value of $f_D(\eta_1, \eta_2, \eta_3)$ decreases as η_3 increases, which reinforces the intuition that a higher probability of a record y having greater than $f_D(\eta_1, \eta_2, \eta_3)$ similarity with r, given $\delta_{aux_y} = \eta_1$ and $S(aux_y, r) \geq \eta_2$, is accompanied by a lower guarantee $f_D(\eta_1, \eta_2, \eta_3)$ of similarity.

Additionally, we observe that, for a constant value of η_3, the value of $f_D(\eta_1, \eta_2, \eta_3)$ increases as γ increases, but the value of γ is still small, and the function also becomes smooth with increasing γ, which implies that small perturbation of rare attributes does not decrease the knowledge of similarity between y and r that is gained from the knowledge of aux_y.

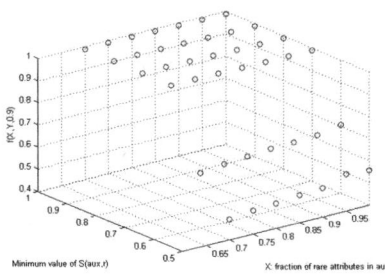

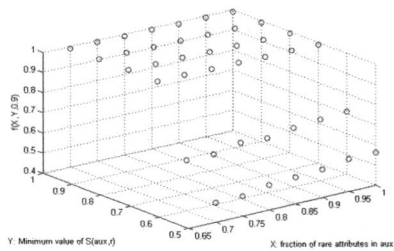

Fig. 3. Value of $f(\eta_1, \eta_2, \eta_3)$ when $\eta_3 =$ 0.9 and $\gamma = 0.07$

Fig. 4. Value of $f(\eta_1, \eta_2, \eta_3)$ when $\eta_3 =$ 0.9 and $\gamma = 0.1$

$f_D(\eta_1, \eta_2, \eta_3)$ **for unperturbed** aux_y**.** We also compute the value of $f_D(\eta_1, \eta_2, \eta_3)$ when $\gamma = 0$, which implies that the auxiliary information has no noise. The results are plotted in Figures 5, 6 for $m = 20$. Figures 5, 6 show the value of $f_D(\eta_1, \eta_2, \eta_3)$ when $(\eta_3 = 0.75, \gamma = 0.0)$ and $(\eta_3 = 0.9, \gamma = 0.0)$ respectively. All these graphs show that $f_D(\eta_1, \eta_2, \eta_3)$ is monotonically increasing in η_1 and η_2, and also tends to 1 as η_1, η_2 increase.

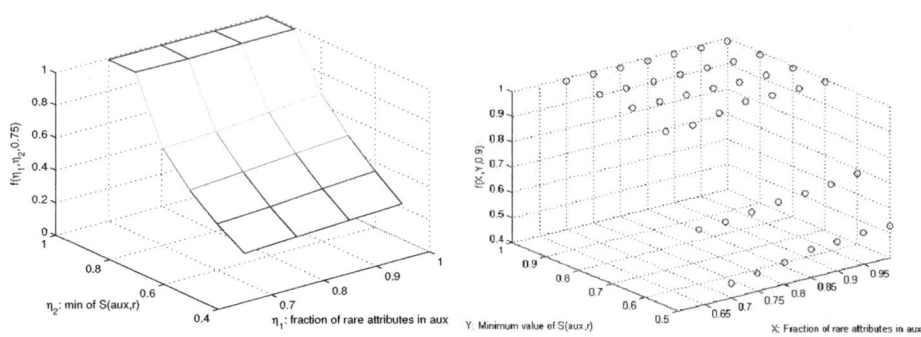

Fig. 5. Value of $f(\eta_1, \eta_2, \eta_3)$ when $\eta_3 =$ 0.75 and $\gamma = 0$

Fig. 6. Value of $f(\eta_1, \eta_2, \eta_3)$ when $\eta_3 =$ 0.9 and $\gamma = 0$

7   Conclusion

We have presented a mathematical analysis of the effectiveness of the Narayanan-Shmatikov weighted algorithm in isolating individuals and carrying out information amplification attacks. Our empirical study of the Netflix database of movie ratings demonstrates that the assumptions about the database used in proving the theorems hold for a substantial fraction of records in the database. Thus, our theorems formally explain why these attacks work on the Netflix database.

Indeed enabling this form of empirical validation without requiring knowledge of the distribution from which the database was drawn was a desideratum for our approach.

Our empirical results for the isolation attack are not as strong as those reported by Narayanan and Shmatikov (72% vs. 84% for parameter settings where a head-to-head comparison was possible). The difference could be caused by the generality of our assumptions. At a technical level, it would be interesting to understand if it is possible to prove an isolation theorem with stronger bounds using different assumptions about the dataset.

The technical result about the information amplification attack is formulated in terms of an abstract function f_D that depends on the database D. Our empirical results demonstrate that for the Netflix database $f_D(\eta_1, \eta_2, \eta_3)$ is monotonically increasing in η_1 and η_2, and also tends to 1 as η_1, η_2 increase. Our theorem predicts that this behavior of f_D implies that the Netflix database is de-anonymizable by the weighted scoring algorithm. It would be interesting to identify a class of distributions from which if databases are drawn they would satisfy this property.

Acknowledgments. We thank Anupam Gupta for suggesting the asymmetric similarity metric. We also thank Arvind Narayanan for useful discussions during the course of this work.

References

1. PACER- Public Access to Court Electronic Records, http://www.pacer.gov (last accessed December 16, 2011)
2. Barbaro, M., Zeller, T.: A Face Is Exposed for AOL Searcher No. 4417749. New York Times (August 09, 2006), http://www.nytimes.com/2006/08/09/technology/09aol.html?pagewanted=all
3. Boreale, M., Pampaloni, F., Paolini, M.: Quantitative Information Flow, with a View. In: Atluri, V., Diaz, C. (eds.) ESORICS 2011. LNCS, vol. 6879, pp. 588–606. Springer, Heidelberg (2011)
4. Dalenius, T.: Towards a methodology for statistical disclosure control. Statistics Tidskrift 15, 429–444 (1977)
5. Dwork, C.: Differential Privacy. In: Bugliesi, M., Preneel, B., Sassone, V., Wegener, I. (eds.) ICALP 2006. LNCS, vol. 4052, pp. 1–12. Springer, Heidelberg (2006)
6. Dwork, C.: Differential Privacy: A Survey of Results. In: Agrawal, M., Du, D.-Z., Duan, Z., Li, A. (eds.) TAMC 2008. LNCS, vol. 4978, pp. 1–19. Springer, Heidelberg (2008), http://dl.acm.org/citation.cfm?id=1791834.1791836
7. Frankowski, D., Cosley, D., Sen, S., Terveen, L., Riedl, J.: You are What You Say: Privacy Risks of Public Mentions. In: Proceedings of the 29th Annual International ACM SIGIR Conference on Research and Development in Information Retrieval, SIGIR 2006, pp. 565–572. ACM, New York (2006), http://doi.acm.org/10.1145/1148170.1148267
8. Hafner, K.: And if You Liked the Movie, a Netflix Contest May Reward You Handsomely. New York Times (October 02, 2006), http://www.nytimes.com/2006/10/02/technology/02netflix.html

9. Li, N., Li, T., Venkatasubramanian, S.: t-closeness: Privacy beyond k-anonymity and l-diversity. In: IEEE 23rd International Conference on Data Engineering, ICDE 2007, pp. 106–115 (April 2007)
10. Machanavajjhala, A., Kifer, D., Gehrke, J., Venkitasubramaniam, M.: L-diversity: Privacy beyond k-anonymity. ACM Trans. Knowl. Discov. Data 1 (March 2007), http://doi.acm.org/10.1145/1217299.1217302
11. Narayanan, A., Shmatikov, V.: Robust De-anonymization of Large Sparse Datasets. In: Proceedings of the 2008 IEEE Symposium on Security and Privacy, pp. 111–125. IEEE Computer Society, Washington, DC (2008), http://dl.acm.org/citation.cfm?id=1397759.1398064
12. Narayanan, A., Shmatikov, V.: Myths and fallacies of personally identifiable information. Communications of the ACM 53, 24–26 (2010)
13. Samarati, P.: Protecting respondents' identities in microdata release. IEEE Trans. on Knowl. and Data Eng. 13, 1010–1027 (2001), http://dl.acm.org/citation.cfm?id=627337.628183
14. Schwarz, H.A.: ber ein Flchen kleinsten Flcheninhalts betreffendes Problem der Variationsrechnung. Acta Societatis Scientiarum Fennicae XV, 318 (1888)
15. Sweeney, L.: Achieving k-anonymity privacy protection using generalization and suppression. Int. J. Uncertainty, Fuzziness and Knowledge-Based System 10, 571–588 (2002), http://dl.acm.org/citation.cfm?id=774544.774553
16. Sweeney, L.: k-anonymity: a Model for Protecting Privacy. Int. J. Uncertain. Fuzziness Knowl.-Based Syst. 10, 557–570 (2002), http://dl.acm.org/citation.cfm?id=774544.774552
17. Xiao, X., Tao, Y.: M-invariance: towards privacy preserving re-publication of dynamic datasets. In: Proceedings of the 2007 ACM SIGMOD International Conference on Management of Data, SIGMOD 2007, pp. 689–700. ACM, New York (2007), http://doi.acm.org/10.1145/1247480.1247556

Appendix

Theorem 1. *Let y denote the target record from given database D. Let aux_y denote (m, γ)-perturbed auxiliary information, uniformly sampled from the attributes in record y. Let $\epsilon > 0$. Then with probability $\geq 1 - g$, a record o can be found in the dataset such that the value of $S(y, o)$ is greater than $1 - 2\gamma - \epsilon$, where $g = e^{-2*\epsilon^2*m}$.*

Proof. Let $x_i(y, r) = T(y(i), r(i))$ for any record r. Therefore, $S(y, r) = \sum_i \frac{x_i(y, r)}{k}$, where $k = |supp(y)|$.

Let $\mathbf{Y_1}, \mathbf{Y_2}, .. \mathbf{Y_m}$ be m random variables which take a value equal to any of the x_j's and are chosen independently. $\mathbf{Z}$ is another random variable defined as $\mathbf{Z} = \frac{\sum_i \mathbf{Y_i}}{m}$ where $i \in \{1, ..., m\}$.

We form the matching set M such that,

$$M = \{r \in D : Score_g(aux_y, r) \geq 1 - \gamma\}$$
$$\text{Using definition of } Score_g(aux_y, r)$$
$$M = \{r \in D : min_{i \in supp(aux_y)} T(aux_y(i), r(i)) \geq 1 - \gamma\}$$
$$M = \{r \in D : \forall i \in supp(aux_y). T(aux_y(i), r(i)) \geq 1 - \gamma\}$$

Also, given $\forall i \in supp(aux_y).T(y(i), aux_y(i)) \geq 1 - \gamma$, we calculate $T(y(i), r(i))$ for any record r in the matching set, and $\forall i \in supp(aux_y)$.

$$T(y(i), r(i)) \triangleq 1 - \frac{|y(i) - r(i)|}{p}$$

$$|y(i) - r(i)| \leq |y(i) - aux_y(i)| + |aux_y(i) - r(i)|$$

$$|y(i) - r(i)| \leq 1 - (1 - p * \gamma) + 1 - (1 - p * \gamma) = 2 * p * \gamma$$

Thus, for any record r in the matching set

$$\forall i \in supp(aux_y).T(y(i), r(i)) \geq 1 - 2\gamma$$

Also, since $\mathbf{Y_i}$ has an uniform distribution

$$E[\mathbf{Y_i}] = x_1(y, r) * \frac{1}{k} + x_2(y, r) * \frac{1}{k} + \cdots + x_k(y, r) * \frac{1}{k} = S(y, r)$$

We show that expectation of $\mathbf{Z}$ is also $S(y, r)$

$$E[\mathbf{Z}] = \frac{\sum_i E[\mathbf{Y_i}]}{m} = \frac{m * E[\mathbf{Y_1}]}{m} = \frac{mS(y, r)}{m} = S(y, r)$$

One-sided Hoeffding bound states that given n independent random variables $\mathbf{X_1}, \mathbf{X_2}, \ldots, \mathbf{X_n}$ where $Pr(\mathbf{X_i} \in [a_i, b_i]) = 1$ and $\bar{\mathbf{X}} = \frac{\mathbf{X_1} + \mathbf{X_2} + \cdots + \mathbf{X_n}}{n}$, the following inequality holds: $Pr[\bar{\mathbf{X}} - E[\bar{\mathbf{X}}] \geq \epsilon] \leq \exp\left(\frac{-2 * \epsilon^2 * n^2}{\sum_{i=1}^{n}(b_i - a_i)^2}\right)$. Using Hoeffding bound for $\mathbf{Z}$ with the observation that $\mathbf{Z}$ takes values in $[0, 1]$ we get

$$Pr[\mathbf{Z} - E[\mathbf{Z}] \geq \epsilon] \leq \exp\left(\frac{-2 * \epsilon^2 * m^2}{\sum_{i=1}^{m}(1 - 0)^2}\right) = \exp(-2 * \epsilon^2 * m)$$

We can consider the complementary event and get

$$Pr[\mathbf{Z} - E[\mathbf{Z}] \leq \epsilon] \geq 1 - \exp(-2 * \epsilon^2 * m)$$

Let $g = e^{-2 * \epsilon^2 * m}$. Therefore, with probability $\geq 1 - g$, z_i (realized value of $\mathbf{Z}$) $\leq E[\mathbf{Z}] + \epsilon$. Thus, with probability $\geq 1 - g$, $E[\mathbf{Z}] \geq z_i - \epsilon$, and by substituting the value of $E[\mathbf{Z}]$ we get that with probability $\geq 1 - g$, $S(y, r) \geq z_i - \epsilon$. Additionally, we have shown that for $r \in M$, $z_i \geq 1 - 2\gamma$ and hence for $r \in M$, $S(y, r) \geq (1 - 2\gamma - \epsilon)$. This implies that the record output by the generic algorithm described above, is guaranteed to have similarity greater than $1 - 2\gamma - \epsilon$ with the target record y, with probability $\geq 1 - g$.

Revisiting Botnet Models and Their Implications for Takedown Strategies

Ting-Fang Yen[1] and Michael K. Reiter[2]

[1] RSA Laboratories, Cambridge, MA
tingfang.yen@rsa.com
[2] University of North Carolina, Chapel Hill, NC
reiter@cs.unc.edu

Abstract. Several works have utilized network models to study peer-to-peer botnets, particularly in evaluating the effectiveness of strategies aimed at taking down a botnet. We observe that previous works fail to consider an important structural characteristic of networks — assortativity. This property quantifies the tendency for "similar" nodes to connect to each other, where the notion of "similarity" is examined in terms of node degree. Empirical measurements on networks simulated according to the Waledac botnet protocol, and on network traces of bots from a honeynet running in the wild, suggest that real-world botnets can be significantly assortative, even more so than social networks. By adjusting the level of assortativity in simulated networks, we show that high assortativity allows networks to be more resilient to takedown strategies than predicted by previous works, and can allow a network to "heal" itself effectively after a fraction of its nodes are removed. We also identify alternative takedown strategies that are more effective, and more difficult for the network to recover from, than those explored in previous works.

1 Introduction

Graph models from network theory have been applied to study properties of real-world networks, including social, biological, and computer networks. Erdös-Rényi random graphs [13] model networks where the edges are created with uniform probability between every pair of nodes. Watts-Strogatz small-world graphs [38] model networks where the diameter of the network is small, i.e., increasing logarithmically with the size of the network. Barabási-Albert scale-free graphs [2] model networks with a few highly connected "hub" nodes and many leaf nodes. These models can be used to analyze the spread of information (or infection) within a network [30,38] and its resilience to node and edge failures [1,9,15], for example.

Recently, several works have also applied graph models from network theory to study peer-to-peer (P2P) botnets [10,11,41,19]. Each node in the network represents an infected host, and edges reflect communications between the hosts. Properties of the graph can quantify the botnet's "usefulness". For instance, the diameter of the network measures the efficiency of bot communications, and

P. Degano and J.D. Guttman (Eds.): POST 2012, LNCS 7215, pp. 249–268, 2012.
© Springer-Verlag Berlin Heidelberg 2012

the size of the largest connected component is the number of bots that are reachable by the attacker and can carry out her instructions. Assuming that P2P botnets are structured according to known models, these works aim to assess the effectiveness of strategies to take down a botnet, i.e., decreasing the botnet's "usefulness". For example, one strategy that was found to be effective for some network topologies is to target nodes with high degree, i.e., that communicate with many hosts [10,11,41].

We observe that previous works applying graph models to P2P botnets do not consider an important property of networks — assortative mixing [25]. Assortativity refers to the tendency for a node to attach to other "similar" nodes, and is commonly examined in terms of a node's degree, i.e., high-degree nodes are likely to be neighbors of other high-degree nodes. This property is also referred to as *degree correlation*. The existence of this correlation between neighboring nodes has been observed in many real-world networks [29,27,25]. More importantly, it has been found to be a property of *growing* networks [5,18], where the network increases in size as nodes join over time, as is true in a botnet as more hosts become infected.

In this work, we show that assortativity plays an important role in network structure, such that neglecting it can lead to an over-estimation of the effectiveness of botnet takedown strategies. By generating networks with varying levels of degree correlation, we demonstrate that a higher level of assortativity allows the network to be more resilient to certain takedown strategies, including those found to be effective by previous works. Moreover, we note that bots are dynamic entities that can react and adapt to changes in the network, and so the botnet can potentially "heal" itself after a fraction of its nodes are removed. We specifically explore cases where nodes can compensate for lost neighbors by creating edges to other nearby nodes, e.g., that are within h hops. This is similar to the behavior of a P2P bot contacting known hosts on its peer-list, which the bot maintains by constant exchanges with its neighbors [4,6,31,16,36]. Our simulations show that the graph can recover significantly after takedown attempts, even when h is small, and that higher levels of assortativity can allow the network to recover more effectively.

Another contribution of this work is in identifying alternative takedown strategies that are more effective than those explored by previous works. Specifically, we show that targeting nodes with both high degree and low clustering coefficient will decrease the connectivity and communication efficiency of the network significantly, and also makes it considerably more difficult for the network to recover from the takedown attempt. We further examine the effectiveness of applying this strategy "locally" where only a subset of nodes and edges is visible, such as when traffic from only a single subnet can be observed.

The rest of this paper is organized as follows. Section 2 describes related work. Section 3 defines assortativity, studies this value in botnets, and describes our algorithm for generating networks with varying levels of assortativity. The effect of assortativity on network resilience and "healing" ability is investigated in Sections 4 and 5. Discussion and conclusions are presented in Sections 6 and 7.

2   Related Work

Botnet models. Several previous works have studied botnets using network models. Cooke et al. [8] described three potential botnet topologies: centralized, P2P, and random, and qualitatively discussed their design complexity, detectability, message latency, and survivability. Other works [19,10] applied theoretical network models to botnets, including Erdös-Rényi random graphs [13], Watts-Strogatz small world graphs [38], and Barabási-Albert scale-free graphs [2]. This allows the effectiveness of takedown strategies to be quantitatively evaluated using graph properties, such as the network diameter, the average shortest distance between pairs of nodes, and the size of the largest connected component. Davis et al. [11] compared Overnet, which is utilized by the Storm botnet [31,16], with random and scale-free networks to justify the choice of structured P2P networks made by bot-masters. They simulated takedown efforts on the networks by removing nodes at random, in descending order of node degree, or in a "tree-like" fashion by identifying nodes reachable from an initial node, and found Overnet to be more resilient than other graph models.

To our knowledge, no previous work on botnet modeling has considered the effect of *degree assortativity* in networks. This property, defined as the correlation coefficient between the degrees of neighboring nodes [25], has been found to be high in many real-world social, biological, and computer networks [26,29]. It has been studied analytically in the statistical physics literature, and found to be an inherent property of *growing* networks where nodes join and edges are created over time [5,18], since older nodes are likely to have higher degree and tend to connect to each other. Studies in the statistical physics domain focus on understanding the underlying interactions between nodes that would result in a network that matches one empirically measured in the real world. By contrast, a network of bots is elusive and difficult to quantify in practice. Making assumptions about the graph structure or node correlation (e.g., that there is none) is thus unfounded.

Network takedown strategies. The resilience of networks to attacks or failures have been explored in the physics branch of complex networks [1,15,9]. A scale-free network, which consists of a few highly-connected "hub" nodes and many "leaf" nodes, has been found to be particularly vulnerable to attacks where high-degree nodes are removed first. A takedown strategy that targets high-degree nodes is also recommended by previous works that studied botnet models [10,11,41], particularly for unstructured P2P networks where there are "super-peers" present.

Other types of takedown efforts on networks have also been explored in the complex networks literature, such as cascaded node removals [37], removing nodes according to their betweenness centrality, or removing edges instead of nodes [15]. These works focus on the resilience of different network topologies, and do not take assortativity into account. Newman et al. [26] studied the prevalence of assortativity in real-world networks. Even though their focus is on measuring and generating assortative networks, they also showed, through simulation, that higher assortativity allows a network to have a larger connected component after a small fraction of high-degree nodes are removed. However, they did not explore other takedown strategies, the effect on other graph properties, or the network's ability to "heal" itself. In this work, we explicitly study the effect of assortativity on network resilience and the ability of dynamic networks (such as P2P botnets) to recover from takedown attempts.

3   Constructing and Measuring Assortative Networks

We first define degree assortativity, following the definition by Newman et al. [25], and perform empirical analyses on the assortativity of real botnets by simulating networks according to the Waledac botnet protocol [6] and examining a portion of the Storm botnet [31,16,36]. We then describe our algorithm for adjusting the level of assortativity in simulated networks, and the metrics we use to quantify the "usefulness" of a network. The metrics are aimed at capturing notions of communication efficiency between nodes and the number of reachable bots, which are likely to be of importance to the bot-master.

3.1   Degree Assortativity

Degree assortativity, defined as the correlation coefficient between the degrees of neighboring nodes, measures the tendency for nodes to be connected to others who are "similar" in terms of their degree. For example, this property is especially significant in social networks, where gregarious people are likely to be friends with each other [27,17]. It is also found to be a property of growing networks, where the network size increases as new nodes join and edges are created [5,18], as is true for botnets as vulnerable nodes become infected.

We define assortativity following the definition of Newman et al. [25]. Let the fraction of nodes in a network graph with degree k be denoted p_k. If we choose an edge from the graph at random, and follow it to one of its ends, the probability that the node at which we arrive has a degree of k is proportional to k. This is because we are more likely to end up at a node with high degree, which has more edges connected to it. To account for the edge from which we arrived, the *remaining degree* of the node is its degree minus one. The probability q_k that we arrive at a node with remaining degree k is then

$$q_k = \frac{(k+1)p_{k+1}}{\sum_{j=0}^{\infty} jp_j} \tag{1}$$

Let $e_{j,k}$ be the probability that a randomly selected edge connects nodes of remaining degree j and k, where $\sum_{j,k} e_{j,k} = 1$. The assortativity γ of the network, being the correlation coefficient between the degrees of neighboring nodes, is

$$\gamma = \frac{1}{\sigma_q^2} \sum_{j,k} jk(e_{j,k} - q_j q_k) \tag{2}$$

where σ_q^2 is the variance of the distribution of q_k, i.e., $\sigma_q^2 = \sum_k k^2 q_k - [\sum_k k q_k]^2$. A higher value of γ indicates that there is higher correlation between the degrees of two neighboring nodes. In a random graph, where every pair of nodes is connected with uniform probability, no correlation exists and $\gamma = 0$.

3.2   Degree Assortativity in Botnets

Even though high assortativity is found in many real-world networks, measuring it in practice can be challenging due to difficulties in observing all interactions between nodes in a large network. This is especially true for P2P botnets, since infected hosts cannot always be identified, and obtaining a comprehensive view of those hosts' communications may require multiple administrative entities to share sensitive information. While researchers have studied P2P botnets via infiltration (e.g., [16]), this provides a limited view of only a subset of the botnet.

We expect that real P2P botnets are likely to be assortative. This is not only because assortativity has been found to be a property of growing networks that increase in size over time (e.g., when vulnerable hosts become infected and join the botnet), but also due to the constant peer-list exchanges that occur between neighboring bots, which makes the "edges" in a botnet far from being random.

We perform two experiments to estimate the level of assortativity in P2P botnets. In the first, we simulate networks where nodes create and delete edges according to the algorithm performed by Waledac bots, as described in previous work that reverse-engineered the Waledac bot binary [4,6]. In the second, we examine network traffic from Storm bots in a honeynet running in the wild.

Waledac botnet simulations. Waledac is a P2P botnet that communicates over the HTTP protocol [4,6,35]. Similar to other P2P bots, each bot maintains a fixed-length list of known peers with which it communicates in order to stay connected to the botnet (and hence to the bot-master). A bot periodically exchanges peer-lists with other peers known to it, i.e., by randomly selecting hosts from its peer-list. This allows the bot to learn about other hosts in the botnet and to remove inactive nodes from its peer-list. As documented by Calvet et al. [6], the Waledac binary comes with a hard-coded list of 200 boot-strapping hosts. As the bot learns about other existing peers, its peer-list grows to a maximum of 500 entries, where each entry includes the IP address of the peer, as well as the time at which activities from that peer was last observed. If the number of known peers exceeds 500, the bot only keeps track of 500 most recently active hosts. During each peer-list exchange, each bot extracts 99 entries from its peer-list, appends its own IP address and the current time to this shortened list, and sends it to a host selected at random from its peer-list. In return, the receiving host also responds with a list of hosts extracted from its own peer-list.

We simulated networks where nodes join and depart over time (e.g., due to hosts becoming infected or patched), creating or deleting edges between each other following the Waledac protocol as described above. Assuming a constant rate of nodes joining the network in each round, we drew each node's lifetime from an exponential distribution [28,21], after which the node was removed from the network. Each simulated network was allowed to evolve this way until the number of online nodes reached 5,000. This number represents a small botnet, and follows the simulation settings in previous work on modeling botnets [10].

From this experiment, we found the assortativity of such networks to be quite high. Over a total of 50 simulation runs, the average assortativity was 0.39 (with a standard deviation of 0.036), which is higher than that of social networks [26]. This suggests that a botnet may be significantly assortative, and highlights the importance of this property in considering botnet models.

Traffic from Storm bots in a honeynet. In addition to our simulations, we also obtained network traffic from a honeynet running in the wild in late 2007 [14]. This dataset consists of a consecutive 24-hour trace from 13 hosts participating in the Storm botnet [31,16,36].

Figure 1 shows the assortativity measured among the 13 Storm bots, where snapshots of their communications were taken on an hourly basis. The "degree" of a bot is represented by 1) the number of distinct source IP addresses from which it receives packets (the in-degree), 2) the number of distinct destination IPs to which it sends packets (the out-degree), or 3) the total number of distinct IPs with which it interacts. Since the rest of the Storm botnet is not directly observable, we calculated the assortativity of the sub-graph that consisted of the 13 Storm bots, i.e., by considering traffic

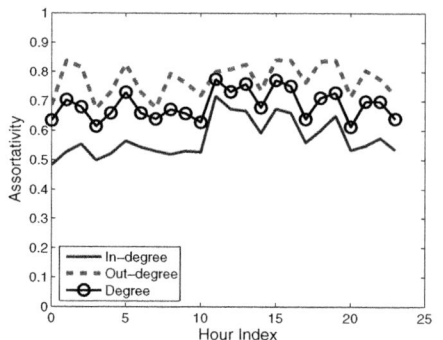

Fig. 1. The assortativity for 13 Storm bots in a honeynet running in the wild

between only the 13 Storm bots. As shown in Figure 1, this value is quite high, ranging from 0.48 to 0.84.

That said, we acknowledge that this limited dataset may not be representative of the actual Storm botnet. For example, the high level of assortativity may be due to certain aspects of the honeynet setup; e.g., the observable bots were placed in the same local network and so may have been more likely to communicate with each other. (Such localized measurements may be all that is available in practice to a network administrator who can observe traffic from only a single network. We will discuss the effectiveness of botnet takedown strategies using only local information in Section 6.)

While we recognize the limitations of the above efforts to evaluate assortativity in today's botnets, the results of our analysis in Sections 4 and 5 suggest that a botnet designer would want his botnet to be assortative for added resilience and recoverability, further buttressing our belief that future botnets will leverage this naturally occurring property.

3.3   Generating Assortative Networks

To study the effect of assortativity on networks, we need to be able to generate networks with varying levels of assortativity. One method for this is to rewire edges in a given network [40]: At each step, select two edges at random, and shuffle them so that the two nodes with larger remaining degrees are connected, and the two nodes with smaller remaining degrees are connected. Repeating this step will result in the network becoming increasingly assortative. However, rewiring causes the shortest path length between nodes to increase rapidly [40], which may bias the comparison between networks with different levels of assortativity.

We apply another method for constructing assortative networks, similar to Newman et al. [26]. This method takes as input the number of nodes in the network, the desired degree distribution p_k, and the edge probabilities $e_{j,k}$. Each node in the network is assigned a degree drawn from p_k. The remaining degree distribution q_k can then be calculated from p_k, and edges are added by connecting each pair of nodes of remaining degrees j and k with probability $e_{j,k}$.

To control the level of assortativity in the resulting network, we specify $e_{j,k}$ as follows. For a fixed value j, assume that $e_{j,k}$ follows a normal distribution centered at j, where the standard deviation σ is the adjustable knob for tuning the level of assortativity. Figure 2 illustrates $e_{j,k}$ centered at j. A smaller σ causes the normal distribution to become more peaked, where nodes with remaining degree j have a higher probability of sharing edges with other nodes of remaining degree close to j, resulting in a more assortative network.

In our simulations, p_k is chosen so that the resulting network is scale-

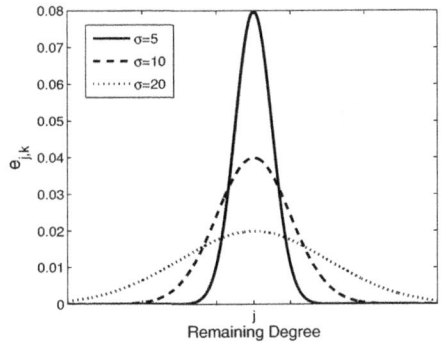

Fig. 2. Edge probabilities $e_{j,k}$ as a normal distribution centered at j with different values for the standard deviation σ

free, specifically, $p_k \sim k^{-3}$. We focus on scale-free networks because it is representative of many real-world networks, including unstructured P2P networks [22]. Empirical analysis by Dagon et al. [10] also suggest that the Nugache P2P botnet [36] has a scale-free structure. We set the number of nodes to 5,000 to represent a small botnet, following the simulation settings in previous work [10]. All of the edges are assumed to be undirected.

3.4   Metrics

We utilize the following two graph properties to quantify the "usefulness" of a botnet: 1) the size of the largest connected component, and 2) the inverse geodesic length. These metrics have been used by Dagon et al. [10] to compare the utility of different botnet topologies, and were also used in analyzing the resilience of various networks in the physics literature [15].

The fraction S of nodes in the largest connected component is an upper bound on the number of bots that are directly under the control of the attacker (assuming that she is part of one of the connected components). The more hosts that can carry out the attacker's commands, the larger the scale of the attack that can be launched, e.g., denial-of-service attacks or spamming.

In addition to controlling many infected hosts, another property that is likely to be of importance to the attacker is the efficiency of communication, i.e., how long it takes for messages to be relayed through the botnet. We measure the number of hops between pairs of nodes for this purpose. Specifically, let N be the total number of nodes, V be the set of nodes, $|V| = N$, and $d(u, v)$ be the length of the shortest path between node u and node v. The average inverse geodesic length [15] is defined as

$$L^{-1} = \frac{1}{N(N-1)} \sum_{u \in V} \sum_{v \neq u, v \in V} \frac{1}{d(u, v)} \tag{3}$$

Measuring the average inverse geodesic length is particularly useful in cases where the graph may be disconnected, since the distance $d(u, v)$ between two nodes u and v that belong to separate connected components would be infinite (and so its contribution to L^{-1} is zero). The larger L^{-1} is, the shorter the distances between nodes, and hence more efficient their communication. In evaluating the effectiveness of network takedown attempts, we are more interested in measuring the *normalized* average inverse geodesic length, which is defined as

$$\hat{L}^{-1} = \frac{\sum_{u \in V} \sum_{v \neq u, v \in V} \frac{1}{d'(u,v)}}{\sum_{u \in V} \sum_{v \neq u, v \in V} \frac{1}{d(u,v)}} \tag{4}$$

where $d'(u, v)$ is the *modified* length of the shortest path between nodes u and v, that is, after takedown efforts or after the network tries to heal itself. Note that both the numerator and denominator in $\hat{L}^{-1}$ are summed over the original set of nodes, V. Nodes that are removed have infinite distance to the rest of the network, the inverse of which is zero, and so do not contribute to the sum in Eqn. 4. The value that $\hat{L}^{-1}$ takes ranges from 0 to 1. A smaller value indicates more disruption to network communication and lower communication efficiency.

We measure $\hat{L}^{-1}$ and S of a network before and after takedown to evaluate the effectiveness of the takedown strategy (Section 4), and also measure them after the network attempts to "heal" itself to assess the effectiveness of recovery mechanisms (Section 5).

4   Network Resilience

In attempts to take down a P2P botnet, network administrators may wish to prioritize their efforts to focus on the more "important" nodes first, i.e., nodes whose removal will cause the most disruption to botnet operation. Using the two metrics described in Section 3.4, we investigate the effectiveness of botnet takedown strategies, and how they are sensitive to the assortativity of the network.

4.1 Uniform and Degree-Based Takedown Strategies

We first focus on strategies explored in previous works that study botnet models [10,11,41,19]:

- **Uniform takedown:** removing nodes from the network by selecting them uniformly at random.
- **Degree-based takedown:** removing nodes from the network in descending order of node degree, that is, targeting high-degree nodes first.

Uniform takedown is similar to the process in which users and network administrators patch infected hosts as they are discovered, without coordinating bot discoveries or patching activities. It has also been used to study random failures in the context of communication networks or biological networks [1]. While most networks are found to be resilient to uniform takedown, many are vulnerable to a degree-based strategy. This targeted takedown strategy is especially effective against scale-free networks, since the few highly-connected "hub" nodes responsible for maintaining the connectivity of the network are removed first, e.g., the "super-peers" that are found in unstructured P2P networks. The degree of a node, interpreted as the number of hosts with which it communicates, has also been used as an indicator of anomalies in network intrusion detection systems (e.g., [23,33,34]). In practice, these takedown strategies do not necessarily require access to the entire network communication graph, but can be applied to takedown efforts within a sub-graph as well, e.g., within a local network. We further discuss implementation challenges in Section 6.

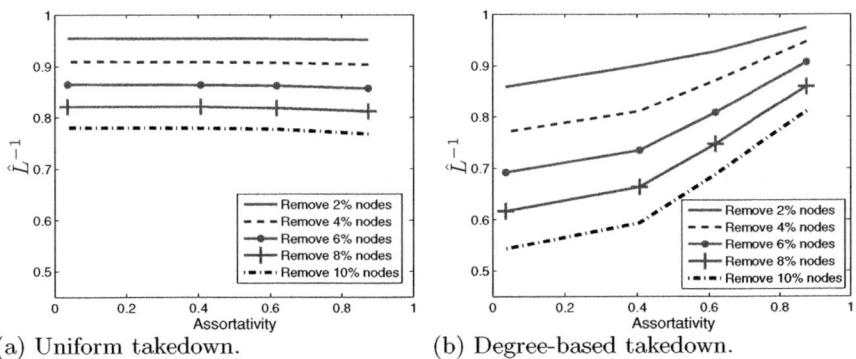

(a) Uniform takedown.   (b) Degree-based takedown.

Fig. 3. The normalized average inverse geodesic length $\hat{L}^{-1}$ after uniform or degree-based takedown strategies

As described in Section 3.3, we adjust the standard deviation σ of the edge probability distribution $e_{j,k}$ to generate networks of varying assortativity. For a scale-free network with 5,000 nodes, we set σ to 1, 5, 10, and 15 to obtain networks covering a range of assortativity from 0.04 to 0.87. Figures 3 and 4 show how networks with varying levels of assortativity respond to uniform and

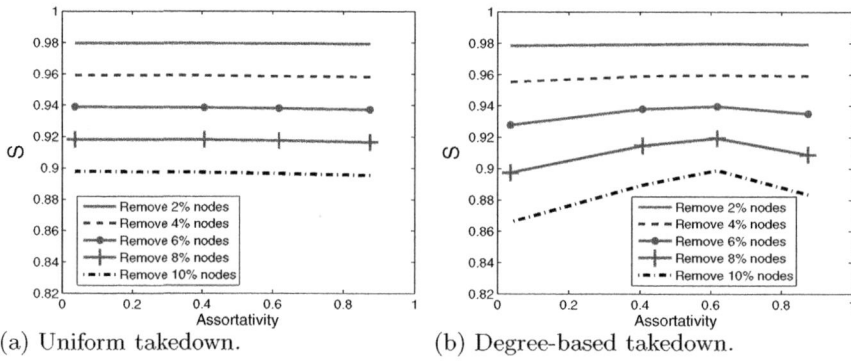

(a) Uniform takedown.　　　　　　(b) Degree-based takedown.

Fig. 4. The average fraction S of nodes in the largest connected component after uniform or degree-based takedown strategies

degree-based takedown, when 2%, 4%, 6%, 8%, or 10% of nodes were removed according to each strategy. The numbers are an average of 50 networks generated for each value of σ. We omit the standard deviations from the plots since they were generally small, that is, within 0.007 for both $\hat{L}^{-1}$ and S.

We find the degree-based strategy to be much more effective at taking down a network compared to uniform takedown, in agreement with previous works. However, as shown in Figure 3(b), the effectiveness of the degree-based strategy is highly dependent on the level of assortativity of the network. A lower assortativity, e.g., toward the left of Figure 3(b), results in the network experiencing a larger decrease in $\hat{L}^{-1}$ after takedown attempts. The difference between the decrease in $\hat{L}^{-1}$ for assortative and non-assortative networks grows as more nodes are removed. A similar phenomenon can be observed in Figure 4(b) for the fraction S of nodes in the largest connected component. With the exception of highly assortative networks (e.g., greater than 0.6), the fraction of nodes retained in the largest connected component increases with the level of assortativity. That is, more bots remain reachable to the attacker in moderately assortative networks.

The higher resilience in assortative networks can be attributed to nodes of similar degree "clustering" together. When the high-degree nodes are removed due to the degree-based strategy, only a connected subset of neighboring nodes are lost in effect. Moreover, since high-degree nodes tend to connect to each other, fewer of their edges are attached to nodes of low degree — who would be prone to isolation if their neighbors were removed. However, this also means that there are fewer high-degree nodes that can act as "bridges" between clusters of nodes with varying degrees. As more high-degree nodes are removed, the loss of those "bridging" nodes eventually cancels out other factors contributing to resilience, and the network can disintegrate, as shown on the far right of Figure 4(b). These discrepancies in how networks are affected by the same takedown strategy underline the importance of taking assortativity into account, both in evaluating takedown strategies and in considering botnet network models.

4.2   Other Takedown Strategies

While the degree-based strategy is much more effective than the uniform strategy, the former is sensitive to the level of assortativity in the network, as shown in Figures 3 and 4. In the search for a takedown strategy that would be effective even for assortative networks, we explore alternative approaches based on other graph properties, described below.

- **Neighborhood connected components:** We define the local neighborhood of a node u to be those nodes reachable within h hops from it. Figure 5(a) shows an example of the neighborhood of node u within three hops, where the edge labels indicate distances to u. If we were to remove u from the network, its local neighborhood would be split into separate "connected components", as shown in Figure 5(b). The number of "connected components" that remains in the neighborhood of a node can be an approximation of its local importance, since communication between components may have to be routed through u. Hence, as an alternative takedown strategy, we remove nodes in descending order of the number of connected components in their local neighborhood. A similar metric has also been used to detect hit-list worms [7].

- **Closeness centrality:** Closeness centrality for a node u is defined as the sum of the inverse geodesic distance from u to all other nodes in the network. A larger value indicates that the node is at a more "centered" location, and has more influence over the spread of information within the network. In this strategy, we remove nodes in descending order of their closeness centrality.

- **Clustering coefficient with degree:** The clustering coefficient measures how dense the connections are between the neighbors of a node. For a node u, it is defined as the number of edges that exist between u's neighbors, divided by the number of possible edges between u's neighbors. In Figure 6, this value for u is 4/10, while that for all other nodes is 1. A smaller value means that the neighbors of u may be disconnected without u. Ignoring nodes with the smallest degrees — in our tests, nodes with degree less than one-fifth of the maximum degree — we remove nodes in increasing order of their clustering coefficient, and among those with the same clustering coefficient, in decreasing order of degree.

Figures 7 and 8 show the normalized average inverse geodesic length $\hat{L}^{-1}$ and the fraction S of nodes in the largest connected component after each of the above takedown strategies, for networks of different levels of assortativity. The results are plotted after removing 2% or 10% of the nodes, and averaged over 50 networks generated for each level of assortativity. The standard deviations are all within 0.02 for both $\hat{L}^{-1}$ and S. Compared with the uniform and degree-based strategies discussed earlier, the clustering coefficient strategy is more effective at decreasing the network communication efficiency, as shown in Figure 7, while the connected components strategy seems more effective at lowering the connectivity of the network, as shown in Figure 8. In both of these cases, the alternative takedown strategy out-performs the degree-based strategy that previous works found to be effective [10,11,41].

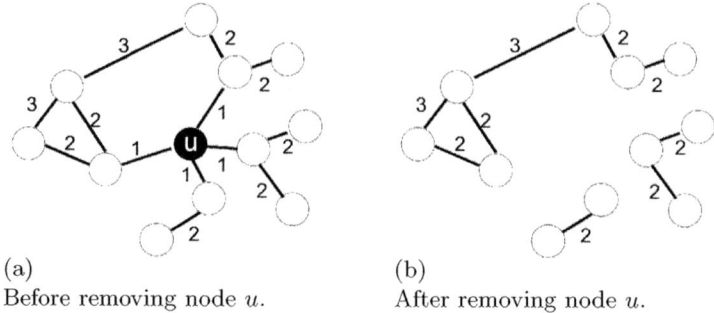

(a)   (b)

Before removing node u.   After removing node u.

Fig. 5. An example of the connected components within the neighborhood of node u.
The edge labels indicate number of hops to u.

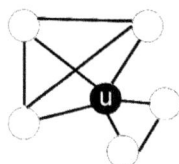

Fig. 6. An example of edges
between neighbors of node u

One of the reasons that the clustering coefficient strategy works well is because nodes that "cluster" together in assortative networks are likely to have higher clustering coefficient as well, since their neighbors also have similar degree. However, while the nodes at the center of a "cluster" may have a clustering coefficient close to 1, this value is likely to be much smaller for those connecting the "cluster" to the rest of the network. For example, all nodes in Figure 6 have a clustering coefficient of 1 except for node u, who turns out to be the "bridge" between the two clusters of degree two and three nodes. The removal of nodes with small clustering coefficient in this strategy is hence likely to lower the communication efficiency within the network.

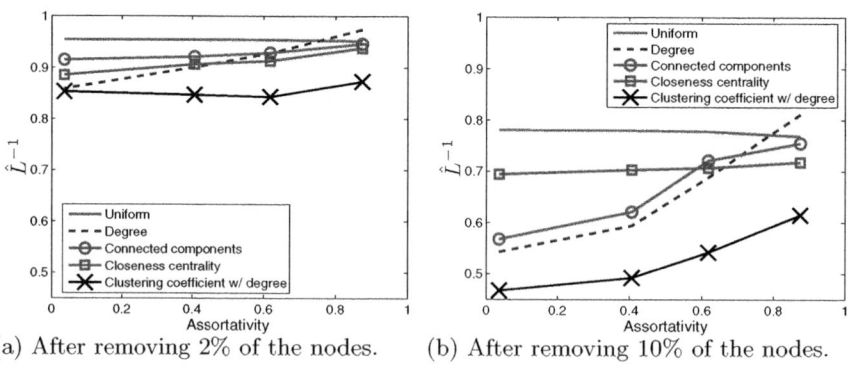

(a) After removing 2% of the nodes.   (b) After removing 10% of the nodes.

Fig. 7. The normalized average inverse geodesic length $\hat{L}^{-1}$ after removing 2% or 10% of the nodes according to each takedown strategy

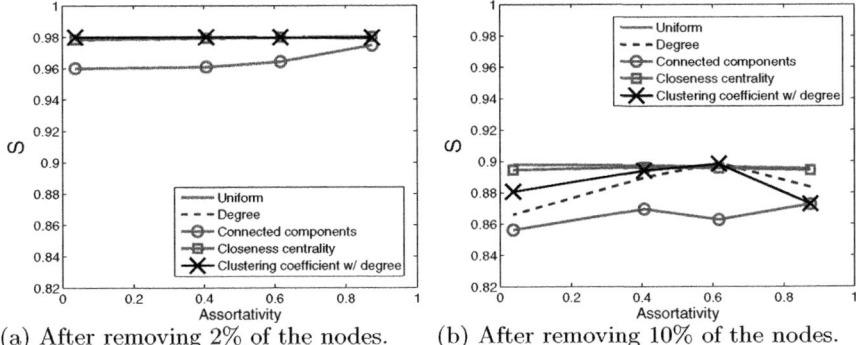

(a) After removing 2% of the nodes.   (b) After removing 10% of the nodes.

Fig. 8. The average fraction S of nodes in the largest connected component after removing 2% or 10% of the nodes according to each takedown strategy

5   Network Recovery

The dynamism inherent in P2P networks means that each individual bot is required to adapt to changes in its surroundings, for example, due to newly infected hosts joining the network or current peers going offline, even without takedowns taking place. Such mechanisms would hence also provide opportunities for the network to *recover* itself, i.e., restoring connectivity or reconstructing shortest paths between nodes, in the face of takedown attempts.

While previous works tend to regard a botnet as a static entity, and evaluate changes to the network immediately after takedown efforts as a measure of their effectiveness, we explicitly consider the ability of dynamic networks to heal themselves. Specifically, we model a recovery process where nodes can "look out" to a distance h and find peers that are within h hops. When a node loses a neighbor, e.g., due to takedown, it compensates for that lost neighbor by creating a new edge to a randomly selected node within distance h from it. This models the edge creation process in a P2P botnet, where nodes discover others that are "close" to it through peer-list exchanges with its neighbors [4,6,31,16,36,35]. The h-neighborhood of a node u hence represents hosts on u's peer-list, to which u looks for maintaining connectivity with the rest of the botnet.

5.1   Recovering from Uniform and Degree-Based Strategies

We first consider the ability of botnets to recover after takedown attempts employing the uniform or degree-based strategies described in Section 4.1. We focus on the $\hat{L}^{-1}$ metric, since it better illustrates the difference between networks of varying levels of assortativity. Figure 9 shows the normalized average inverse geodesic distance $\hat{L}^{-1}$ for networks after they attempt to recover from uniform or degree-based takedown strategies, when 2% or 10% of the nodes are removed. The numbers are averaged over 50 runs for each network, where the standard

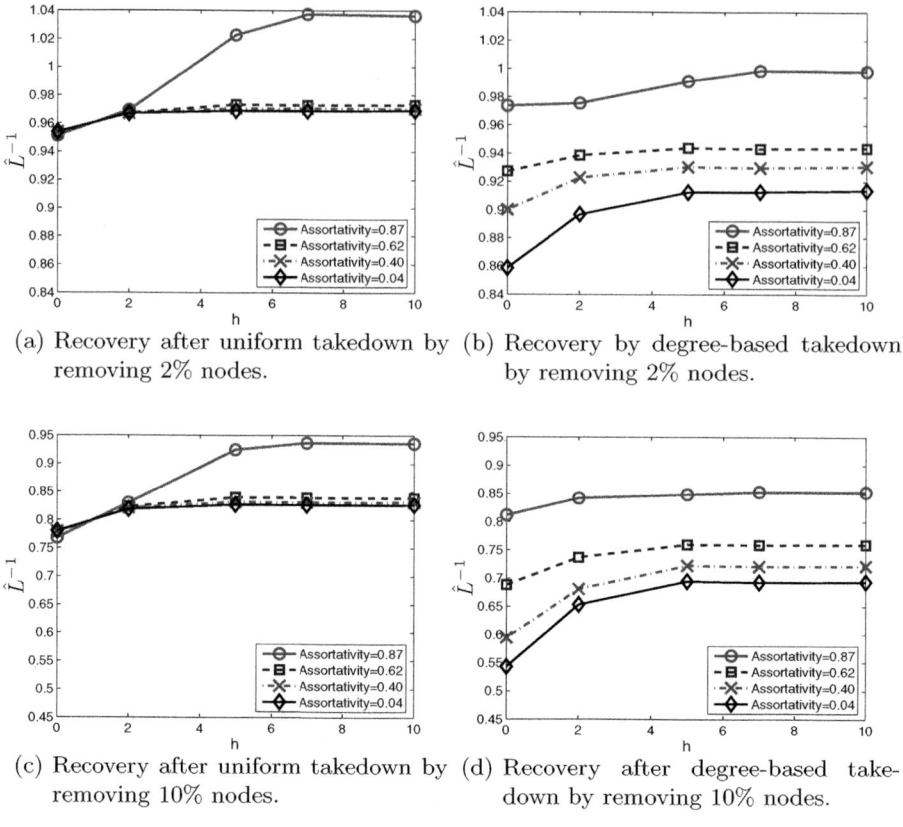

(a) Recovery after uniform takedown by removing 2% nodes.

(b) Recovery by degree-based takedown by removing 2% nodes.

(c) Recovery after uniform takedown by removing 10% nodes.

(d) Recovery after degree-based takedown by removing 10% nodes.

Fig. 9. The normalized average inverse geodesic length after recovering from uniform or degree-based takedown, when 2% or 10% of the nodes are removed, for various values of the look-out distance h

deviations are all below 0.006. The look-out distance h was set to 2, 5, 7, and 10. As h increases, $\hat{L}^{-1}$ increases as well, even reaching above 1 in Figure 9(a), i.e., the shortest distance between nodes becomes even shorter than before the takedown! However, while the increase in $\hat{L}^{-1}$ for networks with lower assortativity falls flat after a small h (even decreasing slightly, as in Figure 9(d)), the increase for networks with higher assortativity continues.

One reason for the continued recovery benefit enjoyed by assortative networks is high-degree nodes "clustering" together, since nodes tend to connect to others of similar degree. A node that is able to reach a high-degree node upon "looking out" is likely to be able to reach other high-degree nodes as well at a similar distance. This increases the probability that a compensation edge attaches to a high-degree node, hence shortening path lengths within the network and resulting in a higher $\hat{L}^{-1}$. This phenomenon is more pronounced in networks recovering from uniform takedown (see Figures 9(a) and 9(c)), since fewer high-degree nodes remain after the degree-based strategy.

5.2   Recovering from Other Takedown Strategies

Figures 10 and 11 show how networks of high and low assortativity recover from those alternative takedown strategies described in Section 4.2, when 2% or 10% of the nodes were removed. The results are an average of 50 networks. The standard deviations are all within 0.009. We observe a trend similar to the recovery from uniform and degree-based strategies, where networks with higher levels of assortativity experience continued recovery benefits with the look-out distance h (Figure 10(a) and 11(a)). Less assortative networks, on the other hand, do not benefit much after a look-out distance of 2 or 3 (Figure 10(b) and 11(b)). Regardless of the takedown strategy, assortative networks have higher communication efficiency after recovery, in terms of $\hat{L}^{-1}$, than less assortative networks.

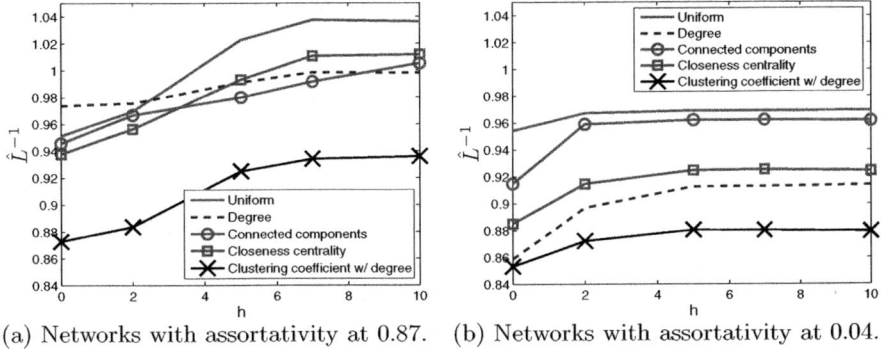

(a) Networks with assortativity at 0.87.   (b) Networks with assortativity at 0.04.

Fig. 10. Recovery for networks of high and low assortativity when 2% of the nodes were removed according to each strategy

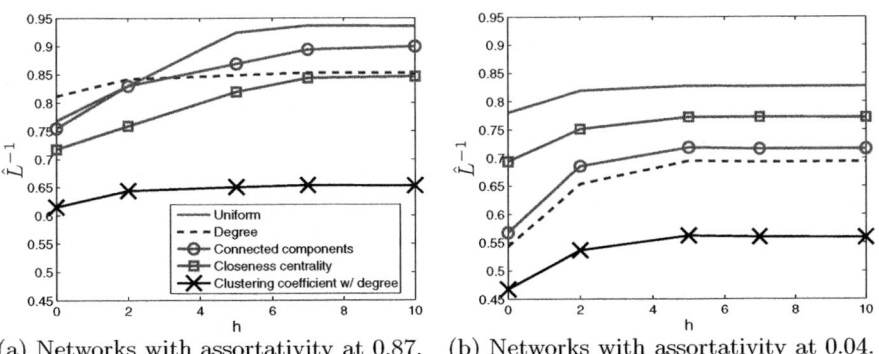

(a) Networks with assortativity at 0.87.   (b) Networks with assortativity at 0.04.

Fig. 11. Recovery for networks of high and low assortativity when 10% of the nodes were removed according to each strategy

In addition to being one of the most effective strategies (see Section 4.2), we also find takedown attempts based on clustering coefficient with degree to be the most difficult one for a network to recover from, as shown by low values of $\hat{L}^{-1}$

in Figures 10 and 11. In fact, when 10% of the nodes were removed from the same network, the $\hat{L}^{-1}$ after recovering from the degree-based and the clustering coefficient strategies can differ by 0.2. This shows that the clustering coefficient strategy can be a better alternative to one based solely on degree.

Besides creating compensation edges, a botnet may try to recover from takedowns by re-structuring itself into alternative topologies that are more resilient. Exploring how bots can perform this effectively in practice is part of future work.

6   Discussion

Applying takedown strategies in practice. Perhaps one of the reasons for the widespread study of the degree-based strategy is that it can be applied easily in practice. For example, if the degree of a node is interpreted as the number of hosts with which it communicates in some time interval, then identifying a node's degree can be performed on the basis of flow records (e.g., Cisco Netflows) that are collected from a router (or routers) that its traffic traverses. Notably, a node's degree can be determined solely by observing traffic to and from it, without requiring knowledge about the entity at the other end of the communication.

Other graph properties, however, may not be so straightforward to measure. For instance, takedown strategies based on clustering coefficient or neighborhood connected components depend on observing communications between the neighbors of a node, and may require collaboration between multiple administrative domains. This can be performed using a method similar to that proposed by Xie et al. to trace the origin of worm propagations [39]. Another approach is to examine the peer-lists an infected host receives from its neighbors, assuming that such data can be captured (i.e., it is not sent encrypted, and full packet capture is enabled on the network). If a node u has two neighbors communicating with each other, those nodes should be listed on each other's peer-lists, and so the fact that they communicate with each other can be inferred by identifying overlaps between u's neighbors and peer-lists sent to u. Of course, in cases where communications between some neighbors of an infected node are visible neither directly nor by inference, takedown strategies requiring this information can be applied considering only those neighbors for which communications are visible.

To examine the effect of applying takedown strategies locally, we generated networks according to the method described in Section 3.3, and partitioned the network randomly into k equal-sized portions. The clustering coefficient with degree strategy (which we find to be the most effective, see Section 4.2) was then applied separately in each partition, i.e., based on only those edges attached to nodes in each partition. Figure 12 shows the normalized average geodesic length $\hat{L}^{-1}$ and the fraction S of nodes in the largest connected component for varying values of k, when 10% of all nodes are removed this way. The numbers were averaged over 50 runs of this experiment. The standard deviations were all within 0.027 for $\hat{L}^{-1}$ and 0.013 for S. As shown in the figure, the takedown strategy becomes less effective as the number of network partitions increases, though the difference is small. For example, splitting highly assortative networks (assortativity at 0.87) into 200 partitions only increases S by 5% compared to the case when the network is not partitioned (i.e., $k =1$). We hence believe that our suggested takedown strategies can be applied with reasonable effectiveness in practice.

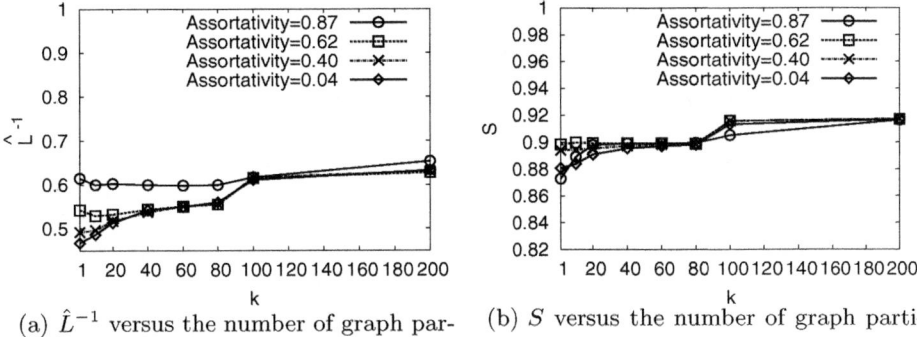

(a) $\hat{L}^{-1}$ versus the number of graph partitions.

(b) S versus the number of graph partitions.

Fig. 12. The fraction S of nodes in the largest connected component and the normalized average inverse geodesic length $\hat{L}^{-1}$ after applying the clustering coefficient with degree takedown strategy locally in each of the k network partitions and removing 10% of the nodes

Modeling networks analytically. Rather than assuming a particular network topology, e.g., random, scale-free, or small-world, or a specific level of assortativity, another approach to modeling networks is to specify a set of actions governing the behavior of nodes at each step in time, and analytically determine properties of the resulting network. This type of growing network models have been used extensively in the physics domain of complex networks [3,24,32,18,12]. Given knowledge of individual bot behaviors and how they interact with each other from P2P bot studies [4,6,31,16,36], it seems likely that analytical network models from the physics literature can be adapted to characterize P2P botnets. In fact, a recent work by Li et al. [20] used this approach to derive the degree distribution of a botnet where new nodes joins the network by "copying" the edges of an existing node that it chooses at random.

However, these analytical approaches do make other assumptions about the underlying network that they attempt to model in order to simplify calculations. Specifically, by assuming that both the age of the network t and the network size N is large, $t \to \infty$, $N \gg 1$, all actions experienced by a node are approximated by the *expected* action, e.g., when a node creates one edge at random, the degree of all other nodes increases by $1/N$, where the denominator N is also replaced by the expected value. These assumptions may not be applicable to botnets in practice, since 1) network administrators will be equally, if not more, concerned about infections in the early stages of a botnet when t is small; 2) botnets have been found to consist of a few hundred or thousand nodes only, and are commonly rented out in small numbers, e.g., for sending spam; 3) to a network administrator managing a local network, N certainly does not grow indefinitely; and 4) approximating aspects of network growth using expected values introduces error that could potentially be magnified by a bot designed counter to assumptions that these approximations imply.

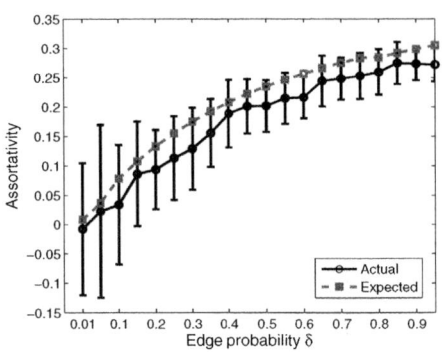

Fig. 13. The expected assortativity, shown in the dashed line, versus the actual average value from simulations, with one standard deviation shown with error bars

As a simple demonstration of the separation between analytical models and actual network growth, we examine a derivation by Callaway et al. [5] of the assortativity of a simple network growth model. In each time step, the model assumes that one node joins the network, and with probability δ an edge forms between two nodes selected at random. Their derivation of the assortativity is based on a rate equation specifying the *expected* increase in the number of edges that connect nodes of remaining degree j and k at each time step, and makes the same assumptions as described above. Figure 13 shows the expected assortativity of the network as approximated by Callaway et al. for various values of δ. The actual average values from simulations are also plotted in the figure, with one standard deviation shown as error bars. To generate these values, we generated 50 networks for each value of δ, and set the number of time steps (i.e., number of nodes) to 1,000. Figure 13 shows that the expected assortativity as predicted by Callaway et al. can differ from the actual average assortativity by an amount that approaches or, in some cases, exceeds one standard deviation. This suggests that the simplifying assumptions typically employed in analytical models may cause nontrivial deviations from practice.

7   Conclusion

Peer-to-peer (P2P) botnets, in contrast to their centralized counterparts, do not have a single point-of-failure and are difficult to take down. Identifying and removing those nodes that are "important" to the connectivity or communication efficiency of a botnet is hence critical to disrupting its operation. Toward this goal, several previous works have modeled P2P botnets using theoretical network models [19,10,11]. These works compare the resilience of various network topologies to uniform or degree-based node removals, and quantify the effectiveness of these takedown strategies using graph properties, including the inverse geodesic length or the fraction of nodes in the largest connected component.

We observe that previous works do not consider an important structural property of networks, namely assortativity. Empirical measurements on networks simulated according to the Waledac botnet protocol and on network traffic from a portion of the Storm botnet suggest that this property can be quite high for botnets in practice. We show that in omitting the presence of assortativity in botnet models, and without considering the effect of dynamic networks actively recovering from node failures, previous works may have over-estimated the effectiveness of recommended takedown strategies. In addition, we identify alternative strategies that are more effective than those in previous works for botnets with high assortativity, and study the application of these strategies in a "local" setting when only a subset of the network is visible.

References

1. Albert, R., Jeong, H., Barabasi, A.L.: Error and attack tolerance of complex networks. Nature 406 (2000)
2. Barabási, A.L., Albert, R.: Emergence of scaling in random networks. Science 286, 509–512 (1999)
3. Barabási, A.L., Albert, R., Jeong, H.: Mean-field theory for scale-free random networks. Physica A 272, 173–187 (1999)
4. Borup, L.: Peer-to-peer botnets: A case study on Waledac. Master's thesis, Technical University of Denmark (2009)
5. Callaway, D.S., Hopcroft, J.E., Kleinberg, J.M., Newman, M.E.J., Strogatz, S.H.: Are randomly grown graphs really random? Phys. Rev. E 64(4), 041902 (2001)
6. Calvet, J., Davis, C.R., Bureau, P.: Malware authors don't learn, and that's good! In: Intl. Conf. Malicious and Unwanted Software (2009)
7. Collins, M.P., Reiter, M.K.: Hit-List Worm Detection and Bot Identification in Large Networks Using Protocol Graphs. In: Kruegel, C., Lippmann, R., Clark, A. (eds.) RAID 2007. LNCS, vol. 4637, pp. 276–295. Springer, Heidelberg (2007)
8. Cooke, E., Jahanian, F., McPherson, D.: The zombie roundup: Understanding, detecting, and disrupting botnets. In: Wksh. Steps to Reducing Unwanted Traffic on the Internet (2005)
9. Crucitti, P., Latora, V., Marchiori, M., Rapisarda, A.: Error and attack tolerance of complex networks. Phys. A 340, 388–394 (2004)
10. Dagon, D., Gu, G., Lee, C.P., Lee, W.: A taxonomy of botnet structures. In: Annual Computer Security Applications Conf. (2007)
11. Davis, C.R., Neville, S., Fernandez, J.M., Robert, J.-M., McHugh, J.: Structured Peer-to-Peer Overlay Networks: Ideal Botnets Command and Control Infrastructures? In: Jajodia, S., Lopez, J. (eds.) ESORICS 2008. LNCS, vol. 5283, pp. 461–480. Springer, Heidelberg (2008)
12. Dorogovtsev, S.N., Mendes, J.F.F.: Scaling properties of scale-free evolving networks: Continuous approach. Phys. Rev. E 63, 056125 (2001)
13. Erdös, P., Rényi, A.: On the evolution of random graphs. Publications of the Mathematical Institute of the Hungarian Academy of Sciences 5, 17–61 (1960)
14. Gu, G., Perdisci, R., Zhang, J., Lee, W.: BotMiner: Clustering analysis of network traffic for protocol- and structure-independent botnet detection. In: USENIX Security Symp. (2008)
15. Holme, P., Kim, B., Yoon, C., Han, S.: Attack vulnerability of complex networks. Phys. Rev. E 65, 056109 (2002)
16. Holz, T., Steiner, M., Dahl, F., Biersack, E., Freiling, F.: Measurements and mitigation of peer-to-peer-based botnets: A case study on Storm worm. In: USENIX Wksh. Large-Scale Exploits and Emergent Threats (2008)

17. Jackson, M.O., Rogers, B.W.: Meeting strangers and friends of friends: How random are social networks? American Economic Review 97(3) (2007)
18. Krapivsky, P., Redner, S.: Organization of growing random networks. Phys. Rev. E 63, 066123 (2001)
19. Li, J., Ehrenkranz, T., Kuenning, G., Reiher, P.: Simulation and analysis on the resiliency and efficiency of malnets. In: Wksh. Principles of Advanced and Distributed Simulation (2005)
20. Li, X., Duan, H., Liu, W., Wu, J.: The growing model of botnets. In: Intl. Conf. Green Circuits and Systems (2010)
21. Liben-Nowell, D., Balakrishnan, H., Karger, D.: Analysis of the evolution of peer-to-peer systems. In: ACM Symp. Principles of Distributed Computing (2002)
22. Matei, R., Iamnitchi, A., Foster, P.: Mapping the Gnutella network. IEEE Internet Computing 6, 50–57 (2002)
23. Mirkovic, J., Prier, G., Reiher, P.: Attacking DDoS at the source. In: IEEE Intl. Conf. Network Protocols (2002)
24. Moore, C., Ghoshal, G., Newman, M.: Exact solutions for models of evolving networks with addition and deletion of nodes. Phys. Rev. E 74, 036121 (2006)
25. Newman, M.: Assortative mixing in networks. Phys. Rev. Lett. 89(20) (2002)
26. Newman, M.: Mixing patterns in networks. Phys. Rev. E 67, 026126 (2003)
27. Newman, M., Park, J.: Why social networks are different from other types of networks. Phys. Rev. E 68, 036122 (2003)
28. Pandurangan, G., Raghavan, P., Upfal, E.: Building low-diameter P2P networks. In: IEEE Symp. Foundations of Computer Science (2001)
29. Pastor-Satorras, R., Vazquez, A., Vespignani, A.: Dynamical and correlation properties of the internet. Phys. Rev. Lett. 87(25) (2001)
30. Pastor-Satorras, R., Vespignani, A.: Epidemic spreading in scale-free networks. Phys. Rev. Lett. 86(14) (2001)
31. Porras, P., Saidi, H., Yegneswaran, V.: A multi-perspective analysis of the Storm (Peacomm) worm. Tech. rep., Computer Science Laboratory, SRI International (2007)
32. Sarshar, N., Roychowdhury, V.: Scale-free and stable structures in complex ad hoc networks. Physical Review E 69(2), 026101 (2004)
33. Schechter, S.E., Jung, J., Berger, A.W.: Fast Detection of Scanning Worm Infections. In: Jonsson, E., Valdes, A., Almgren, M. (eds.) RAID 2004. LNCS, vol. 3224, pp. 59–81. Springer, Heidelberg (2004)
34. Sekar, V., Xie, Y., Reiter, M.K., Zhang, H.: A multi-resolution approach for worm detection and containment. In: Intl. Conf. Dependable Syst. and Netw. (2006)
35. Sinclair, G., Nunnery, C., Kang, B.B.: The Waledac protocol: The how and why. In: Intl. Conf. Malicious and Unwanted Software (2009)
36. Stover, S., Dittrich, D., Hernandez, J., Dietrich, S.: Analysis of the Storm and Nugache trojans: P2P is here. USENIX; Login 32(6) (2007)
37. Watts, D.J.: A simple model of global cascades on random networks. Natl. Acad. Sci. 99(9) (2002)
38. Watts, D.J., Strogatz, S.H.: Collective dynamics of 'small-world' networks. Nature 393 (1998)
39. Xie, Y., Sekar, V., Reiter, M.K., Zhang, H.: Forensic analysis for epidemic attacks in federated networks. In: 14th IEEE Intl. Conf. Network Protocols (2006)
40. Xulvi-Brunet, R., Sokolov, I.: Reshuffling scale-free networks: From random to assortative. Phys. Rev. E 70, 066102 (2004)
41. Yu, J., Li, Z., Hu, J., Liu, F., Zhou, L.: Using simulation to characterize topology of peer to peer botnets. In: Intl. Conf. Computer Modeling and Simulation (2009)

A Game-Theoretic Analysis of Cooperation in Anonymity Networks

Mu Yang[1], Vladimiro Sassone[1], and Sardaouna Hamadou[2]

[1] ECS, University of Southampton, UK
[2] Università Ca' Foscari, Venice, IT

Abstract. Anonymity systems are of paramount and growing importance in communication networks. They rely on users to cooperate to the realisation of an effective anonymity service. Yet, existing systems are marred by the action of 'selfish' free-loaders, so that several cooperation incentives are being proposed.

We propose a game-theoretic model of incentives in anonymity networks based on parametric utility functions, which make it flexible, adaptable and realistic. We then use the framework to analyse the cost of cooperation and the performance of the gold-star incentive scheme in the Crowds protocol.

1 Introduction

Anonymity of electronic communication is rapidly becoming an essential requirement of today's society, in particular as far as tracking web browsing and handheld, mobile devices is concerned. Its importance is increasingly recognised as crucial in many fields of computer-supported human activities, such as e-commerce, web surfing, consumer profiling, personalised advertising. Anonymity is needed both by individuals and organisations who want to keep their identities, interests and activities confidential. Cryptographic techniques, firewalls, VPNs, and similar, can only provide partial protection; indeed, they can only protect the contents of a communication, not its origin, destination and occurrence. This constitutes a problem because in general a lot of potentially sensitive information can be inferred by the mere presence of a communication between two parties. To address this issue, many anonymity systems and protocols have been proposed in the literature. Their purpose is to support anonymous communications, at least to some extent [6,22,11,21]. Since public visibility is the default condition on today's main networks, most notably the Internet, anonymity cannot be enforced by either senders of receivers, but must be created by using messages to hide messages. In fact, the consumers of the anonymity service are at the same time its providers, as they cooperate to generate the network activity that grants anonymity to the system as a whole. Typically, cooperation entails relaying other users' messages in order to create sufficient 'doubt' as to whom the real message originator actually is.

Anonymity systems have a broad range of users, ranging from ordinary citizens who want to avoid being profiled for targeted advertisements, to companies trying to hide information from their competitors, to entities requiring untraceable communication over the Internet. With these many potential users, it would seem that anonymity services based on consumer/provider users will naturally be well-resourced and able to operate

P. Degano and J.D. Guttman (Eds.): POST 2012, LNCS 7215, pp. 269–289, 2012.

efficiently. However, cooperation cannot be taken for granted. Just because functioning as a relay may cost a significant amount of processing power and bandwidth, not all the users are going to be *cooperative*. Some will indeed act *selfishly*, and only use the system to send their messages whilst ignoring the requests to forward others' messages. Obviously, with not enough cooperative users, the systems will hardly operate at all, and will certainly not be able to afford adequate anonymity guarantees. Observe that this is not a trivial problem as it may appear superficially. In fact, as part of the anonymity requirements which lay at their very core, these systems do not monitor their users' behaviours nor their identities, making it virtually impossible to detect selfish users. In other words, even without considering the several documented attacks against anonymity networks (cf. e.g., [15,19,20]), inducing users to cooperate to the anonymity mechanisms is among the most critical aspects of maintaining the security and viability of the network. Due to the demand for strong anonymity from large numbers of cooperative users, it is therefore vital that these systems are able to deploy '*incentives*' to encourage users' cooperation and so make the anonymity provision effective. Some interesting approaches to achieve that have been proposed, such as make running relays easier and provide better forwarding performance [23].

To evaluate whether these approaches are effective, we need a framework which empowers us to analyse them, as well as provide guidelines and some mechanism design principles for incentive schemes. This much we provide in the present paper, exploiting notions and techniques from Game Theory.

Game theory [12] concerns strategic decision-making by rational entities – referred to as *players* – who behave according to a given set of rules – the *game* – with the explicit purpose of maximising their own benefit. Benefits are expressed by *utility functions*, whose value is determined by the players' actions and, ultimately, by their decisions. The '*rationality*' hypothesis is very significant, meaning that players are always capable to choose their actions exactly as required to maximise their utilities. Game theory is an excellent tool to model anonymity networks. In such systems users compete for anonymity services in the way prescribed by specific protocols and, in doing so, they invest their own resources. At the core of their participation in the system is therefore a need to balance their gain in terms of security (viz., the level of anonymity guaranteed to them) and/or performance (viz., the speed at which their transactions are processed) against their costs (e.g., in terms of bandwidth, software, etc). Rationality here is reflected in the micro-economic mechanisms which underpin such cost/benefit decisions.

In this paper we build a game-theoretic framework to study incentive mechanisms in anonymity systems. We model user behaviours (viz., cooperative or selfish) as a non-cooperative game, and compute the equilibrium strategies for the users involved in the game. As games model systems, we rely on game-theoretic principles to predict whether the users will or will not be cooperative, i.e., under exactly what conditions they will participate in the system or just exploit it. We also use the game theoretic notion of *Nash Equilibrium* and *Dominant Equilibrium* to analyse the strategic choices made by different users. Our objective is achieved by considering a rich and flexible set of parameters for users' payoffs, including aspects such as anonymity, cost and performance. In general, a user's utility function $U_i(_-)$ in our framework is a sum of factor functions $\Phi_k(_-)$, each representing on a given payoff relevant to the analysis at hand. Furthermore, such functions can be weighed differently for each individual user, so as to afford great flexibility to the model.

In the paper we apply this framework to a relative simple anonymity scenario: the CROWDS protocol. We show that, if we consider anonymity as the only parameter of importance, then there is exactly one Nash (dominant) equilibrium, whose equilibrium strategy is to behave cooperatively. Whilst this may explain why in standard CROWDS there are no incentives to cooperation, it fails to match the real-world experience that users can indeed behave uncooperatively. In fact, the picture changes radically as soon as we consider the cost of communication as a parameter: as cost is a potent dissuader, users will soon start to contemplate the opportunities of selfishness. We observe that users who constantly behave selfishly enjoy *no anonymity at all*: as they only forward their own messages, there can be no ambiguity whatsoever as to the origin of a message intercepted from one of them. Strategic users will therefore engineer complex strategies whereby cooperative and selfish phases alternate. This leads us straight to our framework of mixed-strategy games, in which we study – both through analysis and simulations – the collective equilibrium behaviour of strategic users. We furthermore focus on the impact on equilibria of environmental parameters such as the number of attackers, the volume of network traffic, etc, and investigate the mechanics they induce on the equilibrium points.

We anticipate that the full power of our model only comes to the forefront when incentive mechanisms are involved: the ability to analyse the dynamics of the users' chosen behaviours – viz., the equilibrium strategies – as contextual parameters vary, make the model suitable to design and analyse incentive mechanisms. To exemplify this, we focus on the *gold-star incentive mechanism* [23], whereby cooperative users are rewarded for their behaviour by enhanced performance, in the form of quicker delivery time for their anonymous messages. Precisely, messages carrying a gold-star are routed with priority over other messages. Users gain 'gold-star' status, i.e., the ability to send gold-star messages, according to whether they "achieved a satisfactory performance for at least R times out of the last V measurements." We conduct for gold-star-incentivised CROWDS the same set of analyses we carried out for CROWDS. In particular, we study the equilibrium strategies as typical parameters vary, and illustrate how at equilibrium a strategic user will be selfish at most with frequency $1 - R/V$. In other terms, our results confirm the effectiveness of the gold-star mechanism as an incentive to cooperation.

To the best of our knowledge, ours is the first application of game-theory to yield an applicable framework to model incentives in anonymity systems. We compare our approach with the existing literature in §6 and assess it in the concluding section §7.

Structure of the paper: §2 and §3 introduce the framework from its game-theoretic foundations. In §4 we present our analysis of CROWDS, and in §5 that of CROWDS extended with the gold-star mechanism. The appendices contain most of the proofs and some of the figures that could not find space in this exposition.

2   Game-Theoretic Incentive Framework

2.1   Strategies and Equilibriums

In anonymity networks, honest users compete for anonymity services with limited resources, such as bandwidth from servers. We model honest users' behaviours in such networks as a non-cooperative game. Each player (user) is a rational agent trying to maximise her own utility and choosing her actions (e.g., cooperative, selfish, etc) strategically. The actions she chooses are so-called *strategies*; the players' chosen *strategies* are drawn from a (finite) set of actions, and determine their utilities. A *dominant strategy* for a player is a strategy which guarantees her an optimal utility irrespective of the strategies chosen by the other players. It is thus natural for a player to adopt a dominant strategy, if any such strategy exists. A game reaches a *dominant-strategy equilibrium* if each player has a dominant strategy. However this may not be possible, since in general a user's utility depends not only on her own strategy, but may be affected by other players' strategies. In such cases, one typically considers a weaker property called *Nash Equilibrium* (NE), which represents a strategy profile in which each player's utility is optimal, given that the other players also play their optimal strategies. We remark that if a dominant strategy equilibrium exists, then at least one Nash Equilibrium does.

2.2   The General Model in Anonymity Systems

We consider an anonymity system of n members $\{1, \ldots, n\}$ where n_h users are honest and the other n_m $(= n - n_h)$ are malicious. Each honest member i has a finite set of strategic actions $\mathcal{A}ct_i$ and we write S_i and U_i for respectively user i's strategies and utilities. Here the U_i depends on several factors which we discuss below. Typically, the set of strategic actions for user i include actions $\mathcal{C}$ and $\mathcal{S}$, respectively for *cooperative* and *selfish*. In this paper, we are only interested in these two actions, thus the set $\mathcal{A}ct_i$ is independent of i. For every user, we then denote $\mathcal{A}ct_i$ simply as $\mathcal{A}ct = \{\mathcal{C}, \mathcal{S}\}$. Here we define $\mathcal{C}$ as the behaviour of forwarding messages for any requests and $\mathcal{S}$ as the behaviour of always refusing others' requests but only forwarding one's own messages. User i will be called *cooperative* or *selfish* user according to whether $S_i = \mathcal{C}$ or $S_i = \mathcal{S}$. Note that cooperative and selfish actions refer to the behaviour of honest users: in the paper, we make the standard assumption that malicious users always act cooperatively in order to be chosen on the honest users' paths and, so, to de-anonymise the system. We leave to future work the investigation of the case where attackers may act selfishly.

Definition 1. *A game Γ with n_h players over anonymity systems of n members consists of a set of utility functions $U_1, \ldots, U_{n_h}$, where $U_i; \mathcal{A}ct^{n_h} \to \mathbb{R}$, the set of real numbers.*

For each $i \in \{1, \ldots, n_h\}$, the utility function $U_i(S_1, \cdots, S_{n_h})$ describes the payoff to user i under each combination of strategies. We assume that the utility functions take the form of a linear combination of factor functions $\Phi_k(\_)$, each accounting for a parameter k relevant to the specific application. That is, using $\rho_{ik} \geq 0$ to indicate the (relative) weight that user i attributes to parameter k, then $\sum_k \rho_{ik} = 1$ and

$$U_i(\_) = \sum_k \rho_{ik} \cdot \Phi_k(\_) \tag{1}$$

In the paper we will only use the factors of *anonymity*, *performance* and *cost*. The former quantifies the value a user attaches to their anonymity, whilst the second to the speed of their network activity. These parameters often need to be traded off against each other, as a higher anonymity level often requires more complex protocols which, as a side effect, reflect in longer delivery times. The ability to give them different weights in the *same* utility function allows i to select their individual strategy to finely balance their payoffs. Similarly, the 'cost' factor measures the importance that i attaches to any payments she incurs for using the anonymity network. We believe these three factors are the most important ones, and as such are sufficient to cover several significant applications, as in this paper; yet, additional factors can easily be included as required.

As honest users will in general vary their behaviour, and not always act according to a fixed strategy S_i, we shall use probabilities to describe the likelihood of i choosing each possible strategy. More precisely, in our context we assume that with probability x_i (resp. $1 - x_i$), user i will act cooperatively (resp. selfishly). Such randomness yields a so called *mixed strategy*. A mixed strategy is said *pure* if $x_i = 0$ or $x_i = 1$, i.e., when i in fact never varies her strategy.

Let $\mathbf{X} = [0, 1]^{n_h}$ be the set of all possible combinations of n_h honest users' mixed strategies. Given a combination of mixed strategies $x = (x_1, \cdots, x_{n_h}) \in \mathbf{X}$, we denote by x_{-i} the combination $(x_1, x_2, \cdots, x_{i-1}, x_{i+1}, \cdots, x_{n_h})$ of $n_h - 1$ mixed strategies obtained from it by removing i's, and, for a mixed strategy y, we let define

$$(x_{-i}; y) \triangleq (x_1, x_2, \cdots, x_{i-1}, y, x_{i+1}, \cdots, x_{n_h}),$$

which differs from x as user i switches from strategy x_i to y.

Since a user action is determined by its mixed strategy x_i, we rewrite his utility U_i as a function from $\mathbf{X}$ to $\mathbb{R}$ and define the notion of equilibrium as follows.

Definition 2. *For Γ a game, a mixed strategy z is a 'best response' for user i to x_{-i} if*

$$U_i(x_{-i}; z) \geq U_i(x_{-i}; y) \quad \text{for all mixed strategies } y.$$

A combination of strategies $x = (x_1, \cdots, x_{n_h}) \in \mathbf{X}$ is a mixed Nash equilibrium if x_i is a best response to x_{-i}, for $i = 1, \ldots, n_h$; the equilibrium is called a pure Nash Equilibrium if every x_i in x is a pure strategy.

Observe that definition above the just formalises the idea that no user can improve their own utility by unilaterally deviating from the mixed strategy combination x.

Following [12], we compute the Nash equilibrium by studying the players' best-response correspondences. From Definition 2, i's utility maximisation problem is

$$\max_{x_i \in [0,1]} U_i(x_{-i}; x_i).$$

3   CROWDS

For the reader's convenience, we report a detailed description of the CROWDS protocol [24]. In this section, we succinctly recall the fundamental mechanism of the protocol, and the related notion of probable innocence. We opt for the algorithmic description below, where aSend(M,D) represents the anonymous send of a message M to a destination D provided by CROWDS, M ⟶ D a standard communication, and {M}$_\kappa$ a link-encryption via a shared symmetric key κ, of which there exists one for each pair of participants in the protocol. The *forwarding probability* p_f is (together with n) the key parameter, as it determines the average length of the forwarding paths.

```
function aSend(M,D)              function Relay(M,D)
  begin                           begin
    j:= Random_Pick({1,...,n})       if(Flip_biased_coin(p_f))
    {Relay(M,D)}_{κ_j} ⟶ j             M ⟶ D
  end                               else
                                       j:= Random_Pick({1,...,n})
                                       {Relay(M,D)}_{κ_j} ⟶ j
                                    endif
                                  end
```

Replies, if any, travel the path in reverse to reach the initiator. This is realised in the obvious way, whereby j sends any reply back to the user she received the corresponding `Relay` message from.

Reiter and Rubin have proposed in [24] a hierarchy of anonymity notions in the context of CROWDS. These range from '*absolute privacy*,' where the attacker cannot perceive the presence of an actual communication, to '*provably exposed*,' where the attacker can prove a sender-and-receiver relationship. Clearly, as most protocols used in practice, CROWDS cannot ensure absolute privacy in presence of attackers or corrupted users, but can only provide weaker notions of anonymity. In particular, in [24] the authors propose an anonymity notion called *probable innocence* and prove that, under some conditions on the protocol parameters, CROWDS ensures the probable innocence property to the originator. Informally, they define it as follows:

> A sender is probably innocent if, from the attacker's point of view, she appears no more likely to be the originator than to not be the originator. (2)

Since anonymity only makes sense for honest users, we define the set of anonymous events as $\mathcal{A} = \{a_1, a_2, \ldots, a_{n_h}\}$, where a_i indicates that user i is the initiator of the message.

We assume that attackers will always deliver a request to forward immediately to the end server, since forwarding it any further cannot help them learn anything more about the identity of the originator. Thus in any given path, there is at most one detected user: the first honest member to forward the message to a corrupt user. Therefore we define the set of observable events as $O = \{o_1, o_2, \ldots, o_{n_h}\}$, where o_j indicates that user j forwarded a message to a corrupt user. In this case we also say that j *is detected* by the attacker. Halpern and O'Neill in [13] formalised condition (2) mathematically as:

$$P(a_i \mid o_j) \leq \frac{1}{2} \quad \text{for all } i, j. \tag{3}$$

Also, it was proved in [24] as one of the fundamental properties of the framework that, under the assumption that each honest user is equally likely to initiate a transaction (which we adopt in this paper too), probable innocence (2) holds if and only if

$$n \geq \frac{p_f}{p_f - 1/2}(n_m + 1) \quad and \quad p_f \geq \frac{1}{2} \tag{4}$$

We remark that the concept of probable innocence was recently generalised in [14] to encompass the frequent situations where attackers have extra knowledge on users. The idea formalised in [14] is that the gain obtained by the attacker by observing an event must be relative to the knowledge that the attacker has of the users independently of that acquired through the protocol (whence the attribute 'extra'). The authors express the extra information in terms of a random variable S with observable values $s_1 \ldots s_\ell$, and the conditional probabilities $p(s_k \mid a_i)$. Probable innocence in presence of extra information can then be expressed by the condition:

$$P(a_i \mid o_j, s_k) \leq \frac{1}{2} \quad \text{for all } i, j, k. \tag{5}$$

4   Cooperation Analysis in CROWDS

We now specialise our general game model to the setting of CROWDS. Our assumptions identify a tractable yet realistic case for us to analyse how different utility factors affect the users' cooperation behaviour.

Honest users. In CROWDS, paths are static, and each user creates only one path per time period. At the end of the period, all existing paths are destroyed, and a new session starts where each user creates a new path for her anonymous communications. The reason for that is that dynamic paths tend to decrease the overall system anonymity. Therefore, we assume that honest users play the following mixed strategies game: (1) at the beginning of each session, each player i chooses her strategy by flipping a coin governed by her mixed strategy x_i, and then acts accordingly for the entire session;[1] (2) selfish users will only cooperate to route their own messages. Observe that this is a reasonable assumption in CROWDS, since messages are received in cleartext, and can therefore be recognised by their originators.

Attackers. As stated earlier, attackers will always cooperate. Moreover, we assume they do not originate messages, as they focus on de-anonymising the system.[2] Finally, we assume that in their attempt to guess the identity of the initiator, the attackers always bet on the previous user on the path, the so-called detected user, because the latter is the most likely initiator (cf. Proposition 4). That is why we measure the anonymity degree of i against such attackers via the popular metric $P(a_i \mid o_i)$, as expressed in (3) above.

4.1   The Anonymity Analysis

Since the purpose of joining an anonymity system is to enjoy anonymous communications, the anonymity payoff is typically a very important factor for honest users. Each

---

[1] We plan to investigate in future work the case when users may flip their behaviour at each interaction, by resorting to more advanced notions from game theory.

[2] We leave to future work the case where attackers may flood part of the network to break some users' anonymity or to perform DOS attacks; for recent work related see, e.g., [10,4,25].

cooperative user contributes to provide anonymity to all users, including herself. We first focus on how cooperation affects the overall anonymity of the system, and then investigate the anonymity payoffs of individual users.

During the creation of a path initiated by user i, both i and the malicious users will forward i's message with probability 1, while a generic honest user j will do so with probability x_j. Thus, i has on average η_i users to pick from for a path, where

$$\eta_i = 1 + \sum_{j \neq i} x_j + n_m,$$

and $\zeta_i = \eta_i - n_m$ of these are honest. We can then prove that Reiter and Rubin's condition (3) to ensure probable innocence to the initiator i becomes as follows.

Proposition 1. *Let $\overline{x_i}$ be the average cooperation probability of users other than i, viz., $(\sum_{j \neq i} x_j)/(n_h - 1)$, and assume $p_f > 1/2$ and that i is cooperative, i.e., $x_i = 1$. Then, i has probable innocence against n_m malicious users if and only if*

$$n \geq \frac{p_f + (1 - \overline{x_i})/2\overline{x_i}}{p_f - 1/2}(n_m + 1).$$

Proposition 1 can be proved similarly to condition (4), with respect to which it expresses a more stringent constraint on n: indeed, as the honest users may behave less cooperatively, there more users are required in the system altogether to guarantee probable innocence against the same number of malicious users.

4.2   Measuring Anonymity Payoffs

Let $A_i(\_)$ denote i's anonymity payoff function, whose value can be computed using the anonymity degree metric $P(a_i \mid o_j)$, as a function of the honest users' mixed strategies. Since the lower the anonymity degree, the better the anonymity guaranteed, we define $A_i(\_)$ to be $(1 - P(a_i \mid o_j))a$, where the parameter a can be used to normalise the value of a 'unit' of anonymity and $a \geq 0$. Let us start by evaluating the probability $P(o_j \mid a_i)$, for which we obtain the following result.[3]

Proposition 2. $P\left(o_j \mid a_i\right) = \begin{cases} \dfrac{n_m}{\eta_i} + \dfrac{n_m p_f}{\eta_i(\eta_i - \zeta_i p_f)} & i = j \\[3mm] \dfrac{n_m p_f}{\eta_i(\eta_i - \zeta_i p_f)}x_j & i \neq j \end{cases}$

Note that $P(o_j \mid a_i)$ does not depend on x_i, that when i is the initiator, the probability of detecting user j is not influenced by i's strategy. This is because that no matter what strategy i chooses, she will forward her own messages with probability 1.

Now, let us compute the probability of detecting a user $P(o_j)$. Assuming a uniform distribution for anonymous events a_i, the following results hold.

Proposition 3. $P(o_j) = \dfrac{1}{n_h}\left(\dfrac{n_m}{\eta_j} + \dfrac{n_m p_f}{\eta_j(\eta_j - \zeta_j p_f)} + \sum_{k \neq j} \dfrac{n_m x_j p_f}{\eta_k(\eta_k - \zeta_k p_f)} \right).$

---

[3] Due to space limitations, the proofs of Prop. 2 and 3 are omitted. We refer the reader to [28].

Proposition 4. $P(a_i \mid o_j)$ *can be expressed as* $P(o_j \mid a_i)P(a_i)/P(o_j)$ *from Proposition 2 and 3.*

It is easy to show that $P(a_i \mid o_i)$ is a decreasing function of x_i and that, in particular, $P(a_i \mid o_i) = 1$ when $x_i = 0$. Therefore, a fully selfish user has zero anonymity degree.

Corollary 1. $\dfrac{\partial P(a_i \mid o_i)}{\partial x_i} \leq 0.$

Since $A_i(\_)$ is a decreasing function of $P(a_i \mid o_i)$, we have $\dfrac{\partial A_i(x)}{\partial x_i} \geq 0$. Therefore, when anonymity is the sole value taken into account, cooperation is the dominant strategy in CROWDS. Why is then the case that in the real world users often opt for the self-ish behaviour? In the following sections, we shall explain this apparent mismatch by investigating the impact on users' behaviour of cost factor.

4.3 The Cost Analysis

To fulfill the forwarding demands of CROWDS, user i incurs a cost $C_i(\_)$ and which can be evaluated as

$$C_i(\_) = C_{i0} + \sum_{j \leq n_h} C_{ij},$$

where C_{i0} is a fixed cost. i.e., incurred whether or not i is involved in any communication, and C_{ij} is the cost incurred for forwarding messages from j.

In the CROWDS protocol, the expected length of a path is

$$E(L) = \frac{p_f}{1 - p_f} + 2.$$

Each path starts with the initiator while the last node is occupied either by a honest user or by an attacker. The path's internal nodes can only be honest users, because once a malicious user is encountered, the previous user is detected and the path terminated. The expected number of internal nodes is $E(L) - 2$. We can then evaluate the average number of times i appears on her own paths as

$$1 + \frac{E(L) - 2}{\zeta_i} + \frac{1}{\eta_i} = 1 + \frac{p_f/(1 - p_f)}{\zeta_i} + \frac{1}{\eta_i}. \tag{6}$$

Similarly, the average number of times i appears on other users' paths is:

$$\frac{p_f \cdot x_i/(1 - p_f)}{\zeta_j} + \frac{1 \cdot x_i}{\eta_j}.$$

Let us now define τ_i as i's network traffic, i.e., the number of the messages sent by i, and c as the cost of forwarding each single one of them. Assuming that all users will incur the same cost c, we can compute the cost of forwarding by summing up the two cost components above and C_{i0}.

Proposition 5. $C_i(x) = C_{i0} + \left(1 + \frac{p_f/(1-p_f)}{\zeta_i} + \frac{1}{\eta_i}\right)\tau_i c + \sum_{j \neq i}\left(\frac{p_f \cdot x_i/(1-p_f)}{\zeta_j} + \frac{1 \cdot x_i}{\eta_j}\right)\tau_j c$

An immediate consequence is that the x_i derivative of cost is greater than zero.

Corollary 2. $\dfrac{\partial C_i(x)}{\partial x_i} = \sum_{j \neq i} \left(\dfrac{\frac{p_f}{1-p_f}(1+\sum_{k \neq i,j} x_k)}{\zeta_j^2} + \dfrac{1+n_m+\sum_{k \neq i,j} x_k}{\eta_j^2} \right) \tau_j c \geq 0 .$

Clearly, an increase in cooperation level will result in an increase in cost. Thus, if only the cost factor is considered, the dominant strategy in CROWDS is to behave selfishly.

4.4   Balancing between Cost and Anonymity in CROWDS

In this section, we apply our game-theoretic model to the CROWDS protocol when users considers both cost and anonymity factors at the same time. We substitute the cost and anonymity from Propositions 4 and 5 in our utility function, and assume that the normalisation factor a and c are such to put both utility factors on a same scale.

$$U_i(\_) = -\rho_{iC} \left[C_{i0} + \left(1 + \frac{p_f/(1-p_f)}{\zeta_i} + \frac{1}{\eta_i} \right) \tau_i c + \sum_{j \neq i} \left(\frac{p_f \cdot x_i/(1-p_f)}{\zeta_j} + \frac{x_i}{\eta_j} \right) \tau_j c \right]$$

$$+ \rho_{iA} \left[1 - \frac{\dfrac{n_m}{\eta_i} + \dfrac{n_m p_f}{\eta_i(\eta_i - \zeta_i p_f)}}{\dfrac{n_m}{\eta_i} + \dfrac{n_m p_f}{\eta_i(\eta_i - \zeta_i p_f)} + \sum_{k \neq i} \dfrac{n_m x_i p_f}{\eta_k(\eta_k - \zeta_k p_f)}} \right] a .$$

$$\tag{7}$$

Differently from the cases of the anonymity and cost utilities, to find the equilibrium points for $U_i(\_)$ appears to be hard, although we know that there always exists in mixed strategies games. Therefore, in order to illustrate the effect on a user's utility of the combination of the two factors, we resort to simulation techniques, focussing on relevant parameters such as, the user strategy x_i, her choice of factor weights ρ_{iC}, and the number of the attackers in the system. The results are illustrated and discussed below.

In the following simulation, we consider $n_h = 100$, $p_f = 0.8$, $c = 0.1$, $C_{i0} = 5$ and $a = 100$. We assume that the cooperation level for users other than i is uniformly distributed and in the range of $[0, 1]$.

Factors' weights. We first show how the weights of the anonymity and cost factors influence i's strategies. Figure 1 shows $U_i(\_)$ as a function of i' strategy x_i, when the weight attributed to cost varies from 0 to 1. Figure 1b represents the projection of Figure 1a's surface onto the x_i axis, for eleven selected values of ρ_{iC} (from 0 to 1 in 1/10 steps); for each such projection π, Figure 1c plots the value of x_i which maximises π, which attempts to visualise the process of choosing the strategy for i.

Observe that as ρ_{iC} increases from 0 to 1, the equilibrium points x_i decreases: a bias towards anonymity leads to a higher cooperation level for user i.

Number of malicious users. We perform a similar analysis as above (but due to lack of space, in the rest of the paper we omit the figures). This confirms that more malicious users result in smaller utilities for i, as i's anonymity payoffs decrease substantially. In particular, when n_m is equal to 10 and 40 respectively, the maximum utility occurs at

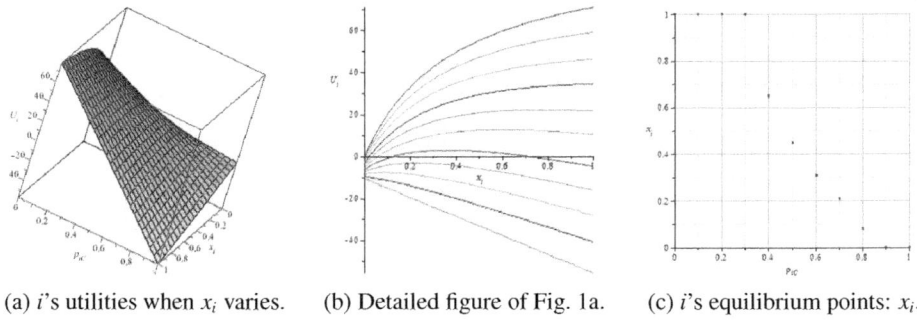

(a) i's utilities when x_i varies.   (b) Detailed figure of Fig. 1a.   (c) i's equilibrium points: x_i.

Fig. 1. $U_i(\_)$ as x_i and ρ_{iC} vary; $(n_m = 10, \tau = 50)$

$x_i = 0.5$, and $x_i = 0.68$ respectively. The values of x_i on equilibrium points are in the range of $[0.4, 0.7]$. Thus the number of malicious users in the system has a minor impact in encouraging or dissuading honest users to behave cooperatively.

Light traffic vs heavy traffic. Regarding the influence of network traffic, in our simulations as the number τ of messages increases from 5 to 80, the utility $U_i(\_)$ decreases considerably, as i incurs a heftier cost. The impact on the value of x_i at the equilibrium points is also significant, covering the interval $[0.35, 1]$. Thus, light traffic encourages the honest users to behave cooperatively more often, whilst heavy traffic pushes them towards selfishness.

Cooperation levels of the honest users other than user i. Here we let $\bar{x}_i$, the average cooperation level of the users other than i, vary from 0 to 1. We find that when the average $\bar{x}_i$ is small, i will tend to behave selfishly to gain more payoff. When instead $\bar{x}_i$ increases, the values of x_i on equilibrium points increase as well. Thus cooperative behaviour of the honest users encourages more cooperative behaviour.

In conclusion, we see that when a user, interested in both anonymity and cost, wants to optimise her utility, she needs to adapt her level of cooperation constantly, as the network topology (e.g., the number of cooperating users and attackers), the traffic level and her own choice of weight factor vary. As cost tend to be a very tangible a value, we can reasonably conclude that it will be a prominent factor for most users. It is therefore very important for anonymity systems to contemplate incentives mechanisms designed to offer tangible benefits to cooperative users. The next section is dedicated to the analysis of the effectiveness of one such mechanism.

5   Adding Incentives: The Analysis of Gold-Star Mechanism

The gold-star mechanism was introduced in Tor [23] to encourage users to act as cooperative relays, and thus enhance the service performance for well-behaved forwarders. We now turn to the *gold-star* incentive mechanism [23] in CROWDS. A request from a user carrying a 'gold star' is given higher priority by other users, i.e., it is always relayed ahead of other traffic. The assignment of gold-star status, in the context of CROWDS, is ruled by the policy *"to have satisfactory cooperation for R times out of the last V measurements."* In accordance with our game in the setting of CROWDS, defined in §4, we assume a measurement is made in each session, and therefore a user obtain a gold-star status if and only if she cooperated in R sessions out of the last V sessions. Let $r = R/V$ be the above ratio. Then a user i will be awarded the gold-star if x_i is greater than or equal to r. We assume that each cooperative user will give priority to gold-star messages even if she is not a gold-star user. There exist mechanisms in the literature to allow anonymous users to accurately and securely report their interactions with their neighbours, whose description in beyond the scope of this paper. Such mechanism will help enforce the gold-star mechanism. Finally, as in its original proposal [23], we assume that the gold-star status are publicly known.

5.1   The Anonymity Analysis with Gold-Star Mechanism

In presence of gold-star mechanism, attackers have an extra information about the initiator due the fact that gold-star status are public. Therefore, we use the anonymity metric encompassing extra knowledge via the conditional probability $P(a_i \mid o_j, s_l)$, as expressed in (5). Here $s_l \in \{s_1, s_2\}$, where $l = 1$ when the message is a gold-star one, and $l = 2$ otherwise.

The correlation between a message status and its initiator, that is the probability $P(s_l \mid a_i)$ is as follows.

$$P(s_1 \mid a_i) = \begin{cases} 1 & x_i \geq r, \\ 0 & x_i < r, \end{cases} \qquad P(s_2 \mid a_i) = \begin{cases} 0 & x_i \geq r, \\ 1 & x_i < r, \end{cases} \qquad (8)$$

Now since for each initiator O and S are independent, from [14], we have

$$P(a_i \mid o_j, s_l) = P(a_i \mid o_j) \frac{P(s_l \mid a_i)}{P(s_l \mid o_j)}.$$

If all honest users are equally likely to initiate a transaction, the probability $P(a_i \mid o_j, s_l)$ can be rewritten as follows.

Proposition 6

$$P(a_i \mid o_j, s_1) = \begin{cases} \dfrac{P(o_j \mid a_i)}{\sum_{x_k \geq r} P(o_j \mid a_k)} & x_i \geq r, \\ 0 & x_i < r, \end{cases} \qquad P(a_i \mid o_j, s_2) = \begin{cases} 0 & x_i \geq r, \\ \dfrac{P(o_j \mid a_i)}{\sum_{x_k < r} P(o_j \mid a_k)} & x_i < r, \end{cases}$$

Now we can prove that the presence of gold-star mechanism reduces the anonymity level of the network. The following indeed holds.

Corollary 3. $P(a_i \mid o_j, s_l) \geq P(a_i \mid o_j)$.

We define GS as the set of users j who have gold-star, i.e., $x_j \geq r$, and GS^c as the complement set of those who do not, $x_j < r$. If user i is the only element in either set, then there is no anonymity guaranteed for i, given malicious users are on the path.

We again define the anonymity payoffs as $A_i(\_) = \left(1 - P(a_i \mid o_i, s_l)\right)a$, the anonymity payoffs for unincentivised CROWDS and gold-star CROWDS are respectively evaluated as

Proposition 7. – *Unincentivised* CROWDS *(cf. Proposition 4):*

$$A_i(\_) = \left(1 - \frac{\dfrac{n_m}{\eta_i} + \dfrac{n_m p_f}{\eta_i(\eta_i - \zeta_i p_f)}}{\dfrac{n_m}{\eta_i} + \dfrac{n_m p_f}{\eta_i(\eta_i - \zeta_i p_f)} + \displaystyle\sum_{k \neq i} \dfrac{n_m x_i p_f}{\eta_k(\eta_k - \zeta_k p_f)}}\right)a$$

– *Gold-star* CROWDS:

$$A_i(\_) = \left(1 - \frac{\dfrac{n_m}{\eta_i} + \dfrac{n_m p_f}{\eta_i(\eta_i - \zeta_i p_f)}}{\dfrac{n_m}{\eta_i} + \dfrac{n_m p_f}{\eta_i(\eta_i - \zeta_i p_f)} + \displaystyle\sum_{k \neq i, k \in \phi(i)} \dfrac{n_m x_i p_f}{\eta_k(\eta_k - \zeta_k p_f)}}\right)a$$

where $\phi(i) = GS$ if $i \in GS$, $\phi(i) = GS^c$ otherwise.

For the unincentivised CROWDS, since $\dfrac{\partial A_i(\_)}{\partial x_i} \geq 0$, behaving cooperatively will bring i maximum anonymity payoffs. However in gold-star CROWDS, $A_i(\_)$ also depends on the number of users in the set which i belongs to. More users in such set leads to better anonymity provided for i. When CROWDS starts out with a small number of gold star relays, i has to behave selfishly more often in order not to be rewarded gold-star, and hence gains more anonymity payoffs.

$A_i(\_)$ is an increasing function depending on x_i in the following two ranges:

– if $0 \leq x_i < r$, then $\dfrac{\partial A_i(\_)}{\partial x_i} \geq 0$;

– if $r \leq x_i \leq 1$, then $\dfrac{\partial A_i(\_)}{\partial x_i} \geq 0$.

We observe that $A_i(\_)$ is a discontinuous function, with a discontinuity at $x_i = r$. Thus maximum points in the two ranges above occur at the extremes, $x_i = r$, and $x_i = 1$, respectively, and the equilibrium behaviour of i will ultimately depend on which of these is larger. If $A_i(x_{-i}; r) \geq A_i(x_{-i}; 1)$, then i will behave according to $x_i = r$ to reach the tipping point and gain the gold-star. If instead $A_i(x_{-i}; r) \leq A_i(x_{-i}; 1)$, then the dominant strategy for i is cooperative.

5.2 The Performance Analysis

We will use $P_i(x_{-i}; 1)$ and $P_i(x_{-i}; 0)$ to denote i's performance payoffs when she behaves cooperative or selfish, respectively. Thus, the expected performance payoff for i can be evaluated as

$$P_i(\_) = P_i(x_{-i}; x_i) = x_i P_i(x_{-i}; 1) + (1 - x_i)P_i(x_{-i}; 0) \tag{9}$$

Following [23], the factor P_i here is interpreted as *forwarding time T_i*: the shorter the forwarding time, the better the system performance. Thus we assume $P_i(\_) = (-T_i)p$ where p represents the benefit of each unit of performance.

For the reader's convenience, we summarise here the notation and names we shall be using in the analysis in the rest of the section.

b: the size of messages sent by initiators;
$f_j^{\mathcal{C}}$: the number of messages waiting at position j in the forwarding path, when the forwarder at j has strategy cooperative ;
$f_j^{\mathcal{C}-\mathcal{S}}$: as above, but excepting the messages sent by selfish users;
n_{ri}: the number of forwarders on the path i initiated;
Q: the bandwidth of each user. Here we assume each user has the same bandwidth.

The total forwarding time T_i for user i is equal to the sum of the forwarding times of all $n_{ri} + 1$ nodes in user i's path. We start by evaluating the expected forwarding time for cooperative users. The first relay is i herself and the forwarding time t_1 is

$$t_1 = \frac{b(f_1^{\mathcal{C}} + 1)}{Q}. \tag{10}$$

The forwarding time of cooperative users at position jth can be computed the same as Eq. 10. The cooperative users appear in the path with the probability $p(j, \mathcal{C}) = 1$ in that selfish users will not forward the messages initiated by the users other than themselves, thus

$$t_j = t_j(\mathcal{C})\, p(j, \mathcal{C}) = \frac{b(f_j^{\mathcal{C}} + 1)}{Q} \times 1.$$

Given that the total forwarding time T_i is equal to $t_1 + \sum_{j=2}^{n_{ri}+1} t_j$, we can express the performance payoffs of cooperative users as follows, where we denote by $\varnothing$ the 'no-incentive' mechanism

$$P_{\varnothing i}(x_{-i}; 1) = -\left(t_1 + \sum_{j=2}^{n_{ri}+1} t_j\right) \cdot p = -\left[\frac{b(f_1^{\mathcal{C}} + 1)}{Q} + \sum_{j=2}^{n_{ri}+1} \frac{b(f_j^{\mathcal{C}} + 1)}{Q}\right]p \tag{11}$$

The payoff function of the selfish user strategy can be evaluated along similar lines; the resulting formula is shown in (12).

$$P_{\varnothing i}(x_{-i}; 0) = -\left(\frac{b}{Q} + \sum_{j=2}^{n_{ri}} \left(\frac{\zeta_i - 1}{\zeta_i} \frac{b(f_j^{\mathcal{C}} + 1)}{Q} + \frac{1}{\zeta_i}\frac{b}{Q}\right) + \frac{\eta_i - 1}{\eta_i} \frac{b(f_j^{\mathcal{C}} + 1)}{Q} + \frac{1}{\eta_i}\frac{b}{Q}\right)p \tag{12}$$

We now turn to the *gold-star* incentive mechanism [23] in CROWDS. The development is similar to that in the above computations. The messages marked with a gold star, sent by cooperative users, have higher priority. There are then $bf_j^{\mathcal{C}-\mathcal{S}}$ KB rather than $bf_j^{\mathcal{C}}$ KB before i's requests at the jth position of the path. Let $\star$ denote the gold-star mechanism, we then evaluate $P_{\star i}(x_{-i}; 1)$ as

$$P_{\star i}(x_{-i}; 1) = -\left(t_1 + \sum_{j=2}^{n_{ri}+1} t_j\right)p = -\sum_{j=1}^{n_{ri}+1} \frac{b(f_j^{\mathcal{C}-\mathcal{S}} + 1)}{Q}p \tag{13}$$

The performance payoff of selfish strategy is shown below in Eq. (14).

$$P_{\star i}(x_{-i}; 0) = - \left(\frac{b}{Q} + \sum_{j=2}^{n_{ri}} \left(\frac{\zeta_i - 1}{\zeta_i} \frac{bf_j^{\mathcal{C}} + b}{Q} + \frac{1}{\zeta_i} \frac{b}{Q} \right) + \frac{\eta_i - 1}{\eta_i} \frac{bf_j^{\mathcal{C}} + b}{Q} + \frac{1}{\eta_i} \frac{b}{Q} \right) p \quad (14)$$

Since the utility $P_i(\_)$ of a fixed user depends on factors that may change very often at different forwarding paths, we instead consider the average payoffs $P_i(x_{-i}; 1)$ and $P_i(x_{-i}; 0)$ of cooperative and selfish users, respectively for each forwarding path. We define $\overline{f^{\mathcal{C}}}$ (resp. $\overline{f^{\mathcal{C}-\mathcal{S}}}$) as the average number of messages (resp. gold-star messages) waiting for a cooperative user. We also define the average n_{ri} as n_r.

According to Eq. (9), we have the performance payoffs for i in unincentivised CROWDS and gold-star CROWDS as

Proposition 8

$$P_{\varnothing i}(x_{-i}; x_i) = -\frac{bp\overline{f^{\mathcal{C}}}x_i}{Q} \left(n_r(1 - \frac{\zeta_i - 1}{\zeta_i}) + \frac{\zeta_i - 1}{\zeta_i} + \frac{1}{\eta_i} \right)$$
$$- \frac{bp}{Q} \left(n_r + 1 + \overline{f^{\mathcal{C}}} \left(\frac{(n_r - 1)(\zeta_i - 1)}{\zeta_i} + \frac{\eta_i - 1}{\eta_i} \right) \right)$$

$$P_{\star i}(x_{-i}; x_i) = \frac{bpx_i}{Q} \left(\overline{f^{\mathcal{C}}} \left(\frac{(n_r - 1)(\zeta_i - 1)}{\zeta_i} + \frac{\eta_i - 1}{\eta_i} \right) - \overline{f^{\mathcal{C}-\mathcal{S}}}(n_r + 1) \right)$$
$$- \frac{bp}{Q} \left(n_r + 1 + \overline{f^{\mathcal{C}}} \left(\frac{(n_r - 1)(\zeta_i - 1)}{\zeta_i} + \frac{\eta_i - 1}{\eta_i} \right) \right)$$

Let α define the ratio $\overline{f^{\mathcal{C}-\mathcal{S}}}/\overline{f^{\mathcal{C}}}$. It actually represents the percentage of users who have gold star among the all honest users, $0 \leq \alpha \leq 1$ in that if α is relatively small, then it reflects not many users are rewarded the gold-star. Then we study the x_i derivative of the performance payoffs, we have

Proposition 9.   – *Unincentivised* CROWDS

$$\frac{\partial P_{\varnothing i}(x_{-i}; x_i)}{\partial x_i} \leq 0$$

– *Gold-star* CROWDS: *if* $\alpha \leq \dfrac{n_r - 1}{n_r + 1} \dfrac{\zeta_i - 1}{\zeta_i} + \dfrac{1}{n_r + 1} \dfrac{\eta_i - 1}{\eta_i}$ *holds, then*

$$\frac{\partial P_{\star i}(x_{-i}; x_i)}{\partial x_i} \geq 0.$$

5.3 Balancing between Performance and Anonymity

By applying our game-theoretic model to the gold-star CROWDS, we consider anonymity and performance factors in this section. We substitute the anonymity and performance payoff equations Proposition 7 and 8 to our utility function, we obtain:

– Unincentivised CROWDS:

$$U_i(\_) = \rho_{iA}\left[1 - \frac{\dfrac{n_m}{\eta_i} + \dfrac{n_m p_f}{\eta_i(\eta_i - \zeta_i p_f)}}{\dfrac{n_m}{\eta_i} + \dfrac{n_m p_f}{\eta_i(\eta_i - \zeta_i p_f)} + \displaystyle\sum_{k \neq i} \dfrac{n_m x_i p_f}{\eta_k(\eta_k - \zeta_k p_f)}}\right] a$$

$$+\rho_{iP}\left(-\frac{bp\overline{f^{\mathbb{C}}}x_i}{Q}\left(n_r(1 - \frac{\zeta_i - 1}{\zeta_i}) + \frac{\zeta_i - 1}{\zeta_i} + \frac{1}{\eta_i}\right)\right.$$

$$\left. -\frac{bp}{Q}\left(n_r + 1 + \overline{f^{\mathbb{C}}}\left(\frac{(n_r - 1)(\zeta_i - 1)}{\zeta_i} + \frac{\eta_i - 1}{\eta_i}\right)\right)\right)$$

– Gold-star CROWDS:

$$U_i(\_) = \rho_{iA}\left[1 - \frac{\dfrac{n_m}{\eta_i} + \dfrac{n_m p_f}{\eta_i(\eta_i - \zeta_i p_f)}}{\dfrac{n_m}{\eta_i} + \dfrac{n_m p_f}{\eta_i(\eta_i - \zeta_i p_f)} + \displaystyle\sum_{k \neq i, k \in \phi} \dfrac{n_m x_i p_f}{\eta_k(\eta_k - \zeta_k p_f)}}\right] a$$

$$+\rho_{iP}\left(\frac{bp x_i}{Q}\left(\overline{f^{\mathbb{C}}}\left(\frac{(n_r - 1)(\zeta_i - 1)}{\zeta_i} + \frac{\eta_i - 1}{\eta_i}\right) - \overline{f^{\mathbb{C}-\mathcal{S}}}(n_r + 1)\right)\right.$$

$$\left. -\frac{bp}{Q}\left(n_r + 1 + \overline{f^{\mathbb{C}}}\left(\frac{(n_r - 1)(\zeta_i - 1)}{\zeta_i} + \frac{\eta_i - 1}{\eta_i}\right)\right)\right)$$

where $\phi(i) = GS$ if $i \in GS$, $\phi(i) = GS^c$ otherwise.

From the above equations, we derive the following proposition.

Proposition 10. *In gold-star* CROWDS, *if* $\alpha \leq \dfrac{n_r - 1}{n_r + 1}\dfrac{\zeta_i - 1}{\zeta_i} + \dfrac{1}{n_r + 1}\dfrac{\eta_i - 1}{\eta_i}$ *holds, then*

$$\frac{\partial U_i(\_)}{\partial x_i} \geq 0 \text{ when } x_i \in [0, r); \qquad \frac{\partial U_i(\_)}{\partial x_i} \geq 0 \text{ when } x_i \in [r, 1],$$

and function $U_i(\_)$ *is discontinuous at the point* $x_i = r$.

We run simulations to illustrate the equilibrium points of i strategies in different situations. We consider $n_h = 100$, $n_r = 3$, $b = 100$, $Q = 500$, $a = 100$ and $p = 1$. We assume the cooperation level for users j other than i is uniformly distributed and in the range of $[0, 1]$. We start with the case of **unincentivised** CROWDS.

Factors' weights. As we did in §4.4, we first show how the weights of the anonymity and performance factors influence i's strategies. In our simulations, as the weight attributed to performance varies from 0 to 1, $U_i(\_)$ varies as a function of i's strategy x_i. As ρ_{iP} keeps increasing from 0 to 1, the equilibrium points x_i decrease. Higher weight towards anonymity factor leads to higher cooperation level of user i.

Number of malicious users. More malicious users result in smaller anonymity but greater performance payoffs for i. In particular, when n_m varies from 2 and 80, the values of x_i on equilibrium points are in the range of $[0.2, 0.43]$. Thus the number of malicious users has a minor impact in encouraging or dissuading cooperation behaviours of honest users.

Light traffic vs heavy traffic. In our simulations, as the average number $\overline{f^e}$ of messages waiting at the forwarders increases from 0 to 10, the utility $U_i(\_)$ decreases, so that i incurs more delivery time. The values of x_i on equilibrium points decrease as well, from 1 to 0.18. Thus, like before, light traffic encourages more frequent cooperation by honest users, while heavy traffic suggests them selfishness.

Cooperation levels of the honest users other than user i. Regarding the influence of users' behaviours, we find that when the average $\overline{x}_j$ is small, i will be willing to behave cooperatively more often to gain more payoff. When $\overline{x}_j$ increases, the values of x_i on equilibrium points decrease until 0.37. Thus, cooperative behaviours of the honest users other than i do not encourage more cooperative behaviours of i.

Moving to analyse *Gold-star* CROWDS, we consider the following parameter settings: $\rho_{iP} = 0.5$, $n_m = 10$, $\overline{f^e} = 3$, $\overline{f^{e-s}} = (1-r)\overline{f^e}$ in our simulations. When r varies as 0.8, 0.7 and 0.6 respectively, the equilibrium points for i are $x_i = 0.8$, $x_i = 0.7$ and $x = 1$, respectively. They are better than those in unincentivised CROWDS.

Note that the first two x_i of equilibrium points are exactly the values of rule r. We find that before x_i increases to r, both the anonymity and performance payoffs increase as x_i increases. Then, when x_i exceeds r, the performance payoff increases further, whilst the anonymity payoff depends on the number of gold-star users. In this simulation, when i gets the gold-star, the anonymity payoff of i is smaller than that when i has not. This is because, since x_j is uniformly distributed and $r = 0.8$, the number of gold-star users is smaller than the number of users without gold-star. Thus by balancing with performance payoffs, i chooses her strategy as $x_i = r$. The third x_i is 1, because from r to 1 the performance payoff keeps increasing while the the anonymity payoff increases as well. On the point $x_i = 1$, the balanced payoffs ($U_i = 38.9139$) of performance and anonymity have exceed the previous maximum payoffs ($U_i(\_) = 34.6699$) where $x_i = 0.6$.

We do simulations by varying n_m, $\overline{f^e}$, and find the shapes of the lines are the same as those of the above simulations. Therefore, as we proved in Proposition 10, i's strategy depends on the comparison of $U_i(\_)$ on $x_i = r$ and $x_i = 1$.

6   Related Work

The anonymity systems and protocols are typically based on a suitable infrastructure for forwarding messages. For instance, the CROWDS protocol [24] requires a set of users or peers willing to route each others' requests. In other cases where they do not directly require 'forwarders' – as e.g. for single-hop web proxies like the *Anonymizer* protocol [3] – they rely on the obfuscation of network traffic provided by the activity of a (large) set of users. The number of users who forward requests or join in the infrastructure determines the anonymity degree of the systems. A point in case is the Tor protocol [9]. Although Tor has built a significant community of volunteer forwarders, if at any time the user-to-relay ratio becomes too small, then all users will be affected, and will receive a lower-security service [23].

To address these problems, researchers in anonymity networks have considered mechanisms to incentivise cooperation [23,16]. The '*gold star*' mechanism in Tor [23] encourages users to act as cooperative relays, by enhancing the service performance for well-behaved forwarders. Indeed, relays which provide a good service to other users get the gold-star reward, and messages sent by gold-star holders are given higher relay priority, i.e. they are always relayed ahead of other traffic. Tor's management algorithms routinely scans existing directory authorities to actively measure each user' performance, and only grant the gold star where appropriate. Users of BRAIDS [16] anonymously 'pay' Tor relays with generic tickets according to the three hierarchical service classes. This allows the users to earn credits which they can redeem against improved traffic performance in Tor. Some mechanisms were proposed to encourage peers to act cooperatively in P2P systems. These include, e.g., payment schemes, which charge for anonymity services and/or reward good user behaviour; and reputation schemes, where users with higher reputation get higher-quality service. PAR [2] and XPay [7] are payment mechanisms: they produce monetary incentives by using e-cash and an online bank. Reputation schemes [8,27,29] use interaction histories to develop trust levels for members in the systems; this encourages trustworthy behaviour and incentives future cooperative behaviours. Some reputation schemes are however incompatible with anonymity systems, as relays cannot always link interactions to users.

In this paper we model user behaviours in the anonymity systems as non-cooperative games. In the context of network security, game-theoretic models have primarily been used to address problems related to free-riding in P2P systems [18] and distributed intrusion detection [5,17,26]. In [18], game theory has been used to characterise peer selfishness and provide incentives for peers to contribute their upload capacities. The work closest to ours is [1], where the authors study incentive systems for four types of users and in doing so lay the foundations for a game-theory approach to modelling anonymity infrastructures. Their model is based on mix-nets [6]. Although quite general, such model cannot accommodate the evaluation of specialised utility functions in the context of specific anonymity protocols. Each player in *loc. cit.* belongs to one of only four types (viz., user, honest node, dishonest node and sender), and in each type all players behave uniformly. Finally, [1] assume that traffic is distributed uniformly across nodes, which clearly may not be a realistic assumption: e.g., in reputation-based networks users are obviously more likely to ask relays with high reputation as forwarders for the messages. In such cases, the anonymity degree differ for each user [25].

7   Conclusion

The effectiveness of anonymity networks depends heavily on the number of cooperative users. In this paper, we investigated the incentives for users to behave cooperative or selfish in such networks. We proposed a game theoretic framework and used it to analyse users' behaviours and also predict what strategies users will choose under different circumstances and according to their exact balance of preferences among factors such as anonymity, performance (message delivery time) and cost. To allow to trade-off against each others quantities as different as cost (measured in, say, dollars) and anonymity (measured in the interval [0,1]), the model uses multiplicative parameters (*viz.*, a and c) to map them to a common or standard scale. Significantly, we also used the model to assess the effectiveness of the gold-star incentive mechanism.

We studied the phenomenon that in the original Crowds protocol users have little incentive to act cooperatively beyond the minimum required to remain probabilistically anonymous, as cooperation incurs a cost which reflects in the user suffering a utility loss. We then investigated the effectiveness of gold-star mechanism when implemented in Crowds. We showed that the gold-star mechanism does create incentives for users to cooperate exactly when the performance incentives cover the cost of forwarding other users' messages. Depending on the amount of performance incentives, users will be willing to be cooperative all the time, or they will choose the Nash equilibrium mixed strategy, which gains them maximum utility. We observed that the mechanism can become de-anonymising when there are not enough gold-star users, as gold-star messages then carry a strong clue about their originators. To factor this in, our analysis used an anonymity measure which takes into account the attackers' extra knowledge, i.e., the a priori knowledge they may acquire besides the protocol. In order for the mechanism to remain effective, the system must therefore enforce a minimum number of gold-star users in the system, and relax the condition for obtaining gold-star status when the threshold is not met. Observe that although the gold-star mechanism was conceived for Tor, in order to keep the paper self-contained, here we have formulated its concepts and mechanisms on Crowds. We expect no major difficulties to translate the present results back to Tor, by applying our game model to the relays, which in fact are the entities the gold-star mechanism was designed for. Also, he plan to validate our model of Tor by comparing the predictions made through it with existing results in the literature (viz., the simulations in the original gold-star paper [23]). We believe that by restricting to relays, we can apply the game-theoretic framework to Tor, and the performance analysis can be translated back. We are currently working on mixed anonymity/performance/cost utilities in Tor, which appears to be more complex.

A cost model alternative to bandwidth is a relay's liability for the traffic emerging from it. This generates interesting issues. For instance it may create a deficit of exit nodes, as relay do not drop messages to save bandwidth, but keep relaying them to avoid liability for their delivery. This is tantamount to a user fiddling with the forwarding parameter p_f, and goes beyond the cooperative vs selfish choice. Our investigation in this paper focused on the cooperative/selfish forwarding behaviours in Crowds, where p_f is fixed and equal for all users. We leave the study of the important *liability* payoff for future work.

Modelling performance payoffs is useful in real-world scenarios, in that it allows researchers to make good and useable predictions with no or only minor resort to simulations. We believe that this is a significant contribution, as simulations can be taxing in terms of computational power as well as time.

Differently from previous work, our utility functions are not limited to anonymity aspects, but are composed of independently-configurable factors which allow us to model different types of users as well as adapt the model to specific applications. This adds a good deal of flexibility to our game model. In particular, it makes the model more suitable for *asymmetric* anonymity systems, i.e., systems where users differ from each other by means of different payoffs and utility functions. Also, we employ our model to study the *Nash strategies* and *dominant strategies* for users in the game. We are not aware of previous work in this line.

In future work, we plan to refine the model and, more specifically, adapt the techniques presented here to *cooperative games* in the presence of irrational players and more complex utilities. This will allow us to take into account more kinds of attack, and model the fact that attacks targeted to specific users may definitely affect their utilities. For instance, a 'denial-of-service' attack will impact adversely the effectiveness of reputation-based incentive mechanisms, whilst the gold-star scheme will suffer from 'intersection attacks' on anonymity. We also plan to compare different anonymity systems, such as, CROWDS, onion routing, Mix-net in our model, to study which incentive schemes are better suited to each of them.

References

1. Acquisti, A., Dingledine, R., Syverson, P.F.: On the Economics of Anonymity. In: Wright, R.N. (ed.) FC 2003. LNCS, vol. 2742, pp. 84–102. Springer, Heidelberg (2003)
2. Androulaki, E., Raykova, M., Srivatsan, S., Stavrou, A., Bellovin, S.M.: PAR: Payment for Anonymous Routing. In: Borisov, N., Goldberg, I. (eds.) PETS 2008. LNCS, vol. 5134, pp. 219–236. Springer, Heidelberg (2008)
3. The anonymizer, http://www.anonymizer.com
4. Borisov, N., Danezis, G., Mittal, P., Tabriz, P.: Denial of service or denial of security? In: Proceedings of the 14th ACM Conference on Computer and Communications Security, CCS 2007, pp. 92–102. ACM, New York (2007)
5. Bye, R., Luther, K., Çamtepe, S.A., Alpcan, T., Albayrak, Ş., Yener, B.: Decentralized Detector Generation in Cooperative Intrusion Detection Systems. In: Masuzawa, T., Tixeuil, S. (eds.) SSS 2007. LNCS, vol. 4838, pp. 37–51. Springer, Heidelberg (2007)
6. Chaum, D.: Untraceable electronic mail, return addresses, and digital pseudonyms. Commun. ACM 24(2), 84–88 (1981)
7. Chen, Y., Sion, R., Carbunar, B.: Xpay: practical anonymous payments for tor routing and other networked services. In: Al-Shaer, E., Paraboschi, S. (eds.) WPES, pp. 41–50. ACM (2009)
8. Damiani, E., di Vimercati, S.D.C., Paraboschi, S., Samarati, P., Violante, F.: A reputation-based approach for choosing reliable resources in peer-to-peer networks. In: Atluri, V. (ed.) ACM Conference on Computer and Communications Security, pp. 207–216. ACM (2002)
9. Dingledine, R., Mathewson, N., Syverson, P.F.: Tor: The second-generation onion router. In: USENIX Security Symposium, pp. 303–320. USENIX (2004)
10. Dingledine, R., Shmatikov, V., Syverson, P.: Synchronous batching: From cascades to free routes, pp. 186–206 (2004)
11. Freedman, M.J., Morris, R.: Tarzan: a peer-to-peer anonymizing network layer. In: ACM Conference on Computer and Communications Security, pp. 193–206 (2002)
12. Fudenberg, D., Tirole, J.: Game Theory. MIT Press (1991)
13. Halpern, J.Y., O'Neill, K.R.: Anonymity and information hiding in multiagent systems. Journal of Computer Security 13(3), 483–512 (2005)
14. Hamadou, S., Palamidessi, C., Sassone, V., ElSalamouny, E.: Probable Innocence in the Presence of Independent Knowledge. In: Degano, P., Guttman, J.D. (eds.) FAST 2009. LNCS, vol. 5983, pp. 141–156. Springer, Heidelberg (2010)

15. Hopper, N., Vasserman, E.Y., Chan-Tin, E.: How much anonymity does network latency leak? ACM Trans. Inf. Syst. Secur. 13(2) (2010)
16. Jansen, R., Hopper, N., Kim, Y.: Recruiting new tor relays with braids. In: Al-Shaer, E., Keromytis, A.D., Shmatikov, V. (eds.) ACM Conference on Computer and Communications Security, pp. 319–328. ACM (2010)
17. Liu, Y., Comaniciu, C., Man, H.: Modelling misbehaviour in ad hoc networks: a game theoretic approach for intrusion detection. IJSN 1(3/4), 243–254 (2006)
18. Ma, R., Lee, S., Lui, J., Yau, D.: A game theoretic approach to provide incentive and service differentiation in P2P networks. ACM SIGMETRICS Performance Evaluation Review 32(1), 189–198 (2004)
19. McLachlan, J., Tran, A., Hopper, N., Kim, Y.: Scalable onion routing with Torsk. In: Al-Shaer, E., Jha, S., Keromytis, A.D. (eds.) ACM Conference on Computer and Communications Security, pp. 590–599. ACM (2009)
20. Murdoch, S.J., Danezis, G.: Low-cost traffic analysis of tor. In: IEEE Symposium on Security and Privacy, pp. 183–195. IEEE Computer Society (2005)
21. Nambiar, A., Wright, M.: Salsa: a structured approach to large-scale anonymity. In: Juels, A., Wright, R.N., di Vimercati, S.D.C. (eds.) ACM Conference on Computer and Communications Security, pp. 17–26. ACM (2006)
22. Neff, C.A.: A verifiable secret shuffle and its application to e-voting. In: ACM Conference on Computer and Communications Security, pp. 116–125 (2001)
23. "Johnny" Ngan, T.-W., Dingledine, R., Wallach, D.S.: Building Incentives into Tor. In: Sion, R. (ed.) FC 2010. LNCS, vol. 6052, pp. 238–256. Springer, Heidelberg (2010)
24. Reiter, M.K., Rubin, A.D.: Crowds: Anonymity for web transactions. ACM Trans. Inf. Syst. Secur. 1(1), 66–92 (1998)
25. Sassone, V., Hamadou, S., Yang, M.: Trust in Anonymity Networks. In: Gastin, P., Laroussinie, F. (eds.) CONCUR 2010. LNCS, vol. 6269, pp. 48–70. Springer, Heidelberg (2010)
26. Lye, K.W., Wing, J.M.: Game strategies in network security. Int. J. Inf. Sec. 4(1-2), 71–86 (2005)
27. Xiong, L., Liu, L.: Peertrust: Supporting reputation-based trust for peer-to-peer electronic communities. IEEE Trans. Knowl. Data Eng. 16(7), 843–857 (2004)
28. Yang, M., Sassone, V., Hamadou, S.: A game-theoretic analysis of cooperation in anonymity networks. Extended version of this paper available at,
http://eprints.ecs.soton.ac.uk/23091
29. Zhou, R., Hwang, K.: Powertrust: A robust and scalable reputation system for trusted peer-to-peer computing. IEEE Trans. Parallel Distrib. Syst. 18(4), 460–473 (2007)

Deciding Selective Declassification of Petri Nets

Eike Best[1] and Philippe Darondeau[2]

[1] Parallel Systems, Department of Computing Science
Carl von Ossietzky Universität Oldenburg, D-26111 Oldenburg, Germany
eike.best@informatik.uni-oldenburg.de
[2] INRIA, Centre Rennes - Bretagne Atlantique
Campus de Beaulieu, F-35042 Rennes Cedex
Philippe.Darondeau@inria.fr

Abstract. This paper considers declassification, as effected by *down-grading* actions D, in the context of *intransitive non-interference* encountered in systems that consist of *high-level* (secret) actions H and *low-level* (public) actions L. In a previous paper, we have shown the decidability of a strong form of declassification, by which D contains only a single action $d \in D$ declassifying all H actions at once. The present paper continues this study by considering *selective declassification*, where each transition $d \in D$ can declassify a subset $H(d)$ of H. The decidability of this more flexible, application-prone declassification framework is proved in the context of (possibly unbounded) Petri nets with possibly infinite state spaces.

1   Introduction

This work has been inspired by papers by Gorrieri et al., especially [2,5], which contain structurally defined security properties for Petri nets describing systems with high-level (secret) and low-level (public) transitions. In particular, the NDC property (non-distinguishability with respect to composition [2]) defines security in terms of parallel compositions with (almost) arbitrary other systems. While this is an intuitively appealing concept, it is desirable, for formally handling it, to obtain a characterisation based on transition systems. In [1], we provided such a characterisation and we used it in order to prove the decidability of NDC for (possibly unbounded) Petri nets. Moreover, we extended this investigation to the property INI (intransitive non-interference) defined in [5], which generalises the NDC property to systems exhibiting downgrading actions in addition to secret and public ones. The idea is that downgrading actions *declassify* (i.e., turn public) previously executed secret activity. In [1], the decidability of such a property was obtained as well.

The downgrading technique defined in [5,1] appears to be quite coarse, however, in the sense that a single downgrading action declassifies the entire set of secret actions. As suggested e.g. in [5], *selective* downgrading is more likely to be of practical interest. In this approach, declassification can be targeted selectively towards subsets of high-level actions (not necessarily the whole set). Thus, a subset of high-level actions may be associated with every downgrading action, and

P. Degano and J.D. Guttman (Eds.): POST 2012, LNCS 7215, pp. 290–308, 2012.

those subsets may differ from one downgrading action to the next. [1] contains neither a definition of such systems, nor any investigation of their decidability. These gaps are closed in the present paper.

2   Basic Definitions and Decidability Results

A *PT-net* is a triple $N = (P, T, F)$, where P and T are *finite* disjoint sets of vertices, called *places* and *transitions*, respectively, and $F \colon (P \times T) \cup (T \times P) \to \mathbb{N}$ is a set of directed edges with non-negative integer weights. A place p is said to be in *ordinary self-loop* with a transition t if $F(p, t) = 1$ and $F(t, p) = 1$.

A *marking* of N is a map $M \colon P \to \mathbb{N}$. A transition $t \in T$ is *enabled* at a marking M (notation: $M[t\rangle$) if $M(p) \geq F(p, t)$ for all places $p \in P$. If t is enabled at M, then it can *be fired*, leading to the new marking M' (notation: $M[t\rangle M'$) defined by $M'(p) = M(p) + F(t, p) - F(p, t)$ for all $p \in P$. These definitions are extended inductively to transition sequences $\sigma \in T^*$: for the empty sequence ε, $M[\varepsilon\rangle$ and $M[\varepsilon\rangle M$ are always true; for a non-empty sequence σt with $t \in T$, $M[\sigma t\rangle$ (or $M[\sigma t\rangle M'$) iff $M[\sigma\rangle M''$ and $M''[t\rangle$ (or $M''[t\rangle M'$, respectively) for some M''. A marking M' is *reachable* from a marking M if $M[\sigma\rangle M'$ for some $\sigma \in T^*$. The set of markings reachable from M is denoted by $[M\rangle$.

Let V be any alphabet. For words $w, v \in V^*$ and a set of letters $U \subseteq V$, let $w \sim_U v$ denote the fact that the projection of w onto letters of U equals the projection of v onto letters of U. A (transition-) *labelling* of a net (P, T, F) is a function $\lambda \colon T \to V \uplus \{\varepsilon\}$. Transitions t with $\lambda(t) \in V$ are called *visible*, while those with $\lambda(t) = \varepsilon$ are called *invisible*. The function λ can be extended to $\lambda \colon T^* \to V^*$ as follows: $\lambda(\varepsilon) = \varepsilon$ and $\lambda(\sigma t) = \lambda(\sigma)\lambda(t)$. The label ε here plays the role of the empty word in V^*.

In later parts of the paper, several behavioral notions will be investigated. Such notions usually depend both on some marking and on the labelling of a net. As it is normally clear from the context which marking and which labelling are meant, we will often take the liberty of denoting by N variously some net (P, T, F) or some marked net (P, T, F, M_0) or some marked labelled net (P, T, F, M_0, λ).

Let N denote a net with initial marking M_0 and labelling λ. The (prefix) language of N is the set of words

$$L(N) \;=\; \{w \in V^* \mid \exists \text{ firing sequence } M_0[\sigma\rangle \text{ such that } \lambda(\sigma) = w\}.$$

Two (initially marked and labelled) nets N_1, N_2 are called *language-equivalent* iff $L(N_1) = L(N_2)$. A labelling λ is called *plain* if $\lambda(t) \in V$ for all t, i.e., all transitions are visible. A labelling λ is called *injective* if $\lambda(t_1) = \lambda(t_2) \in V$ implies $t_1 = t_2$. In an injectively labelled net, the labels of the visible transitions can be identified with these transitions, and the rest of the transitions are invisible. In the main part of this paper, we will be concerned exclusively with injective labellings, so that it will be sufficient to designate the subset of transitions that are to be considered as visible. In particular, we can then just use the terminology "N_1 and N_2 are language-equivalent with respect to some set of transitions V".

We shall need the following known decidability results. Their proofs and original sources can be found in [11].

1. Given a net N and a place s. It is decidable whether there exists a reachable marking M with $M(s) > 0$.
2. Given two labelled nets N_1 and N_2 where N_2 is plainly and injectively labelled. It is decidable whether $L(N_1) \subseteq L(N_2)$. A stronger statement is the following:
3. Given two labelled nets N_1 and N_2 where N_2 is plainly and injectively labelled, and a regular language K. It is decidable whether $(L(N_1) \cap K) \subseteq L(N_2)$.

3   Noninterference Properties, and Previous Results

An (injectively labelled) net is called *HL* if its set of transitions T is partitioned as $T = H \uplus L$ where transitions in H are invisible (i.e., ε-labelled) and are called *high-level* transitions, while transitions in L are visible (i.e., every $t \in L$ is labelled by t, its own name) and are called *low-level* transitions. An *HL*-net is called H-net (L-net) if it only has high-level (low-level, respectively) transitions, i.e., if $T = H$ (respectively, $T = L$). Let $U \subseteq T$ be a set of transitions of N. Then $N \setminus U$ is the net obtained from N by erasing all transitions U and their surrounding arrows. Suppose that N and N' have disjoint sets of places, but not necessarily disjoint sets of transitions. Then $N|N'$ is the net obtained from N and N' by identifying (or "merging") their common transitions.

The next definition originates from [2], and it was the starting point of our investigations.

Definition 1. Non-deducibility on compositions (NDC)

Let N be an (initially marked) *HL*-net with $T = H \uplus L$. N has property NDC iff $N \setminus H$ and $(N|N') \setminus (H \setminus H')$ are language-equivalent, for any H-net N' whose place set is disjoint from that of N and whose set of transitions $T' = H'$ is disjoint from L.   □

In [1], the NDC property was characterised as follows:

Theorem 1. Characterisation of the NDC property

A net N is NDC if and only if N and $N \setminus H$ are language-equivalent (with respect to the set L of visible transitions).   □

An (injectively labelled) net is called *HLD* if its set of transitions T is partitioned as $T = H \uplus L \uplus D$, where H and L denote the set of high-level and low-level transitions, respectively, and D denotes the set of downgrading (or declassifying) transitions. Transitions in H are considered invisible while transitions in $L \cup D$ are considered visible.

The next definition stems from [5].

Definition 2. INTRANSITIVE NON-INTERFERENCE (INI)

Let N be an *HLD*-net with $T = H \uplus L \uplus D$ and with initial marking M_0. N has property INI iff $(N \setminus D, M)$ has the property NDC for $M = M_0$ and for any marking M such that $M_0[vd\rangle M$ in N for some sequence $v \in T^*$ and some downgrading transition $d \in D$. □

This captures the idea that as soon as some d occurs, all the previously invisible (secret) H actions become visible (i.e., no longer secret). In [1], the following facts were proved about Property INI. (Actually, Theorem 2 follows directly from Theorem 1.)

Theorem 2. CHARACTERISATION OF THE INI PROPERTY

An HLD-net (N, M_0) is INI if and only if $(N \setminus D, M)$ and $((N \setminus (H \cup D), M)$ are language-equivalent for $M = M_0$ and for any marking M such that $M_0[vd\rangle M$ in N for some sequence $v \in T^*$ and some downgrading transition $d \in D$. □

Theorem 3. DECIDABILITY OF THE INI PROPERTY

Given an HLD-net N, it is decidable whether N has Property INI. □

4   Selective Non-interference

Next, Definition 2 will be refined in order to account for selective declassification. Assume, to that end, that every transition $d \in D$ has some associated set of high-level transitions $H(d) \subseteq H$, and denote such nets as *sd* (for *selective declassification*). The idea is that an occurrence of d declassifies all previously executed transitions in $H(d)$, but no other high-level transitions.

Definition 3. INI WITH SELECTIVE DECLASSIFICATION (INISD)

An *sd-HLD*-net N with $T = H \uplus L \uplus D$ and with initial marking M_0 has property INISD iff for any firing sequence of the form:

$$M_0[w_0 d_1 w_1 d_2 \ldots d_{n-1} w_{n-1} d_n w_n\rangle,$$
$$\text{where } d_1, \ldots, d_n \in D;$$
$$\text{for all } j \in \{1, \ldots, n\}, d_j \text{ does not occur in } w_j d_{j+1} \ldots d_n w_n; \quad (1)$$
$$\text{and}\{d_1, \ldots, d_n\} \text{ is the set of all declassifying}$$
$$\text{actions occurring in the sequence}$$

there exists a corresponding firing sequence of the form

$$M_0[v_0 d_1 v_1 d_2 \ldots d_{n-1} v_{n-1} d_n v_n\rangle \quad (2)$$

with similar properties, such that for every $i \in \{0, \ldots, n\}$:

$$v_i \in L_i^* \text{ and } w_i \sim_{L_i} v_i, \text{ where } L_i = L \cup D \cup \left(\bigcup_{i < k \leq n} H(d_k) \right). \quad □$$

According to the conditions in (1), the *last* occurrence of any declassifying action d_k inside the sequence

$$w \; = \; w_0 d_1 w_1 d_2 \ldots d_{n-1} w_{n-1} d_n w_n$$

is singled out as being critical. Before that last occurrence, all occurrences of transitions in $H(d_k)$ are declassified by this d_k. After that last occurrence, they may either be declassified by some other d action, or still be secret. For this reason, $H(d_k)$ is included in L_i, for every $i < k$. The definition stipulates that the sequences v_i required to exist by (2) must be the projections of w_i onto L_i. Transitions left out of these projections are just those H-transitions which are *not* declassified later in w. In order to understand this definition better, it is perhaps helpful to scan w mentally from right to left; once d_k occurs in such a scan, no *previously* occurring $H(d_k)$-transition is to be considered as secret.

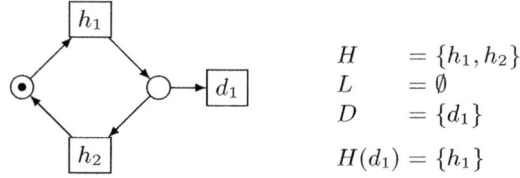

$$\begin{aligned} H &= \{h_1, h_2\} \\ L &= \emptyset \\ D &= \{d_1\} \\ H(d_1) &= \{h_1\} \end{aligned}$$

Fig. 1. An *sd-HLD*-Petri net which is not INISD

For the sake of illustration, consider the net shown in Figure 1 and the sequence

$$M_0[\underbrace{h_1 h_2 h_1}_{w_0} d_1\rangle.$$

We have $L_0 = \{d_1, h_1\}$ and $L_1 = \{d_1\}$. If we wanted to prove the INISD property, we would need to find a sequence $M_0[v_0 d_1\rangle$ such that $v_0 \in L_0^*$ and $w_0 \sim_{L_0} v_0$. As the projection of w_0 onto L_0 is $h_1 h_1$, we would thus need to check whether $h_1 h_1 d_1$ is firable. However, since this is not the case, the net does not have the INISD property. Informally, by "seeing $h_1 h_1 d_1$", an observer can sense something secret, namely that some non-declassified high-level action (in this case, h_2) must have occurred.

Consider Figure 2 for a slightly more involved example. Some government (place "gov") is engaged in two types of diplomatic activity, secret ones (transitions h_1, h_1') and top secret ones (transitions h_2, h_2'), producing an unknown (and unlimited) amount of documents on the corresponding places. At any point, it may be decided to declassify some information. This is done either by declassifying only secret information, without also declassifying top secret information (transition d_1), or by declassifying all informations, be they top secret or just

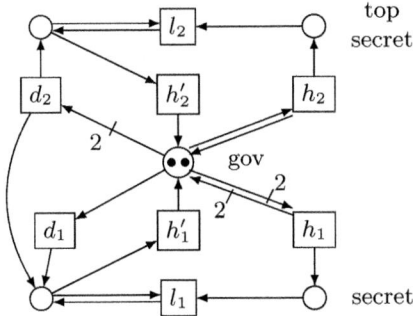

$$H(d_2) = \{h_1, h'_1, h_2, h'_2\} \text{ and } H(d_1) = \{h_1, h'_1\}$$

Fig. 2. Another non-INISD Petri net

secret (transition d_2). After d_1-declassification, visible secret-reading activity (transition l_1) may be started, or, alternatively, secret activity may be restarted by h'_1, which at the same time disables l_1. After d_2-declassification, both types of reading (l_1 and l_2) may be started, or, alternatively, disabled by their corresponding h'_1 or h'_2 actions (i.e.: restart of secret and top secret activity, respectively). Note that more h_1-secrets may only be produced if *both* restart actions h'_1 and h'_2 have occurred.

A sequence not disproving the INISD property. Consider the first line of (3):

$$
\begin{aligned}
w &= \underbrace{h_1 h_1 h_2 d_1 h_2 l_1 h'_1 h_1}_{w_0}\, d_2\, \underbrace{l_2 h'_2 l_1 h'_1 h_2}_{w_1}\, d_1\, \underbrace{l_1}_{w_2} \\
v &= \underbrace{h_1 h_1 h_2 d_1 h_2 l_1 h'_1 h_1}_{v_0}\, d_2\, \underbrace{l_2 l_1 h'_1}_{v_1}\, d_1\, \underbrace{l_1}_{v_2}
\end{aligned}
\tag{3}
$$

Then w is of the form (1), and we compute $L_0 = \{l_1, l_2, d_1, d_2, h_1, h'_1, h_2, h'_2\}$, $L_1 = \{l_1, l_2, d_1, d_2, h_1, h'_1\}$, and $L_2 = \{l_1, l_2, d_1, d_2\}$. A corresponding v of the form (2), which is firable, is shown in the second line of (3). Note that the declassifying transition d_1 may be fired twice in a row, in which case the transition h'_1 needs to be fired also twice in a row to actually let secret activity be restarted.

A sequence disproving the INISD property. Consider $w' = d_2 h'_2 d_1$. We compute the same sets L_0, L_1, L_2 as for w. If the net were INISD, there would exist a firable sequence $v' = v'_0 d_2 v'_1 d_1 v'_2$ satisfying (2) of Definition 3, where v'_1 is the projection of h'_2 onto L_1, that is, $v'_1 = \varepsilon$. However, such a sequence does not exist. Hence, the net does not satisfy the INISD property. This problem hinges on the fact that some "visible" lower level activity (d_1-declassification) is made partially dependent on some top secret activity (the h'_2 event), and therefore, the latter is detectable when it should not be.

Definition 3 has been adopted as an unostentatious extension of Definition 2. In particular, there are the following special cases. If $D = \emptyset$, then in view of

Theorem 1, Definition 3 amounts to Definition 1. If $H(d) = H$ for every $d \in D$, then Definition 3 reduces to Definition 2. When comparing the INISD property to other properties of information control flow, we did not find any equivalent one, but several related ones. This will be discussed in more detail in Section 8.

5   Decidability of the INISD Property

As properties of systems described by *sd-HLD* Petri nets seem to be quite sensitive to design decisions, it would be nice if one could use an algorithm to check automatically whether a system satisfies the INISD property or not. Next, it will be shown that such an algorithm exists.

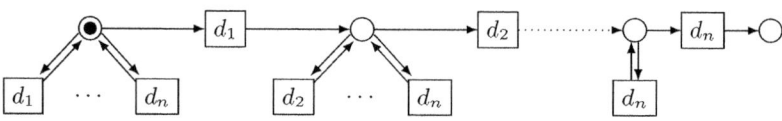

Fig. 3. The net $N[d_1 \ldots d_n]$

Theorem 4. Property INISD is decidable

Given an sd-HDL-net N, it is decidable whether N has Property INISD.

Proof: First note that the $d_1, \ldots, d_n$ in Definition 3 are mutually distinct, because every one of them is the *last* of its kind in the firing sequence considered in (1). Therefore, the set Σ of sequences $d_1 \ldots d_n \in D^*$ such that some firing sequence $M_0[w_0 d_1 w_1 d_2 \ldots d_n w_n\rangle$ exists and satisfies the conditions stated in (1) is finite, since D is finite and there are only finitely many repetition-free sequences over D. For repetition-free sequences $d_1 \ldots d_n$, membership in Σ can be decided effectively by the following algorithm:

- Let $d_1 \ldots d_n \in D^*$ with $\forall 1 \leq i, j \leq n: i \neq j \Rightarrow d_i \neq d_j$ be given.
- Consider the net $N[d_1 \ldots d_n]$ depicted in Figure 3.
- For each $d_i \in \{d_1, \ldots, d_n\}$, replicate the *unique* transition d_i of N as many times as needed to obtain the same number of transitions d_i in N and in $N[d_1 \ldots d_n]$ (all replicas have similar flow relations).
- For each $d_i \in \{d_1, \ldots, d_n\}$, glue the d_i-transitions of N and $N[d_1 \ldots d_n]$ pairwise.
- If a marking can be reached such that the final place of $N[d_1 \ldots d_n]$ carries a token, then $d_1 \ldots d_n$ belongs to Σ, otherwise it does not.

This implies by the results recalled in section 2 that the finite set Σ can be effectively constructed. Note the special case $n = 0$ (hence $d_1 \ldots d_n = \varepsilon$). The final place in $N[\varepsilon]$ equals the initial place, which is marked initially. Hence the empty sequence is trivially checked by the above algorithm as belonging to Σ (as indeed it should, by the definition of Σ).

Next, consider some fixed sequence $d_1 \ldots d_n \in \Sigma$. We will define two Petri nets, $N_1[d_1 \ldots d_n]$ and $N_2[d_1 \ldots d_n]$. Both nets are derivatives from N, the given *HDL*-net. We shall use these pairs of nets (one pair for each sequence $d_1 \ldots d_n \in \Sigma$) in order to reduce the INISD property to Petri net language inclusion.

The idea of this construction is as follows. *L*-actions, which are visible, will simply always be left intact. *D*-actions d will be duplicated into a tilde-adorned variant $\tilde{d}$, which will denote the *last* occurrence of d, and plain d, which will denote all other occurrences. Also, *H*-actions h will be duplicated into $\tilde{h}$ and plain h. The latter are invisible as before, while the former will denote declassified actions, which are made visible by being declassified.

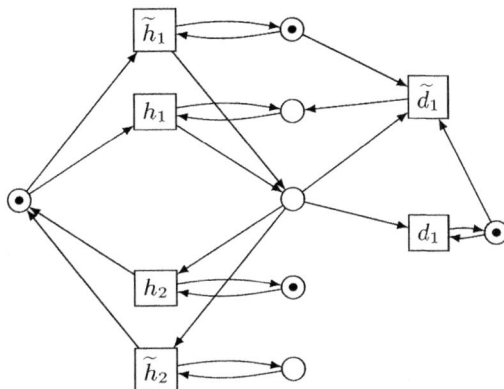

Fig. 4. $N_1[d_1]$, for the net shown in Figure 1

Definition of $N_1[d_1 \ldots d_n]$:

1. Copy all the places of N into $N_1[d_1 \ldots d_n]$.
2. Copy all *L*-transitions (with the same flow relations) from N to $N_1[d_1 \ldots d_n]$.
3. Copy all *H*-transitions (with the same flow relations) from N to $N_1[d_1 \ldots d_n]$. From each $h \in H$, make a copy $\tilde{h}$ with the same flow relations as h.
4. Copy all transitions $\{d_1, \ldots, d_n\} \subseteq D$ from N to $N_1[d_1 \ldots d_n]$ and for every d_j ($1 \le j \le n$), make a copy $\tilde{d_j}$ with the same flow relations as d_j.
5. For every h and $\tilde{h}$, add control places p_h and $p_{\tilde{h}}$ in ordinary self-loop with h and $\tilde{h}$, respectively. Put one token on p_h iff $h \notin \bigcup_{1 \le j \le n} H(d_j)$, and one token on $p_{\tilde{h}}$ iff $h \in \bigcup_{1 \le j \le n} H(d_j)$.
6. For every $\tilde{d_j}$, add a one-token control place q_j in ordinary self-loop with $\tilde{d_j}$.
7. Add flow relations with the following effect: $\tilde{d_j}$ disables d_j by emptying q_j; furthermore, if h is in the set $H(d_j) \setminus \bigcup_{j < k \le n} H(d_k)$ then $\tilde{d_j}$ disables transition $\tilde{h}$ by emptying $p_{\tilde{h}}$ and enables transition h by filling p_h.
8. Synchronise this net (by the | operation defined above) with the net $\tilde{N}[d_1 \ldots d_n]$ as follows: ⊙→[$\tilde{d_1}$]→○→[$\tilde{d_2}$]→ $\cdots$ →[$\tilde{d_n}$]→○

The set of visible transitions of $N_1[d_1 \ldots d_n]$ are defined as
$$X = L \cup \{d_1, \ldots, d_n\} \cup \{\tilde{d}_1, \ldots, \tilde{d}_n\} \cup \{\tilde{h} \mid h \in H\},$$
i.e., all transitions except those in H. The result of this construction, applied to the net shown in Figure 1 and with the sequence d_1, is shown in Figure 4.

Definition of $N_2[d_1 \ldots d_n]$:

1. Create $N_1[d_1 \ldots d_n]$.
2. Delete all transitions h and all places p_h for $h \in H$, as well as their surrounding arcs.

All transitions of $N_2[d_1 \ldots d_n]$ are defined to be visible. (This set of transitions happens to be the same set X as above.) The result of this construction, applied to the net shown in Figure 1 and with the sequence d_1, is shown in Figure 5.

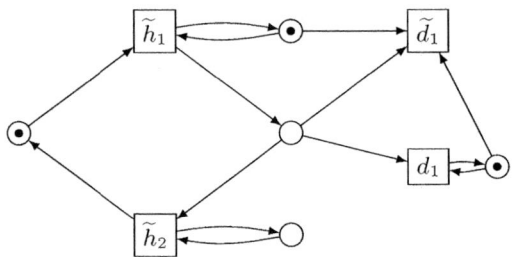

Fig. 5. $N_2[d_1]$, for the net shown in Figure 1

Note that because of the requirements formulated in Definition 3, in (1), there can be no D-action whatsoever in w_n, at most action d_n in w_{n-1}, at most actions d_n and d_{n-1} in w_{n-2}, and so on, until in w_0 there could be any number of actions from $\{d_1, \ldots, d_n\}$ but no other D-actions. It is with a view to this that, in both nets $N_1[d_1 \ldots d_n]$ and $N_2[d_1 \ldots d_n]$, $\tilde{d}_j$ disables d_j and actions in $D \setminus \{d_1, \ldots, d_n\}$ do not appear.

To finish the proof, we show that the following two statements are equivalent:

A : N has the INISD property.

B : $L(N_1[\varepsilon]) \subseteq L(N_2[\varepsilon])$,

   and for every $\sigma = d_1 \ldots d_n \in \Sigma$ with $n \geq 1$:
   $$L(N_1[d_1 \ldots d_n]) \cap (X^* \tilde{d}_n L^*) \subseteq L(N_2[d_1 \ldots d_n])$$
   where X is the set of visible transitions of $N_1[d_1 \ldots d_n]$.

The claim of the theorem follows, because **B** can be checked effectively by the results recalled in section 2. Note, to this end, that $X^* \tilde{d}_n L^*$ is a regular language.

($\mathbf{A} \Rightarrow \mathbf{B}$): Assume that N is INISD. Let $\sigma = d_1 \ldots d_n$ be any sequence from Σ. We distinguish two cases, $n = 0$ and $n \geq 1$.
Case $n = 0$: We prove $L(N_1[\varepsilon]) \subseteq L(N_2[\varepsilon])$.

Let $x \in L(N_1[\varepsilon])$. Then there is some sequence τ, firable in $N_1[\varepsilon]$, such that x is the projection of τ on X^*, with $X = L \cup \{\tilde{h} \mid h \in H\}$. In particular, x does not contain any downgrading transitions. By the construction of $N_1[\varepsilon]$, τ does not contain any transition d or $\tilde{d}$ with $d \in D$, nor any $\tilde{h}$-transitions. So, the sequence τ is also firable in N, and moreover, $x \in L^*$. Setting $w = w_0 = w_n = \tau$, w is of the form (1). By the INISD property, there exists some $v = v_0$, firable in N, such that v_0 is the projection of w_0 onto $L \cup D$, hence onto L. By the construction of $N_2[\varepsilon]$, v_0 is firable in $N_2[\varepsilon]$ as well. But $v_0 = x$, because both x and v_0 are the projection on L^* of $w_0 = \tau \in (H \cup L)^*$. Since v_0 is firable in $N_2[\varepsilon]$, so is x. This implies that $x \in L(N_2[\varepsilon])$, and since x was arbitrary, we get a proof of $L(N_1[\varepsilon]) \subseteq L(N_2[\varepsilon])$.

Case $n \geq 1$: We prove $L(N_1[d_1 \ldots d_n]) \cap (X^*\tilde{d}_n L^*) \subseteq L(N_2[d_1 \ldots d_n])$.

Let $x \in L(N_1[d_1 \ldots d_n]) \cap (X^*\tilde{d}_n L^*)$. Then there is some sequence τ, firable in $L(N_1[d_1 \ldots d_n])$, such that x is the projection of τ on X^*, and moreover, x contains $\tilde{d}_n$ at some point and only transitions from L after the last $\tilde{d}_n$. By the construction of $N_1[d_1 \ldots d_n]$ (more precisely, item 8. in that construction), τ contains all of $\tilde{d}_1, \ldots, \tilde{d}_n$, in that order, and each $\tilde{d}_i$ exactly once. Therefore, τ can be split as follows:

$$\tau = \tau_0 \tilde{d}_1 \tau_1 \tilde{d}_2 \ldots \tilde{d}_{n-1} \tau_{n-1} \tilde{d}_n \tau_n$$

such that τ_n contains no d nor any $\tilde{d}$ with $d \in D$, τ_{n-1} contains at most some d_n transitions, and so on, thus providing a sequence of the form (1).

In going from τ to x by projecting τ on X^*, at most some high-level transitions h *without tilde* are erased. By item 7. of the construction of $N_1[d_1 \ldots d_n]$, such high-level transitions h may occur *only after* the last declassifying $\tilde{d}_j$ for which $h \in H(d_j)$ holds. Before such a $\tilde{d}_j$, high-level transitions $h \in H(d_j)$ can only occur (if at all) in the form $\tilde{h}$. Let $w = plain(\tau)$ be the sequence obtained from τ by removing the tildes from all actions $\tilde{h}$ and $\tilde{d}$, but leaving the sequence unchanged otherwise. Then by the construction of $N_1[d_1 \ldots d_n]$ (as it essentially - disregarding the tildes - does not add any behaviour to N), w is firable in N. Taking account of the splitting of τ, let $w_i = plain(\tau_i)$, for $0 \leq i \leq n$, and hence

$$w = w_0 d_1 w_1 d_2 \ldots d_{n-1} w_{n-1} d_n w_n.$$

By the properties just explained, w conforms to the requirements associated with (1). Therefore, by the INISD property, a sequence v conforming to (2) exists. More precisely, there exists

$$v = v_0 d_1 v_1 d_2 \ldots d_{n-1} v_{n-1} d_n v_n$$

such that v is firable in N and every v_i arises from w_i by erasing (only) those high-level transitions h that do not belong to $\bigcup_{i<k\leq n} H(d_k)$. Let τ' be the sequence obtained from v by putting back tildes on all remaining high level transitions and on the last occurrence of each declassifying action $d \in D$. Then τ' is firable in $N_2[d_1 \ldots d_n]$, because the firing in N of any high-level transition h occurring in v_i is faithfully simulated by the firing of the corresponding $\tilde{h}$ in $N_2[d_1 \ldots d_n]$.

This is so because, for any such high-level transition h, necessarily, $h \in H(d_j)$ for some $j > i$, and by item 8. in the construction of $N_2[d_1 \ldots d_n]$, the transition $\widetilde{d}_j$ cannot have been fired earlier.

Now by the above construction, τ' is the same as x. This shows that x is firable in $N_2[d_1 \ldots d_n]$, ending the proof of $(\mathbf{A} \Rightarrow \mathbf{B})$.

$(\mathbf{B} \Rightarrow \mathbf{A})$: In order to prove the INISD property from $(\mathbf{B})$, let

$$w \;=\; w_0 d_1 w_1 d_2 \ldots d_{n-1} w_{n-1} d_n w_n$$

be any sequence, firable in N and satisfying the conditions stated in (1). We show that a related sequence $v = v_0 d_1 v_1 d_2 \ldots d_{n-1} v_{n-1} d_n v_n$ satisfying (2) exists such that $v_i \in L_i^*$ and $w_i \sim_{L_i} v_i$ for all i. Again, we distinguish the cases $n = 0$ and $n \geq 1$.

Case $n = 0$: Then $w = w_0 = w_n$, and no D action occurs in w. By construction of $N_1[\varepsilon]$, w is firable in $N_1[\varepsilon]$. (Note that in $N_1[\varepsilon]$, a token is on p_h but not on $p_{\widetilde{h}}$.) Let v be the projection of w onto X (which by the above, is the same as the projection of w onto L). By $L(N_1[\varepsilon]) \subseteq L(N_2[\varepsilon])$, coming from $(\mathbf{B})$, and since all transitions of $N_2[\varepsilon]$ are visible, v is firable in $N_2[\varepsilon]$. But since the L-firing sequences of $N_2[\varepsilon]$ agree with those of N, v is also firable in N. So, (2) is satisfied with $v_0 = v$.

Case $n \geq 1$: By the construction of $N_1[d_1 \ldots d_n]$, and because w is firable in N, the sequence

$$\widetilde{w}_0 \widetilde{d}_1 \widetilde{w}_1 \widetilde{d}_2 \ \ldots \ \widetilde{d}_n \widetilde{w}_n$$

is firable in $N_1[d_1 \ldots d_n]$, where for $0 \leq i \leq n$, $\widetilde{w}_i$ is as w_i, except that every $h \in \bigcup_{i < k \leq n} H(d_k)$ (in w_i) is replaced by $\widetilde{h}$.

For every $0 \leq i \leq n$, let $\widetilde{v}_i$ be the projection of $\widetilde{w}_i$ onto X. By $(\mathbf{B})$,

$$\widetilde{v} \;=\; \widetilde{v}_0 \widetilde{d}_1 \widetilde{v}_1 \widetilde{d}_2 \ \ldots \ \widetilde{d}_n \widetilde{v}_n$$

is firable in $N_2[d_1 \ldots d_n]$. Let v_i be the same as $\widetilde{v}_i$, where each $\widetilde{h}$ is replaced by h. By the constructions of $N_1[d_1 \ldots d_n]$, $\widetilde{v}_i$ and v_i, no $h \in H(d_i)$ occurs in the sequence $v_i d_{i+1} \ldots d_n v_n$. Hence, by the construction of $N_2[d_1 \ldots d_n]$,

$$v \;=\; v_0 d_1 v_1 d_2 \ldots d_n v_n$$

which is a firing sequence of N, satisfies the requirements of (2).   □

As an illustration of this theorem, let us apply $(\mathbf{B})$ to prove that the net shown in Figure 1 is not INISD. Consider

$$\tau \;=\; \widetilde{h}_1 h_2 \widetilde{h}_1 \widetilde{d}_1 \quad \text{in } N_1[d_1] \text{ (see Figure 4)}.$$

The projection of τ on X^* is $\sigma = \widetilde{h}_1 \widetilde{h}_1 \widetilde{d}_1$. By comparing Figures 4 and 5, one can see that σ is in $L(N_1[d_1]) \cap (X^* \widetilde{d}_1 L^*)$ but not in $L(N_2[d_1])$. This captures net-theoretically the fact that for $w = h_1 h_2 h_1 d_1$, firable in N and satisfying (1), no corresponding $v = v_0 d_1$, firable in N and satisfying (2), exists such that $v_0 \in L_0^*$ and $v_0 \sim_{L_0} h_1 h_2 h_1$, where $L_0 = L \cup D \cup H(d_1) = \{d_1, h_1\}$.

6   Undecidability for Non-plain or Non-injective Labellings

One might consider extensions of this work in several directions. One possibility is to relax the assumption of injectivity of net labelling maps. A second possibility is to replace downgrading actions D by (completely) invisible actions I which are neutral with respect to non-interference, thus considering HLI-net with $T = H \uplus L \uplus I$. By neutral, we mean that on the one hand, such actions have no downgrading effect, and on the other hand, it is not required from low actions not to reveal the firing of these invisible actions. Alternatively, one may add neutral actions I as a fourth class of actions, i.e., consider $HLDI$-net with $T = H \uplus L \uplus D \uplus I$. The former extension would make a kind of bridge with language based security. The latter extensions would be ideal for considering non-interference in multi-agent systems, where the global alphabet of the system is partitioned to $T = H_a \uplus L_a \uplus D_a \uplus I_a$ in as many ways as there are agents a in the system (neutral actions I play essentially the same role as N-events in Mantel's taxonomies [7,8,9]).

Unfortunately, in all cases considered, we obtain undecidability instead of decidability results. The underlying net-theoretic reason is that a statement quoted in section 2, namely

> For two labelled nets N_1 and N_2 where N_2 is plainly *and* injectively labelled, it is decidable whether $L(N_1) \subseteq L(N_2)$,

changes into

> For two labelled nets N_1 and N_2, it is undecidable whether $L(N_1) \subseteq L(N_2)$ even if N_2 is assumed to be plainly *or* injectively labelled,

i.e., as soon as the precondition of N_2 being plainly and injectively labelled is omitted.

Before proceeding to prove these negative results, we propose an extended definition of NDC which, for the sake of simplicity, is based on Theorem 1 instead of Definition 1. Similar extensions could be proposed for INI or INISD, but this is not necessary since the undecidability of NDC for PT-nets with non-plain or non-injective labelling entails similar results for INI or INISD.

Definition 4. NON-DEDUCIBILITY ON COMPOSITIONS FOR LABELLED NETS

Let $N = (P, T, F)$ be a PT-net with initial marking M_0 and labelling map $\lambda \colon T \to H \uplus L \uplus \{\varepsilon\}$. N has property NDC iff N and $N \setminus \lambda^{-1}(H)$ are language-equivalent with respect to the set of labels L.   □

In the above definition, $I = \lambda^{-1}(\{\varepsilon\})$ is the set of completely invisible transitions. We will prove first the undecidability of NDC for PT-nets with plain but non-injective labelling, i.e., such that $\lambda(t) \neq \varepsilon$ for all $t \in T$ but possibly $\lambda(t) = \lambda(t')$ for $t \neq t'$.

Theorem 5

Given a PT-net N with a plain but non-injective labelling $\lambda \colon T \to H \uplus L \uplus \{\varepsilon\}$, it is undecidable whether N has Property NDC.

Proof: Let $N_1 = (P_1, T_1, F_1)$ and $N_2 = (P_2, T_2, F_2)$ be two plainly labelled PT-nets with initial markings $M_{0,1}, M_{0,2}$ and labelling maps $\lambda_1 : T_1 \to L$ and $\lambda_2 : T_2 \to L$. Without loss of generality, assume that P_1, T_1, P_2, T_2 are pairwise disjoint. Let $\{M_{0,2}[t_i\rangle M_{i,2} \mid i = 1 \dots n\}$ be the set of possible firings from the initial marking of N_2. Embed N_1 and N_2 in a larger net N with two new places p_0, p_0' and $n+1$ new transitions t_0 and $t_1', \dots, t_n'$ as follows. Initially, p_0 contains one token, places $p \in P_1$ contain $M_{0,1}(p)$ tokens, and all other places are empty. All transitions of N_1 are set in ordinary self-loops with the place p_0', hence they cannot be fired from the initial marking of N. The transition t_0, labelled with $\lambda(t_0) = h \in H$, transfers the missing token from p_0 to p_0', thus enabling N_1 to execute. On the other hand, for each transition $M_{0,2}[t_i\rangle M_{i,2}$ of N_2, N has a corresponding transition t_i', labelled with $\lambda(t_i') = \lambda_2(t_i)$, that takes the token from p_0 and loads the marking $M_{i,2}$ in the places of N_2. Clearly, the initial transition in a run of N determines whether this run simulates a run of N_1 or a run of N_2, and such simulations cannot interfere. Now let $\lambda(t) = \lambda_1(t)$ for $t \in T_1$, and $\lambda(t) = \lambda_2(t)$ for $t \in T_2$. Then, by definition, N has the property NDC if and only if $L(N_1) \subseteq L(N_2)$, and this is undecidable.   □

We next show that NDC is undecidable for HLI-nets.

Theorem 6

Given a PT-net N with an injective but non-plain labelling map $\lambda : T \to H \uplus L \uplus \{\varepsilon\}$, it is undecidable whether N has Property NDC.

Proof: Let $N_1 = (P_1, T_1, F_1)$ and $N_2 = (P_2, T_2, F_2)$ be two PT-nets with initial markings M_1, M_2 and injective labelling maps $\lambda_1 : T_1 \to L \uplus \{\varepsilon\}$ and $\lambda_2 : T_2 \to L \uplus \{\varepsilon\}$. W.l.o.g., assume that L is included in the ranges of λ_1 and λ_2, and let $I_1 = \lambda_1^{-1}(\varepsilon)$ and $I_2 = \lambda_2^{-1}(\varepsilon)$. W.l.o.g., assume also that P_1 and P_2 are disjoint.

Construct from N_1 and N_2 a new PT-net N as follows. First, one makes the fusion, for each $l \in L$ of the two transitions of N_1 and N_2 labelled with l, respectively. Let L denote the resulting set of transitions of N. Second, one adds four places p_{00}, p_0, p_1, p_2 and four transitions i_0, h, i_1, i_2, yielding a global set of transitions $H \cup I \cup L$ with $H = \{h\}$ and $I = I_1 \cup I_2 \cup \{i_0, i_1, i_2\}$. The initial marking of N is the joint extension M of M_1 and M_2 defined with $M(p_{00}) = 1$ and $M(p_0), M(p_1), M(p_2) = 0$. The net N inherits all flow relations from N_1 and N_2. The other flow relations are as follows (see Figure 6). First, one sets $F(p_{00}, i_0) = F(i_0, p_0) = F(i_0, p_1) = 1$ and $F(p_{00}, h) = F(h, p_0) = F(h, p_2) = 1$. Second, one sets $F(p_1, i_1) = F(i_1, p_1) = 1$, $F(p_2, i_2) = F(i_2, p_2) = 1$, and $F(p_0, t) = F(t, p_0) = 1$ for every transition $t \in L \cup I_1 \cup I_2$. Finally, one sets $F(i_1, p) = 1$ for every place p originated from N_1 (but not from N_2) and $F(i_2, p) = 1$ for every place p originated from N_2 (but not from N_1).

At the start, only i_0 or h can be fired. After i_0 has fired, i_1 may be fired at any time and as often as desired, hence the language generated by N after firing i_0 is equal to the language of N_2 (recall that only the transitions in L are visible). After h has fired, i_2 may be fired at any time and as often as desired, hence the language generated by N after firing h is equal to the language of N_1.

Now, the language of $N \setminus H$ (or $N \setminus \{h\}$) is clearly equal to the language of N_2. Therefore, N is NDC if and only if $L(N_1) \cup L(N_2) = L(N_2)$, i.e., $L(N_1) \subseteq L(N_2)$, and this cannot be decided. $\qquad\square$

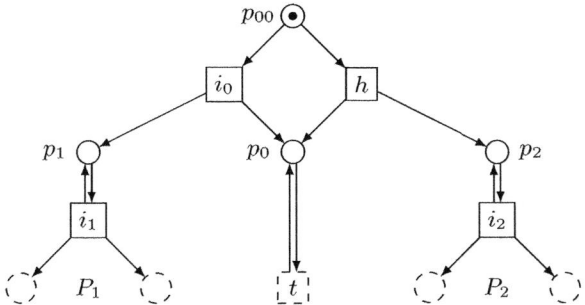

Fig. 6. The construction of N in the proof of Theorem 6

7   Another Example

Consider the HDI-net shown in Fig. 7, where $H(d_i) = \{h_i\}$ for $i = 1 \ldots 3$. The outer circuit comprised of places p_1, p_2, p_3 and low transitions l_1, l_2, l_3 is followed clockwise by sheep, that cannot move from p_i to $p_{(i+1) \bmod 3}$ (low transition $l_{(i+1) \bmod 3}$) unless the place $r_{(i+1) \bmod 3}$ is marked (this place controls a gate and it is marked when the gate is open). Initially, there are two sheep in place p_2, and the gates r_3 and r_1 are open. Sheep may reproduce in place p_2. The central place is occupied by a number of wolves (in the system shown in the figure, there is only one of them). Each wolf may use one of high transitions h_i to hide in the corresponding place q_i and wait there for catching sheep in place p_i. In order to (perhaps) increase chances of success, when using transition h_i, a wolf opens the gate r_i if not already open (so that prey can come in), and tries to close the gate $r_{(i+1) \bmod 3}$ (so that prey cannot escape). When a wolf hides in q_i and there is sheep in p_i, the wolf can catch prey and come back to the central place.

The question is to decide whether this net has the INISD property, meaning that the sheep can oppose no strategy to the wolves and cannot ever know that they will be caught until this actually happens. The answer is that the net is not INISD, as $l_3 l_1 h_2 l_2$ is friable but $l_3 l_1 l_2$ is not.

The example may be modified in various ways as follows. If there are two or more wolves, then the net is still not INISD, for the same reason. If there are three open gates initially, then the net is not INISD, since $l_3 l_1 h_1 d_1 l_3 l_1 h_2 l_2$ can be executed, but $l_3 l_1 h_1 d_1 l_3 l_1 l_2$ cannot. If only one gate is open initially, three cases can be distinguished. With gate 3 open, $l_3 h_2 d_2 h_1 l_1$ can be executed and $l_3 h_2 d_2 l_1$ cannot be executed; hence the net is not INISD. With gate 2 open, gate 3 gets closed forever and no low action can take place (only h_1 can fire);

hence the net is INISD. With gate 1 open, $h_3 l_3$ can be executed but l_3 cannot be executed; hence the net is not INISD. If all gates are deconstructed (i.e.: places r_1, r_2, r_3 and all their surrounding arrows are deleted), then the net becomes INISD. Finally, if transition $+$ is deleted, the same reasonings continue to apply.

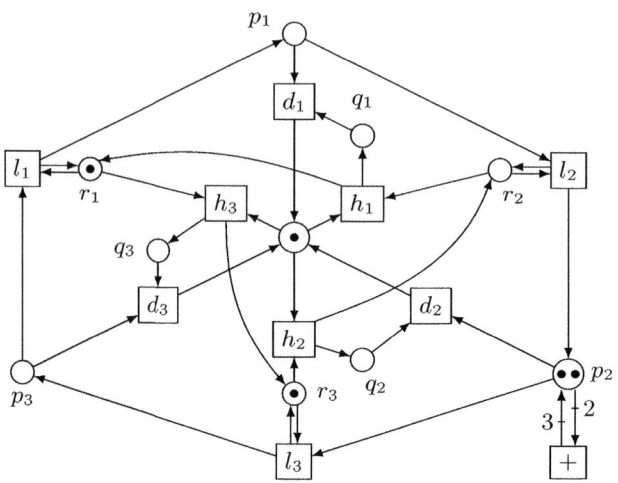

Fig. 7. An HDI-net

8 INISD and Information Flow Security

In this section, the connection between INISD (Definition 3 in section 4) and information flow control will be examined. In particular, Definition 3 will be compared with the definitions of intransitive noninterference studied in [9] and in [10], respectively. First, we show that Definition 3 may be explained alternatively in terms of security domains and the intransitive purge function introduced by Haigh and Young [6] and reformulated by van der Meyden [10].

8.1 Equivalent Reformulation of Definition 3

Let N be an *sd-HLD*-net with $T = H \uplus L \uplus D$ as in section 4. For $d \in D$, let $H(d)$ denote the set of high-level actions declassified by d. Let $\equiv_D$ and $\equiv_H$ be the equivalence relations on D and H defined by

$$d \equiv_D d' \quad \text{iff} \quad H(d) = H(d')$$
$$\text{and} \quad h \equiv_H h' \quad \text{iff} \quad \forall d \in D : h \in H(d) \iff h' \in H(d).$$

For $t \in T$, let the security domain $dom(t)$ of t be defined by $dom(t) = L$ if $t \in L$, $dom(t) = [t]_{\equiv_D}$ if $t \in D$, and $dom(t) = [t]_{\equiv_H}$ if $t \in H$. Let $\mathcal{D}$ be the set of security domains L or $[d]_{\equiv_D}$ or $[h]_{\equiv_H}$. Consider the intransitive security policy $\rightarrowtail\; \subseteq \mathcal{D} \times \mathcal{D}$ defined by

$$
\begin{aligned}
x &\rightarrowtail x && \text{for all } x \in \mathcal{D} \\
[d]_{\equiv_D} &\rightarrowtail L && \text{for all } d \in D \\
[h]_{\equiv_H} &\rightarrowtail [d]_{\equiv_D} && \text{for all } d \in D \text{ and } h \in H(d).
\end{aligned}
$$

For two security domains x and x', $x \rightarrowtail x'$ means that information may legally flow from x to x'. Finally, consider van der Meyden's *ipurge* function defined as follows for $w \in T^*$, $t \in T$, and for any subset X of security domains:

$$
ipurge_X(w\,t) \;=\; \textbf{if } (\exists x \in X \colon dom(t) \rightarrowtail x) \;\textbf{ then } \; (ipurge_{X\cup\{dom(t)\}}(w))\,t
$$
$$
\textbf{else } \quad ipurge_X(w)
$$

Letting $Tr = \{w \in T^* \mid M_0[w\rangle\}$ be the set of firing sequences of N, condition INISD may be reformulated equivalently as follows:

$$
\forall w \in Tr, v \in (L \cup H)^* \colon wv \in Tr \Rightarrow
$$
$$
\exists w' \in Tr, v' \in L^* \colon w'v' \in Tr \wedge (ipurge_{\{L\}}(w) = ipurge_{\{L\}}(w')) \wedge v \sim_L v'.
$$

8.2 Mantel's Framework [9]

According to Mantel's definition of (possibly intransitive) flow policies given in [9], the above defined structure $(\mathcal{D}, \rightarrowtail)$ may be interpreted as $(\mathcal{D}, \rightsquigarrow_V, \rightsquigarrow_N, \not\rightsquigarrow)$ where for all $x, x' \in \mathcal{D}$:

$$
\begin{aligned}
x &\rightsquigarrow_V x' && \text{if } x \rightarrowtail x' \\
x &\not\rightsquigarrow x' && \text{if } x = [h]_{\equiv_H} \text{ and } (x' = L \text{ or } (x' = [d]_{\equiv_D} \text{ and } h \notin H(d))) \\
x &\rightsquigarrow_N x' && \text{if neither } x \rightsquigarrow_V x' \text{ nor } x \not\rightsquigarrow x'.
\end{aligned}
$$

The relation $x \rightsquigarrow_N x'$ means that it is not considered important whether information flows or does not flow from x to x'.

In this alternative framework, Mantel proposes two basic security properties: IBSD (Intransitive Backwards Strict Deletion of confidential events) and IBSIA (Intransitive Backwards Strict Insertion of confidential events), parametric on a subset of security domains $\mathcal{D}' \subseteq \mathcal{D}$, and applicable to a set of traces Tr. (In our case, Tr would simply again be the set of firing sequences.) We sketch below (without completely defining IBSD) an explanation why the property INISD studied in this paper has only a relatively loose relationship with IBSD, or more precisely, with the conjunction of IBSD$_{\mathcal{D}'}$ for all subsets $\mathcal{D}'$ of $\mathcal{D}$ containing L and not containing $[h]_{\equiv_H}$ for any $h \in H$. The reader is referred to [9] for the full definition of IBSD.

Given a fixed $\mathcal{D}' \subseteq \mathcal{D}$, for any transition $t \in T$, let $t \in V$ ("t is visible") if $\exists x' \in \mathcal{D}' \colon dom(t) \rightsquigarrow_V x'$, and $t \in C$ ("t is confidential") if $\forall x' \in \mathcal{D}' \colon dom(t) \not\rightsquigarrow x'$. The property IBSD$_{\mathcal{D}'}(Tr)$ may then be expressed in the following form (where the crucial predicate φ is left unspecified):

$$
\forall wtv \in Tr \colon \; t \in C \wedge \varphi(v) \;\Rightarrow\; \exists v' \in T^* \colon wv' \in Tr \wedge \varphi(v') \wedge v \sim_V v'.
$$

IBSD serves here to check that there is no illegal information flow inside the net N, even though such flows of information cannot be detected by any external observer. Indeed, for a fixed $\mathcal{D}' \subseteq \mathcal{D}$, the prefix w of wtv in the expression of IBSD is in general different from $ipurge_{\mathcal{D}'}(w)$, i.e., it cannot be observed from outside. In our definition of INISD, we have taken the opposite stance which, for IBSD, would consist of requiring instead:

$$\forall wtv \in Tr\colon \ t \in C \wedge \varphi(v) \ \Rightarrow$$
$$\exists w'v' \in T^*\colon \ w'v' \in Tr \wedge (ipurge_{\mathcal{D}'}(w){=}ipurge_{\mathcal{D}'}(w')) \wedge \varphi(v') \wedge v \sim_V v'.$$

8.3   Van der Meyden's Framework [10]

IP-security (short for *intransitive purge security*) [6,10] is closer to the intransitive noninterference (INISD) model which we have presented in this paper. IP-security may be expressed as the conjunction for all security domains $x \in \mathcal{D}$ of the property

$$\forall w, w' \in Tr\colon \ ipurge_{\{x\}}(w) = ipurge_{\{x\}}(w') \ \Rightarrow \ obs_x(w) = obs_x(w')$$

where obs_x is a fixed family of observation functions parametric on security domains. However, INISD does not coincide with IP-security. Even though IP-security stipulates that observing an existing trace w cannot afford more information than $ipurge_{\{x\}}(w)$, which is the maximal legal information, more information can be inferred without effective information flow. Indeed, IP-security does not stipulate, for a given trace w, that there exist other traces w' such that $ipurge_{\{x\}}(w) = ipurge_{\{x\}}(w')$. In the extreme case where w is alone in its equivalence class with respect to the purge function, $obs_x(w)$ reveals all of w. In our definition of INISD, like in IBSD, we have taken a different stance which, instead of IP-security, would consist of requiring:

$$\forall w \in Tr\colon \ ipurge_{\{L\}}(w) \in Tr\,,$$

Like IP-security, INISD suffers from a limitation pointed out and overcome by van der Meyden who proposed for this purpose two other security properties called TA-security and TO-security in [10]. The considered limitation lays in that, in case $h_1 \in H(d_1)$ and $h_2 \in H(d_2)$, if h_1 and d_1 are concurrent with h_2 and d_2 in the net N, the order in which the transitions h_1 and h_2 have been executed may nevertheless be revealed by a firing sequence of the form $\dots h_1 \dots h_2 \dots d_1 \dots d_2$. The proof techniques that we have developed for deciding INISD rely on the use of the sequential firing rule of Petri nets, and they do not address this limitation. Different techniques should be discovered for modifying INISD accordingly in a truly concurrent framework. We feel that Petri nets, being a privileged model for true concurrency, are well equipped for this future (and possibly quite exciting) task.

9   Conclusion

The only other decidability results of trace-based security properties for infinite-state systems we know about are described in [1,3,4]. Of these papers, [1] is a direct predecessor of the present one. The result of [3] and its relation to [1] (and therefore also to the present paper) has already been discussed in [1]. The main results of the paper [4], which came to our attention only after [1] had been published, concern the *un*decidability of several of the security properties described in [8] for pushdown systems. These sets of results are not directly comparable, since pushdown languages and Petri net languages are not comparable either. At the end of [4], we also find a decidability result. This result pertains to a very restricted system model. More precisely, it is shown there that a property called "weak non-inference", which falls neither into Mantel's framework [7,8] nor into the NDC/INI/INISD framework of the present paper, and which is undecidable even for finite-state systems, becomes decidable for pushdown systems if one limits both the set of visible actions and the set of secret actions to cardinality 1. Nevertheless, the approaches in the present paper and in [4] lead to the question (which is so far open, to our knowledge), as to which – if any – of the many trace-based transitive security properties of [7,8] are actually decidable for unbounded Petri nets, and to a similar question for the intransitive security policies discussed in section 8.

Acknowledgements. The authors would like to thank several anonymous reviewers for their comments, and in particular, one of them for detecting a technical mistake in Figure 2. A remark of this reviewer also prompted the discussion contained in section 8.

References

1. Best, E., Darondeau, P., Gorrieri, R.: On the Decidability of Non Interference over Unbounded Petri Nets. In: Chatzikokolakis, K., Cortier, V. (eds.) Proceedings 8th International Workshop on Security Issues in Concurrency, SecCo. EPTCS, vol. 51, pp. 16–33 (2010), http://dx.doi.org/10.4204/EPTCS.51.2
2. Busi, N., Gorrieri, R.: Structural Non-Interference in Elementary and Trace Nets. Mathematical Structures in Computer Science 19(6), 1065–1090 (2009), doi:10.1017/S0960129509990120
3. Dam, M.: Decidability and Proof Systems for Language-based Noninterference Relations. In: Proc. POPL 2006, pp. 67–78 (2006), doi:10.1145/1111037.1111044
4. D'Souza, D., Holla, R., Kulkarni, J., Ramesh, R.K., Sprick, B.: On the Decidability of Model-Checking Information Flow Properties. In: Sekar, R., Pujari, A.K. (eds.) ICISS 2008. LNCS, vol. 5352, pp. 26–40. Springer, Heidelberg (2008)
5. Gorrieri, R., Vernali, M.: On Intransitive Non-interference in Some Models of Concurrency. In: Aldini, A., Gorrieri, R. (eds.) FOSAD 2011. LNCS, vol. 6858, pp. 125–151. Springer, Heidelberg (2011), http://dx.doi.org/10.1007/978-3-642-23082-0_5
6. Haigh, T.J., Young, W.D.: Extending the noninterference versions of MLS for SAT. IEEE Trans. on Software Engineering SE-13(2), 141–150 (1987)
7. Mantel, H.: Possibilistic Definitions of Security - an Assembly Kit. In: Proc. of the 13th IEEE Computer Security Foundations Workshop, Cambridge, UK, July 3-5, pp. 185–199 (2000)

8. Mantel, H.: A Uniform Framework for the Formal Specification and Verification of Information Flow Security. PhD Thesis, Universität des Saarlandes (2003)
9. Mantel, H.: Information Flow Control and Applications - Bridging a Gap. In: Oliveira, J.N., Zave, P. (eds.) FME 2001. LNCS, vol. 2021, pp. 153–172. Springer, Heidelberg (2001)
10. van der Meyden, R.: What, Indeed, Is Intransitive Noninterference? In: Biskup, J., López, J. (eds.) ESORICS 2007. LNCS, vol. 4734, pp. 235–250. Springer, Heidelberg (2007)
11. Wimmel, H.: Entscheidbarkeit bei Petri Netzen - Überblick und Kompendium, p. 239. Springer, Heidelberg (2008),
http://dx.doi.org/10.1007/978-3-540-85471-5

Enforceable Security Policies Revisited*

David Basin[1], Vincent Jugé[2], Felix Klaedtke[1], and Eugen Zălinescu[1]

[1] Institute of Information Security, ETH Zurich, Switzerland
[2] MINES ParisTech, France

Abstract. We revisit Schneider's work on policy enforcement by execution monitoring. We overcome limitations of Schneider's setting by distinguishing between system actions that are controllable by an enforcement mechanism and those actions that are only observable, that is, the enforcement mechanism cannot prevent their execution. For this refined setting, we give necessary and sufficient conditions on when a security policy is enforceable. To state these conditions, we generalize the standard notion of safety properties. Our classification of system actions also allows one, for example, to reason about the enforceability of policies that involve timing constraints. Furthermore, for different specification languages, we investigate the decision problem of whether a given policy is enforceable. We provide complexity results and show how to synthesize an enforcement mechanism from an enforceable policy.

1 Introduction

Security policies come in all shapes and sizes, ranging from simple access-control policies to complex data-usage policies governed by laws and regulations. Given their diversity and their omnipresence in regulating processes and data usage in modern IT systems, it is important to have a firm understanding of what kinds of policies can be enforced and to have general tools for their enforcement.

Most conventional enforcement mechanisms are based on some form of execution monitoring. Schneider [29] began the investigation of which kinds of security policies can be enforced this way. In Schneider's setting, an execution monitor runs in parallel with the target system and observes the system's actions just before they are carried out. In case an action leads to a policy violation, the enforcement mechanism terminates the system. Schneider's results on the enforceability of security policies has spurred various research, both practical and theoretical, on developing and analyzing runtime enforcement mechanisms. For instance, Erlingsson and Schneider [12,13] implement and evaluate enforcement mechanisms based on monitoring. Ligatti and others [24–26] propose more powerful models for enforcement, which can not only terminate a system but also insert and suppress system actions, and they analyze the classes of properties that can be described by such models.

In this paper, we refine Schneider's setting, thereby overcoming several limitations. To explain the limitations, we first summarize Schneider's findings. Schneider [29] shows that only those security policies that can be described by a safety

---

* This work was partly supported by Google Inc.

P. Degano and J.D. Guttman (Eds.): POST 2012, LNCS 7215, pp. 309–328, 2012.
© Springer-Verlag Berlin Heidelberg 2012

property [1, 23, 27] on traces are enforceable by execution monitoring. Roughly speaking, (1) inspecting the sequence of system actions is sufficient to determine whether it is policy compliant and (2) nothing bad ever happens on a prefix of a satisfying trace.[1] History-based access-control policies, for example, fall into this class of properties. Furthermore, Schneider defines so-called security automata that recognize the class of safety properties and that "can serve as the basis for an enforcement mechanism" [29, Page 40]. However, Schneider's conditions for enforceability are necessary but not sufficient. In fact, there are safety properties that are not enforceable. This is already pointed out by Schneider [29, Page 41].

We provide a formalization of enforceability for mechanisms similar to Schneider's [29], i.e., monitors that observe system actions and that terminate systems in case of a policy violation. A key aspect of our formalization is that we distinguish between actions that are only observable and those that are also controllable: An enforcement mechanism cannot terminate the system when observing an only-observable action. In contrast, it can prevent the execution of a controllable action by terminating the system. An example of an observable but not controllable action is a clock tick, since one cannot prevent the progression of time. With this classification of system actions, we can derive that, e.g., availability policies with hard deadlines, which require that requests are processed within a given time limit, are not enforceable although they are safety properties. Another example is administrative actions like assigning roles or permissions to users. Such actions change the system state and can be observed but not controlled by most (sub)systems and enforcement mechanisms. However, a subsystem might permit or deny other actions, which it controls, based on the system's current state. Therefore the enforceability of a policy for the subsystem usually depends on this distinction.

In contrast to Schneider, we give also sufficient conditions for the existence of an enforcement mechanism in our setting with respect to a given trace property. This requires that we first generalize the standard notion of safety [1] to account for the distinction between observable and controllable actions. Our necessary and sufficient conditions provide a precise characterization of enforceability that we use for exploring the realizability of enforcement mechanisms for security policies. For different specification languages, we present decidability results for the decision problem that asks whether a given security policy is enforceable. In case of decidability, we also show how to synthesize an enforcement mechanism for the given policy. In particular, we prove that the decision problem is undecidable for context-free languages and PSPACE-complete for regular languages. Moreover, we extend our decidability result by giving a solution to the realizability problem where policies are specified in a temporal logic with metric constraints.

Summarizing, we see our contributions as follows. We overcome limitations of Schneider's setting on policy enforcement based on execution monitoring [29]. First, we distinguish between controllable and observable system actions when monitoring executions. Second, we give conditions for policy enforcement based

---

[1] Note that a trace property must also be a decidable set to be enforceable, as remarked later by Viswanathan [32] and Hamlen et al. [18].

on execution monitoring that are necessary and also sufficient. These two refinements of Schneider's work allow us to reason about the enforceability of policies that, for instance, involve timing constraints. We also provide results on the decidability of the decision problem of whether a policy is enforceable with respect to different specification languages.

We proceed as follows. In Section 2, we define our notion of enforceability. In Section 3, we relate it to a generalized notion of safety. In Section 4, we analyze the realizability problem for different specification languages. In Sections 5 and 6, we discuss related work and draw conclusions.

2   Enforceability

In this section, we first describe abstractly how enforcement mechanisms monitor systems and prevent policy violations. Afterwards, we define our notion of enforceability.

2.1   Policy Enforcement Based on Execution Monitoring

We take an abstract view of systems and their behaviors similar to Schneider [29] and others [24–26], where executions are finite or infinite sequences over an alphabet Σ. We assume that a system execution generates such a sequence incrementally, starting from the empty sequence ε. In the following, we also call these sequences *traces*. Possible interpretations of the elements in Σ are system actions, system states, or state-action pairs. Their actual meaning is irrelevant for us. However, what is important is that each of these elements is finitely represented and visible to a system observer, and that policies are described in terms of these elements. For convenience, we call the elements in Σ *actions*. Furthermore, we assume that the actions are classified as being either *controllable* actions $C \subseteq \Sigma$ or only *observable* actions $O \subseteq \Sigma$, with $O = \Sigma \setminus C$.

Our abstract system architecture for equipping a system S with an enforcement mechanism E is as follows. Before S executes an action $a \in \Sigma$, E intercepts it and checks whether a's execution violates the given policy P. If the execution of a leads to a policy violation and a is controllable, E terminates S. Otherwise, E does not intervene and S successfully executes a. Note that if the execution of a leads to a policy violation but a is only observable, E detects the violation but cannot prevent it. Hence, in this interaction between S and E, we extend Schneider's setting [29] by distinguishing between controllable and observable actions.

We conclude the description of this system architecture with the following remarks. First, in process algebras like CSP and CCS, S and E are modeled by processes over the action set Σ, and their interaction is the synchronous composition of processes. See, for example, [6], where it is assumed that all actions are controllable. The composed system deadlocks in case of policy violation. Since we distinguish between controllable and observable actions, the process modeling E must always be able to engage in actions in O. Second, instead of assuming that system actions are solely generated by the system S, the enforcement mechanism E can generate observable actions, which are internal and invisible to S.

For instance, the enforcement mechanism can have its own internal clock, which generates clock ticks. Third, instead of action interception and system termination, we could require that S sends a query to E whether executing an action $a \in C$ is authorized. E sends then a permit-or-deny message back to S who proceeds according to E's answer: in case of permit, S executes the action and in case of deny, S continues with an alternative action for which S might need to send a request to E prior to executing it. When executing an action in O, S notifies E of its execution. With this kind of interaction, E's function is similar to a policy decision point (PDP) in standard access-control architectures like XACML.

As pointed out by Schneider [29], a necessary condition for enforcing a policy by execution monitoring is that policy compliance is determined by the observed trace. We therefore require that a policy P is a *property of traces*, i.e., $P \subseteq \Sigma^* \cup \Sigma^\omega$, where Σ^* is the set of finite sequences over Σ and Σ^ω is the set of infinite sequences over Σ. We also write Σ^∞ for $\Sigma^* \cup \Sigma^\omega$. Since systems might not terminate—in fact, they often should not terminate—we also consider infinite traces, which describe system behaviors in the limit.

Another necessary condition for enforceability is that the decision of whether the enforcement mechanism E terminates the system S cannot depend on possible future actions [29]. This point is reflected in how and when E checks policy compliance in its interaction with S: E's decision depends on whether τa is in P, where a is the intercepted action and τ is the trace of the previously executed actions.

Additionally, although implicit in Schneider's work [29], there are *soundness* and *transparency* requirements for an enforcement mechanism [11, 18, 24, 25]. Soundness means that the enforcement mechanism must prevent system executions that are not policy compliant. Transparency means that the enforcement mechanism must not terminate system executions that are policy compliant. These requirements clearly restrict the class of trace properties that can be enforced by the interaction described above between S and E.

2.2   Formalization

Checking whether the execution of an action is policy compliant is at the core of any enforcement mechanism. The maximum information available to check is the intercepted action a together with the already executed trace τ. Our formalization of enforceability requires the existence of a Turing machine that carries out these checks. In particular, for every check, the Turing machine must terminate, either accepting or rejecting the input τa. Accepting the input means that executing a is policy compliant whereas rejecting τa means that a's execution leads to a policy violation. We do not formalize the interaction between the enforcement mechanism and the system and how actions are intercepted.

Prior to formalizing enforceability, we first introduce the following definitions. For a sequence $\sigma \in \Sigma^\infty$, we denote the set of its prefixes by $\text{pre}(\sigma)$ and the set of its finite prefixes by $\text{pre}_*(\sigma)$, i.e., $\text{pre}_*(\sigma) := \text{pre}(\sigma) \cap \Sigma^*$. The *truncation* of $L \subseteq \Sigma^*$ is $\text{trunc}(L) := \{\sigma \in \Sigma^* \mid \text{pre}(\sigma) \subseteq L\}$ and its *limit closure* is $\text{cl}(L) := L \cup \{\sigma \in \Sigma^\omega \mid \text{pre}_*(\sigma) \subseteq L\}$. Note that $\text{trunc}(L)$ is the largest subset of L that is prefix-closed and $\mathrm{cl}(L)$ contains, in addition to the sequences in L, the infinite sequences whose finite prefixes are all elements of L. Furthermore, for $L \subseteq \Sigma^*$ and $K \subseteq \Sigma^\infty$, we define $L \cdot K := \{\sigma\tau \in \Sigma^\infty \mid \sigma \in L \text{ and } \tau \in K\}$. For generality, we formalize enforceability relative to a *trace universe* U, which is a nonempty prefix-closed subset of Σ^∞.

Definition 1. *Let Σ be a set of actions. The property of traces $P \subseteq \Sigma^\infty$ is enforceable in the trace universe $U \subseteq \Sigma^\infty$ with the observable actions in $O \subseteq \Sigma$, (U, O)-enforceable for short, if there is a deterministic Turing machine $\mathcal{M}$ with the following properties, where $A \subseteq \Sigma^*$ is the set of inputs accepted by $\mathcal{M}$:*
(i) $\mathcal{M}$ halts on the inputs in $(\mathrm{trunc}(A) \cdot \Sigma) \cap U$.
(ii) $\mathcal{M}$ accepts the inputs in $(\mathrm{trunc}(A) \cdot O) \cap U$.
(iii) $\mathrm{cl}(\mathrm{trunc}(A)) \cap U = P \cap U$.
(iv) $\varepsilon \in A$.

Intuitively, with property (i) we ensure that whenever the enforcement mechanism E checks whether τa is policy compliant by using the Turing machine $\mathcal{M}$ (when intercepting the action $a \in \Sigma$), then E obtains an answer from $\mathcal{M}$. Note that we require that the trace τ produced so far by the system S is in $\mathrm{trunc}(A)$ and not in A, since if there is a prefix of τ that is not accepted by $\mathcal{M}$, then E would have terminated S earlier. Furthermore, we are only interested in traces in the universe U. Property (ii) states that $A \supseteq (\mathrm{trunc}(A) \cdot O) \cap U$ and we guarantee with it that a finite trace τa with $a \in O$ is policy compliant provided that $\tau a \in U$ and τ is policy compliant. Property (iii) relates the policy P with the inputs accepted by $\mathcal{M}$. Note that $\mathrm{cl}(\mathrm{trunc}(A)) \cap U \subseteq P \cap U$ formalizes the soundness requirement for an enforcement mechanism and $\mathrm{cl}(\mathrm{trunc}(A)) \cap U \supseteq P \cap U$ formalizes the transparency requirement. With property (iv) we ensure that the system S is initially policy compliant.

We illustrate Definition 1 by determining whether the following two policies are enforceable.

Example 2. The policy P_1 requires that whenever there is a *fail* action then there must not be a *login* action for at least 3 time units. The policy P_2 requires that every occurrence of a *request* action must be followed by a *deliver* action within 3 time units provided the system does not stop in the meanwhile. We give their trace sets below. We assume, for the ease of exposition, that actions do not happen simultaneously and whenever time progresses by one time unit, the system sends a *tick* action to the enforcement mechanism. However, more than one action can be executed in a single time unit.

Let Σ be the action set $\{tick, fail, login, request, deliver\}$. The trace universe $U \subseteq \Sigma^\infty$ consists of all infinite traces containing infinitely many *tick* actions and their finite prefixes. This models that time does not stop. We define P_1 as the complement with respect to U of the limit closure of

$$\{a_1 \ldots a_n \in \Sigma^* \mid \text{there are } i, j \in \{1, \ldots, n\} \text{ with } i < j \text{ such that } a_i = fail,$$
$$a_j = login, \text{ and } a_{i+1} \ldots a_{j-1} \text{ contains 3 or fewer } tick \text{ actions}\}$$

and P_2 as the complement with respect to U of the limit closure of

$\{a_1 \ldots a_n \in \Sigma^* \mid$ there are $i, j \in \{1, \ldots, n\}$ with $i < j$ such that $a_i = request$ and
$\qquad a_{i+1} \ldots a_j$ contains no $deliver$ action and more than 3 $ticks\}$.

A $tick$ action is only observable by an enforcement mechanism since the enforcement mechanism cannot prevent the progression of time. It is also reasonable to assume that $fail$ actions are only observable since otherwise an enforcement mechanism could prevent the failure from happening in the first place. Hence we define $O := \{tick, fail\}$.

It is straightforward to define a Turing machine $\mathcal{M}$ as required in Definition 1, showing that P_1 is (U, O)-enforceable. Intuitively, whenever the enforcement mechanism observes a $fail$ action, it prevents all $login$ actions until it has observed sufficiently many $tick$ actions. This requires that $login$ actions are controllable, whereas the actions $tick$ and $fail$ need only be observed by the enforcement mechanism.

The set of traces P_2 is not (U, O)-enforceable. The reason is that whenever an enforcement mechanism observes a $request$ action, it cannot terminate the system in time to prevent a policy violation when no $deliver$ action occurs within the given time bound. This is because the enforcement mechanism cannot prevent the progression of time. More precisely, assume that there exists a Turing machine $\mathcal{M}$ required in Definition 1, which must accept the trace $request\ tick^3 \in P_2 \cap U$. But then, by condition (ii) of Definition 1, it also must accept the trace $request\ tick^4 \notin P_2 \cap U$.

Natural questions that arise from Definition 1 are (1) for which class of trace properties does such a Turing machine $\mathcal{M}$ exist, (2) for which specification languages can we decide whether such a Turing machine $\mathcal{M}$ exists, and (3) when a policy is enforceable, can we synthesize from its given description an enforcement mechanism? We investigate these questions in the next two sections.

3   Relation between Enforceability and Safety

In this section, we characterize the class of trace properties that are enforceable with respect to Definition 1. To provide this characterization, we first generalize the standard notions of safety properties [1, 19].

3.1   Generalizing Safety

According to Lamport [23], a safety property intuitively states that nothing bad ever happens. A widely accepted formalization of this intuition, from Alpern and Schneider [1], is as follows: the set $P \subseteq \Sigma^\omega$ is ω-safety if

$$\forall \sigma \in \Sigma^\omega.\ \sigma \notin P \rightarrow \exists i \in \mathbb{N}.\ \forall \tau \in \Sigma^\omega.\ \sigma^{<i}\tau \notin P,$$

where $\sigma^{<i}$ denotes the prefix of σ of length i. In particular, $\sigma^{<0}$ is the empty sequence ε. Alpern and Schneider's definition takes only infinite sequences into account. Their definition, however, straightforwardly generalizes to finite and infinite sequences: the set $P \subseteq \Sigma^\infty$ is ∞-*safety* if

$$\forall \sigma \in \Sigma^\infty. \; \sigma \notin P \to \exists i \in \mathbb{N}. \; \forall \tau \in \Sigma^\infty. \; \sigma^{<i}\tau \notin P \, ,$$

where $\sigma^{<i} = \sigma$ if σ is finite and $i \in \mathbb{N}$ is greater than or equal to σ's length.

Note that ω-safety is not directly related to enforceability, since an enforcement mechanism monitors finite traces and ω-safety restricts the infinite traces in a set of traces. Moreover, note that ω-safety and ∞-safety differ even on sets of infinite sequences. For instance, the set $\{a\} \cdot \Sigma^\omega$ is ω-safety, since for every infinite sequence σ that does not start with a, no extension of $\sigma^{<1}$ is in $\{a\} \cdot \Sigma^\omega$. However, $\{a\} \cdot \Sigma^\omega$ is not ∞-safety, since we can extend the empty sequence, which is not in $\{a\} \cdot \Sigma^\omega$, by an infinite sequence τ that starts with the letter a. In general, whenever a policy $P \subseteq \Sigma^\infty$ is ∞-safety, the set $P \cap \Sigma^\omega$ of its infinite traces is ω-safety, whereas the converse is invalid.

In Definition 3 below, we give our generalized notion of safety, which is parametric in the universe U. The sets Σ^ω and Σ^∞ used in the definitions for ω-safety and ∞-safety are just two instances for U. This generalization is similar to Henzinger's [19] definitions of safety and liveness, which extends the classical safety-liveness classification for properties of untimed systems [1] to real-time settings. Furthermore, our definition is parametric in the set $O \subseteq \Sigma$. Intuitively, if a trace $\sigma \in U$ violates P, then this violation must be caused by a finite prefix of σ not ending with an element in O.

Definition 3. *Let $U \subseteq \Sigma^\infty$ and $O \subseteq \Sigma$. The set $P \subseteq \Sigma^\infty$ is (U, O)-safety if*

$$\forall \sigma \in U. \; \sigma \notin P \to \exists i \in \mathbb{N}. \; \sigma^{<i} \notin \Sigma^* \cdot O \land \forall \tau \in \Sigma^\infty. \; \sigma^{<i}\tau \notin P \cap U \, .$$

In the following examples, we illustrate this generalized notion of safety.

Example 4. Both the policies P_1 and P_2 from Example 2 are ∞-safety. If a trace τ violates P_1 then the violation can be pinpointed to a position where a *login* action is executed, i.e., there is some $i \geq 1$ with $\tau^{<i-1} \in P_1$, $\tau^{<i} \notin P_1$, and $\tau^{<i}$ ends with a *login* action. No matter how we extend $\tau^{<i}$, the extension still violates P_1. Analogously for P_2, policy violations are caused by *tick* actions instead of *login* actions.

However, P_1 is (U, O)-safety and P_2 is not (U, O)-safety, where U and O are as in Example 2. A violation of P_1 is caused by executing a *login* action, i.e., $\tau \in P_1$ and $\tau \, login \notin P_1$. We cannot extend such an execution so that the resulting extended trace is policy compliant. For P_2, a violation is caused by a *tick*. Here, the prefix excluding this *tick* action can be extended to a trace that is in P_2. Namely, we discharge the *request* action in the prefix by adding a *deliver* action.

Example 5. Recall the trace universe $U \subseteq \Sigma^\infty$ from Example 2, where $\Sigma = \{tick, fail, login, request, deliver\}$. It consists of the infinite traces with infinitely many *tick* actions and their finite prefixes. The trace property "always eventually a *tick* action," formalized as follows, is not safety:

$$P := \{\varepsilon\} \cup \{a_0 \ldots a_n \in \Sigma^* \mid n \in \mathbb{N} \text{ and } a_n = tick\} \cup$$
$$\{a_0 a_1 \cdots \in \Sigma^\omega \mid \text{for all } i \in \mathbb{N}, \text{ there is some } j \in \mathbb{N} \text{ with } j \geq i \text{ and } a_j = tick\} \, .$$

When considering only the infinite traces, the trace property $P \cap \Sigma^\omega$ is not ω-safety. In fact, according to Alpern and Schneider [1], $P \cap \Sigma^\omega$ is a liveness property.

P is also not $(U, \emptyset)$-safety since any nonempty trace $a_0 \ldots a_n$ with $a_n \neq tick$ is in $U \setminus P$ and can be extended to the trace $a_0 \ldots a_n\ tick$, which is in $P \cap U$. However, when we exclude finite traces from U, then P is $(U \cap \Sigma^\omega, \emptyset)$-safety, since $P \cap \Sigma^\omega = U \cap \Sigma^\omega$.

Lemma 6 below characterizes (U, O)-safety in terms of prefix sets and limit closures. For a set of sequences $L \subseteq \Sigma^\infty$, we abbreviate $\bigcup_{\sigma \in L} \mathrm{pre}(\sigma)$ by $\mathrm{pre}(L)$ and $\bigcup_{\sigma \in L} \mathrm{pre}_*(\sigma)$ by $\mathrm{pre}_*(L)$.

Lemma 6. *Let $U \subseteq \Sigma^\infty$ be a trace universe and $O \subseteq \Sigma$. The set $P \subseteq \Sigma^\infty$ is (U, O)-safety iff $\mathrm{cl}(\mathrm{pre}_*(P \cap U) \cdot O^*) \cap U \subseteq P$.*

Proof. We rephrase Definition 3 in terms of set containment, from which we conclude the stated equivalence.

We first show that the set $P \subseteq \Sigma^\infty$ is (U, O)-safety iff $\forall \sigma \in U.\ \sigma \notin P \rightarrow \mathrm{pre}_*(\sigma) \not\subseteq \mathrm{pre}_*(P \cap U) \cdot O^*$. We start with the left to right implication. Suppose that P is (U, O)-safety and let $\sigma \in U$. Assume that $\sigma \notin P$. Then there is an index $i \in \mathbb{N}$ such that (1) $\sigma^{<i} \notin \Sigma^* \cdot O$ and (2) $\sigma^{<i}\tau \notin P \cap U$, for all $\tau \in \Sigma^\infty$. (2) establishes that $\sigma^{<i} \notin \mathrm{pre}_*(P \cap U)$ and, together with (1), that $\sigma^{<i} \notin \mathrm{pre}_*(P \cap U) \cdot O^*$. As $\sigma^{<i} \in \mathrm{pre}_*(\sigma)$, we obtain that $\mathrm{pre}_*(\sigma) \not\subseteq \mathrm{pre}_*(P \cap U) \cdot O^*$. We now prove the right to left implication. Let $\sigma \in U \setminus P$. Then $\mathrm{pre}_*(\sigma) \not\subseteq \mathrm{pre}_*(P \cap U) \cdot O^*$, and thus there is an index $i \in \mathbb{N}$ such that $\sigma^{<i} \notin \mathrm{pre}_*(P \cap U) \cdot O^*$. Let $\sigma_1, \sigma_2 \in \Sigma^*$ be such that $\sigma^{<i} = \sigma_1 \sigma_2$, $\sigma_1 \notin \Sigma^* \cdot O$, and $\sigma_2 \in O^*$. Hence $\sigma_1 \notin \mathrm{pre}_*(P \cap U)$, that is $\sigma_1\tau \notin P \cap U$, for all $\tau \in \Sigma^\infty$. It follows that P is (U, O)-safety.

The statement $\forall \sigma \in U.\ \sigma \notin P \rightarrow \mathrm{pre}_*(\sigma) \not\subseteq \mathrm{pre}_*(P \cap U) \cdot O^*$ is equivalent to $\forall \sigma \in U.\ \sigma \in P \leftarrow \mathrm{pre}_*(\sigma) \subseteq \mathrm{pre}_*(P \cap U) \cdot O^*$. Since $\mathrm{pre}_*(P \cap U) \cdot O^*$ is prefix-closed, it is also equivalent to $\forall \sigma \in U.\ \sigma \in P \leftarrow \sigma \in \mathrm{cl}(\mathrm{pre}_*(P \cap U) \cdot O^*)$, i.e., $\mathrm{cl}(\mathrm{pre}_*(P \cap U) \cdot O^*) \cap U \subseteq P$. □

Note that $P \cap U \subseteq \mathrm{cl}(\mathrm{pre}_*(P \cap U) \cdot O^*) \cap U$, for any sets $P, U \subseteq \Sigma^\infty$ and $O \subseteq \Sigma$. Therefore, $P \subseteq \Sigma^\infty$ is (U, O)-safety iff $\mathrm{cl}(\mathrm{pre}_*(P \cap U) \cdot O^*) \cap U = P \cap U$.

3.2   Characterizing Enforceability

In the following, we generalize Schneider's [29] statement that ∞-safety is a necessary condition for a security policy to be enforceable by execution monitoring. First, we distinguish between controllable actions C and observable actions O. Second, we take a trace universe U into account. In Schneider's setting, $U = \Sigma^\infty$ and $O = \emptyset$. Third, we show that a policy $P \subseteq \Sigma^\infty$ must satisfy additional conditions to be enforceable. Finally, we show that our conditions are not only necessary, but also sufficient.

Theorem 7. *Let $U \subseteq \Sigma^\infty$ be a trace universe such that $U \cap \Sigma^*$ is a decidable set and let $O \subseteq \Sigma$. The set $P \subseteq \Sigma^\infty$ is (U, O)-enforceable iff the following conditions are satisfied:*

(1) P is (U, O)-safety,
(2) $\mathrm{pre}_*(P \cap U)$ is a decidable set, and
(3) $\varepsilon \in P$.

Proof. We start with the implication from left to right. Assume that $P \subseteq \Sigma^\infty$ is (U, O)-enforceable. Let $A \subseteq \Sigma^*$ be the set of inputs accepted by a Turing machine $\mathcal{M}$ determined by Definition 1. The set A satisfies the following properties: (a) $(\mathrm{trunc}(A) \cdot O) \cap U \subseteq A$, (b) $\mathrm{cl}(\mathrm{trunc}(A)) \cap U = P \cap U$, and (c) $\varepsilon \in A$.

First, we prove that P is (U, O)-safety. Let $\sigma \in U$ be a trace such that $\sigma \notin P$. Then, from (b), we have that $\sigma \notin \mathrm{cl}(\mathrm{trunc}(A))$. Hence there is an index $i \in \mathbb{N}$ such that $\sigma^{<i} \notin A$. Let i be the minimal index with this property. Then $i > 0$ and all proper prefixes of $\sigma^{<i}$ are in A, and hence $\sigma^{<i-1}$ is in $\mathrm{trunc}(A)$. Let $a \in \Sigma$ be such that $\sigma^{<i} = \sigma^{<i-1}a$. We have that $a \notin O$, as otherwise, from (a), $\sigma^{<i} \in A$, which is a contradiction. Hence $\sigma^{<i} \notin \Sigma^* \cdot O$. Moreover, as $\sigma^{<i} \notin A$, for any trace $\tau \in \Sigma^\infty$, we have that $\sigma^{<i}\tau \notin \mathrm{cl}(\mathrm{trunc}(A))$, that is, $\sigma^{<i}\tau \notin P$. This shows that σ satisfies the right hand side of the implication in Definition 3. Hence P is (U, O)-safety.

Second, note that A is not necessarily decidable, as $\mathcal{M}$ need not halt on all inputs in Σ^*. Since $U \cap \Sigma^*$ is decidable by assumption, there is a Turing machine $\mathcal{M}_U$ that terminates on Σ^* and that accepts $U \cap \Sigma^*$. Let $\mathcal{M}_{\mathrm{trunc}}$ be the following Turing machine. For an input $\sigma \in \Sigma^*$, $\mathcal{M}_{\mathrm{trunc}}$ executes steps 1 to 5 until it either accepts or rejects σ:

1. if $\mathcal{M}_U$ rejects σ, then $\mathcal{M}_{\mathrm{trunc}}$ rejects σ;
2. if $\sigma = \varepsilon$, then $\mathcal{M}_{\mathrm{trunc}}$ accepts σ;
3. if n is the length of σ and $\mathcal{M}_{\mathrm{trunc}}$ rejects $\sigma^{<n-1}$, then $\mathcal{M}_{\mathrm{trunc}}$ rejects σ;
4. if $\mathcal{M}$ accepts σ, then $\mathcal{M}_{\mathrm{trunc}}$ accepts σ;
5. otherwise, $\mathcal{M}_{\mathrm{trunc}}$ rejects σ.

It follows by induction over the length of σ that $\mathcal{M}_{\mathrm{trunc}}$ halts on σ and that $\mathcal{M}_{\mathrm{trunc}}$ accepts σ iff $\sigma \in \mathrm{trunc}(A) \cap U$. Therefore, $\mathrm{trunc}(A) \cap U$ is decidable. We have $\mathrm{pre}_*(P \cap U) = \mathrm{pre}_*(\mathrm{cl}(\mathrm{trunc}(A)) \cap U) = \mathrm{trunc}(A) \cap U \cap \Sigma^*$. Because both $\mathrm{trunc}(A) \cap U$ and $U \cap \Sigma^*$ are decidable, so is $\mathrm{pre}_*(P \cap U)$.

Third, as $\varepsilon \in A$ and $\varepsilon \in U$, we have $\varepsilon \in \mathrm{cl}(\mathrm{trunc}(A)) \cap U = P \cap U \subseteq P$.

We now prove the implication from right to left. Assume that P is (U, O)-safety, $\mathrm{pre}_*(P \cap U)$ is a decidable set, and $\varepsilon \in P$. We prove properties (i)–(iv) of Definition 1. As $\mathrm{pre}_*(P \cap U)$ is decidable, there is a Turing machine that halts on all inputs in Σ^* and accepts the set $A := \mathrm{pre}_*(P \cap U)$. Property (i) follows trivially. Property (iv) is also immediate as $\varepsilon \in P \cap U$. As $A = \mathrm{pre}_*(P \cap U)$ is prefix-closed, $\mathrm{trunc}(A) = A = \mathrm{pre}_*(P \cap U)$. It remains to be shown that (ii) $(\mathrm{pre}_*(P \cap U) \cdot O) \cap U \subseteq \mathrm{pre}_*(P \cap U)$ and (iii) $\mathrm{cl}(\mathrm{pre}_*(P \cap U)) \cap U = P \cap U$. By Lemma 6, and since P is (U, O)-safety, we have:

- $(\mathrm{pre}_*(P \cap U) \cdot O) \cap U \subseteq \mathrm{cl}(\mathrm{pre}_*(P \cap U) \cdot O^*) \cap U \cap \Sigma^* = P \cap U \cap \Sigma^* \subseteq \mathrm{pre}_*(P \cap U)$;
- $P \cap U \subseteq \mathrm{cl}(\mathrm{pre}_*(P \cap U)) \cap U \subseteq \mathrm{cl}(\mathrm{pre}_*(P \cap U) \cdot O^*) \cap U = P \cap U$.

Therefore, P is (U, O)-enforceable. $\qquad\square$

4   Realizability

In this section, we investigate the realizability problem for enforcement mechanisms for security policies. We examine this problem for two policy specification formalisms, based on automata and temporal logic.

4.1   Automata-Based Specification Languages

Automata may be used to give direct, operational specifications of security policies [24, 25, 29]. For instance, Schneider [29] introduces security automata as a formalism for specifying and implementing the decision making of enforcement mechanisms. Given a deterministic security automaton $\mathcal{A}$, the enforcement mechanism E stores $\mathcal{A}$'s current state and whenever E intercepts an action, it updates the stored state using $\mathcal{A}$'s transition function. If there is no outgoing transition and the action is controllable, then E terminates the system. Nondeterministic security automata are handled analogously by storing and updating finite sets of states. In this case, E terminates the system if the set of states becomes empty during an update.

Roughly speaking, if all actions are controllable then the existence of a security automaton specifying a policy implies that the policy is enforceable. This is because security automata characterize the class of trace properties that are ∞-safety. However, if there are actions that are only observable, the existence of a security automaton is insufficient to conclude that the policy is enforceable. Additional checks are needed. We show that these checks can be carried out algorithmically for policies described by finite-state automata. In contrast to security automata, a finite-state automaton has a finite set of states and a finite alphabet, and not all its states are accepting. Furthermore, we delimit the boundary between decidability and undecidability by showing that for a more expressive automata model, namely, pushdown automata, the realizability problem is undecidable.

We start by defining pushdown and finite-state automata. Since trace properties are sets of finite and infinite sequences, we equip the automata with two sets of accepting states, one for finite sequences and the other for infinite sequences.

A *pushdown automaton (PDA)* $\mathcal{A}$ is a tuple $(Q, \Sigma, \Gamma, \delta, q_{\mathrm{I}}, F, B)$, where (1) Q is a finite set of states, (2) Σ is a finite nonempty alphabet, (3) Γ is a finite stack alphabet with $\# \in \Gamma$, (4) $\delta : Q \times \Sigma \times \Gamma \to 2^{Q \times \Gamma^*}$ is the transition function, where $\delta(q, a, b)$ is a finite set, for all $q \in Q$, $a \in \Sigma$, and $b \in \Gamma$, (5) $q_{\mathrm{I}} \in Q$ is the initial state, (6) $F \subseteq Q$ is the set of accepting states for finite sequences, and (7) $B \subseteq Q$ is the set of accepting states for infinite sequences. The *size* of $\mathcal{A}$, denoted by $\|\mathcal{A}\|$, is the cardinality of Q.

A *configuration* of $\mathcal{A}$ is a pair (q, u) with $q \in Q$ and $u \in \Gamma^*$. A *run* of $\mathcal{A}$ on the finite sequence $a_0 \ldots a_{n-1} \in \Sigma^*$ is a sequence of configurations (q_0, u_0) $(q_1, u_1) \ldots (q_n, u_n)$ with $(q_0, u_0) = (q_{\mathrm{I}}, \#)$ and for all $i \in \mathbb{N}$ with $i < n$, it holds that $u_i = vb$, $(q_{i+1}, w) \in \delta(q_i, a_i, b)$, and $u_{i+1} = vw$, for some $v, w \in \Gamma^*$ and $b \in \Gamma$. The run is *accepting* if $q_n \in F$. Runs over infinite sequences are defined analogously. The infinite sequence $(q_0, u_0)(q_1, u_1) \cdots \in (Q \times \Gamma^*)^\omega$ is a *run* on

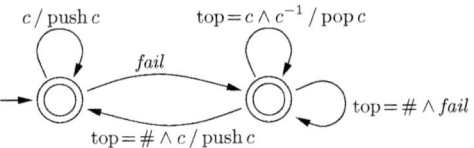

Fig. 1. Pushdown automaton, where c ranges over the elements in C

the infinite sequence $a_0 a_1 \cdots \in \Sigma^\omega$ if $(q_0, u_0) = (q_I, \#)$ and for all $i \in \mathbb{N}$, it holds that $u_i = vb$, $(q_{i+1}, w) \in \delta(q_i, a_i, b)$, and $u_{i+1} = vw$, for some $v, w \in \Gamma^*$ and $b \in \Gamma$. The run is *accepting* if it fulfills the Büchi acceptance condition, i.e., for every $i \in \mathbb{N}$, there is some $j \in \mathbb{N}$ with $j \geq i$ and $q_j \in B$. In other words, the run visits a state in B infinitely often. We define $L(\mathcal{A}) := L_*(\mathcal{A}) \cup L_\omega(\mathcal{A})$, where

$$L_\circ(\mathcal{A}) := \{\sigma \in \Sigma^\circ \mid \text{there is an accepting run of } \mathcal{A} \text{ on } \sigma\},$$

for $\circ \in \{*, \omega\}$.

We say that $\mathcal{A}$ is a *finite-state automaton (FSA)* if its transitions do not depend on the stack content, i.e., $\delta(q, a, b) = \delta(q, a, b')$, for all $q \in Q$, $a \in \Sigma$, and $b, b' \in \Gamma$. In this case, we may omit the stack alphabet Γ and assume that δ is of type $Q \times \Sigma \to 2^Q$. Runs over finite and infinite sequences simplify then to sequences in Q^* and Q^ω, respectively.

PDAs are more expressive than FSAs, as illustrated by the following example.

Example 8. Let C and C^{-1} be finite nonempty sets of actions with $C^{-1} = \{c^{-1} \mid c \in C\}$. That is, every action $c \in C$ has a corresponding "undo" action $c^{-1} \in C^{-1}$. Consider the policy stating that whenever a *fail* action is executed the system must backtrack before continuing. That is, consider the language $L := \text{pre}(F^* \cdot C^\omega) \cup F^\omega$ over the alphabet $\Sigma := C \cup C^{-1} \cup \{fail\}$, with $F := \{c_1 \ldots c_n \, fail \, c_n^{-1} \ldots c_1^{-1} \mid n \in \mathbb{N} \text{ and } c_1, \ldots, c_n \in C\}$, where the superscripts $*$ and ω denote here the finite and infinite concatenation of languages, respectively. The PDA in Figure 1, where both states are accepting for both finite and infinite sequences, recognizes this language. However, no FSA accepts this language.

Observe that this policy is $(\Sigma^\infty, \emptyset)$-enforceable. Indeed, the conditions in Theorem 7 are satisfied: (1) L contains the empty sequence, (2) $\text{pre}_*(L) = F^* \cdot (C^* \cup C^* \cdot F)$ is decidable, and (3) $\text{cl}(\text{pre}_*(L)) = F^\omega \cup F^* \cdot (C^\infty \cup C^* \cdot F) = L$ is $(\Sigma^\infty, \emptyset)$-safety. The policy is not $(\Sigma^\infty, \{fail\})$-enforceable, since an enforcement mechanism must terminate the system when intercepting the second *fail* action in the trace $c_1 c_2 \, fail \, c_2^{-1} \, fail \, c_1^{-1}$.

We now turn to the decision problem of checking whether a policy given as a PDA or FSA is enforceable. In each case, we first analyze the related decision problem of checking whether a policy is a safety property.

Theorem 9. *Let Σ be the alphabet $\{0, 1\}$. It is undecidable to determine for a PDA $\mathcal{A}$ with alphabet Σ whether $L(\mathcal{A})$ is $(\Sigma^\infty, \emptyset)$-safety.*

Proof. Recall that the universality problem for context-free grammars is undecidable [20]. That means, we cannot decide if $L_*(\mathcal{A}) = \Sigma^*$, for a given PDA $\mathcal{A}$.

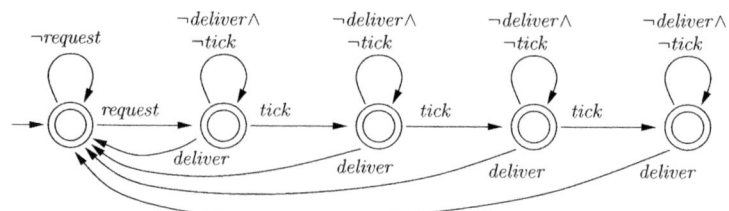

Fig. 2. Finite-state automaton

Given a PDA $\mathcal{A}$, we build a PDA $\mathcal{A}'$ with $L(\mathcal{A}') = L(\mathcal{A}) \cup \Sigma^\omega$. Thus we have that $L(\mathcal{A}') = L_*(\mathcal{A}) \cup \Sigma^\omega$ and $\mathrm{cl}(\mathrm{pre}_*(L(\mathcal{A}'))) = \Sigma^\infty$. Then, from Lemma 6, $L(\mathcal{A}')$ is $(\Sigma^\infty, \emptyset)$-safety iff $L_*(\mathcal{A}) = \Sigma^*$. □

Theorem 10. *Let Σ be the alphabet $\{0,1\}$. It is undecidable to determine for a PDA $\mathcal{A}$ with alphabet Σ whether $L(\mathcal{A})$ is $(\Sigma^\infty, \emptyset)$-enforceable.*

Proof. From $\mathcal{A}$ we build a PDA $\mathcal{A}'$ with $L(\mathcal{A}') = L(\mathcal{A}) \cup \Sigma^\omega \cup \{\varepsilon\}$. Note that $\mathrm{pre}_*(L(\mathcal{A}')) = \Sigma^*$ is decidable and that $\varepsilon \in L(\mathcal{A})$. Moreover, one can decide whether $\varepsilon \in L_*(\mathcal{A})$ but not whether $L_*(\mathcal{A}) = \Sigma^*$. Hence one cannot decide whether $\Sigma^* = L_*(\mathcal{A}) \cup \{\varepsilon\}$. By Theorem 7, the language $L(\mathcal{A}')$ is $(\Sigma^\infty, \emptyset)$-enforceable iff $L(\mathcal{A}')$ is $(\Sigma^\infty, \emptyset)$-safety iff $\Sigma^* = L_*(\mathcal{A}) \cup \{\varepsilon\}$. □

It is straightforward to define FSAs that recognize the languages P_1 and P_2 from Example 2. For instance, the FSA depicted in Figure 2 recognizes P_2. Since this FSA is deterministic, it is easy to check that the recognized language is not (U, O)-safety and therefore also not (U, O)-enforceable, where U and O are as in Example 2. There is a state from which the observable *tick* action leads to nonacceptance of the input sequence. In general, the problem is PSPACE-complete as shown in Corollary 12 below.

Theorem 11. *Let $\mathcal{U}$ be an FSA over the alphabet Σ such that $L(\mathcal{U})$ is a trace universe and let $O \subseteq \Sigma$. The decision problem of determining, for an FSA $\mathcal{A}$ over Σ, whether $L(\mathcal{A})$ is $(L(\mathcal{U}), O)$-safety, is PSPACE-complete.*

Proof. Recall that the universality problem for FSAs, that is, deciding whether $L_*(\mathcal{A}) = \Sigma^*$ for a given FSA $\mathcal{A}$, is PSPACE-complete [20].

Given an FSA $\mathcal{A}$, we build an FSA $\mathcal{A}'$ with $L(\mathcal{A}') = L(\mathcal{A}) \cup \Sigma^\omega$. As in the proof of Theorem 9, $L(\mathcal{A}')$ is $(\Sigma^\infty, \emptyset)$-safety iff $L_*(\mathcal{A}) = \Sigma^*$. This proves that checking whether $L(\mathcal{A}')$ is $(L(\mathcal{U}), O)$-safety is PSPACE-hard.

To establish membership in PSPACE, we first show how to build, for a given FSA $\mathcal{X} = (Q, \Sigma, \delta, q_1, F, B)$, two FSAs $\mathcal{Y}$ and $\mathcal{Z}$ such that $L(\mathcal{Y}) = \mathrm{pre}_*(L(\mathcal{X}))$ and, if $L(\mathcal{X}) \cap \Sigma^* = \mathrm{pre}_*(L(\mathcal{X}))$ then $L(\mathcal{Z}) = \mathrm{cl}(L(\mathcal{X}) \cap \Sigma^*)$:

- Let B' be the set of states $q \in B$ that are on a cycle in $\mathcal{X}$. Let $F_{\mathcal{Y}}$ be the set of states $q \in Q$ for which there is a path in $\mathcal{X}$ starting in q and ending in a state of $F \cup B'$. The FSA $\mathcal{Y} := (Q, \Sigma, \delta, q_1, F_{\mathcal{Y}}, \emptyset)$ accepts the language $L(\mathcal{Y}) = \mathrm{pre}_*(L(\mathcal{X}))$.
- If $\mathrm{pre}_*(L(\mathcal{X})) = L(\mathcal{X}) \cap \Sigma^*$, the FSA $\mathcal{Z} := (Q, \Sigma, \delta, q_1, F, F)$ accepts the language $L(\mathcal{Z}) = \mathrm{cl}(L(\mathcal{X}) \cap \Sigma^*)$.

Consider an FSA $\mathcal{A}$. Using the two previous constructions, we build an FSA $\mathcal{A}'$ whose size is polynomial in $\|\mathcal{A}\|$, such that $L(\mathcal{A}') = \mathrm{cl}(\mathrm{pre}_*(L(\mathcal{A}) \cap L(\mathcal{U})) \cdot O^*) \cap L(\mathcal{U})$. Note that $\|\mathcal{U}\|$ is a constant, as $\mathcal{U}$ is fixed. By Lemma 6 $L(\mathcal{A})$ is $(L(\mathcal{U}), O)$-safety iff $L(\mathcal{A}') \subseteq L(\mathcal{A})$. Since the inclusion problem for FSAs is in PSPACE [16], our problem is therefore also in PSPACE. $\qquad\square$

Corollary 12. *Let $\mathcal{U}$ be an FSA over the alphabet Σ such that $L(\mathcal{U})$ is a trace universe and let $O \subseteq \Sigma$. The decision problem of determining, for an FSA $\mathcal{A}$ over Σ, whether $L(\mathcal{A})$ is $(L(\mathcal{U}), O)$-enforceable, is PSPACE-complete.*

Proof. The proof is similar to that of Theorem 10, the statement being an easy consequence of Theorems 7 and 11. $\qquad\square$

4.2 Logic-Based Specification Languages

Temporal logics are prominent specification languages for expressing properties on traces [28]. In the following, we consider a linear-time temporal logic with future and past operators, and metric constraints [2,22].

We fix a finite set $\mathcal{P}$ of propositions, where we assume that they are classified into observable propositions $O \subseteq \mathcal{P}$ and controllable propositions $\mathcal{P} \setminus O$. The syntax of the metric linear-time temporal logic MLTL is given by the grammar

$$\varphi ::= true \mid p \mid \neg\varphi \mid \varphi \vee \varphi \mid \bullet_I \varphi \mid \bigcirc_I \varphi \mid \varphi \, \mathsf{S}_I \, \varphi \mid \varphi \, \mathsf{U}_I \, \varphi,$$

where p ranges over the propositions in $\mathcal{P}$ and I ranges over the nonempty intervals over $\mathbb{N}$, i.e., subsets of the form $\{n, n+1, \ldots, m\}$ and $\{n, n+1, \ldots\}$ with $n, m \in \mathbb{N}$ and $n \leq m$. The *size* of a formula φ, denoted by $\|\varphi\|$, is the number of φ's subformulas plus the sum of the representation sizes of the interval bounds occurring in φ, which are $\lceil \log(1 + \max I) \rceil$ for a finite interval I, and $\lceil \log(1 + \min I) \rceil$ for an infinite interval I.

We use standard syntactic sugar. For instance, $\varphi \wedge \psi$ abbreviates $\neg(\neg\varphi \vee \neg\psi)$, $\Diamond_I \varphi$ abbreviates $true \, \mathsf{U}_I \varphi$, and $\Box_I \varphi$ abbreviates $\neg \Diamond_I (\neg\varphi)$. We drop the interval attached to a temporal operator if it is $\mathbb{N}$ and we use constraints like $\leq n$ and $\geq n$ to describe intervals of the form $\{0, 1, \ldots, n\}$ and $\{n, n+1, \ldots\}$, respectively. Furthermore, we use standard conventions concerning the binding strength of operators to omit parentheses. For instance, $\neg$ binds stronger than $\wedge$, which in turn binds stronger than $\vee$. Boolean operators bind stronger than temporal ones.

The truth value of a formula φ is defined over timestamped sequences, where time is monotonically increasing and progressing. To formalize this, we introduce the following notation. We denote the length of a sequence σ by $|\sigma|$ and the letter at the $(i+1)$st position in σ by σ_i, where $i \in \mathbb{N}$ with $i < |\sigma|$. We define T as the set that consists of the sequences $t \in \mathbb{N}^\infty$ with the following properties:

(i) For each $i, j \in \mathbb{N}$ with $i \leq j < |t|$, $t_i \leq t_j$.
(ii) If t is infinite then for each $k \in \mathbb{N}$, there is an integer $i \in \mathbb{N}$ with $t_i \geq k$.

Furthermore, for sequences $\sigma \in (2^\mathcal{P})^\infty$ and $t \in T$ with $|\sigma| = |t|$, we define $\sigma \otimes t$ as the sequence of length $|\sigma|$ with $(\sigma \otimes t)_i := (\sigma_i, t_i)$, for $i \in \mathbb{N}$ with $i < |\sigma|$. For $L \subseteq (2^\mathcal{P})^\infty$, we define $L \otimes T := \{\sigma \otimes t \mid \sigma \in L, \ t \in T, \text{ and } |\sigma| = |t|\}$.

For $\sigma \in (2^{\mathcal{P}})^{\infty}$, $t \in T$, and $i \in \mathbb{N}$ with $|\sigma| = |t|$ and $i < |\sigma|$, we define the relation $\models$ inductively over the formula structure:

$$\sigma, t, i \models true$$
$$\sigma, t, i \models p \quad \text{iff} \quad p \in \sigma_i$$
$$\sigma, t, i \models \neg\varphi \quad \text{iff} \quad \sigma, t, i \not\models \varphi$$
$$\sigma, t, i \models \varphi \vee \psi \quad \text{iff} \quad \sigma, t, i \models \varphi \text{ or } \sigma, t, i \models \psi$$
$$\sigma, t, i \models \bullet_I \varphi \quad \text{iff} \quad i > 0 \text{ and } t_i - t_{i-1} \in I \text{ and } \sigma, t, i - 1 \models \varphi$$
$$\sigma, t, i \models \bigcirc_I \varphi \quad \text{iff} \quad i < |\sigma| - 1 \text{ and } t_{i+1} - t_i \in I \text{ and } \sigma, t, i + 1 \models \varphi$$
$$\sigma, t, i \models \varphi \, \mathsf{S}_I \, \psi \quad \text{iff} \quad \text{there is an integer } j \in \mathbb{N} \text{ with } j \leq i \text{ such that}$$
$$t_i - t_j \in I \text{ and } \sigma, t, j \models \psi \text{ and}$$
$$\sigma, t, k \models \varphi, \text{ for all } k \in \mathbb{N} \text{ with } j < k \leq i$$
$$\sigma, t, i \models \varphi \, \mathsf{U}_I \, \psi \quad \text{iff} \quad \text{there is an integer } j \in \mathbb{N} \text{ with } i \leq j < |\sigma| \text{ such that}$$
$$t_j - t_i \in I \text{ and } \sigma, t, j \models \psi \text{ and}$$
$$\sigma, t, k \models \varphi, \text{ for all } k \in \mathbb{N} \text{ with } i \leq k < j$$

Finally, for a formula φ, we define $L(\varphi) := \{\varepsilon\} \cup \{\sigma \otimes t \in (2^{\mathcal{P}})^{\infty} \otimes T \mid \sigma, t, 0 \models \varphi\}$. We also define $L_{\omega}(\varphi)$ and $L_*(\varphi)$ that consist of the infinite and finite sequences in $L(\varphi)$, respectively. Note that different semantics exist for linear-time temporal logics over finite traces [10], each with their own artifacts. Since our semantics is not defined for the empty sequence, we include it in $L(\varphi)$.

The time model over which MLTL's semantics is defined is discrete and point-based. See Alur and Henzinger's survey [2] for an overview of alternative time models and their relationships. We briefly justify our chosen time model. The use of the discrete time domain $\mathbb{N}$ instead of a dense time domain like $\mathbb{Q}_{\geq 0}$ or even $\mathbb{R}_{\geq 0}$ is justified by the fact that clocks with arbitrarily fine precision do not exist in practice. The choice of a point-based time model is justified by our action-based view of system executions, where an action happens at some point in time. Furthermore, an enforcement mechanism does not continuously monitor the system but only at specific points in time.

Example 13. We return to the policies from Example 2. Let $\mathcal{P}$ be the proposition set $\{fail, login, request, deliver\}$. The formula

$$\varphi_1 := \square \, fail \rightarrow \square_{\leq 3} \neg login$$

formalizes the first policy and the second policy is formalized by the formula

$$\varphi_2 := \square \, request \rightarrow \diamondsuit_{\leq 3}(deliver \vee \neg \bigcirc true).$$

The trace properties described by φ_1 and φ_2 differ from the trace properties P_1 and P_2 from Example 2 in the following respects. First, the progression of time in P_1 and P_2 was explicitly modeled by *tick* actions. In $L(\varphi_1)$ and $L(\varphi_2)$ time is modeled by timestamping the letters in the sequences in $(2^{\mathcal{P}})^{\infty}$. We only consider timestamped sequences that adequately model time, i.e., the sequences in the trace universe $(2^{\mathcal{P}})^{\infty} \otimes T$, which is a subset of $(2^{\mathcal{P}} \times \mathbb{N})^{\infty}$. Second, the traces in Example 2 contained only one system action at a time. Here, we consider traces in which multiple system actions can happen at the same point in time. Instead of using the trace universe $(2^{\mathcal{P}})^\infty \otimes T$, we can alternatively use the trace universe $\mathcal{P}^\infty \otimes T$ by filtering out the traces where a letter $(a, t) \in 2^{\mathcal{P}} \times \mathbb{N}$ occurs and a is not a singleton. However, the trace universe $\mathcal{P}^\infty \otimes T$ is more restrictive.

The trace properties described by φ_1 and φ_2 match the trace properties P_1 and P_2 from Example 2 with respect to enforceability. Here $O = \{\mathit{fail}\}$ and a letter $(a, t) \in 2^{\mathcal{P}} \times \mathbb{N}$ is only observable iff a does not contain any controllable actions, that is, iff $a = \emptyset$ or $a = \{\mathit{fail}\}$. To see, for instance, that $L(\varphi_2)$ is not enforceable, consider the trace $\sigma = (\{\mathit{request}\}, 0)$ and the letter $a = (\emptyset, 4)$. Then $\sigma \in L(\varphi_2)$ and $\sigma a \notin L(\varphi_2)$, while a is only observable.

In general, we assume that $a \in 2^{\mathcal{P}}$ is observable if $a \subseteq O$. In other words, $a \in 2^{\mathcal{P}}$ is controllable if it contains at least one controllable proposition. In particular, the empty set is not controllable. We define $\hat{O} := \{a \in 2^{\mathcal{P}} \mid a \subseteq O\}$.

In the remainder of this section, we analyze the complexity of two related realizability problems where policies are specified in MLTL. We start with the realizability problem for the untimed fragment of MLTL, which we call LTL. The interval attached to a temporal operator occurring in a formula of this fragment is $\mathbb{N}$. Hence, an LTL formula does not specify any timing constraints and, instead of $(2^{\mathcal{P}})^\infty \otimes T$, we consider trace universes that are subsets of $(2^{\mathcal{P}})^\infty$.

Lemma 14. *Let $O \subseteq \mathcal{P}$ and let $\mathcal{U}$ be an FSA such that $L(\mathcal{U}) \subseteq (2^{\mathcal{P}})^\infty$ is a trace universe. The decision problem of checking for an LTL formula φ whether $L(\varphi)$ is $(L(\mathcal{U}), \hat{O})$-enforceable is PSPACE-complete.*

Proof. By Theorem 7 we have that $L(\varphi)$ is $(L(\mathcal{U}), \hat{O})$-enforceable iff $L(\varphi)$ is $(L(\mathcal{U}), \hat{O})$-safety: note that $\varepsilon \in L(\varphi)$ by definition and $\mathrm{pre}_*(L(\varphi) \cap L(\mathcal{U}))$ is regular, hence decidable. Hence it suffices to show that determining whether $L(\varphi)$ is $(L(\mathcal{U}), \hat{O})$-safety is PSPACE-complete.

We first prove that the problem is PSPACE-hard. Recall that the satisfiability problem for LTL over infinite sequences is PSPACE-complete [30]. Given an LTL formula φ, we define $\varphi' := \varphi \vee \Diamond \neg \bigcirc \mathit{true}$. Then $L(\varphi') = L(\varphi) \cup (2^{\mathcal{P}})^*$. Moreover, using Lemma 6, we have that $L(\varphi')$ is $((2^{\mathcal{P}})^\infty, \emptyset)$-safety iff $L_\omega(\varphi) = (2^{\mathcal{P}})^\omega$ iff $L_\omega(\neg \varphi) = \emptyset$. Hence determining if $L(\varphi)$ is $((2^{\mathcal{P}})^\infty, \emptyset)$-safety is PSPACE-hard.

To show membership in PSPACE, let φ be an LTL formula of size $n \in \mathbb{N}$. There exist FSAs $\mathcal{A}$ and $\mathcal{A}'$ with $L(\mathcal{A}) = L(\varphi)$, $L(\mathcal{A}') = L(\neg \varphi)$, and $\|\mathcal{A}\|, \|\mathcal{A}'\| \in 2^{O(n)}$. These two FSAs can be obtained by straightforwardly extending the translations of LTL over infinite sequences into nondeterministic Büchi automata [8, 31]. Using standard automata constructions and the constructions from the proof of Theorem 11, we build an FSA $\mathcal{B}$ with $\|\mathcal{B}\| \in 2^{O(n)}$ and $L(\mathcal{B}) = L(\mathcal{A}') \cap L(\mathcal{U}) \cap \mathrm{cl}(\mathrm{pre}_*(L(\mathcal{A}) \cap L(\mathcal{U})) \cdot \hat{O}^*) \setminus \{\varepsilon\}$. It follows that $L(\varphi)$ is $(L(\mathcal{U}), \hat{O})$-safety iff $\mathrm{cl}(\mathrm{pre}_*(L(\varphi) \cap L(\mathcal{U})) \cdot \hat{O}^*) \cap L(\mathcal{U}) \subseteq L(\varphi)$ iff $L(\mathcal{B}) = \emptyset$. Since the emptiness problem for FSAs is in NLOGSPACE [21] and since we can construct $\mathcal{B}$ on the fly, our problem is in PSPACE. □

If $L(\varphi)$ is $(L(\mathcal{U}), \hat{O})$-enforceable, we can use the FSA $\mathcal{U}$ and the FSA $\mathcal{A}$ constructed in the proof of Lemma 14 to obtain an enforcement mechanism for $L(\varphi)$. Namely, we construct the product automaton $\mathcal{C}$ of $\mathcal{U}$ and $\mathcal{A}$ that accepts the intersection of $L(\mathcal{U})$ and $L(\mathcal{A})$. The enforcement mechanism E initially stores the singleton set consisting of $\mathcal{C}$'s initial state. Whenever E intercepts a system action $a \in 2^{\mathcal{P}}$, it updates this set by determining the successor states of the stored states using $\mathcal{C}$'s transition function. We remove from the updated set the states from which we do not accept any sequence. E terminates the system if the set becomes empty provided that the intercepted action a is controllable. Otherwise, it continues by intercepting the next system action.

Theorem 15. *Let $O \subseteq \mathcal{P}$ and let $\mathcal{U}$ be an FSA such that $L(\mathcal{U}) \subseteq (2^{\mathcal{P}})^\infty$ is a trace universe. The decision problem of checking for an MLTL formula φ whether $L(\varphi)$ is $(L(\mathcal{U}) \otimes T, \hat{O} \times \mathbb{N})$-enforceable is EXPSPACE-complete.*

Proof. Let $tick \notin \mathcal{P}$ be a new proposition modeling clock ticks. Let $\Sigma := 2^{\mathcal{P}}$, $\overline{\Sigma} := 2^{\mathcal{P} \cup \{tick\}}$, $U_T := L(\mathcal{U}) \otimes T$, and $\mathcal{T} := \Sigma^\infty \otimes T$. We first map each MLTL formula φ to an LTL formula $\overline{\varphi}$, each FSA $\mathcal{A}$ to an FSA $\overline{\mathcal{A}}$, and each trace τ in $\mathcal{T}$ to a trace $\overline{\tau}$ in $\overline{\Sigma}^\omega$ such that
- $\tau \in L(\varphi)$ iff $\overline{\tau} \in L(\overline{\varphi})$ and
- $\tau \in L(\mathcal{A})$ iff $\overline{\tau} \in L(\overline{\mathcal{A}})$.

For a trace $\tau = \sigma \otimes t$ in $\mathcal{T}$, we define the trace $\overline{\tau}$ in $\overline{\Sigma}^\infty$ as follows:
- if τ is infinite, then $\overline{\tau} := \{tick\}^{t_0} \sigma_0 \{tick\}^{d_1} \sigma_1 \{tick\}^{d_2} \sigma_2 \ldots$,
- if $\tau = \varepsilon$, then $\overline{\tau} := \{tick\}^\omega$, and
- if $\tau \neq \varepsilon$ is finite, then $\overline{\tau} := \{tick\}^{t_0} \sigma_0 \{tick\}^{d_1} \sigma_1 \{tick\}^{d_2} \sigma_2 \ldots \sigma_{|\tau|-1} \{tick\}^\omega$,

where $d_i := t_i - t_{i-1}$, $\{tick\}^i$ is the sequence $\{tick\} \ldots \{tick\}$ of length i and $\{tick\}^\omega$ is the infinite sequence $\{tick\}\{tick\}\ldots$. For a set of traces $L \subseteq \mathcal{T}$, we abbreviate by $\overline{L}$ the set $\{\overline{\tau} \in \overline{\Sigma}^\infty \mid \tau \in L\}$. Note that this mapping is one-to-one, so that it induces a bijection from L to $\overline{L}$.

For an MLTL formula φ, we define the formulas $\ulcorner \varphi \urcorner$ and $\overline{\varphi}$ as follows:

- $\ulcorner true \urcorner := true$,
- $\ulcorner p \urcorner := p$ if $p \in \mathcal{P}$,
- $\ulcorner \neg \varphi \urcorner := \neg \ulcorner \varphi \urcorner$,
- $\ulcorner \varphi \vee \psi \urcorner := \ulcorner \varphi \urcorner \vee \ulcorner \psi \urcorner$,
- $\ulcorner \bigcirc_I \varphi \urcorner := \ulcorner \bigcirc_I true \urcorner \wedge \ulcorner \bigcirc \varphi \urcorner$ if $I \neq \mathbb{N}$ and $\varphi \neq true$,
- $\ulcorner \bigcirc_I true \urcorner := \bigcirc(tick \wedge \ulcorner \bigcirc_{I-1} true \urcorner)$ if $0 \notin I$, where $I - 1 := \{t - 1 \mid t \in I\}$,
- $\ulcorner \bigcirc_{[0,a]} true \urcorner := \bigcirc(\neg tick \vee \ulcorner \bigcirc_{[0,a-1]} true \urcorner)$ if $a \geq 1$,
- $\ulcorner \bigcirc_{[0,0]} true \urcorner := \bigcirc \neg tick$,
- $\ulcorner \bigcirc \varphi \urcorner := \bigcirc(tick \mathbin{\mathsf{U}} (\neg tick \wedge \ulcorner \varphi \urcorner))$,
- $\ulcorner \varphi \mathbin{\mathsf{U}}_I \psi \urcorner := (\neg tick \wedge \ulcorner \varphi \urcorner) \mathbin{\mathsf{U}} (tick \wedge \bigcirc(\ulcorner \varphi \mathbin{\mathsf{U}}_{I-1} \psi \urcorner))$ if $0 \notin I$,
- $\ulcorner \varphi \mathbin{\mathsf{U}}_{[0,a]} \psi \urcorner := (\neg tick \wedge \ulcorner \varphi \urcorner) \mathbin{\mathsf{U}} ((\neg tick \wedge \ulcorner \psi \urcorner) \vee (tick \wedge \bigcirc(\ulcorner \varphi \mathbin{\mathsf{U}}_{[0,a-1]} \psi \urcorner)))$ if $a \geq 1$,
- $\ulcorner \varphi \mathbin{\mathsf{U}}_{[0,0]} \psi \urcorner := (\neg tick \wedge \ulcorner \varphi \urcorner) \mathbin{\mathsf{U}} (\neg tick \wedge \ulcorner \psi \urcorner)$,
- $\ulcorner \varphi \mathbin{\mathsf{U}} \psi \urcorner := (tick \vee \ulcorner \varphi \urcorner) \mathbin{\mathsf{U}} (\neg tick \wedge \ulcorner \psi \urcorner)$,
- $\ulcorner \bullet_I \varphi \urcorner$ and $\ulcorner \varphi \mathbin{\mathsf{S}}_I \psi \urcorner$ are defined analogously to $\ulcorner \bigcirc_I \varphi \urcorner$ and $\ulcorner \varphi \mathbin{\mathsf{U}}_I \psi \urcorner$,
- $\overline{\varphi} := (\Box\, tick) \vee (tick \mathbin{\mathsf{U}} (\neg tick \wedge \ulcorner \varphi \urcorner))$.

For an FSA $\mathcal{A} = (Q, \Sigma, \delta, q_I, F, B)$, we define the FSA $\overline{\mathcal{A}} := (\overline{Q}, \overline{\Sigma}, \overline{\delta}, \overline{q}_I, \overline{F}, \overline{B})$ with $\overline{Q} := Q \times \{0, 1, 2\}$, $\overline{q}_I := (q_I, 0)$, $\overline{F} := \emptyset$, $\overline{B} := (B \times \{0\}) \cup (F \times \{2\})$, and for any $q \in Q$, $i \in \{0, 1, 2\}$, and $a \in \overline{\Sigma}$,

$$\overline{\delta}((q,i),a) := \begin{cases} \{(q',0) \mid q' \in \delta(q,a)\} & \text{if } a \in \Sigma \text{ and } i \in \{0,1\}, \\ \{(q,1),(q,2)\} & \text{if } a = \{tick\} \text{ and } i = 0, \\ \{(q,i)\} & \text{if } a = \{tick\} \text{ and } i \in \{1,2\}, \\ \emptyset & \text{otherwise.} \end{cases}$$

It is easy to check that $\tau \in L(\mathcal{A}) \otimes T$ iff $\overline{\tau} \in L(\overline{\mathcal{A}}) \cap \overline{T}$. In addition, by induction over φ, one verifies that $\sigma, t, i \models \varphi$ iff $\overline{\tau}, i+t_i \models \ulcorner \varphi \urcorner$ for all $i < |\tau|$, where $\tau = \sigma \otimes t$. Therefore, $\tau \in L(\varphi)$ iff $\overline{\tau} \in L(\overline{\varphi})$.

Note that $\overline{T} = L(\theta) \cap \overline{\Sigma}^{\omega}$, where $\theta := (\Box \Diamond tick) \wedge \Box(tick \rightarrow \bigwedge_{p \in \mathcal{P}} \neg p)$. Then $\overline{U_T} = L(\overline{\mathcal{U}}) \cap \overline{T}$. Moreover, $U_T \cap (\Sigma \times \mathbb{N})^*$ is decidable, and a finite trace τ in U_T is in $\mathrm{pre}_*(L(\varphi))$ iff $\overline{\tau}^{<|\tau|+t_{|\tau|-1}}$ is in $\mathrm{pre}_*(L(\overline{\varphi}) \cap \overline{T})$. Since $\mathrm{pre}_*(L(\overline{\varphi}) \cap \overline{T})$ is decidable, so is $\mathrm{pre}_*(L(\varphi) \cap U_T)$. Thus $L(\varphi)$ is $(U_T, \hat{O} \times \mathbb{N})$-enforceable iff $L(\varphi)$ is $(U_T, \hat{O} \times \mathbb{N})$-safety.

Recall now that the satisfiability problem for MLTL with infinite timed words is EXPSPACE-hard [3]. Given an MLTL formula φ, we define the formula $\varphi' := \varphi \vee \Diamond \neg \bigcirc true$. We have $L(\varphi') = L(\varphi) \cup (\mathcal{T} \cap (\Sigma \times \mathbb{N})^*)$. $L(\varphi')$ is $(U_T, \hat{O} \times \mathbb{N})$-safety iff $L_\omega(\varphi) = \mathcal{T} \cap (\Sigma \times \mathbb{N})^\omega$ iff $L_\omega(\neg \varphi) = \emptyset$. This proves that checking whether $L(\varphi)$ is $(U_T, \hat{O} \times \mathbb{N})$-safety is EXPSPACE-hard.

To prove membership in EXPSPACE, consider an MLTL formula φ of size $n \in \mathbb{N}$. It is easy to see by induction over φ that $\|\overline{\varphi}\| \in 2^{O(n)}$. Moreover, note that $\overline{\mathcal{T} \cap (\Sigma \times \mathbb{N})^\omega} = L(\theta') \cap \overline{\Sigma}^\omega$, where $\theta' := \theta \wedge (\Box \Diamond \neg tick)$. For convenience, we also let $O_t := O \cup \{tick\}$ and $S_\varphi := \mathrm{cl}(\mathrm{pre}_*(L(\varphi) \cap U_T) \cdot (\hat{O} \times \mathbb{N})^*) \cap U_T$. We have that S_φ is mapped to $\overline{S_\varphi} = \left(\mathrm{pre}_*(L(\overline{\varphi}) \cap \overline{U_T}) \cdot \hat{O}_t^{\overline{\omega}} \cup (\mathrm{cl}(\mathrm{pre}_*(L(\overline{\varphi}) \cap \overline{U_T})) \cap L(\theta')) \right) \cap \overline{U_T}$. Therefore, $L(\varphi)$ is $(U_T, \hat{O} \times \mathbb{N})$-enforceable iff $\overline{S_\varphi} \subseteq L(\overline{\varphi})$.

As in the proof of Theorem 11, we build an FSA $\mathcal{B}$ of size $2^{2^{O(n)}}$ such that $L(\mathcal{B}) = \overline{S_\varphi} \cap L(\neg \overline{\varphi})$. Then $L(\varphi)$ is $(U_T, \hat{O} \times \mathbb{N})$-enforceable iff $L(\mathcal{B}) = \emptyset$. As the emptiness problem for FSAs is in NLOGSPACE [21] and since we can build $\mathcal{B}$ on the fly, checking whether $L(\varphi)$ is $(U_T, \hat{O} \times \mathbb{N})$-safety is in EXPSPACE. $\Box$

If $L(\varphi)$ is $(L(\mathcal{U}) \otimes T, \hat{O} \times \mathbb{N})$-enforceable, we can use—similar to the LTL case—the FSAs $\overline{\mathcal{U}}$ and $\overline{\mathcal{A}}$ from the proof of Theorem 15 to obtain an enforcement mechanism E. We construct the product automaton $\mathcal{C}$ accepting $L(\overline{\mathcal{U}}) \cap L(\overline{\mathcal{A}})$. The enforcement mechanism E initializes the state set to the singleton set consisting of $\mathcal{C}$'s initial state. Additionally, E stores the current timestamp, which is initially 0. Whenever E intercepts a system action $(a,t) \in 2^{\mathcal{P}} \times \mathbb{N}$, it performs the following updates on the state set and the current timestamp.

1. E updates the state set with respect the progression of time, i.e., E determines the states reachable by the sequence $tick^d$, where d is the difference of the timestamp t and the stored timestamp.
2. E stores t as the current timestamp.
3. E updates the state set with respect to the system action a.
4. E removes the states from the state set from which $\mathcal{C}$ does not accept any sequence.

E terminates the system if the state set becomes empty and the intercepted action a is controllable. Otherwise, it continues by intercepting the next action.

5   Related Work

Schneider [29] initiated the study of which security policies are enforceable. He showed that every security policy enforceable by execution monitoring must be a property of traces and an ∞-safety property. Furthermore, he introduced an automata model, called security automata, that recognizes ∞-safety properties. Fong [15] analyzed classes of security policies that can be recognized by shallow-history automata, a restricted class of security automata. Hamlen et. al [18] related the policies that can be enforced by program rewriting to those that can be recognized by security automata. Ligatti et al. [24, 25] introduced edit automata, which are transducers with infinitely many states. Edit automata can recognize trace properties that are not ∞-safety. However, it remains unclear how to use edit automata as enforcement mechanisms, in particular, how an edit automaton and a system interact with each other in general. Ligatti and Reddy [26] recently introduced mandatory-result automata for enforcement and analyzed their expressive power. In contrast to edit automata, mandatory-result automata have an interface for interacting with a system. Namely, a mandatory-result automaton obtains requests from the system and sends outputs back to the system. Before sending output, it can interact with the execution platform. Falcone et al. [14] study the trace properties that can be recognized by security, edit, and shallow-history automata in terms of the safety-progress hierarchy [7] of regular languages and classical finite-state automata models.

All the above works assume that all system actions are controllable. In contrast, we distinguish between actions that are controllable and those that are only observable by an enforcement mechanism. Furthermore, the above works also do not consider the realizability of an enforcement mechanism from a policy description and its computational complexity. Note that classifications of system actions, signals, and states with a flavor similar to ours are common in other areas like control theory and software testing. However, to the best of our knowledge, this is the first such investigation in the domain of policy enforcement.

Recently, the problem of checking whether system behaviors are compliant with security policies, regulations, and laws has attracted considerable attention. This problem is simpler than policy enforcement, since one need only detect and report policy violations. Monitoring approaches have proved useful here, based either on offline [17] or online [4] algorithms. See also [5].

Another generalization of the standard definition of safety [1] has been recently given by Ehlers and Finkbeiner [9]. They distinguish between the inputs and outputs of a reactive system. The corresponding decision problems are EXPTIME-complete and 2EXPTIME-complete when the properties are given as automata and LTL formulas, respectively. Since enforcement mechanisms based on execution monitoring do not produce outputs, their generalization does not apply to our setting. However, a combination of their safety generalization and ours seems promising when considering more powerful enforcement mechanisms like those based on mandatory-result automata [26].

6 Conclusion

We have refined Schneider's setting for policy enforcement based on execution monitoring by distinguishing between controllable and observable system actions. This allows us to reason about enforceability in systems where not all actions can be controlled, for example, the passage of time. Using our characterization, we have provided, for the first time, both necessary and sufficient conditions for enforceability. We have also examined the problem of determining whether a specified policy is enforceable, for different specification languages, and provided results on the complexity of this realizability decision problem.

As future work, we will investigate the realizability problem for more powerful enforcement mechanisms and for more expressive specification languages, such as those not limited to finite alphabets. We would also like to provide tool support for synthesizing enforcement mechanisms from declarative policy specifications.

References

1. Alpern, B., Schneider, F.B.: Defining liveness. Inform. Process. Lett. 21(4), 181–185 (1985)
2. Alur, R., Henzinger, T.A.: Logics and Models of Real Time: A Survey. In: Huizing, C., de Bakker, J.W., Rozenberg, G., de Roever, W.-P. (eds.) REX 1991. LNCS, vol. 600, pp. 74–106. Springer, Heidelberg (1992)
3. Alur, R., Henzinger, T.A.: A really temporal logic. J. ACM 41(1), 181–203 (1994)
4. Basin, D., Harvan, M., Klaedtke, F., Zălinescu, E.: Monitoring usage-control policies in distributed systems. In: Proceedings of the 18th International Symposium on Temporal Representation and Reasoning, pp. 88–95. IEEE Computer Society (2011)
5. Basin, D., Klaedtke, F., Müller, S.: Monitoring security policies with metric first-order temporal logic. In: Proceedings of the 15th ACM Symposium on Access Control Models and Technologies, pp. 23–33. ACM Press (2010)
6. Basin, D., Olderog, E.-R., Sevinç, P.E.: Specifying and analyzing security automata using CSP-OZ. In: Proceedings of the 2007 ACM Symposium on Information, Computer and Communications Security, pp. 70–81. ACM Press (2007)
7. Chang, E.Y., Manna, Z., Pnueli, A.: Characterization of Temporal Property Classes. In: Kuich, W. (ed.) ICALP 1992. LNCS, vol. 623, pp. 474–486. Springer, Heidelberg (1992)
8. Dax, C., Klaedtke, F., Lange, M.: On regular temporal logics with past. Acta Inform. 47(4), 251–277 (2010)
9. Ehlers, R., Finkbeiner, B.: Reactive safety. In: Proceedings of 2nd International Symposium on Games, Logics and Formal Verification. Electronic Proceedings in Theoretical Computer Science, vol. 54, pp. 178–191 (2011), eptcs.org
10. Eisner, C., Fisman, D., Havlicek, J., Lustig, Y., McIsaac, A., Van Campenhout, D.: Reasoning with Temporal Logic on Truncated Paths. In: Hunt Jr., W.A., Somenzi, F. (eds.) CAV 2003. LNCS, vol. 2725, pp. 27–39. Springer, Heidelberg (2003)
11. Erlingsson, Ú.: The inlined reference monitor approach to security policy enforcement. PhD thesis, Cornell University, Ithaca, NY, USA (2004)
12. Erlingsson, Ú., Schneider, F.B.: SASI enforcement of security policies: A retrospective. In: Proceedings of the 1999 Workshop on New Security Paradigms, pp. 87–95. ACM Press (1999)

13. Erlingsson, Ú., Schneider, F.B.: IRM enforcement of Java stack inspection. In: Proceedings of the 2000 IEEE Symposium on Security and Privacy, pp. 246–255. IEEE Computer Society (2000)

14. Falcone, Y., Mounier, L., Fernandez, J.-C., Richier, J.-L.: Runtime enforcement monitors: composition, synthesis, and enforcement abilities. Form. Methods Syst. Des. 38(2), 223–262 (2011)

15. Fong, P.W.: Access control by tracking shallow execution history. In: Proceedings of the 2004 IEEE Symposium on Security and Privacy, pp. 43–55. IEEE Computer Society (2004)

16. Garey, M.R., Johnson, D.S.: Computers and Intractability: A Guide to the Theory of NP-Completeness. W.H. Freeman and Company (1979)

17. Garg, D., Jia, L., Datta, A.: Policy auditing over incomplete logs: Theory, implementation and applications. In: Proceedings of the 18th ACM Conference on Computer and Communications Security, pp. 151–162. ACM Press (2011)

18. Hamlen, K.W., Morrisett, G., Schneider, F.B.: Computability classes for enforcement mechanisms. ACM Trans. Progr. Lang. Syst. 28(1), 175–205 (2006)

19. Henzinger, T.A.: Sooner is safer than later. Inform. Process. Lett. 43(3), 135–141 (1992)

20. Hopcroft, J.E., Ullman, J.D.: Introduction to Automata Theory, Languages and Computation. Addison-Wesley (1979)

21. Jones, N.D.: Space-bounded reducibility among combinatorial problems. J. Comput. Syst. Sci. 11(1), 68–85 (1975)

22. Koymans, R.: Specifying real-time properties with metric temporal logic. Real-Time Syst. 2(4), 255–299 (1990)

23. Lamport, L.: Proving the correctness of multiprocess programs. IEEE Trans. Software Eng. 3(2), 125–143 (1977)

24. Ligatti, J., Bauer, L., Walker, D.: Edit automata: enforcement mechanisms for run-time security policies. Int. J. Inf. Secur. 4(1-2), 2–16 (2005)

25. Ligatti, J., Bauer, L., Walker, D.: Run-time enforcement of nonsafety policies. ACM Trans. Inform. Syst. Secur. 12(3) (2009)

26. Ligatti, J., Reddy, S.: A Theory of Runtime Enforcement, with Results. In: Gritzalis, D., Preneel, B., Theoharidou, M. (eds.) ESORICS 2010. LNCS, vol. 6345, pp. 87–100. Springer, Heidelberg (2010)

27. Paul, M., Siegert, H.J., Alford, M.W., Ansart, J.P., Hommel, G., Lamport, L., Liskov, B., Mullery, G.P., Schneider, F.B.: Distributed Systems—Methods and Tools for Specification: An Advanced Course. LNCS, vol. 190. Springer, Heidelberg (1985)

28. Pnueli, A.: The temporal logic of programs. In: Proceedings of the 18th Annual Symposium on Foundations of Computer Science, pp. 46–57. IEEE Computer Society (1977)

29. Schneider, F.B.: Enforceable security policies. ACM Trans. Inform. Syst. Secur. 3(1), 30–50 (2000)

30. Sistla, A.P., Clarke, E.M.: The complexity of propositional linear temporal logic. J. ACM 32(3), 733–749 (1985)

31. Vardi, M.Y., Wolper, P.: Reasoning about infinite computations. Inf. Comput. 115(1), 1–37 (1994)

32. Viswanathan, M.: Foundations for the run-time analysis of software systems. PhD thesis, University of Pennsylvania, Philadelphia, PA, USA (2000)

Towards Incrementalization of Holistic Hyperproperties

Dimiter Milushev and Dave Clarke

IBBT-DistriNet, KU Leuven, Heverlee, Belgium

Abstract. A *hyperproperty* is a set of sets of finite or infinite traces over some fixed alphabet and can be seen as a very generic system specification. In this work, we define the notions of *holistic* and *incremental* *hyperproperties*. Systems specified holistically tend to be more intuitive but difficult to reason about, whereas incremental specifications have a straightforward verification approach. Since most interesting security-related hyperproperties are in the syntactic class of holistic hyperproperties, we introduce the process of *incrementalization* to convert holistic specifications into incremental ones. We then present three incrementalizable classes of holistic hyperproperties and a respective verification method.

1 Introduction

The problem of verifying that a system adheres to some given security policy has been an active research area for several decades. Substantial progress has been made in the verification of security policies that can be expressed as *properties*— first-order predicates over system execution traces. Well-known examples of such progress include the abundance of logics for system specification and the success story of automata-based model checking [7,8,18]. Unfortunately properties are not expressive enough to capture a large class of security policies, such as secure information flow and noninterference.

In an attempt to remedy this and provide a uniform theory of security policies, Clarkson and Schneider formalized security policies as *hyperproperties* [9]. A *hyperproperty* is a second-order predicate over system execution traces, or, in other words, a set of sets of execution traces. Hyperproperties generalize properties and are expressive enough to capture not only secure information flow and noninterference, but also many other interesting policies on systems [9]. Intuitively, a hyperproperty is the set of systems permitted by some policy. (In contrast, a property is the set of runs a system must satisfy.) Although arising in the context of security, hyperproperties are not necessarily limited to security policies; they can be seen as very general and expressive system specifications. Quality of Service (QoS) and Service Level Agreement (SLA) properties can be expressed as hyperproperties.

Clarkson and Schneider specify a class of security-related hyperproperties as first-order predicates on sets of traces [9], using universal and existential quantifiers over traces in a candidate set T, as well as relations on those traces. We call

P. Degano and J.D. Guttman (Eds.): POST 2012, LNCS 7215, pp. 329–348, 2012.

the hyperproperties in this syntactic class *holistic* as they talk about whole traces at once; their specifications tend to be straightforward, but they are difficult to reason about, exemplified by the fact that no general approach to verifying such hyperproperties exists, to the best of our knowledge. To address this problem, we adopt a coalgebraic perspective on systems and hyperproperty specifications and propose to model systems as coalgebras of the functor $GX = 2 \times (1 + X)^A$; this is useful as in their nature, coalgebras and coinductive predicates are "incremental". Intuitively, systems correspond to trees, where the initial state of a system is mapped to the root of the corresponding tree and possible executions build the branches; incremental hyperproperties reason about such trees. Our contributions are firstly formal definitions of the classes of *holistic* and *incremental* hyperproperties, secondly introduction of the notion of *incrementalization* and its application to three classes of holistic hyperproperties, and finally an illustration of the verification approach for incremental hyperproperties.

The rest of the paper is structured as follows. Section 2 provides some background material. Section 3 introduces and formalizes the notions of holistic and incremental hyperproperties and Section 4 presents the incrementalization of three classes of holistic hyperproperties. Section 5 presents a verification method for incremental hyperproperties. Finally, Sections 6 and 7 are left for the related work and conclusion. The proofs can be found in the technical report [21].

2   Background

This section provides the necessary background. Fix a finite alphabet A of abstract observations. A *string* is a finite sequence of elements of A. The set of all strings over A is denoted A^*. A *stream* of A's is an infinite sequence of elements of A. The set of all streams over A is $A^\omega = \{\sigma \mid \sigma : \{0, 1, 2, \ldots\} \to A\}$. A stream σ can be specified in terms of its first element $\sigma(0)$ and its stream derivative σ', given by $\sigma'(n) = \sigma(n + 1)$; these operators are also known as *head* and *tail*. A *trace* is a finite or infinite sequence of elements of A. The set of all traces over A is denoted $A^\infty = A^* \cup A^\omega$. Let 2 be any two element set, for instance the one given as $2 = \{true, false\}$. A *system* is a set of traces. The set of all systems is $\mathsf{Sys} = 2^{A^\infty}$, the set of infinite systems is $\mathsf{Sys}_\omega = 2^{A^\omega}$.

Clarkson and Schneider present a theory of policies based on properties and hyperproperties [9]. A *property* is a set of traces. The set of all properties is $\mathsf{Prop} = 2^{A^\infty}$. A *hyperproperty* is a set of sets of traces or equivalently a set of properties. The set of all hyperproperties is $\mathsf{HP} = 2^{2^{A^\infty}} = 2^{\mathsf{Prop}} = 2^{\mathsf{Sys}}$. Note that our definition, unlike the original one, does not require all traces to be infinite; as a result termination-sensitive definitions can be expressed in a more natural fashion. The *satisfaction relation for hyperproperties* $\models \,\subseteq \mathsf{Sys} \times 2^{\mathsf{Prop}}$ is defined as $C \models \boldsymbol{H} \;\widehat{=}\; C \in \boldsymbol{H}$. Although $\mathsf{Sys} = \mathsf{Prop}$, we use both names for emphasis.

We now present an example hyperproperty, a variant of *noninterference*. Let $\tau \notin A$ represent unobservable elements of a trace. Let $A_\tau = A \cup \{\tau\}$ and assume predicates *low* and *high* on elements of A such that *low* is equivalent to $\neg high$. Coinductively define function $ev_L : A^\infty \to A_\tau^\infty$ to filter out "high" events:

$$\frac{}{ev_L(\epsilon) = \epsilon} \qquad \frac{ev_L(x) = y \quad high(a)}{ev_L(a \cdot x) = \tau \cdot y} \qquad \frac{ev_L(x) = y \quad low(a)}{ev_L(a \cdot x) = a \cdot y}$$

Next define *weak trace equivalence* $\approx \subseteq A_\tau^\infty \times A_\tau^\infty$ as:

$$\frac{}{\epsilon \approx \epsilon} \qquad \frac{x \approx y}{\tau \cdot x \approx y} \qquad \frac{x \approx y}{x \approx \tau \cdot y} \qquad \frac{x \approx y}{a \cdot x \approx a \cdot y}$$

Predicate $no_H : A_\tau^\infty \to 2$ states that there are no high events in a trace:

$$\frac{}{no_H(\epsilon)} \qquad \frac{low(a) \quad no_H(x)}{no_H(a \cdot x)}$$

Finally define *noninterference* as

$$NI = \{T \in \mathsf{Sys} \mid \forall t_0 \in T (\exists t_1 \in T (no_H(t_1) \wedge ev_L(t_0) \approx t_1))\}.$$

For every trace t_0 in a candidate set T the definition of NI requires a low-equivalent modulo weak-bisimulation trace t_1 such that $no_H(t_1)$ is in T. This definition of noninterference is similar in spirit to *strong non-deterministic non-interference* (*NNI*), originally proposed by Focardi and Gorrieri [13]. The major difference is that NI does not distinguish between inputs and outputs; thus it is in a sense stronger than similar definitions that guard the confidentiality of high inputs only (*NI* ensures the confidentiality of high events, which implies confidentiality of high inputs). Additionally, *NNI* is defined over elements of 2^{A^*}, whereas *NI* over elements of Sys; finally, *NNI* uses string equality whereas *NI* uses a form of weak-bisimulation.

Example 1 (Noninterference). Given $A = \{a, b, c\}$, where $high(a)$, $high(c)$, $low(b)$ hold. Consider system $C = \{\sigma, \gamma\}$, where $\sigma = (abc)^\omega$, $\gamma = b^\omega$. Note that $no_H(\gamma) = true$, $ev_L(\sigma) \approx b^\omega$ and $ev_L(\gamma) = b^\omega$ hold. From these we deduce:

1. for σ there exists $t \in C$ s.t. $no_H(t) \wedge ev_L(\sigma) \approx t$, namely $t = \gamma$.
2. for γ there exists $t \in C$ s.t. $no_H(t) \wedge ev_L(\gamma) \approx t$, namely $t = \gamma$.

Hence $C \models NI$: system C satisfies NI as well as variants of *NNI*.

The former definition of noninterference is relatively abstract. In order to additionally illustrate the practical significance of the proposed approach, we also work with *reactive noninterference* [5], a variant of Zdancewic and Myers's definition of *observational determinism* [30] for reactive systems. Without loss of generality, assume that A may be partitioned into A_i and A_o, corresponding to input and output events. Following the original work [5], assume that systems are input-total; moreover, assume that every input event produces some finite or infinite output trace. The model assumes that a system waits for input in some consumer state; whenever an input event is received, the system produces a finite or infinite output trace; if the output trace was finite, the system returns to a consumer state, waiting for further events; otherwise it diverges. For the sake of illustration, we consider deterministic reactive systems. Formally, a *deterministic reactive system* RS can be modeled as the set of traces produced by a function $f_{RS} : A_i^\infty \to A^\infty$. Let $f_i : A_i \to A_o^\infty$ be a function, taking one input event and producing some output trace. Function f_{RS} can be defined coinductively as:

$$\frac{}{f_{RS}(\epsilon) = \epsilon} \qquad \frac{f_i(a) = \sigma \qquad \sigma \in A^* \qquad f_{RS}(r) = \sigma_m}{f_{RS}(a \cdot r) = a \cdot \sigma \cdot \sigma_m} \qquad \frac{f_i(a) = \sigma \qquad \sigma \in A^\omega}{f_{RS}(a \cdot r) = a \cdot \sigma}$$

Let *FRS* be the set of deterministic reactive systems that can be characterized by a functional input-output relation. Let $x \approx_L y$ denote $ev_L(x) \approx ev_L(y)$, and $\approx_{L_i}$ and $\approx_{L_o}$ be analogous definitions for input and output events, respectively; similarly $x \approx_H y$ denotes $ev_H(x) \approx ev_H(y)$ and $x \approx_{H_i} y$ is the restriction to inputs. *Reactive noninterference* [5] can be defined as a hyperproperty as follows:

$$RN = \{ T_f \in FRS \mid \forall t_0, t_1 \in T_f (t_0 \approx_{L_i} t_1 \to t_0 \approx_L t_1) \},$$

where $T_f = \{ t \in A^\infty \mid \exists \sigma \in A_i^\infty (f(\sigma) = t) \}$. Note that the relation $t_0 \approx_L t_1$ is on whole traces, not on output traces as it is typically defined. This is because $t_0 \approx_L t_1$ implies $t_0 \approx_{L_o} t_1$, as L_o is a subset of L and the way traces are generated.

Unlike batch-job program models, where all program inputs are available at the start of execution and all program outputs are available at program termination, reactive programs receive inputs and send outputs to their environment during execution. RIMP [5] is a language geared towards writing reactive systems, allowing agents to interact with the system by sending and receiving messages. Messages are typically considered secret to certain agents and public to others. Inputs in RIMP are natural numbers sent over channels and outputs are natural numbers over channels or a tick (τ), signifying an internal action. The channels model users or security levels in some security lattice; typically, *L* and *H* model the low and high channel respectively. The detailed syntax and semantics of RIMP are available in the original paper [5]. The following RIMP program illustrates reactive noninterference:

```
1   input chH(x) {i := x;}
2   input chL(x) {if i <= x then  output chL(0);
3                 else output chL(1);}
```

Program 1.1. Simple program in RIMP

Let $\sigma_{in} = [ch_H^i(0), ch_L^i(0)]$ and $\gamma_{in} = [ch_H^i(1), ch_L^i(0)]$ be input strings. Clearly $\sigma_{in} \approx_{L_i} \gamma_{in}$. The traces are $\sigma = [ch_H^i(0), \tau, \tau, ch_L^i(0), \tau, ch_L^o(0), \tau]$ and $\gamma = [ch_H^i(1), \tau, \tau, ch_L^i(0), \tau, ch_L^o(1), \tau]$; because they are not weak trace equivalent at *L*, it follows that P is not secure, i.e. $P \not\models RN$.

2.1   Partial Automata, Coalgebras and Languages à la Rutten [26]

A *partial automaton* with input alphabet *A* is defined *coalgebraically* as a 3-tuple $\langle S, o, t \rangle$, where set *S* is the possibly infinite state space of the automaton, the observation function $o : S \to 2$ says whether a state is accepting or not, and the partial function $t : S \to (1 + S)^A$ gives the transition structure. Notation S^A stands for the set of functions with signature $A \to S$; $1 + S$ is notation used for the set $\{\bot\} \cup S$: whenever the function $t(s)$ is undefined, it is the constant function mapping every undefined symbol from *A* to $\bot$; if $t(s)$ is defined for some $a \in A$, then $t(s)(a) = s'$ gives the next state. The symbol $\delta \notin A$ is used to represent *deadlock*. An automaton is in a *deadlock* state s_δ if for all $a \in A$, $t(s_\delta)(a) = \bot$ (the transition function is undefined).

Let $A^* \cdot \delta = \{w \cdot \delta \mid w \in A^*\}$ be the set of finitely deadlocked words. The collection of all languages acceptable by partial automata is $A_\delta^\infty = A^* \cup (A^* \cdot \delta) \cup A^\omega$; note that this can also be seen as a set of sequences i.e. a property, but since any property can be lifted to a hyperproperty [9] there is no inconsistency. Let the truncation of an infinite word $w = a_1 a_2 a_3 \ldots$ to the first n ($n \in \mathbb{N}$) letters be denoted $w[n] = a_1 \ldots a_n$. For words $w \in A^*$ and sets $L \subseteq A_\delta^\infty$, define the *w-derivative* of L to be $L_w = \{v \in A_\delta^\infty \mid w \cdot v \in L\}$. Define a set $L \subseteq A_\delta^\infty$ to be *closed* if for all words w in A^ω, $w \in L \iff \forall n \geq 1, L_{w[n]} \neq \emptyset$. Define a set $L \subseteq A_\delta^\infty$ to be *consistent* if for all words w in A_δ^∞, $\delta \in L_w \iff L_w = \{\delta\}$. The *language of a partial automaton* is a non-empty, closed and consistent subset of A_δ^∞. The set of all such languages is

$$\mathcal{L} = \{L \mid L \subseteq A_\delta^\infty, L \text{ is non-empty, closed and consistent}\}.$$

Any state of a partial automaton accepts some language having three kinds of words: firstly, all finite words that leave the automaton in an accepting state, secondly, all infinite words that cause the automaton to run indefinitely and thirdly, words that lead to a deadlock state. Intuitively, the language of a partial automaton is the language accepted by the start state.

The set $\mathcal{L}$ can be thought of as an automaton $\mathcal{L} = \langle \mathcal{L}, o_\mathcal{L}, t_\mathcal{L} \rangle$ [26]:

$$o_\mathcal{L}(L) = \begin{cases} \textit{true} & \text{if } \epsilon \in L \\ \textit{false} & \text{if } \epsilon \notin L \end{cases} \qquad t_\mathcal{L}(L)(a) = \begin{cases} L_a & \text{if } L_a \neq \emptyset \\ \bot & \text{if } L_a = \emptyset. \end{cases}$$

A bisimulation between two automata $S_1 = \langle S, o, t \rangle$ and $S_2 = \langle S', o', t' \rangle$ is a relation $R \subseteq S \times S'$ s.t. for all s in S, s' in S' and a in A

$$s \, R \, s' \implies o(s) = o'(s') \bigwedge t(s)(a) \, (1 + R) \, t'(s')(a).$$

Condition $t(s)(a) \, (1+R) \, t'(s')(a)$ holds iff either $t(s)(a) = \bot$ and $t'(s')(a) = \bot$ or $t(s)(a) \, R \, t'(s')(a)$. The maximal bisimulation $\sim$ is the union of all bisimulation relations.

The automaton $\mathcal{L} = \langle \mathcal{L}, o_\mathcal{L}, t_\mathcal{L} \rangle$ satisfies the coinduction proof principle [26]. In other words, for all languages L and K in $\mathcal{L}$ we have: $L \sim K \iff L = K$.

Coalgebras of the polynomial functor $G : \textit{Set} \to \textit{Set}$, given by $GX = 2 \times (1 + X)^A$, will be called *G-coalgebras* or *G-systems*. As partial automata are in one-to-one correspondence with G-coalgebras [26], all the theory presented here is applicable to G-coalgebras.

2.2   Systems — From Sets of Traces to G-Coalgebras

This section shows that the model of systems as sets of traces can be converted into a tree/coalgebra/partial automaton model; the latter model is more convenient and well-studied. This is an important prerequisite to incrementalization: the conversion of system specifications on sets of traces to specifications on trees.

Let F be an arbitrary functor $F : Set \rightarrow Set$. An F-coalgebra is *final* if there is a unique homomorphism from any other F-coalgebra to it. A set of traces can be seen not only as a property or system, but also as a language, and as a G-coalgebra, which itself can be either seen as a partial automaton or as a tree. A *tree* is obtained from a language by continuously taking derivatives with respect to elements of A. Conversely, the language of a tree is given by the paths from the root that either end at a marked node or continue forever. The different perspectives are illustrated in Fig. 1; note that ellipses indicate infinite repetition of the string that has occurred so far. Combined with Rutten's observation [26] that the set of all languages is a final coalgebra, this allows the use of coalgebra and coinduction for reasoning about hyperproperties. We next describe the transition from sets of traces to G-coalgebras.

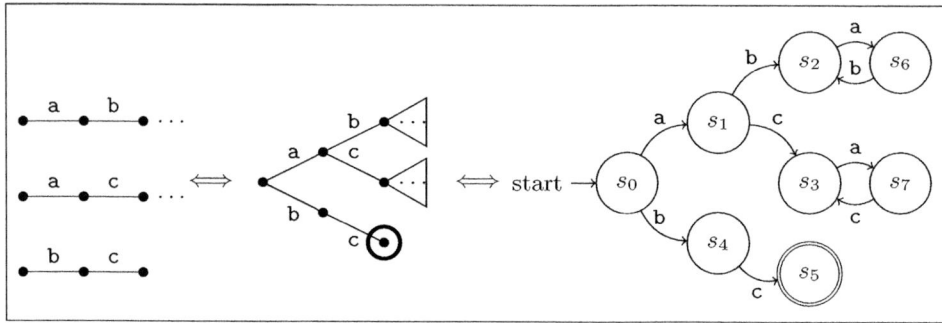

Fig. 1. Equivalent representations of $M = \{(ab)^{\omega}, (ac)^{\omega}, bc\}$ over $A = \{a, b, c\}$: traces, trees and G-coalgebras. The branches of the tree are labelled with elements of the alphabet A, its accepting nodes are marked with a circle.

The functor G has the final coalgebra $\mathcal{L}$. The *coinductive definition principle* gives a way to define maps from arbitrary G-coalgebras into the final G-coalgebra. We use the principle to convert an arbitrary set of traces into a G-coalgebra. To this end, take the state space to be $\mathsf{Sys} = 2^{A^{\infty}}$, the set of all possible sets of traces. Any pair $\langle o, t \rangle$ with signatures $o : \mathsf{Sys} \rightarrow 2$ and $t : \mathsf{Sys} \rightarrow (1 + \mathsf{Sys})^A$ induces a unique homomorphism $h : \mathsf{Sys} \rightarrow \mathcal{L}$ that makes the following diagram commute:

$$
\begin{array}{ccc}
\mathsf{Sys} & \xdashrightarrow{\;!h\;} & \mathcal{L} \\
{\scriptstyle\langle o,t\rangle}\downarrow & & \downarrow{\scriptstyle\langle o_{\mathcal{L}}, t_{\mathcal{L}}\rangle} \\
2 \times (1 + \mathsf{Sys})^A & \xdashrightarrow{\;G(h)\;} & 2 \times (1 + \mathcal{L})^A
\end{array}
$$

Thus the homomorphism h would map any set of traces $s \in \mathsf{Sys}$ to a unique element in the final coalgebra $\mathcal{L}$. Since the elements of the final coalgebra can be seen as trees, we say that h maps a set of traces to the root of a unique tree in $\mathcal{L}$, corresponding precisely to the set of traces.

We now define a particular pair $\langle o, t \rangle$ allowing us to switch perspective from seeing a system as a set of traces to seeing it as a G-coalgebra. Let $C \in \mathsf{Sys}$, $a \in A$ and $\sigma \in A^\infty$. Define an auxiliary function $test : \mathsf{Sys} \to (A \to 2)$ as follows:

$$test_a(C) \; \widehat{=} \; \exists \, \sigma. \sigma \in C \land \sigma(0) = a.$$

The functions o and t can be readily defined as follows:

$$o(C) \; \widehat{=} \; \epsilon \in C \qquad t(C)(a) \; \widehat{=} \; \begin{cases} \{\sigma' \mid \sigma(0) = a\} & \text{if } test_a(C) \\ \bot & \text{if } \neg test_a(C). \end{cases}$$

This function pair induces a unique element of the final coalgebra $\mathcal{L}$, corresponding to the inclusion of Sys in $\mathcal{L}$. Clearly every set $S \in \mathsf{Sys}$ is closed and consistent. As a result we may conclude that $\mathsf{Sys} \subseteq \mathcal{L}$.

In summary, any system defined as a set of traces can be uniquely seen as an element (without deadlock states) of the final G-coalgebra, defining its behaviour.

3   Holistic and Incremental Hyperproperties

One of the crucial steps towards verification is finding the class of *incrementalizable* holistic hyperproperties. To that end, we need a formalism for reasoning about holistic and incremental specifications. In this section, we give syntactic definitions of *holistic* and *incremental* hyperproperties. The logical languages used are based on *Least Fixed Point Logic (LFP)* [6] — an extension of first order logic by addition of least and greatest fixed point operators. The new logical languages are holistic hyperproperty logic $\mathcal{HL}$, in which most interesting security hyperproperties are expressible, and incremental hyperproperty logic $\mathcal{IL}$. The key difference between the languages is that the former has only coinductive predicates over streams, whereas the latter has only coinductive predicates over systems. In both cases hyperproperties are defined over systems.

3.1   Holistic Hyperproperty Logic $\mathcal{HL}$

Clarkson and Schneider specify hyperproperties as first-order predicates on sets of traces [9], using universal and possibly existential quantification over traces ($\forall t \in T$, $\exists t \in T$) in a candidate set T, as well as relations on tuples of traces. The hyperproperty *NI* (Section 2) is one example. Next, we propose the logical language $\mathcal{HL}$ to formalize hyperproperties specified in this style.

First, we give a grammar for coinductive predicates over streams, a substantial part of $\mathcal{HL}$. Let x range over a set of variables, a over elements of A, p_i over predicates in some set P and X over predicate variables. To define the logic we use standard, trace-manipulation primitives: for any $\sigma \in A^\infty$, $\sigma(0)$ gives the first element (head) of the stream and σ' gives the stream derivative (tail). As usual, $cons : A \times A^\infty \to A^\infty$ is a constructor for streams. The predicates in P have signatures: $p_i : A^{n_i} \to 2$ and $= : A \times A \to 2$. Terms are given as

$$t ::= x \mid \epsilon \mid cons(a, t) \mid t(0) \mid t'$$

and coinductive predicates have the following syntax:

$$\phi_0 ::= p(\bar{t}) \mid X(\bar{t}) \mid \bot \mid \neg\phi_0 \mid \phi_0 \wedge \phi_0,$$

where X can occur only positively in ϕ_0. As usual $\top = \neg\bot$, $\phi \vee \psi = \neg(\neg\phi \wedge \neg\psi)$ and the implication $\phi \rightarrow \psi$ is $\neg\phi \vee \psi$.

Second, define *holistic hyperproperty logic* $\mathcal{HL}$ with the following syntax:

$$\phi_1 ::= \bot \mid \neg\phi_1 \mid \phi_1 \wedge \phi_1 \mid \exists x.\phi_1 \mid x \in X \mid \nu X(\bar{x}).\phi_0.$$

As usual $\forall x.\phi = \neg(\exists x.\neg\phi)$ and $\nu X(\bar{x}).\phi_0$ denotes the greatest fixed point; also note that $x \in X$ iff $X(x) = true$. It is well-known that each coinductive predicate in this language corresponds to a final coalgebra in a category of relations [22]. A *holistic hyperproperty* is a set of sets of traces expressible in $\mathcal{HL}$.

For example, consider defining hyperproperty *FLIP*, assuring that for every stream in a candidate set, its element-wise opposite is also in the set. Start by defining the predicate $flip \subseteq A^\omega \times A^\omega$, relating each stream over $A = \{0,1\}$ to its element-wise opposite:

$$flip \;\hat{=}\; \nu X(x,y).(\neg(y(0) = x(0)) \wedge X(x',y')).$$

Then, the simple hyperproperty *FLIP* can be given in $\mathcal{HL}$ as:

$$FLIP(X) \;\hat{=}\; \forall x_0 \in X \; \exists x_1 \in X.flip(x_0,x_1).$$

The proposed logic is fairly general as it captures most security-relevant hyperproperties from the original hyperproperties paper [9]; the noteworthy exceptions are service level agreement (SLA) polices such as mean response time (*MRT*), time service factor and percentage uptime. Formal verification of systems with respect to such policies is an inherently difficult problem [9]: for instance, consider *MRT* as a property; it is generally not clear how to find the mean of a sequence of infinite number of response times in a trace because the series might be diverging; moreover, if *MRT* is seen as a hyperproperty, an additional problem arises, namely that the cardinality of the set of traces might be infinite. We do not address SLA policies in this work.

Next, we present three illustrative examples. First, consider McLean's formulation of a policy called *generalized noninterference* [20] for non-deterministic systems. Informally, the policy states that any high-level behavior is compatible with any low level view of the system. The definition of *GNI* in $\mathcal{HL}$ is

$$GNI(X) \;\hat{=}\; \forall x_0 \in X \; \forall x_1 \in X \; \exists x_2 \in X.x_2 \approx_{\mathrm{H_i}} x_0 \wedge x_2 \approx_{\mathrm{L}} x_1.$$

Note that $\approx_{\mathrm{H_i}}$ and $\approx_{\mathrm{L}}$ can be defined coinductively and are based on the coinductively defined functions ev_H and ev_L respectively; the latter are not in $\mathcal{HL}$. However, note that combining ev_H and ev_L with $\approx$ gives coinductive predicates.

Second, consider the definition of termination insensitive observational determinism [30]:

$$OD(X) \;\hat{=}\; \forall x_0 \in X \; \forall x_1 \in X.(x_0(0) =_{\mathrm{L}} x_1(0) \rightarrow x_0 \approx_{\mathrm{L}} x_1),$$

where $=_L$ is an indistinguishability relation on initial program states. Note that the alphabet A is abstract and except events its elements may also be states, as is the case in this example. Third, note that the former definition of OD implies a batch-job model, but for the reactive model of computation, we give the reformulation to RN from Section 2:

$$RN(X) \triangleq \forall x_0 \in X \; \forall x_1 \in X.(x_0 \approx_{L_i} x_1 \rightarrow x_0 \approx_L x_1).$$

Note that this is one particular definition of termination-insensitive observational determinism. By modifying the definitions of the relation on traces, other flavors of the definitions (e.g. termination-sensitive, time-sensitive) can be obtained.

3.2 Incremental Hyperproperty Logic $\mathcal{IL}$

Incremental hyperproperties can be expressed in a fragment of LFP, called $\mathcal{IL}$ logic. Let y range over a set of tree variables, a, b over alphabet elements and I over predicate variables.

To define the logic, we use the system manipulation primitives $o : \mathsf{Sys} \rightarrow 2$, $(-)_a : \mathsf{Sys} \rightarrow \mathsf{Sys}+1$ and $test_a : \mathsf{Sys} \rightarrow 2$ for each $a \in A$: these are the observation, transition and auxiliary $test$ function (see Section 2.2) in the final G-coalgebra. The predicates are $p_i : A^{n_i} \rightarrow 2$, $= : A \times A \rightarrow 2$, o and $test_a$. The terms are

$$T ::= y \mid a \mid T_a.$$

Formulae in $\mathcal{IL}$ have the following syntax:

$$\psi ::= \nu I(\overline{y}).\phi \qquad \phi ::= I(\overline{T}) \mid \bot \mid \neg\phi \mid \phi \wedge \phi \mid \exists a.\phi \mid a \in A \mid p(\overline{T}),$$

where I can occur only positively in ϕ and all occurrences of T_a must be guarded by $test_a(T)$. As an example, consider the coinductive tree predicate $FLIP'(X,Y)$, giving the incremental version of $FLIP$ defined as:

$$FLIP' \triangleq$$
$$\nu I(X,Y).(\forall a \in A.test_a(X) \rightarrow (\exists b \in A.test_b(Y) \wedge \neg(b = a) \wedge I(X_a, Y_b))).$$

Let Sys^n be the n-ary Cartesian power of Sys. Define an *incremental hyperproperty* to be the greatest fixed point of a monotone function over Sys^n, expressible in $\mathcal{IL}$. In other words, it is a coinductive tree predicate. A hyperproperty $H \in \mathcal{HL}$ is *incrementalizable* iff there exists an $H' \in \mathcal{IL}$ such that for all $T \in \mathsf{Sys}$ we have that $H'(\overline{T}) \equiv H^k(\overline{T})$, where $H^k(\overline{T})$ is an equivalent definition of $H(T)$ on k copies of T. Examples of incrementalizable hyperproperties can be found in Section 4.

The logic is general enough to capture the incremental hyperproperties we are aware of. The long term goal of this work is to *characterize the class of incrementalizable hyperproperties*. As a first step towards this goal, we incrementalize three classes of hyperproperties.

4   Incrementalization of Holistic Hyperproperties

In this section, we outline and illustrate a syntactic approach to incrementalization for three classes of holistic hyperproperties. We give a detailed explanation of the process for the first class.

At a high level, incrementalization of a holistic hyperproperty H, based on trace predicates c_i ($i \in \mathbb{N}$), amounts to finding a coinductive predicate H' and a functional $\Psi_{H'}$ such that H' is the greatest fixed point of $\Psi_{H'}$ (i.e. $H' = \Psi_{H'}(H') = \nu\Psi_{H'}$) and $H(X)$ iff $H'(X, \dots, X)$ holds. In essence, we lift the fixed point operator, defining coinductive trace predicates in a holistic specification, to the outermost level in an incremental specification. The techniques used include generalizing the definition of H to n parameters, unfolding H and rewriting it using derivatives, unfolding the coinductive definitions c_i, swapping quantifiers, rearranging expressions and folding the holistic definition. This process results in an incremental definition equivalent to H. An incremental hyperproperty, based on a monotone function, corresponds closely to a bisimulation-like notion, from which a verification methodology immediately suggests itself (see Section 5).

4.1   Incrementalization of PHH

Let c be a pointwise, coinductive predicate [22] defined as follows: for $x, y \in A^\infty$ and some functional $R \subseteq A \times A$ (i.e. R can be seen as a function)

$$c \triangleq \nu X(x,y).(x = y = \epsilon) \vee ((x(0) \ R \ y(0)) \wedge X(x',y')).$$

Let PHH be the class of *pointwise, holistic hyperproperties* defined in $\mathcal{HL}$:

$$\mathsf{PHH}(X) \triangleq \forall x \in X \ \exists y \in X.c(x,y).$$

Generalize PHH to take a pair of systems as a parameter as follows:

$$\mathsf{PHH}^2(X,Y) \triangleq \forall x \in X \ \exists y \in Y.c(x,y).$$

Clearly, we have that for all $T \in \mathsf{Sys}$, $\mathsf{PHH}(T)$ iff $\mathsf{PHH}^2(T,T)$. Each of the following lemmas is one or more steps of the incrementalization process. First, unfold the holistic definition of PHH^2.

Lemma 1. *The predicate* $\mathsf{PHH}^2(X,Y)$ *holds iff*

$$\epsilon \in X \rightarrow \epsilon \in Y \bigwedge (\forall a \in A \ \forall w \in A^\infty. \ aw \in X \rightarrow$$
$$\exists b \in A \ \exists u \in A^\infty.bu \in Y \wedge a \ R \ b \wedge c(aw,bu)).$$

Second, rewrite the definition using derivatives and unfold the coinductive definition of c once.

Lemma 2. *The predicate* $\mathsf{PHH}^2(X,Y)$ *holds iff*

$$o(X) \rightarrow o(Y) \bigwedge (\forall a \in A. \ test_a(X) \rightarrow (\forall w \in A^\infty. \ w \in X_a \rightarrow$$
$$\exists b \in A. \ a \ R \ b \wedge test_b(Y) \wedge \exists u \in A^\infty. \ u \in Y_b \wedge c(w,u))).$$

Third, swap the quantifiers $\exists b$ and $\forall w$; this can be done as b depends only on a.

Lemma 3. *The predicate* $\mathsf{PHH}^2(X, Y)$ *holds iff*

$$o(X) \to o(Y) \bigwedge (\forall a \in A.\ test_a(X) \to (\exists b \in A.\ a\ R\ b \wedge test_b(Y) \wedge$$
$$(\forall w \in A^\infty.\ w \in X_a \to \exists u \in A^\infty.\ u \in Y_b \wedge c(w, u)))).$$

Fourth, rearrange the resulting expression and fold the definition of PHH^2.

Lemma 4. *The predicate* $\mathsf{PHH}^2(X, Y)$ *holds iff*

$$o(X) \to o(Y) \bigwedge (\forall a \in A.\ test_a(X) \to \exists b \in A.\ test_b(Y) \wedge a\ R\ b\ \wedge \mathsf{PHH}^2(X_a, Y_b)).$$

Finally, define the incremental hyperproperty PIH^2 as follows:

$$\mathsf{PIH}^2 \ \widehat{=}\ \nu I(X, Y).\ (o(X) \to o(Y)$$
$$\bigwedge (\forall a \in A.\ test_a(X) \to \exists b \in A.\ test_b(Y) \wedge a\ R\ b \wedge I(X_a, Y_b))).$$

Theorem 1 (Incrementalization of PHH^2). *For all* $X, Y \in \mathsf{Sys}$, *we have that* $\mathsf{PHH}^2(X, Y)$ *iff* $\mathsf{PIH}^2(X, Y)$.

Corollary 1. *For all* $T \in \mathsf{Sys}$, *we have that* $\mathsf{PHH}(T)$ *iff* $\mathsf{PIH}^2(T, T)$.

4.2 Incrementalization of SHH

As illustrated in Section 3.1, a number of security policies can be based on coinductive predicates on traces. We present the incrementalization of SHH — a class of such security-relevant, holistic hyperproperties defined on infinite systems in Sys_ω. This type of definitions claim that a system is secure if the set of traces is closed under removal of high events (see, for instance, [20]). Let $p : A \to 2$ be a predicate and $f : A \to A$ a function. Define a coinductive predicate $\sim_\mathrm{p} : A^\omega \times A^\omega \to 2$ as follows:

$$\frac{p(a) \quad p(b) \quad x \sim_\mathrm{p} y \quad b = f(a)}{a \cdot x \sim_\mathrm{p} b \cdot y} \qquad \frac{\neg p(a) \quad p(b) \quad x \sim_\mathrm{p} b \cdot y}{a \cdot x \sim_\mathrm{p} b \cdot y}$$
$$\frac{p(a) \quad \neg p(b) \quad a \cdot x \sim_\mathrm{p} y}{a \cdot x \sim_\mathrm{p} b \cdot y}$$

Define a coinductive predicate $p_s : A^\omega \to 2$, generalizing no_H from Section 2:

$$\frac{p(a) \quad p_s(x)}{p_s(a \cdot x)}$$

Let T, X, Y range over Sys_ω. Define SHH as follows:

$$\mathsf{SHH}(X) \ \widehat{=}\ \forall x \in X\ \exists y \in X.\ p_s(y) \wedge x \sim_\mathrm{p} y$$

In order to work with only one predicate, combine p_s and $\sim_p$ into a new coinductive predicate c_1:

$$c_1 \; \hat{=} \; \nu X(x,y).$$
$$((p(x(0)) \wedge p(y(0)) \wedge f(x(0)) = y(0) \wedge X(x',y')) \vee (\neg p(x(0)) \wedge X(x',y)))).$$

Lemma 5. *For all $s,t \in A^\omega$, we have that $(p_s(t) \wedge s \sim_p t) \rightarrow c_1(s,t)$.*

To define this class, an additional restriction on Sys_ω is needed. We work only with systems satisfying the property $P_{\square\lozenge} = \{t \in A^\omega \mid t \models \square\lozenge p\}$, based on temporal logic modalities *eventually* ($\lozenge$) and *always* ($\square$) [23].

Lemma 6. *For all $s,t \in P_{\square\lozenge}$, we have that $c_1(s,t) \rightarrow (p_s(t) \wedge s \sim_p t)$.*

Now, we will work with an equivalent definition of SHH by Lemmas 5 and 6:

$$\mathsf{SHH}(X) \iff \forall x \in X \; \exists y \in X. \; c_1(x,y).$$

Property SHH can be generalized as follows:

$$\mathsf{SHH}^2(X,Y) \; \hat{=} \; \forall x \in X \; \exists y \in Y. \; c_1(x,y).$$

Clearly, for all $T \in \mathsf{Sys}_\omega$, it is the case that $\mathsf{SHH}(T)$ iff $\mathsf{SHH}^2(T,T)$. Incrementalization allows us to derive the following version of SIH^2:

$$\mathsf{SIH}^2 \; \hat{=} \; \nu I(X,Y). \; (\forall a \in A. \; test_a(X) \wedge p(a) \rightarrow test_{f(a)}(Y) \wedge I(X_a, Y_{f(a)})$$
$$\bigwedge \forall a \in A. \; test_a(X) \wedge \neg p(a) \rightarrow I(X_a, Y)).$$

Theorem 2 (Incrementalization of SHH^2). *For all $X,Y \in P_{\square\lozenge}$, we have that $\mathsf{SHH}^2(X,Y)$ iff $\mathsf{SIH}^2(X,Y)$.*

Corollary 2. *For all $T \in P_{\square\lozenge}$, we have that $\mathsf{SHH}(T)$ iff $\mathsf{SIH}^2(T,T)$.*

Next, we give some intuition about the restriction for systems to be in the class $P_{\square\lozenge}$ and argue that it is reasonable. First, note that the predicate $p : A \rightarrow 2$ could be thought of as denoting the visibility of events to agents at a certain security level. Let us call events for which p evaluates to true p-*events*, dually there are $\neg p$-*events*. Intuitively, many security-relevant systems (e.g. reactive systems such as servers) have infinite traces and can be characterized as follows: each trace has some p-event appearing eventually, and that happens infinitely often. These are the type of properties we expect from a server, for instance: each request needs to be eventually serviced and that should happen infinitely often. The latter is captured by the property $P_{\square\lozenge}$. $P_{\square\lozenge}$ is a liveness property (informally always possible and possibly infinite), as defined by Alpern and Schneider [3]: formally, such a liveness property is given as follows: $\forall \alpha \in A^* \; \exists \beta \in A^\omega . \alpha\beta \models \square\lozenge p$.

Thus, the restriction on systems to be in the $P_{\square\lozenge}$ class is not severe as it actually captures a large class of interesting systems. These are indefinitely running systems in which security is a concern at any point in time.

4.3 Incrementalization of OHH

There are other security policies (such as *timing-sensitive, termination-sensitive noninterference* [2]) based on coinductive predicates on traces. We present the incrementalization of OHH, a class of security-relevant, holistic hyperproperties defined on systems in Sys. Recall that $p : A \to 2$ is a predicate and $f : A \to A$ a function. Define $\sim_{\text{pt}} : A^\infty \times A^\infty \to 2$ on finite or infinite streams:

$$\frac{}{\epsilon \sim_{\text{pt}} \epsilon} \qquad \frac{p(a) \quad p(b) \quad x \sim_{\text{pt}} y \quad b = f(a)}{a \cdot x \sim_{\text{pt}} b \cdot y} \qquad \frac{\neg p(a) \quad \neg p(b) \quad x \sim_{\text{pt}} y}{a \cdot x \sim_{\text{pt}} b \cdot y}$$

Let $\sim_{\text{pt}_i}$ be the natural restriction of the relation on input elements in A_i. Let T, X, Y range over Sys. Define OHH as follows:

$$\text{OHH}(X) \;\hat{=}\; \forall x \in X \; \forall y \in X. \; (x \sim_{\text{pt}_i} y \to x \sim_{\text{pt}} y).$$

Again, we can generalize OHH to take a pair of systems as a parameter as follows:

$$\text{OHH}^2(X, Y) \;\hat{=}\; \forall x \in X \; \forall y \in Y. \; (x \sim_{\text{pt}_i} y \to x \sim_{\text{pt}} y).$$

Incrementalization allows to derive the following version of OHH^2:

$$\text{OIH}^2 \;\hat{=}\; \nu I(X, Y). \; (o(X) \leftrightarrow o(Y)$$
$$\bigwedge \forall a \in A_i. \; test_a(X) \wedge p(a) \wedge test_{f(a)}(Y) \to I(X_a, Y_{f(a)})$$
$$\bigwedge \forall a \in A_o \; \forall b \in A_o. \; test_a(X) \wedge p(a) \wedge test_b(Y) \wedge p(b) \to$$
$$b = f(a) \wedge I(X_a, Y_{f(a)})$$
$$\bigwedge \forall a \in A \; \forall b \in A. \; test_a(X) \wedge \neg p(a) \wedge test_b(Y) \wedge \neg p(b) \to I(X_a, Y_b)).$$

Theorem 3 (Incrementalization of OHH^2). *For all $X, Y \in$ Sys, we have that* $\text{OHH}^2(X, Y)$ *iff* $\text{OIH}^2(X, Y)$.

Corollary 3. *For all $T \in$ Sys, we have that* $\text{OHH}(T)$ *iff* $\text{OIH}^2(T, T)$.

An interesting, security-related hyperproperty in OHH is weak time-sensitive noninterference [2]. To formalize it, first define its key ingredient $\sim_{\text{ts}}$:

$$\frac{}{\epsilon \sim_{\text{ts}} \epsilon} \qquad \frac{x \sim_{\text{ts}} y \quad low(a)}{a \cdot x \sim_{\text{ts}} a \cdot y} \qquad \frac{x \sim_{\text{ts}} y \quad high(a) \quad high(b)}{a \cdot x \sim_{\text{ts}} b \cdot y}$$

Note that this definition guarantees that both traces terminate in an equal number of steps and are low-view indistinguishable, or both diverge and are still low-view indistinguishable. Thus, the definition is also *termination-sensitive*. Let $\sim_{\text{ts}_i}$ be the same as $\sim_{\text{ts}}$, but restricted to inputs. Finally, define *weak time-sensitive noninterference*:

$$WTSNI(X) \;\hat{=}\; \forall x \in X \; \forall y \in X. (x \sim_{\text{ts}_i} y \to x \sim_{\text{ts}} y).$$

5   Verification of Incremental Hyperproperties

First, recall some fixed point theory. Let $\Psi : \mathcal{P}(X_1 \times \ldots \times X_n) \to \mathcal{P}(X_1 \times \ldots \times X_n)$ be a monotone operator over the complete lattice of set-theoretic n-ary relations on the Cartesian product of sets X_i, $i \in 1..n$, and $gfp(\Psi)$ be the greatest fixed point of Ψ. For any $\overline{x} = (x_1, \ldots, x_n) \in X_1 \times \ldots \times X_n$ and $R \subseteq X_1 \times \ldots \times X_n$ the following principle is sound:

$$\frac{R(\overline{x}) \qquad R \subseteq \Psi(R)}{gfp(\Psi)(\overline{x})}$$

This is the *Tarski coinduction principle* [17], generalised to an n-ary relation.

Due to the nature of incrementalization, the original holistic definition H becomes irrelevant for verification. Instead, the resulting coinductive predicate H' has to be verified to show that H holds. One way to do this is via theory established by Niqui and Rutten [22]. For a coinductive predicate H', they introduce H'-*simulations* which are to coinductive predicates as bisimulations are to equality. Formally an H'-simulation is an n-ary relation R such that $R \subseteq \Psi_{H'}(R)$: an H'-simulation corresponds closely to a respective monotone operator $\Psi_{H'}$ (see Section 3.2) whose greatest fixed point is H'. Thus, finding an H'-simulation for the system of interest will be sufficient for showing that H' holds.

Verification of an incremental hyperproperty would typically have two steps. First, find an appropriate notion of H'-simulation. Second, find a specific H'-simulation for the system of interest. Showing that there is no H'-simulation implies that the predicate does not hold. The second step can be automatic, adapting techniques from automata-based model checking. The soundness of this verification methodology follows directly from Tarski's coinduction principle [17].

Theorem 4. *The predicate $H'(x_1, \ldots, x_k)$ on G-systems $\langle S_i, \alpha_i, x_i \rangle$ for $i \in 1..k$ holds iff there exists some H'-simulation Q s.t. the k-tuple of the start states $\langle x_1, \ldots, x_k \rangle \in Q$.*

It should be noted that Theorem 4 is not constructive: it does not give an algorithm for finding H'-simulations. Nevertheless, automata-based model checking techniques provide a practical means to compute or approximate the greatest fixed point of a monotone operator. There are well-known iterative schemata for computing the greatest fixed points on a complete lattice [29]. Typically, the bottom and top elements of the lattice are the empty set and the powerset of the state space S, the partial order relation is set inclusion. When approximating (or calculating for finite state spaces) the greatest fixed point one starts with S and iteratively applies the functional Ψ. Formally $\Psi^0 = id$ and $\Psi^{n+1} = \Psi \circ \Psi^n$ where id is the identity function and operator $\circ$ denotes composition. The greatest fixed point of Ψ can be found as follows: $\nu\Psi = \bigcap_{n \geq 0} \Psi^n(S)$. The technique needs adaptation in order to accommodate our different state space, namely $S_1 \times \ldots \times S_k$. Finding efficient algorithms for deciding whether concrete coinductive predicates hold has not been explored yet and is left for future work. Nevertheless, the fact that different notions of bisimilarity can be decided more efficiently than language equivalence on finite transition systems [1] is promising.

5.1   Sample Hyperproperties in **PHH**

Consider the holistic hyperproperty *FLIP* from Section 3.1, which is in the class PHH. Therefore, we can instantiate the incremental definition of PIH^2 and find the appropriate notion of *FLIP'*-simulation: a relation Q is a *FLIP'*-simulation whenever, if $y_1 \, Q \, y_2$, then

$$o(y_1) \to o(y_2)$$
$$\bigwedge \forall a \in A. \ test_a(y_1) \to \exists b \in A. \ test_b(y_2) \land b = \neg a \land t(y_1)(a) \, Q \, t(y_2)(b).$$

Note that we rely on the fact that there is a unique map from G-coalgebras to trees. Now, take the system ζ_1 represented by the automaton in Fig. 2a. Relation $Q = \{(s_0, s_0), (s_0, s_1), (s_1, s_0)\}$ is the needed *FLIP'*-simulation and thus $\zeta_1 \models FLIP$.

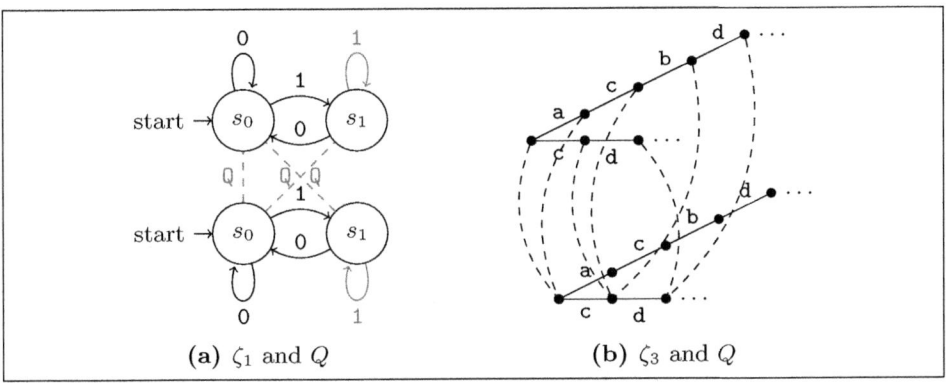

(a) ζ_1 and Q **(b)** ζ_3 and Q

Fig. 2. Illustration of *FLIP'*-simulation in (a) and *NI'*-simulation in (b)

Let ζ_2 be the system resulting from the removal of the transition from state s_1 to itself (gray transition in Fig. 2a). We show that there is no *FLIP'*-simulation Q such that $\langle s_0, s_0 \rangle \in Q$. To that end, assume there were such Q. By the assumption and the definition of *FLIP'*-simulation we have that the pair $\langle t(s_1)(1), t(s_0)(0) \rangle$ should be in Q (and in every *FLIP'*-simulation). This is not the case as $t(s_1)(1) = \bot$, whereas $t(s_0)(0) = s_0$. This is a contradiction and thus there is no Q that is a *FLIP'*-simulation and $\langle s_0, s_0 \rangle \in Q$. Thus $\zeta_2 \not\models FLIP$.

5.2   Sample Hyperproperties in **SHH**

Consider *NI* from Section 2 on systems satisfying $P_{\square\lozenge}$, which is in the class SHH. Hence we can instantiate the definition of SIH^2 and get an incremental definition of *NI*, called as usual *NI'* and corresponding to an *NI'*-simulation: a relation Q such that if $y_1 \, Q \, y_2$, then

$$\forall a \in A. \ (test_a(X) \land low(a) \to test_a(Y) \land t(y_1)(a) \, Q \, t(y_2)(a))$$
$$\bigwedge \forall a \in A. \ (test_a(X) \land high(a) \to t(y_1)(a) \, Q \, y_2).$$

Next, consider alphabet $A = \{a, b, c, d\}$ and define predicate $high$ as $high(a)$, $high(b), \neg high(c), \neg high(d)$. Take the system $\zeta_3 = \{(acbd)^\omega, (cd)^\omega\}$ (see Fig. 2b). Let $Q = \{(T, T), (T_a, T), (T_{ac}, T_c), (T_{acb}, T_c), (T_{acbd}, T_{cd}), (T_c, T_c), (T_{cd}, T_{cd})\}$. Q is an NI'-simulation such that $\langle T, T \rangle \in Q$ and thus we conclude that $\zeta_3 \models NI$.

5.3 Sample Hyperproperties in OHH

Recall hyperproperty $WTSNI$ from the class OHH. We can get an incremental definition, corresponding to a $WTSNI'$-simulation: a relation Q s.t. if $y_1 \; Q \; y_2$

$$o(y_1) \leftrightarrow o(y_2)$$

$$\bigwedge \forall a \in A_i. \; test_a(X) \wedge low(a) \wedge test_a(Y) \rightarrow t(y_1)(a) \; Q \; t(y_2)(a)$$

$$\bigwedge \forall a \in A_o \; \forall b \in A_o. \; test_a(X) \wedge low(a) \wedge test_b(Y) \wedge low(b) \rightarrow$$
$$a = b \wedge t(y_1)(a) \; Q \; t(y_2)(a)$$

$$\bigwedge \forall a \in A \; \forall b \in A. test_a(X) \wedge high(a) \wedge test_b(Y) \wedge high(b) \rightarrow$$
$$t(y_1)(a) \; Q \; t(y_2)(b).$$

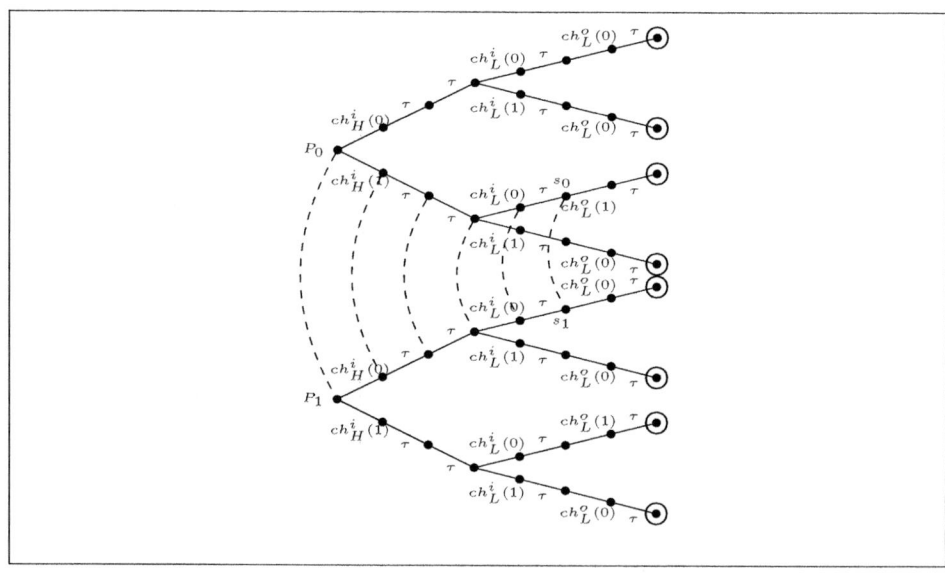

Fig. 3. Illustration of the lack of $WTSNI'$-simulation for Program 1.1

To illustrate the applicability of our abstract notions to programs, consider the RIMP Program 1.1, also called P. Two copies of the program (P_0 and P_1) are presented visually in Fig. 3. We show that there is no $WTSNI'$-simulation

Q such that $\langle P_0, P_1 \rangle \in Q$; to that end assume there were such a Q; states that should be related in any $WTSNI'$-simulation are connected by the dashed line. By the assumption and the definition of $WTSNI'$-simulation, it follows that $\langle t(P_0)(ch_H^i(1)), t(P_1)(ch_H^i(0)) \rangle \in Q$. This process continues until the pair $\langle s_0, s_1 \rangle$ is reached. The definition requires that $ch_L^o(1) = ch_L^o(0)$, by the rule for low outputs. This is a contradiction, thus there is no Q that is a $WTSNI'$-simulation and $\langle P_0, P_1 \rangle \in Q$. Hence $P \not\models WTSNI$. Note that Program 1.1 is also insecure with respect to other, less strict definitions, such as RN (see Section 2).

To illustrate that this definition is termination-sensitive, consider Program 1.2, also called P_2, which is termination-insensitive noninterferent. To see this, let $\sigma_{in} = [ch_H^i(1)]$ and $\gamma_{in} = [ch_H^i(0)]$ be input strings. Clearly, $\sigma_{in} \approx_L \gamma_{in}$ and the resultant traces are $\sigma = [ch_H^i(1), \tau, \tau, \tau, ch_L^o(0), \tau]$ and $\gamma = [ch_H^i(0), \tau, \tau, \tau, \ldots]$. Since $\sigma \approx_L \gamma$, and these are all traces, it follows that P_2 is secure. The application of the theory to this example is relatively straightforward and left to the reader.

```
1   input ch_H(x) {i:=x; if i = 0 then while 1 do skip};
2   output ch_L(0);
```

Program 1.2. Termination-sensitive interferent program in RIMP

6   Related Work

Clarkson and Schneider show that labelled transition systems can be encoded as sets of traces [10]. They argue that bisimulation-based hyperproperties, notably Focardi and Gorrieri's *bisimulation nondeducibility on composition* (*BNDC*), can be converted into trace sets. This is in effect the opposite to what we suggest. We propose going from trace sets to state-based systems because the latter are well-understood and enjoy well-established verification techniques, as well as mature verification tools. It is arguable, but we believe that such an approach is more natural and generic enough to work for a large number of applications.

That incrementalization is useful can be seen from recent work on noninterference for reactive systems [5]; Bohannon et al. start with a holistic definition of reactive noninterference and convert it into a relation on program states that they call *ID-bisimulation*; they effectively make the definition incremental. The authors use that latter incremental definition in order to prove that well-typed RIMP programs are secure. They also show that an *ID-bisimulation* implies the high level, holistic policy.

At first sight, incrementalization is somewhat similar to *unwinding* [14]. As Goguen and Meseguer describe it, unwinding is the process of translating a security policy first into local constraints on the transition system that inductively guarantee that the policy is satisfied and second in a finite set of lemmas; any system that satisfies the lemmas is guaranteed to satisfy the policy. The main difference to our work is that unwinding is still a trace based property, whereas incrementalization results in coinductive predicates and reasoning on trees. In addition, incrementalization gives an equivalent definition of the hyperproperty, whereas unwinding gives only a logically sufficient condition.

It turns out that incremental hyperproperties are inherently related to Mantel's work on unwinding of possibilistic security properties [19]. He proposes a modular framework in which most well-known security properties can be composed from a set of *basic security properties* (BSPs); he also presents unwinding conditions for most BSPs. His unwinding conditions are specified locally on states of the system (inspired by Rushby's work [25]) as opposed to the more traditional global (trace-based) unwinding conditions. These unwinding conditions can be seen as simulation relations on system states and in that sense are similar to our incremental security hyperproperties. A major difference is that Mantel's traces are only finite, i.e. his systems are in 2^{A^*}. Mantel also shows that the unwinding conditions for his BSPs are generally sound and only complete for a restricted class of models, in which any event is either high or low. In summary, Mantel's unwinding conditions can be seen as instances of incremental hyperproperties on finite systems.

Recent work [12] has proposed an automata-theoretic technique for model checking the possibilistic information flow hyperproperties from Mantel's framework [19] on finite state systems. To that end the authors show how to model check Mantel's BSPs, which are the building blocks of the respective holistic hyperproperties. This is a nice theoretical result, supporting our thesis that incremental hyperproperties are amenable to model checking. On the negative side, the authors show that the model checking problem is undecidable for the class of pushdown systems. Although using unwinding conditions (simulation relations), the proposed model checking approach is based on deciding set inclusion on regular languages. The latter question can be answered by standard automata-theoretic techniques. Such an approach is not directly applicable to hyperproperties, because the presence of infinite traces means that the languages (sets of traces) under consideration are not regular.

Also in recent work, Huisman and Blondeel [16] give a modal μ-calculus characterization of two determinism-based notions of information flow: observational determinism and eager trace equivalence [24]. Their characterization is based on a self-composed model [4,11] of the transition system induced by the program of interest; effectively the program would be executed in parallel with itself. The major differences to our framework is that we are not restricted to deterministic systems, thus we can handle more security-relevant hyperproperties.

There has been a substantial amount of work on verifying other specific hyperproperties, most notably of secure information flow from both the language-based security [28] and process calculi security [13,27] communities. Language-based secure information flow has traditionally relied on information flow type systems, with a recent trend to incorporate program logics or a combination of both [28,4,11,15]. There have also been attempts to address noninterference using results from process algebra [27,13]. Common for this line of work is formalizing different definitions of security and showing that they all depend on some notion of equivalence of processes, e.g. strong, weak, power bisimulation.

7   Conclusion

This work presents a formal classification of hyperproperties into holistic and incremental ones. It furthermore motivates the shift from a holistic to an incremental approach to hyperproperty specifications, dictated by the fact that the incremental approach has a clearer verification methodology. We argue that identifying the class of hyperproperties that are incrementalizable and finding a generic methodology for incrementalization of holistic hyperproperties are important problems. We propose a generic framework and techniques to explore the process of incrementalization and the usefulness of the resulting incremental hyperproperties. We identify three classes of incrementalizable hyperproperties. Future work will explore the problems presented here as well as techniques for model checking incremental hyperproperties.

Acknowledgements. We would like to thank Frank Piessens and José Proenca for valuable comments on drafts of this paper. We also thank the anonymous reviewers for their constructive feedback.

References

1. Aceto, L., Ingolfsdottir, A., Srba, J.: The Algorithmics of Bisimilarity. In: Advanced Topics in Bisimulation and Coinduction, pp. 100–172. Cambridge University Press (2011)
2. Agat, J.: Transforming out timing leaks. In: Proceedings of the 27th ACM SIGPLAN-SIGACT Symposium on Principles of Programming Languages, POPL 2000, pp. 40–53. ACM, New York (2000)
3. Alpern, B., Schneider, F.B.: Defining liveness. Technical report, Ithaca, NY, USA (1984)
4. Barthe, G., D'Argenio, P.R., Rezk, T.: Secure information flow by self-composition. In: CSFW 2004: Proceedings of the 17th IEEE Workshop on Computer Security Foundations, p. 100. IEEE Computer Society, Washington, DC (2004)
5. Bohannon, A., Pierce, B.C., Sjöberg, V., Weirich, S., Zdancewic, S.: Reactive noninterference. In: Proceedings of the 16th ACM Conference on Computer and Communications Security, CCS 2009, pp. 79–90. ACM, New York (2009)
6. Bradfield, J., Stirling, C.: Modal mu-calculi. In: Handbook of Modal Logic, pp. 721–756. Elsevier (2007)
7. Clarke, E.M., Emerson, E.A., Sistla, A.P.: Automatic verification of finite-state concurrent systems using temporal logic specifications. ACM Transactions on Programming Languages and Systems 8(2), 244–263 (1986)
8. Clarke Jr., E.M., Grumberg, O., Peled, D.A.: Model checking. MIT Press, Cambridge (1999)
9. Clarkson, M.R., Schneider, F.B.: Hyperproperties. In: CSF 2008: Proceedings of the 2008 21st IEEE Computer Security Foundations Symposium, pp. 51–65. IEEE Computer Society, Washington, DC (2008)
10. Clarkson, M.R., Schneider, F.B.: Hyperproperties. Journal of Computer Security 18, 1157–1210 (2010)
11. Darvas, Á., Hähnle, R., Sands, D.: A Theorem Proving Approach to Analysis of Secure Information Flow. In: Hutter, D., Ullmann, M. (eds.) SPC 2005. LNCS, vol. 3450, pp. 193–209. Springer, Heidelberg (2005)

12. D'Souza, D., Holla, R., Raghavendra, K.R., Sprick, B.: Model-checking trace-based information flow properties. Journal of Computer Security 19, 101–138 (2011)
13. Focardi, R., Gorrieri, R.: A taxonomy of security properties for process algebras. Journal of Computer Security 3(1), 5–34 (1995)
14. Goguen, J.A., Meseguer, J.: Unwinding and inference control. In: IEEE Symposium on Security and Privacy, p. 75 (1984)
15. Hähnle, R., Pan, J., Rümmer, P., Walter, D.: Integration of a Security Type System into a Program Logic. In: Montanari, U., Sannella, D., Bruni, R. (eds.) TGC 2006. LNCS, vol. 4661, pp. 116–131. Springer, Heidelberg (2007)
16. Huisman, M., Blondeel, H.-C.: Model-Checking Secure Information Flow for Multi-threaded Programs. In: Mödersheim, S., Palamidessi, C. (eds.) TOSCA 2011. LNCS, vol. 6993, pp. 148–165. Springer, Heidelberg (2012)
17. Lenisa, M.: From set-theoretic coinduction to coalgebraic coinduction: some results, some problems. Electronic Notes in Theoretical Computer Science, 19 (1999)
18. Manna, Z., Pnueli, A.: The temporal logic of reactive and concurrent systems. Springer-Verlag New York, Inc., New York (1992)
19. Mantel, H.: Unwinding Possibilistic Security Properties. In: Cuppens, F., Deswarte, Y., Gollmann, D., Waidner, M. (eds.) ESORICS 2000. LNCS, vol. 1895, pp. 238–254. Springer, Heidelberg (2000)
20. McLean, J.: A general theory of composition for a class of possibilistic properties. IEEE Transactions on Software Engineering 22(1), 53–67 (1996)
21. Milushev, D., Clarke, D.: Towards incrementalization of holistic hyperproperties: extended version. Technical Report CW 616, Katholieke Universiteit Leuven (December 2011)
22. Niqui, M., Rutten, J.: Coinductive predicates as final coalgebras. In: Matthes, R., Uustalu, T. (eds.) Proceedings of the 6th Workshop on Fixed Points in Computer Science, FICS 2009, Coimbra, Portugal, September 12-13, pp. 79–85 (2009)
23. Pnueli, A.: The temporal semantics of concurrent programs. In: Proceedings of the International Sympoisum on Semantics of Concurrent Computation, pp. 1–20. Springer, London (1979)
24. Roscoe, A.W.: CSP and determinism in security modelling. In: Proceedings of the 1995 IEEE Symposium on Security and Privacy, SP 1995, pp. 114–127. IEEE Computer Society, Washington, DC (1995)
25. Rushby, J.: Noninterference, transitivity and channel-control security policies. Technical report (1992)
26. Rutten, J.J.M.M.: Automata and Coinduction (an Exercise in Coalgebra). In: Sangiorgi, D., de Simone, R. (eds.) CONCUR 1998. LNCS, vol. 1466, pp. 194–218. Springer, Heidelberg (1998)
27. Ryan, P.Y.A., Schneider, S.A.: Process algebra and non-interference. Journal of Computer Security 9(1/2), 75–103 (2001)
28. Sabelfeld, A., Myers, A.C.: Language-based information-flow security. IEEE Journal on Selected Areas in Communications 21(1), 5–19 (2003)
29. Stirling, C.: Modal and temporal properties of processes. Springer-Verlag New York, Inc., New York (2001)
30. Zdancewic, S., Myers, A.C.: Observational determinism for concurrent program security. In: IEEE Computer Security Foundations Workshop, p. 29 (2003)

Type-Based Analysis of PKCS#11 Key Management*

Matteo Centenaro, Riccardo Focardi, and Flaminia L. Luccio

DAIS, Università Ca' Foscari Venezia, Italy
{mcentena,focardi,luccio}@dsi.unive.it

Abstract. PKCS#11, is a security API for cryptographic tokens. It is known to be vulnerable to attacks which can directly extract, as cleartext, the value of sensitive keys. In particular, the API does not impose any limitation on the different roles a key can assume, and it permits to perform conflicting operations such as asking the token to wrap a key with another one and then to decrypt it. Fixes proposed in the literature, or implemented in real devices, impose policies restricting key roles and token functionalities. In this paper we define a simple imperative programming language, suitable to code PKCS#11 symmetric key management, and we develop a type-based analysis to prove that the secrecy of sensitive keys is preserved under a certain policy. We formally analyse existing fixes for PKCS#11 and we propose a new one, which is type-checkable and prevents conflicting roles by *deriving* different keys for different roles.

1 Introduction

PKCS#11, also known as Cryptoki, defines a widely adopted API for cryptographic tokens [18]. It provides access to cryptographic functionalities while, in principle, providing some security properties. More specifically, the value of keys stored on a PKCS#11 device and tagged as *sensitive* should never be revealed outside the token, even when connected to a compromised host. Unfortunately, PKCS#11 is known to be vulnerable to attacks that break this property [4,8,10].

An application initiates a *session* with a PKCS#11 compliant device by first supplying a PIN, and then accessing the functionalities provided by the token. There may be various *objects* stored in the token, such as cryptographic keys and certificates. Objects are referenced via *handles* to permit, e.g., that a cryptographic key is used without necessarily knowing its value: we can ask a token to encrypt some data just providing a handle to the encryption key. The value of a key is one of the *attributes* of the enclosing object. There are other attributes to specify the various roles a key can assume: each different API call can, in fact, require a different role. For example, decryption keys are required to have attribute CKA_DECRYPT set, while key-encrypting keys, i.e., keys used to encrypt other keys, must have attribute CKA_WRAP set.

---

* Work partially supported by the RAS Project *"TESLA: Techniques for Enforcing Security in Languages and Applications"*.

P. Degano and J.D. Guttman (Eds.): POST 2012, LNCS 7215, pp. 349–368, 2012.

The attacks on PKCS#11 we consider in this paper are at the API level [1,2,3,4,7,8,10,16], i.e., the attacker is assumed to control the host on which the token is connected and to perform any sequence of (legal) API calls. The crucial functionalities of PKCS#11 are the ones for exporting and importing sensitive keys, called C_WrapKey and C_UnwrapKey. The former performs the encryption of a key under another one, giving as output the resulting ciphertext, and the latter performs the corresponding decrypt and import into the token. They allow for exporting and reimporting keys, in an encrypted form. Note that, having a wrapping key (CKA_WRAP) which can also be used for decryption (CKA_DECRYPT) is dangerous and leads to the following simple 'wrap-decrypt' API-level attack:

```
h_myKey = C_GenerateKey({CKA_DECRYPT, CKA_WRAP});
wrapped = C_WrapKey(h_sensitiveKey, h_myKey);
leak = C_Decrypt(wrapped, h_myKey);
```

First, we ask the token to generate a new key with attributes CKA_DECRYPT, CKA_WRAP set. Then, we use this key to wrap an existing sensitive key referenced by h_sensitiveKey. Finally, we ask the token to decrypt the resulting ciphertext using again the freshly generated key. Since it is the same key used for wrapping, we obtain the value of the sensitive key in the clear.

A recent work [4] has shown that the state of the art in PKCS#11 security tokens is rather poor: many existing commercially available devices are vulnerable to attacks similar to the above one; the secured ones, instead, prevent the attacks by completely removing wrapping functionalities. However, it has been shown that the API can be 'patched' without necessarily cutting down so much on its functionalities [4,10]: this can be done by (*i*) imposing a policy on the attributes so that a key cannot be used for conflicting operations; (*ii*) limiting the way attributes can be changed so to avoid that conflicting attributes are set at two different instants; (*iii*) either adding a wrapping format which binds attributes to wrapped keys [10] or limiting very carefully the usage of imported keys to a subset of non-critical functions [4].

In our opinion, formal tools to reason about the security of different implementations of PKCS#11 APIs, such as Tookan [4], are fundamental to help developers and hardware producers to detect and better understand the causes of the bugs affecting the implementations, and they are very important for the testing of new patches.

Our contribution. In this paper we (*i*) define a simple imperative programming language, suitable to code PKCS#11 APIs for symmetric key management; (*ii*) formalize a Dolev-Yao attacker and API security in this setting; (*iii*) present a type system to statically enforce API security; (*iv*) propose a new fix for PKCS#11 based on key-diversification; (*v*) apply the type system to validate our new fix and one previously proposed in [4,5]. We only consider functions for encryption/decryption of data and wrap/unwrap of keys as these are the most relevant ones for what concerns API-level attacks.

The language is, by itself, an original contribution as PKCS#11 is typically modelled following a 'black-box' approach: each API function takes some input values and a (representation of a) device, and returns new values possibly modifying the device state. This is done in one step, disregarding the internal single steps (see, e.g., [10]). Our target is to perform a language-based analysis of the API specification, and this requires that APIs are specified as sequences of internal commands and lower level calls to the device. The attacker is modelled in a classic Dolev-Yao style: he can perform any cryptographic operation once he knows the corresponding key. He can also execute any API call passing, as parameters, values that he knows, and incrementing his knowledge with the returned value. API security requires that sensitive keys that are not already known by the attacker, and *always-sensitive* keys (special sensitive keys that have been generated inside the token) will never be disclosed to the attacker.

Our type system statically enforces API security by checking that keys can only be wrapped using *trusted* keys and every key has a clear, unambiguous role. Typing is parametrized with respect to a policy dictating the possible attributes that can be simultaneously set on a key and the ones that are set when unwrapping/importing a new key in a device. We prove that type-checked APIs are secure against a Dolev-Yao attacker. Using the proposed type system we analyse the Secure Templates fix proposed in [4,5], and we prove it secure. We then propose a new patch, based on key-diversification, a standard cryptographic technique to derive a new key from a known one. Our idea, is to explicitly require that keys for different roles will always be different. To the best of our knowledge, key-diversification has previously never been adopted as a systematic mechanism to secure key management of cryptographic tokens. We finally prove that this new patch type-checks.

Related work. The most established work on formal analysis of PKCS#11 is [10]. In this paper, it is given a model of a fragment of PKCS#11 and a model-checking procedure to look for possible attack sequences. Interesting abstractions to reduce state explosion and to analyse unbounded fresh data have been given in [14]. In [4], the theory has been engineered into Tookan, a tool for the analysis of real devices. The tool is able to build a formal model of a real token, perform model-checking and try the theoretical attacks on a real device. Once the model is extracted from the token, it is also possible to try new fixes are check again for existing attacks.

Our present contribution extends this line of research by exploring a language-based, static analysis technique that allows for proving the security of PKCS#11 APIs and their fixes. We in fact intend to integrate this type-based analysis in Tookan. The contribution is also in the line of other type-based analyses on different settings: For what concerns Bank APIs in [6] it is studied the security of PIN managements Hardware Security Modules and it is given a type system to prove their security; in [11] we have given a type system for the security of rechargeable disposable RFID tickets.

A recent line of research [12,13] investigates models of PKCS#11 based on first-order linear time logic extended by past operators. The motivation is, again, to check the security of the PKCS#11 configuration, but the underlying model is completely different. A comparison between the two models is for sure an interesting future issue.

In [15] Keighren, Aspinall, and Steel propose a type system to check information flow properties for cryptographic operations in security APIs. There seem to be many differences with our contribution: (*i*) the target property is different: Here we consider confidentiality of sensitive keys while in [15] the authors investigate *noninterference*, a much stronger property. In this sense their result is more in the line of [6]; (*ii*) their model is very general and allows for reasoning on cryptographic operations so that the wrap/decrypt attack is modelled as a forbidden information flow from secret to public. No language is given to express internal commands. Our language allows for specifying PKCS#11 key management APIs at a fine granularity, and the same attack is prevented by avoiding conflicting roles for the same key. This is why we can avoid the complex treatment of noninterference and only focus on key confidentiality; (*iii*) Keighren, Aspinall, and Steel only considers confidentiality and do not treat integrity (or trust) that is one of the crucial ingredient of our analysis: only trusted keys should be used to wrap sensitive keys. A more detailed comparison will be the subject of future work.

Paper structure. The paper is organized as follows. In section 2 we introduce the simple imperative language for PKCS#11 key management, the attacker model and the notion of API security; in section 3 we present the type system statically enforcing API security; in section 4 we type-check known implementations of PKCS#11 key management APIs, and we propose our new fix based on key-diversification, which we prove to be secure. We conclude in section 5.

2   A Language for PKCS#11 Key Management

In this section we first introduce a simple imperative language suitable to specify PKCS#11 key management APIs. We then formalize the attacker model and define API security.

Values. We let $\mathcal{C}$ and $\mathcal{G}$, with $\mathcal{C} \cap \mathcal{G} = \emptyset$, respectively be the set of atomic *constant* and *fresh* values. The former is used to model any public data, including non-sensitive keys; the latter models the generation of new fresh values such as sensitive keys. We associate to $\mathcal{G}$ an extraction operator $g \leftarrow \mathcal{G}$, representing the extraction of the first 'unused' value g from $\mathcal{G}$. Extracted values are always different: two, even non-consecutive, extractions $g \leftarrow \mathcal{G}$ and $g' \leftarrow \mathcal{G}$ are always such that $g \neq g'$. We let *val* range over the set of all atomic values $\mathcal{C} \cup \mathcal{G}$ and we define values v as follows:

$$v ::= val \mid enc(v, v') \mid dec(v, v') \mid kdf(v, v')$$

where $enc(v, v')$ and $dec(v, v')$ denote value v respectively encrypted and decrypted under key v', and $kdf(v, v')$ represents a new key obtained via diversification from a value v and another key v'. Key diversification may be implemented in many different ways. For example, using the encryption scheme, we can directly obtain $kdf(v, v')$ as $enc(v, v')$. We explicitly represent decrypted values in order to model situations in which a wrong key is used to decrypt an encrypted value: for example, the decryption under v' of $enc(v, v')$ will give, as expected, value v; instead, the decryption under v' of $enc(v, v'')$, with $v'' \neq v'$ will be explicitly represented as $dec(enc(v, v''), v')$. This allows us to model a cryptosystem with no integrity check, as the one used in PKCS#11 for symmetric keys: decrypting with a wrong key never gives a failure.

Expressions. Our language is composed of a core set of expressions for manipulating the above values. Expressions are based on a set of variables $\mathcal{V}$ ranged over by x, and have the following syntax:

$$e ::= x \mid \mathsf{enc}(e, x) \mid \mathsf{dec}(e, x) \mid \mathsf{kdf}(val, x)$$

The explicit tag val will simplify typing for key diversification. A memory $\mathsf{M} : x \mapsto v$ is a partial mapping from variables to values and $e \downarrow^{\mathsf{M}} v$ denotes that the evaluation of the expression e in memory M leads to value v. Let $e \downarrow^{\mathsf{M}} v$ and $\mathsf{M}(x) = v'$. The semantics of expressions follows:

$$x \downarrow^{\mathsf{M}} \mathsf{M}(x) \qquad \text{if } \mathsf{M}(x) \text{ is defined}$$

$$\mathsf{enc}(e, x) \downarrow^{\mathsf{M}} enc(v, v')$$

$$\mathsf{dec}(e, x) \downarrow^{\mathsf{M}} \begin{cases} v'' & \text{if } v = enc(v'', v') \\ dec(v, v') & \text{otherwise} \end{cases}$$

$$\mathsf{kdf}(val, x) \downarrow^{\mathsf{M}} kdf(val, v')$$

The modeled encryption mechanism does not perform any integrity check on the messages, so the decryption of a ciphertext under a wrong key gives $dec(v, v')$.

Templates. Properties and capabilities of keys are described by templates, ranged over by T, represented as a set of *attributes*. When a certain attribute is contained in a template T we will say that the attribute is set, it is unset otherwise. A key can be *sensitive*, and a sensitive key can also be *always-sensitive* if it has been generated (as a sensitive key) by a secure device. These two properties are described by the attributes S (sensitive), and A (always-sensitive). Four attributes identify the capabilities of a key: data encryption (E) and decryption (D), wrap (W) and unwrap (U), i.e., encryption and decryption of other keys. Formally, a template T is a subset of $\{S, A, E, D, W, U\}$ under the constraint $S \notin T$ implies $A \notin T$, i.e., non-sensitive keys can never be always-sensitive.

APIs and tokens. An API is specified as a set $\mathcal{A} = \{\mathsf{a}_1, \ldots, \mathsf{a}_n\}$ of functions, each one composed of simple sequences of assignment commands:

```
a ::= λx₁, . . . , xₖ.c
c ::= x := e | x := f | return e | c₁; c₂
f ::= getObj(y) | checkTemplate(y, T) | genKey(T) | importKey(y, T)
```

We will only consider API commands in which return e can only occur as the last command. Internal functions f represent operations that can be performed on the underlying devices. Note that these functions are used to implement the APIs and are not directly available to the users. Intuitively, getObj retrieves the plaintext value of a key stored in the device, given its handle y; checkTemplate is similar but it additionally queries the template of the stored key: if the key template 'matches', i.e., is a superset of, the given one T, the key is returned; genKey generates a key with template T; finally, importKey imports a new key with plaintext value y and template T. The first two functions fail (i.e., are stuck) if the given handle does not exists or refers to a key with a wrong template. A call to an API a $= \lambda x_1, \ldots, x_k.$c, written a$(v_1, \ldots, v_k)$, binds $x_1, \ldots, x_k$ to values $v_1, \ldots, v_k$, executes c and outputs the value given by return e.

Example 1 (PKCS#11 C_WrapKey command). The language introduced is suitable to implement PKCS#11 commands. Each API command will be modeled as a procedure reading inputs from pre-defined variables and returning a value as output. The following is a possible specification of the wrap command. It takes the handles of a key to be wrapped and the one pointing to the wrapping key (whose flags W and S have to be set, as it has to be a sensitive wrapping key) returning an encrypted byte-stream. For the sake of readability, we will always write a$(x_1, \ldots, x_k)$ c in place of a $= \lambda x_1, \ldots, x_k.$c to specify an API function:

$$
\begin{aligned}
&\text{C\_WrapKey}(h\_key,\ h\_w) \\
&\quad w := \text{checkTemplate}(h\_w,\ \{S, W\}); \\
&\quad k := \text{getObj}(h\_key); \\
&\quad \text{return } enc(k, w);
\end{aligned}
$$

Device keys are modelled by the handle-map H $: g \mapsto (v, T)$, a partial mapping from the atomic (generated) values to pairs of keys and templates. Each key has a handle to be referred with, and a template. Notice that we do not distinguish between one or many devices: we consider all keys available to the API as a unique 'universal' PKCS#11 token. This corresponds to a worst-case scenario in which attackers can simultaneously access all existing tokens. Notice, also, that this does not limit the multiple presence of the same key value under different handles or templates, as for example, with H$(g) = (v, T)$ and H$(g') = (v, T')$.

An API command c working on a memory M and handle-map H is noted as $\langle$M, H, c$\rangle$. Semantics is reported in Table 1, where ϵ denotes the empty API. We explain the first rule for assignment $x := e$: it evaluates expression e on M and stores the results in variable x, noted M$[x \mapsto v]$. In case x is not defined in M the domain of M is extended to include the new variable, otherwise the value stored in x is overwritten. Other rules are similar in spirit. Notice that genKey and importKey also modify the handle-map. The last rule is for API calls on an handle-map H: parameter values are assigned to variables of an empty memory M$_\epsilon$, i.e., a memory with no variables mapped to values (recall memories are partial functions); then, the API commands are executed and the return value is given as a result of the call. This is noted a$(v_1, \ldots, v_k) \downarrow^{\text{H,H}'} v$ where H$'$ is the resulting handle map. Notice that at this API level we do not observe memories

Table 1. API Semantics

$$\frac{e \downarrow^{\mathsf{M}} v}{\langle \mathsf{M}, \mathsf{H}, x := e \rangle \to \langle \mathsf{M}[x \mapsto v], \mathsf{H}, \varepsilon \rangle} \qquad \frac{H(\mathsf{M}(y)) = (v, T)}{\langle \mathsf{M}, \mathsf{H}, x := \mathsf{getObj}(y) \rangle \to \langle \mathsf{M}[x \mapsto v], \mathsf{H}, \varepsilon \rangle}$$

$$\frac{H(\mathsf{M}(y)) = (v, T') \quad T \subseteq T'}{\langle \mathsf{M}, \mathsf{H}, x := \mathsf{checkTemplate}(y, T) \rangle \to \langle \mathsf{M}[x \mapsto v], \mathsf{H}, \varepsilon \rangle}$$

$$\frac{g, g' \leftarrow \mathcal{G}}{\langle \mathsf{M}, \mathsf{H}, x := \mathsf{genKey}(T) \rangle \to \langle \mathsf{M}[x \mapsto g], \mathsf{H}[g \mapsto (g', T)], \varepsilon \rangle}$$

$$\frac{g \leftarrow \mathcal{G}}{\langle \mathsf{M}, \mathsf{H}, x := \mathsf{importKey}(y, T) \rangle \to \langle \mathsf{M}[x \mapsto g], \mathsf{H}[g \mapsto (\mathsf{M}(y), T)], \varepsilon \rangle}$$

$$\frac{\langle \mathsf{M}, \mathsf{H}, c_1 \rangle \to \langle \mathsf{M}', \mathsf{H}', \varepsilon \rangle}{\langle \mathsf{M}, \mathsf{H}, c_1; c_2 \rangle \to \langle \mathsf{M}', \mathsf{H}', c_2 \rangle} \qquad \frac{\langle \mathsf{M}, \mathsf{H}, c_1 \rangle \to \langle \mathsf{M}', \mathsf{H}', c_1' \rangle}{\langle \mathsf{M}, \mathsf{H}, c_1; c_2 \rangle \to \langle \mathsf{M}', \mathsf{H}', c_1'; c_2 \rangle}$$

$$\frac{\mathsf{a} = \lambda x_1, \ldots, x_k.\mathsf{c} \quad \langle \mathsf{M}_\epsilon[x_1 \mapsto v_1 \ldots x_k \mapsto v_k], \mathsf{H}, \mathsf{c} \rangle \to \langle \mathsf{M}', \mathsf{H}', \mathsf{return}\ e \rangle \quad e \downarrow^{\mathsf{M}'} v}{\mathsf{a}(v_1, \ldots, v_k) \downarrow^{\mathsf{H}, \mathsf{H}'} v}$$

that are, in fact, used internally by the device to execute the function. The only exchanged data are the input parameters and the return value.

Example 2 (Semantics of C_WrapKey*).* To illustrate the semantics, we now show the transitions of the C_WrapKey command specified above. Suppose that the device associates the handle g to $(v, \{A, S, E, D\})$ and g' to $(v', \{S, W, U\})$. We consider a memory M where all the variables are set to zero except for h_key and h_w which store respectively g and g', i.e., $\mathsf{M} = \mathsf{M}_\epsilon[h\_key \mapsto g, h\_w \mapsto g']$. Then it follows,

$$\langle \mathsf{M}, \mathsf{H}, w := \mathsf{checkTemplate}(h\_w, \{S, W\}); k := \mathsf{getObj}(h\_key); \mathsf{return}\ \mathsf{enc}(k, w) \rangle$$
$$\to \langle \mathsf{M}[w \mapsto v'], \mathsf{H}, k := \mathsf{getObj}(h\_key); \mathsf{return}\ \mathsf{enc}(k, w) \rangle$$
$$\to \langle \mathsf{M}[w \mapsto v', k \mapsto v], \mathsf{H}, \mathsf{return}\ \mathsf{enc}(k, w) \rangle$$

which gives C_WrapKey$(g, g') \downarrow^{\mathsf{H}, \mathsf{H}} enc(v, v')$ meaning that the value returned invoking the wrap command is thus the encryption of v under v'. Obviously, this is safe as long as v' is not know outside the device, otherwise a user knowing the raw value of the key used to wrap could retrieve v by simply computing $\mathsf{dec}(enc(v, v'), v')$.

Attacker Model. We now formalize the attacker in a classic Dolev-Yao style. In particular, the attacker knowledge $\mathcal{K}(V)$ deducible from a set of values V is defined as the least superset of V such that $v, v' \in \mathcal{K}(V)$ implies

(1) $enc(v, v') \in \mathcal{K}(V)$;
(2) $kdf(v, v') \in \mathcal{K}(V)$;
(3) if $v = enc(v'', v')$ then $v'' \in \mathcal{K}(V)$;
(4) if $v \neq enc(v'', v')$ then $dec(v, v') \in \mathcal{K}(V)$.

Given a handle map H, representing tokens, and an API $\mathcal{A} = \{a_1, \ldots, a_n\}$, the attacker can invoke any API function giving any of the known values as a parameter. The returned value is then added to the knowledge. Formally, an attacker configuration is represented as $\langle H, V \rangle$ and evolves as follows:

$$\frac{a \in \mathcal{A} \quad v_1, \ldots, v_k \in \mathcal{K}(V) \quad a(v_1, \ldots, v_k) \downarrow^{H, H'} v}{\langle H, V \rangle \rightsquigarrow_{\mathcal{A}} \langle H', V \cup \{v\} \rangle}$$

We assume that the attacker initially knows an arbitrary subset V_0 of the constant atomic values $\mathcal{C}$ and we consider an initial empty handle map H_0. In the following, we use the standard notation $\rightsquigarrow_{\mathcal{A}}^*$ to note multi-step reductions.

API security. The main property required by PKCS #11: "Sensitive keys cannot be revealed in plaintext off the token" [18, page 30], is modelled by requiring that sensitive keys, that are not already known by the attacker, should never be learned by the attacker. Moreover, we formalize the intuitive property that always-sensitive keys and all keys derived from them, are never known by the attacker. This will be useful to guarantee that such keys have not been imported by the attacker and can be trusted.

Formally, sensitive keys are the ones that only appear in the handle map with the attribute sensitive set. Always-sensitive keys additionally have the always-sensitive attribute set.

Definition 1 (Sensitive and always-sensitive values). *Let val be an atomic value and H a handle-map. If val is such that $H(g) = (val, T)$ implies $S \in T$ we say that val is sensitive in H. If we additionally have that $H(g) = (val, T)$ implies $A \in T$ we say that val is always-sensitive in H.*

The definition of API security follows.

Definition 2 (API Security). *Let $\mathcal{A}$ be an API. We say that $\mathcal{A}$ is secure if for all reductions $\langle H_0, V_0 \rangle \rightsquigarrow_{\mathcal{A}}^* \langle H, V \rangle \rightsquigarrow_{\mathcal{A}}^* \langle H', V' \rangle$ and for all atomic values val we have*

1. *$val \notin \mathcal{K}(V)$ and val is sensitive in H imply $val \notin \mathcal{K}(V')$;*
2. *val is always-sensitive in H implies $val, \mathrm{kdf}(v, val) \notin \mathcal{K}(V) \cup \mathcal{K}(V')$.*

3   Type System

We enforce the security of an API through a type system requiring that (i) every key has a clear, unambiguous role, and (ii) keys can only be wrapped using trusted keys. This latter idea is, in fact, suggested in PKCS#11 v2.20 [18]: CKA_TRUSTED keys are added by the security officer in a protected environment. Keys with the CKA_WRAP_WITH_TRUSTED attribute (that we do not model here) set can only be wrapped via such security officer keys. In fact, here it is like we were assuming that CKA_WRAP_WITH_TRUSTED is always set.

Our type system generalizes this idea of trusted keys by also including the ones generated by the device (always-sensitive). Even in this case, in fact, we

Table 2. Typing templates

$$\frac{A \notin T, S \in T \quad \neg data(T) \vee wrap(T)}{\vdash T : \mathsf{Any}} \qquad \frac{A \notin T, S \in T \quad data(T) \quad \neg wrap(T)}{\vdash T : \mathsf{Data}}$$

$$\frac{A, S \in T \quad data(T) \quad \neg wrap(T)}{\vdash T : \mathsf{TData}} \qquad \frac{A, S \in T \quad \neg data(T) \quad wrap(T)}{\vdash T : \mathsf{Wrap}}$$

$$\frac{A, S \in T \quad data(T) \Leftrightarrow wrap(T)}{\vdash T : \mathsf{Seed}} \qquad \frac{A, S \notin T}{\vdash T : \mathsf{Un}}$$

are guaranteed that their value has never appeared as plain-text outside the device. This will allow us to propose and analyse configurations in which always-sensitive keys can be exchanged by users. This is not allowed for trusted security officer keys. In the following we will then use the word trusted to refer to a key that is guaranteed to be unknown to the attacker. We will use the attribute always-sensitive to capture this fact, but we could easily extend the analysis to incorporate the above discussed attribute trusted. We consider the following types.

$$\rho ::= \mathsf{Any} \mid \mathsf{Data} \mid \mathsf{TData} \mid \mathsf{Wrap} \mid \mathsf{Seed} \mid \mathsf{Un}$$
$$\tau ::= \rho \mid \mathsf{Wrap}[\rho]$$

Intuitively, Any is the top type including all possible data and keys; type Data and TData are, respectively, for secret and trusted keys used to encrypt and decrypt data; Wrap is for trusted wrapping keys, i.e., keys used to encrypt

other keys, and Seed is for trusted keys used to derive other keys via diversification; $\mathsf{Wrap}[\rho]$ is for trusted wrapping keys transporting keys of type ρ, obtained via diversification from some (trusted) seed; finally, Un represents untrusted values. Types are related by a subtyping relation $\leq$ depicted on the right. Notice that the level of secrecy can only grow while the level of trust can only decrease. Promoting a type via subtyping, in fact, should not compromise security. This will be proved in lemma 1 below.

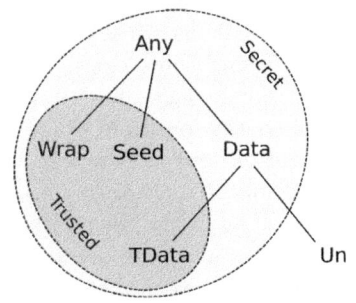

Typing keys. We now describe how PKCS#11 key templates are converted to key types. Key templates represent the 'types' of the keys stored in the devices. Attributes describe how keys are supposed to be used and which security properties the device enforces on them.

First we notice that attribute sensitive (S) indicates that the key should be regarded as secret. If, additionally, always-sensitive (A) is set we know that the key is trusted. In fact, the always-sensitive PKCS#11 attribute cannot be set by a user when generating or unwrapping a key (see [18], Table 15 footnotes 4 and 6). This attribute is meant to be automatically managed by the tamper resistant token whenever a key is generated as sensitive. Data and wrapping keys are instead determined by attributes E,D and W,U, respectively. We require that these pairs of attributes cannot coexists on data and wrapping keys, so to disambiguate key roles. Trusted keys that are neither wrapping not data keys are considered seeds while sensitive keys with mixed roles, e.g., E plus W, are given type Any.

We let $data(T)$ be $E \in T \vee D \in T$ and $wrap(T)$ be $W \in T \vee U \in T$. Types for keys are derived through the judgment $\vdash T : \tau$ formalized in Table 2. It is easy to see that any possible template is associated to exactly one type: non-sensitive keys are typed as Un; sensitive but not always-sensitive keys are typed Data if they have at least E or D set, and Any otherwise; always-sensitive keys are typed TData if they have E or D set, otherwise they are typed Wrap or Seed depending on the presence of W and U. Notice that no wrapping untrusted keys are allowed, in fact secret non-data keys are typed as Any.

The following lemma states that subtyping does not compromise the security of keys: non-sensitive keys can be regarded as sensitive and always-sensitive keys can be regarded as just sensitive ones. Intuitively, it is safe to increase the level of secrecy and decrease the level of trust.

Lemma 1 (Subtyping preserves security). *Let* $\vdash T : \rho$ *and* $\vdash T' : \rho'$ *with* $\rho \leq \rho'$. *Then* $S \in T$ *implies* $S \in T'$ *and* $A \in T'$ *implies* $A \in T$.

Proof. $S \in T$ implies that $\rho \neq$ Un meaning that $\rho' \neq$ Un. Since Un is the only type for non-sensitive templates we have the thesis. Let $A \in T'$. We have $\rho' \in \{$Wrap, TData, Seed$\}$ which implies $\rho \in \{$Wrap, TData, Seed$\}$ giving the thesis.

Security policy. As we have already discussed in the introduction, PKCS#11 security tokens present different flaws, it is thus very important to fix them by imposing some extra security policies on them. In [4] it has been observed that real devices often limit the possible templates of keys, in order to have more control on their usage. It is possible that different operations such as key generation and key import restrict templates in different ways. At the level of static analysis, we abstract away the exact point where restrictions happen, and we consider $\mathbb{T}$ the set of all possible templates of keys.

Another very important aspect is to be clear about which keys are wrapped and unwrapped as the standards do not add any information about the template when encrypting a key with another one (one solution to this is, in fact, to add wrapping formats [9], solution which is however out of the standard). Types are useful here, as we can just establish a default type transported by wrapping keys. As we will see, thus this is limiting, it is however possible to rise the number of transported types via key diversification.

A security policy is thus defined as a pair $(\mathbb{T}, \rho)$, where $\mathbb{T}$ is the set of all possible templates of keys, and ρ is the default type for wrapped keys.

Expressions. In order to type expressions and commands we introduce a typing environment $\Gamma : x \mapsto \tau$ which maps variables to their respective types. Type judgment for expressions is noted $\Gamma \vdash_\rho e : \tau$ meaning that expression e is of type τ under Γ and assuming ρ as the default type for wrapped keys.

Table 3. Typing expressions

$$[var] \ \frac{\Gamma(x) = \tau}{\Gamma \vdash_\rho x : \tau} \quad [sub] \ \frac{\Gamma \vdash_\rho e : \tau' \quad \tau' \le \tau}{\Gamma \vdash_\rho e : \tau} \quad [kdf\text{-}w] \ \frac{\Gamma \vdash_\rho x : \mathsf{Seed}}{\Gamma \vdash_\rho \mathsf{kdf}(\mathsf{w}_{\rho'}, x) : \mathsf{Wrap}[\rho']}$$

$$[kdf\text{-}d] \ \frac{\Gamma \vdash_\rho x : \mathsf{Seed}}{\Gamma \vdash_\rho \mathsf{kdf}(\mathsf{d}, x) : \mathsf{Data}} \quad [kdf\text{-}un] \ \frac{\Gamma \vdash_\rho x : \mathsf{Un} \quad v = \mathsf{w}_{\rho'}, \mathsf{d}}{\Gamma \vdash_\rho \mathsf{kdf}(v, x) : \mathsf{Un}}$$

$$[enc] \ \frac{\Gamma \vdash_\rho x : \mathsf{Data} \quad \Gamma \vdash_\rho e : \mathsf{Un}}{\Gamma \vdash_\rho \mathsf{enc}(e, x) : \mathsf{Un}} \quad [dec] \ \frac{\Gamma \vdash_\rho x : \mathsf{Data} \quad \Gamma \vdash_\rho e : \mathsf{Un}}{\Gamma \vdash_\rho \mathsf{dec}(e, x) : \mathsf{Un}}$$

$$[wrap] \ \frac{\Gamma \vdash_\rho x : \mathsf{Wrap} \quad \Gamma \vdash_\rho e : \rho}{\Gamma \vdash_\rho \mathsf{enc}(e, x) : \mathsf{Un}} \quad [unwrap] \ \frac{\Gamma \vdash_\rho x : \mathsf{Wrap} \quad \Gamma \vdash_\rho e : \mathsf{Un}}{\Gamma \vdash_\rho \mathsf{dec}(e, x) : \rho}$$

$$[wrap\text{-}div] \ \frac{\Gamma \vdash_\rho x : \mathsf{Wrap}[\rho'] \quad \Gamma \vdash_\rho e : \rho'}{\Gamma \vdash_\rho \mathsf{enc}(e, x) : \mathsf{Un}} \quad [unwrap\text{-}div] \ \frac{\Gamma \vdash_\rho x : \mathsf{Wrap}[\rho'] \quad \Gamma \vdash_\rho e : \mathsf{Un}}{\Gamma \vdash_\rho \mathsf{dec}(e, x) : \rho'}$$

$$[enc\text{-}any] \ \frac{\Gamma \vdash_\rho x : \mathsf{Any} \quad \Gamma \vdash_\rho e : \mathsf{Un} \quad \rho \ne \mathsf{Wrap}}{\Gamma \vdash_\rho \mathsf{enc}(e, x) : \mathsf{Un}} \quad [dec\text{-}any] \ \frac{\Gamma \vdash_\rho x : \mathsf{Any} \quad \Gamma \vdash_\rho e : \mathsf{Un}}{\Gamma \vdash_\rho \mathsf{dec}(e, x) : \mathsf{Any}}$$

Typing rules are reported in Table 3. Rules [*var*] and [*sub*] are standard and derives types directly from Γ (for variables) or via subtyping. Rules [*kdf-w*] and [*kdf-d*] state that given a seed x we can derive a new wrapping key of type $\mathsf{Wrap}[\rho']$ as $\mathsf{kdf}(\mathsf{w}_{\rho'}, x)$, and a new data key as $\mathsf{kdf}(\mathsf{d}, x)$. Notice that we use values $\mathsf{w}_{\rho'}$ and d as tags to diversify keys, we can thus consider them as constant values established a-priori to this purpose. We do not assume any secrecy on them: security of this operation is given by the trusted seed x. Rule [*kdf-un*] allows for diversification from untrusted seeds, always generating an untrusted key. Rules [*enc*] and [*dec*] are for data encryption and decryption, and only work on untrusted values. Rules [*wrap*] and [*unwrap*] are more interesting: given a wrapping key we can wrap/unwrap other keys of type ρ, the default wrapping type specified in the security policy. Rules [*wrap-div*] and [*unwrap-div*] are similar but work on type ρ' given by the above rule [*kdf-w*]: diversification is in fact useful to obtain keys that can wrap keys of various types, as we will see in the case studies of section 4. Finally, rules [*enc-any*] and [*dec-any*] are conservative rules for cryptographic operation using generic keys of type Any. The former states that it is safe to encrypt with such keys as far as the default import type is not Wrap, otherwise we would be able to encrypt a broken key and then unwrap/import it as trusted in the device. The latter allows for decryption if the resulting value is considered of type Any. In section 4 we will see an example of application of these extremely conservative rules.

APIs. We now type APIs via the judgment $\Gamma \vdash_{\mathbb{T}, \rho} \mathsf{c}$ meaning that c is well-typed under Γ and the policy $\mathbb{T}, \rho$. The judgment is formalized in Table 4. Rules [*assign*] and [*seq*] are standard, and they amount to recursively type the expression and

Table 4. Typing APIs

$$[API] \frac{\forall a \in \mathcal{A} \quad \Gamma \vdash_{\mathbb{T},\rho} a}{\Gamma \vdash_{\mathbb{T},\rho} \mathcal{A}} \quad [assign] \frac{\Gamma(x) = \tau \quad \Gamma \vdash_\rho e : \tau}{\Gamma \vdash_{\mathbb{T},\rho} x := e} \quad [seq] \frac{\Gamma \vdash_{\mathbb{T},\rho} c_1 \quad \Gamma \vdash_{\mathbb{T},\rho} c_2}{\Gamma \vdash_{\mathbb{T},\rho} c_1 ; c_2}$$

$$[getobj] \frac{\Gamma(x) = \mathsf{Any} \quad \Gamma \vdash_\rho y : \mathsf{Un}}{\Gamma \vdash_{\mathbb{T},\rho} x := \mathsf{getObj}(y)} \quad [checktmp] \frac{\Gamma(x) = \mathsf{LUB}(T,\mathbb{T}) \quad \Gamma \vdash_\rho y : \mathsf{Un}}{\Gamma \vdash_{\mathbb{T},\rho} x := \mathsf{checkTemplate}(y, T)}$$

$$[genkey] \frac{\Gamma(x) = \mathsf{Un} \quad T \in \mathbb{T}}{\Gamma \vdash_{\mathbb{T},\rho} x := \mathsf{genKey}(T)} \quad [impkey] \frac{\Gamma(x) = \mathsf{Un} \quad \vdash T : \tau \quad \Gamma \vdash_\rho y : \tau \quad T \in \mathbb{T}}{\Gamma \vdash_{\mathbb{T},\rho} x := \mathsf{importKey}(y, T)}$$

$$[return] \frac{\Gamma \vdash_\rho e : \mathsf{Un}}{\Gamma \vdash_{\mathbb{T},\rho} \mathsf{return}\ e} \quad [function] \frac{\Gamma \vdash_\rho x_1 : \mathsf{Un} \quad \ldots \quad \Gamma \vdash_\rho x_k : \mathsf{Un} \quad \Gamma \vdash_{\mathbb{T},\rho} c}{\Gamma \vdash_{\mathbb{T},\rho} \lambda x_1, \ldots, x_k.c}$$

the sequential sub-part of a program, respectively. Rule $[getobj]$ states that when getting a key from the token with no template check, we need to be conservative and assign the result to a variable of type Any. In fact, we cannot deduce any specific usage or security level for the obtained key; rule $[checktmp]$, instead, approximates the type of the obtained key by getting the least upper bound of all types for templates T' matching T, i.e., such that $T \subseteq T'$:

$$\mathsf{LUB}(T, \mathbb{T}) = \bigsqcup \{\tau' \mid \exists T' \in \mathbb{T}.T \subseteq T' \wedge \vdash T' : \tau'\}$$

Rule $[genkey]$ checks that the template for the new key is in the set of the admitted template $\mathbb{T}$, while $[impkey]$ additionally checks that the type of the imported value is consistent with the given template. Rules $[return]$ and $[function]$ state that the return value and the parameter of an API call must be untrusted. In fact they are the interface to the external, possibly malicious users. Finally, by rule $[API]$ we have that an API is well-typed if all of its functions are well-typed.

3.1 Type Soundness

We give a notion of value well-formedness in order to track the value integrity at run-time. The judgment is based on a mapping $\Theta : val \mapsto \rho$ from atomic values to types, excluding $\mathsf{Wrap}[\rho]$ that is derived for diversified non-atomic keys. Tags $\mathsf{w}_{\rho'}$ and d for key diversification are implicitly assumed to be untrusted, i.e., $\Theta(\mathsf{w}_{\rho'}) = \Theta(\mathsf{d}) = \mathsf{Un}$. Rules are given in Table 5 and follow very closely the ones of Table 3 used for expressions.

Definition 3 (Well-formedness). $\Gamma, \Theta \vdash_{\mathbb{T},\rho} \mathsf{M}, \mathsf{H}$ *if*

- $\Gamma, \Theta \vdash_{\mathbb{T},\rho} \mathsf{M}$, *i.e.,* $\mathsf{M}(x) = v$, $\Gamma(x) = \tau$ *implies* $\Theta \vdash_\rho v : \tau$,
- $\Theta \vdash_{\mathbb{T},\rho} \mathsf{H}$, *i.e.,* $\mathsf{H}(v') = (v, T)$, $\vdash T : \tau$ *implies* $\Theta \vdash_\rho v : \tau$ *and* $T \subseteq \mathbb{T}$

We now prove that if we only give the attacker untrusted atomic values, all the values he will be able to derive (according to section 2) will also be untrusted. Intuitively, having type Un is a necessary condition for a well-formed value to be deducible by the attacker. The following holds:

Table 5. Value well-formedness

$$[atom] \frac{\Theta(val) = \rho'}{\Theta \vdash_\rho val : \rho'} \quad [sub] \frac{\Theta \vdash_\rho v : \tau' \quad \tau' \leq \tau}{\Theta \vdash_\rho v : \tau} \quad [kdf\text{-}w] \frac{\Theta \vdash_\rho v : \mathsf{Seed}}{\Theta \vdash_\rho kdf(\mathsf{w}_\rho, v) : \mathsf{Wrap}[\rho]}$$

$$[kdf\text{-}d] \frac{\Theta \vdash_\rho v : \mathsf{Seed}}{\Theta \vdash_\rho kdf(\mathsf{d}, v) : \mathsf{Data}} \quad [kdf\text{-}un] \frac{\Theta \vdash_\rho v, v' : \mathsf{Un}}{\Theta \vdash_\rho kdf(v', v) : \mathsf{Un}}$$

$$[enc] \frac{\Theta \vdash_\rho v : \mathsf{Data} \quad \Theta \vdash_\rho v' : \mathsf{Un}}{\Theta \vdash_\rho enc(v', v) : \mathsf{Un}} \quad [dec] \frac{\Theta \vdash_\rho v : \mathsf{Data} \quad \Theta \vdash_\rho v' : \mathsf{Un} \quad v' \neq enc(v'', v)}{\Theta \vdash_\rho dec(v', v) : \mathsf{Un}}$$

$$[wrap] \frac{\Theta \vdash_\rho v : \mathsf{Wrap} \quad \Theta \vdash_\rho v' : \rho}{\Theta \vdash_\rho enc(v', v) : \mathsf{Un}} \quad [unwrap] \frac{\Theta \vdash_\rho v : \mathsf{Wrap} \quad \Theta \vdash_\rho v' : \mathsf{Un} \quad v' \neq enc(v'', v)}{\Theta \vdash_\rho dec(v', v) : \rho}$$

$$[wrap\text{-}div] \frac{\Theta \vdash_\rho v : \mathsf{Wrap}[\rho'] \quad \Theta \vdash_\rho v' : \rho'}{\Theta \vdash_\rho enc(v', v) : \mathsf{Un}} \quad [unwrap\text{-}div] \frac{\Theta \vdash_\rho v : \mathsf{Wrap}[\rho'] \quad \Theta \vdash_\rho v' : \mathsf{Un} \quad v' \neq enc(v'', v)}{\Theta \vdash_\rho dec(v', v) : \rho'}$$

$$[enc\text{-}any] \frac{\Theta \vdash_\rho v : \mathsf{Any} \quad \Theta \vdash_\rho v' : \mathsf{Un} \quad \rho \neq \mathsf{Wrap}}{\Theta \vdash_\rho enc(v', v) : \mathsf{Un}} \quad [dec\text{-}any] \frac{\Theta \vdash_\rho v : \mathsf{Any} \quad \Theta \vdash_\rho v' : \mathsf{Un} \quad v' \neq enc(v'', v)}{\Theta \vdash_\rho dec(v', v) : \mathsf{Any}}$$

Proposition 1. *Let $\Theta \vdash_{\mathsf{T},\rho} H$ and let V be a set of atomic values such that $val \in V$ implies $\Theta(val) = \mathsf{Un}$. Then, $v \in \mathcal{K}(V)$ implies $\Theta \vdash_\rho v : \mathsf{Un}$.*

Proof. By an easy induction on the length of the derivation of values in $\mathcal{K}(V)$. For length 0 we trivially have that $v \in V$ which gives the thesis. We assume the proposition holds for length i and we prove it for length $i + 1$. We show case $enc(v, v') \in \mathcal{K}(V)$ because of $v, v' \in \mathcal{K}(V)$. The other cases are analogous. By rule $[enc]$ and observing that $\mathsf{Un} \leq \mathsf{Data}$ we obtain the thesis.

Next lemma proves that we can never type a value with two types that are not related via subtyping. As a consequence, we have that trusted values can never be typed as untrusted and vice-versa.

Lemma 2. $\Theta \vdash_\rho v : \tau$ *and* $\Theta \vdash_\rho v : \tau'$ *implies* $\tau \leq \tau'$ *or* $\tau' \leq \tau$.

Proof. By an easy induction on the (sum of the) length of the derivations of $\Theta \vdash_\rho v : \tau$ and $\Theta \vdash_\rho v : \tau'$. Base case is length 0 and trivially gives $\tau = \tau' = \Theta(v)$. We show once case of the inductive step. Suppose $v = kdf(v', v'')$. We have three different rules for typing v: $[kdf\text{-}w], [kdf\text{-}d], [kdf\text{-}un]$. For example, types Data and $\mathsf{Wrap}[\tau]$ given by the first two rules are unrelated, however the typed values differ for a tag which excludes the case. More interestingly, Un and $\mathsf{Wrap}[\tau]$ are also unrelated but, by induction, we know that the key v should be typed with two related types, which is not the case since Seed and Un are not in the subtyping relation. Other cases follow similarly.

This last lemma states that evaluating an expression of type τ on a well-formed memory, gives a value of type τ.

Lemma 3. *Let $\Gamma \vdash_\rho e : \tau$ and $e \downarrow^M v$. If $\Gamma, \Theta \vdash_{T,\rho} M$ then it holds $\Theta \vdash_\rho v : \tau$.*

Proof. By induction on the structure of e. Base case is when e is x. Thesis directly follows by memory well-formedness. For the inductive step, in some cases we use Lemma 2: for example, when dealing with decryption [*dec*] we might have a value encrypted under the right key that we know to type Un. Now looking at the possible cases in Table 5 we see that the encrypted values can be obtained in different ways, but the information about the type of the key (Data) allows us to pick either [*enc*] or [*enc-any*], both of which prove the plaintext to be of type Un as required. Other cases follow analogously.

We now give a subject-reduction result stating that well-typed programs remain well-typed at run-time and preserve memory and handle-map well-formedness.

Theorem 1. *Let $\Gamma, \Theta \vdash_{T,\rho} M, H$ and $\Gamma \vdash_{T,\rho} c$. If $\langle M, H, c \rangle \rightarrow \langle M', H', c' \rangle$ then*

(i) *if $c' \neq \varepsilon$ then $\Gamma \vdash_{T,\rho} c'$;*
(ii) *$\exists \Theta' \supseteq \Theta$ such that $\Gamma, \Theta' \vdash_{T,\rho} M', H'$.*

Proof. (Sketch.) Proof of item (i) is by trivial induction on the structure of c. In fact almost all commands reduce to ε. Item (ii) is again by induction on the structure of c: for expressions we just apply Lemma 3. For genKey and importKey the returned handle and the new key are fresh names that we add to Θ in order to type the new memory (this is why we have Θ' in the thesis). Template T is checked to be compatible with respect to $\mathbb{T}$, and the type of the imported key value is checked to be the same as the one derived from the template. getObj assigns to type Any so there is nothing to prove, while checkTemplate approximates the type of the key using a least upper bound which guarantees that the value can be typed the same as the variable x via subtyping.

We can now state the main result of the paper: well-typed APIs are secure, according to definition 2.

Theorem 2. *Let $\Gamma \vdash_{T,\rho} \mathcal{A}$. Then $\mathcal{A}$ is secure.*

Proof. We first prove, by induction on the length of reduction $\langle H_0, V_0 \rangle \rightsquigarrow^*_{\mathcal{A}} \langle H, V \rangle$, that there exists Θ such that $\Theta \vdash_{T,\rho} H$ and $\Theta \vdash_\rho v : $ Un for each $v \in V$.

Base case is length 0, meaning that $H_0 = H$ and $V_0 = V$. If we take Θ such that $\Theta(v) = $ Un for each $v \in V_0$, since H is empty, we easily obtain the thesis.

For the inductive case we have $\langle H_0, V_0 \rangle \rightsquigarrow^*_{\mathcal{A}} \langle H_n, V_n \rangle \rightsquigarrow_{\mathcal{A}} \langle H, V \rangle$. By inductive hypothesis there exists Θ such that $\Theta \vdash_{T,\rho} H_n$ and $\Theta(v) = $ Un for each $v \in V_n$. We consider the last step $\langle H_n, V_n \rangle \rightsquigarrow_{\mathcal{A}} \langle H, V \rangle$. By definition, this is due to a call to a function $a \in \mathcal{A}$. In particular, we have $a(v_1, \ldots, v_k) \downarrow^{H_n, H} v$ with $v_1, \ldots, v_k \in \mathcal{K}(V)$ and $V = V_n \cup \{v\}$. This, in turns, happens because $a = \lambda x_1, \ldots, x_k.c$ and $\langle M_\epsilon[x_1 \mapsto v_1 \ldots x_k \mapsto v_k], H_n, c \rangle \rightarrow \langle M', H, $ return $e \rangle$ with $e \downarrow^{M'} v$. From $\Gamma \vdash_{T,\rho} \mathcal{A}$ we have $\Gamma \vdash_{T,\rho} a$ which requires $\Gamma \vdash_\rho x_1 : $ Un $\ldots$ $\Gamma \vdash_\rho x_k : $ Un and $\Gamma \vdash_{T,\rho} c$. Since $x_1, \ldots, x_k$ are the only variables in the domain of $M_0 = M_\epsilon[x_1 \mapsto v_1 \ldots x_k \mapsto v_k]$, we easily obtain that $\Gamma, \Theta \vdash_{T,\rho} M_0$. We have proved that $\Gamma, \Theta \vdash_{T,\rho} M_0, H$

and $\Gamma \vdash_{T,\rho} c$, thus by Theorem 1 we obtain $\Gamma \vdash_{T,\rho}$ return e and $\exists \Theta' \supseteq \Theta$ such that $\Gamma, \Theta' \vdash_{T,\rho} M', H$. Now, $\Gamma \vdash_{T,\rho}$ return e requires $\Gamma \vdash_\rho e : \mathsf{Un}$, by Lemma 3 we have $\Theta' \vdash_\rho v : \mathsf{Un}$ which gives the thesis.

We have proved that there exists Θ such that $\Theta \vdash_{T,\rho} H$ and $\Theta \vdash_\rho v : \mathsf{Un}$ for each $v \in V$. For item 1, if $\Theta \vdash_\rho val : \mathsf{Un}$, meaning that $\Theta(val) = \mathsf{Un}$, since we have $val \notin \mathcal{K}(V)$ and val is sensitive, we can change Θ into $\tilde{\Theta} = \Theta[val \mapsto \mathsf{Data}]$ while preserving $\tilde{\Theta} \vdash_{T,\rho} H$ and $\tilde{\Theta} \vdash_\rho v : \mathsf{Un}$ for each $v \in V$. In fact, if S appears in all the templates for value val and val is different from all values in V, we have that its type is never required to be Un, since none of the templates will be typed as Un. Notice that $\tilde{\Theta}(val) = \mathsf{Data}$ implies that $\tilde{\Theta} \nvdash_\rho val : \mathsf{Un}$. We consider now $\langle H, V \rangle \leadsto_A^* \langle H', V' \rangle$. By following the same proof scheme as above, we can prove that $\Theta' \vdash_{T,\rho} H'$ and $\Theta' \vdash_\rho v : \mathsf{Un}$ for each $v \in V'$ with $\Theta' \supseteq \tilde{\Theta}$. Thus, $\Theta'(val) = \mathsf{Data}$ meaning that $\Theta' \nvdash_\rho val : \mathsf{Un}$. From Proposition 1 we obtain that $val \notin \mathcal{K}(V')$ which gives the thesis.

For item 2, we have that that all templates of val are typed with one of $\mathsf{Wrap}, \mathsf{TData}, \mathsf{Seed}$. This, by lemma 2, implies $\Theta \nvdash_\rho val : \mathsf{Un}$ which by Proposition 1 gives $val \notin \mathcal{K}(V)$. We can now apply item 1 to obtain $val \notin \mathcal{K}(V')$. Recall, in fact, we have assumed that $A \in T$ implies $S \in T$.

4   Type-Based Analysis

In this section we consider different implementations of (a subset of) PKCS#11 API and we analyse them using our type-based approach. We only consider the functions for encryption/decryption of data and wrap/unwrap of keys.

RSA PKCS#11 Standard. We show that an implementation of PKCS#11 that exactly follows the standard, fails to type-check, as expected, since it is known to be vulnerable to attacks. This is useful to show how these attacks can be prevented by statically requiring a precise unambiguous role for each key, as done by our type system.

The API is defined in the RSA standard, which specifies what are the input parameters and the result of each function. C_Encrypt takes a byte-stream and a handle to a key having the encrypt (E) flag set, and returns an encrypted byte-stream. Similarly C_Decrypt takes a byte-stream and decrypts it using the key pointed by the given handle, with the decrypt (D) flag set; it then returns to the user the decrypted message:

C_Encrypt(*data*, *h_key*)	C_Decrypt(*data*, *h_key*)
$k := $ checkTemplate(*h_key*, $\{E\}$)	$k := $ checkTemplate(*h_key*, $\{D\}$);
return enc(*data*, k);	return dec(*data*, k);

C_WrapKey takes the handle of a key to be wrapped and the one pointing to the wrapping key, having the wrap (W) flag set, and returns an encrypted byte-stream. The unwrap command (C_UnwrapKey) reads a byte-stream, decrypts it using a key having the unwrap (U) flag set, imports the resulting key in the device and returns a handle to it. The standard allows the user to specify the template for the new key. In this example, we assume the key is imported as sensitive (S).

```
C_WrapKey(h_key, h_w)                    C_UnwrapKey(data, h_w)
    w := checkTemplate(h_w, {W})             w := checkTemplate(h_w, {U})
    k := getObj(h_key);                      k := dec(data, w);
    return enc(k, w);                        return importKey(k, {S});
```

The standard does not impose any rule on the usage of encrypt, decrypt, wrap and unwrap attributes. Thus the policy is the most permissive one, i.e., $\mathbb{T}$ is the set of all the possible templates T. In section 1 we have seen an attack that exploits C_Decrypt and C_WrapKey. We now show that the latter does not type-check, confirming that we cannot prove the security of the API. Command return $\text{enc}(k, w)$ requires $\Gamma \vdash_\rho$ return $\text{enc}(k, w)$: Un. Command $k := \text{getObj}(h\_key)$ requires that $\Gamma \vdash_\rho k$: Any. Typing $w := \text{checkTemplate}(h\_w, \{W\})$ requires w to have type $\text{LUB}(\{W\}, \mathbb{T}) = \text{Any}$ since the permissive policy allows for templates with mixed roles such as $\{S, E, D, W, U\}$. Since there is no rule for typing expressions of type Any with key of type Any we can never obtain $\Gamma \vdash_\rho$ return $\text{enc}(k, w)$: Un, giving a contradiction.

Secure Templates. We now analyse and prove the security of a fix proposed in [4,5]. Note that, it is the first proposed patch that does not require the addition of any cryptographic mechanisms to the standard. The idea is to limit the set of admissible attribute combinations for keys in order to avoid that they ever assume conflicting roles at creation time. This is configurable at the level of the specific PKCS#11 operation. For example, different secure templates can be defined for different operations such as key generation and unwrapping.

More precisely, the fix includes three templates for the key generation command: a wrap and unwrap one for importing/exporting other keys, here mapped into $\{A, S, W, U\}$ with type Wrap; an encrypt and decrypt template for cryptographic operations, here encoded as $\{S, E, D\}$ with type Data and an empty template, corresponding to $\{\}$, i.e., Un. The unwrap command is instead allowed to set either an empty template or one which has the unwrap and encrypt attributes set and the wrap and decrypt ones unset. This is a mixed-role template that corresponds to type Any that we pick as the default unwrapping type ρ.

We use the policy $\mathbb{T}$ such that $T \in \mathbb{T}$ and $\{W\} \in T$ implies $T = \{A, S, W, U\}$, moreover $\{D\} \in T$ implies $T = \{S, E, D\}$, i.e., wrapping and decryption keys are respectively encoded with the unique templates $\{A, S, W, U\}, \{S, E, D\}$. With such a policy, whenever a checkTemplate expression queries a handle for a decryption key $(\{D\})$ then the type returned is Data, since the only matching template is $\{S, E, D\}$. When we query for an encryption key $(\{E\})$ then the type returned is Any since, for example, $\{S, E, U\} \in \mathbb{T}$. When querying for a wrapping key $(\{W\})$ the result will be typed as Wrap since the only template satisfying the query is $\{A, S, W, U\}$. Finally, when querying for an unwrapping key $(\{U\})$ the results is Any since, again, $\{S, E, U\} \in \mathbb{T}$. We now show that the standard API as defined above type-checks under the above more restrictive policy. Recall that we let $\rho = \text{Any}$, i.e., the default type for wrapped key is Any.

```
C_Encrypt(data, h_key)
  k := checkTemplate(h_key, {E})   (Γ(k) = Any)
  return enc(data, k);              (Γ ⊢_ρ enc(data, k) : Un)

C_Decrypt(data, h_key)
  k := checkTemplate(h_key, {D})   (Γ(k) = Data)
  return dec(data, k);              (Γ ⊢_ρ dec(data, k) : Un)

C_WrapKey(h_key, h_w)
  w := checkTemplate(h_w, {W})     (Γ(w) = Wrap)
  k := getObj(h_key);              (Γ(k) = Any)
  return enc(k, w);                (Γ ⊢_ρ enc(k, w) : Un)

C_UnwrapKey(data, h_w)
  w := checkTemplate(h_w, {U})     (Γ(w) = Any)
  k := dec(data, w);               (Γ(k) = Any)
  return importKey(k, {S, E, U});  (Γ ⊢_ρ importKey(k, {S, E, U}) : Un)
```

By theorem 2 we have that this fix is secure and never leaks sensitive and always-sensitive keys. It strongly limits, however, the set of possible templates, and this could be an issue if an application in use on a given system fails to obey such requirements. On the other hand, compatibility with other devices is not broken, since the implementation of the above functions is the same as in the standard. However, even if interoperability is guaranteed, the usage of an unsafe token would obviously expose the keys to attacks.

Finally, notice that the patch is presented here in an extended version: originally it allowed the generation of sensitive keys only, we instead let non-sensitive keys to be accepted by the policy.

Key Diversification. We present a novel fix to PKCS#11. The idea is to use key diversification to avoid the same key to be used for conflicting purposes. This ensures that the same key will never be used for encrypting and decrypting both data and other keys. The fix is completely transparent to the user as far as all the devices implement it. It must be noted, in fact, that a key wrapped by a token implementing this patch cannot be correctly imported by one acting as described by the standard, i.e., not using key diversification (and vice versa). The same holds for encrypted data. To the best of our knowledge, this is the only patch that correctly enforces the security of sensitive keys and, at the same time, is transparent to existing applications.

We define a policy that allows for templates typed as Seed, Any, Data, Un. Formally $\mathbb{T} = \{T \mid \vdash T : \rho$ and $\rho \in \{\text{Seed}, \text{Any}, \text{Data}, \text{Un}\}$ }. We now specify the fixed functions and the typing for each variable/expression.

```
C_Encrypt(data, h_key)
  k := checkTemplate(h_key, {A, S})  (Γ(k) = Seed)
  dk := kdf(d, k);                   (Γ(dk) = Data)
  return enc(data, dk);              (Γ ⊢_ρ enc(data, dk) : Un)
```

> C_Decrypt($data$, h_key)
> $k := \mathsf{checkTemplate}(h\_key, \{A, S\})$ $(\Gamma(k) = \mathsf{Seed})$
> $dk := \mathsf{kdf}(\mathsf{d}, k);$ $(\Gamma(dk) = \mathsf{Data})$
> return $\mathsf{dec}(data, dk);$ $(\Gamma \vdash_\rho \mathsf{dec}(data, dk) : \mathsf{Un})$

Notice, in particular, that $\Gamma \vdash_\rho \mathsf{checkTemplate}(h\_key, \{A, S\})$: Seed since $\mathsf{LUB}(\{A, S\}, \mathbb{T}) = \mathsf{Seed}$. In fact, Seed is the only type in T with A set (we have excluded from the policy Wrap and TData).

Key diversification allows to choose at run-time the wrapping and unwrapping of different kind of keys: different instances of each command will be provided, each of them using a different tag when diversifying the seed retrieved from the device. Since the code is exactly the same, we just parametrize it on the tag value w_ρ. With $T_{\rho'}$ we identify a template such that $\mathsf{LUB}(T_{\rho'}, \mathbb{T}) = \rho'$. For $\rho' = \mathsf{Seed}, \mathsf{Any}, \mathsf{Data}$ we respectively have $T_{\rho'} = \{A, S\}, \{S\}, \{S, E, D\}$. Wrap and unwrap are specified an typed as follows:

> C_WrapKey$^{\mathsf{w}_{\rho'}}$(h_key, h_w)
> $w := \mathsf{checkTemplate}(h\_w, \{A, S\})$ $(\Gamma(w) = \mathsf{Seed})$
> $k := \mathsf{checkTemplate}(h\_w, T_{\rho'})$ $(\Gamma(k) = \rho')$
> $dk := \mathsf{kdf}(\mathsf{w}_{\rho'}, w);$ $(\Gamma(dk) = \mathsf{Wrap}[\rho'])$
> return $\mathsf{enc}(k, dk);$ $(\Gamma \vdash_\rho \mathsf{enc}(k, dk) : \mathsf{Un})$

> C_UnwrapKey$^{\mathsf{w}_{\rho'}}$($data$, h_w)
> $w := \mathsf{checkTemplate}(h\_w, \{A, S\})$ $(\Gamma(w) = \mathsf{Seed})$
> $dk := \mathsf{kdf}(\mathsf{w}_{\rho'}, w);$ $(\Gamma(dk) = \mathsf{Wrap}[\rho'])$
> $k := \mathsf{dec}(data, dk);$ $(\Gamma(k) = \rho')$
> return $\mathsf{importKey}(k, T_{\rho'});$ $(\Gamma \vdash_\rho \mathsf{importKey}(k, T_{\rho'}) : \mathsf{Un})$

Since the API type-checks, by theorem 2 we have that it is secure and never leaks sensitive and always-sensitive keys. Notice that, since it is possible to exchange seeds we have that new wrapping keys can be easily shared between users. Notice also that, in practice, the parameter w_ρ needs to be somehow fixed, in order to have a single implementation of wrap and unwrap commands. The way this value is picked is not relevant, since we prove that all these instances are secure even if they coexist on the device. For example, it might be derived at run-time from the CKA_UNWRAP_TEMPLATE attribute which specifies, for each wrapping key, the template to be assigned to the unwrapped key.

5   Conclusions

We have presented a type system to statically enforce the security of PKCS#11 key management APIs. We believe that a formal tool working at the language-level might help developers and hardware producers to better understand the crucial issues and limits affecting the design and implementation of this standard. For example, we have shown that C_Decrypt and C_WrapKey commands cannot be both type-checked if implemented as prescribed by the standard [18]. More precisely, it has been shown that the requirements on the templates of the keys used to perform such operations are not enough restrictive to avoid keys having conflicting purposes. Thus, failing to type-check corresponds, in this case, to the intuitive problematic issue, well understood by developers and hardware producers, of conflicting roles assigned to a single key.

We have also presented a new fix to PKCS#11, based on key diversification: Intuitively, the token avoids conflicting roles for one key by diversifying it depending on the actual role. We have type-checked both this new fix and the 'secure templates' one [4,5], formally proving their security.

Starting from version 2.20, RSA added to the standard the new attribute CKA_WRAP_WITH_TRUSTED, that could potentially be used to prevent the API-level attacks discussed in this work. However, a big limitation is that trusted keys, i.e., keys whose CKA_TRUSTED attribute is set, may be imported into a token only by a security officer, a special privileged user operating in a protected environment. Moreover, in order to prevent attacks on a sensitive key, it is required that its CKA_WRAP_WITH_TRUSTED attribute is set, meaning that it can only be wrapped under a key imported by the security officer. Here we have generalized this idea of wrapping keys only under trusted keys. We have used the always-sensitive attribute, even if the standard does not foresee any special usage for it, in order to show that what is important is 'trust', and not who has imported the key: a key that has always been sensitive (and has never been known by the attacker) can be considered trusted the same as one imported by the security officer. So, intuitively, in our model the always-sensitive and trusted attributes collapse into the A attribute. This allows for dynamically exchanging new always-sensitive, trusted keys, wrapped under the one initially imported by the security officer.

Quite surprisingly, in [18] RSA does not discuss any security implication of the two new attributes and does not provide any guideline about how to correctly use them to prevent attacks (in fact, attacks are not mentioned even in the most recent draft of the standard [19]). There are, instead, many problematic issues that need to be considered. We give a partial list here: (i) trusted keys should be non-extractable, i.e., not wrappable even under another trusted key. This is to avoid they are unwrapped with a different template and then leaked; (ii) a sensitive key with CKA_WRAP_WITH_TRUSTED set might be wrapped under a trusted key and then unwrapped with CKA_WRAP_WITH_TRUSTED unset, making it attackable; (iii) trusted keys should not have conflicting roles (such as wrap and decrypt). While this might be obvious, it is not a good idea to leave the security officer the freedom of freely configuring such crucial keys. Our type-based analysis solves all the above issues by enforcing a controlled usage of roles and templates for keys.

The extension to public-key cryptography and the implementation of the key diversification fix on a software emulated token are left as a future work. As already done for the secure template patch [4,5] the starting point for the implementation would be the open-source project openCryptoki [17].

Acknowledgements. We would like to thank the anonymous reviewers for their helpful comments and suggestions.

References

1. Anderson, R.: The Correctness of Crypto Transaction Sets. In: Christianson, B., Crispo, B., Malcolm, J.A., Roe, M. (eds.) Security Protocols 2000. LNCS, vol. 2133, pp. 125–127. Springer, Heidelberg (2001),
http://www.cl.cam.ac.uk/ftp/users/rja14/protocols00.pdf
2. Bond, M.: Attacks on Cryptoprocessor Transaction Sets. In: Koç, Ç.K., Naccache, D., Paar, C. (eds.) CHES 2001. LNCS, vol. 2162, pp. 220–234. Springer, Heidelberg (2001)
3. Bond, M., Anderson, R.: API level attacks on embedded systems. IEEE Computer Magazine 34(10), 67–75 (2001)
4. Bortolozzo, M., Centenaro, M., Focardi, R., Steel, G.: Attacking and fixing PKCS#11 security tokens. In: Proceedings of the 17th ACM Conference on Computer and Communications Security (CCS), pp. 260–269. ACM (2010)
5. Bortolozzo, M., Centenaro, M., Focardi, R., Steel, G.: CryptokiX: a cryptographic software token with security fixes. In: Proceedings of the 4th International Workshop on Analysis of Security APIs (ASA), Edinburgh, UK (July 2010)
6. Centenaro, M., Focardi, R., Luccio, F.L., Steel, G.: Type-Based Analysis of PIN Processing APIs. In: Backes, M., Ning, P. (eds.) ESORICS 2009. LNCS, vol. 5789, pp. 53–68. Springer, Heidelberg (2009)
7. Clayton, R., Bond, M.: Experience Using a Low-Cost FPGA Design to Crack DES Keys. In: Kaliski Jr., B.S., Koç, Ç.K., Paar, C. (eds.) CHES 2002. LNCS, vol. 2523, pp. 579–592. Springer, Heidelberg (2003)
8. Clulow, J.: On the Security of PKCS #11. In: Walter, C.D., Koç, Ç.K., Paar, C. (eds.) CHES 2003. LNCS, vol. 2779, pp. 411–425. Springer, Heidelberg (2003)
9. Delaune, S., Kremer, S., Steel, G.: Formal analysis of PKCS#11. In: Proceedings of the 21st IEEE Computer Security Foundations Symposium (CSF 2008), Pittsburgh, PA, USA, pp. 331–344. IEEE Computer Society Press (June 2008)
10. Delaune, S., Kremer, S., Steel, G.: Formal analysis of PKCS#11 and proprietary extensions. Journal of Computer Security 18(6), 1211–1245 (2010)
11. Focardi, R., Luccio, F.L.: Secure Recharge of Disposable RFID Tickets. In: Barthe, G. (ed.) FAST 2011. LNCS, vol. 7140, pp. 85–99. Springer, Heidelberg (2012)
12. Fröschle, S.B., Sommer, N.: Reasoning with Past to Prove PKCS#11 Keys Secure. In: Degano, P., Etalle, S., Guttman, J. (eds.) FAST 2010. LNCS, vol. 6561, pp. 96–110. Springer, Heidelberg (2011)
13. Fröschle, S., Sommer, N.: Concepts and Proofs for Configuring PKCS#11. In: Barthe, G. (ed.) FAST 2011. LNCS, vol. 7140, pp. 131–147. Springer, Heidelberg (2012)
14. Fröschle, S.B., Steel, G.: Analysing PKCS#11 Key Management APIs with Unbounded Fresh Data. In: Degano, P., Viganò, L. (eds.) ARSPA-WITS 2009. LNCS, vol. 5511, pp. 92–106. Springer, Heidelberg (2009)
15. Keighren, G., Aspinall, D., Steel, G.: Towards a Type System for Security APIs. In: Degano, P., Viganò, L. (eds.) ARSPA-WITS 2009. LNCS, vol. 5511, pp. 173–192. Springer, Heidelberg (2009)
16. Longley, D., Rigby, S.: An automatic search for security flaws in key management schemes. Computers and Security 11(1), 75–89 (1992)
17. openCryptoki, http://sourceforge.net/projects/opencryptoki/
18. RSA Security Inc., v2.20. PKCS #11: Cryptographic Token Interface Standard (June 2004)
19. RSA Security Inc., Draft v2.30. PKCS #11: Cryptographic Token Interface Standard (July 2009), http://www.rsa.com/rsalabs/node.asp?id=2133

A Certificate Infrastructure for Machine-Checked Proofs of Conditional Information Flow

Torben Amtoft[1], Josiah Dodds[2], Zhi Zhang[1], Andrew Appel[2],
Lennart Beringer[2], John Hatcliff[1], Xinming Ou[1], and Andrew Cousino[1]

[1] Kansas State University, CIS Department, 234 Nichols Hall, Manhattan KS 66506
{tamtoft,zhangzhi,hatcliff,xou,acousino}@ksu.edu
[2] Princeton University, Dept. of Comp. Sci., 35 Olden Street, Princeton NJ 08540
{jdodds,appel,eberinge}@cs.princeton.edu

Abstract. In previous work, we have proposed a compositional framework for stating and automatically verifying complex conditional information flow policies using a relational Hoare logic. The framework allows developers and verifiers to work directly with the source code using source-level code contracts. In this work, we extend that approach so that the algorithm for verifying code compliance to an information flow contract emits formal certificates of correctness that are checked in the Coq proof assistant. This framework is implemented in the context of SPARK – a subset of Ada that has been used in a number of industrial contexts for implementing certified safety and security critical systems.

1 Introduction

Network and embedded security devices have complex information flow policies that are crucial to fulfilling device requirements. We have previously explained [1, §1] how devices (such as "separation kernels") developed following the MILS (Multiple Independent Levels of Security) architecture must be certified to very stringent criteria such as Common Criteria EAL 6/7 and DCID 6/3, and that many previous information-flow analyses (based on type systems) are too weak to specify these systems; the notion of *conditional information flow* is needed. We have also explained [2] that in these real applications, one must be able to trace information flow through individual array elements, rather than "contaminating" the entire array whenever an assignment is done.

SPARK (a safety-critical subset of Ada) is being used by various organizations, including Rockwell Collins[1] and the US National Security Agency (NSA) [3], to engineer information assurance systems including cryptographic controllers, network guards, and key management systems. To guarantee analyzability and conformance to embedded system resource bounds, SPARK does not include pointers and heap-based data. Thus, SPARK programs use arrays and for-loops to implement complex data structures. SPARK provides automatically checked procedure annotations that specify information flows (dependences) between procedure inputs and outputs. In the certification process, these annotations play a key role in justifying conformance to information flow and

---

[1] See the 2006 press release at http://212.113.201.96/sparkada/pdfs/
praxis_rockwell_final_pr.pdf

P. Degano and J.D. Guttman (Eds.): POST 2012, LNCS 7215, pp. 369–389, 2012.

separation policies relevant to MILS development; however, the standard SPARK annotation language is too weak to express the flow policies needed to verify/certify many real embedded information assurance applications.

Due to the lack of precision in SPARK and other conventional language-based security frameworks, policy adherence arguments are often reduced to informal claims substantiated by manual inspections that are time-consuming, tedious, and error-prone. Some past certification efforts have created models of software code in theorem provers and proved that the models of code comply with security policies. While this strategy can provide high degrees of confidence and support very precise policy declarations, it has the disadvantages of (a) leaving "trust gaps" between source code and models (their correspondence has in past efforts been only manually verified by inspection), (b) requiring intensive manual efforts, and (c) inhibiting developers from proceeding with information flow specification and verification during the development process.

In our previous work [2,1] we extended SPARK's procedure annotations to conditional information flow and fine-grained treatment of structured data, necessary for the automatic analysis and verification of many programs, and we developed a compositional framework for stating and automatically verifying complex array-oriented and conditional information flow policies using a relational Hoare logic. Although our Secure Information Flow Logic (SIFL) is language-neutral, we have chosen to cast our work as an enhancement to the SPARK information flow framework. Indeed, this work has been inspired by challenge problems provided by our industrial collaborators at Rockwell Collins who are using SPARK on several projects.

Here we extend our framework with new functionality to generate machine-checkable proofs of the information-flow properties that it derives. Our framework is *much* more automated than tactical theorem-proving in a proof assistant. In our framework, engineers work directly with the source code using code contracts to specify/check with greater precision than in conventional language-based information flow frameworks. We believe that most units (e.g., procedures) of real embedded applications can be handled directly by our analysis—and those units that cannot may smoothly be handed off to verification in a proof assistant; the compositional nature of our system will eventually allow the whole system to be checked end-to-end in the proof assistant.

Contributions: (a 50+ pages technical report describing the details of the approach, as well as Coq proofs for evidence soundness, is available at [4].)

- We enhance our previously developed precondition-generation algorithm for SIFL assertions to emit *evidence* that program units conform to their (conditional) information flow contracts. This evidence can be viewed as an application of rules of a relational logic for information flow that encodes the algorithm's reasoning steps.
- We provide an implementation of the evidence-emitting precondition generation algorithm for SPARK.
- We encode the derived logic in Coq, and prove it sound with respect to an operational semantics for a core subset of SPARK. We thus have a foundational machine-checked proof that whenever our evidence-checker accepts evidence about a program, then that program really does conform to the given information flow policy.
- We evaluate the framework on a collection of methods from embedded applications, including applications from industrial research projects.

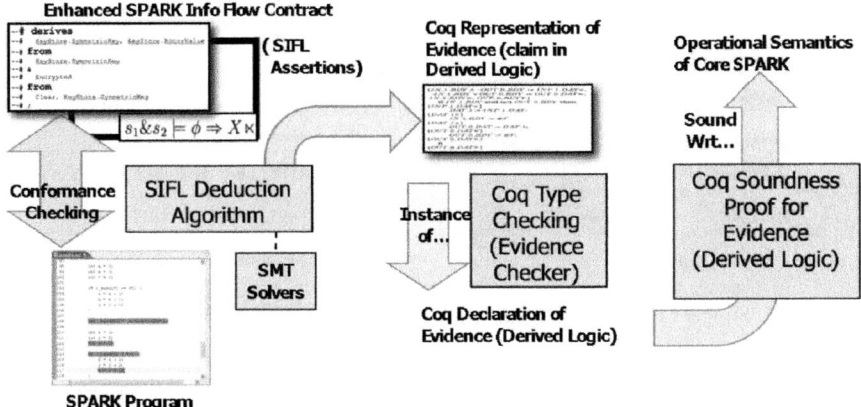

Fig. 1. Structure of Information Flow Evidence Generation and Checking

2   Background

SPARK is a safety critical subset of Ada developed by Altran Praxis and supported by AdaCore. SPARK provides (a) an annotation language for writing functional as well as information-flow software contracts, and (b) automated static analyses and semi-automated proof assistants for proving absence of run-time exceptions, and confor-mance of code to contracts. SPARK has been used to build a number of high-assurance systems; Altran Praxis is currently using it to implement the next generation of the UK air traffic control system. We are using SPARK due to our strong collaborative ties with Rockwell Collins, who uses SPARK to develop safety and security critical components of a number of embedded systems.

Figure 1 illustrates the structure of our SIFL contract checking and evidence gen-eration framework. An Eclipse-based integrated development environment allows pro-grammers to develop information-assurance applications in SPARK. Our logic-based approach allows us to extend the SPARK information-flow contract language to include support for conditional information flow and quantified flow policies that describe flows through individual components of arrays. Behind the scenes, the enhanced SPARK infor-mation flow contracts are represented using relational *agreement assertions* (explained below). Our tool framework includes a precondition generation algorithm for agreement assertions that allows us to infer SIFL contracts or check user-supplied contracts; in the latter mode, preconditions are inferred from postconditions, and then the tool checks that the user-supplied preconditions imply the inferred preconditions. The precondition generation algorithm uses a collection of SMT solvers via the Sireum Topi interface (www.sireum.org). As the precondition generation executes, it builds evidence, in the form of a Coq data structure, that relates postconditions to generated preconditions. This language of evidence is a relational Hoare logic derived from the basic reason-ing steps in the algorithm. Coq type checking acts as an "evidence checker" confirming that the evidence emitted by the algorithm is indeed well-formed. The Coq evidence representation is proved sound in Coq wrt. an operational semantics for an imperative language representing core features of SPARK. Thus, given a SPARK program and a

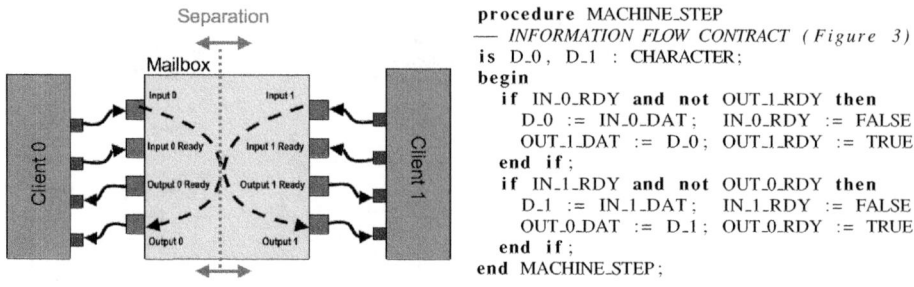

Fig. 2. Simple MLS Guard - mailbox mediates communication between partitions

SIFL contract, if the contract checking algorithm produces evidence that type checks in Coq, we have a machine-checked proof that the program's behavior (as defined by the operational semantics) conforms to the information-flow contract.

Observe that the precondition generator is not part of the trusted code base and hence in principle might fail to produce well-typed evidence, but we are exploring (cf. the end of Sect. 4) an implementation of the precondition generator inside Coq. Once verified, this Gallina implementation cannot fail to produce valid evidence.

Figure 2 illustrates the conceptual information flows in a fragment of a simplistic MLS (Multiple Levels of Security) component, described in our earlier work [1]. Rockwell Collins engineers constructed this example to illustrate, to NSA and industry representatives, the specification and verification challenges facing the developers of MLS software. The "Mailbox" component in the center of the diagram mediates communication between two client processes – each running on its own partition in the separation kernel. *Client 0* writes data to communicate in the memory segment *Input 0* that is shared between *Client 0* and the mailbox, then it sets the *Input 0 Ready* flag. The mailbox process polls its ready flags; when it finds that, *e.g.*, *Input 0 Ready* is set and *Output 1 Ready* is cleared (indicating that *Client 1* has already consumed data deposited in the *Output 1* slot in a previous communication), then it copies the data from *Input 0* to *Output 1* and clears *Input 0 Ready* and sets *Output 1 Ready*. The communication from *Client 1* to *Client 0* follows a symmetric set of steps. The actions to be taken in each execution frame are encoded in SPARK by the MACHINE_STEP procedure of Fig. 2.

While upper levels of the MILS architecture require reasoning about lattices of security levels (*e.g.*, *unclassified*, *secret*, *top secret*), the policies of infrastructure components such as separation kernels and guard applications usually focus on data separation policies (reasoning about flows between components of program state), and we restrict ourselves to such reasoning in this paper.

Figure 3(a) displays a fragment of an information flow contract for the mailbox example written in our contract language that enhances the original SPARK contract language with the ability to specify conditional information flows. This specification states from which input values (and under which conditions) the final values of OUT_0_DAT and OUT_1_DAT are *derived*. For example, OUT_0_DAT always derives from IN_1_RDY and OUT_0_RDY because these "guarding variables" determine whether or not the body of the conditional that assigns to OUT_0_DAT is executed, i.e., OUT_0_DAT is control dependent on IN_1_RDY and OUT_0_RDY. In addition, the final value of OUT_0_DAT depends

```
—# derives                                      { IN_1_RDY ∧ ¬OUT_0_RDY ⇒ IN_1_DAT⋉,
—# OUT_0_DAT from                                 ¬IN_1_RDY ∨ OUT_0_RDY ⇒ OUT_0_DAT⋉,
—#      IN_1_DAT when                              IN_1_RDY⋉, OUT_0_RDY⋉ }
—#      (IN_1_RDY and not OUT_0_RDY),   1. if IN_1_RDY and not OUT_0_RDY then
—#      OUT_0_DAT when                           { IN_1_DAT⋉ }
—#      (not IN_1_RDY or OUT_0_RDY),    2.   DATA_1 := IN_1_DAT;
—#      OUT_0_RDY, IN_1_RDY &                    { DATA_1⋉ }
—# OUT_1_DAT from                        3.   IN_1_RDY := false;
—#      IN_0_DAT when                            { DATA_1⋉ }
—#      (IN_0_RDY and not OUT_1_RDY),   4.   OUT_0_DAT := DATA_1;
—#      OUT_1_DAT when                           { OUT_0_DAT⋉ }
—#      (not IN_0_RDY or OUT_1_RDY),    5.   OUT_0_RDY := true;
—#      OUT_1_RDY, IN_0_RDY                      { OUT_0_DAT⋉ }
                                        6. end if;
                                            { OUT_0_DAT⋉ }
              (a)                                         (b)
```

Fig. 3. (a) Fragment of conditional information flow contract. (b) Corresponding derivation with SIFL assertions.

on the initial value of IN_1_DAT when the flag IN_1_RDY is set and the flag OUT_0_RDY is cleared; otherwise, it depends on the initial value of OUT_0_DAT.

The derives clauses in SPARK, like most formal specification mechanisms for information flow, are unconditional (e.g., they do not include the when clauses illustrated in Figure 3). Thus, they cannot distinguish the flag variables as guards nor phrase the conditions under which the guards allow information to pass or be blocked. This means that guarding logic, which is central to many security applications including those developed at Rockwell Collins, *is completely absent from the checkable specifications* in SPARK. In general, the lack of ability to express *conditional* information flow not only inhibits automatic verification of guarding logic specifications, but also results in imprecision which cascades and builds throughout the specifications in the application.

To capture conditional information flow as well as other forms of information that cannot be specified in SPARK, we have been building [1,2] on a reasoning framework based on *conditional* agreement assertions, also called *2-assertions*, originally introduced by Amtoft and Banerjee [5]. These SIFL assertions are of the form $\phi \Rightarrow E\kappa$, where ϕ is a boolean expression and E is any kind of expression (to be defined in the next section), which is satisfied by a pair of stores if either at least one of them does not satisfy ϕ, or they agree on the value of E:

Definition 1. $s_1 \& s_2 \models \phi \Rightarrow E\kappa$ *iff* $[\![E]\!]_{s_1} = [\![E]\!]_{s_2}$ *whenever* $s_1 \models \phi$ *and* $s_2 \models \phi$.

We use $\theta \in \mathbf{twoAssn}$ to range over 2-assertions. For $\theta = (\phi \Rightarrow E\kappa)$, we call ϕ the antecedent of θ and write $\phi = ant(\theta)$, and we call E the consequent of θ and write $E = con(\theta)$. We use $\Theta \in \mathcal{P}(\mathbf{twoAssn})$ to range over sets of 2-assertions, with conjunction implicit. Thus, $s \& s_1 \models \Theta$ iff $\forall \theta \in \Theta : s \& s_1 \models \theta$. We often write $E\kappa$ for $true \Rightarrow E\kappa$, and often write θ for the singleton set $\{\theta\}$.

Fig. 3(b) illustrates a simple derivation using SIFL assertions that answers the question: what is the source of information flowing into variable OUT_0_DAT? The natural way to read the derivation is from the bottom up (since our algorithm works "backwards"). Thus, for OUT_0_DAT⋉ to hold after execution of P, we must have DATA_1⋉ before line 4 (since data flows from DATA_1 to OUT_0_DAT), IN_1_DAT⋉ before line 2 (since data flows from IN_1_DAT to DATA_1), and before line 1 IN_1_RDY⋉ and

OUT_0_RDY⋉ (since they *control* which branch of the condition is taken), along with conditional assertions. The precondition shows, just as we would expect, that the value of OUT_0_DAT depends *unconditionally* on IN_1_RDY and OUT_0_RDY, and *conditionally* on IN_1_DAT and OUT_0_DAT.

3   Evidence Representations

One of our primary goals in this paper is to design *evidence* terms η whose types correspond to triples: if we can establish that η has type $\{\Theta\}\ C\ \{\Theta'\}$ then the command C has information flow property given by precondition Θ and postcondition Θ' where both are sets of *2-assertions*. Intuitively, evidence represents the primary reasoning steps taken in the precondition generation algorithm when constructing a derivation such as the one displayed in Fig. 3(b). We shall need several auxiliary kinds of evidence, described later but summarized below:

$\vdash \eta : \{\Theta\}\ C\ \{\Theta'\}$	η shows C has information flow pre/post-condition Θ/Θ'
$\vdash \nu : \phi \overset{C}{\Leftarrow} \phi'$	ν shows ϕ is NPC for ϕ' wrt. C
$\vdash \iota : \phi \Rightarrow_1 \phi'$	ι shows ϕ logically implies ϕ'
$\vdash \tau : \Theta \Rightarrow_2 \Theta'$	τ shows the 2-assertions in Θ logically imply Θ'
$\vdash \mu : C\ \mathsf{mods\_only}\ X$	μ shows C modifies at most X

3.1   Preliminaries

We shall now describe our language, sufficient to represent the primary features of SPARK. We shall consider only one-dimensional[2] arrays, and model such an array as a total mapping from integers into integers that is zero except for a finite number of places; we do thus not try to model array bounds which is an orthogonal issue and we assume that SPARK development tools have been applied to prove that there are no index range nor arithmetic overflow violations.

Basic Syntax. Commands C are given by the abstract syntax

$$C ::= \mathbf{skip} \mid C\ ;C \mid \mathbf{assert}(B) \mid x := A \mid h := H \mid \mathbf{if}\ B\ \mathbf{then}\ C\ \mathbf{else}\ C$$
$$\mid\ \mathbf{while}\ B\ \mathbf{do}\ C \mid \mathbf{for}\ q \leftarrow 1\ \mathbf{to}\ m\ \mathbf{do}\ C$$

In **for** $q \leftarrow 1$ **to** m **do** C we require q and m to be different identifiers, neither modified by C. We use x (and y, z) to range over scalar identifiers, h to range over array identifiers, and z, w to range over either kind of identifier; we use A to range over arithmetic expressions, B and ϕ to range over boolean expressions which are also called *1-assertions*, H to range over array expressions, and E to range over any kind of expression. Those are given by the syntax

$$A ::= c \mid x \mid A\ \mathsf{op}\ A \mid H[A]$$
$$B ::= A\ \mathsf{bop}\ A \mid \mathit{true} \mid \mathit{false} \mid B \wedge B \mid B \vee B \mid \neg B$$
$$H ::= h \mid Z \mid H\{A\ :\ A\}$$

---

[2] Multi-dimensional arrays are supported in the complete SPARK language, but they are not yet supported in our theory nor in our tool implementation.

where c ranges over constants, op ranges over binary arithmetic operators, bop ranges over binary comparison operators, and Z denotes the array which is zero everywhere. Note that an array identifier can be assigned an arbitrary array expression but we will typically only do a one-place update: we use the standard notation $h[A_0] := A$ as a shorthand for $h := h\{A_0 : A\}$.

Semantics. A value is just an integer in Int. Thus a store s is a (partial) mapping from scalar identifiers into values, and from array identifiers into total functions in Int $\to$ Int where we shall use a to range over members of that function space. Then $[\![A]\!]_s$ denotes the value resulting from evaluating A in store s, $[\![H]\!]_s$ denotes the function resulting from evaluating H in store s, and $[\![B]\!]_s$ denotes the boolean resulting from evaluating B in store s. We we say that s satisfies ϕ, written $s \models \phi$, iff $[\![\phi]\!]_s =$ True. Below, we shall list the semantic clauses that deal with arrays (the other clauses are straightforward):

$$[\![H[A]]\!]_s = [\![H]\!]_s([\![A]\!]_s) \qquad\qquad [\![Z]\!]_s = \lambda n.0$$
$$[\![H\{A_0 : A\}]\!]_s = [[\![H]\!]_s \mid [\![A_0]\!]_s \mapsto [\![A]\!]_s]$$

We write $s\ [\![C]\!]\ s'$ if the command C transforms the store s into store s'. For example, $s\ [\![h := H]\!]\ s'$ iff for some a we have $a = [\![H]\!]_s$ and $s' = [s \mid h \mapsto a]$.

Given C and s, there exists at most one s' such that $s\ [\![C]\!]\ s'$ holds; if C is a **while** loop that loops on s or an **assert** command that fails then no such s' will exist.

In **for** loops, we allow zero iterations and let the final value of the counter q be one above the bound; then one can prove that a **for** loop can be expressed as a **while** loop: for all s and s', $s\ [\![\textbf{for}\ q \leftarrow 1\ \textbf{to}\ m\ \textbf{do}\ C]\!]\ s'$ iff $s\ [\![q := 1\ ;\ C_w]\!]\ s'$ where C_w is given by **while** $q \leq m$ **do** $(C\ ;\ q := q + 1)$.

To analyze **for** loops, we could thus rely on an analysis for **while** loops, but we shall present (Sect. 3.6) a specialized analysis of **for** loops that often gives more precise information than analyzing the equivalent **while** loop would have done.

3.2   Evidence

We shall provide rules, numbered below from (1) to (12), for inferring judgements of the form $\vdash \eta : \{\Theta\}\ C\ \{\Theta'\}$. Each rule corresponds to an evidence construct and is designed so as to enable the following soundness property:

Theorem 2. *Assume that* $\vdash \eta : \{\Theta\}\ C\ \{\Theta'\}$. *Then* $\models \{\Theta\}\ C\ \{\Theta'\}$.

Here $\models \{\Theta\}\ C\ \{\Theta'\}$ denotes the desired semantic soundness result: if $s_1 \& s_2 \models \Theta$, and $s_i\ [\![C]\!]\ s_i'$ for $i = 1, 2$, then $s_1' \& s_2' \models \Theta'$. Also, evidence has unique type: if $\vdash \eta : \{\Theta_i\}\ C_i\ \{\Theta_i'\}$ for $i = 1, 2$ then $\Theta_1 = \Theta_2$, $C_1 = C_2$, and $\Theta_1' = \Theta_2'$.

Syntax-Directed Evidence. For each syntactic construct there is a corresponding piece of evidence. For the most basic constructs, the inference rules are listed in Fig. 4. (For space reasons, we omit the evidence for **while** loops, and we postpone **for** loops until Sect. 3.6.) We let $\text{add}_B^\wedge(\Theta)$ denote the result of conjoining B to the antecedent of each assertion in Θ: $\text{add}_B^\wedge(\Theta) = \{\text{add}_B^\wedge(\theta) \mid \theta \in \Theta\}$ where $\text{add}_B^\wedge((\phi \Rightarrow E\bowtie)) = (\phi \wedge B) \Rightarrow E\bowtie$.

$$\overline{\vdash \mathsf{SkipE}(\Theta) \,:\, \{\Theta\}\ \mathbf{skip}\ \{\Theta\}} \tag{1}$$

$$\frac{\vdash \eta_1 \,:\, \{\Theta_1\}\ C_1\ \{\Theta\} \qquad \vdash \eta_2 \,:\, \{\Theta\}\ C_2\ \{\Theta_2\}}{\vdash \mathsf{SeqE}(\eta_1, \eta_2) \,:\, \{\Theta_1\}\ C_1\,;C_2\ \{\Theta_2\}} \tag{2}$$

$$\overline{\vdash \mathsf{AssignE}(\Theta, x, A) \,:\, \{\Theta[A/x]\}\ x := A\ \{\Theta\}} \tag{3}$$

$$\overline{\vdash \mathsf{HAssignE}(\Theta, h, H) \,:\, \{\Theta[H/h]\}\ h := H\ \{\Theta\}} \tag{4}$$

$$\overline{\vdash \mathsf{AssertE}(\Theta, B) \,:\, \{\mathsf{add}_B^{\wedge}(\Theta)\}\ \mathbf{assert}(B)\ \{\Theta\}} \tag{5}$$

Fig. 4. Simple rules for syntax-directed evidence

Before presenting the rule for conditionals, we need to introduce the notion of "necessary precondition" (NPC). We say that ϕ is a NPC for ϕ' wrt. C if whenever $s\ [\![C]\!]\ s'$ and $s' \models \phi'$ then $s \models \phi$. It is easy to see that the set of NPCs for given C and ϕ' forms a *Moore family* (closed under arbitrary conjunction) and hence there exists a smallest (strongest) NPC, which is equal to $wp(C, \phi')$ with wp denoting "weakest precondition" (satisfied by a store s if there exists s' with $s\ [\![C]\!]\ s'$ and $s' \models \phi'$). It may be infeasible to compute $wp(C, \phi')$ exactly but then any *weaker* assertion (and trivially *true*) can be used as NPC. We use ν to range over evidence for NPC, described in Sect. 3.3.

The general rule for a conditional $C = \mathbf{if}\ B\ \mathbf{then}\ C_1\ \mathbf{else}\ C_2$ is

$$\frac{\Theta = \{\phi \Rightarrow E\bowtie\} \qquad \vdash \eta_i \,:\, \{\Theta_i\}\ C_i\ \{\Theta\}\ (i=1,2) \qquad \vdash \nu \,:\, \phi_0 \overset{C}{\Leftarrow} \phi}{\vdash \mathsf{CondE}(\eta_1, \eta_2, \nu, B) \,:\, \{\mathsf{add}_B^{\wedge}(\Theta_1) \cup \mathsf{add}_{\neg B}^{\wedge}(\Theta_2) \cup \{\phi_0 \Rightarrow B\bowtie\}\}\ C\ \{\Theta\}} \tag{6}$$

which demands the postcondition to be a singleton; if not, we decompose it and then recombine using the UnionE evidence construct (9). The assertion $\phi_0 \Rightarrow B\bowtie$ occurring in the precondition expresses that if two runs must agree on the consequent E then they must also agree on the test B; this may be too restrictive if E is not modified by either branch in which case we can instead use the ConseqNotModE evidence construct (11).

We now look back at the derivation in Fig. 3(b). The analysis of the command in line 4 was done using rule (3), with $x = $ OUT_0_DAT and $A = $ DATA_1 and $\Theta = $ OUT_0_DAT$\bowtie$, giving the precondition $\Theta[A/x] = $ DATA_1$\bowtie$. The analysis of the conditional in line 1 was done using rule (6), with $B = ($IN_1_RDY $\wedge\ \neg$OUT_0_RDY$)$ and using evidence η_1 for the analysis of C_1 (the lines 2–5) and evidence η_2 for the analysis of C_2 (**skip**), both with postcondition $\Theta = $ OUT_0_DAT$\bowtie$. From $\Theta_1 = $ IN_1_DAT$\bowtie$ and $\Theta_2 = $ OUT_0_DAT$\bowtie$, and from *true* being a NPC for *true*, we get the precondition

$$\Theta_0 = \{\ (\mathit{true} \wedge (\text{IN\_1\_RDY} \wedge \neg\text{OUT\_0\_RDY})) \Rightarrow \text{IN\_1\_DAT}\bowtie,$$
$$(\mathit{true} \wedge \neg(\text{IN\_1\_RDY} \wedge \neg\text{OUT\_0\_RDY})) \Rightarrow \text{OUT\_0\_DAT}\bowtie,$$
$$\mathit{true} \Rightarrow (\text{IN\_1\_RDY} \wedge \neg\text{OUT\_0\_RDY})\bowtie\}$$

Non-Syntax Directed Evidence. Some additional evidence constructs are given by the inference rules listed in Fig. 5 which we shall now explain and motivate.

The rules (7,8) allow us to strengthen the precondition or weaken the postcondition; here τ is evidence (described in Sect. 3.3) for *2-implication*: if $\vdash \tau \,:\, \Theta \Rightarrow_2 \Theta'$ then Θ logically implies Θ' (that is, for all stores s_1, s_2, if $s_1 \& s_2 \models \Theta$ then $s_1 \& s_2 \models \Theta'$).

$$\frac{\vdash \eta : \{\Theta''\} \, C \, \{\Theta'\} \qquad \vdash \tau : \Theta \Rightarrow_2 \Theta''}{\vdash \mathsf{PreImplyE}(\tau, \eta) : \{\Theta\} \, C \, \{\Theta'\}} \tag{7}$$

$$\frac{\vdash \eta : \{\Theta\} \, C \, \{\Theta''\} \qquad \vdash \tau : \Theta'' \Rightarrow_2 \Theta'}{\vdash \mathsf{PostImplyE}(\eta, \tau) : \{\Theta\} \, C \, \{\Theta'\}} \tag{8}$$

$$\frac{\vdash \eta_1 : \{\Theta_1\} \, C \, \{\Theta_1'\} \qquad \vdash \eta_2 : \{\Theta_2\} \, C \, \{\Theta_2'\}}{\vdash \mathsf{UnionE}(\eta_1, \eta_2) : \{\Theta_1 \cup \Theta_2\} \, C \, \{\Theta_1' \cup \Theta_2'\}} \tag{9}$$

$$\frac{\vdash \mu : C \text{ mods\_only } X \qquad \mathsf{fv}(\Theta) \cap X = \emptyset}{\vdash \mathsf{NotModE}(\mu, \Theta) : \{\Theta\} \, C \, \{\Theta\}} \tag{10}$$

$$\frac{\vdash \mu : C \text{ mods\_only } X \qquad \vdash \nu : \phi \overset{\mathcal{C}}{\Leftarrow} \phi' \qquad \mathsf{fv}(E) \cap X = \emptyset}{\vdash \mathsf{ConseqNotModE}(\mu, \nu, E) : \{\phi \Rightarrow E \ltimes\} \, C \, \{\phi' \Rightarrow E \ltimes\}} \tag{11}$$

$$\frac{\vdash \eta : \{\Theta\} \, C \, \{\Theta'\} \qquad \vdash \nu : \phi \overset{\mathcal{C}}{\Leftarrow} \phi'}{\vdash \mathsf{AntecStrongerE}(\eta, \nu) : \{\mathsf{add}_\phi^\wedge(\Theta)\} \, C \, \{\mathsf{add}_{\phi'}^\wedge(\Theta')\}} \tag{12}$$

Fig. 5. Rules for non-syntax-directed evidence

Two derivations may be combined using (9) which can trivially be generalized to an evidence construct combining an arbitrary number of elements: $\mathsf{UnionE}(\eta_1 \ldots \eta_n)$.

The rule (10) allows a simple treatment of 2-assertions when no identifier is modified; it uses evidence μ for not-modification: if $\vdash \mu : C \text{ mods\_only } X$ then all identifiers[3] possibly modified by C are included in X. We shall not represent such evidence explicitly, since not-modification is a syntactic property which can be checked easily by a simple Gallina function in Coq. Again looking back at the derivation in Fig. 3(b), we observe that line 5 could have been analyzed using rule (3) but can also be analyzed using rule (10) which is particularly powerful if applied to a whole block of code. For example, for the program in Figure 2, the precondition (shown in Figure 3) of the second conditional does not contain any identifiers that are modified by the first conditional, and hence by a single application of (10) can be shown to be also the precondition of the whole program.

Another rule (11) addresses the more general case where antecedents, but not consequents, may be modified. We then need to ensure that whenever two post-states are required to agree on the consequent, also the two pre-states are required to agree on the consequent. This is expressed using the notion of NPC, which is also used in (12) to allow us to make pre-and postconditions "more conditional", by strengthening the antecedents.

3.3   Auxiliary Evidence

Evidence for 2-Implication. In order to justify the simplication of assertions, or showing that a user-supplied precondition is correct in that it implies the precondition generated

---

[3] If C modifies just one entry of h then h has to be included in X. This may seem very imprecise, but we shall present (in Sect. 3.6) an analysis that in many cases does allow us to get precise information about how individual array elements are affected by **for** loops.

$$\frac{\Theta \supseteq \Theta_0}{\vdash \mathsf{Superset2I}(\Theta, \Theta_0) \; : \; \Theta \; \Rightarrow_2 \; \Theta_0} \tag{13}$$

$$\frac{\text{for all } \phi \Rightarrow E \ltimes \; \in \Theta, \text{ there exists no } s \text{ with } s \models \phi}{\vdash \mathsf{Vacuous2I}(\Theta) \; : \; \emptyset \; \Rightarrow_2 \; \Theta} \tag{14}$$

$$\frac{\mathsf{fv}(E) = \emptyset}{\vdash \mathsf{Const2I}(E, \phi) \; : \; \emptyset \; \Rightarrow_2 \; (\phi \Rightarrow E \ltimes)} \tag{15}$$

$$\frac{\vdash \tau_1 \; : \; \Theta_1 \; \Rightarrow_2 \; \Theta_1' \qquad \vdash \tau_2 \; : \; \Theta_2 \; \Rightarrow_2 \; \Theta_2'}{\vdash \mathsf{Union2I}(\tau_1, \tau_2) \; : \; \Theta_1 \cup \Theta_2 \; \Rightarrow_2 \; \Theta_1' \cup \Theta_2'} \tag{16}$$

$$\frac{\vdash \tau_1 \; : \; \Theta_1 \; \Rightarrow_2 \; \Theta' \qquad \vdash \tau_2 \; : \; \Theta_2 \; \Rightarrow_2 \; \Theta' \qquad \Theta = (\Theta_2 \setminus \Theta_1') \cup \Theta_1}{\vdash \mathsf{Trans2I}(\tau_1, \tau_2) \; : \; \Theta \; \Rightarrow_2 \; \Theta'} \tag{17}$$

$$\frac{\vdash \iota \; : \; \phi \; \Rightarrow_1 \; \phi'}{\vdash \mathsf{Contravar2I}(\iota, E) \; : \; \{\phi' \Rightarrow E \ltimes\} \; \Rightarrow_2 \; \{\phi \Rightarrow E \ltimes\}} \tag{18}$$

$$\frac{E \text{ is of the form } E_1 \text{ op } E_2 \text{ or } E_1 \text{ bop } E_2 \text{ or } E_1 \wedge E_2 \text{ or } E_1 \vee E_2 \text{ or } \neg E_1}{\vdash \mathsf{BinOp2I}(E, \phi) \; : \; \{\phi \Rightarrow E_1 \ltimes, \phi \Rightarrow E_2 \ltimes\} \; \Rightarrow_2 \; \{\phi \Rightarrow E \ltimes\}} \tag{19}$$

Fig. 6. Rules for 2-implication evidence

by our inference algorithm, we need evidence that a given assertion set logically implies another assertion set. Such evidence can be built using a number of constructs (more might be added) whose inference rules are listed in Fig. 6.

Here (13) says that any set of 2-assertions logically implies a smaller set, while (14) allows us to discard (replace by the empty set) 2-assertions that are vacuously true, and (15) allows us to discard 2-assertions whose consequent are constants.

Derivations can be combined "horizontally" by (16) which easily can be generalized to take an arbitrary number of arguments, and "vertically" by (17) which as a special case (when $\Theta_1' = \Theta_2$) has the "standard" transitivity rule.

The rule (18) allows us to lift simplications on antecedents to simplifications on 2-assertions, and expresses that 2-implication is contravariant in the antecedent; here ι ranges over evidence (described later) for logical implication: if $\vdash \iota \; : \; \phi \; \Rightarrow_1 \; \phi'$ then ϕ logically implies ϕ' (that is, whenever $s \models \phi$ then also $s \models \phi'$). For example, for the precondition Θ_0 computed above, one can easily verify that

$$true \wedge \big(\text{IN\_1\_RDY} \wedge \neg\text{OUT\_0\_RDY} \big) \Rightarrow \text{IN\_1\_RDY} \wedge \neg\text{OUT\_0\_RDY}$$
$$true \wedge \neg\big(\text{IN\_1\_RDY} \wedge \neg\text{OUT\_0\_RDY} \big) \Rightarrow \neg\big(\text{IN\_1\_RDY} \wedge \neg\text{OUT\_0\_RDY} \big)$$

and hence rule (18), together with rule (16), allows us to simplify Θ_0 to

$$\Theta_0' = \{ \; (\text{IN\_1\_RDY} \wedge \neg\text{OUT\_0\_RDY}) \Rightarrow \text{IN\_1\_DAT} \ltimes, \neg(\text{IN\_1\_RDY} \wedge \neg\text{OUT\_0\_RDY}) \Rightarrow \text{OUT\_0\_DAT} \ltimes,$$
$$(\text{IN\_1\_RDY} \wedge \neg\text{OUT\_0\_RDY}) \ltimes \}.$$

Complex consequents can be decomposed using (19). For example, we can split the last consequent of Θ_0' to reach the final precondition of the code segment:

$$\Theta_0'' = \{ \; (\text{IN\_1\_RDY} \wedge \neg\text{OUT\_0\_RDY}) \Rightarrow \text{IN\_1\_DAT} \ltimes, \neg(\text{IN\_1\_RDY} \wedge \neg\text{OUT\_0\_RDY}) \Rightarrow \text{OUT\_0\_DAT} \ltimes,$$
$$\text{IN\_1\_RDY} \ltimes, \text{OUT\_0\_RDY} \ltimes \}.$$

Evidence for Necessary Precondition. Recall that we need, for the rules (6) and (11) and (12), evidence ν such that if $\vdash \nu : \phi \overset{C}{\Leftarrow} \phi'$ then whenever $s \ [\![C]\!] \ s'$ and $s' \models \phi'$ then also $s \models \phi$. To build such evidence, we use one construct for each language construct, with one extra to make a shortcut when the command does not modify the 1-assertion. Two typical rules are listed below:

$$\frac{\vdash \nu_1 : \phi_1 \overset{C_1}{\Leftarrow} \phi \qquad \vdash \nu_2 : \phi_2 \overset{C_2}{\Leftarrow} \phi}{\vdash \mathsf{CondNPC}(\nu_1, \nu_2, B) : (\phi_1 \wedge B) \vee (\phi_2 \wedge \neg B) \overset{\text{if } B \text{ then } C_1 \text{ else } C_2}{\Leftarrow} \phi} \tag{20}$$

$$\frac{\vdash \nu : \phi_0 \overset{C}{\Leftarrow} \phi \qquad \vdash \iota_0 : \phi_0 \wedge B \Rightarrow_1 \phi \qquad \vdash \iota_1 : \phi' \wedge \neg B \Rightarrow_1 \phi}{\vdash \mathsf{WhileNPC}(\nu, \iota_0, \iota_1) : \phi \overset{\text{while } B \text{ do } C}{\Leftarrow} \phi'} \tag{21}$$

Evidence for Logical Implication. We have two kinds of evidence:

1. rules that resemble axiomatization of propositional logic;
2. the evidence $\mathsf{CheckLI}(\phi, \phi')$ which says that "a decision procedure has verified that ϕ logically implies ϕ'".

3.4   Manipulating 2-Assertions

It is often useful to transform a set of 2-assertions into a set which is "simpler" and which satisfies certain properties; for example, to analyze a **while** loop (or a method call), all (modified) consequents in the postcondition must be identifiers. Ideally, we would like the result to be equivalent to the original (like Θ_0' to Θ_0 in the previous example), but often it will be strictly stronger (as is Θ_0'' when $(E_1 \wedge \neg E_2) \ltimes$ is decomposed into $E_1 \ltimes$ and $E_2 \ltimes$). Hence[4] our overall approach does in general *not* calculate the *weakest* precondition.

We have written an algorithm that transforms a set of 2-assertions Θ' into a more manageable form, as may be required by the command C for which Θ' is the postcondition, while producing evidence that the result is at least as strong as the original. The algorithm as input also takes a set X, to be thought of as the identifiers that are modified by C. The algorithm returns τ, and also Θ_u (assertions whose *consequents* are <u>un</u>modified) and Θ_n, such that $\vdash \tau : \Theta_n \cup \Theta_u \Rightarrow_2 \Theta'$ and

- all array expressions inside Θ_n and Θ_u are identifiers; thus there are no occurrences of Z or $H\{A_0 : A\}$ which may be introduced by rule (4) but hamper readability;
- all assertions in Θ_n are of the form $\phi \Rightarrow w \ltimes$ or of the form $\phi \Rightarrow h[A] \ltimes$, as is required if C is a **while** or **for** loop;
- if $\phi \Rightarrow E \ltimes \in \Theta_u$ then $\mathrm{fv}(E) \cap X = \emptyset$;
- if $\phi \Rightarrow h[A] \ltimes \in \Theta_n$ then $\mathrm{fv}(A) \cap X = \emptyset$;
- if $\phi_1 \Rightarrow E \ltimes \in \Theta_n$ and $\phi_2 \Rightarrow E \ltimes \in \Theta_n$ then $\phi_1 = \phi_2$.

3.5   Generating Evidence

For any command and postcondition, it is possible to compute a precondition, together with evidence that the resulting triple is indeed semantically sound. To help with that,

---

[4] Another reason is the approximation needed to efficiently handle loops.

we need an algorithm **NpcEvdGen** generating evidence for necessary precondition. For the nonlooping constructs, such an algorithm is straightforward to write, but for a **while** loop a *precise* analysis involves guessing an invariant; we expect that we might be able to use some of the emerging tools for finding loop invariants even though our perspective is dual.

We shall first present a *nondeterministic* algorithm **EvdGen** such that for all commands C (without **while** and **for**) and postconditions Θ, a call **EvdGen**(C, Θ) returns evidence η such that $\vdash \eta : \{\Theta_0\}\, C\, \{\Theta\}$ for some Θ_0. Below we list the possible actions of **EvdGen**, the applicability of which depend on the form of C and/or Θ.

Decompose Postcondition. The enabling condition is that Θ has at least two elements. Let Θ_1', Θ_2' be nonempty disjoint sets such that $\Theta = \Theta_1' \cup \Theta_2'$. For each $i \in \{1..2\}$, recursively call **EvdGen**(C, Θ_i') to produce η_i such that $\vdash \eta_i : \{\Theta_i\}\, C\, \{\Theta_i'\}$ for some Θ_i. Define $\eta = \mathsf{UnionE}(\eta_1, \eta_2)$; we thus have $\vdash \eta : \{\Theta_1 \cup \Theta_2\}\, C\, \{\Theta\}$.

Push Through Postcondition. The enabling condition is that $\mathrm{fv}(\Theta) \cap X = \emptyset$ where X is such that $\vdash \mu : C\ \mathsf{mods\_only}\ X$ for some μ. Then we can define $\eta = \mathsf{NotModE}(\mu, \Theta)$ and achieve $\vdash \eta : \{\Theta\}\, C\, \{\Theta\}$.

Push Through Consequent of Postcondition. The enabling condition is that Θ is a singleton $\{\phi' \Rightarrow E\ltimes\}$, and that $\mathrm{fv}(E) \cap X = \emptyset$ with X such that $\vdash \mu : C\ \mathsf{mods\_only}\ X$ for some μ. Let $\nu = \mathbf{NpcEvdGen}(C, \phi')$. There thus exists ϕ with $\vdash \nu : \phi \overset{C}{\Leftarrow} \phi'$. Now define $\eta = \mathsf{ConseqNotModE}(\mu, \nu, E)$ and get $\vdash \eta : \{\phi \Rightarrow E\ltimes\}\, C\, \{\Theta\}$.

Syntax-Directed Actions. Two typical cases are as follows:

If $C = x := A$ then **EvdGen**(C, Θ) returns $\mathsf{AssignE}(\Theta, x, A)$.

If $C = \mathbf{if}\ B\ \mathbf{then}\ C_1\ \mathbf{else}\ C_2$, and Θ is a singleton $\{\phi' \Rightarrow E\ltimes\}$, we for each $i \in \{1, 2\}$ recursively call **EvdGen**(C_i, Θ) to produce η_i such that $\vdash \eta_i : \{\Theta_i\}\, C_i\, \{\Theta\}$ for some Θ_i, and call **NpcEvdGen**(C, ϕ') to compute ν such that for some ϕ we have $\vdash \nu : \phi \overset{C}{\Leftarrow} \phi'$. We then return $\eta = \mathsf{CondE}(\eta_1, \eta_2, \nu, B)$ which by the typing rules satisfies the desired $\vdash \eta : \{\Theta_0\}\, C\, \{\Theta\}$ for some Θ_0.

Properties of **EvdGen**. The precondition Θ_0 for an assignment statement $x := A$ depends only on the postcondition Θ, but not on the kind of evidence that was chosen; we will always have $\Theta_0 = \Theta[A/x]$. However, we do *not* have a similar result for conditionals $C = \mathbf{if}\ B\ \mathbf{then}\ C_1\ \mathbf{else}\ C_2$: for example, if E is not modified by C then **EvdGen**(C, Θ) may either produce evidence of the form $\mathsf{CondE}(\eta_1, \eta_2, \nu, B)$ whose type has a precondition containing an assertion with B as consequent, or evidence of the form $\mathsf{ConseqNotModE}(\mu, \nu, E)$ whose type does not have that property.

We thus need to restrict the non-determinism present in the definition of **EvdGen**. For conditionals, syntax-directed evidence CondE should only be generated when the postcondition is a singleton whose consequent has been modified. For other constructs, we may be free either to split the postcondition or to apply the syntax-directed rules directly. The advantage of the former is that then the evidence provides fine-grained information about which preconditions come from which postconditions. The advantage of the latter is that then the evidence becomes more compact.

3.6 For Loops

We shall introduce 3 extra evidence constructs:

$$\eta ::= \ldots \mid \mathsf{ForAsWhileE}(\eta, \mu) \mid \mathsf{ForPolyE}(\ldots) \mid \mathsf{InstantiateE}(\eta, \mu, A)$$

Here $\mathsf{ForAsWhileE}$ just analyzes a **for** loop as a **while** loop; this involves splitting an assertion $\phi \Rightarrow h[A]\Bowtie$ into $\phi \Rightarrow h\Bowtie$ and $\phi \Rightarrow A\Bowtie$ and thus we lose any information about individual array elements.

We shall now present a method, first given in [2] which contains further motivation and examples, that in certain cases allows us to reason about individual array elements. To do so in a finite way, we need the concept of *polymorphic identifiers*. Those may occur in pre/post conditions but never in commands; we shall use u to range over them. We shall extend $\models \{\Theta\}\ C\ \{\Theta'\}$ to cover the case where Θ and/or Θ' contains a polymorphic identifier u: then $\models \{\Theta\}\ C\ \{\Theta'\}$ holds iff $\models \{\Theta[c/u]\}\ C\ \{\Theta'[c/u]\}$ holds for all constants c. We have the inference rule

$$\frac{\vdash \eta : \{\Theta\}\ C\ \{\Theta'\} \qquad \vdash \mu : C\ \mathsf{mods\_only}\ X \qquad \mathrm{fv}(A) \cap X = \emptyset}{\vdash \mathsf{InstantiateE}(\eta, \mu, A)\ :\ \{\{A\Bowtie\} \cup \Theta[A/u]\}\ C\ \{\Theta'[A/u]\}}$$

which is applicable not just when C is a **for**-loop. We shall design $\mathsf{ForPolyE}$ such that

$$\vdash \mathsf{ForPolyE}(\ldots)\ :\ \{\Theta\}\ \mathbf{for}\ q \leftarrow 1\ \mathbf{to}\ m\ \mathbf{do}\ C\ \{h[u]\}$$

if certain requirements, to be motivated and detailed below, are fulfilled. Let μ with $\vdash \mu : C\ \mathsf{mods\_only}\ X$ where $q, m \notin X$, and a polymorphic identifier u, be given.

Index Sets. There must exist a set of arithmetic expressions, $\{A_j \mid j \in J\}$ with $\mathrm{fv}(A_j) \cap X = \emptyset$, such that for all array assignments $h := H$ in C there exists j and A such that $H = h\{A_j : A\}$ (and thus the assignment may be written $h[A_j] := A$).

Linearity. We shall assume, as is very often the case for practical applications, that each A_j is a linear function in q. That is, there exists integer constants (or identifiers not in X) $b_j \neq 0$ and k_j such that A_j is given by $b_j q + k_j$. Then for each $j \in J$, we define

$$A'_j = \frac{u - k_j}{b_j}$$
$$\phi_j = (u - k_j) \bmod b_j = 0\ \wedge\ u - k_j \geq b_j\ \wedge\ u - k_j \leq m b_j$$

with the intention that whereas A_j computes an index value from the iteration number, A'_j computes the iteration number from the index value while ϕ_j denotes the set of index values, as formalized by the following properties (to be suitably quantified):

1. if $c = [\![A_j]\!]_{[s|q \rightarrow i]}$ for $i \in \{1 \ldots s(m)\}$ then $[\![A'_j[c/u]]\!]_s = i$.
2. $s \models \phi_j[c/u]$ iff $c \in \{[\![A_j]\!]_{[s|q \rightarrow i]} \mid i \in \{1 \ldots s(m)\}\}$.

Local Preconditions. For all $j \in J$, there must exists η_j and Θ_j such that

1. $\vdash \eta_j : \{\Theta_j\} \, C \, \{h[A_j] \ltimes\}$ with $u \neq \mathrm{fv}(\Theta_j)$
2. $\mathrm{fv}(\Theta_j) \cap X \subseteq \{h\}$
3. if h occurs in Θ_j it is in a context of the form $h[A]$ where for all $j' \in J$, all $i, i' \in \{1 \ldots s(m)\}$, all stores s: if $[\![A]\!]_{[s|q \to i]} = [\![A_{j'}]\!]_{[s|q \to i']}$ then $i \leq i'$.

Requirement 2 excludes loop-carried dependencies in the body such as $h[q] := x; x := y$ in which case $h[1]$ depends on the initial value of x while $h[2]$, $h[3]$,... depends on the initial value of y. Requirement 3 is designed to exclude loop-carried dependencies *within* the array h; it is possible to list some cases that are easily checkable and which each is a *sufficient condition* for this requirement to hold:

1. when J is a singleton $\{j\}$, and the only occurrence of h in Θ_j is in the context $h[bq + k]$ where $b \geq b_j$ and $b \geq 1$ and $k \geq k_j$;
2. when $b_j = 1$ for all $j \in J$, and if h occurs in some Θ_j it is in a context of the form $h[A]$ with A of the form $q + c$ where c satisfies:

$$\forall j \in J : \; c \geq k_j \text{ or } c \leq k_j - m.$$

Both conditions will accept a loop body containing (only) $h[q] := h[q + 1]$ and reject a loop body containing $h[q] := h[q - 1]$.

We are now ready to construct the precondition Θ, as the union of

BOUND $\{true \Rightarrow m \ltimes\}$
INDEX $\{true \Rightarrow w \ltimes \mid w \in \cup_{j \in J} \mathrm{fv}(A_j) \setminus \{q\}\}$
OUTSIDE $\{\bigwedge_{j \in J} \neg \phi_j \Rightarrow h[u] \ltimes\}$
UPDATED for each $j \in J$, the set $\mathrm{add}_{\phi_j}^{\wedge}(\Theta_j[A_j'/q])$.

Here BOUND ensures that the two runs agree on the number of iterations, while IN-DEX ensures that the two runs agree on which indices are updated. For an index that might not be updated, the two runs must agree on the original value, as expressed by OUTSIDE. But for an index that may be updated, we apply the computed preconditions, as expressed by UPDATED.

Example. As in [2], we can analyze a **for** loop whose body swaps[5] $h[q]$ and $h[q + m]$ and where we therefore have $J = \{1, 2\}$, $A_1 = q$, $A_2 = q + m$, $b_1 = b_2 = 1$, $k_1 = 0$, and $k_2 = m$. We compute $\phi_1 = u \geq 1 \wedge u \leq m$, $\phi_2 = u - m \geq 1 \wedge u - m \leq m$, $A_1' = u$, and $A_2' = u - m$; we also get $\Theta_1 = \{h[q + m] \ltimes\}$ and $\Theta_2 = \{h[q] \ltimes\}$. The abovementioned sufficient condition 2 amounts to the 4 claims

$$0 \geq 0 \text{ or } 0 \leq 0 - m \qquad\qquad 0 \geq m \text{ or } 0 \leq m - m$$
$$m \geq 0 \text{ or } m \leq 0 - m \qquad\qquad m \geq m \text{ or } m \leq m - m$$

which are all easily verified. Hence we may generate the expected precondition

$$\{ \, m \ltimes, \; (u < 1 \vee u > 2m) \Rightarrow h[u] \ltimes,$$
$$1 \leq u \leq m \Rightarrow h[u + m] \ltimes, \; m + 1 \leq u \leq 2m \Rightarrow h[u - m] \ltimes \, \}.$$

---

[5] Since each position participates in at most one swap there is no loop-carried dependency.

4 Machine-Checked Evidence and Soundness Overview

We now discuss how the evidence constructors of the previous section are represented and proven sound in Coq. Our technical report [4] provides detailed correctness proofs for all the evidence constructors. At the time of writing, we have completed the corresponding formalization of the proofs in Coq for assignments, conditionals, arrays, polymorphic tuples and almost all of the **for** loop, and we do not anticipate problems completing the remaining soundness proofs (remainder of **for** plus **while**).

4.1 Representation of Evidence

Our representation of evidence is based on deep embeddings of the language and the logic in Coq, using type-respecting categories of variables (e.g. SkalVar), expressions Expr (separated into arithmetic, boolean and array expressions AExpr, BExpr, HExpr), and Commands. Based on these definitions, we define expression evaluation and the operational semantics in direct correspondence to the definitions in Section 3; for example, Opsem s C t means that command C transforms state s into state t.

A 2-assertion is made up of a BExpr and an Expr:

Definition TwoAssn :=prod BExpr Expr.

Abbreviating the type of lists of 2-assertions as TwoAssns, we introduce the inductive type of pre/postconditions as

Inductive assns :=
| Assns : TwoAssns $\rightarrow$ TwoAssns $\rightarrow$ assns
| APoly : (AExpr $\rightarrow$ assns)$\rightarrow$ assns.

Here, the first constructor carries a precondition/postcondition pair and will be used for standard triples. The second constructor allows the assertions to be parametrized by a shared variable, and will be required for implementing for-loops.

Evidence takes the form of an inductive proposition with constructors corresponding to the rules in Figures 4 and 5.

Inductive TEvid (X: list SkalVar) : Command $\rightarrow$ assns $\rightarrow$ Prop :=
| TSkipE ... | TAAssignE ... | TCondE ...
...

For example, the constructor for TAAssignE,

| TAAssignE : $\forall \Theta$ x A, TEvid X (Assign x (AExp A)) (Assns(TwoAssnsSubstA Θ x A) Θ)

is a direct translation of rule (3), where TwoAssnsSubstA Θ x A represents the substitution (code omitted) of arithmetic expression A for x in the 2-assertion Θ.

Evidence for conditionals (rule 6) is translated similarly; the rule takes three explicit arguments of evidence type, one for each possible outcome of the branch, and one for the necessary precondition.

| TCondEN: $\forall \{\Theta_1 \ \phi \ \text{E} \ \Theta_2 \ \Theta' \ \text{C1 C2} \ \phi_0\}$
    (η_1: TEvid X C1 (Assns Θ_1 [(ϕ, E)])) (η_2: TEvid X C2 (Assns Θ_2 [(ϕ, E)]))
    B (ν : NPCEvid X ϕ_0 (Cond B C1 C2) ϕ),
    andIntoTheta Θ_1 B ++ andIntoTheta Θ_2 (NotExpr B) ++ [(ϕ_0, BExp B)] = Θ' $\rightarrow$
    allVarsIn (BFv ϕ_0) X =true $\rightarrow$ TEvid X (Cond B C1 C2) (Assns Θ' [(ϕ, E)])

We have evidence forms declared for all syntax but while and for loops, and we have also declared constructors for all the rules mentioned in Fig. 5. There are similar inductive types and accompanying soundness proofs for NPC, 1-implication, 2-implication and expression equivalence. Rules representing decision-procedure-validated evidence such as CheckLI are currently axiomatically admitted, although future work will aim to verify the output of decision procedures using methods similar to [6].

4.2   Soundness

The soundness of constructed evidence terms rests on the interpretation of 2-assertions

Definition twoSatisfies(s_1 s_2:State) (asn: TwoAssn) := **let** (ϕ, E) = asn **in**
    BEval ϕ s_1 = Some true $\rightarrow$ BEval ϕ s_2 = Some true $\rightarrow$ (Eval E s_1 = Eval E s_2)

which corresponds to the informal definition given earlier in the paper.[6] The interpretation is naturally extended to lists of 2-assertions (where Forall is the universal quantification over list elements, taken from the Coq library):

Definition twoAssnsInterpretation (s_1 s_2: State) (a:TwoAssns) : Prop :=
    Forall (twoSatisfies s1 s2) a.

We are now ready to model the definition (Sect. 3.2) of the predicate $\models \{\Theta\}\ C\ \{\Theta'\}$.

Definition validHoareTriple (X: list SkalVar) C (asns: assns): Prop :=
match asns **with**
| Assns pre post $\Rightarrow$ $\forall$ s s' t t',
                ($\forall$ x, In x X $\rightarrow$ $\exists v_1$, lookup s x = Some v_1 $\wedge$ $\exists v_2$, lookup s' x = Some v_2) $\rightarrow$
                Opsem s C t $\rightarrow$ Opsem s' C t' $\rightarrow$
                twoAssnsInterpretation s s' pre $\rightarrow$ twoAssnsInterpretation t t' post
| ...
end.

Our soundness statement (Theorem 2 in Sect. 3) is formulated as follows.

Theorem soundness : $\forall$ X C asns, TEvid X C asns $\rightarrow$ (validHoareTriple X C asns).

Whenever we apply this soundness result to a defined concrete piece of evidence, the type of the resulting construction explicitly witnesses the validity of the triple. For example, applying the soundness result to a piece of evidence named assignEvid

Definition evidSound := soundness _ _ _ assignEvid.

guarantees our intended security property in that it yields a term of type

validHoareTriple X cmd (Assns pre post).

Performing the proof of the soundness theorem constitutes a major engineering task even once all the definitions are set up correctly. As an indication of the effort, the Coq code has around 2300 lines of soundness proof and only 590 lines of trusted definitions; it formalizes a manual correctness proof in [4] which is about 5.5 pages from about 610 lines of LATEX source.

---

[6] This direct correspondence between informal and formal definitions is crucial, as the formal definitions introduced here form part of the trusted code base of our system.

In order to address the concern that certificates may be unacceptably large, we have also explored an implementation of the precondition generator inside Coq, in the style of proof-by-reflection. Our precondition generator consists of a Gallina function

Fixpoint generatePrecondition (c:Command) (post:TwoAssns)
   (X: list SkalVar): (TwoAssns $*$ list SkalVar) := ...

with defining clauses that closely resemble Figures 4 and 5. The soundness theorem

Theorem generatePreconditionEvidence: $\forall$ C Y X Z post pre, allVarsIn X Y = true$\rightarrow$
(pre, X) = generatePrecondition C post Z $\rightarrow$ TEvid Y C (Assns pre post).

expresses that any result (pre, X) from a call to generatePrecondition yields evidence for the triple made up from the inferred precondition and the supplied command and postcondition. Thus, evidence terms need not be explicitly constructed, as valid evidence can be constructed automatically for any command and postcondition.

5 Evaluation

We summarize our initial experience in applying our SIFL deduction engine for evidence generation. The SIFL precondition generation algorithm supports assignments, conditionals, arrays, **for** and **while** loops, polymorphic flow contracts, and procedure calls. We tested this implementation on procedures from a collection of embedded applications (an Autopilot, a Minepump, a Water Boiler monitor, and a Missile Guidance system – all developed outside of our research group), and a collection of small programs that we developed ourselves to highlight common array idioms that we discovered in information assurance applications. Approximately 6-15 procedures from each of these examples were selected due to having the richest control flow and loop structures. The security-critical sections to be certified from code bases in this domain are often relatively small, *e.g.*, roughly 1000 LOC (non-comment lines of code) for a Rockwell Collins high assurance guard and 3000 LOC for an (undisclosed) device certified by Naval Research Labs researchers [7]. The average LOC per procedure in our examples is 22. In this evaluation, we focused on running the tool in a mode that infers information flow contracts. For each procedure P, and each output variable w, the algorithm analyzes the body wrt. post-condition $w\bowtie$. All experiments were run under JDK 1.6 on a 2x2.6 GHz Quad Core Intel Xeon Mac Pro with 32 GB of RAM.

We were most interested in evaluating (a) the size of the generated evidence, (b) the number and structure of assertions in the inferred precondition (for the purpose of minimizing its size), (c) the time required for the algorithm to infer a contract and generate evidence, and (d) the time required for Coq to type-check (i.e., establish the correctness) of the evidence. In the subsequent paragraphs, we shall summarize the outcomes for the first 3 measures (see [4] for detailed data and evidence outputs for all examples we considered); for (d), no procedure required more than 3 seconds.

In contrast to other proof-carrying code applications such as mobile code, contract size is not as significant an issue in our context since contracts are not being transmitted or checked at run-time. Instead, the focus is on leveraging contracts for greater assurance in the certification process. We consider three different metrics for the size of evidence: the number of evidence constructors, the total number of Coq abstract syntax tree (AST) nodes (which captures the size of assertion expressions and program ASTs in the evidence), and the number of bytes in the text file holding the evidence. For the full version of the mailbox example of Section 2 which has 24 LOC, the generated evidence includes 318 evidence constructors, 3729 Coq AST nodes, and 89 KB of text. For a slightly longer example (30 LOC) from the autopilot codebase that has one of the longest analysis run-times, the presence of four conditions leads to larger generated evidence due to more conditional preconditions: 326 evidence constructors, 19461 Coq AST nodes, and 211 KB of text. Our current contract representation includes the syntax tree of the program as well as the 2-assertions generated between each command. Thus, many program expressions are repeated numerous times across the evidence structure for a procedure. There is significant opportunity to optimize the size by, e.g., common subexpression elimination.

Initial examination of the generated preconditions identified a number of minimization opportunities (e.g., simplifying assertions of the form $true \land \phi \Rightarrow E\kappa$ to $\phi \Rightarrow E\kappa$ or removing a 2-assertion when it is implied by another within the precondition). In the mailbox example, there are 52 AST nodes in the precondition for OUT_0_DAT without minimization and 28 when minimization applied. Our current strategy for expressing minimization includes many fine-grained reasoning steps using the rules of Figure 6. Thus, the number of evidence constructors in the OUT_0_DAT derivation actually increases from 25 to 83. Potentially, this can be reduced by making the Coq checker "smarter" by having it do more manipulation of logical expressions without direct instruction from the evidence generator.

The time required for processing a procedure ranged from 3 to 140 secs. As previously discussed, the correctness of minimization of assertions was validated with calls to SMT solvers. The repeated calls to the SMT solvers were the dominating factor in the time required to infer contracts, and we have not yet devoted any effort to optimize this. Many of the minimization steps can be implemented using simple syntactic checks, and we are in the process of implementing and proving correct a minimizer in Coq that will allow us to dramatically reduce the number of SMT solver calls. Experimental results from our earlier work [1] in which we used only syntactic scans to minimize showed that inference for almost all the procedures could be completed in less than a second. Our approach is compositional which greatly aids scalability when considering the overall time requirements for a complete application.

6   Related Work

Bergeretti and Carré [8] present a compositional method for inferring and checking dependencies among variables in SPARK programs. That approach is flow-sensitive, unlike most security type systems [9] that rely on assigning a security level ("high" or "low") to each variable. Chapman and Hilton [10] present an approach, now implemented in the latest SPARK release, for extending SPARK information flow contracts with lattices of security levels and enhancing the SPARK Examiner accordingly.

Agreement assertions (inherently flow-sensitive) were introduced in [11] and later extended in [5] to introduce conditional agreement assertions (for a heap-manipulating language). In [1] that approach was applied to the (heap-free) SPARK setting and worked out extensively, with an algorithm for computing loop invariants and with reports from an implementation; then arrays were handled in subsequent work [2].

Our evidence-checker is an example of the proof-carrying code paradigm [12]; it is *foundational* [13] in that the rules used by the evidence checker are themselves proved sound with a machine-checked proof. Although the original PCC generated proofs mainly via type-checking, more recently the PCC paradigm has been extended to policies of mobile code concerning resource consumption and information flow [14,15]. Certificate generation for such systems was obtained by formalizing static analyses (refined type systems or abstract interpretation frameworks) either directly at the level of virtual machine code, or by providing compiler-mediated interpretations of appropriate high-level analyses [16,17,18]. Wildmoser and Nipkow developed verified VCGens for bytecode for a deeply embedded assertion language for bytecode [19]. In the context of abstract-interpretation-based PCC, Besson et al. [20] employed certificates in the form of strategies for (re-)recomputing fixed points at the consumer side.

Techniques for reducing the size of evidence representations using oracles [21] and small witnesses [22] developed into *reflective* PCC [15] where the evidence checker (or even a partial evidence reconstruction algorithm) is implemented in the tactic language of the proof assistant, and proved sound by the principle of reflection. We have found (cf. Section 4) that our current evidence checker permits this approach.

In addition to direct justification of static analyses wrt. operational semantics, several of the above-mentioned formalizations employ program logics and/or VCGen's as intermediate representations. In order to employ these for the verification of information flow, the relational nature of information flow security must be taken into account, either by direct use of relational program logics [23], or by suitable encodings [24,25] in nonrelational logics based on the idea of self-composition [26,27].

In contrast to (typically not foundationally validated) efforts to relax baseline security policies to more permissive notions (e.g. declassification), our conditional information flow analysis aims to improve the precision and trustworthiness of static analysis results for the baseline policy, in the setting of an existing domain-specific tool flow methodology. Dufay, Felty, and Matwin [28] and Terauchi and Aiken [29] provide tool support for the verification of noninterference based on self-composition. In [28], the Krakatoa/Why verification framework is extended by variable-agreement assertions and corresponding loop annotations, and emits verification conditions in Coq that are typically interactively discharged by the user. In [29], information inherent in type systems for noninterference is exploited to limit the application of the program-duplication to smaller subphrases, obtaining self-composed programs that are better amenable to fully automated state-space-exploring techniques. Neither system produces foundationally validated and independently checkable artefacts of evidence relating the source program to user-level specifications, and it is at present unclear whether either could be extended to support conditional information flow policies.

7 Conclusions and Future Work

By implementing an evidence emitting algorithm and an associated evidence checking framework in Coq, we have provided a solution that allows developers to work at source level to specify/check rich information flow contracts while still enabling machine-checked proofs that source code implementations conform to contracts. This work puts in place a crucial element of our larger vision for end-to-end security assurance – namely, the ability eventually to leverage our other work on formally verified compilers [30] to provide a tool chain that enables us to prove that *deployed executable code* conforms to complex information flow policies stated as source-level contracts. Our next steps include adding a higher-level information flow policy specification language on top of our framework, enlarging the subset of SPARK that our tools can handle, and engineering a connection to the CompCert verified compiler stack [31]. We are also working with our industrial partners to evaluate our tools on additional examples.

Acknowledgements. This work is funded in part by the Air Force Office of Scientific Research (FA9550-09-1-0138), and by Rockwell Collins whose engineers David Hardin, David Greve, Ray Richards, and Matt Wilding we would like to thank for feedback on earlier versions of this work. We would also like to thank the anonymous referees for useful and detailed comments.

References

1. Amtoft, T., Hatcliff, J., Rodríguez, E., Robby, Hoag, J., Greve, D.A.: Specification and Checking of Software Contracts for Conditional Information Flow. In: Cuellar, J., Sere, K. (eds.) FM 2008. LNCS, vol. 5014, pp. 229–245. Springer, Heidelberg (2008)
2. Amtoft, T., Hatcliff, J., Rodríguez, E.: Precise and Automated Contract-Based Reasoning for Verification and Certification of Information Flow Properties of Programs with Arrays. In: Gordon, A.D. (ed.) ESOP 2010. LNCS, vol. 6012, pp. 43–63. Springer, Heidelberg (2010)
3. Barnes, J., Chapman, R., Johnson, R., Widmaier, J., Cooper, D., Everett, B.: Engineering the Tokeneer enclave protection software. In: Proceedings of the IEEE International Symposium on Secure Software Engineering (ISSSE 2006). IEEE Press (2006)
4. Amtoft, T., Dodds, J., Zhang, Z., Appel, A., Beringer, L., Hatcliff, J., Ou, X., Cousino, A.: A certificate infrastructure for machine-checked proofs of conditional information flow (2012), http://santos.cis.ksu.edu/papers/Amtoft-al-POST12/
5. Amtoft, T., Banerjee, A.: Verification condition generation for conditional information flow. In: 5th ACM Workshop on Formal Methods in Security Engineering (FMSE 2007), pp. 2–11. George Mason University, ACM (2007)
6. Armand, M., Faure, G., Grégoire, B., Keller, C., Théry, L., Werner, B.: A Modular Integration of SAT/SMT Solvers to Coq through Proof Witnesses. In: Jouannaud, J.-P., Shao, Z. (eds.) CPP 2011. LNCS, vol. 7086, pp. 135–150. Springer, Heidelberg (2011)
7. Heitmeyer, C.L., Archer, M., Leonard, E.I., McLean, J.: Formal specification and verification of data separation in a separation kernel for an embedded system. In: 13th ACM Conference on Computer and Communications Security (CCS 2006), pp. 346–355 (2006)
8. Bergeretti, J.F., Carré, B.A.: Information-flow and data-flow analysis of while-programs. ACM Transactions on Programming Languages and Systems 7, 37–61 (1985)
9. Volpano, D.M., Smith, G.: A Type-Based Approach to Program Security. In: Bidoit, M., Dauchet, M. (eds.) CAAP 1997, FASE 1997, and TAPSOFT 1997. LNCS, vol. 1214, pp. 607–621. Springer, Heidelberg (1997)
10. Chapman, R., Hilton, A.: Enforcing security and safety models with an information flow analysis tool. ACM SIGAda Ada Letters XXIV, 39–46 (2004)
11. Amtoft, T., Banerjee, A.: Information Flow Analysis in Logical Form. In: Giacobazzi, R. (ed.) SAS 2004. LNCS, vol. 3148, pp. 100–115. Springer, Heidelberg (2004)

12. Necula, G.C.: Proof-carrying code. In: POPL 1997, pp. 106–119. ACM Press (1997)
13. Appel, A.W.: Foundational proof-carrying code. In: LICS 2001. IEEE Computer Society (2001)
14. Sannella, D., Hofmann, M., Aspinall, D., Gilmore, S., Stark, I., Beringer, L., Loidl, H.W., MacKenzie, K., Momigliano, A., Shkaravska, O.: Mobile resource guarantees. In: van Eekelen, M.C.J.D. (ed.) Revised Selected Papers from the Sixth Symposium on Trends in Functional Programming (TFP 2005), Intellect, pp. 211–226 (2007)
15. Barthe, G., Crégut, P., Grégoire, B., Jensen, T., Pichardie, D.: The MOBIUS Proof Carrying Code Infrastructure. In: de Boer, F.S., Bonsangue, M.M., Graf, S., de Roever, W.-P. (eds.) FMCO 2007. LNCS, vol. 5382, pp. 1–24. Springer, Heidelberg (2008)
16. Beringer, L., Hofmann, M., Momigliano, A., Shkaravska, O.: Automatic Certification of Heap Consumption. In: Baader, F., Voronkov, A. (eds.) LPAR 2004. LNCS (LNAI), vol. 3452, pp. 347–362. Springer, Heidelberg (2005)
17. Albert, E., Puebla, G., Hermenegildo, M.V.: Abstraction-Carrying Code. In: Baader, F., Voronkov, A. (eds.) LPAR 2004. LNCS (LNAI), vol. 3452, pp. 380–397. Springer, Heidelberg (2005)
18. Barthe, G., Pichardie, D., Rezk, T.: A Certified Lightweight Non-interference Java Bytecode Verifier. In: De Nicola, R. (ed.) ESOP 2007. LNCS, vol. 4421, pp. 125–140. Springer, Heidelberg (2007)
19. Wildmoser, M., Nipkow, T.: Asserting Bytecode Safety. In: Sagiv, M. (ed.) ESOP 2005. LNCS, vol. 3444, pp. 326–341. Springer, Heidelberg (2005)
20. Besson, F., Jensen, T.P., Pichardie, D.: Proof-carrying code from certified abstract interpretation and fixpoint compression. Theor. Comput. Sci. 364, 273–291 (2006)
21. Necula, G.C., Rahul, S.P.: Oracle-based checking of untrusted software. In: POPL 2001, pp. 142–154 (2001)
22. Wu, D., Appel, A.W., Stump, A.: Foundational proof checkers with small witnesses. In: Proceedings of the 5th International ACM SIGPLAN Conference on Principles and Practice of Declarative Programming (PPDP 2003), pp. 264–274. ACM (2003)
23. Benton, N.: Simple relational correctness proofs for static analyses and program transformations. In: Jones, N.D., Leroy, X. (eds.) POPL 2004, pp. 14–25. ACM (2004)
24. Beringer, L., Hofmann, M.: Secure information flow and program logics. In: CSF 2007, pp. 233–248. IEEE Computer Society (2007)
25. Beringer, L.: Relational Decomposition. In: van Eekelen, M., Geuvers, H., Schmaltz, J., Wiedijk, F. (eds.) ITP 2011. LNCS, vol. 6898, pp. 39–54. Springer, Heidelberg (2011)
26. Darvas, Á., Hähnle, R., Sands, D.: A Theorem Proving Approach to Analysis of Secure Information Flow. In: Hutter, D., Ullmann, M. (eds.) SPC 2005. LNCS, vol. 3450, pp. 193–209. Springer, Heidelberg (2005)
27. Barthe, G., D'Argenio, P.R., Rezk, T.: Secure information flow by self-composition. In: 17th IEEE Computer Security Foundations Workshop (CSFW-17 2004), pp. 100–114. IEEE Computer Society (2004)
28. Dufay, G., Felty, A.P., Matwin, S.: Privacy-Sensitive Information Flow with JML. In: Nieuwenhuis, R. (ed.) CADE 2005. LNCS (LNAI), vol. 3632, pp. 116–130. Springer, Heidelberg (2005)
29. Terauchi, T., Aiken, A.: Secure Information Flow as a Safety Problem. In: Hankin, C., Siveroni, I. (eds.) SAS 2005. LNCS, vol. 3672, pp. 352–367. Springer, Heidelberg (2005)
30. Appel, A.W.: Verified Software Toolchain. In: Barthe, G. (ed.) ESOP 2011. LNCS, vol. 6602, pp. 1–17. Springer, Heidelberg (2011)
31. Leroy, X.: Formal certification of a compiler back-end or: programming a compiler with a proof assistant. In: POPL 2006, pp. 42–54 (2006)

PTaCL: A Language for Attribute-Based Access Control in Open Systems

Jason Crampton[1] and Charles Morisset[1,2,*]

[1] Information Security Group,
Royal Holloway, University of London,
Egham, Surrey TW20 0EX, U.K.
Jason.Crampton@rhul.ac.uk
[2] Security Group,
Istituto di Informatica e Telematica (IIT), C.N.R.,
Via Giuseppe Moruzzi, 1, 56124 Pisa, Italy
Charles.Morisset@iit.cnr.it

Abstract. Many languages and algebras have been proposed in recent years for the specification of authorization policies. For some proposals, such as XACML, the main motivation is to address real-world requirements, typically by providing a complex policy language with somewhat informal evaluation methods; others try to provide a greater degree of formality – particularly with respect to policy evaluation – but support far fewer features. In short, there are very few proposals that combine a rich set of language features with a well-defined semantics, and even fewer that do this for authorization policies for attribute-based access control in open environments. In this paper, we decompose the problem of policy specification into two distinct sub-languages: the policy target language (PTL) for target specification, which determines when a policy should be evaluated; and the policy composition language (PCL) for building more complex policies from existing ones. We define syntax and semantics for two such languages and demonstrate that they can be both simple and expressive. PTaCL, the language obtained by combining the features of these two sub-languages, supports the specification of a wide range of policies. However, the power of PTaCL means that it is possible to define policies that could produce unexpected results. We provide an analysis of how PTL should be restricted and how policies written in PCL should be evaluated to minimize the likelihood of undesirable results.

Keywords: Target, Policy, Composition, PCL, PTL, PTaCL.

1 Introduction

One of the fundamental security services in computer systems is *access control*, a mechanism for constraining the interaction between (authenticated) users and

* Work partially supported by EU FP7-ICT project NESSoS (Network of Excellence on Engineering Secure Future Internet Software Services and Systems) under the grant agreement n. 256980.

P. Degano and J.D. Guttman (Eds.): POST 2012, LNCS 7215, pp. 390–409, 2012.

protected resources. Generally, access control is implemented by an authorization service, which includes an *authorization decision function* (ADF) for deciding whether a user request to access a resource (an "access request") should be permitted or not. In its simplest form an authorization decision function either returns an allow or a deny decision.

Many access control models and systems are *policy-based*, in the sense that a request for access to protected resources is evaluated with respect to a policy that defines which requests are authorized. Many languages have been proposed for the specification of authorization policies, perhaps the best known being XACML [3,8,14]. However, it is generally acknowledged that XACML suffers from having poorly defined and counterintuitive semantics [12,13]. More formal approaches have provided well-defined semantics and typically use "policy operators" to construct complex policies from simpler sub-policies [1,4,17]. However, such approaches tend to support fewer "features" than XACML.

In a "closed" information system – one in which all authorized users are known to the system – it is possible to authenticate users of the system and to ascribe an identity to processes associated with those users. Hence, access control decisions and the policies that inform those decisions can be based on user identifiers.

Increasingly, it is necessary to define authorization policies for "open" systems, where we must make access control decisions based on user attributes, rather than identities. Hence, access request formats need to change from the user-centric subject-object-action triples of classical access control models [2,9], although such request formats are still widely used in the specification of access control models and authorization policy languages [3,4,8,14,17].

An authorization policy is typically defined by a target, a set of child policies and a decision-combining algorithm. The target, either implicitly or explicitly, identifies a set of requests. The policy is said to be "applicable" if the access request belongs to (or "matches") the target. If a policy is applicable, then its child policies are evaluated and the results returned by those child policies are combined using the decision-combining algorithm.

Informally, a policy may be regarded as a tree, in which the leaf nodes return a "conclusive" decision (allow or deny). If a request does not match the target of a leaf policy then the evaluation of that policy returns a "not applicable" decision. Hence, the set of possible decisions is 3-valued.

However, it may be the case that it is not possible to evaluate request applicability: perhaps the simplest case arises when the request is malformed. But once the request format is extended to accommodate attribute-based access control, the problem of evaluating the applicability of a request becomes even more acute. In other words, the result of request applicability is not necessarily binary: in particular, we must include a value that represents that some error has occurred while trying to evaluate request applicability. Naturally, extending the set of results that can be returned when evaluating request applicability means that we need to reconsider policy evaluation.

We believe that existing proposals for authorization policy languages suffer from at least one of the following problems:

- no support for attribute-based requests (and hence attribute-based authorization policies);
- a lack of formality in the definition of target and policy evaluation, leading to ambiguity about the meaning of policies;
- a poor understanding of the way in which attribute-based requests, targets and policies interact.

Our main objective is to define a policy language that addresses the same problem space as XACML 3.0 [15] while retaining the formality of recent work on policy algebras [1,4,5,6,17]. XACML (eXtensible access control markup language) is a standardized language: XACML 2.0 was ratified in 2005; XACML 3.0 will add support for attribute-based access control and policy administration. More specifically, our objectives are:

- to define a request format that is appropriate for attribute-based authorization policies;
- to define a syntax for specifying policy targets;
- to formally define an evaluation method for those targets that is sufficiently robust to withstand deliberate attempts to exploit the greater freedom provided by our request format;
- to define a syntax for policies, which makes use of the policy target language;
- to formally define an evaluation method for those policies that is able to handle errors in target evaluation gracefully and securely.

In this paper, we develop two distinct languages for completely defining authorization policies. Roughly speaking, our goals are to combine support for the wide variety of policies that can be defined in more informal approaches such as XACML with the more formal semantics with which policy algebras are furnished. Our policy target language (PTL) provides a syntax for specifying policy targets, while our policy composition language (PCL), provides a language for combining policies (that is, constructing policy trees). Together, we call this PTaCL, read "p-tackle", to denote *policy target and composition language*. We also provide "authorization policy semantics", which enable us to ascribe a meaning to a policy for a given request. That meaning is determined by the target semantics and the composition semantics.

The main contribution of this work is therefore the definition of PTaCL, which, although far simpler syntactically than XACML 2.0 and 3.0, can express any desired target or policy, thanks to the functional completeness of PTL and PCL. We specify precisely how to evaluate any target and policy expressed in PTaCL, thus providing the basis for a low-level language into which XACML policies, for example, could be compiled and evaluated. Moreover, we identify the problem of *attribute-hiding attacks*, where a user deliberately suppresses attributes in order to gain favorable authorization decisions, and we propose different restrictions on the definition of a target in order to avoid such attacks. We note that such attacks are not peculiar to PTaCL; they are a potential problem for any attribute-based access control mechanism. We believe we are the first to identify and, therefore, propose mitigation strategies for, this type of attack.

In the next section, we define our request format and illustrate some of the challenges introduced by attribute-based access control. Then, in Section 3, we define the syntax and evaluation method for targets. In Section 4, we define policy syntax and evaluation. In this section, we reflect on the problems that might arise because of the more flexible request format we use and explain how those problems inform the development of PTaCL. We also explain how PTL can be restricted to provide certain guarantees about the decisions returned by policy evaluation, thereby addressing the problem of attribute-hiding attacks. We conclude the paper with a discussion of related work and some ideas for future work.

2   Attribute-Based Requests

The simplest authorization policy languages assume that an access request comprises three identifiers: the requester, the resource to which access is requested, and the type of the requested interaction (such as read, write, etc), often known as subject, object and action, respectively. The authorization decision function (ADF) associated with a given language will take that request and an authorization policy as input and return a decision. For more complex languages, the ADF may require additional information, such as the roles or security groups associated with a user, in order to make a decision. These attributes may be "pushed" with the request or "pulled" from authoritative information sources (such as the policy information points in the XACML architecture). The increasingly "open" nature of distributed computer systems, where the user population is not known in advance, requires authorization languages that are not based on user identities. For this reason, attribute-based access control (ABAC) and languages that support ABAC are expected to become increasingly important.

PTaCL comprises two sub-languages: PTL for target specification and PCL for policy specification. Policies written in PTaCL are used to evaluate access requests that may contain arbitrary attributes associated with users, resources and actions.

We model a request as a set of name-value pairs, where each name specifies an attribute and each value specifies a value for the corresponding attribute. In the simplest situation, for example, we might have attribute names such as subject, object and action, and a request might have the form

$$\{(\texttt{subject}, \mathit{alice}), (\texttt{object}, \mathit{test.txt}), (\texttt{action}, \mathit{read})\}.$$

The above request is no different from the usual view of an access request as a subject-object-action triple. However, the request format described above is not limited to requests of this form and can be used to represent requests that do not contain identifiers for subjects, objects and actions. We could, for example, have a request of the form

$$\{(\texttt{role}, \mathit{nurse}), (\texttt{object}, \mathit{test.txt}), (\texttt{action}, \mathit{read})\}.$$

An attribute name may appear multiple times in the request; the above request could include multiple role identifiers, for example. The use of some set of name-value pairs, rather than the fixed format subject-object-action triples (as used in XACML 2.0 [14] and most other policy languages), means that we can specify targets and requests with greater freedom than is usually the case. However, the greater freedom with which requests can be specified also means that we have to take greater care in the specification of policies.

As an example, we consider a simplified instance of the Chinese Wall policy, where a company A defines a policy to protect a set of confidential resources. Informally, this policy states that if a user is working for A, then she can access the (confidential) resource o, unless she is also working for B, the direct competitor of A, in which case the access is denied. We consider the following requests:

$$r_1 = \{(\texttt{employer}, A), (\texttt{confidential}, true)\};$$
$$r_2 = \{(\texttt{employer}, A), (\texttt{employer}, B), (\texttt{confidential}, true)\};$$
$$r_3 = \{(\texttt{confidential}, false)\};$$
$$r_4 = \{(\texttt{confidential}, true)\}.$$

Informally, an ABAC policy defines a set of atomic policies (or rules), where each atomic policy describes the subset of requests to which it applies – the policy's *target* – and the decision to take when it is applicable. When a request does not belong to the policy's target, then this policy is non-applicable, which has a different meaning from saying that the request is denied. The decisions returned by the evaluation of the atomic policies are then combined together using decision combination operators.

For instance, the policy enforced by the company A should comprise two rules, the second of which is applicable to all requests and returns allow. The first rule is applicable if the request contains ($\texttt{confidential}$, *true*), and in this case, if the user works for A, then it is allowed, unless she also works for B, in which case it is denied. The two rules are combined using a deny-overrides combination operator. The first rule would not be applicable to request r_3 and hence the request would be allowed. The first rule would be applicable to the remaining requests. Therefore, the evaluation of r_1 would return allow, while the evaluation of request r_2 would return deny.

Note that if the user is able to *suppress* the element ($\texttt{employer}$, B) in r_2, then the resulting request would be allowed. We call such a situation a *partial attribute hiding attack*, where, by hiding some of her attributes, a user is able to obtain a more favorable authorization decision. A second possibility is for the user to suppress all the employer attributes. Hence, we might wish to insist that if the resource is confidential, then the request *must* contain information about the employer(s) of the requesting user, otherwise the evaluation of the request should fail. In particular, r_4 must not be allowed, returning either deny or some appropriate evaluation-error decision.

We now describe PTaCL, which provides mechanisms to tackle the issues raised by this simple example, in particular by considering attribute requests instead of subject-object-action requests; by distinguishing between optional and mandatory attributes; and by stating two properties of monotonicity, thus allowing the detection of policies vulnerable to partial attribute hiding attacks.

3   Targets

We first define a syntax for targets. Then, in Section 3.1, we will define how to evaluate a target with respect to a request. We define three types of *atomic target*:

- null_T is a target;
- n is a target, where n is an attribute name;
- (n, v, f) is a target, where n is an attribute name, v is an attribute value and f is a binary predicate.

The most usual predicate is likely to be a test for (string) equality, but other predicates, such as $\leqslant, <, \geqslant$ and $>$, are possible. For ease of exposition, we assume throughout that all attributes are of type string and that f is string equality; henceforth we omit f from the definition of an atomic target.

We build more complex targets by defining two binary target operators, and_T and or_T, and two unary target operators, opt_T and not_T. Let t, t_1 and t_2 be targets. Then the following terms are also targets:

$$\mathsf{opt}_T\, t, \quad \mathsf{not}_T\, t, \quad (t_1\, \mathsf{and}_T\, t_2) \quad \text{and} \quad (t_1\, \mathsf{or}_T\, t_2).$$

The operators opt_T and not_T bind more tightly than and_T and or_T: $\mathsf{opt}_T\, t\, \mathsf{and}_T\, t'$, for example, is interpreted as $(\mathsf{opt}_T\, t)\, \mathsf{and}_T\, t'$, rather than $\mathsf{opt}_T(t\, \mathsf{and}_T\, t')$. As we will see in Section 3.1, the semantics of or_T and and_T are provided by associative, commutative binary operators on the set of target evaluation decisions, so we can (and will) omit brackets from expressions of the form $(t_1\, \mathsf{or}_T\, (t_2\, \mathsf{or}_T \ldots \mathsf{or}_T\, t_k))$ and $(t_1\, \mathsf{and}_T\, (t_2\, \mathsf{and}_T \ldots \mathsf{and}_T\, t_k))$.

In Section 4, we will define similar operators for policies and use a subscript P to distinguish them from target operators. When no ambiguity can occur we will omit the subscripts T and P.

3.1   Evaluation

A target is evaluated with respect to a request, represented as a set of name-value pairs (as described in Section 2). Informally, a request is said to "match" an atomic target if the name of one of the attribute pairs in the request is the same as the name defined in the atomic target and the predicate f evaluated at v and the corresponding value in the request is true. If no such pair exists in the request, then the request does not match the target.

The "universal" target null is matched by all requests; the target n is matched by all requests that include an attribute pair (n, v) for any value v; the target (n, v) is matched by any request that includes the specific attribute pair (n, v). The target employer, for example, is matched by requests r_1 and r_2 defined in Section 2 but not by the requests r_3 and r_4.

⊓	1_T	0_T	$\perp_T$
1_T	1_T	0_T	$\perp_T$
0_T	0_T	0_T	$\perp_T$
$\perp_T$	$\perp_T$	$\perp_T$	$\perp_T$

(a)

⊔	1_T	0_T	$\perp_T$
1_T	1_T	1_T	$\perp_T$
0_T	1_T	0_T	$\perp_T$
$\perp_T$	$\perp_T$	$\perp_T$	$\perp_T$

(b)

$\tilde{\sqcap}$	1_T	0_T	$\perp_T$
1_T	1_T	0_T	$\perp_T$
0_T	0_T	0_T	0_T
$\perp_T$	$\perp_T$	0_T	$\perp_T$

(c)

$\tilde{\sqcup}$	1_T	0_T	$\perp_T$
1_T	1_T	1_T	1_T
0_T	1_T	0_T	$\perp_T$
$\perp_T$	1_T	$\perp_T$	$\perp_T$

(d)

X	$\neg X$	$\sim X$
1_T	0_T	1_T
0_T	1_T	0_T
$\perp_T$	$\perp_T$	0_T

(e)

Fig. 1. Binary and unary operators on the target decision set $\{1_T, 0_T, \perp_T\}$

In addition, we may wish to distinguish the case where the request does not include the attribute name at all from the case where the attribute name was found, but with a value that does not match. Consider the atomic target (employer, B): then request r_1 has a matching attribute name (employer), but $A \neq B$; in contrast, requests r_3 and r_4 do not include any matching attribute.

Informally, a request must match both t_1 and t_2 for it to match target (t_1 and t_2), while a request is only required to match one of t_1 and t_2 for it to match target (t_1 or t_2). By default, a request is required to match a target t; we can relax this requirement, while retaining the possibility of matching t, by writing opt t.

More formally, we define the set of target evaluation decisions Dec_T to be $\{1_T, 0_T, \perp_T\}$, where $\perp_T$ denotes that a request does not include the attribute name, 1_T denotes that a request matches an atomic target, and 0_T denotes that a request includes the attribute name but the predicate doesn't hold.[1]

We define the binary operators $\sqcap$, $\sqcup$, $\tilde{\sqcap}$ and $\tilde{\sqcup}$ on $\{1_T, 0_T, \perp_T\}$ in Fig. 1. These operators correspond to the weak and strong Kleene operators [11], respectively. We also define two unary operators $\neg$ and $\sim$ in Fig. 1. Finally, we define the total order $1_T > 0_T > \perp_T$ on Dec_T and let $\dot{\sqcup}$ denote the least upper bound operator on this ordered set.

Given a request q, we write $[\![t]\!]_T(q)$ to denote the evaluation of t with respect to q. That is, $[\![t]\!]_T(q) \in \mathsf{Dec}_T$. As for target operators, we will omit the subscript T where no ambiguity can arise. First, we define, for all requests q and for all attributes n and all values v,

$$[\![\mathsf{null}]\!](q) = 1_T \qquad \text{and} \qquad [\![n]\!](\emptyset) = [\![(n,v)]\!](\emptyset) = \perp_T.$$

We then define the evaluation of targets n and (n, v) recursively.

$$[\![n]\!](\{(n',v')\} \cup q) = \begin{cases} 1_T & \text{if } n = n' \\ [\![n]\!](q \setminus \{(n',v')\}) & \text{otherwise.} \end{cases}$$

---

[1] We will use analogous notation for policy-evaluation decisions, where 1_P will denote an "allow" decision and 0_P will denote a "deny" decision. The symbol $\perp$ will be used to denote an evaluation error condition in the context of targets and "not-applicable" in the context of policies.

$$[\![(n,v)]\!](\{(n',v')\} \cup q) = \begin{cases} 1_T & \text{if } n = n', \, v = v' \\ 0_T \sqcup [\![(n,v)]\!](q) & \text{if } n = n', \, v \neq v' \\ [\![(n,v)]\!](q \setminus \{(n',v')\}) & \text{otherwise.} \end{cases}$$

Note that, for all q, $[\![n]\!](q)$ is either 1_T or $\perp_T$. In evaluating (n, v), we compare each element of the request with the atomic target and do one of the following: we return 1_T if a match is found; if the attribute name matches but the predicate doesn't hold then we record the fact that the attribute name matched and continue processing; otherwise, we simply continue processing.

Since $\sqcup$ is a supremum operator, it is commutative and associative and hence can be applied to any non-empty subset of Dec_T without ambiguity. Hence, for a non-empty request $q = \{(n_1, v_1), \dots (n_k, v_k)\}$, it is easy to see that we have

$$[\![n]\!](q) = \sqcup \{[\![n]\!](\{(n_i, v_i)\}) : 1 \leqslant i \leqslant k\};$$
$$[\![(n,v)]\!](q) = \sqcup \{[\![(n,v)]\!](\{(n_i, v_i)\}) : 1 \leqslant i \leqslant k\}.$$

In other words, we can evaluate the applicability of a request with respect to a target by splitting the request into single name-value pairs and evaluating each of these requests separately. This, in turn, suggests that the evaluation of requests can be parallelized, with different target evaluation functions (TEFs) specialized for the evaluation of requests for particular attribute names.

We then define the semantics of $\mathsf{not}\,t$, $\mathsf{opt}\,t$, t_1 and t_2 and t_2 or t_2 as follows:

$$[\![\mathsf{not}\,t]\!](q) = \neg[\![t]\!](q) \qquad [\![t_1 \text{ and } t_2]\!](q) = [\![t_1]\!](q) \sqcap [\![t_2]\!](q)$$
$$[\![\mathsf{opt}\,t]\!](q) = \sim[\![t]\!](q) \qquad [\![t_1 \text{ or } t_2]\!](q) = [\![t_1]\!](q) \sqcup [\![t_2]\!](q)$$

Here we see that opt modifies the target t by converting a $\perp_T$ decision (missing attribute) into a 0_T decision (attribute not matched). The target $\mathsf{opt}\,\mathsf{role}$, for example, evaluates to 1_T if a request contains a role attribute pair and evaluates to 0_T (rather than $\perp_T$) if no such pair is present in the request.

It is important to note that the semantics for the and operator are provided by weak conjunction $\sqcap$, not by $\tilde{\sqcap}$. The point here is that a target is specified as part of a policy and it should not be possible to force target evaluation to return 0_T when the target is a conjunction and at least one of the conjuncts is mandatory. (Had we combined targets using $\tilde{\sqcap}$, if t_1 were to evaluate to 0_T and t_2 were to evaluate to $\perp_T$, then $t_1 \tilde{\sqcap} t_2$ would evaluate to 0_T, not the desired $\perp_T$.)

3.2   Interface Targets

An atomic target of the form (n, v) requires that a particular attribute value must appear in a request (to obtain a match). Such targets are little different conceptually from those defined in XACML 2.0 and other authorization languages and are, therefore, of limited novelty or interest here.[2]

---

[2] Targets in XACML 2.0 only consider subjects, objects and actions; targets in the draft XACML 3.0 do consider other types of attributes.

In contrast, targets of the form n, have not previously been seen in the literature on authorization languages (to the best of our knowledge). A target of the form n can be used to define a target that enforces a "request interface": a target of the form

$$\mathsf{opt}(n_1 \text{ and } n_2 \text{ and } \ldots \text{ and } n_k),$$

for example, only matches a request that contains particular named attributes (corresponding to $n_1, \ldots, n_k$); the evaluation of a request that doesn't contain all the required attributes will evaluate to 0_T (because of the opt). In this way, we can construct a target that "guards" conventional subject-object-action policies and others that can respond to requests containing other types of attributes.

More complex "mixed" interfaces can also be constructed. An access control list is a type of access control data structure that is widely used in operating systems. The target for a policy used to represent an access control list for object *test.txt* would have the form

$$\mathsf{opt}((\mathsf{object}, \textit{test.txt}) \text{ and } \mathsf{subject} \text{ and } \mathsf{action}),$$

so that only requests that specify the desired object as well as including some subject and action would match.

3.3   On Functional Completeness

By way of motivation, we first observe that it might be useful to be able to define "conditional" interface targets, where the presence of one attribute in a request requires the presence of some other attribute. Suppose, for example, we have two attribute names n_1 and n_2. If a request doesn't contain attribute n_1 then the evaluation of the target should be 0_T. If, however, a request does contain n_1 then it must contain n_2. In other words, we have the following "match table", where the row headers indicate the values taken by the evaluation of n_1 and the column headers indicate the values taken by n_2.

	1_T	$\perp_T$
1_T	1_T	$\perp_T$
$\perp_T$	0_T	0_T

By inspection of the match tables in Fig. 1, we see that the above table could be represented by the target $\sim x \,\tilde{\sqcap}\, y$, where x and y denote the evaluation of n_1 and n_2, respectively. However, the semantics of and are given by the operator $\sqcap$. Hence, it would be useful to demonstrate that our chosen target operators opt, not, or and and are functionally complete. In particular, we would prefer to define the interface target described above in terms of our existing operators, rather than having to introduce another type of target conjunction.

We now prove that for all n and any function $f : \mathrm{Dec}_T^n \to \mathrm{Dec}_T$, f can be constructed using the constants 1_T, 0_T and $\perp_T$ and the operators opt, not and or. We obtain this property by proving that the three-valued logic expressed over the set $\{0_T, 1_T, \perp_T\}$ and defined by the operators $\tilde{\sqcup}$, $\neg$ and $\sim$ is functionally complete, re-using a result of Jobe [10], stated below.

$\bullet$	3	2	1	E_1	E_2
3	3	2	1	3	1
2	2	2	1	1	2
1	1	1	1	2	3

(a) Over the set $\{3,2,1\}$

$\bullet$	1_T	$\perp_T$	0_T	E_1	E_2
1_T	1_T	$\perp_T$	0_T	1_T	0_T
$\perp_T$	$\perp_T$	$\perp_T$	0_T	0_T	$\perp_T$
0_T	0_T	0_T	0_T	$\perp_T$	1_T

(b) Over the set $\{1_T, \perp_T, 0_T\}$

Fig. 2. Jobe's 3-valued logic

Theorem 1 (Jobe 1962). *The three-valued logic E expressed over the set $\{1,2,3\}$ and defined by the operators $\bullet, E_1$ and E_2, given in Fig. 2(a), is functionally complete.*

Corollary 1. *The three-valued logic expressed over the set $\{0_T, 1_T, \perp_T\}$ and defined by the operators $\tilde{\sqcup}, \neg$ and $\sim$ is functionally complete.*

Proof. We first define the operator $\tilde{\sqcap}$ from $\tilde{\sqcup}$ and $\neg$: for any $X_1, X_2 \in \mathsf{Dec_T}$, $(X_1 \tilde{\sqcap} X_2) = \neg(\neg X_1 \tilde{\sqcup} \neg X_2)^3$.

We can clearly see from Fig. 2(b), that the operator $\tilde{\sqcap}$ is identical to $\bullet$ and $\neg$ is identical to E_1. Therefore, we only need to define a unary operator that swaps the values of 0_T and $\perp_T$ while leaving 1_T unchanged. We write $\updownarrow$ to denote such an operator. The table below demonstrates that $\updownarrow X$ is equivalent to $(X \tilde{\sqcup} \perp_T) \tilde{\sqcap} (\sim(X \tilde{\sqcup} \neg X))$.

X	$X \tilde{\sqcup} \perp_T$	$\neg X$	$X \tilde{\sqcup} \neg X$	$\sim(X \tilde{\sqcup} \neg X)$	$\updownarrow X$
1_T	1_T	0_T	1_T	1_T	1_T
0_T	$\perp_T$	1_T	1_T	1_T	$\perp_T$
$\perp_T$	$\perp_T$	$\perp_T$	$\perp_T$	0_T	0_T

We can therefore conclude that the logic defined over the set $\{0_T, 1_T, \perp_T\}$ by the operators $\tilde{\sqcup}, \neg$ and $\sim$ is functionally complete.

For instance, the operator and can be built directly from or and not, since we can define the operator $\sqcap$ from $\tilde{\sqcup}$ and $\neg$. Indeed, for any $x, y \in \mathsf{Dec_T}$, we have the following equivalences:

$$x \sqcap y = (x \tilde{\sqcap} y) \tilde{\sqcup} ((x \tilde{\sqcap} \neg x) \tilde{\sqcup} (y \tilde{\sqcap} \neg y))$$
$$x \sqcup y = (x \tilde{\sqcup} y) \tilde{\sqcap} ((x \tilde{\sqcup} \neg x) \tilde{\sqcap} (y \tilde{\sqcup} \neg y))$$

We also have $x \dot{\sqcup} y = (x \tilde{\sqcup} (\sim y)) \tilde{\sqcap} ((\sim x) \tilde{\sqcup} y)$, where $\dot{\sqcup}$ is the supremum operator used to define the evaluation of an atomic target.

---

[3] Note that we also have the expected equivalence $(X_1 \tilde{\sqcup} X_2) = \neg(\neg X_1 \tilde{\sqcap} \neg X_2)$.

4   Policies

PTaCL policies are defined inductively. Let $d \in \{1_P, 0_P\}$, and let p, p_1 and p_2 be policies. Then

- d is a policy;
- $\text{not}_P \, p$ – the *negation* of policy p – is a policy, which returns 1_P if p returns 0_P and vice versa;
- $\text{dbd}_P \, p$ – the *deny-by-default* of policy p – is a policy, which returns 1_P if p returns 1_P and returns 0_P otherwise;
- $p_1 \, \text{and}_P \, p_2$ – the *conjunction* of two policies p_1 and p_2 – is a policy;
- (t, p) – the *restriction* of policy p to a target t – is a policy.

We discuss policy evaluation in detail in Section 4.1.

A *policy tree* is a convenient way of visualizing a policy and can be constructed recursively from a policy. The policy d is represented as a tree comprising a single node. The policy $p_1 \, \text{and}_P \, p_2$ is represented as a tree comprising a root node labelled and_P and two child sub-trees representing p_1 and p_2. Policies of the form (t, p), $\text{dbd}_P \, p$ and $\text{not}_P \, p$ are represented as trees comprising a root node labelled t, dbd_P and not_P, respectively, a single child sub-tree representing p. An illustrative policy tree representing the policy

$$\text{dbd}_P(t_5, \text{not}_P(t_3, (t_1, 1_P) \, \text{and}_P \, (t_2, 0_P)) \, \text{and}_P \, (t_4, 1_P))$$

is shown in Fig. 3(a) (on page 402). To save space, we have "absorbed" the nodes labelled and_P into their respective parents (t_3 and t_5).

4.1   Policy Evaluation

The evaluation of a policy with respect to a request q returns $\perp_P$ if the policy is not applicable to the request: that is, the evaluation of the policy's target with respect to q returned 0_T. However, it may be the case that the evaluation of a target returns neither 1_T nor 0_T, instead returning $\perp_T$. The possibility of target evaluation failing is considered in XACML [14] and in the work of Li *et al.* [12] and of Crampton and Huth [6]. The methods used to handle such failures assume that target evaluation failures arise because of unexpected failures in hardware, software or network connectivity and, accordingly, make a best effort to construct a conclusive decision for the request.

Our target language is expressly designed to support flexible request formats for open environments. As a result, our language explicitly includes the possibility that target evaluation may not be possible (if, for example, attributes are missing). Hence, target evaluation may fail, not because of "benign" failures, but because a user may withhold attributes in an attempt to force an error in target evaluation and thereby circumvent policy evaluation. Therefore, we must ensure that no advantage is gained by a malicious user who deliberately suppresses information when making an access request.[4]

---

[4] We also note the possibility that the user may not wish to divulge certain attributes when making an application request.

Our approach is to consider all possible decisions that might have arisen had target evaluation not failed. In other words, policy evaluation may return a set of decisions. We shall see that imposing appropriate restrictions on targets and using a "conservative" method of deriving a single decision from a set of decisions, will enable us to guarantee that a malicious user obtains no advantage by withholding attribute information.

We recall the operators $\neg$, $\sim$ and $\tilde{\sqcap}$ on $\mathsf{Dec_T}$ (as shown in Fig. 1) and define the same operators on $\mathsf{Dec_P} = \{1_\mathsf{P}, 0_\mathsf{P}, \bot_\mathsf{P}\}$. We extend the unary operators to $X \subseteq \mathsf{Dec_P}$, writing $\neg X$ to denote the set $\{\neg x : x \in X\}$ and $\sim X$ to denote the set $\{\sim x : x \in X\}$; and we extend $\tilde{\sqcap}$ on $\mathsf{Dec_P}$ to sets $X, Y \subseteq \mathsf{Dec_P}$, writing $X \tilde{\sqcap} Y$ to denote the set $\{x \tilde{\sqcap} y : x \in X, y \in Y\}$.

Informally, the evaluation of targeted policy (t, p) for a request q proceeds in the following way.

1. If t evaluates to 1_T, we then inductively evaluate p (see below)
2. If t evaluates to 0_T, we return $\{\bot_\mathsf{P}\}$
3. Otherwise, we evaluate p and take the union of the resulting set of decisions with $\{\bot_\mathsf{P}\}$[5]

We write $\llbracket p \rrbracket_\mathsf{P}(q)$ to denote the evaluation of policy p with respect to a request q, where

$$\llbracket d \rrbracket_\mathsf{P}(q) = \{d\};$$
$$\llbracket \mathsf{not_P}\, p \rrbracket_\mathsf{P}(q) = \neg(\llbracket p \rrbracket_\mathsf{P}(q));$$
$$\llbracket \mathsf{dbd_P}\, p \rrbracket_\mathsf{P}(q) = \sim(\llbracket p \rrbracket_\mathsf{P}(q))$$
$$\llbracket (p_1\ \mathsf{and_P}\ p_2) \rrbracket_\mathsf{P}(q) = \llbracket p_1 \rrbracket_\mathsf{P}(q) \tilde{\sqcap} \llbracket p_2 \rrbracket_\mathsf{P}(q);$$

$$\llbracket (t, p) \rrbracket_\mathsf{P}(q) = \begin{cases} \llbracket p \rrbracket_\mathsf{P}(q) & \text{if } \llbracket t \rrbracket_\mathsf{T}(q) = 1_\mathsf{T}, \\ \{\bot_\mathsf{P}\} & \text{if } \llbracket t \rrbracket_\mathsf{T}(q) = 0_\mathsf{T}, \\ \{\bot_\mathsf{P}\} \cup \llbracket p \rrbracket_\mathsf{P}(q) & \text{otherwise.} \end{cases}$$

Consider the policy depicted in Fig. 3(a) and suppose that $\llbracket t_1 \rrbracket(q) = \llbracket t_4 \rrbracket(q) = \llbracket t_5 \rrbracket(q) = 1_\mathsf{T}$, $\llbracket t_2 \rrbracket(q) = 0_\mathsf{T}$ and $\llbracket t_3 \rrbracket(q) = \bot_\mathsf{T}$. The evaluation of this policy is shown in Fig. 3(c). Note that the evaluation of the sub-tree with root t_3 considers the union of two sets of decisions because $\llbracket t_3 \rrbracket(q) = \bot_\mathsf{T}$. Note also that the strong conjunction $\tilde{\sqcap}$ has the effect of preferring the $\bot_\mathsf{P}$ decision to the 1_P decision. For those familiar with previous related work, this may seem an unusual way in which to combine policy decisions. We discuss this in more detail in the next section and, in Section 4.3, we will discuss ways in which more familiar decision-combining operators can be defined. Finally, note that the policy does evaluate to a single decision (0_P) for this request, although there is no reason in general for this to occur. However, it is easy to establish the following result.

Lemma 2. *Let p be a policy whose policy tree contains targets $t_1, \ldots, t_k$ and let q be a request. If $\llbracket t_i \rrbracket(q) \neq \bot_\mathsf{T}$ for all i, then $\llbracket p \rrbracket(q) = \{x\}$ for some $x \in \mathsf{Dec_P}$.*

---

[5] In other words, the evaluation of p in this case considers the decisions that would have been returned if the request had been applicable and if the request had not been applicable.

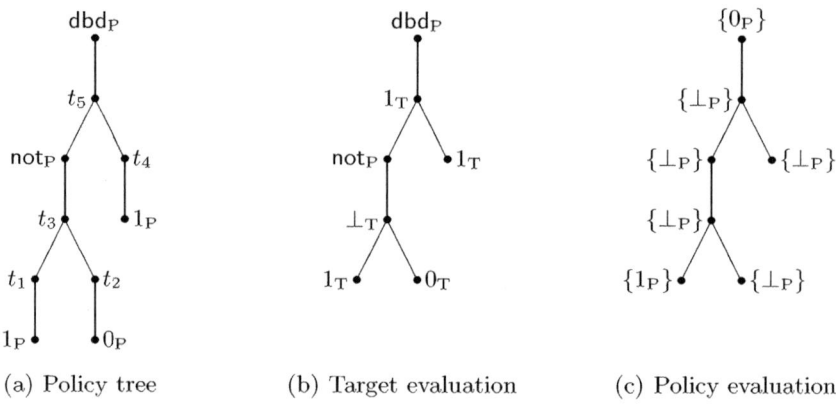

(a) Policy tree   (b) Target evaluation   (c) Policy evaluation

Fig. 3. Evaluating a PTaCL policy

In other words, if the applicability of all targets referenced by a policy can be determined for a request q, our evaluation semantics will return a unique authorization decision. The proof is a straightforward induction on the depth of the policy tree.

Finally, we note that the functional completeness for the target language also holds for our policy language, because opt_T and dbd_P have identical properties, as do not_T and not_P. However, it is also important to realize that the interpretation of $\perp_T$ and $\perp_P$ are quite different: the former indicates that the request supplied insufficient information to evaluate target applicability, whereas $\perp_P$ indicates that a policy is irrelevant to the evaluation of a request. Henceforth, we will omit the subscript from $[\![\cdot]\!]_P$ and the PTL operators, although, for clarity, we will retain the subscripts on decisions.

4.2   On the Non-monotonicity of Targets

The language we use for targets and the way in which targets are evaluated means that, for some target t, there may exist requests q and q' such that $q' \subseteq q$, $[\![t]\!](q') = 0_T$ and $[\![t]\!](q) = 1_T$. This feature of the language means that withholding attributes may provide some advantage to a malicious user: if we have a policy $p = (t, p')$ such that $[\![p']\!](q) = 0_P$, and $[\![t]\!](q) = 1_T$, then $[\![p]\!](q) = 0_P$; if, however, $[\![t]\!](q) = 0_T$, then $[\![p]\!](q) = \perp_P$. In other words, it might be possible for a malicious user to turn a 0_P decision into a $\perp_P$ decision by suppressing certain attributes. For brevity, we refer to this as the non-monotonicity of targets. Hence, we might reasonably regard $\perp_P$ as a potentially dangerous policy decision. (This view of $\perp_P$ is quite different from the interpretation used by other policy languages and algebras.) It is this view that informs our use of $\tilde{\sqcap}$ to combine policy decisions, which means that $\perp_P \tilde{\sqcap} 1_P$ is defined to be $\perp_P$ rather than 1_P.

Similarly, a user can force a target to evaluate to $\perp_T$ (rather than 0_T or 1_T) by withholding attributes. It is for this reason, that policy evaluation considers the possibility that a target might have been matched or not matched when target evaluation returns $\perp_T$.

Following from the above discussion, we would like to prove a result of the form: *Let p be a policy whose policy tree contains targets $t_1, \ldots, t_k$ and let q be a request. Then for any $q' \subseteq q$, $[\![p]\!](q) \subseteq [\![p]\!](q')$.* Informally, this result states that if a request contains less information, then the result of evaluating the policy is more uncertain. Then the authorization decision point can have a decision-set "resolution strategy" that returns a single final decision. Such a strategy should be "conservative" in the sense that the larger decision sets should be treated with more caution. The obvious strategy of this nature is: for $X \subseteq \text{Dec}_P$, we return 1_P if $X = \{1_P\}$ and 0_P otherwise.

However, it is easy to see that the above result does not hold, because of the functional completeness of our target language. In particular, we can create an operator $\oplus$ such that $\perp_T \oplus \perp_T = 1_T$ and $1_T \oplus \perp_T = \perp_T$. Now consider the target $t = (n_1, v_1) \oplus (n_2, v_2)$, and the requests $q_1 = \{(n_1, v_1)\}$ and $q_2 = \{\}$. Then

$$[\![t]\!](q_1) = 1_T \oplus \perp_T = \perp_T \quad \text{and} \quad [\![t]\!](q_2) = \perp_T \oplus \perp_T = 1_T.$$

Now consider the policy $p = (t, 1_P)$: we have $[\![p]\!](q_1) = \{\perp_P, 1_P\}$ and $[\![p]\!](q_2) = \{1_P\}$, providing a counter-example to the desired result. In other words, there are good reasons to restrict our target language so that only "well-behaved" targets can be defined. Specifically, we would like to restrict our target language so that all targets have the following property:

Definition 3. *A target t is* monotonic *if for all requests q and for every $q' \subseteq q$, $[\![t]\!](q') \in \{\perp_T, [\![t]\!](q)\}$.*

Then we have the following result (all the proofs of this paper are given in [7] and have been encoded in the proof assistant Isabelle/Isar[6]).

Theorem 4. *Let p be a policy whose policy tree contains* monotonic *targets $t_1, \ldots, t_k$ and let q be a request. Then for any $q' \subseteq q$, $[\![p]\!](q) \subseteq [\![p]\!](q')$.*

The obvious questions to ask now are: Which of our target operators are monotonic? And does composition of monotonic target operators preserve monotonicity?

We say that an operator is monotonic if, given monotonic targets as inputs, it returns a monotonic target. We prove in [7] that the operators not, and and or are monotonic, as well as the operators corresponding to $\bar{\sqcap}$ and $\sqcup$. However, the operator opt is not monotonic, since it can transform a $\perp_T$ into a 0_T.

Unfortunately (and somewhat unexpectedly), an atomic target is not, in general, monotonic. To see this, note that a request can contain several pairs with the same attribute name. (A request might, for example, enumerate all the roles with which the requester is associated.) Removing one occurrence from this set of pairs can change the evaluation of the request from 1_T to 0_T. This situation corresponds to a partial hiding of attribute values: that is, the ability for a user or an attribute server to remove only some values for a given attribute. In practice,

---

[6] http://isg.rhul.ac.uk/~jason/isabelle/ptacl.thy

such a situation is quite hard to detect and to prevent. However, let us assume that an attribute server works in an "all-or-nothing mode": that is, either it returns all the values for a given attribute, or none. With this assumption, for two requests q and q' such that $q' \subseteq q$ and for any attribute name n such that $(n, v) \in q'$ and $(n, v') \in q$, then $(n, v') \in q'$. With such an assumption, it is easy to see that any atomic target is monotonic, and it follows that any target built using the operators and, or and not is monotonic.

Such an assumption might not always hold, in particular when there is little control over the attribute servers. Therefore, we now consider an alternative, weaker notion of monotonicity, defined below.

Definition 5. *A target t is* weakly monotonic *if for all requests q and for every $q' \subseteq q$, $[\![t]\!](q') \preccurlyeq [\![t]\!](q)$, where we define $\bot_T \prec 0_T \prec 1_T$.*

The operators $\sim, \sqcap, \sqcup$ and $\tilde{\sqcup}$ preserve the weak monotonicity, as proven in [7], but the operators $\neg$ and $\tilde{\sqcap}$ do not. Moreover, since any atomic target is clearly weakly monotonic, any target built using any combination from the operators $\sim, \sqcap, \sqcup$ and $\tilde{\sqcup}$ is also weakly monotonic. Although we cannot prove a result as strong as Theorem 4, we can prove the following result (the proof of which can be found in [7]).

Theorem 6. *Let p be a policy whose policy tree contains weakly monotonic targets $t_1, \ldots, t_k$ and let q be a request.*
  1. *If p is constructed from the operators* not *and* and*, then for any $q' \subseteq q$, if $[\![p]\!](q') = \{d\}$, with $d \in \{1_P, 0_P\}$, then $[\![p]\!](q) = [\![p]\!](q')$.*
  2. *If p is constructed from the operators* dbd *and* and*, then for any $q' \subseteq q$, if $[\![p]\!](q') = \{1_P\}$, then $[\![p]\!](q) = \{1_P\}$.*

One consequence of Theorem 6 is that if a partial request is allowed, then the full request would have been allowed too, and therefore an attacker has no advantage in hiding some attribute values. However, this result requires a "conservative" resolution strategy: that is, request q is only allowed if and only if $[\![p]\!](q) = \{1_P\}$.

4.3   Decision Operators

We now discuss other ways in which decisions from sub-policies might be combined. Following Crampton and Huth [6], we restrict attention to *idempotent* and *well-behaved* decision operators.

Definition 7. *Let $\oplus : \text{Dec}_P \times \text{Dec}_P \to \text{Dec}_P$ be a decision operator.*
  - *If $x \oplus x = x$ for all $x \in \text{Dec}_P$, then we say $\oplus$ is* idempotent*.*
  - *If $x \oplus \bot_P = x = \bot_P \oplus x$ for all $x \in \text{Dec}_P$, then we say $\oplus$ is a $\cup$-operator.*
  - *If $x \oplus \bot_P = \bot_P = \bot_P \oplus x$ for all $x \in \text{Dec}_P$, then we say $\oplus$ is an $\cap$-operator.*
  - *We say $\oplus$ is* well-behaved *if it is either a $\cup$- or an $\cap$-operator.*

Informally, a ∪-operator ignores policies that evaluate to $\perp_P$ by returning a conclusive decision (that is, a decision that belongs to $\{1_P, 0_P\}$) if either operand returns a conclusive decision. XACML, for example, assumes that all operators are ∪-operators. In contrast, a ∩-operator only returns a conclusive decision if both arguments are conclusive decisions. An operator of this nature is used by Bonatti *et al.* in their policy algebra [4].

Intuitively, it seems reasonable to assume that a policy decision operator is idempotent: if two policies return the same decision d, then we would expect that the composition of those policies would also return d. An idempotent, well-behaved decision operator is uniquely defined by the choices of $x \oplus \perp_P$, $1_P \oplus 0_P$ and $0_P \oplus 1_P$: the remaining values are fixed because the operator is idempotent and well-behaved (as shown in Fig. 4 for an idempotent ∪-operator $\oplus$).

If we assume that $\oplus$ is commutative, then there are only three choices for an idempotent ∪-operator (and three choices for an idempotent ∩-operator). And if we assume that $1_P \oplus 0_P \in \{1_P, 0_P\}$, then there are only two choices for a commutative, idempotent ∪-operator; both these operators are shown in Fig. 4, labeled as $\text{and}_\cup$ and $\text{or}_\cup$. Analogous operators $\text{and}_\cap$ and $\text{or}_\cap$ can be defined by making the obvious adjustments to the bottom row and rightmost column of the tables for $\text{and}_\cup$ and $\text{or}_\cup$, respectively.

The operators $\text{and}_\cup$ and $\text{and}_\cap$ are rather similar to logical conjunction, while $\text{or}_\cup$ and $\text{or}_\cap$ are rather similar to logical disjunction, respectively. Our decision operators play a similar role to the conflict resolution strategies or policy-combining algorithms used in policy algebras and XACML. Such strategies are used to resolve discrepancies in the results returned by different sub-policies. In particular, $\text{and}_\cup$ has the same effect as the "deny-overrides" conflict resolution strategy: namely, if one sub-policy returns 0_P, then the combined decision is 0_P. Similarly, $\text{or}_\cup$ has the same effect as the "allow-overrides" strategy.

The most widely used non-commutative conflict resolution strategy is "first-applicable", which we denote by $\triangleright$. The operator $\triangleright$ is defined in Fig. 4(d): note, in particular, $1_P \triangleright 0_P = 1_P$ and $0_P \triangleright 1_P = 0_P$.[7] The first-applicable operator is commonly used in firewall rulesets as well as in policy algebras and XACML. The other idempotent, well-behaved, non-commutative operator such that $1_P \oplus 0_P \in \{1_P, 0_P\}$ and $0_P \oplus 1_P \in \{1_P, 0_P\}$ is what might be called "last-applicable", denoted by $\triangleleft$, where $x \triangleleft y = y$ if $y \in \{1_P, 0_P\}$ and is equal to x otherwise. This operator does not appear to be widely supported or used.

We now show how to define the operators $\text{or}_\cap$, $\text{and}_\cap$, $\text{or}_\cup$, $\text{and}_\cup$ and $\triangleright$ from the PTL operators not, dbd and and. Since the logic $(\{1_P, 0_P, \perp_P\}, \text{not}, \text{dbd}, \text{and})$ is functionally complete, we can directly reuse the definitions of the operators given in Fig. 1. Clearly, $\text{or}_\cap$ and $\text{and}_\cap$ are directly given by $\sqcup$ and $\sqcap$, respectively. Moreover, the operator $\text{or}_\cup$ corresponds to the supremum operator over the total order $1_P > 0_P > \perp_P$, so we can re-use the operator $\dot{\sqcup}$ defined in Section 3.3. The operator $\text{and}_\cup$ is defined as follows:

$$x \text{ and}_\cup y = \text{not}((\text{not } x) \text{ or}_\cup (\text{not } y))$$

---

[7] Note that a first-applicable ∩-operator is vacuous, as it would be equivalent to a unary, identity operator.

$\oplus$	1_P	0_P	$\perp_P$
1_P	1_P	x	1_P
0_P	y	0_P	0_P
$\perp_P$	1_P	0_P	$\perp_P$

(a) Idempotent

$and_\cup$	1_P	0_P	$\perp_P$
1_P	1_P	0_P	1_P
0_P	0_P	0_P	0_P
$\perp_P$	1_P	0_P	$\perp_P$

(b) Conjunction

$or_\cup$	1_P	0_P	$\perp_P$
1_P	1_P	1_P	1_P
0_P	1_P	0_P	0_P
$\perp_P$	1_P	0_P	$\perp_P$

(c) Disjunction

$\triangleright$	1_P	0_P	$\perp_P$
1_P	1_P	1_P	1_P
0_P	0_P	0_P	0_P
$\perp_P$	1_P	0_P	$\perp_P$

(d) First-applicable

Fig. 4. Decision tables for idempotent $\cup$-operators on $\{1_P, 0_P, \perp_P\}$

In order to define the operator $\triangleright$, we first introduce the operator abd ("allow-by-default"), which transforms $\perp_P$ into 1_P, and is defined by $\mathsf{abd}\,x = \mathsf{not}(\mathsf{dbd}(\mathsf{not}\,x))$. The definition of $\triangleright$ is then given by:

$$x \triangleright y = (\mathsf{abd}(x \,\tilde{\cup}\, (\mathsf{not}\,x))) \,\tilde{\cap}\, (x \,\mathsf{or}_\cup\, y)$$

Finally, $x \triangleleft y$ is equivalent to $y \triangleright x$. Henceforth, we will use the operators defined above as syntactic sugar. Notice that our definitions of $\mathsf{or}_\cup$, $\mathsf{and}_\cup$ and $\triangleright$ all require the three PTL operators for their construction. Hence, a policy containing the standard XACML operators does not satisfy the requirements of Theorem 6, so we need to rely on the all-or-nothing assumption.

Finally, we note that the operators and, $\mathsf{and}_\cup$ and $\mathsf{and}_\cap$ can be regarded as defining a greatest lower bound operator for suitable choices of ordering on Dec_P; similarly $\mathsf{or}_\cup$ and $\mathsf{or}_\cap$ define least upper bound operators. These orderings are summarized in Table 1.

Table 1. Decision operators and orderings on Dec_P

Operator	Ordering
and	$0_P < \perp_P < 1_P$
$and_\cup$	$0_P < 1_P < \perp_P$
$and_\cap$	$\perp_P < 0_P < 1_P$
$or_\cup$	$\perp_P < 0_P < 1_P$
$or_\cap$	$0_P < 1_P < \perp_P$

The fact that each of the orderings is a total order means that and, $\mathsf{and}_\cup$ and $\mathsf{and}_\cap$ take the minimum of their operands, while $\mathsf{or}_\cup$ and $\mathsf{or}_\cap$ take the maximum of their operands. This, in turn, means that all four operators can be extended to n-ary operators (for any natural number $n > 1$).

5   Related Work

It is important to note that PTaCL is neither intended to fix XACML nor to provide formal semantics for XACML policy evaluation. Rather, PTaCL is a language that seeks to provide rigorous, alternative solutions to the same problems that motivated the development of XACML. Our work is also influenced by the work of Li *et al.* [12] and of Crampton and Huth [6] on using a set of decisions, rather than a single decision, to define the result of policy evaluation.

Although there is a substantial body of work on policy specification [1,4,5,13,17], this prior work assumes a very restricted format for access requests and targets. To the best of our knowledge, there is no previous work on a formal language for target specification and evaluation, let alone the consideration of missing attributes names. Both the ratified standard XACML 2.0 [14] and the draft XACML 3.0 [15], acknowledge that attributes may be missing from a request. However, the treatment of target evaluation in such circumstances is, like much of the XACML standard, rather informal. Moreover, the XACML target syntax is unnecessarily complicated and does not support interface targets. Finally, the XACML target syntax only provides operators that are equivalent to the strong conjunction and strong disjunction (in the 3-value Kleene logic), thereby limiting the expressive power of XACML. On the other hand, the functional completeness of PTL means that any XACML target can be represented in PTL.

The work on policy algebras varies in the operators that are supported, the set of decisions that can arise as a result of policy evaluation, and the extent to which policy evaluation can cope with failures in target evaluation. Ni *et al.*, for example, provide a functional complete policy algebra [13], where policy evaluation returns a single decision from the set $\{1_P, 0_P, \perp_P\}$. The functional completeness of PCL means that we can express any operators that we might wish to. In particular, we can express all XACML policy-combining algorithms. Structurally, our atomic policies correspond to rules in XACML, while our policy trees correspond to policies and policy sets. Crampton and Huth [6] extend the work of Li *et al.* on policy evaluation in the presence of target evaluation failure [12], where policy evaluation returns a set of decisions. Our treatment of policy evaluation is rather similar to this earlier work, although the way in which we resolve a set of decisions to a single decision that is enforced by the AEF is completely different, due to the suspicion with which we choose to treat the $\perp_P$ decision.

An important contribution of this paper is the recognition that providing support for attribute-based access control and greater freedom for request formats leads to the potential for attribute hiding by malicious users. By manipulating requests in this way, it may be possible to circumvent the expected or intended policy semantics. Existing work that supports attribute-based access control, such as XACML 3.0 and that of Rao *et al.* [16], does not consider such possibilities and hence may be vulnerable to "attribute-hiding attacks". Consider, for example, the PTL policy $p = (1_P \text{ and}_\cup ((n, v), 0_P))$ – which corresponds to an XACML policy with two rules combined using the deny-overrides operator – and two requests $q = \{(n, v), (n, v')\}$ and $q' = \{(n, v')\}$. Then $[\![p]\!](q) = 0_P$ while $[\![p]\!](q') = 1_P$: that is, by hiding some information, a more favorable answer is obtained. Theorem 6 suggests that such behavior is to be expected because we require all three PTL operators to represent $\text{and}_\cup$.

6   Concluding Remarks

Attribute-based access control, rather than the traditional identity-based access control that is deployed extensively in closed systems, is likely to become increasingly important in loosely coupled and open computing environments. This paper introduces PTaCL, an expressive language for the definition of attribute-based authorization policies. PTaCL can represent all commonly used policy composition operators (indeed it can represent any desired operator) and, to the best of our knowledge, PTaCL is the first language with a concise syntax for policy targets and a precise semantics for their evaluation.

Nevertheless, PTaCL is rather simple syntactically, which enables us to identify and propose solutions to the problem of attribute hiding. Such an issue is problematic in the context of open and distributed systems, and is not addressed in the literature, which define composition operators to favor conclusive decisions over a not-applicable decision. Having identified the problem, we propose two approaches to address this issue, formally justifying each of them: either forbidding optional targets, assuming the attribute servers to work in an "all-or-nothing mode" and adopting a conservative evaluation; or constraining more strictly the definition of the targets and the definition of the policies. The second approach does not make any assumption about the behavior of the attribute servers, but the standard policy composition operators can no longer be used. We propose other operators that are resilient to attribute hiding and differ from the standard ones in the way in which they handle the not-applicable decision. These "new" operators actually correspond to the strong conjunction and strong disjunction defined in the original Kleene three-valued logic.

There are many opportunities for future work. Clearly, when the evaluation of a request returns more than one decision, it implies that some attributes are missing in the request, and PTaCL should be extended in order for the set of the decisions to also indicate which attributes are missing. Hence, the entity in charge of collecting the attributes, for instance the Context Handler in the XACML architecture. Hence, a useful extension to the operational semantics of PTaCL would be to extend the return type of PCL so that the response includes a list of missing attribute names. PCL can be similarly extended in order to support obligations, that can be returned in addition to a set of decisions (as in XACML).

These extensions naturally lead to the problem of understanding and formalizing the complete access control architecture, and in particular to the question of *attribute privacy*. Indeed, in practice, a reason for a missing attribute can be because the source responsible for providing its value considered that this value was too sensitive to be shared. In such a case, the evaluation of the policy, or part of it, needs to be delegated to the attribute source. However, the possible presence of multiple, sensitive and conflicting sources makes it a non-trivial problem to solve. We believe that by completely formalizing the notion of attribute and its treatment by the policy decision point, PTaCL paves the way to address the problem of attribute privacy.

References

1. Backes, M., Dürmuth, M., Steinwandt, R.: An Algebra for Composing Enterprise Privacy Policies. In: Samarati, P., Ryan, P.Y.A., Gollmann, D., Molva, R. (eds.) ESORICS 2004. LNCS, vol. 3193, pp. 33–52. Springer, Heidelberg (2004)
2. Bell, D., LaPadula, L.: Secure computer systems: Unified exposition and Multics interpretation. Technical Report MTR-2997, Mitre Corporation (1976)
3. Bertino, E., Castano, S., Ferrari, E.: Author-$\mathcal{X}$: A comprehensive system for securing XML documents. IEEE Internet Computing 5(3), 21–31 (2001)
4. Bonatti, P., De Capitani Di Vimercati, S., Samarati, P.: An algebra for composing access control policies. ACM Transactions on Information and System Security 5(1), 1–35 (2002)
5. Bruns, G., Huth, M.: Access-control policies via Belnap logic: Effective and efficient composition and analysis. In: Proceedings of the 21st IEEE Computer Security Foundations Symposium, pp. 163–176 (2008)
6. Crampton, J., Huth, M.: An Authorization Framework Resilient to Policy Evaluation Failures. In: Gritzalis, D., Preneel, B., Theoharidou, M. (eds.) ESORICS 2010. LNCS, vol. 6345, pp. 472–487. Springer, Heidelberg (2010)
7. Crampton, J., Morisset, C.: Ptacl: A language for attribute-based access control in open systems. CoRR, abs/1111.5767 (2011), http://arxiv.org/abs/1111.5767
8. Damiani, E., De Capitani di Vimercati, S., Paraboschi, S., Samarati, P.: A fine-grained access control system for XML documents. ACM Transactions on Information and System Security 5(2), 169–202 (2002)
9. Harrison, M., Ruzzo, W., Ullman, J.: Protection in operating systems. Communications of the ACM 19(8), 461–471 (1976)
10. Jobe, W.: Functional completeness and canonical forms in many-valued logics. Journal of Symbolic Logic 27(4), 409–422 (1962)
11. Kleene, S.: Introduction to Metamathematics. D. Van Nostrand, Princeton, NJ (1950)
12. Li, N., Wang, Q., Qardaji, W., Bertino, E., Rao, P., Lobo, J., Lin, D.: Access control policy combining: Theory meets practice. In: Proceedings of 14th ACM Symposium on Access Control Models and Technologies, pp. 135–144 (2009)
13. Ni, Q., Bertino, E., Lobo, J.: D-algebra for composing access control policy decisions. In: Proceedings of 2009 ACM Symposium on Information, Computer and Communications Security, pp. 298–309 (2009)
14. OASIS. eXtensible Access Control Markup Language (XACML) Version 2.0, OASIS Committee Specification (Tim Moses, editor) (2005)
15. OASIS. eXtensible Access Control Markup Language (XACML) Version 3.0, OASIS Committee Specification 01 (Erik Rissanen, editor) (2010)
16. Rao, P., Lin, D., Bertino, E., Li, N., Lobo, J.: An algebra for fine-grained integration of XACML policies. In: Proceedings of the 14th ACM Symposium on Access Control Models and Technologies, pp. 63–72. ACM, New York (2009)
17. Wijesekera, D., Jajodia, S.: A propositional policy algebra for access control. ACM Transactions on Information and System Security 6(2), 235–286 (2003)

A Core Calculus for Provenance

Umut A. Acar[1], Amal Ahmed[2], James Cheney[3], and Roly Perera[1]

[1] Max Planck Institute for Software Systems
{umut,rolyp}@mpi-sws.org
[2] Indiana University
amal@cs.indiana.edu
[3] University of Edinburgh
jcheney@inf.ed.ac.uk

Abstract. Provenance is an increasing concern due to the revolution in sharing and processing scientific data on the Web and in other computer systems. It is proposed that many computer systems will need to become provenance-aware in order to provide satisfactory accountability, reproducibility, and trust for scientific or other high-value data. To date, there is not a consensus concerning appropriate formal models or security properties for provenance. In previous work, we introduced a formal framework for provenance security and proposed formal definitions of properties called disclosure and obfuscation.

This paper develops a core calculus for provenance in programming languages. Whereas previous models of provenance have focused on special-purpose languages such as workflows and database queries, we consider a higher-order, functional language with sums, products, and recursive types and functions. We explore the ramifications of using traces based on operational derivations for the purpose of comparing other forms of provenance. We design a rich class of provenance views over traces. Finally, we prove relationships among provenance views and develop some solutions to the disclosure and obfuscation problems.

1 Introduction

Provenance, or meta-information about the origin, history, or derivation of an object, is now recognized as a central challenge in establishing trust and providing security in computer systems, particularly on the Web. Essentially, provenance management involves instrumenting a system with detailed monitoring or logging of auditable records that help explain how results depend on inputs or other (sometimes untrustworthy) sources. The security and privacy ramifications of provenance must be understood in order to safely meet the needs of users that desire provenance without introducing new security vulnerabilities or compromising the confidentiality of other users.

The lack of adequate provenance information can cause (and has caused) major problems, which we call *provenance failures* [11]. Essentially, a provenance failure can arise either from failure to *disclose* some key provenance information to users (for example, if a years-out-of-date story causes investors to panic about a company's financial stability [7]), or from failure to *obfuscate* some sensitive provenance information (for example, if a Word document is published with supposedly secret contributors' identities logged in its change history [27]). To address these problems, a number of forms

P. Degano and J.D. Guttman (Eds.): POST 2012, LNCS 7215, pp. 410–429, 2012.

of provenance have been proposed for different computational models, including *why* and *where* provenance [6], *dependency* provenance [9], and a variety of other ad hoc techniques [3,24].

Prior work on provenance and security. Our previous work [9] appears to have been the first to explicitly relate information-flow security to a form of provenance, called *dependency provenance*. Provenance has been studied in language-based security by Cirillo et al. [13] and by Swamy et al. [26,25]. Both focus on specifying and enforcing security policies involving provenance tracking alongside many other concerns, and not on defining provenance semantics or extraction techniques. Work on secure auditing [21,19] and expressive programming languages for security is also related, but this work focuses on explicitly manipulating proofs of authorization or evidence about protocol or program runs rather than automatically deriving or securing provenance information.

There is also some work directly addressing security for provenance [12,8,15]. Chong [12] gave candidate definitions of *data security* and *provenance security* using a trace semantics, based in part on an earlier version of our trace model. Davidson et al. [15] studied privacy for provenance in scientific workflows, focusing on complexity lower bounds. Cheney [8] gave an abstract framework for provenance, proposed definitions of properties called *obfuscation* and *disclosure*, and discussed algorithms and complexity results for instances of this framework including finite automata, workflows, and the semiring model of database provenance [18].

In this paper, we build on prior work on provenance security by studying the disclosure and obfuscation properties of different forms of provenance in the context of a higher-order, pure, functional language. To illustrate what we mean by provenance, we present examples of programming with three different forms of provenance in Transparent ML (TML), a prototype implementation of the ideas of this paper.

1.1 Examples

Where-provenance. Where-provenance [6,5] identifies at most one source location from which a part of the output was copied. For example, consider the following TML session:

```
- f [(1,2), (4,3), (5,6)];
val it = [(5,6), (3,4), (1,2)]
```

Without access to the source code, one can guess that f is doing something like

$$reverse \circ (map\ (\lambda(x,y).\text{if } x < y \text{ then } (x,y) \text{ else } (y,x)))$$

However, by providing where-provenance information, the system can explain whether the numbers in the result were copied from the input or constructed in some other way:

```
- trace (f [(1@L1,2@L2),(4@L3,3@L4),(5@L5,6@L6)]);
it = <trace> : ({L1:int,...}, (int*int) list) trace
- where it;
val it = [(5@L5,6), (3@L4,4), (1@L1,2)]
```

This shows that f contrives to copy the first elements of the returned pairs but construct the second components.

Dependency provenance. Dependency provenance [9] is an approach that tracks a set of all source locations on which a result depends. For example, if we have:

```
- g [(1,2,3), (4,5,6)];
val it = [6,6] : int list
```

we again cannot tell much about what g does. By tracing and asking for dependency provenance, we can see:

```
- trace (g [(1@L1,2@L2,3@L3),(4@L4,5@L5,6@L6)]);
val it = <trace> : ({L1:int,...}, int list) trace
- dependency it;
val it = [6@{L1,L2,L3}, 6@{L1,L2,L3}]
```

This suggests that g is simply summing the first triple and returning the result twice, without examining the rest of the list. We can confirm this as follows:

```
- trace (g ((1@L1,2@L2,3@L3)::[]@L));
val it = <trace> : ({L1:int,...}, int list) trace
- dependency it;
val it = [6@{L1,L2,L3}]
```

The fact that L does not appear in the output confirms that g does not look further into the list.

Expression provenance. A third common form of provenance is an expression graph or tree that shows how a value was computed by primitive operations. For example, consider:

```
- (h 3, h 4, h 5)
val it = (6,24,120);
```

We might conjecture that h is actually the factorial function. By tracing h and extracting expression provenance, we can confirm this guess (at least for the given inputs):

```
- trace (h (4@L));
val it = <trace> : ({L:int}, int) trace
- expression it;
val it = 24@{L * (L-1) * (L-2) * (L-3)  * 1}
```

In this case where-provenance and dependency provenance would be uninformative since the result is not copied from, and obviously depends on, the input.

This kind of provenance is used extensively in *workflow* systems often used in e-science [20], where the main program is a high-level process coordinating a number of external (and often concurrent) program or RPC calls, for example, image-processing steps or bulk data transformations, which we could model by adding primitive image-processing operations and types to our language. Thus, even though the above examples use fine-grained primitive operations, this model is also useful for coarse-grained provenance-tracking.

Provenance security. The three models of provenance above represent useful forms of provenance that might increase users' trust or confidence that they understand the results of a program. However, if the underlying data, or the structure of the computation, is sensitive, then making this information available may lead to inadvertent vulnerabilities, by making it possible for users to infer information they cannot observe directly. This is a particular problem if we wish to disclose part of the result of a program, and provenance that justifies part of the result, while keeping other parts of the program's execution, input, or output confidential. As a simple example, consider a program if $x \neq 1$ then (y, y) else (z, w). If x is sensitive, but z and w happen to both equal 42, then it is safe to reveal the result $(42, 42)$. However, any of the above forms of provenance make it possible to distinguish which branch was taken because the two different copies of 42 in z and w will have different provenance. Thus, if the provenance information is released then a principal can infer that the second branch was taken, and hence, $x = 1$. In technical terms, we cannot *disclose* any of the above forms of provenance for the result while *obfuscating* the fact that $x = 1$.

1.2 Summary

Contributions. In this paper, we build on, and refine, the provenance security framework previously introduced by Cheney [8]. We introduce a core language with replayable execution traces for a call-by-value, higher-order functional language, and make the following technical contributions:

– Refined definitions of obfuscation and disclosure (Sec. 2).
– A core calculus defining traced execution for a pure functional programming language (Sec. 3).
– A generic provenance extraction framework that includes several previously-studied forms of provenance as instances (Sec. 4).
– An analysis of disclosure and obfuscation guarantees provided by different forms of provenance, including techniques based on slicing execution traces (Sec. 5).

Outline. Section 2 briefly recapitulates the framework introduced by Cheney [8] and refines some definitions. We present the (standard) syntax and tracing semantics of TML in Section 3. In Section 4 we introduce a framework for querying and extracting provenance views from traces, including the three models discussed above. Section 5 presents our main results about disclosure, obfuscation, and trace slicing. Section 6 presents related work and Section 7 concludes.

2 Background

We recapitulate the main components of the provenance security framework of Cheney [8]. The framework assumes a given set of *traces* $\mathcal{T}$, together with a collection $\mathcal{Q}$ of possible *trace queries* $Q : \mathcal{T} \to \mathbb{B}$. These represent properties of traces that the system designer may want to protect or that legitimate users or attackers of the system may want to learn. In the previous paper, we considered refinements to take into account the knowledge of the principals about the possible system behaviors. In this paper, we assume that all traces $\mathcal{T}$ are considered possible by all principals, for simplicity.

For each principal A, fix a set Ω_A of the possible *provenance views* offered to A, and a function $P_A : \mathcal{T} \to \Omega_A$ mapping each trace to A's provenance view of the trace. For the purposes of this paper, we do not consider interactions among multiple principals, so we typically consider only one principal and omit the A subscripts. We may write $(\Omega, P : \mathcal{T} \to \Omega)$ or just (Ω, P) for a provenance view. Also, we sometimes write $Q : \Omega \to \mathbb{B}$ for a provenance query, that is, a query on a provenance view.

Given this framework, we proposed the following definitions:

Definition 1 (Disclosure). *A query Q is* disclosed *by a provenance view (Ω, P) if for every $t, t' \in \mathcal{T}$, if $P(t) = P(t')$ then $Q(t) = Q(t')$.*

In other words, disclosure means that there can be no traces t, t' that have the same provenance view but where one satisfies the query and the other does not.

Definition 2 (Obfuscation). *A query Q is* obfuscated *by a provenance view (Ω, P) if for every t in $\mathcal{T}$, there exists $t' \in \mathcal{T}$ such that $P(t) = P(t')$ and $Q(t) \neq Q(t')$.*

Thus, obfuscation is not exactly the opposite of disclosure; instead, it means that for every trace there is another trace with the same provenance view but different Q-value. This means that a principal that has access to the provenance view but not the trace cannot be certain that Q is satisfied or not satisfied by the underlying trace.

The definitions above turn out to be too strong; in this paper we will also consider some weaker versions of disclosure and obfuscation.

Definition 3. *We say that $P : \mathcal{T} \to \Omega$ positively discloses $Q : \mathcal{T} \to \mathbb{B}$ via query $Q' : \Omega \to \mathbb{B}$ if for every t, if $Q'(P(t))$ then $Q(t)$.*

In other words, positive disclosure means that there is a query Q' on the provenance that safely overapproximates Q on the underlying trace. If $Q'(P(t))$ holds then we know $Q(t)$ holds but otherwise we may not learn anything about t.

Definition 4. *We say that P positively obfuscates $Q : \mathcal{T} \to \mathbb{B}$ if for every t satisfying Q there exists a trace t' falsifying Q such that $P(t) = P(t')$.*

In other words, positive obfuscation means that the provenance never reveals that Q holds of the trace, but it may reveal that Q fails. This weaker notion is useful for asserting that sensitive data is protected: if the sensitive data is not present in the trace then it is harmless to reveal this, but if the sensitive data is present then the provenance should hide enough information to make its presence uncertain.

Dual notions of negative disclosure and obfuscation can be defined as positive disclosure or obfuscation of $\neg Q$ respectively.

Proposition 1. *If P both positively discloses and negatively discloses Q via Q', then P discloses Q. Similarly, if P both positively and negatively obfuscates Q then P obfuscates Q.*

In the previous paper, we gave several examples of instances of this framework. Here, for illustration, we just review one such instance, given by finite automata.

Types	$\tau ::=$	$b \mid \tau_1 \times \tau_2 \mid \tau_1 + \tau_2 \mid \tau_1 \to \tau_2 \mid \mu\alpha.\tau \mid \alpha$
Type contexts	$\Gamma ::=$	$[x_1 : \tau_1, \ldots, x_n : \tau_n]$
Code pointers	$\kappa ::=$	$f(x).e$
Matches	$m ::=$	$\{\mathtt{inl}(x_1).e_1; \mathtt{inr}(x_2).e_2\}$
Values	$v ::=$	$c \mid (v_1, v_2) \mid \mathtt{inl}(v) \mid \mathtt{inr}(v) \mid \mathtt{roll}(v) \mid \langle \kappa, \gamma \rangle$
Expressions	$e ::=$	$c \mid x \mid \oplus(\bar{e}) \mid \mathtt{let}\ x = e_1\ \mathtt{in}\ e_2$
		$\mid\ (e_1, e_2) \mid \mathtt{fst}(e) \mid \mathtt{snd}(e) \mid \mathtt{inl}(e) \mid \mathtt{inr}(e)$
		$\mid\ \mathtt{roll}(e) \mid \mathtt{unroll}(e) \mid \mathtt{fun}\ \kappa \mid \mathtt{case}\ e\ \mathtt{of}\ m \mid (e\ e')$
Traces	$T ::=$	$c \mid x \mid \oplus(\overline{T}) \mid \mathtt{let}\ x = T_1\ \mathtt{in}\ T_2$
		$\mid\ (T_1, T_2) \mid \mathtt{fst}(T) \mid \mathtt{snd}(T) \mid \mathtt{inl}(T) \mid \mathtt{inr}(T)$
		$\mid\ \mathtt{roll}(T) \mid \mathtt{unroll}(T) \mid \mathtt{fun}\ \kappa$
		$\mid\ \mathtt{case}\ T \triangleright_{\mathtt{inl}} x.T_1 \mid \mathtt{case}\ T \triangleright_{\mathtt{inr}} x.T_2 \mid (T_1\ T_2) \triangleright_\kappa f(x).T$
Environments	$\gamma ::=$	$[x_1 \mapsto v_1, \ldots, x_n \mapsto v_n]$

Fig. 1. Abstract syntax of Core TML

Example 1 (Automata provenance framework). The set of traces $\mathcal{T}_M$ of an automaton $M = (\Sigma, Q, q_0, \delta, F)$ is the set $Q(\Sigma Q)^*$ of alternating sequences of states and alphabet letters. The queries are simply regular subsets of $\mathcal{T}_M$. The provenance views are given by finite-state transducers. We showed that disclosure is decidable for all queries and views and that obfuscation is decidable for all queries and views whose range is finite. It is unknown whether obfuscation is decidable in the general case.

We now proceed to instantiate the framework with traces generated by a much richer language, with corresponding notions of trace query and provenance view.

3 Core Language

We will develop a core language for provenance based on a standard, typed, call-by-value, pure language, called Transparent ML, or TML. The syntax of TML types, expressions, traces, and other syntactic classes is shown in Figure 1. We include standard constructs for dealing with binary pairs, binary sums, recursive types, and recursive functions; more general constructs such as records, datatypes, or simultaneous recursive functions can of course be handled without difficulty. In $f(x).e$, both f and x are variable names; f is the name of the recursively defined function while x is the name of the argument.

We abbreviate functional terms of the form $f(x).e$ using the letter κ, when convenient; similarly, we often abbreviate the expression $\{\mathtt{inl}(x_1).e_1; \mathtt{inr}(x_2).e_2\}$ as m. We sometimes refer to κ or m as a *code pointer* or *match pointer* respectively; in a fixed program, there are a fixed finite number of such terms and so we can share them instead of explicitly copying them when used in traces.

$$\boxed{\gamma, e \Downarrow v, T}$$

$$\frac{}{\gamma, x \Downarrow \gamma(x), x} \qquad \frac{}{\gamma, c \Downarrow c, c} \qquad \frac{}{\gamma, \mathtt{fun}\,\kappa \Downarrow \langle \kappa, \gamma \rangle, \mathtt{fun}\,\kappa} \qquad \frac{\gamma, \overline{e} \Downarrow \overline{v}, \overline{T}}{\gamma, \oplus(\overline{e}) \Downarrow \hat{\oplus}(\overline{v}), \oplus(\overline{T})}$$

$$\frac{\gamma, e_1 \Downarrow v_1, T_1 \qquad \gamma, e_2 \Downarrow v_2, T_2}{\gamma, (e_1, e_2) \Downarrow (v_1, v_2), (T_1, T_2)} \qquad \frac{\gamma, e \Downarrow (v_1, v_2), T}{\gamma, \mathtt{fst}(e) \Downarrow v_1, \mathtt{fst}(T)}$$

$$\frac{\gamma, e \Downarrow v, T}{\gamma, \mathtt{inl}(e) \Downarrow \mathtt{inl}(v), \mathtt{inl}(T)} \qquad \frac{\gamma, e_1 \Downarrow v_1, T_1 \qquad \gamma[x \mapsto v_1], e_2 \Downarrow v_2, T_2}{\gamma, \mathtt{let}\ x = e_1\ \mathtt{in}\ e_2 \Downarrow v_2, \mathtt{let}\ x = T_1\ \mathtt{in}\ T_2}$$

$$\frac{\gamma, e \Downarrow v, T}{\gamma, \mathtt{roll}(e) \Downarrow \mathtt{roll}(v), \mathtt{roll}(T)} \qquad \frac{\gamma, e \Downarrow \mathtt{roll}(v), T}{\gamma, \mathtt{unroll}(e) \Downarrow v, \mathtt{unroll}(T)}$$

$$\frac{(\mathtt{inl}(x_1).e_1 \in m) \qquad \gamma, e \Downarrow \mathtt{inl}(v), T \qquad \gamma[x_1 \mapsto v], e_1 \Downarrow v_1, T_1}{\gamma, \mathtt{case}\ e\ \mathtt{of}\ m \Downarrow v_1, \mathtt{case}\ T \triangleright_{\mathtt{inl}} x_1.T_1}$$

$$\frac{(\mathtt{inr}(x_2).e_2 \in m) \qquad \gamma, e \Downarrow \mathtt{inr}(v), T \qquad \gamma[x_2 \mapsto v], e_2 \Downarrow v_2, T_2}{\gamma, \mathtt{case}\ e\ \mathtt{of}\ m \Downarrow v_2, \mathtt{case}\ T \triangleright_{\mathtt{inr}} x_2.T_2}$$

$$\frac{\gamma, e_1 \Downarrow \langle \kappa, \gamma' \rangle, T_1}{(\kappa = f(x).e) \qquad \gamma, e_2 \Downarrow v_2, T_2 \qquad \gamma'[f \mapsto \langle \kappa, \gamma' \rangle, x \mapsto v_2], e \Downarrow v, T}{\gamma, (e_1\ e_2) \Downarrow v, (T_1\ T_2) \triangleright_\kappa f(x).T}$$

Fig. 2. Dynamic semantics of Core TML: selected rules for expression evaluation

3.1 Dynamic Semantics

We augment a standard large-step operational semantics for TML by adding a parameter T, which records a trace of the evaluation of the expression. The judgment $\gamma, e \Downarrow v, T$ says that in environment γ, expression e evaluates to value v with trace T. (Traces were defined in Figure 1.) Many of the trace forms are isomorphic to the corresponding expression forms. The exceptions are the case and application evaluation rules. In either case, the first argument is evaluated to determine what expression to evaluate to obtain the final result. For case traces, we record the trace of the case scrutinee and the taken branch. Traces can contain free variables and so we re-bind the variable in the trace of the taken branch. Similarly for an application we record the traces of the function subexpression and the argument subexpression, and also record the trace of the evaluation of the body of the function. Again, since the body trace can mention the function and argument names as free variables, we re-bind these variables.

We want to emphasize at this point that we do not necessarily expect that implementations routinely construct fully detailed traces along the above lines. Rather, the trace semantics is proposed here as a candidate for the most detailed form of provenance we will consider. Recording and compressing or filtering relevant information from traces in an efficient way is beyond the scope of this paper.

Trace Replay. We equip traces with a semantics that relates them to expressions. We write $\gamma, T \curvearrowright v$ for the *replay* relation that reruns a trace on an environment (possibly different from the one originally used to construct T). The rules for most trace forms are the same as the standard rules for evaluating the corresponding expression forms.

$$\boxed{\gamma, T \curvearrowright v}$$

$$\frac{\gamma, T \curvearrowright \mathtt{inl}(v) \qquad \gamma[x_1 \mapsto v], T_1 \curvearrowright v_1}{\gamma, \mathtt{case}\ T \triangleright_{\mathtt{inl}} x_1.T_1 \curvearrowright v_1} \qquad \frac{\gamma, T \curvearrowright \mathtt{inr}(v) \qquad \gamma[x_2 \mapsto v], T_2 \curvearrowright v_2}{\gamma, \mathtt{case}\ T \triangleright_{\mathtt{inr}} x_2.T_2 \curvearrowright v_2}$$

$$\frac{\gamma, T_1 \curvearrowright \langle \kappa, \gamma' \rangle \qquad \gamma, T_2 \curvearrowright v_2, T_2' \qquad \gamma'[f \mapsto \langle \kappa, \gamma' \rangle, x \mapsto v_2], T \curvearrowright v}{\gamma, (T_1\ T_2) \triangleright_\kappa f(x).T \curvearrowright v}$$

Fig. 3. Dynamic semantics of Core TML: selected rules for trace replay

Figure 3 shows the rules for replaying case and application traces. Essentially, these rules require that the same control flow branches are taken as in the original run. If the input environment is different enough that the same branches cannot be taken, then replay fails.

3.2 Basic Properties of Traces

In this section, we identify key properties of traces, including type safety, and the consistency and fidelity properties that characterize how traces record the evaluation of an expression.

Determinacy and Type Safety. We employ a standard type system for expressions, with straightforward extensions to handle traces. Determinacy of typechecking and type-safety can be established for expression evaluation and trace replay. Types do not play a significant role in the main technical results, however, so we elide the details.

Consistency and Fidelity. We say that a trace T is *consistent* with an environment γ if there exists v such that $\gamma, T \curvearrowright v$. Evaluation produces consistent traces, and replaying a trace on the same input yields the same value:

Theorem 1 (Consistency). *If* $\gamma, e \Downarrow v, T$ *then* $\gamma, T \curvearrowright v$.

Furthermore, the trace produced by evaluation is faithful to the original expression, in the sense that whenever the trace can be successfully replayed on a different input, the result (and its trace) is the same as what we would obtain by rerunning e from scratch, and the resulting trace is the same as well. We call this property *fidelity*.

Theorem 2 (Fidelity). *If* $\gamma, e \Downarrow v, T$ *and* $\gamma', T \curvearrowright v'$ *then* $\gamma', e \Downarrow v', T$.

4   Provenance Views and Trace Queries

4.1   Provenance Extraction

Many previous approaches to provenance can be viewed as performing a form of *annotation propagation*. The idea is to decorate the input with annotations (often, initially, unique identifiers) and propagate the annotations through the evaluation. For example, in where-provenance, annotations are optional tags that can be thought of as pointers showing where output data was copied from in the source [6,5]. Other techniques, such

$$\begin{aligned}
\mathsf{F}(x, \widehat{\gamma}) &= \widehat{\gamma}(x) \\
\mathsf{F}(\mathtt{let}\ x = T_1\ \mathtt{in}\ T_2, \widehat{\gamma}) &= \mathsf{F}(T_2, \widehat{\gamma}[x \mapsto \mathsf{F}(T_1, \widehat{\gamma})]) \\
\mathsf{F}(c, \widehat{\gamma}) &= c^{\mathsf{F}_c} \\
\mathsf{F}(\oplus(T_1, \ldots, T_n), \widehat{\gamma}) &= (\oplus(v_1, \ldots, v_n))^{\mathsf{F}_\oplus(a_1, \ldots, a_n)} \\
&\quad \text{where}\ v_i^{a_i} = \mathsf{F}(T_i, \widehat{\gamma}) \\
\mathsf{F}((T_1, T_2), \widehat{\gamma}) &= (\mathsf{F}(T_1, \widehat{\gamma}), \mathsf{F}(T_2, \widehat{\gamma}))^\perp \\
\mathsf{F}(\mathtt{fst}(T), \widehat{\gamma}) &= v_1^{\mathsf{F}_1(a,b)} \\
&\quad \text{where}\ (v_1^b, \widehat{v}_2)^a = \mathsf{F}(T, \widehat{\gamma}) \\
\mathsf{F}(\mathtt{inl}(T), \widehat{\gamma}) &= \mathtt{inl}(\mathsf{F}(T, \widehat{\gamma}))^\perp \\
\mathsf{F}((\mathtt{case}\ T) \triangleright_{\mathtt{inl}} x.T_1, \widehat{\gamma}) &= v^{\mathsf{F}_L(a,b)} \\
&\quad \text{where}\ \mathtt{inl}(\widehat{v})^a = \mathsf{F}(T, \widehat{\gamma}) \\
&\quad \text{and}\ v^b = \mathsf{F}(T_1, \widehat{\gamma}[y \mapsto \widehat{v}]) \\
\mathsf{F}(\mathtt{fun}\ \kappa, \widehat{\gamma}) &= \langle \kappa, \widehat{\gamma} \rangle^{\mathsf{F}_\kappa} \\
\mathsf{F}((T_1\ T_2) \triangleright_\kappa f(x).T, \widehat{\gamma}) &= v^{\mathsf{F}_{\mathtt{app}}(a,b)} \\
&\quad \text{where}\ \langle \kappa, \widehat{\gamma}' \rangle^a = \mathsf{F}(T_1, \widehat{\gamma}) \\
&\quad \text{and}\ \widehat{v}_2 = \mathsf{F}(T_2, \widehat{\gamma}) \\
&\quad \text{and}\ v^b = \mathsf{F}(T, \widehat{\gamma}'[f \mapsto \langle \kappa, \widehat{\gamma}' \rangle^a, x \mapsto \widehat{v}_2])
\end{aligned}$$

Fig. 4. Generic extraction (selected rules)

as why-, how-, dependency, and workflow provenance, can also be defined in terms of annotation propagation [18,17,4,10].

Based on this observation, we define a provenance extraction framework in which values are decorated with annotations and extraction functions take traces and return annotated values that can be interpreted as useful provenance information. We apply this framework to specify several concrete annotation schemes and extraction functions.

Extraction framework. Let A be an arbitrary set of *annotations* a, which we usually assume includes a blank annotation $\perp$ and a countably infinite set of identifiers $\ell \in Loc$, called *locations*. We define *A-annotated values* $\widehat{v}$ (or just *annotated values*, when A is clear) using the following grammar:

$$\widehat{v} ::= v^a \qquad \widehat{\gamma} ::= [x_1 \mapsto \widehat{v}_1, \ldots, x_n \mapsto \widehat{v}_n]$$
$$v ::= c \mid (\widehat{v}_1, \widehat{v}_2) \mid \mathtt{inl}(\widehat{v}) \mid \mathtt{inr}(\widehat{v}) \mid \langle \kappa, \widehat{\gamma} \rangle \mid \mathtt{roll}(\widehat{v})$$

We write $\widehat{\gamma}$ for *annotated environments* mapping variables to annotated values. We define an erasure function $|\widehat{v}|$ that maps each annotated value to an ordinary value by erasing the annotations. Similarly, $|\widehat{\gamma}|$ is the ordinary environment obtained by erasing the annotations from the values of $\widehat{\gamma}$.

We will define a family of provenance extraction functions $\mathsf{F}(T, \widehat{\gamma})$ that take a trace T and an environment $\widehat{\gamma}$ and return an annotated value. Each such F can be specified by giving the following annotation-propagation functions:

$$\mathsf{F}_c, \mathsf{F}_\kappa : A$$
$$\mathsf{F}_1, \mathsf{F}_2, \mathsf{F}_L, \mathsf{F}_R, \mathsf{F}_{\mathtt{app}}, \mathsf{F}_{\mathtt{unroll}} : A \times A \to A$$
$$\mathsf{F}_\oplus : A \times \cdots \times A \to A$$

Each function shows how the annotations involved in the corresponding computational step propagate to the result. For example, $F_1(a, b)$ gives the annotation on the result of a fst-projection, where a is the annotation on the pair and b is the annotation of the first element. Figure 4 shows how to propagate annotations through a trace given basic annotation-propagation functions.

Remark 1. The extraction framework hard-wires the behavior of certain operations such as let, inl(), inr(), and application. It would also be possible to extend the framework to provide to customize their behavior; however, this functionality is not needed by any of the forms of provenance in this paper, and it is not clear whether there are natural provenance models that require them.

Theorem 3. *Every generic provenance extraction function is compatible with replay: that is, for any $\widehat{\gamma}, T, v$, if $|\widehat{\gamma}|, T \curvearrowright v$ then $|F(T, \widehat{\gamma})| = v$.*

Where-provenance. Where-provenance can be defined via an annotation-propagating semantics where annotations are either labels ℓ or the blank annotation $\bot$. We define the where-provenance semantics $W(T, \widehat{\gamma})$ using the following annotation-propagation functions:

$$W_c, W_\kappa = \bot$$
$$W_1, W_2, W_L, W_R, W_{\text{app}}, W_{\text{unroll}} = \lambda(x, y).y$$
$$W_\oplus = \lambda(a_1, \ldots, a_n).\bot$$

Essentially, these functions preserve the annotations of data that are copied, and annotate computed or constructed data with $\bot$. This semantics is similar to that in Buneman et al. [5] and previous treatments of where-provenance in databases, adapted to TML.

Theorem 4. *Suppose $|\widehat{\gamma}|, e \Downarrow v', T$. If an annotated value v^a appears in $W(T, \widehat{\gamma})$ with annotation $a \neq \bot$, then v^a is an exact copy (including any nested annotations) of a part of $\widehat{\gamma}$.*

Expression provenance. To model expression provenance, we consider *expression annotations* t consisting of labels ℓ, blanks $\bot$, constants c, or primitive function applications $\oplus(t_1, \ldots, t_n)$. We define expression-provenance extraction $E(T, \widehat{\gamma})$ in much the same way as W, with the following differences:

$$E_c = c \qquad E_\oplus(t_1, \ldots, t_n) = \oplus(t_1, \ldots, t_n)$$

It would also be straightforward to define a translation from traces to provenance graphs (for example, Open Provenance Model graphs [23]).

The correctness property for expression provenance states that the expression annotation correctly recomputes the value it annotates.

Theorem 5. *Suppose $|\widehat{\gamma}|, e \Downarrow v', T$, where each subvalue in $\widehat{\gamma}$ is annotated with a copy of itself. If an annotated value v^e appears in $E(T, \widehat{\gamma})$ with $e \neq \bot$, then e is a closed expression evaluating to $|v|$.*

Dependency provenance. To extract dependency provenance, we will use annotations ϕ that are sets of source locations $\{\ell_1, \ldots, \ell_n\}$. Initial annotations consist of distinct singleton sets $\{\ell\}$. We define $D(T, \widehat{\gamma})$ using the following propagation functions:

$$D_c, D_\kappa = \emptyset$$
$$D_1, D_2, D_L, D_R, D_{\text{app}}, D_{\text{unroll}} = \lambda(x, y).x \cup y$$
$$D_\oplus = \lambda(a_1, \ldots, a_n).a_1 \cup \cdots \cup a_n$$

This semantics is based on the dynamic provenance tracking semantics given by Cheney et al. [9], generalized to TML.

This definition satisfies the *dependency-correctness* property introduced in [9]. This property requires an auxiliary relation $\approx_\ell$ that says that two annotated values are equal except possibly at parts labeled by ℓ, whose straightforward definition we omit. Then we can show:

Theorem 6. *Suppose* $|\widehat{\gamma}|, e \Downarrow v, T$ *and* $\widehat{\gamma}' \approx_\ell \widehat{\gamma}$ *and* $|\widehat{\gamma}'|, e \Downarrow v', T'$. *Then we have* $D(T, \widehat{\gamma}) \approx_\ell D(T', \widehat{\gamma}')$.

This says that the label of a value in the input propagates to all parts of the output where changing the value can have an impact on the result.

Path annotations. For annotations to be useful when the full input is unavailable, we consider annotations where the locations ℓ are *paths* that uniquely address parts of the input environment. We write $\text{path}(\gamma)$ for the environment γ with each component annotated with the path to that component. More generally, we define $\text{path}_p(\gamma)$ as $[x_1 := \text{path}_{p.x}(\gamma(x_1)), \ldots, x_n := \text{path}_{p.x_n}(\gamma(x_n))]$ where $\text{path}_p(v)$ is defined as follows:

$$\text{path}_p(c) = c^p$$
$$\text{path}_p((v_1, v_2)) = (\text{path}_{p.1}(v_1), \text{path}_{p.2}(v_2))^p$$
$$\text{path}_p(\text{inl}(v)) = \text{inl}(\text{path}_{p.1}(v))^p$$
$$\text{path}_p(\text{inr}(v)) = \text{inr}(\text{path}_{p.1}(v))^p$$
$$\text{path}_p(\langle \kappa, \gamma \rangle) = \langle \kappa, \text{path}_p(\gamma) \rangle^p$$

For example, $\text{path}([x = (1, 2), y = \text{inl}(4)]) = [x = (1^{x.1}, 2^{x.2})^x, y = \text{inl}(4^{y.\text{inl}})^y]$.

4.2   Patterns, Partial Traces, and Trace Queries

We introduce patterns for values, environments and traces. The syntax of patterns (pattern environments) is similar to that of values (respectively environments), extended with special *holes*:

$$p ::= c \mid (p_1, p_2) \mid \text{inl}(p) \mid \text{inr}(p) \mid \text{roll}(p) \mid \langle \kappa, \rho \rangle \mid \Diamond \mid \square$$
$$\rho ::= [x_1 \mapsto p_1, \ldots, x_n \mapsto p_n]$$

Patterns actually denote binary relations on values. The hole symbol $\square$ denotes the total relation, while the exact-match symbol $\Diamond$ denotes the identity relation. (The $\Diamond$ pattern is used in backward disclosure slicing.)

$$\boxed{v \approx_p v}$$

$$\frac{}{v \approx_\Box v'} \qquad \frac{}{v \approx_\Diamond v} \qquad \frac{}{c \approx_c c} \qquad \frac{v_1 \approx_{p_1} v_1' \qquad v_2 \approx_{p_2} v_2'}{(v_1, v_2) \approx_{(p_1, p_2)} (v_1', v_2')}$$

$$\frac{v \approx_p v' \qquad C \in \{\mathtt{inl}, \mathtt{inr}, \mathtt{roll}\}}{C(v) \approx_{C(p)} C(v')} \qquad \frac{\gamma \approx_\rho \gamma'}{\langle \kappa, \gamma \rangle \approx_{\langle \kappa, \rho \rangle} \langle \kappa, \gamma' \rangle}$$

$$\gamma \approx_\rho \gamma' \iff \forall x \in \mathrm{dom}(\rho). \, \gamma(x) \approx_{\rho(x)} \gamma'(x)$$

Fig. 5. Equality modulo patterns

$$\Box \sqcup p = p \sqcup \Box = p \qquad \Diamond \sqcup p = p \sqcup \Diamond = p[\Diamond / \Box]$$
$$(p_1, p_2) \sqcup (p_1', p_2') = (p_1 \sqcup p_1', p_2 \sqcup p_2') \qquad c \sqcup c = c$$
$$C(p) \sqcup C(p') = C(p \sqcup p') \qquad C \in \{\mathtt{inl}, \mathtt{inr}, \mathtt{roll}\}$$
$$\langle \kappa, \rho \rangle \sqcup \langle \kappa, \rho' \rangle = \langle \kappa, \rho \sqcup \rho' \rangle$$
$$(\rho \sqcup \rho')(x) = \begin{cases} \rho(x) \sqcup \rho'(x) & x \in \mathrm{dom}(\rho) \cup \mathrm{dom}(\rho') \\ \rho(x) & x \in \mathrm{dom}(\rho) \backslash \mathrm{dom}(\rho') \\ \rho'(x) & x \in \mathrm{dom}(\rho') \backslash \mathrm{dom}(\rho) \end{cases}$$

Fig. 6. Least upper bounds of patterns and environments

We say that v matches v' modulo p (written $v \approx_p v'$) if v and v' match the structure of p, and are equal at corresponding positions denoted by $\Diamond$. Moreover, we say $p \sqsubseteq v$ if $v \approx_p v$, and we write $p \sqcup p'$ for the least upper bound (join) of two patterns. Rules defining $\approx_p$ and $\sqcup$ are given in Figures 5 and 6.

When $p \sqsubseteq v$, we write $v|_p$ for the pattern obtained by replacing all of the $\Diamond$-holes in p with the corresponding values in v. For example, $(1, 2)|_{(\Diamond, \Box)} = (1, \Box)$. Similarly, we write $\gamma|_\rho$ for $[x_1 = \gamma(x_1)|_{\rho(x_1)}, \ldots, x_n = \gamma(x_n)|_{\rho(x_n)}]$.

We also consider partial traces, usually written S, which are trace expressions where some subexpressions have been replaced with $\Box$:

$$S ::= \cdots \mid \Box$$

As with patterns, we write $S \sqsubseteq T$ to indicate that T matches S, that is, S can be made equal to T by filling in some holes.

For the purpose of disclosure and obfuscation analysis, we will consider the "traces" to be triples (γ, T, v) where T is consistent with γ and v, that is, $\gamma, T \curvearrowright v$. We refer to such a triple as a consistent triple. Furthermore, to analyze forms of provenance based on annotation we will consider consistent annotated triples $(\hat{\gamma}, T, \hat{v})$ where $\hat{v} = \mathsf{F}(T, \hat{\gamma})$. We consider trace or provenance queries built out of partial values and partial traces. We will later also consider queries derived from different forms of provenance, based on annotated triples.

Definition 5. *1. Let $\phi(\gamma)$ be a predicate on input environments. An* input query $\mathsf{IN}\gamma.\phi(\gamma)$ *is defined as* $\{(\gamma, T, v) \mid \gamma, T \curvearrowright v \text{ and } \phi(\gamma)\}$. *As a special case, we write* IN_ρ *for* $\mathsf{IN}\gamma.(\rho \sqsubseteq \gamma)$.

2. *Let $\phi(v)$ be a predicate on output values. An* output query $\mathsf{OUT}v.\phi(v)$ *is defined as* $\{(\gamma, T, v) \mid \gamma, T \curvearrowright v \text{ and } \phi(v)\}$. *As a special case, we write* $\mathsf{OUT}_p = \mathsf{OUT}v.(p \sqsubseteq v)$.

5   Disclosure and Obfuscation Analysis

5.1   Disclosure

We first consider properties disclosed by various forms of provenance considered above. Both where-provenance and expression provenance disclose useful information about the input. Dependency provenance does not disclose input information in an easy-to-analyze way, but is useful for obfuscation, as discussed later.

For where-provenance, we consider input queries $Q_{v_0,\ell} = \mathsf{IN}\gamma. (\gamma.\ell = v_0)$ and output queries $Q'_{v_0,\ell} = \mathsf{OUT}v. (v.\ell = v_0)$, where ℓ is a path and v_0 is a value. Such a query tests whether the value at a given path in γ or v matches the provided value.

Theorem 7. *The provenance view* $(\gamma, T, v) \mapsto \mathsf{W}(T, \mathsf{path}(\gamma))$ *positively discloses* $Q_{v_0,\ell}$ *via* $Q'_{v_0,\ell}$.

For expression-provenance, let $\gamma(t)$ be the result of evaluating t in γ with all paths ℓ replaced by their values $\gamma.\ell$ in γ. We consider queries $Q_{t,v_0} = \mathsf{IN}\gamma. (\gamma(t) = v_0)$, where t is an expression provenance annotation and v_0 is a value. Such a query tests whether evaluating an expression e over γ yields the specified value. For example, $\mathsf{IN}\gamma. \ x.1 + y.2 = 4$ holds for $\gamma = [x = (1, 2), y = (2, 3)]$, because $\gamma(x.1) + \gamma(y.2) = 1 + 3 = 4$. We also consider output queries $Q'_{t,v_0} = \mathsf{OUT}v. (\hat{v_1}^t$ appears in v and $|\hat{v_1}| = v_0)$, that simply test whether an annotated copy of v_0 appears in the output with annotation t.

Theorem 8. *The provenance view* $(\gamma, T, v) \mapsto \mathsf{E}(T, \mathsf{path}(\gamma))$ *positively discloses* Q_{t,v_0} *via* Q'_{t,v_0}.

Expression provenance and where-provenance are also related in the following sense:

Theorem 9. *Where-provenance is computable from expression-provenance.*

Proof. Where-provenance annotations can be extracted from expression-provenance annotations by mapping locations ℓ to themselves and all other expressions to $\bot$.

Note that this implies that for a function like "factorial", the where-provenance of the output is always $\bot$. Hence, any query disclosed by where-provenance is disclosed by expression-provenance, and any query obfuscated by expression-provenance is also obfuscated by where-provenance.

We now consider a form of *trace slicing* that takes a partial output value and removes information from the input and trace that is not needed to disclose the output. We show that such *disclosure slices* also disclose generic provenance views (Theorem 11). Thus, disclosure slices form a quite general form of provenance in their own right.

Definition 6. *Let* $\gamma, T \Downarrow v$, *and suppose* $S \sqsubseteq T$ *and* $\rho \sqsubseteq \gamma$. *We say* (ρ, S) *is a disclosure slice with respect to partial value p if for all* $\gamma' \sqsupseteq \rho$ *and* $T' \sqsupseteq S$ *such that if* $\gamma', T' \curvearrowright v'$, *we have* $p \sqsubseteq v$ *iff* $p \sqsubseteq v'$.

$$\boxed{p, T \xrightarrow{\text{disc}} S, \rho}$$

$$\square, T \xrightarrow{\text{disc}} \square, [] \qquad p, x \xrightarrow{\text{disc}} x, [x \mapsto p] \qquad p, c \xrightarrow{\text{disc}} c, [] \qquad \langle \kappa, \rho \rangle, \text{fun } \kappa \xrightarrow{\text{disc}} \text{fun } \kappa, \rho$$

$$\frac{}{\langle \kappa', \rho \rangle, \text{fun } \kappa \xrightarrow{\text{disc}} \text{fun } \kappa', \square} \qquad \frac{p_2, T_2 \xrightarrow{\text{disc}} S_2, \rho_2[x \mapsto p_1] \qquad p_1, T_1 \xrightarrow{\text{disc}} S_1, \rho_1}{p_2, \text{let } x = T_1 \text{ in } T_2 \xrightarrow{\text{disc}} \text{let } x = S_1 \text{ in } S_2, \rho_1 \sqcup \rho_2}$$

$$\frac{\Diamond, T_1 \xrightarrow{\text{disc}} S_1, \rho_1 \quad \cdots \quad \Diamond, T_n \xrightarrow{\text{disc}} S_n, \rho_n}{p, \oplus(T_1, \ldots, T_n) \xrightarrow{\text{disc}} \oplus(S_1, \ldots, S_n), \rho_1 \sqcup \cdots \sqcup \rho_n}$$

$$\frac{p_1, T_1 \xrightarrow{\text{disc}} S_1, \rho_1 \qquad p_2, T_2 \xrightarrow{\text{disc}} S_2, \rho_2}{(p_1, p_2), (T_1, T_2) \xrightarrow{\text{disc}} (S_1, S_2), \rho_1 \sqcup \rho_2} \qquad \frac{(p, \square), T \xrightarrow{\text{disc}} S, \rho}{p, \text{fst}(T) \xrightarrow{\text{disc}} \text{fst}(S), \rho}$$

$$\frac{p, T \xrightarrow{\text{disc}} S, \rho}{\text{inl}(p), \text{inl}(T) \xrightarrow{\text{disc}} \text{inl}(S), \rho} \qquad \frac{p, T \xrightarrow{\text{disc}} S, \rho}{\text{inl}(p), \text{inr}(T) \xrightarrow{\text{disc}} \text{inr}(\square), []}$$

$$\frac{p, T \xrightarrow{\text{disc}} S, \rho}{\text{roll}(p), \text{roll}(T) \xrightarrow{\text{disc}} \text{roll}(S), \rho} \qquad \frac{\text{roll}(p), T \xrightarrow{\text{disc}} S, \rho}{p, \text{unroll}(T) \xrightarrow{\text{disc}} \text{unroll}(S), \rho}$$

$$\frac{p_1, T_1 \xrightarrow{\text{disc}} S_1, \rho_1[x_1 \mapsto p] \qquad \text{inl}(p), T \xrightarrow{\text{disc}} S, \rho}{p_1, \text{case } T \triangleright_{\text{inl}} x_1.T_1 \xrightarrow{\text{disc}} \text{case } S \triangleright_{\text{inl}} x_1.S_1, \rho \sqcup \rho_1}$$

$$\frac{p, T \xrightarrow{\text{disc}} S, \rho[f \mapsto p_1, x \mapsto p_2] \qquad p_1 \sqcup \langle \kappa, \rho \rangle, T_1 \xrightarrow{\text{disc}} S_1, \rho_1 \qquad p_2, T_2 \xrightarrow{\text{disc}} S_2, \rho_2}{p, (T_1 \ T_2) \triangleright_\kappa f(x).T \xrightarrow{\text{disc}} (S_1 \ S_2) \triangleright_\kappa f(x).S, \rho_1 \sqcup \rho_2}$$

$$\frac{fvs(\kappa) = \{x_1, \ldots, x_n\}}{\Diamond, \text{fun } \kappa \xrightarrow{\text{disc}} \text{fun } \kappa, [x_1 \mapsto \Diamond, \ldots, x_n \mapsto \Diamond]} \qquad \frac{\Diamond, T_1 \xrightarrow{\text{disc}} S_1, \rho_1 \qquad \Diamond, T_2 \xrightarrow{\text{disc}} S_2, \rho_2}{\Diamond, (T_1, T_2) \xrightarrow{\text{disc}} (S_1, S_2), \rho_1 \sqcup \rho_2}$$

$$\frac{\Diamond, T \xrightarrow{\text{disc}} S, \rho}{\Diamond, \text{inl}(T) \xrightarrow{\text{disc}} \text{inl}(S), \rho} \qquad \frac{\Diamond, T \xrightarrow{\text{disc}} S, \rho}{\Diamond, \text{inr}(T) \xrightarrow{\text{disc}} \text{inr}(S), \rho} \qquad \frac{\Diamond, T \xrightarrow{\text{disc}} S, \rho}{\Diamond, \text{roll}(T) \xrightarrow{\text{disc}} \text{roll}(S), \rho}$$

Fig. 7. Disclosure slicing (selected rules)

Note that by this definition, minimal disclosure slices exist (since there are finitely many slices) but need not be unique. For example, both $\square \vee \text{true}$ and $\text{true} \vee \square$ are disclosure slices showing that $\text{true} \vee \text{true}$ evaluates to true, but $\square \vee \square$ is not a disclosure slice.

Figure 7 shows selected rules defining a disclosure slicing judgment $p, T \xrightarrow{\text{disc}} \rho, S$. Basically, the idea is to push a partial value backwards through a trace to obtain a partial input environment and trace slice. The partial input environment is needed to handle local variables in traces; for example, in the rule for let, we first slice through the body of the let, then identify the partial value showing the needed parts of the let-bound value, and use that to slice backwards through the first subtrace. Slicing for application traces is similar, but more complex due to the closure environments. Note also that the special $\Diamond$ patterns are used to slice backwards through primitive operations even when we do not know the values of the inputs or results. (Another possibility is to annotate the traces of primitive operations with these values.)

Lemma 1. *If $\gamma, T \curvearrowright v$ then for any $p \sqsubseteq v$ there exists $S \sqsubseteq T$ and $\rho \sqsubseteq \gamma$ such that $p, T \xrightarrow{\text{disc}} S, \rho$. Moreover, there is a unique least such S and ρ.*

We choose a function $\text{Disc}_p(\gamma, T, v)$ on consistent triples (γ, T, v) whose value is $(\gamma|_\rho, S)$ where $p, T \xrightarrow{\text{disc}} S, \rho$ and S, ρ are the least slices (obtained by determinizing the slicing algorithm by applying the first, hole-propagating rule greedily before any other rule). The idea is that we slice using the rules in Figure 7 and then transform ρ by filling in all $\Diamond$-holes with the corresponding values in γ. Note that the v parameter is irrelevant and is included only so that Disc_p is a uniform function from consistent triples to slices.

To prove the correctness of this disclosure slicing algorithm, we need a stronger notion of equivalence. Recall the definition of $v \approx_p v'$ as shown in Figure 5. Using this relation, we can prove the correctness of the slicing relation as follows:

Lemma 2. *Assume $\gamma, T \curvearrowright v$ and $p, T \xrightarrow{\text{disc}} S, \rho$.*

1. *If $p \sqsubseteq v$ then for all $\gamma' \approx_\rho \gamma$ and $T' \sqsupseteq S$, if $\gamma', T' \Downarrow v'$ then $v' \approx_p v$.*
2. *If $p \not\sqsubseteq v$ then for all $\gamma' \approx_\rho \gamma$ and $T' \sqsupseteq S$, if $\gamma', T' \Downarrow v'$ then $p \not\sqsubseteq v'$.*

Proof. Both parts follow by induction on the structure of slicing derivations.

Correctness follows as a consequence of the above two properties.

Theorem 10. Disc_p *discloses* OUT_p.

Proof. Suppose $\text{Disc}_p(\gamma, T, v) = \text{Disc}_p(\gamma', T', v')$. Then $(\gamma|_\rho, S) = (\gamma'|_{\rho'}, S')$ where $p, T \xrightarrow{\text{disc}} S, \rho$ and $p, T' \xrightarrow{\text{disc}} S', \rho'$. Hence, $S = S'$ and $\gamma|_\rho = \gamma'|_{\rho'}$, which in turn implies $\gamma \approx_\rho \gamma'$. Suppose that $\text{OUT}_p(\gamma, T, v)$ holds; that is, $p \sqsubseteq v$. Then by Lemma 2(1), $v' \approx_p v$ so $p \sqsubseteq v'$. Conversely, suppose $p \not\sqsubseteq v$. Then by Lemma 2(2), we have $p \not\sqsubseteq v'$.

Disclosure from slices. Finally, we link disclosure for value patterns to disclosure for generic provenance views. Essentially, we show that for any F, the disclosure slice for p positively discloses the F-provenance annotations of values matching p. Informally, this means that disclosure slices provide a highly general form of provenance specialized to a part of the output: one can compute and reveal the disclosure slice and others can then compute any generic provenance view from the slice, without rerunning the original computation or consulting input data or subtraces that are dropped in the slice.

Theorem 11. *Assume $|\widehat{\gamma}|, T \curvearrowright v$ and $p \sqsubseteq v$. Suppose $p, T \xrightarrow{\text{disc}} S, \rho$. Suppose that F is a generic extraction function. Then the annotations associated with p in $\text{F}(T, \widehat{\gamma})$ can be correctly extracted from S using only input parts needed by ρ. That is, suppose we have $\widehat{\gamma} \approx_\rho \widehat{\gamma}'$ (lifting $\approx_-$ to annotated values in the obvious way) and $T' \sqsupseteq S$, where $|\widehat{\gamma}'|, T' \curvearrowright v'$. Then we have $\text{F}(T, \widehat{\gamma}) \approx_p \text{F}(T', \widehat{\gamma}')$.*

5.2 Obfuscation

We now consider obfuscating properties of traces. We first consider what can be obfuscated by the standard provenance views. Where-provenance, essentially, obfuscates anything that can never be copied to the output or affect the control flow of something that is copied to the output. Similarly, expression provenance obfuscates any part of the input that never participates in expression annotations. In both cases, we can potentially learn about parts of the input that affected control flow, however. For example, if $x = 1$ then 1 else y does not obfuscate the value of x in either model, provided y comes from the input, since we can inspect the annotation of the result to determine that $x = 1$ or $x \neq 1$.

Given that we want to ensure obfuscation, we consider conservative techniques that accept (or construct) only provenance views that successfully obfuscate, but may reject some views or construct views that are unnecessarily opaque.

There are several ways to erase information from traces (or other provenance views) to ensure obfuscation of input properties. One way is to re-use the static analysis of dependency provenance (in [9], for example) to identify parts of the output that suffice to make it impossible to guess sensitive parts of the input. Alternatively we can use dynamic dependency provenance to increase precision, by propagating dependency tracking information from the input to the output.

This is similar to using static analysis or dynamic labels for information flow security; the difference is one of emphasis. In information flow security, we usually identify high- or low-security *locations* and try to certify that high-security data does not affect the computation of low-security data; here, instead, we identify a high-security *property* of the trace (e.g. that the input satisfies a certain formula) and try to determine what parts of the output do not depend on sensitive inputs, and hence can be safely included in the provenance view. However, these techniques do not provide guidance about what parts of the *trace* can be safely included in the provenance view.

Here, we develop an alternative approach based on traces. Consider a pattern $\rho \sqsubseteq \gamma$ that erases all information that is considered sensitive. We construct an *obfuscation slice* by re-evaluating T on ρ as much as possible, to compute a sliced trace S and partial value p. We erase parts of T and of the original output value that depend on the erased parts of ρ. Thus, any part of the trace or output value that remains in the obfuscation slice is irrelevant to the sensitive part of the input, and cannot be used to guess it.

Figure 8 shows a syntactic algorithm for computing obfuscation slices as described above. Many rules are essentially generalizations of the rules for evaluation to allow for partial inputs, outputs and traces. The rules of interest, near the bottom of the figure, show how to handle attempts to compute that encounter holes in places where a value constructor is expected. When this happens, we essentially propagate the hole result and return a hole trace. This may be unnecessarily aggressive for some cases, but is necessary for the case and application traces where the trace form gives clues about the control flow.

We define $\mathrm{Obf}_\rho(\gamma, T, v)$ as (p, S) where $\rho, T \xrightarrow{\text{obf}} p, S$. We can show that this is total for well-formed, $\Diamond$-free traces and input environments.

Lemma 3. *If* $\gamma, T \curvearrowright v$ *and* $\rho \sqsubseteq \gamma$ *and* $\rho, T \xrightarrow{\text{obf}} p, S$ *then* $p \sqsubseteq v$ *and* $S \sqsubseteq T$.

$$\boxed{\rho, T \xrightarrow{\text{obf}} p, S}$$

$$\rho, x \xrightarrow{\text{obf}} \rho(x), x \qquad \rho, c \xrightarrow{\text{obf}} \rho(x), c \qquad \rho, \mathtt{fun}\ \kappa \xrightarrow{\text{obf}} \langle \kappa, \rho \rangle, \mathtt{fun}\ \kappa$$

$$\frac{\rho, T_1 \xrightarrow{\text{obf}} p_1, S_1 \qquad \rho[x \mapsto p_1], T_2 \xrightarrow{\text{obf}} p_2, S_2}{\rho, \mathtt{let}\ x = T_1\ \mathtt{in}\ T_2 \xrightarrow{\text{obf}} p_2, \mathtt{let}\ x = S_1\ \mathtt{in}\ S_2}$$

$$\frac{\rho, T_1 \xrightarrow{\text{obf}} v_1, S_1 \quad \cdots \quad \rho, T_n \xrightarrow{\text{obf}} v_n, S_n}{\rho, \oplus(T_1, \ldots, T_n) \xrightarrow{\text{obf}} \oplus(v_1, \ldots, v_n), \oplus(S_1, \ldots, S_n)}$$

$$\frac{\rho, T_1 \xrightarrow{\text{obf}} p_1, S_1 \qquad \rho, T_2 \xrightarrow{\text{obf}} p_2, S_2}{\rho, (T_1, T_2) \xrightarrow{\text{obf}} (p_1, p_2), (S_1, S_2)} \qquad \frac{\rho, T \xrightarrow{\text{obf}} (p_1, p_2), S}{\rho, \mathtt{fst}(T) \xrightarrow{\text{obf}} p_1, \mathtt{fst}(S)}$$

$$\frac{\rho, T \xrightarrow{\text{obf}} p, S}{\rho, \mathtt{inl}(T) \xrightarrow{\text{obf}} \mathtt{inl}(p), \mathtt{inl}(S)} \qquad \frac{\rho, T \xrightarrow{\text{obf}} \mathtt{inl}(p), S \qquad \rho[x_1 \mapsto p], T_1 \xrightarrow{\text{obf}} p_1, S_1}{\rho, \mathtt{case}\ T \rhd_{\mathtt{inl}} x_1.T_1 \xrightarrow{\text{obf}} p_1, \mathtt{case}\ S \rhd_{\mathtt{inl}} x_1.S_1}$$

$$\frac{\rho, T \xrightarrow{\text{obf}} p, S}{\rho, \mathtt{roll}(T) \xrightarrow{\text{obf}} \mathtt{roll}(p), \mathtt{roll}(S)} \qquad \frac{\rho, T \xrightarrow{\text{obf}} \mathtt{roll}(p), S}{\rho, \mathtt{unroll}(T) \xrightarrow{\text{obf}} p, \mathtt{unroll}(S)}$$

$$\frac{\rho, T_1 \xrightarrow{\text{obf}} \langle \kappa, \rho_0 \rangle, S_1 \qquad \rho, T_2 \xrightarrow{\text{obf}} p_2, S_2 \qquad \rho[f \mapsto \langle \kappa, \rho_0 \rangle, x \mapsto p_2], T \xrightarrow{\text{obf}} p, S}{\rho, (T_1\ T_2) \rhd_\kappa f(x).T \xrightarrow{\text{obf}} p, (S_1\ S_2) \rhd_\kappa f(x).S}$$

$$\frac{\rho, T_i \xrightarrow{\text{obf}} \square, S_i}{\rho, \oplus(T_1, \ldots, T_n) \xrightarrow{\text{obf}} \square, \square} \qquad \frac{\rho, T \xrightarrow{\text{obf}} \square, S}{\rho, \mathtt{fst}(T) \xrightarrow{\text{obf}} \square, \square} \qquad \frac{\rho, T \xrightarrow{\text{obf}} \square, S}{\rho, \mathtt{unroll}(T) \xrightarrow{\text{obf}} \square, \square}$$

$$\frac{\rho, T \xrightarrow{\text{obf}} \square, S}{\rho, \mathtt{case}\ T \rhd_{\mathtt{inl}} x_1.T_1 \xrightarrow{\text{obf}} \square, \square} \qquad \frac{\rho, T_1 \xrightarrow{\text{obf}} \square, S_1}{\rho, (T_1\ T_2) \rhd_\kappa f(x).T \xrightarrow{\text{obf}} \square, \square}$$

Fig. 8. Obfuscation slicing (selected rules)

Lemma 4. *If* $\gamma, e \Downarrow v, T$ *and* $\rho \sqsubseteq \gamma$ *and* $\rho, T \xrightarrow{\text{obf}} p, S$ *then for all* $\gamma' \sqsupseteq \rho$, *if* $\gamma', e \Downarrow v', T'$ *then* $\rho, T' \xrightarrow{\text{obf}} p, S$.

Theorem 12. *For traces generated by terminating expressions, and* ρ *with holes of nonsingular types, and* $\rho' \sqsupseteq \rho$, *we have* Obf_ρ *positively obfuscates* $\mathsf{IN}_{\rho'}$.

Proof. Suppose $\mathsf{IN}_{\rho'}$ holds of (γ, T, v) where $\rho' \sqsupseteq \rho$. Then $\rho \sqsubseteq \rho' \sqsubseteq \gamma$. Moreover, since the inclusion is strict, ρ must contain holes that can be replaced with different values, so there exists another $\gamma' \sqsupseteq \rho$ that differs from ρ'. Since T was generated by a terminating expression, we know that $\gamma', e \Downarrow v', T'$ can be derived for some v', T'. By Lemma 4 (and the easily-verified determinacy of $\xrightarrow{\text{obf}}$) we know that $\rho, T' \xrightarrow{\text{obf}} p, S$, hence $\mathsf{Obf}_\rho(\gamma', T', v') = (p, S) = \mathsf{Obf}_\rho(\gamma, T, v)$, as required.

5.3   Discussion

The analysis in section 5.1 gives novel characterizations of what information is disclosed by where-provenance and expression provenance. Essentially, where-provenance discloses information about what parts of the input are copied to the output, while expression provenance additionally discloses information about how parts of the input can be combined to compute parts of the output. The analysis in section 5.1 also shows (in a formal sense) that where-provenance and expression provenance are closely related: one can obtain where-provenance from expressions simply by erasure. Moreover, we can obtain a number of intermediate provenance models based on transductions over expression-provenance annotations.

The disclosure slicing algorithm is based on an interesting insight (which we are exploring in concurrent work on slicing): at a technical level, the information we need for program comprehension via slicing (to understand how a program has evaluated its inputs to produce outputs) is quite similar to what we need for provenance. Although we have identified connections between provenance and slicing before [9], our disclosure and obfuscation slicing algorithms provide further evidence of this close connection.

6 Related Work

There is a huge, and growing, literature on provenance [3,10,24,22], but there is little work on formal models of provenance and none on provenance in a general-purpose higher-order language. Due to space limits, we confine our comparison to closely related work on formal techniques for provenance, and on related ideas in programming languages and language-based security. We refer the interested reader to the aforementioned surveys for more information on provenance in workflows and databases, and to [11,8] for further discussion of prior work on provenance security.

Provenance. This work differs from previous work on provenance in databases in several important ways. First, we consider a general purpose, higher-order language, whereas previous work considers database query languages of limited expressiveness (e.g., monotone query languages), which include unordered collection types with monadic iteration operations but not sum types, recursive types or first-class functions. Second, we aim to record traces adequate to answer a wide range of provenance queries in this general setting, whereas previous work has focused on particular kinds of queries (e.g., where-provenance [6,5], why-provenance [6], how-provenance [18,17]).

Provenance has also been studied extensively for scientific workflow systems [3,24,14]. Most work in this area describes the provenance tracking behavior of a system through examples and does not give a formal semantics that could be used to prove correctness properties. An exception is Hidders et al. [20], which is the closest workflow provenance work to ours. They model workflows using a core database query language extended with nondeterministic, external function calls, and partially formalize a semantics of *runs*, or sets of triples (γ, e, v) labeling an operational derivation tree.

Other related topics. Our trace model is partly inspired by previous work on self-adjusting computation [1], where execution traces are used to efficiently recompute functional programs under arbitrary modifications to their inputs. Provenance-like ideas have also appeared in the context of bidirectional computation [2]. Dimoulas et al. study correctness properties for *blame* in contracts based on semantic properties that, they suggest, may be related to provenance [16]. However, to our knowledge no formal relationships between provenance and self-adjusting computation, bidirectional computation, or blame have been developed.

7   Conclusions

While the importance of understanding provenance and its security characteristics has been widely documented, to date there has been little work on formal modeling of either provenance or provenance security. In this paper, we elaborate upon the ideas introduced in previous work [8], by instantiating the formal framework proposed there with a general-purpose functional programming language and a natural notion of execution traces. We showed how more conventional forms of provenance can be extracted from such traces via a generic provenance extraction mechanism. Furthermore, we studied the key notions of disclosure and obfuscation in this context. In the process we identified weaker *positive* and *negative* variants of disclosure and obfuscation, based on the observation that the original definitions seem too strong to be satisfied often in practice. Our main results include algorithms for *disclosure slicing*, which traverses a trace backwards to retain information needed to certify how an output was produced, and *obfuscation slicing*, which reruns a trace on partial input (excluding sensitive parts of the input), yielding a partial trace and partial output that excludes all information that could help a principal learn sensitive data.

To summarize, our main contribution is the development of a general model of provenance in the form of a core calculus that instruments runs of programs with detailed execution traces. We validated the design of this calculus by showing that traces generalize other known forms of provenance and by studying their disclosure and obfuscation properties. There are many possible avenues for future work, including:

- identifying richer languages for defining trace queries or provenance views
- developing and implementing effective algorithms for trace slicing, and relating these to program slicing
- extending trace and provenance models to handle references, exceptions, input/output, concurrency, nondeterminism, communication, etc.

References

1. Acar, U.A., Blelloch, G.E., Harper, R.: Adaptive functional programming. ACM Trans. Program. Lang. Syst. 28(6), 990–1034 (2006)
2. Bohannon, A., Foster, J.N., Pierce, B.C., Pilkiewicz, A., Schmitt, A.: Boomerang: resourceful lenses for string data. In: POPL, pp. 407–419. ACM, New York (2008)
3. Bose, R., Frew, J.: Lineage retrieval for scientific data processing: a survey. ACM Comput. Surv. 37(1), 1–28 (2005)
4. Buneman, P., Cheney, J., Tan, W.-C., Vansummeren, S.: Curated databases. In: PODS, pp. 1–12 (2008)
5. Buneman, P., Cheney, J., Vansummeren, S.: On the expressiveness of implicit provenance in query and update languages. ACM Transactions on Database Systems 33(4), 28 (2008)

6. Buneman, P., Khanna, S., Tan, W.-C.: Why and Where: A Characterization of Data Provenance. In: Van den Bussche, J., Vianu, V. (eds.) ICDT 2001. LNCS, vol. 1973, pp. 316–330. Springer, Heidelberg (2000)
7. Carey, S., Rogow, G.: UAL shares fall as old story surfaces online. Wall Street Journal (September 2008),
   `http://online.wsj.com/article/SB122088673--738010213.html`
8. Cheney, J.: A formal framework for provenance security. In: CSF, pp. 281–293. IEEE (2011)
9. Cheney, J., Ahmed, A., Acar, U.A.: Provenance as dependency analysis. Mathematical Structures in Computer Science 21(6), 1301–1337 (2011)
10. Cheney, J., Chiticariu, L., Tan, W.C.: Provenance in databases: Why, how, and where. Foundations and Trends in Databases 1(4), 379–474 (2009)
11. Cheney, J., Chong, S., Foster, N., Seltzer, M., Vansummeren, S.: Provenance: A future history. In: OOPSLA Companion (Onward! 2009), pp. 957–964 (2009)
12. Chong, S.: Towards semantics for provenance security. In: Workshop on the Theory and Practice of Provenance (2009), Informal online proceedings:
   `http://www.usenix.org/events/tapp09/`
13. Cirillo, A., Jagadeesan, R., Pitcher, C., Riely, J.: TAPIDO: Trust and Authorization Via Provenance and Integrity in Distributed Objects (Extended Abstract). In: Gairing, M. (ed.) ESOP 2008. LNCS, vol. 4960, pp. 208–223. Springer, Heidelberg (2008)
14. Davidson, S.B., Freire, J.: Provenance and scientific workflows: challenges and opportunities. In: SIGMOD, New York, NY, USA, pp. 1345–1350 (2008)
15. Davidson, S.B., Khanna, S., Milo, T., Panigrahi, D., Roy, S.: Provenance views for module privacy. In: PODS, pp. 175–186 (2011)
16. Dimoulas, C., Findler, R.B., Flanagan, C., Felleisen, M.: Correct blame for contracts: no more scapegoating. In: POPL, pp. 215–226. ACM, New York (2011)
17. Foster, J.N., Green, T.J., Tannen, V.: Annotated XML: queries and provenance. In: PODS, pp. 271–280 (2008)
18. Green, T.J., Karvounarakis, G., Tannen, V.: Provenance semirings. In: PODS, pp. 31–40 (2007)
19. Guts, N., Fournet, C., Zappa Nardelli, F.: Reliable Evidence: Auditability by Typing. In: Backes, M., Ning, P. (eds.) ESORICS 2009. LNCS, vol. 5789, pp. 168–183. Springer, Heidelberg (2009)
20. Hidders, J., Kwasnikowska, N., Sroka, J., Tyszkiewicz, J., Van den Bussche, J.: A Formal Model of Dataflow Repositories. In: Cohen-Boulakia, S., Tannen, V. (eds.) DILS 2007. LNCS (LNBI), vol. 4544, pp. 105–121. Springer, Heidelberg (2007)
21. Jia, L., Vaughan, J.A., Mazurak, K., Zhao, J., Zarko, L., Schorr, J., Zdancewic, S.: Aura: a programming language for authorization and audit. In: ICFP, New York, NY, USA, pp. 27–38 (2008)
22. Moreau, L.: The foundations for provenance on the web. Foundations and Trends in Web Science 2(2-3) (2010)
23. Moreau, L., et al.: The open provenance model core specification (v1.1). Future Generation Computer Systems 27(6), 743–756 (2010)
24. Simmhan, Y., Plale, B., Gannon, D.: A survey of data provenance in e-science. SIGMOD Record 34(3), 31–36 (2005)
25. Swamy, N., Chen, J., Fournet, C., Strub, P.-Y., Bhargavan, K., Yang, J.: Secure distributed programming with value-dependent types. In: ICFP, pp. 266–278 (2011)
26. Swamy, N., Corcoran, B.J., Hicks, M.: Fable: A language for enforcing user-defined security policies. In: IEEE Symposium on Security and Privacy, pp. 369–383 (2008)
27. Varghese, S.: UK government gets bitten by Microsoft Word. Sydney Morning Herald (July 2003),
   `http://www.smh.com.au/articles/2003/07/02/1056825430340.html`

Author Index